The Adams Papers

C. JAMES TAYLOR, EDITOR IN CHIEF

SERIES II

Adams Family Correspondence

Adams Family Correspondence

MARGARET A. HOGAN, C. JAMES TAYLOR,
CELESTE WALKER, ANNE DECKER CECERE,
GREGG L. LINT, HOBSON WOODWARD,
MARY T. CLAFFEY
EDITORS

Volume 7 • *January 1786 – February 1787*

THE BELKNAP PRESS
OF HARVARD UNIVERSITY PRESS
CAMBRIDGE, MASSACHUSETTS
AND LONDON, ENGLAND
2005

Printed in the United States of America

Funds for editing *The Adams Papers* were originally furnished by Time, Inc., on behalf of *Life*, to the Massachusetts Historical Society, under whose supervision the editorial work is being done. Further funds were provided by a grant from the Ford Foundation to the National Archives Trust Fund Board in support of this and four other major documentary publications. In common with these and many other enterprises like them, *The Adams Papers* has continued to benefit from the guidance and cooperation of the National Historical Publications and Records Commission, chaired by the Archivist of the United States, which from 1975 to the present has provided this enterprise with major financial support. Important additional funds were supplied from 1980 to 1993 by The Andrew W. Mellon Foundation, The J. Howard Pew Freedom Trust, and The Charles E. Culpeper Foundation through the Founding Fathers Papers, Inc. Since 1993, *The Adams Papers* has received major support from the National Endowment for the Humanities, and matching support from The Packard Humanities Institute, through the Founding Fathers Papers, Inc., and from The Charles Francis Adams Charitable Trust, The Florence J. Gould Foundation, The Lyn and Norman Lear Fund, and an anonymous donor. Any views, findings, conclusions, or recommendations expressed in this publication do not necessarily reflect those of the National Endowment for the Humanities.

∞ This volume meets all ANSI/NISO Z39.48–1992 standards for permanence.

Library of Congress Cataloging in Publication Data

Cataloging in Publication data available from the Library of Congress.

ISBN 0-674-00400-0 (v. 1–2)
ISBN 0-674-00405-1 (v. 3–4)
ISBN 0-674-00406-X (v. 5–6)
ISBN 0-674-01574-6 (v. 7)

This edition of *The Adams Papers*

is sponsored by the MASSACHUSETTS HISTORICAL SOCIETY

to which the ADAMS MANUSCRIPT TRUST

by a deed of gift dated 4 April 1956

gave ultimate custody of the personal and public papers

written, accumulated, and preserved over a span of three centuries

by the Adams family of Massachusetts

The Adams Papers

The acorn and oakleaf device on the preceding page is redrawn from a seal cut for John Quincy Adams after 1830. The motto is from Cæcilius Statius as quoted by Cicero in the First Tusculan Disputation: *Serit arbores quæ alteri seculo prosint* ("He plants trees for the benefit of later generations").

Contents

Descriptive List of Illustrations

John Adams first met Dr. Joseph Warren (1741–1775) in April 1764 when Warren inoculated him against smallpox. The two became friends as they worked together for independence, though Warren took a more radical stand than Adams. Warren made his mark with orations on the 1772 and 1775 anniversaries of the Boston Massacre and was responsible for dispatching Paul Revere and William Dawes on their nighttime rides of 18 April 1775. As a general in the Continental Army, Warren dodged enemy fire on 17 June 1775 to join American troops in the Battle of Bunker Hill. During the conflict he was killed by a musket ball to the head. British soldiers buried his body on the battlefield, but it was later exhumed and interred under King's Chapel (John Adams to Abigail Smith, [*13 April 1764*], and note 2, vol. 1:28, 29; *Sibley's Harvard Graduates*, 14:513, 515–516, 519–520, 525–526).

John Trumbull (1756–1843), the son of Connecticut governor Jonathan Trumbull, was a nineteen-year-old adjutant in the First Regiment of the Connecticut militia when he witnessed the battle from a post five miles away on the Roxbury Heights. A few miles to the southeast on Penn's Hill in Braintree, Abigail Adams and seven-year-old John Quincy Adams also watched the Charlestown engagement. The next day, Abigail wrote to her husband in Philadelphia to lament the death of Warren on "perhaps the decisive Day . . . on which the fate of America depends" (Abigail Adams to John Adams, 18 June 1775, and note 3, vol. 1:222, 223–224; *Sibley's Harvard Graduates*, 18:331, 334; Theodore Sizer, ed., *The Autobiography of Colonel John Trumbull: Patriot-Artist, 1756–1843*, N.Y., 1970, p. 17–19).

The young officer on Roxbury duty would pursue a postwar career as an artist, apprenticed to Benjamin West. Trumbull completed his *Death of General Warren at the Battle of Bunker's Hill* in early 1786 in London. Upon seeing it, Abigail wrote that "my Blood Shiverd," while Abigail 2d told her brother that "it is enough to make ones hair to stand on End" (Abigail Adams to Elizabeth Smith Shaw, 4 March 1786; Abigail Adams 2d to John Quincy Adams, 22 Jan. 1786, both below).

English artisans refused to engrave *Death of General Warren* because it glorified an American victory, so Trumbull, with the help of John Adams and Thomas Jefferson, produced an engraving on the Continent. Probably because the work's theme offended English sensibilities, the engraving was a commercial failure. Two copies of the print now hang in the Adams family "Old House" at the Adams National Historical Park, gifts from the artist to John Quincy in 1826 (Theodore Sizer, *The Works of Colonel John Trumbull: Artist of the American Revolution*, rev. edn., New Haven, Conn., 1967, fig. 145; Jefferson, *Papers*, 10:250).

Courtesy of the Yale University Art Gallery Trumbull Collection.

2. PLAYBILL FOR GEN. JOHN BURGOYNE'S *THE HEIRESS* 23

John Burgoyne (1722–1792) was a 62-year-old retired general of the British Army seven years removed from his defeat at Saratoga when he began writing *The Heiress* on a Lancashire retreat in 1784. The play debuted as an anonymous work on 14 January 1786 at the Drury Lane Theatre, though as Abigail Adams 2d suggested a week later, the London press was already reporting that it was "said to be written by Genl Burgoine" (to John Quincy Adams, 22 Jan. 1786, below). After the drama made an impressive debut, Burgoyne revealed his authorship despite the risk that—as he told a friend—"the change of my design will be imputed to vanity" (quoted in James Lunt, *John Burgoyne of Saratoga*, N.Y., 1975, p. 323–324).

While two earlier dramas by Burgoyne had enjoyed modest success, *The Heiress* played an outstanding initial run of 31 nights and returned to the stage the following season. Based in part on Denis Diderot's *Le Père de Famille*, Burgoyne's comedy of manners contrasts the conceited and wealthy Miss Alscrip with the graceful and poor Miss Alton. Miss Alscrip is set to inherit a fortune, but through a series of comedic turns Miss Alton is revealed as the true heiress. The revelation allows the refined Lord Gayville to marry his true love, Miss Alton, rather than the coarse Miss Alscrip to whom he was formerly engaged. An element of the play's initial success was the presence of popular actors Thomas King and Elizabeth Farren in leading roles. At his death in 1792, Burgoyne's obituary gave equal billing to his career as a playwright and his military accomplishments, noting especially his "much celebrated comedy," *The Heiress* (Lunt, *Burgoyne of Saratoga*, p. 324–325, 327; Gerald Howson, *Burgoyne of Saratoga: A Biography*, N.Y., 1979, p. 282–284; E. Cobham Brewer, *The Reader's Handbook*, rev. edn., London, 1902, p. 409).

Courtesy of the University of Bristol Theatre Collection, England.

3. ABIGAIL BROMFIELD ROGERS, BY JOHN SINGLETON COPLEY, 1786 38

When Abigail Adams 2d visited the London studio of artist John Singleton Copley in February 1786, she found Abigail Bromfield Rogers (1753–1791) sitting for a portrait (Abigail Adams 2d to John Quincy Adams, 9 Feb. 1786, below). A stunning image was taking form on Copley's canvas, where the 32-year-old Rogers was depicted against a dramatic landscape and sky as a lady promenading in a flowing satin dress trimmed with lace, complemented by an oversized hat bedecked with ribbons and ostrich plumes. (Frank W. Bayley, *A Sketch of the Life and a List of Some of the Works of John Singleton Copley*, Boston, 1910, p. 84).

Abigail Bromfield Rogers was the daughter of Henry Bromfield, a merchant of Boston and London. Abigail's mother, Margaret Fayerweather Bromfield, died of smallpox when her daughter was eight years old, and a year later Abigail's father married Hannah Clarke of Boston. In 1769 Hannah Clarke's sister married John Singleton Copley. Thus, the painter of the London portrait was the step-uncle of his subject (Daniel Denison Slade, "The Bromfield Family," *NEHGR*, 26[1872]:38–39; John B. Carney, "In Search of Fayerweather: The Fayerweather Family of Boston," *NEHGR*, 145[1991]:66–67; Martha Babcock Amory, *The Domestic and Artistic Life of John Singleton Copley*, Boston, 1882, p. 20).

Abigail Bromfield married Boston merchant Daniel Denison Rogers on 15 October 1781. John and Abigail Adams and the Rogerses were acquainted with each other before the Rogers family moved from Boston to Europe in 1782. During their time together in London, the couples became intimate friends. The Copleys moved in the same circle and became especially close to Abigail Bromfield Rogers during a 1785 scarlet-fever epidemic when Rogers took care of three of the Copleys' children while the parents nursed two others, both of whom eventually died ("Genealogical Memoir of the Family of Rev. Nathaniel Rogers," *NEHGR*, 5[1851]:330; *NEHGR*, 145[1991]:67; Abigail Adams to John Adams, 17 July 1782, and note 1, vol. 4:343, 348; Amory, *Domestic and Artistic Life*, p. 106–107; Abigail Adams 2d to John Quincy Adams, 22 Jan. 1786, and note 47, below).

The Adamses were saddened by the Rogerses' departure for America shortly after Abigail Bromfield Rogers sat for her portrait. "He is a worthy Man, and she one of the best and most amiable of women," Abigail Adams wrote to Mary Smith Cranch. "There is not an other family who could have left London that I should have so much mist, go and See her my sister when she arrives. You will find her one of those gentle Spirits in whom very little alteration is necessary to fit for the world of Spirits, and her Husband seems to be made on purpose for her" (21 March 1786, below).

Courtesy of the Fogg Art Museum, Harvard University Art Museums. Gift of Paul C. Cabot, Treasurer of Harvard University, 1948–1965, and Mrs. Cabot.

4. "WIFE & NO WIFE — OR — A TRIP TO THE CONTINENT," BY JAMES GILLRAY, 1786 69

On a 1784 ramble in the park, a 21-year-old Prince of Wales sighted a 27-year-old Maria Anne Smythe Weld Fitzherbert riding in her carriage. The prince was immediately infatuated and initiated a pursuit of Fitzherbert, which in the coming years would rock the monarchy and supply ample fodder for newspaper printers and caricaturists alike.

The daughter of Royalist Roman Catholic parents, Fitzherbert (1756–1837) had already been twice widowed by the age of 24. When she arrived on the London scene in March 1784, she immediately drew the attention of the city's elite bachelors—among them the future George IV of England. Fitzherbert was unmoved by the ardent pursuit of the prince. In desperation he stabbed himself, prompting her to flee to the Continent. He pursued her there and successfully pressed his case. In December 1785 the couple signed a letter of marriage in a secret ceremony in the bride's drawing room. The prince then shocked the royal family and the public by beginning to treat Fitzherbert as his wife, violating protocol by not seeking the king's permission and possibly forfeiting his crown, as specified in the Act of Settlement, by marrying a Roman Catholic.

Caricaturists soon joined the fray, and James Gillray's "Wife & No Wife" appeared on 27 March. In addition to depicting a cartoonish prince and his bride, Gillray drew in Lord Frederick North asleep in the guise of a coachman and Edmund Burke marrying the couple in the robes of a Jesuit. Charles James Fox is shown giving away the bride, holding her wrist as the prince places a ring on her finger. Fox became deeply embroiled in the "Fitzherbert follies" in April 1787 when he announced in the House of Commons, after a false assurance by the prince, that no marriage ceremony had ever taken place. Fitzherbert remained at court living openly with the prince even after his marriage to Caroline of Brunswick in 1795, only retiring to Brighton after a final falling-out with the prince in 1803 (Shane Leslie, *Mrs. Fitzherbert: A Life Chiefly from Unpublished Sources*, London, 1939, p. 1, 3, 12, 15, 16–17, 19–20, 64; Mary Dorothy George, *Catalogue of the Political and Personal Satires Preserved in the Department of Prints and Drawings in the British Museum*, 11 vols. in 12, London, 1938, 6:293; Stanley Ayling, *George the Third*, N.Y., 1972, p. 317, 341; *DNB*).

Courtesy of the National Portrait Gallery, London.

5. COL. WILLIAM STEPHENS SMITH, BY MATHER BROWN, 1786 219

When Col. William Stephens Smith (1755–1816) introduced himself to Abigail Adams in May 1785 as the secretary to the American legation in London, she thought him "a Modest worthy Man." The 29-year-old decorated veteran of the Revolution took an immediate interest in her daughter, Abigail Adams 2d, who at the age of nineteen was nearing the end of a troubled engagement to Royall Tyler. By the middle of the summer, the senior Abigail hinted to Smith that her daughter's engagement might be broken, and Smith withdrew for a tour of Prussia. Abigail 2d dismissed Tyler in August, and in December Smith returned to initiate a courtship. To the great happiness of all the Adamses, the couple wed on 11 June 1786 (Abigail Adams to Thomas Jefferson, 6 June 1785, vol. 6:170; vol. 5:xxxviii–xxxix; Abigail Adams to Mary Smith Cranch, 13 June 1786, and note 4, below).

Smith was the son of a wealthy New York merchant and graduated from the College of New Jersey (Princeton) in 1774. During the Revolution, he rose through the ranks, serving with distinction at Harlem Heights, Throgs Neck, and Trenton. As an aide to George Washington, he supervised the 1783 British evacuation of New York. In the spring of 1785, Congress appointed him to the

London diplomatic post, and he arrived in the city one day before the Adamses arrived from Auteuil on 26 May (*DAB*; vol. 5:xxxix; vol. 6:172–173).

In the summer of 1785 the Adamses sat for portraits by artist Mather Brown, an American studying in the London studio of Benjamin West. Abigail 2d was particularly pleased with the one of herself, describing it to John Quincy as "a very tasty picture." After Abigail 2d and Smith married, Smith sat for a companion portrait to that of his wife. Both paintings now belong to the Adams National Historical Park (Dorinda Evans, *Mather Brown: Early American Artist in England*, Middletown, Conn., 1982, p. 195, 228–229; Abigail Adams 2d to John Quincy Adams, 4 July 1785, and note 29, vol. 6:216, 222).

Courtesy of the United States Department of the Interior, National Park Service, Adams National Historical Park, Quincy, Massachusetts.

6. "VIEW OF THE BRIDGE OVER CHARLES RIVER," 1789 226

As early as 1713 Bostonians had mulled the construction of a bridge between Boston and Charlestown to replace the ferry that had operated since 1630. The opposition of Harvard College (which owned the ferry) and the difficulty of building a span strong enough to withstand tidal currents and ice floes thwarted plans until 1785 when the legislature approved a charter for the Charles River Bridge Company. The company consisted of 87 shareholders, including John Hancock, Thomas Russell, and Nathaniel Gorham. The shareholders agreed to assume the costs and risks of construction in exchange for the right to collect tolls for forty years (a term later extended to seventy years).

Construction was begun in the spring of 1785 and completed in thirteen months. The bridge was a marvel of eighteenth-century engineering. Seventy-five oak columns supported a span 1,503 feet long and 42 feet wide. A thirty-foot-wide drawbridge in the middle could be raised by two men, and lamps illuminated walkways along each rail. The bridge eliminated what had been an eight-mile detour to Brookline and was put into immediate use by pedestrians, coaches, wagons, and cattle-drivers. In the first four days alone, 500 vehicles and horses passed through the gates, paying tolls ranging from three pence to a shilling. Interest in the bridge was still strong in September 1789 when the illustration reproduced here appeared in *Massachusetts Magazine* (1:533).

The opening of the new bridge was timed to coincide with the eleventh anniversary of the Battle of Bunker Hill on 17 June 1786 and was a grand event. Dignitaries paraded with artisans who had built the span and attended a banquet on the site of the battle. "I never saw such a vast crowd of people in my life, they poured in from every part of the country," Lucy Cranch wrote her aunt Abigail Adams in London. "The Bridge looks beautifully in the evening, there are 40 lamps on it." John Quincy Adams took a different view of the celebrations, refusing to attend what he considered an affront to the memory of the fallen. "I do not think this was a proper place for revelling and feasting," he wrote his sister. "The idea of being seated upon the bones of a friend, I should think would have disgusted many" (Lucy Cranch to Abigail Adams, 24 June 1786; John Quincy Adams to Abigail Adams 2d, 18 May 1786, both below).

Shareholders of the Charles River Bridge Company realized enormous returns. At the end of four decades, initial investments of £100 (about $333) returned profits of $7,000. The company enjoyed a monopoly until 1828 when the legislature voted to build another bridge despite the promise of exclusivity in the 1785 charter. The company litigated the matter in federal court, and a landmark decision by the U.S. Supreme Court affirmed the state's right to disregard the previous decree due to an overriding public interest (Stanley I. Kutler, *Privilege and Creative Destruction: The Charles River Bridge Case*, N.Y., 1971, 1–3, 6–13; *Boston Gazette*, 26 June 1786; Boston *Independent Chronicle*, 22 June 1786).

Courtesy of the Massachusetts Historical Society.

7. "THE BOSOM FRIENDS," 1786 260

"This is the Season of the Year in which London is a desert, even fashion languishes," Abigail Adams wrote to Elizabeth Cranch on 18 July. "I however inclose you a Print of the Bosom Friends. When an object is to be ridiculed, tis generally exagerated. The print however does not greatly exceed some of the most fashionable Dames."

The caricature Abigail enclosed was published by Samuel W. Fores on 28 May and depicted a trio of London women with the exaggerated profiles that marked the silhouette of the day. The "pouter pigeon" look was a short-lived trend of a fashion era known for its constantly changing designs. Also depicted are oversized hairdressings, a longer-lived and more frequently lampooned fashion element of the era (Mary Dorothy George, *Catalogue of Political and Personal Satires Preserved in the Department of Prints and Drawings in the British Museum*, London, 1938, 6:380–381; Diana Donald, *The Age of Caricature: Satirical Prints in the Reign of George III*, New Haven, Conn., 1996, p. 87, 90).

The reign of George III is rightly called the Age of Caricature, and fashion and culture were popular subjects. In addition to providing entertainment and warning women on what looks to avoid, caricatures were moral statements about the excesses of fashion. An underlying theme of condemnation was not lost on Abigail Adams, who told Elizabeth Cranch that Americans should not emulate the women of London. "Pray does the fashion of Merry *thoughts*, *Bustles* and *protuberances* prevail with you," Abigail wrote. "I really think the English more ridiculous than the French in this respect. They import their fashions from them; but in order to give them the mode Anglois, they divest them both of taste and Elegance. Our fair Country women would do well to establish fashions of their own; let Modesty be the first, ingredient, neatness the second and Economy the third. Then they cannot fail of being Lovely without the aid of olympian dew, or Parissian Rouge" (Donald, *The Age of Caricature*, p. 85–86, 89, 93; Abigail Adams to Elizabeth Cranch, 18 July 1786, below).

Courtesy of the Trustees of the Baker Baker Estate and Durham University Library, England.

8. "MARGARET NICHOLSON ATTEMPTING TO ASSASSINATE HIS MAJESTY KING GEORGE III," 1786 301

Margaret Nicholson, a delusional 36-year-old daughter of a Durham barber, approached George III as he stepped down from his carriage at St. James' Palace on 2 August. She carried a rolled document that appeared to be a petition, but when she was within reach she attempted to stab the king with an ivory-handled dessert knife. The knife broke on her second thrust, and the king escaped with only slight damage to his waistcoat (*DNB*).

"She was immediately taken," Abigail Adams 2d reported in a letter to John Quincy Adams later that day. "His Majesty tis said desired she might not be Hurt as he was not injurd. This request prevented her being torn in peices by the Guards and she was taken into Custody and is said to be Insane. . . . She has since been examined, and is to be tried in a few days. It is Supposd She will be Confind in a priests Mad House for Life." Nicholson was examined by the Privy Council, declared insane, and committed to Bethlehem (Bedlam) Hospital, where she resided until her death in 1828. William Stephens Smith reported to the Adamses on 8 August that "Margaret Nicholson is still in confinement and furnishes Paragraphs and Prints," one of which, published by Carington Bowles, is reproduced here (*DNB*; Abigail Adams Smith to John Quincy Adams, 27 July 1786; William Stephens Smith to John and Abigail Adams, 8 Aug. 1786, both below).

While the king was unruffled by the attack, Queen Charlotte and the couple's children were overcome. "It was an evening of grief and horror to his family," a contemporary observer wrote. "Nothing was listened to, scarce a word was spoken; the Princesses wept continually; the Queen, still more deeply struck, could only, from time to time, hold out her hand to the King, and say, 'I have you yet!'" The public was equally moved and crowded the royal family's carriage shouting huzzas when the king and queen toured Kew Gardens on 8 August. "I shall always love little Kew for this," Queen Charlotte reportedly told her husband (Christopher Hibbert, *George III: A Personal History*, N.Y., 1998, p. 227; John Brooke, *King George III*, N.Y., 1972, p. 315).

Courtesy of the National Portrait Gallery, London.

9. THE AMSTERDAM EXCHANGE, BY HERMANUS PETRUS SCHOUTEN, 1783 337

"The exchange is a large Square surrounded with piazza," Abigail Adams wrote to Mary Smith Cranch after she was taken by a friend to see the financial center of Amsterdam. "Here from 12 till two oclock, all and every person who has buisness of any kind to transact meet here, sure of finding the person he wants, and it is not unusal to see ten thousand persons collected at once. I was in a Chamber above the exchange, the Buz from below was like the Swarming of Bees" (12 Sept. 1786, below).

When Abigail visited the Exchange, or Bourse, in August 1786 it was almost two centuries old and a hub of the commerce of the city, region, and continent. Amsterdam commissioned architect Hendrick de Keyser to construct the building in 1608, sending him first to London to study the design of the stock exchange there. De Keyser built an open-air courtyard surrounded by a Mannerist Flemish colonnade and accented with a clock tower that chimed the opening and closing of trading. Shops filled the second level. The Amstel River flowed beneath the building through five stone arches high enough to permit the passage of boats.

By 1835 the crowding that Abigail described had overwhelmed the De Keyser building, and it was replaced with a structure designed by Jan David Zocher. That too proved inadequate and was replaced in 1903 by the present exchange of Hendrik Petrus Berlage. The Berlage building, now a concert hall, featured brick, iron, stained glass, and ornamental scuplture and exerted a strong influence on architectural design in Amsterdam in the early twentieth century (Knopf Guides, *Amsterdam*, N.Y., 1993, p. 132–133; Geert Mak, *Amsterdam*, translated by Philipp Blom, Cambridge, Mass., 2000, p. 102).

Hermanus Petrus Schouten (1747–1822) sketched the De Keyser exchange three years before Abigail's visit. Schouten, a Dutch draftsman of German ancestry, was a leading producer of topographical drawings of Amsterdam during the 1780s and 1790s. His detailed and precise drawings of the city's buildings and streets reflected his esteem for the seventeenth-century painter Jan van der Heyden (Ton Geerts, "Hermanus Petrus Schouten," *The Dictionary of Art*, ed. Jane Turner, N.Y., 1996, 28:166–167).

Courtesy of the Municipal Archives of Amsterdam, Netherlands.

10. THE ROYAL CRESCENT, BATH, BY THOMAS MALTON JR., 1777 449

"What I think the beauty of Bath; is the Cressent," Abigail Adams wrote her sister after visiting the city in early 1787. "The front consists of a range of Ionic Colums on a rustick basement. The Ground falls gradually before it, down to the River Avon about half a miles distance, and the rising Country on the other side of the River holds up to it a most delightfull prospect. The Cressent takes its name from the form in which the houses Stand; all of which join. There is a parade and street before them a hundred foot wide and nothing in front to obstruct this Beautifull prospect" (Abigail Adams to Mary Smith Cranch, 20 Jan. 1787, below).

The majestic 500-foot curved Royal Crescent is considered one of the great pieces of eighteenth-century architecture. Built between 1766 and 1774 by John Wood the Younger, the thirty attached private houses stand fifty feet high and are faced with 114 columns. The houses were built one at a time and sweep in a near-perfect arc. While the nearby Circus of John Wood the Elder was the crowning achievement of a period of architectural development that preceded the Seven Years' War, his son's Royal Crescent represents the pinnacle of a second period of expansion during the 1760s and 1770s. The buildings became the centerpieces of Bath's Upper Town, a new city center to the north of the original city. The architectural renaissance of the eighteenth century paralleled a cultural rebirth that saw Bath transformed from a traditional walled town to a fashionable resort for wealthy nobles and heads of state (James Crathorne, *The Royal Crescent Book of Bath*, London, 1998, p. 74, 75, 77; Barry Cunliffe, *The City of Bath*, New Haven, Conn., 1986, p. 134; David Gadd, *Georgian Summer: Bath in the Eighteenth Century*, Bath, 1971, p. 83–85, 104).

The Royal Crescent appears frequently in English fiction. Baroness Emmuska Orczy had her fictional Scarlet Pimpernel reside in the Royal Crescent no. 16, and Charles Dickens had Mr. Pickwick stay in a Royal Crescent townhouse in *The Pickwick Papers*. The building also appears in the works of Jane Austen and Henry Fielding (Crathorne, *Royal Crescent Book of Bath*, p. 81).

Courtesy of the Victoria Art Gallery, Bath and North East Somerset Council, Bath, England, and Bridgeman Art Library.

Introduction

Continuing the saga of the Adams family, volume 7 of the *Adams Family Correspondence* covers the period between January 1786 and February 1787, during which time John, Abigail, and their daughter Abigail 2d (Nabby) resided in London, while John Quincy, Charles, and Thomas Boylston pursued studies at Harvard College in Massachusetts. The ongoing separation of the family was becoming increasingly difficult for all of them but led to a particularly rich correspondence revealing the Adamses' perspectives on both intimate family matters and major national and world events. In nearly 200 letters sent back and forth over a mere fourteen months, the Adamses discussed births and deaths, marriages and schooling, literature and theater, the intricacies of international politics in Europe and the complexities of domestic life in Braintree—whatever was on the mind of various immediate and extended family members.

As in previous volumes, Abigail Adams remains the central figure in this set of correspondence. Nearly three-quarters of the letters are either to or from Abigail—68 from her and another 67 to her. A substantial portion of those were between Abigail and her sisters, Mary Smith Cranch and Elizabeth Smith Shaw, to whom she conveyed her most intimate and unguarded thoughts, believing, as she wrote to her son, that "never was there a stronger affection than that which binds in a threefold cord your Mamma and her dear sisters. Heaven preserve us to each other for many Years to come."[1] The sisters, having shared experiences as wives and mothers, could write to one another in ways they could not to children or spouses. During this period when John and Abigail were only rarely separated and consequently not writing letters to one another, the relationships among the three sisters provide the central core of the family correspondence.

Abigail maintained copious communications with numerous other friends and family beyond her sisters, a labor she sometimes found burdensome: "I dare not reckon the Number I have to write; least I should feel discouraged in the attempt." Although maintain-

[1] AA to JQA, 16 Feb. 1786, below.

ing such a large correspondence was time consuming, she still took care to revise her letters substantially in both content and style, as extant drafts demonstrate. Abigail even used her insomnia to advantage in pursuing such an active letter-writing life: two nights after her daughter's wedding, unable to sleep, she sat up at "four oclock morg" to write her sister news of the event.[2]

But Abigail is by no means the only family correspondent represented in these pages. Abigail 2d and John Quincy continued to write their "journal-letters" to one another, adding paragraphs day by day in diary fashion as they chronicled their activities in London and Cambridge, respectively. John Adams also participated in the family correspondence, of course, but his public letter-writing, along with work on his three-volume *A Defence of the Constitutions* toward the end of 1786, distracted him from family matters and significantly reduced the total number of letters he wrote to the family in this period. Still, he managed to find time to write occasionally to his children, to his brother-in-law Richard Cranch, to Abigail's uncle Cotton Tufts, and, of course, to Abigail during the brief periods when travel separated them.

1. THE ADAMSES IN LONDON

Since 1785, John, Abigail, and Abigail 2d had lived in London while John served as the United States' minister plenipotentiary to Great Britain. At the same time, John, along with Thomas Jefferson, had been commissioned to negotiate commercial treaties for the United States with a number of different countries, including Portugal, Prussia, and the Barbary States, not to mention Britain itself. The job of negotiating a commercial treaty with the British was thankless. John received little support from the moribund Continental Congress and had few indications that any progress was likely, particularly given the United States' own reluctance to live up to the terms of the Treaty of Paris that ended the Revolution. America's failure to pay its debts and respond to loyalist land claims as required by the peace treaty gave Britain ample opportunity to refuse to negotiate until the United States addressed such issues. Furthermore, lingering resentments in the wake of Britain's defeat made John's position uncomfortable in London society. Abigail noted in one letter home that "the Laws of Nations require civility

[2] AA to Lucy Cranch, 20 July 1786; AA to Mary Smith Cranch, 13 June 1786, both below.

towards Publick Ministers. This we receive, but our Country is vilifye'd by every hireling scribler." She went on to describe the snubbing John received from the Royal Academy, which refused to invite him to their annual dinner, contrary to the custom of inviting all foreign ministers. Worse yet, in the wake of Margaret Nicholson's attempted stabbing of George III, Abigail 2d reported to her brother that "it has been observed in the Papers, that Mr Adams left the Kingdom [for the Netherlands] the very day after the attempt was made up on his Majestys Life. These people are below contempt."[3]

Beyond such obvious slights, both Abigail and her daughter found London society superficial and tiring. The endless cycle of visiting and the evening parties of card games and meaningless conversation—an almost ritualized routine—bored them. Even visits with royalty failed to interest them. Describing their attendance at the celebration of the queen's birthday, Abigail 2d mocked her meeting with George III, commenting that she and Abigail "at last got into the room, and situated ourselvs, so that the King spoke to us very soon. He has askd me one question for these three Months—(*do you get out much this weather*) instructive, improving, indeed." Apart from the danger of being "squeezed to death between the post of the door, and half a dozen great Hoops" from ladies' dresses at these social affairs, Nabby found little about them entertaining. The insipid quality of such activities, combined with the social snubs, left Abigail to lament, "Do not laugh at us my dear sister, may you never know what it is to be in the midst of the World, and yet feel alone. Here are we four, and no more. Do you know that company is widely different from Society?"[4]

Still, despite the professional difficulties and the personal distaste for London society, the Adamses made the most of their time in Great Britain, continuing to enjoy the London theater; attending parties and dinners, particularly with other expatriate Americans; and visiting many of Britain's famed estates. They particularly favored travel and used the opportunities caused by lulls in diplomatic activity to see more of Great Britain, both together and separately. In April, John went off with Thomas Jefferson, who was visiting from Paris, to tour English gardens. John's departure marked a milestone for the couple: as Abigail wrote to her sister, "This is the first Tour he has made since I first came abroad, during which time we have lived longer unseperated, than we have ever done before

[3] AA to Charles Storer, 22 May 1786; AA2 to JQA, 27 July 1786, both below.

[4] AA2 to JQA, 9 Feb. [1786]; AA to Mary Smith Cranch, 4 July 1786, both below.

since we were married."[5] Other trips included visits to Windsor Castle and to Thomas Brand Hollis' estate, The Hyde, in Essex.

In August, Abigail and John ventured even further abroad. John had to travel to The Hague to sign the Prussian-American Treaty, and Abigail decided to accompany him. This was Abigail's first and only trip to the Netherlands, the scene of some of John's greatest diplomatic successes. Abigail, as always, had much to say about the entire nation, from its "singular appearance" and bad roads to the monotony of its countryside: "There is a silence and a dead calm which attends travelling through this Country, the objects which present themselves are meadows, Trees, and Canals, Canals Trees, and meadows, such a want of my *dear variety*, that I really believe an English Robber would have animated me." But she also found much to admire, including clean cities and the "politeness and attention" of its people, which she believed exceeded that of all the other places she had visited. Moreover, Abigail used the opportunity of her visit to comment on the United States' relative neglect of its relationship with the Dutch, a particular affront to Abigail given John's central role in creating that friendship.[6]

Besides travel, one major family event did much to break the Adamses' routine in London and dominate the family's correspondence for a time: Nabby's marriage to William Stephens Smith in June. The first child to marry, Abigail 2d had met Smith the previous summer when he became secretary to her father upon their move to London. While Smith apparently quickly developed an affection for Nabby, she was still formally engaged to Royall Tyler at the time. At Abigail's urging, Smith left for Prussia in the summer of 1785 to give Nabby an opportunity to resolve the situation with Tyler, whom she subsequently dismissed because of what the family perceived as his ongoing neglect of Nabby and their relationship. When Smith returned to London in late 1785, the relationship with Nabby blossomed and they became formally engaged.[7]

Despite Abigail 2d's dismissal of Royall Tyler, he remained an important and frequent topic in family letters, especially since he continued to board at the home of Mary and Richard Cranch in Braintree. The lingering insult of his alleged mistreatment of Nabby,

[5] AA to Mary Smith Cranch, 6 April 1786, below.

[6] For AA's descriptions of the Netherlands, see her letters to AA2 of [*11*], 15, and 23 Aug. 1786, and to Mary Smith Cranch of 12 Sept. 1786, all below.

[7] For an extended discussion of the relationship between AA2 and Royall Tyler, see vol. 5:xxiv–xxv, xxxviii–xxxix.

combined with the widespread rumors of his fathering an illegitimate child with Elizabeth Hunt Palmer, made him the source of numerous attacks, especially from Mary Cranch, who had always opposed his relationship with Nabby. Even as Cranch claimed to be indifferent to Tyler and glad to have the family rid of him, she continued to write about him at great length, attacking both his unfaithfulness to Nabby and his overall character.[8]

Abigail too criticized Tyler, though she clearly felt more ambivalence about him than Mary Cranch did, generally condemning his behavior but not necessarily his whole character. She wrote to Charles Storer (another would-be suitor of Nabby's) about Tyler: "I wish the Gentleman well. He has good qualities, indeed he has, but he ever was his own Enemy." Abigail was more concerned with Nabby's character and with assuring her family that Nabby had acted with the utmost propriety in becoming engaged again so quickly after her dismissal of Tyler. Relieved by John Quincy's indication that Nabby's "conduct meets the approbation of her Friends" back in Massachusetts, Abigail turned her focus to praising Nabby's new beau, who she believed "possesst all those qualifications necessary to make a faithfull and agreeable companion."[9]

Abigail found her daughter's marriage a mixed blessing: She was pleased with Nabby's choice for a husband, describing him as "a Gentleman esteemed by all who know him, and equally beloved by his Friends and acquaintance," but distressed by the Smiths' decision to move out of Grosvenor Square and set up house on their own. Lonely in a foreign country, with few intimate friends, Abigail found it hard to be separated from her only daughter, even if by only a few blocks. She noted that "tho they dine with us every day, it feels very Lonesome I assure you." John too struggled with this transition; as Abigail reported, "The morning after they went to housekeeping Mr Adams went into his Libriary after Breakfast, and I into my chamber where I usually spend my forenoons. Mr A commonly takes his daily walk about one oclock, but by eleven he came into my room with his Hat and cane, 'and a Well I have been to See them: what said I could not you stay till your usual Hour, no I could

[8] Nearly all of Mary Smith Cranch's letters to AA contain some reference to Tyler with varying degrees of vitriol. See, for example, those of 9 Feb. 1786, 22 March 1786, [21] May 1786, and 2 July 1786, all below. For the charge of an affair between Tyler and Elizabeth Hunt Palmer, see Mary Smith Cranch to AA, 24 Sept. 1786, and 8 and 9 Oct. 1786, all below.

[9] AA to Charles Storer, 22 May 1786; AA to JQA, 16 Feb. 1786, both below. For an extended discussion of the development of AA2's relationship with WSS from her mother's perspective, see AA to Mary Smith Cranch, 13 June 1786, below.

not he replied, I wanted to go before Breakfast.'"[10] Equally distressing to Abigail and John was the prospect of a more distant, permanent separation when both the Adamses and the Smiths returned to the United States. In all likelihood, the Smiths would go back to William's home state of New York, while John and Abigail planned to return to their native Massachusetts.

Abigail 2d herself is relatively silent on her engagement, hinting at it only obliquely in letters to her brother, though the crucial letter in which she announced her engagement to John Quincy has apparently been lost. Always more circumspect than her mother in writing about herself, Nabby characteristically gives only brief comments on her new status, though she does describe herself as "perfectly Contented." By fall, Nabby was pregnant with the Adamses' first grandchild, born in early April 1787, and Abigail was deeply engrossed in preparations for the event. She informed her sister that "we have advised col Smith to give up his House and return here again, as it will be vastly inconvenient to me to have her out of the family, no sister no cousin no Aunt who could be at all with her."[11] Her regret that her sisters and nieces were unavailable to help with preparations speaks to the communal nature of childbirth at the time and further highlights the isolation and lack of close female companionship Abigail felt in London.

By early 1787, the Adamses spoke frequently of returning to the United States within the year. The lengthy silences from the Continental Congress had grated for many months, and in January, John sent formal notice to that body of his intentions to come home. At the same time, Abigail openly speculated to her sisters about the timing of her return.[12] After three years in Europe, whatever excitement or novelty she had found from travel abroad had clearly ended. She had been given ample opportunity to compare Europe and America—a subject she took to heart and frequently dwelled on in her letters—and she found Europe wanting. Abigail longed for home, even as she dreaded a possible separation from daughter Nabby, especially with the birth of her first grandchild impending. What would make that separation bearable for John and Abigail, however, was their reunion with John Quincy, Charles, and Thomas Boylston.

[10] AA to Mary Smith Cranch, 13 June 1786 and 4 July 1786, both below.

[11] AA2 to Elizabeth Cranch, 18 July 1786; AA to Mary Smith Cranch, 20 Jan. 1787, both below.

[12] JA wrote to Congress on 24 Jan. 1787 (PCC, No. 84, VI, f. 392–395); see AA to Mary Smith Cranch, 25 Feb. 1787, below.

2. THE ADAMSES IN MASSACHUSETTS

Back in Massachusetts, the three Adams sons focused on their education. John Quincy had returned from Europe in May 1785, enduring his own separation from his parents and sister in order that he might attend Harvard. While his years of travel in Europe—including a stint as secretary to Francis Dana, then U.S. minister plenipotentiary in Russia—had amply prepared him for college, John Quincy still felt compelled to devote considerable energy to studying for his entrance examinations to his father's alma mater. Harvard required examination on a set list of books; any other knowledge was irrelevant for admission, so John Quincy threw himself into mastering the appropriate material. His aunt Elizabeth Shaw, with whom he stayed during this period, noted that he would allow nothing "but Sickness or Death to impede his Course" of study. He routinely stayed up until one in the morning working, causing Shaw to worry that he might damage his health from excessive reading. Fortunately, he passed his examinations without incident in March 1786, moved to Cambridge, and began his Harvard career, joining his brother Charles, who was already attending the school.[13]

Once accepted at Harvard, John Quincy found the school something of a disappointment. His busy schedule included a mix of lectures by professors and recitations to tutors by the students in an array of traditional liberal arts subjects, interspersed with studying and preparation for the next round of classes. The "sameness" of his routine frustrated him: "like a horse in a mill, I am going continually the same round." He also complained about the quality of his professors, many of whom he deemed pompous, ignorant, or both. Even the president of the college, Joseph Willard, did not emerge unscathed from John Quincy's sharp pen: "The reputation of the President is that of a man of great learning, without partiality in favor of any scholars in particular . . . but he has very little knowledge of mankind, and is consequently exceedingly stiff and pedantic, and has made himself ridiculous at times." Many of the tutors, usually young bachelors and themselves recent graduates from Harvard, had the difficult task of teaching material they had learned only recently. Nonetheless, despite his misgivings and complaints, John Quincy found that "all in all, I am strongly confirmed, in your Opin-

[13] Elizabeth Smith Shaw to AA, 2 Jan. 1786; Mary Smith Cranch to AA, 9 Feb. 1786; and JQA to AA2, 15 March 1786, all below.

ion, that this University is upon a much better plan, than any I have seen in Europe."[14]

As in previous volumes of the *Family Correspondence*, the two younger Adams sons play only a limited role. No extant letters from either Charles or Thomas Boylston exist for this period, though references in Abigail's and John's letters clearly indicate that they were writing to their parents in London, at least occasionally. The editors can only speculate as to why those letters have been lost, when the family preserved most other correspondence from these years. It seems unlikely that Abigail or John would have separated Charles' and Thomas' letters from the others they kept; the letters of the two younger brothers were more likely lost or destroyed later on, perhaps by Charles Francis Adams in his work editing the family papers in the nineteenth century, or even by John himself after his falling-out with his son Charles in the 1790s.

Furthermore, only five letters *to* either Charles or Thomas for this time frame still exist, all printed below. Here, the possibility of accidental loss is more plausible; neither Thomas nor Charles seems to have held on to his correspondence with the same care as their older brother or parents. Given the lengthy period of separation between parents and children, it is also likely that John and Abigail simply continued to view their two youngest children as just that—children—and consequently were less inclined to confide in them or write to them in the great detail they did to their eldest son and to Abigail's sisters and other adult relatives.

Charles and Thomas do appear somewhat more frequently as the subject of correspondence, particularly in letters from Abigail's sisters, with whom both brothers stayed on various occasions. Elizabeth Shaw and her husband Rev. John Shaw had served as surrogate parents to Thomas since before Abigail's departure for Europe and spoke of him with great warmth and affection, encouraging Abigail and John to feel the same. John Shaw was also Thomas' tutor, preparing him for the admissions examinations, which Thomas successfully completed in the summer of 1786, thus joining his two elder brothers at Harvard. Likewise, the Cranches played host to all three Adams brothers during the various university vacations. Mary Cranch wrote feelingly of her joy at their presence in her home, even if it was only for short periods of time: "I long for their vacancys to commence as much, and I believe more than they do. We

[14] JQA to AA2, 1 April 1786; JQA to AA2, 15 March 1786; and JQA to JA, 2 April 1786, all below. See also JQA to AA2, [25] April 1786 and 18 May 1786, both below.

have a bustling time tis true and have work enough to do to repair the damages of their late session and prepare them for the next, but the chearfulness they infuse is a full compensation for all that is done for them." Between arranging their housing at school and sewing their clothes during the vacations, worrying over their health and chiding them to better behavior, the Cranches and Shaws saw to it that all of the Adams brothers were well cared for within a loving extended family.[15]

3. UNREST IN AMERICA

While the Adams brothers worked relatively peacefully toward their degrees at Harvard, events elsewhere in America were causing considerable turmoil—especially in western Massachusetts, where Shays' Rebellion became the most important event of this time period. A rural protest movement that began as early as 1784 but gained significant momentum by the fall of 1786, Shays' Rebellion was a response by farmers in western Massachusetts to the problem of growing debt. A combination of severe economic depression and sharp increases in taxes by the state of Massachusetts had caused financial difficulties for these people, and the state's General Court only exacerbated the situation by demanding that all taxes be paid in hard currency. Among the demands of those participating in the revolt were lower taxes, paper money, an end to debt foreclosures, court reforms, and lower salaries for public officials in order to reduce state expenses. While it began as a peaceful movement, its failure to achieve any of its goals through petitions and legal means eventually led to armed attempts to prevent courts from sitting. Gov. James Bowdoin responded by sending an army under Gen. Benjamin Lincoln to defend the courts and suppress the rebellion. The army successfully crushed the insurgency in late January 1787.[16]

The Adamses were no supporters of the rebellion and followed the unfolding events with a mix of fear and disgust. Interestingly, of all the Adamses, Abigail reacted the most strongly to Shays' Rebel-

[15] Mary Smith Cranch to AA, [*21*] May 1786, below. For examples of Elizabeth Shaw's and Mary Cranch's attitudes toward CA and TBA, see, for instance, Shaw to AA, 18 March 1786 and 23 July 1786, and Cranch to AA, 9 Feb. 1786 and 14 July 1786, all below.

[16] Numerous book-length histories of Shays' Rebellion have been written over the years, beginning with George Richards Minot, *The History of the Insurrections, in Massachusetts, in the Year MDCCLXXXVI, and the Rebellion Consequent Thereon*, Worcester, Mass., 1788 (rpt. N.Y., 1971). For more recent analysis of the rebellion, see David P. Szatmary, *Shays' Rebellion: The Making of an Agrarian Insurrection*, Amherst, Mass., 1980, and Leonard L. Richards, *Shays's Rebellion: The American Revolution's Final Battle*, Phila., 2002.

lion. She had little patience with a "lawless Banditti" who would oppose Massachusetts' government, arguing that the changes they suggested would "create themselves a Tyrant e'er long." A loyal wife, she reacted furiously to any challenge to the state constitution her husband had so carefully crafted just a few years before. She blamed the increase of debt in Massachusetts and throughout the United States on too much love of luxury, a fundamental misunderstanding on her part of the very real economic difficulties the rebelling farmers faced but a belief not inconsistent with her overarching concern for excessive American debt. Having lived in Britain, Abigail wrote, "I have very different Ideas of the wealth of my Countrymen, to what I had when I left it. Much of that wealth has proved falacious and their debts exceed their property. Economy and industery may retrive their affairs. I know that the Country is capable of great exertions but in order to this, they must curtail their Ideas of Luxery and refinement." She even debated this subject with no less a figure than Thomas Jefferson, who held a much more sanguine view of events: "The spirit of resistance to government is so valuable on certain occasions, that I wish it to be always kept alive. . . . I like a little rebellion now and then. It is like a storm in the Atmosphere." In the end, Abigail remained unswayed by Jefferson's perspective and strongly endorsed a military solution to the rebellion; as the volume closes, she waited impatiently for word from Massachusetts that the danger had passed.[17]

In the end, Shays' Rebellion had little immediate impact on the well-being of the Adams family. The insurgents never reached Cambridge, despite fears they might try to prevent the sitting of the court there, and after their military rout, the rebellion petered out as a force in Massachusetts. But it became symbolic of wider problems with the American political system. Abigail, on the frontlines of diplomatic efforts in Europe, foresaw the increasing danger of a weak central government for the United States. "Do the united States wish to become the Scorn of Europe and the laughing Stock of Nations," she asked, "by withholding from Congress those powers which would enable them to act in concert, and give vigor and strength to their proceedings."[18] She saw firsthand how the ineffectiveness of the Continental Congress limited John's ability to fulfill

[17] AA to Mary Smith Cranch, 25 Feb. 1787; AA to JQA, 22 Nov. 1786; AA to Mary Smith Cranch, 21 May 1786; AA to Thomas Jefferson, 29 Jan. 1787; Thomas Jefferson to AA, 22 Feb. 1787, all below.

[18] AA to JQA, 20 March 1786, below.

his commissions and experienced routinely the difficulties caused by Congress' lack of money and clarity of policy. Her views, of course, were also underscored by her interpretation of Shays' Rebellion. If the United States had had a more coherent economic plan that discouraged excessive consumption, she felt, such a rebellion would never have occurred in the first place. She was not alone. A consensus was slowly emerging on the need for reform of the government in order to insure its ultimate stability and the United States' ability to compete on the world stage. This set the stage for the Constitutional Convention that was due to open in Philadelphia in just a few months' time.

4. NOTES ON EDITORIAL METHOD

The editors of *Adams Family Correspondence* are guided by the editorial principles outlined in the "Notes on Editorial Method" sections of volumes 1 (p. xli–xlviii), 3 (p. xxxvii–xlii), and 5 (p. lviii–lxiii). A few policy changes have been implemented, however, since the publication of volumes 5 and 6.

The most substantial change is one of form. Beginning with the present volume, *Adams Family Correspondence* volumes will no longer be published in pairs. This and each future volume will be an independent entity containing an introduction, a guide to editorial apparatus, a list of omitted documents, a chronology, and an index. The editors believe that readers will find fully complemented volumes easier to use.

The editors continue to select letters for the *Adams Family Correspondence* that explore the thought, reveal the character, and narrate the action of the Adamses in their domestic life. Letters written to and from John and Abigail Adams and their children on domestic matters are generally included. The principle exceptions are letters written to and from John on public matters, even if the correspondents are members of the Adamses' extended family. Those letters are reserved for publication in Series III, *Papers of John Adams*, and are not included in the List of Omitted Documents.

Letters exchanged between relatives outside of the immediate family (including the spouses of John and Abigail's children) are printed here only if they contribute unusual insight into the domestic lives of the Adams family. Such letters are omitted silently. The List of Omitted Documents in each volume includes only letters written to and from John and Abigail and their children on domestic matters that have been omitted because they are routine or repetitive.

The editors continue to rely whenever possible on the recipient's copies of letters as the most reliable source of the texts that actually passed from writer to reader. When recipient's copies are not available, letterbook copies, drafts, transcripts, or published collections are used. Descriptive notes list all forms of each letter considered in collation and describe how each was used in the preparation of the published text.

In some instances, the editors have been fortunate enough to have access both to recipient's copies and to drafts of individual letters. When this has occurred, the two versions have been compared for significant differences in style and content, which are noted in the annotation. More minor differences of style, such as subtle rewording or changes to capitalization, spelling, or punctuation, are not noted. Archival location information for both versions is always provided for readers who wish to examine more closely the differences between them.

Finally, to incorporate a slightly more literal rendering of the text, the following adjustments in editorial policy have been made:

Capitalization of proper names and geographical terms follows that in the manuscript.

Abbreviations and contractions are preserved as found throughout the document unless confusion or misunderstanding may result. The ampersand (&) is retained in the form of &c. (for *etc.*), in the names of firms, and in polite closings; elsewhere it is rendered as *and*.

Punctuation following all abbreviations and contractions is rendered as in the manuscript.

Volume 7 of the *Adams Family Correspondence* contains 189 printed letters and 20 omitted letters chronicling the lives of the Adamses. This material, however, does not stand in isolation. It should be read in conjunction with the comments of John Adams in his *Diary and Autobiography*, 3:181–203, and with the *Diary of John Quincy Adams*, 1:381–415 and 2:1–167, which provides particularly vivid discussion of the months John Quincy spent with the Shaws and his school life at Harvard. Future volumes of the *Papers of John Adams* will also supplement the family correspondence of this period by documenting John Adams' public writings, which highlight his work on various treaty negotiations and his ongoing service as U.S. minister plenipotentiary to Great Britain.

Acknowledgments

This volume of the Adams Papers has been long in production and would never have been completed without the assistance of many more people than those listed on the title page.

Former editors Richard Alan Ryerson and Laura Graham made important contributions to the annotation of the volume, and Jennifer Shea, our former editorial assistant, helped in various ways in the early stages of the book. Assistant editor Jessie M. Rodrique and transcriber Paul Tsimahides, both current members of the Adams Papers staff, provided valuable assistance in the final production of the volume and with indexing. We are also grateful to our intern Emma Hennessey for her work on the project. Ann-Marie Imbornoni copyedited the entire book with grace and precision.

Many people contributed to the research behind this book. We particularly wish to thank Edward B. Doctoroff, Head of Administrative Services Division at Harvard's Widener Library; Stephen Nonack, Head of Reference at the Boston Athenæum; and the reference staffs at Harvard's Houghton and Lamont libraries, Radcliffe's Schlesinger Library, and the Rare Books and Manuscripts Department of the Boston Public Library. In Great Britain, Eric Stockdale graciously did last-minute research for us on newspaper references. Closer to home, Patty Smith of the Adams National Historical Park, Quincy, Mass., assisted us with the illustrations for the volume.

As with previous volumes, Kevin Krugh, Kenneth Krugh, and Steven Lee of Technologies 'N Typography in Merrimac, Mass., did an admirable job typesetting the volume. At Harvard University Press, we thank John Walsh, Assistant Director for Design and Production; Lisa Roberts, Paperback Manager; and Kathleen McDermott, Editor, History and Social Sciences, for all of their assistance with the publication and marketing of the book.

The Massachusetts Historical Society continues to provide this project with the use of its unparalleled collections and the unstinting support of its knowledgeable staff. In particular, we thank William M. Fowler Jr., Director; Peter Drummey, Stephen T. Riley

Librarian; Conrad E. Wright, Worthington C. Ford Editor of Publications; Brenda M. Lawson, Associate Librarian and Curator of Manuscripts; Mary E. Fabiszewski, Senior Cataloger; Kimberly Nusco, Reference Librarian; Megan Milford and Rakashi Khetarpal, Assistant Reference Librarians; Elsa Villanueva, Library Assistant; Jennifer Smith, Photographic Services; Thomas Blake, Digital Projects Production Specialist; Chris Coveney, Information Systems Manager; Christopher A. Carberry, Operations Manager; and James P. Harrison III, Custodian. Finally, we also greatly appreciate the contributions made by the Adams Papers Administrative Committee to the success of this project.

Guide to Editorial Apparatus

The first three sections (1–3) of this Guide list, respectively, the arbitrary devices used for clarifying the text, the code names for designating prominent members of the Adams family, and the symbols describing the various kinds of manuscript originals used or referred to, which are employed throughout *The Adams Papers* in all its series and parts. The final three sections (4–6) list, respectively, only those symbols designating institutions holding original materials, the various abbreviations and conventional terms, and the short titles of books and other works that occur in volume 7 of the *Adams Family Correspondence*.

1. TEXTUAL DEVICES

The following devices will be used throughout *The Adams Papers* to clarify the presentation of the text.

[. . .]	One word missing or illegible.
[. . . .]	Two words missing or illegible.
[. . . .][1]	More than two words missing or illegible; subjoined footnote estimates amount of missing matter.
[ ]	Number or part of a number missing or illegible. Amount of blank space inside brackets approximates the number of missing or illegible digits.
[roman]	Conjectural reading for missing or illegible matter. A question mark is inserted before the closing bracket if the conjectural reading is seriously doubtful.
⟨*italic*⟩	Canceled matter.
[*italic*]	Editorial insertion.
‖roman‖	Text editorially decoded.

2. ADAMS FAMILY CODE NAMES

First Generation

JA	John Adams (1735–1826)
AA	Abigail Adams (1744–1818), *m.* JA 1764

Second Generation

AA2	Abigail Adams (1765–1813), daughter of JA and AA, *m.* WSS 1786
WSS	William Stephens Smith (1755–1816), brother of Mrs. CA
JQA	John Quincy Adams (1767–1848), son of JA and AA
LCA	Louisa Catherine Johnson (1775–1852), *m.* JQA 1797
CA	Charles Adams (1770–1800), son of JA and AA
Mrs. CA	Sarah Smith (1769–1828), sister of WSS, *m.* CA 1795

TBA	Thomas Boylston Adams (1772–1832), son of JA and AA
Mrs. TBA	Ann Harrod (1774?–1845), *m.* TBA 1805

Third Generation

GWA	George Washington Adams (1801–1829), son of JQA and LCA
JA2	John Adams (1803–1834), son of JQA and LCA
Mrs. JA2	Mary Catherine Hellen (1806?–1870), *m.* JA2 1828
CFA	Charles Francis Adams (1807–1886), son of JQA and LCA
ABA	Abigail Brown Brooks (1808–1889), *m.* CFA 1829
ECA	Elizabeth Coombs Adams (1808–1903), daughter of TBA and Mrs. TBA

Fourth Generation

LCA2	Louisa Catherine Adams (1831–1870), daughter of CFA and ABA, *m.* Charles Kuhn 1854
JQA2	John Quincy Adams (1833–1894), son of CFA and ABA
CFA2	Charles Francis Adams (1835–1915), son of CFA and ABA
HA	Henry Adams (1838–1918), son of CFA and ABA
MHA	Marian Hooper (1842–1885), *m.* HA 1872
MA	Mary Adams (1845–1928), daughter of CFA and ABA, *m.* Henry Parker Quincy 1877
BA	Brooks Adams (1848–1927), son of CFA and ABA

Fifth Generation

CFA3	Charles Francis Adams (1866–1954), son of JQA2
HA2	Henry Adams (1875–1951), son of CFA2
JA3	John Adams (1875–1964), son of CFA2

3. DESCRIPTIVE SYMBOLS

The following symbols will be employed throughout *The Adams Papers* to describe or identify in brief form the various kinds of manuscript originals.

D	Diary (Used only to designate a diary written by a member of the Adams family and always in combination with the short form of the writer's name and a serial number, as follows: D/JA/23, i.e., the twenty-third fascicle or volume of John Adams' manuscript Diary.)
Dft	draft
Dupl	duplicate
FC	file copy (Ordinarily a copy of a letter retained by a correspondent *other than an Adams,* for example, Jefferson's press copies and polygraph copies, since all three of the Adams statesmen systematically entered copies of their outgoing letters in letterbooks.)
Lb	Letterbook (Used only to designate Adams letterbooks and always in combination with the short form of the writer's name and a serial number, as follows: Lb/JQA/29, i.e., the twenty-ninth volume of John Quincy Adams' Letterbooks.)
LbC	letterbook copy (Letterbook copies are normally unsigned, but

	any such copy is assumed to be in the hand of the person responsible for the text unless it is otherwise described.)
M	Miscellany (Used only to designate materials in the section of the Adams Papers known as the "Miscellany" and always in combination with the short form of the writer's name and a serial number, as follows: M/CFA/32, i.e., the thirty-second volume of the Charles Francis Adams Miscellany—a ledger volume mainly containing transcripts made by CFA in 1833 of selections from the family papers.)
MS, MSS	manuscript, manuscripts
RC	recipient's copy (A recipient's copy is assumed to be in the hand of the signer unless it is otherwise described.)
Tr	transcript (A copy, handwritten or typewritten, made substantially later than the original or other copies such as duplicates, file copies, or letterbook copies that were made contemporaneously.)
Tripl	triplicate

4. LOCATION SYMBOLS

CSmH	Huntington Library
CtY	Yale University
DLC	Library of Congress
DSI	Smithsonian Institution
ICN	Newberry Library
InU	Indiana University
M-Ar	Massachusetts Archives
MB	Boston Public Library
MH-H	Houghton Library, Harvard University
MHi	Massachusetts Historical Society
MQA	Adams National Historical Park
MSaE	Peabody Essex Museum
MWA	American Antiquarian Society
MiU-C	Clements Library, University of Michigan
NhD	Dartmouth College
NhHi	New Hampshire Historical Society
NjP	Princeton University
NHi	New-York Historical Society
NN	New York Public Library
NNMus	Museum of the City of New York
PHi	Historical Society of Pennsylvania
ViU	University of Virginia

5. OTHER ABBREVIATIONS AND CONVENTIONAL TERMS

Adams Papers

Manuscripts and other materials, 1639–1889, in the Adams Manuscript Trust collection given to the Massachusetts Historical Society in 1956 and enlarged by a few additions of family papers since then. Citations in the present edition are simply by date of the original document if the original is in the main chronological series of the Papers and therefore readily found in the microfilm edition of the Adams Papers (see below).

Adams Papers Editorial Files

Other materials in the Adams Papers editorial office, Massachusetts Historical Society. These include photoduplicated documents (normally cited by the location of the originals), photographs, correspondence, and bibliographical and other aids compiled and accumulated by the editorial staff.

Adams Papers, Adams Office Files

The portion of the Adams manuscripts given to the Massachusetts Historical Society by Thomas Boylston Adams in 1973.

Adams Papers, Microfilms

The corpus of the Adams Papers, 1639–1889, as published on microfilm by the Massachusetts Historical Society, 1954–1959, in 608 reels. Cited in the present work, when necessary, by reel number. Available in research libraries throughout the United States and in a few libraries in Canada, Europe, and New Zealand.

The Adams Papers

The present edition in letterpress, published by The Belknap Press of Harvard University Press. References to earlier volumes of any given unit take this form: vol. 2:146. Since there will be no overall volume numbering for the edition, references from one series, or unit of a series, to another will be by title, volume, and page; for example, JA, *D&A*, 4:205.

PCC

Papers of the Continental Congress. Originals in the National Archives: Record Group 360. Microfilm edition in 204 reels. Usually cited in the present work from the microfilms, but according to the original series and volume numbering devised in the State Department in the early nineteenth century; for example, PCC, No. 93, III, i.e., the third volume of series 93.

PRO

Public Record Office, London.

Thwing Catalogue, MHi

Annie Haven Thwing, comp., Inhabitants and Estates of the Town of Boston, 1630–1800; typed card catalogue, with supplementary bound typescripts, in the Massachusetts Historical Society. Published on CD-ROM with Annie Haven Thwing, *The Crooked and Narrow Streets of Boston 1630–1822*, Massachusetts Historical Society and New England Historical and Genealogical Society, 2001.

6. SHORT TITLES OF WORKS FREQUENTLY CITED

AA, *Letters*, ed. CFA, 1840
Letters of Mrs. Adams, the Wife of John Adams. With an Introductory Memoir by Her Grandson, Charles Francis Adams, Boston, 1840.

AA, *Letters*, ed. CFA, 1848
Letters of Mrs. Adams, the Wife of John Adams. With an Introductory Memoir by Her Grandson, Charles Francis Adams, 4th edn., rev. and enl., Boston, 1848.

AA2, *Jour. and Corr.*
Journal and Correspondence of Miss Adams, Daughter of John Adams, . . . Edited by Her Daughter [Caroline Amelia (Smith) de Windt], New York and London, 1841–[1849]; 3 vols.
Note: Vol. [1], unnumbered, has title and date: *Journal and Correspondence of Miss Adams*, 1841; vol. 2 has title, volume number, and date: *Correspondence of Miss Adams . . . Vol. II,* 1842; vol. [3] has title, volume number, and date: *Correspondence of Miss Adams . . ., Vol. II,* 1842, i.e., same as vol. 2, but preface is signed "April 3d, 1849," and the volume contains as "Part II" a complete reprinting from same type, and with same pagination, of vol. 2 (i.e., "Vol. II"), above, originally issued in 1842.

Adams, *Geneal. History of Henry Adams*
Andrew N. Adams, *A Genealogical History of Henry Adams, of Braintree, Mass., and His Descendants*, Rutland, Vt., 1898; 1 vol. in 2.

AFC
Adams Family Correspondence, ed. L. H. Butterfield, Marc Friedlaender, Richard Alan Ryerson, and others, Cambridge, 1963– .

Amer. Phil. Soc., *Procs.*
American Philosophical Society, *Proceedings of the American Philosophical Society Held at Philadelphia for Promoting Useful Knowledge*, Philadelphia, 1838– .

Appletons' Cyclo. Amer. Biog.
James Grant Wilson and John Fiske, eds., *Appletons' Cyclopædia of American Biography*, New York, 1887–1889; 6 vols.

Billias, *Elbridge Gerry*
George Athan Billias, *Elbridge Gerry: Founding Father and Republican Statesman*, New York, 1976.

Biographia Dramatica
David Erskine Baker and others, eds., *Biographia Dramatica; or, A Companion to the Playhouse*, London, 1764–1812; 3 vols. in 4.

Boston Directory, [year]
Boston Directory, issued annually with varying imprints.

Boston, [vol. no.] *Reports*
City of Boston, *Annual Reports of the Record Commissioner of Boston* [title varies], Boston, 1876–1909; 39 vols.

Braintree Town Records
Records of the Town of Braintree, 1640 to 1793, ed. Samuel A. Bates, Randolph, Mass., 1886.

Cambridge Modern Hist.
The Cambridge Modern History, Cambridge, Eng., 1902–1911; repr. New York, 1969; 13 vols.

Catalogue of JA's Library
Catalogue of the John Adams Library in the Public Library of the City of Boston, Boston, 1917.

CFA, *Diary*
Diary of Charles Francis Adams, ed. Aïda DiPace Donald, David Donald, Marc Friedlaender, L. H. Butterfield, and others, Cambridge, 1964– .

DAB
Allen Johnson and Dumas Malone, eds., *Dictionary of American Biography*, New York, 1928–1936; repr. New York, 1964; 20 vols. plus index and supplements.

Dict. de la noblesse
François Alexandre Aubert de La Chesnaye-Desbois and —— Badier, *Dictionnaire de la noblesse*, Paris, 3d edn., 1863–1876; 19 vols.

Dipl. Corr., 1783–1789
The Diplomatic Correspondence of the United States of America, from . . . 1783, to . . . 1789, [ed. William A. Weaver], repr. edn., Washington, D.C., 1837 [actually 1855]; 3 vols.

DNB
Leslie Stephen and Sidney Lee, eds., *The Dictionary of National Biography*, repr. ed., London, 1959–1960; 22 vols. plus supplements.

Doc. Hist. Ratif. Const.
The Documentary History of the Ratification of the Constitution, ed. Merrill Jensen, John P. Kaminski, Gaspare J. Saladino, and others, Madison, Wis., 1976– .

Essex Inst., *Hist. Colls.*
Historical Collections of the Essex Institute, 1859– .

Evans
Charles Evans and others, comps., *American Bibliography: A Chronological Dictionary of All Books, Pamphlets and Periodical Publications Printed in the United States of America* [1639–1800], Chicago and Worcester, Mass., 1903–1959; 14 vols.

Fleet's Pocket Almanack [year]
A Pocket Almanack for the Year of Our Lord [1780–1801] . . . Calculated Chiefly for the Use of the Commonwealth of Massachusetts . . . To Which Is Annexed, The Massachusetts Register [title varies], Boston: T. and J. Fleet, 1779–1800; 22 vols.

Franklin, *Papers*
The Papers of Benjamin Franklin, ed. Leonard W. Labaree, William B. Willcox, Claude A. Lopez, Barbara B. Oberg, Ellen R. Cohn, and others, New Haven, Conn., 1959– .

Grandmother Tyler's Book
Grandmother Tyler's Book: The Recollections of Mary Palmer Tyler (Mrs. Royall Tyler), 1775–1866, ed. Frederick Tupper and Helen Tyler Brown, New York and London, 1925.

Greene, *Papers*
The Papers of General Nathanael Greene, ed. Richard K. Showman, Dennis Conrad, and others, Chapel Hill, N.C., 1976– .

Harvard Quinquennial Cat.
Harvard University, *Quinquennial Catalogue of the Officers and Graduates 1636–1930*, Cambridge, 1930.

Heitman, *Register Continental Army*
Francis B. Heitman, comp., *Historical Register of Officers of the Continental Army during the War of the Revolution*, new edn., Washington, D.C., 1914.

Hoefer, *Nouv. biog. générale*
Jean Chrétien Ferdinand Hoefer, ed., *Nouvelle biographie générale depuis les temps les plus reculés jusqu'à nos jours*, Paris, 1852–1866; 46 vols.

JA, *D&A*
Diary and Autobiography of John Adams, ed. L. H. Butterfield and others, Cambridge, 1961; 4 vols.

JA, *Defence of the Const.*
John Adams, *A Defence of the Constitutions of Government of the United States of America*, London, 1787–1788; 3 vols.

JA, *Legal Papers*
Legal Papers of John Adams, ed. L. Kinvin Wroth and Hiller B. Zobel, Cambridge, 1965; 3 vols.

JA, *Papers*
Papers of John Adams, ed. Robert J. Taylor, Gregg L. Lint, and others, Cambridge, 1977– .

JA, *Works*
The Works of John Adams, Second President of the United States: with a Life of the Author, ed. Charles Francis Adams, Boston, 1850–1856; 10 vols.

JCC
Journals of the Continental Congress, 1774–1789, ed. Worthington C. Ford and others, Washington, D.C., 1904–1937; 34 vols.

Jefferson, *Papers*
The Papers of Thomas Jefferson, ed. Julian P. Boyd, Charles T. Cullen, John Catanzariti, Barbara B. Oberg, and others, Princeton, N.J., 1950– .

Jefferson's Memorandum Books
Jefferson's Memorandum Books: Accounts, with Legal Records and Miscellany, 1767–1826, ed. James A. Bear Jr. and Lucia C. Stanton (*The Papers of Thomas Jefferson*, Second Series), Princeton, N.J., 1997; 2 vols.

JQA, *Diary*
Diary of John Quincy Adams, ed. David Grayson Allen, Robert J. Taylor, and others, Cambridge, 1981– .

JQA, *Memoirs*
Memoirs of John Quincy Adams, Comprising Portions of His Diary from 1795 to 1848, ed. Charles Francis Adams, Philadelphia, 1874–1877; 12 vols.

London Encyclopædia
Ben Weinreb and Christopher Hibbert, eds., *The London Encyclopædia*, 1983; repr., Bethesda, Md., 1986.

London Past and Present
Henry B. Wheatley, *London Past and Present: Its History, Associations, and Traditions*, London, 1891; 3 vols.

London Stage, 1776–1800
The London Stage, 1660–1800: A Calendar of Plays, Entertainments and Afterpieces Together with Casts, Box-Receipts and Contemporary Comment, Part 5: 1776–1800, ed. Charles Beecher Hogan, Carbondale, Ill., 1968; 3 vols.

Mass., *Acts and Laws*
Acts and Laws of the Commonwealth of Massachusetts [1780–1805], Boston, 1890–1898; 13 vols.

MHS, *Colls.*, *Procs.*
Massachusetts Historical Society, *Collections* and *Proceedings*.

Miller, *Treaties*
Treaties and Other International Acts of the United States of America, ed. Hunter Miller, Washington, D.C., 1931–1948; 8 vols.

Namier and Brooke, *House of Commons*
Sir Lewis Namier and John Brooke, eds., *The House of Commons, 1754–1790*, London, 1964; 3 vols.

NEHGR
New England Historical and Genealogical Register.

OED
The Oxford English Dictionary, 2d ed., Oxford, 1989; 20 vols.

Pattee, *Old Braintree*
William S. Pattee, *A History of Old Braintree and Quincy, with a Sketch of Randolph and Holbrook*, Quincy, Mass., 1878.

PMHB
Pennsylvania Magazine of History and Biography.

Princetonians
James McLachlan, Richard A. Harrison, Ruth L. Woodward, Wesley Frank Craven, and J. Jefferson Looney, *Princetonians: A Biographical Dictionary*, Princeton, N.J., 1976–1991; 5 vols.

Repertorium
Repertorium der diplomatischen Vertreter aller Länder seit dem Westfälischen Frieden (1648), ed. Ludwig Bittner and others, Oldenburg, &c., 1936–1965; 3 vols.

Sabine, *Loyalists*
Lorenzo Sabine, *Biographical Sketches of Loyalists of the American Revolution*, ed. Gregory Palmer, rev. edn., Westport, Conn., 1984.

Sibley's Harvard Graduates
John Langdon Sibley, Clifford K. Shipton, Conrad Edick Wright, Edward W. Hanson, and others, *Biographical Sketches of Graduates of Harvard University, in Cambridge, Massachusetts* [title varies], Cambridge and Boston, 1873– .

Smith, *Letters of Delegates*
Letters of Delegates to Congress, 1774–1789, ed. Paul H. Smith and others, Washington, D.C., 1976–2000; 26 vols.

Sprague, *Annals Amer. Pulpit*
William B. Sprague, *Annals of the American Pulpit; or Commemorative Notices of Distinguished American Clergymen of Various Denominations*, New York, 1857–1869; 9 vols.

Washington, *Diaries*
The Diaries of George Washington, ed. Donald Dean Jackson and Dorothy Twohig, Charlottesville, Va., 1976–1979; 6 vols.

Washington, *Papers, Confederation Series*
The Papers of George Washington: Confederation Series, ed. W. W. Abbot and others, Charlottesville, Va., 1992–1997. 6 vols.

Young, *Night Thoughts*
Edward Young, *The Complaint; or, Night-Thoughts on Life, Death, and Immortality*.

VOLUME 7

Family Correspondence

January 1786 – February 1787

Adams Family Correspondence

Elizabeth Smith Shaw to Abigail Adams

Haverhill Janry. 2d 1786

Yes! My Dear Sister, Mr. and *Mrs Allen* are just gone from here, and carried away my Betsy Smith to tarry a few Days with them.[1]

After sleeping four years, he rose up like a Lion. He kept the Carpenters to work upon his House, till nine Clock at Night, and before the new painted and papered Rooms were really fit to go into, he harnessed two Horses, put them into a Sleigh, and set out on Friday the 9th. of December for Boston.—A Friday you will say was an unlucky Day in our American Calendar.[2] And so it proved to Mr Allen, for by that time he had got to Woburn the Snow had left him, and to her Friends he appeared almost as ridiculous as old Trunian, when he set out upon a like Expedition,[3] for *they* had no Idea of there being any Snow with us.

But small Things will never discourage those who are acting wisely, and are performing what they esteem their Duty in the fullfilling of their Engagments—And it did not dishearten Mr Allen—for upon Sabbath Evening 11th instant, between the Hours of 7. and 8 their marriage Vows were plighted.—The Ceremony was performed by our Friend Mr J. Eliot, at her Brother Austins. Dr Welsh and Lady, Uncle Smiths Family, and some of Mr Austins Relations formed a Circle of about twenty.[4] Mrs Austin made forty weight of excellant Plumb-Cake, and which I was favoured with a nice Piece. But I have distributed it about in so many Parcels for the young Folks to sleep upon, that they might have a sweet peep into Futurity, that I have not even a Crum left to enrich my Letter with, but I dare say the News will be a sweet Morsel to you, who have felt so interested for the Honour, and the Happiness of our Cousin.

A Monday Mr Allen hired a Chaise at Charlestown, tied on the superfluous Horse at the side of the other, and arrived safe at their own House in Bradford eleven Clock in the Evening. I sent for them to keep Thansgiving with me, but it was cold and difficult geting over the River, and Mr Peabody[5] was there and preached for him, so they both chose to keep Thansgiving at Home. And a joyful one it was to her.

Mr Shaw, and I, went over to pay our Respects to them the 16th, and found them quite in the Family Way. Her Furniture was decent and very pretty. Mr Allen appeared very good and kind, and much more tranquil, and easy than I had seen him for some time past. Mrs Allen full of Joy, and Gratitude—And can we my Sister wonder at it.—To be bereaved of our Parents, and to have the place of our nativity laid in Ashes—and to be wholly dependant upon our Sisters, though they may be ever so kind, is not a Situation to be desired.[6] Now she is blessed with a Friend—with a Protector. One who can rejoice with her in Prosperity—and one to whom she can look up, and claim Assistance—"the Temple of his Arms,"[7] even in the most distressing Scenes of Life.

You will excuse my giving you so circumstantial an Account of this Affair, as I know she is a Person you have a great regard for, and have always enquired particularly about her.

Jan. 8th

I have to acknowledge the Receipt of a kind Letter from you dated .[8] By that, I find that your Station is not in every respect agreeable to you. There is hardly anything more humiliating, and mortifying than to be placed in an Office, knowing, and feeling the importance of it, and not be furnished with the Means to maintain its Honour, and Dignity.[9]

As to the News Paper Squibs, I know you rise above them—and stand collected in a consciousness of your own Integrity, though Malice, Pride, and Envy throw these envenomed Darts. [Exal]ted Stations are a Mark for the publick Eye to shoot at—and Addison says, that Censure is a Tax, which a man pays the Publick for being eminent.[10]

I am both grieved, and disappointed that my Cousin Charles cannot spend the Vacation here. I wrote to him to come home in the Sleigh, with White and Walker[11] if it was possible and told him he could not be more welcome at Grosvenor Square, than he would be to our House, though I will allow your feelings might be somewhat keener, were you really to see him there.

I do not doubt but he can be happy at Braintree, yet while his

Brothers are here, he has not got that feeling Heart I have thought him possessed of, if he does not find himself drawn *hither*, by the bands of Relationship, and the still stronger Cords of Love.

It has been suggested, that he might probably hinder his Brother JQA from pursuing his Studies. They need not have feared that, for he is too much *engaged* to suffer any thing but Sickness or Death to impede his Course.

I intend to write to the Doctor,[12] and I hope Mr Shaw, and I shall have the pleasure of seeing the three dear Brothers together again. They are all well—Mr JQA is not quite so fleshy[13] as when he first arrived, he can afford to spare a little Flesh. Mr Shaw received the Treatise upon Education,[14] and desires his most respectful regards may be accepted by Dr Adams for [his] kind remembrance. My Letter must go to[night,] Lyde sails in a Day or two. May this Letter find you, and *Yours* in the enjoyment of Health—and may every revolving Year be crowned with Blessings, ever prays your affectionate Sister

Eliza Shaw

RC (Adams Papers); addressed: "Mrs: A. Adams. Grosvenor Square. London."; endorsed by AA2: "Mrs Shaw jany 2d 1786"; text lost where the seal was removed has been supplied from the Dft (DLC:Shaw Family Papers).

[1] Elizabeth (Betsy) Smith (1771–1854), daughter of AA's brother William Smith Jr., had been staying with her aunt Elizabeth Shaw.

[2] The editors have not determined the meaning of this reference.

[3] Como. Hawser Trunnion, a character in Tobias Smollett's *The Adventures of Peregrine Pickle*, who, though retired, maintained a nautical lifestyle while living on land and navigated the route to his wedding by consulting a compass (E. Cobham Brewer, *The Reader's Handbook*, rev. edn., London, 1902).

[4] Present for the long-awaited marriage of the Rev. Jonathan Allen to Elizabeth Kent, AA's first cousin, were the bride's sisters Anna Kent Austin and Abigail Kent Welsh; their husbands, Nathaniel Austin and Dr. Thomas Welsh; Rev. John Eliot, pastor of the New North Church; and Isaac Smith Sr., the bride's uncle. Smith's family probably included his wife Elizabeth Storer, and their children, William, Elizabeth, and Mary (Mrs. Samuel Alleyne Otis). Isaac Smith Jr., a minister, was in Haverhill, filling in for Rev. John Shaw, who preached for Rev. Allen in Bradford (Thomas Bellows Wyman, *The Genealogies and Estates of Charlestown, 1629–1818*, 2 vols., Boston, 1879, 2:571; JQA, *Diary*, 1:369).

[5] Probably the Rev. Stephen Peabody of Atkinson, N.H. His wife, Mary Haseltine, was originally from Bradford, Mass. (*Sibley's Harvard Graduates*, 17:210).

[6] Ebenezer Kent died in 1776 and his wife Anna Smith died in 1781. The Kents lost their home and other property in the burning of Charlestown during the Battle of Bunker Hill, 17–18 June 1775 (Isaac Smith Sr. to JA, 24 June 1775, vol. 1:227, 230).

[7] Edward Moore, "Fable VIII. The Lawyer, and Justice," *Poems, Fables, and Plays*, London, 1756, line 28.

[8] Blank in MS. AA's last two letters to Elizabeth Smith Shaw are dated ca. 15 Aug. and 15 Sept. 1785 (vol. 6:280, 361).

[9] AA had written to JQA about the criticism in the English newspapers of the lack of U.S. monetary support for JA's ministerial position (11, 23 Aug. 1785, vol. 6:261, 296). JQA was living and studying at the Shaw's when he received the letters.

[10] The quotation "Censure is the tax a man pays to the public for being eminent" is from Jonathan Swift's *Thoughts on Various Subjects*, though it was widely quoted by

others, including Joseph Addison.

[11] Leonard White and Samuel Walker, CA's roommate at Harvard College (JQA, *Diary*, 1:316).

[12] Cotton Tufts.

[13] "Fat" in Dft.

[14] Not identified, but enclosed in AA to Elizabeth Smith Shaw, 15 Sept. 1785 (vol. 6:362).

Elizabeth Storer Smith to Abigail Adams

Janury 3d 1786

Notwithstanding the unconquerable aversion I ever had to writing I cannot forbear taking up my Pen, to Congratulate my dear Neice on the new year, and to thank her for her favour by the Welcome hand of my Nephew,[1] who is return'd I hope uncorupted, I do not wonder you wisht to keep him with you, I think he is very agreable. Your Journal and Letters to your friends have ever afforded me great Pleasure, and I look on my self under greater Obligation as your Correspondence is so large.

I am glad to find you still retain such an affection to your Native Place, notwithstanding the number of gay Senes which sorounde you, I make no doubt it would be pleasing to you, as well as to all your Conections, to have you with Mr and Miss A return to us again. I have slept but three nights at Brantree since my dear friend absence, it realy looks so Melancholy, I cannot take that pleasure I used to when you was their, I hope you will enliven it again with your Company, the pleasure we feel at seeing our Friends return, in a great measure make up for the pain of separation.

I wish it was in my power to write any thing entertaining, but as I seldom go abroad in Winter, I know but little besides what passes in my one familey, and there is no Matches going on the too Old Bacheldors[2] still continue so.

Mrs Gill has latly had a letter from Mrs Hollowell informing her Capt H. and she had been a Journey and there health is much better, I am sorry their is any impedient in the way to your visiting Mrs H. as I know you would both be happy in each others acquaintance.[3]

Please to remember my love to Miss Hobart, I am much obliged to her for enquiering after me, she is Sister to Mrs Vasal and formaly lived with Madam Steel one of my most agreable Neighbours, I should be glad to see her and Mr Vasal's familey in Boston again.[4]

So our friend Thomas B.[5] begins to think he shall not live here always, as he has so good an opinion of your Uncle I wish he would leave him a handsome legasy, I think he ought to for the care he took of his intrest when he was out of town.

How does my good friend Mrs Rogers has she recovered her health, give my love to her, I sinserely sympathize with her in the death of her amiable Mama:[6] O how many kind friends have we been calld to part with since you left us, and whose turn it may be next God only knows, but may we all be prepared for this Change and meet again in the World above to part no more is the sinsere wish of Your Affectonate Aunt
Elizabeth Smith

PS. Mr and Mrs Otis are well and send their love to you and Mr and miss Adams. My love to Cousin Nabby I sinserely wish her happy.

RC (Adams Papers).

[1] AA's letter of 29 Aug. 1785 was one of those carried by Charles Storer, when he returned to America in November (vol. 6:314, 458).

[2] Undoubtedly her two sons, Isaac Jr., 36, and William, 30.

[3] AA thought she should restrict her visits to loyalist refugees to avoid complicating JA's position as minister to Great Britain. Rebecca Boylston Gill and Mary Boylston Hallowell were sisters, and cousins of JA's mother. Capt. Benjamin Hallowell served as the provincial commissioner of the customs before he left Boston in 1776 (Sabine, *Loyalists*).

[4] Anne Hubbard (Hobart) was the sister of Margaret Hubbard Vassall, who left Boston for England in 1775 with her husband William. In Boston, Hubbard probably had boarded with Margaret Nelson Steel (Edward Warren Day, comp., *One Thousand Years of Hubbard History, 866 to 1895*, N.Y., 1895, p. 185; Thwing Catalogue, MHi).

[5] Formerly of Boston, Thomas Boylston, a merchant, was also a cousin of JA's mother and brother of Rebecca and Mary.

[6] Abigail Bromfield Rogers' stepmother, Hannah Clarke Bromfield, of Boston, died in Aug. 1785 (vol. 6:385, 395).

Cotton Tufts to Abigail Adams

Dear Cousin ⟨*Weymouth*⟩ Boston Jany 5. 1786

I have to thank you for your Communications of Sept and Octob. which came to Hand.[1] And I have many Things which I wish to write but must confine myself to some few matters that have relation to your Affairs. Your Bro Adams informs me that he has your Note for £30. I wish to know whether you would have me discharge it. I this day paid your Mohr. Hall 5 Dolrs. for the ft. Quarter having deferered it to this Time in order to begin the Payments with the Year. Your Tenant Mr Pratt has been so unfortunate in the Year past as to lose with the Horn Distemper one of the largest Oxen—2 Cows, and one Hog with a Distemper of which a Number have died. I have thoughts of making him a Consideration in the Settlement of Acctts. as the loss will be heavy to him and I presume it will not be disagreable to you. I have received the 17 Guineas by Mr Charles Storer (5 delivered him and 12 by the Way of Dr. Crosby). I informed you that I had laid out for Mr Adams Upwards of £100 in Consoledated Notes[2]—and have followed your Directions [by?] your Son John, a more particular Acctt. of the whole, I shall give you in my Next. I wish you to attend to the matter relative to Doanes Acctt.[3] and send me an Answer—and from Time to Time give me a dish of Politices for I assure you that your Intelligence is very acceptable. What shall I do should it be found necessary to call for a Surrender of Account Books Papers &c in the Hands of a certain Attorney.[4] I have found it necessary for a long while to call for the Completion of this and that Business &c which is not very pleasing to one who wishes to have Business dispatched with Care and punctuality and Speed. However I hope I have got Matters into a tolerable good Train. There is not a little rejoicing here at the Breaking off a Correspondence between the young Folks. As soon as I get Leisure I shall write you a long Letter which the Necessity of my returning home this Forenoon and a Snow Storm coming on prevents.

Be so kind as to forward the Letter to Mr Elwerthy.[5] Remember me to Mr Adams and Cousin. Charles is well—now at Braintree being the Winter Vacation, your other Children were well last Week. Adieu. Yr Friend &c

C Tufts

RC (Adams Papers); endorsed: "Dr Tufts Janry 5 1786."

[1] 16 Sept. and 5 Oct. 1785 (vol. 6:363, 407).

[2] See vol. 5:292, 293.

[3] For Tufts' previous attempt to collect money owed JA by the heirs of Elisha Doane (d. 1783), JA's client in the 1777 admiralty case of Penhallow v. The *Lusanna*, see vol. 6:426, 427. For the details of the case, see JA, *Legal Papers*, 2:352–395.

[4] AA gave JA's account books to Royall Tyler in 1783, hoping he could collect some of the old debts. Tufts' concern about the return of JA's books and papers stems from AA2's ending her engagement to Tyler in Aug. 1785 (AA to JA, 3 Jan. 1784, vol. 5:292; AA2 to Royall Tyler, [*ca. 11 Aug. 1785*], vol. 6:262).

[5] James Elworthy, a London merchant, was married to Elizabeth Cranch, a niece of AA's brother-in-law Richard Cranch (AA to Elizabeth Smith Shaw, 28 July 1784, vol. 5:406).

Abigail Adams to Cotton Tufts

Dear Sir

London Janry 10th. 1786

A Boston paper which reachd us by way of Newyork informd me of the Death of my dear Aunt 3 weeks before I received the melancholy account from your own Hand.[1]

From your last Letters and those, of my other Friends, I was led to fear, that I should never see her more; I feel my Dear Sir all that Sympathy for your loss, which a tender affection and the recollection of her amiable Life, and benevolent conduct inspires. Altho her tender state of Health confined her wholy to her own domestick abode, the benevolence of her Heart extended to all the sons and daughters of affliction of whatever kindred or Country, her liberal hand was streached out to the needy and upon her tongue was the Law of kindness. Notwithstanding her bodily infirmities prevented her personal labour, yet she looked well to the Ways of her Household.[2]—Blessed be her Memory, and let this falling Tear the tribute of my affection towards her be dried away by the firm belief of her happy destination; and her releasment from all those infirmities which was her School of trial whilst she inhabitted Mortality, and through which, (by the accounts of my Friends) she rose refined to a World of Spirits.

Thanks to our Benificient Creator who tho he has constituted us subject to mortality has given us the broad Basis of a future happy existance to build our hopes upon, and the best grounded assurcance, that we shall obtain it; by persueing the dictates of our consciences, in the excercise of Love to God; and good will to man.

> "No Man too largely from Heav'n's love can hope
> If what is hop'd he labours to secure"[3]

Mr Adams will write to you soon, and will I suppose give You some state of political affairs.

With regard to Domestick, I have some things to mention in confidence and Friendship. I am happy to find that the return of my son has met the approbation of his Friends. His kind reception from them, he speaks of; with gratefull pleasure and heartfelt satisfaction. I hope he will continue to merit their Esteem. You add Sir to my satisfaction by the account you give, of my son Charles.[4] Heaven Gaurd him from the snares and temptations of vice. The kind care and good advice of my Friends will not I hope be lost upon any of my children. Tommy is not yet launchd into the wide world; the good example and principles which he constantly hears and sees, will make such lasting and abideing impression upon his mind, as to secure him I hope from the practise of vice whenever he is call'd out into the World. Can Life afford a higher satisfaction to a Parent than that of seeing their Children persueing the paths of virtue and rectitude? It is a pleasure which the Almighty himself enjoied, when he lookd upon the Works which his hands had formed and pronounced that all was Good.

My daughter sir has not been less solicitious to conduct herself with propriety, and to secure the approbation of her own mind, and that of her Friends in the step she took last fall, I hope no unkind censure with [*will*] fall upon her in concequence of it. I think proper to acquaint you Sir in very explicit terms, that she is now addrest by a Gentleman of unexceptionable Character, both in publick and private Life.[5] In the Army which he enterd at the commencment of the War, he distinguishd himself by his Bravery his intrepidity and his Humanity, of which he has the amplest testimony from General Sullivan and Washington.[6] By the latter and by congress he was appointed to inspect the evacuation of Newyork, and afterwards received a comission of Secretary of Legation to this Court. He possess as high a sense of honour, and as independant a Spirit as any man I ever knew; and these Ideas appear to be founded upon principals of Religion and Morality. We have every reason to beleive that his Character will bear the strickest Scrutiny. Against this Gentleman we could have no objection, excepting a wish that a longer time might have elapsed before any thing of the kind had been tenderd from any quarter. But as the parties were agree'd, Col Smith conceived that he should be guilty both of a breach of his own honour; and the laws of hospitality, without an immediate parental sanction, which he has solicited and obtaind.

I own I cannot but feel for the situation of a Gentleman who has by his own folly and indiscretion lost all hopes of a connextion where he once lookd for it. It is not permitted us to look into futurity, nor can we say with certainty what will be the Lot of any one, but I own both before I came to this Country and not less so since, I was trembling for the fate of a dear and only daughter. I thought time would fully develope and try Characters, and upon that I relied; keeping my anxiety as much as possible in my own bosom. I however wish all happiness to the Gentleman, he has virtues and amiable qualities, and may be much happier connected with many other families than he could have been in ours because he had certain habits which would never accord with mr A's sentiments and principals. Capt Young yet lies at Portsmouth, and we have only a part of our Letters. I shall write more, by the first direct conveyance. In the mean time I am with tender affection Yours AA

RC (Adams Papers); addressed by WSS: "Doctor Tufts Boston"; endorsed: "Mrs. Abigail Adams Jany. 10. 1786 Recd Via New York & Favd of Rufus King Esq May. 19."

[1] Lucy Quincy Tufts died 30 Oct. 1785 (Tufts to AA, 16 Nov. 1785, vol. 6:457).

[2] Proverbs, 31:27.

[3] Young, *Night Thoughts*, Night IX, lines 443–444.

[4] To JA, 6 Oct. 1785 (vol. 6:412).

[5] Col. William Stephens Smith (WSS) of New York, secretary of the U.S. legation in

Great Britain, formally expressed the seriousness of his intentions regarding AA2 in a letter to AA of 29 Dec. 1785 (vol. 6:508–509).

[6] Probably the certificates of honorable service given to WSS by Gens. John Sullivan and George Washington (13 Oct. 1779 and 24 June 1782, respectively, MHi:DeWindt Coll.).

Cotton Tufts to Abigail Adams

My Dear Friend Weymouth Jany. 12. 1786

I wrote to you last Week by Capt Lyde, expecting that He would have sailed the next Day. I find that He is still here And as Mr. Jenks the Bearer hereof, is going in his Vessell I am loth to omit the favourable opportunity of writing by Him.[1] I propose to send by Him Our December Magazine, in which you will find a succinct Accountt of the Proceedings of the Genl Court in their last Session and what Measures will probably be taken for the Supply of our Treasury and the Payment of continental Interest.[2] The Delay in the States to supply the continental Treasury gives me great Pain. Something more effectual must be done, and common Danger I suppose will lead to it. But How in the mean Time our foreign Ministers are to be paid, foreign Debts, Tributes to the Barbarians &c I know not. Lamb it is said has at length arrived in Europe.[3] He is said to be a Person of a Droll Character and those that pretend to know the Man represent his Abilities and Prudence not in the most promising Light. Have you ever seen a certain Col. Norton (by wh[om] I sent some Letters to you last spring). He is now I suppose in England soliciting Payment for the stock taken from Nantucket and Dukes County by the British Forces in the late War. He has been to England several Times on this Errand, and it would be a satisfaction to know whether He is not by this Time thoroughly *Anglified*. As I sat in Senate with Him, I have some Curiosity to discover what Part He takes in the whale Fishery. For as his Business lays with the British Ministry it is not improbable, that He will be tampered with.[4]

Do you know whether my Brors Son Simon is in England, I was in the year past informed that he was going from St. Augustine to London, the House of Champion & Dickinson he was formerly connected with, and if in London information may be had of them, should it lay in your Way, I wish you to enquire him out. I am been told that He wishes to return, but conscious to himself of the inoffensive part which he has acted, that he does not incline to return untill the way is fully open.[5]

Tho I have heretofore had orders from Mr. Adams to draw to a larger Amount than I have already done, yet It would be agreable to be informed from Time to Time, what sums I may with your Convenience draw for. Bills will fetch at least 5 pr. Ct. above par. The Expences of your Children, Repairs of Buildings &c for the current year will exceed your Incomes here by at least £100 Lawful Money. The Payment of the Interest of your Loan office Notes, will be uncertain both with respect to Time and Value, when paid Certificates will be given for the Interest, which will not be converted into Specie without discount as I imagine. Last year I received a years Interest in Certificates and with great Exertions I finally turned them into the Hands of a Collector who gave me his promisory Note for the full Value of them, Certificates of the same kind are now sold at a Discount of near 40 pr Ct. About £90 of the £100 which I drew in Favour of Mr Samll Eliot was converted into public and private Securities, from the public (I purchased,) there will arise an Interest of £18 ann—but this Interest will not be paid earlier than a year hence, as the Treasurys is much in Arrears. Sloanes Bond has been sued and Execution is now against him. I expect we must take the Lands.[6] I had despaired of Lamberts Debt, but am informed that there is a Prospect of recovering it.[7] The Collection of Debts is a tryall of Patience and when Recourse is had to Law the process is tedious—and I apprehend more expensive and lengthy than need be.—The amazing sums of Money which are sent to England by every Vessell that goes from hence renders Cash very scarce and makes me almost wish that the intercourse was cut off.

Dr. Gordon has wrote a History of the American Revolution which will be printed in 4 Vols. Octo.[8] I have not as yet heard where it is to be printed, but I suspect in Scotland. Subscriptive Papers are handed about here—the Type and Paper are elegant.

As Mr. Jenks will probably deliver this to you, youll be able from Him to get Intelligence of what passes amongst us, he is very intelligent and is much respected in Salem, and should you have occasion to write on his return you may rely on his Care. I forgot to mention, that a piece of Linnen will be of use to yr Children in the coming summer, perchaps some of the Captains would take a piece in their Chests.

Wishing every Blessing I am yr—

RC (Adams Papers).

[1] Cotton Tufts had been the guardian of John Jenks (1751–1817) after the death of his father. A surgeon's mate in 1778–1779, Jenks became a Salem merchant (vol. 3:114, 163; Essex Inst., *Hist. Colls.*, 3 [April 1861]:94).

[2] *The Boston Magazine* reported that Con-

gress had assessed Massachusetts $448,854 "for the services of the present year, and for paying one years interest on the foreign and domestic debt." The General Court proceedings also listed Massachusetts' debt at £1,468,554.7.5 with the annual interest for the year £88,112.13.3, "and that by a calculation which had been formed, an annual tax of 200,000£ would cancel the whole debt, both principal and interest, in fifteen years, and at the same time, pay the ordinary charges of government" (*The Boston Magazine*, Dec. 1785, p. 474–475).

[3] John Lamb spent several months in transit carrying the commissions, given to him by John Jay on 11 March 1785, directing JA, Franklin, and Jefferson to negotiate with the Barbary powers. He arrived in London around 24 Sept. (vol. 6:265, 383).

[4] Col. Beriah Norton traveled on the *Active* with AA in 1784 (vol. 5:359–360). On his long-term efforts seeking redress for damages done by the British during their raid on Martha's Vineyard in 1778, see Charles Edward Banks, *The History of Martha's Vineyard*, 3 vols., Boston, 1911–1925, repr. Edgartown, Mass., 1966, 1:384–403. Cotton Tufts was not alone in his suspicions of Norton's patriotism (same, 1:398, 403).

[5] Simon Tufts Jr. (1750–1802), a Boston storeowner, left for Halifax with the British Army in 1776, later making his way to London. He was proscribed as a loyalist by the Massachusetts Act of 16 Oct. 1778 and never did return to the United States (*Sibley's Harvard Graduates*, 16:540–542).

[6] In a quitclaim dated 17 April, David Sloan released to JA eleven acres of land in Braintree's New South Precinct, now Randolph. In Tufts' account of properties he describes the transaction as "arising from Sloanes Mortgagd and is but of little Value" ("List of private papers, . . . left at JA's decease, 20 July 1826"; "An Account of the Real Estate . . . lying in Braintree and Milton," [*post* 1787?]; both Adams Papers, Microfilms, Reel No. 607; Pattee, *Old Braintree*, p. 290–291).

[7] Tufts' hopes were not realized. In June 1787 he ordered the high sheriff of Lincoln County (now part of Maine) to sue Lambert unless he received the money immediately (to AA, 30 June, Adams Papers).

[8] Rev. William Gordon's *The History of the Rise, Progress, and Establishment of the Independence of the United States of America* was published in London in 1788 (*DAB*).

Edward Baldwin to Abigail Adams

Madam — Saint James's Market 17th. January 1786

Understanding that through the means of some improper and unjust Conduct in your Servants you have had reason to doubt the honesty of some of your Trades-people and as such have come to a determination of changing them. I beg leave to observe, that, truly sensible of my own Integrity throughout the whole time I have had the satisfaction of serving you, the very first moment that I heard of your being dissatisfied with me, which was about Ten days since and which was respecting a deficiency in the Weight of some Meat which your Cook came down to my Shop and informed me of I immediately sett off to your House to re-weigh the same when I found missing a piece of Brisket of Beef and a piece of Gravey Beef which prevented my reweighing the Meat, but the fact really is, that, at that time as well as all others ever since I have had the pleasure of serving you the Weight was full and just and every Article charged hath been at all times truly and faithfully delivered agreeable to the Orders I have received—I have endeavourd, personally to have the satisfaction of Acquitting myself to you in this Business but could not obtain an opportunity, your Servants seemed averse to it, however I hope and trust I shall acquire such my wish herein, as, whether you shall be kind enough to continue to indulge me with the happiness of serving your House or not, it behoves me as a Trades-man to support the Character of an Honest Man. Begging pardon for the Trouble I here give you, and thanking you for the favours I have already received, take the liberty to Subscribe myself, Madam, Your much Obliged and very humble Servant

Edward Baldwin
Butcher

RC (Adams Papers).

Abigail Adams 2d to John Quincy Adams

No. 11

Sunday January 22d. 1786

I have taken my pen, to frame an appology to you my Dear Brother. There are so many that offer themselvs to me, that I am almost at a loss, which to avail myself of as most sattisfactory to you—should I tell you that no opportunity of forwarding my Letter to you had been the cause of my silence since the 9th of December[1] or that not having received any answer to my many long Letters I had determined to wait till I should hear again from you, or, that time and opportunity had not rendered it possible for me to write, or that my acquaintance had become so numerious and my time so much employd in visitting and festing [them?] that I could find no moment unoccupied enough to collect my scattered ideas and arange them for your perusal. Some of these and many of the Like I could collect and perhaps you might be sattisfied but to none of these causes is my silence to be attributed, but has arrisen, from not knowing how to explain the cause to you, in such a manner as to gaurd you from surprise—and I am even at this moment equally at a loss—so I will enclose you a profile of a friend of your sisters as an introduction to the Gentleman to your acquaintance and perhaps he may tell you the Whole Story.[2]

My journal has been a little interrupted but I [shall?] indeavour to continue it, as well as relate to you [wh]atever may have passd worth your knowing since my Last. We have formd some new acquaintances, but none that are very interesting. We dined once at a Mr Penns, who was formerly Governor of Pensylvania and who Married a Lady in America.[3] She has a sister Miss Masters who Lives with her, that is much celebrated for her beauty, and much admired for her expectations and an American Gentleman told me he thought her the handsomest Women he had sien in England.[4] With these prepossessions in her favour, I went into Company where She was. I did not arraign the taste of the Gentleman, but I had sat half an hour before I could be convinced that Miss Masters was [present?]. It is said that She is a fine bold beauty, two ideas that in my mind are incompatiable; I thought this description applicable to her.

But bold her Mien unguarded roved her Eye, and her flushd cheek confessd at nearer view the borrowd blushes of an artfull die.[5]

I am sure she would not have please your fancy. She is a particular friend of Mrs Binghams and you may judge of her.

Miss Hamilton of whom I have spoken to you,[6] was, present at the same time and the contrast much in her favour, but this Lady with all the deli[cate] softness and sweetness of unconscious beauty, will not attract the admiration of your sex, half so much as the other whom I have described to you. It must be acknowledged that your tastes are strongly degenerated. Mr P— seems to affect more roughness of Character than you even find general in this County, but professes to be an American in his principles. Mrs P, as ugly, Masculine and withot one trait of the amiable femal Character. In fine I was dasgusted with their manners, and appearance, and a gentleman observd, to me that he had not heard, such Language, in Thre years, as he had at table in one hour—yet it was polite fashionable and in Short without it they would have thought themselvs unGenteel. The Company were the family we visitted Mr and Mrs Pen, Mrs and Miss Masters Mr Hamilton and Miss H, Mr Chew, Pappa Mamma myself Mr Smith and Mr Humphries.

We have been visitted by a Mrs Lamar[7] as an American, and we received an invitation to a small party at her House the week before last. To give you some idea of society here, I will describe this visit, at Eight o clock we went, Mamma myself and Col S. Pappa did not choose to go. The Lady received us at the Doer, inquired after our Health lamented her disappotment in not seeing his Excellency, ordered us a Cup of tea, and askd whether we would play Whist or Commerce.[8] In this way She receives the Whole Company, you take your seat, drink your tea, and must soon conclude to play either Whisth or Commerce or subject yourself to an inquirey from every person in Company why you do not. I long attemted to plead ignorance of Cards, or of any Game, and in every company but this I have kept to my resolution of not playing, but I found it singular, and if the Company was small the Lady of the House thought herself obliged to set still to keep me company, so this Eve I engaged in Commerce, and fortunately, in this circle of fifty People, got seated at a table with Mr and Ms West[9] Miss Hamilton and Mr Smith. In the course of the evening you are offerd cake and lemonade, and at Ten or Eleven your Carriage is announced, you finish your Game, make a curtsey to the Lady of the House and come away, without noticeing any other Person in Company, or perhaps, knowing any creature [only?] you go, with company. This is the manner of visitting, and a most stupid one it is, yet it may be unavoidable. Where one is obliged to have a large acquaintance it is impossible not to mix your Company, and in such numerous circle, any general conversation is impossible. You must get into parties and, where you are all strangers, they must substitute cards for amusement. They do not oblige you to play high, tho every one must play something, half a crown a game is the usual sum, at some Houses Half a Guinea. But young Ladies play Commerce, which is tottally a game of Chance and a most insipid One too. Here you put one two or three shillings to the Pool and run your chance of gaining or loosing. There are no other games, at present fashionable.

This is the most fashionable Way of visitting here for these People who cannot afford to give dinners may make a figure in this way. It costs you only a little Cake and lemonade, fire and Candeles. Your company pays a shilling a Person for the Cards, that is, they who ever Leave a shilling a Person under the candelestick for the Cards, which is a perquisite of the servants who supply them. Custom reconciles any thing in this Way, but to me it appears a most abominable one.[10]

jany 30th 1786.

More than a week ago, I made an effort to continue my journal, and succeeded thus far when I was interrupted by Madame Binghams being anounced and every day since I have thought of resuming my pen, but waited in hopes to hear from you by the arrival of Young. And to our great joy we received a Number of Letters by his ship, but those which he has in his possession, we have not yet recieved. I have one from you my Dear Brother but it is no latter than the 3d.[11] of September and tho I was extremely gratified with it yet I was not sattisfied that there was none Later, and hope yet I shall find one. I will go on with my journal[12] till the receipt of Your Letter, and then notice it.

Mr and Mrs Bingham called to pay their respects.[13] I allways used to observe in Paris that when this Gentleman had any point to sollicit he allways discovered it by his attention to visit, &c—and from his movements now I judge that he wishes to be presented at Court. They *say*, they shall go to America in the Month of March. Mr B. called one Morning last week and told us, that Mrs B. was perfectly sattisfied with going, indeed she would not stay if she were to follow her own wishes, that all her ideas were American. This Morning we congratulated her upon, the change of her inclination from last year, but she, denied it all, and declared that necessity was her only motive. They have spent three Months at the Hague and she is very much charmed and delighted with it. To be sure the Publick amusements are not equal to Paris but then there is so much good society, and She so much admired, that it would be ingratitude not to be pleased. He wonders, that Congress shold make so many appointments there, without being sure of there being accepted, thinks it a great disadvantage to our Country, and such is his *Patriotism*, that were it offered to him, I guess he would not refuse.[14]

This Evening Mamma, myself, Mr Smith and Mr Humphryes, went to visit Mrs Paradise,[15] at one of her Evening parties. There were I believe forty People crouded into two [rooms?], not too large for a dozen. Ladies and Gentlemen, Stars and Garters, ribbands, and Medals—in Short such a collection as, might be descriptive of the Tower of Babel, for there were some from all Nations English Americans Spanish French Portugeese Polloneesse Venetians Russians, and, the duce knows who. We arrived rather late and had not a choice of seats. I took one next to a Mrs Coswey, an Italian who is rather a singular Character she paintts and her subjects are the most sungular that one can imagine. I saw the last year in the Exbition of painting several of her performances. One was a *Dream*, another the deludge, the mos[t] extreordinary things, that imagination could form.[16] She speaks English Italian and French vastly well, it is said, Plays and sings, well, but has nevertheless, the foibles, which attend these accomplishments. I sat by her the Evening and was witness to sollicidute from all most Every Person in the [room?], to her to Play, and sing, and of her absolute refusall. She was sick had a voilent Cold and had not sung for a forght night. At last after every one had given over there sollicitude she, followed her own inclincation and play and sang till she came away. Now I think a Woman is never excuseable for such a Conduct uless like Miss Mayhew,[17] she has an ineshaustable fund of Wit and good Humour to display upon the occasion, which this Lady had not. She is one of those soft gentle pretty Women, whose Compliance with the request of the company would please more than her Airs could possibly give her importance. She has Musical parties at her own House on Monday Evenings. We have no acquaintance tho General Pauolia,[18] whom you know from report I suppose was there. He appears to be about sixty years of age, light Complexion red Hair, and discovers no simtoms of greatness, or Extraordinary quallities. But were I to attempt to describe the various Characters that were present I shold tire myself, and you also.

When one wishes to see singularity in all its forms it is only necessary to visit this family, for in themselvs they are, extremely so, and we find like all others of their acquaintance that civility is only to be preserved by ceremony and distance.

Monday the 23d.

Pappa and Mr Smith dined at Mr Penns. This was a Political dinner, at the request of, Lord Shelbure who was present with Lord Abingdon. These People you know are supposed to be in the opposition and this was the day before the meeting of Parliament. I believe Pappa was not extremely sattisfied, with thier sentiments with respect *to US* at least. He thinks they have no decided system. But this is Politicks.

Tuesday, 24th.

This day the Parliament meets and the King delivered his speach from the Throne. Sir Clement Cottril Domir [*Dormer*] Master of the cerimonies, sent your Mamma word that if she wished to see this cerimony he would secure her places. But we had engaged company to dine and feared we should be detaind too late, but we might have gone for his Majesty came out at half after three. Our Company were Mr and Mrs West Mr West Junr[19] Mr Trumble, who has finished his battle of Bunkers Hill, and I assure you it is a most terible thing if the expression may be allowed to express, a good performance. I went to see it the other Morning and I was frozen, it is enough to make ones hair to stand on End. The moment of the

Piece is when General Warren is slain and the scene, is dreadfully beautifull, or rather dreadfully expressive. It is to be engraved, and will secure to him imortal reputation. He is now upon the Death of Montgomory.[20] Mr and Miss Hamilton Miss Hollowell,[21] and a Mr Ansty an Englishman, a Lawyer and a Member of Parliament, who is appointed to go out to America to assertain the claims of the Royalists. He was introduced to Pappa by My Lord Carmarthen and Pappa has given him letters to the Governors of all the states, and others to Members of Congress.[22] He has calld upon Pappa once before but I did not then see him and today was the first time and without Hessitation I can say that he is the handsomest, politest best bred Englishman I have yet seen. In short I doubted whether he really was an Englishman his manners were perfectly easy and polite and he was the admiration of the Company. I was sorry that I had not any letter written for you to forward by him as he intends visiting Boston soon after his arrival. Your Mamma has written by him to your Aunt Cranch. If I had have thought more of it I would at least have given him a Letter of introduction to you, for I really think him *a Phenominon*. His family live at Bath and he leaves London on sunday, for thence and goes in the Packet which will sail the first Wedensday in Februry. Mr Humphrys and Mr Smith finishd our circle. These gentlemen however we call a part of our own family for they dine with us, every day when [they are] not otherwise engaged. I often wish for you my Brother to make a sixth, at Table and in every scene. I miss you and wish for you, but to no purpose. I have not had a game of romps since the 12th of *May*[23] and doubt whether I ever shall again. We amuse ourselvs with battledoors, Chess, Cards and &c. Mr Humphries is having his last Poem published[24] if he should present one to me I shall forward it to you. He says that he likes Engld better than he expected he has met with no incivilities of any kind, and he finds them a civiler People than he expected. He now waits for Mrs Siddons to appear and to hear the debates in Parliament before he makes his exit. Pappa tills him he shall be quite in the deepts when he goes—and sometimes proposes to him in jest that they should go together to Algiers to make a Treaty. Mr Barclays movements are so slow that it does not appear that he will get there before next summer, he was appointed in October, and he had not left Paris the begining of January.[25] Lamb and Randall, are I suppose nearly arrived, at Algiers, but from all accounts there does not seem to be much prospect of their succeeding, from the total incapacity of the former. Indeed all who are concernd in the affair, fear that this effort will be inaffectual which is very unfortunate.[26] Pappa says, that he suspects that the Emperior of Morroco, will suppose his dignity insulted by receiving only persons deputized by those who Congress Commisioned, and he does not know but he shall have to go himsellf in the spring if this should be the case. I confess I am not sure that he would not go. I have offered to accompany him but you know I did to Madrid,[27] but I suspect I shall see no more of the One than the other. This however is *entree Nous.*

Wedensday 25th

Mamma and myself were out in the Morning to visit Mr Smith at Clapham, whom I have mentioned formerly to you, as an agreeable family who have shown us many civilities.[28] We had an invitation to a ball and supper at ther House the last week. Pappa you know, dislikes going himself into such companies and Mamma nor myself do not like to go by ourselvs, so we did not accept the invitation. Mrs Smith was so polite as to request Mamma to put me under her Care, for the Eve, but I thought it best not to go. Mr Humphryes and Mr Smith were there and gave us a very cleaver account of it. The latter does not dance, ⟨*but Plays, and*⟩. On our return we called at Madame Binghams but were not admitted and I suppose were we to go every day in the week it would be the sam thing. They have taken a ⟨*small*⟩ House, but by no means, superb, and I suppose do not propose seeing Company at all.

Fryday 27th

Mamma and myself were out all the Morning. We are much engaged at present in preparing our dresses for the Birth day, which has been put off from the 18 of jany, to the 9th of February on account of the long Mourning for the Queens Brother and sister which has kept al London in sable for two Months past.[29] The Princess Elizabbeth has been very much indisposed for a long time her Life has been dispaird of but She is better at Present. *Appropo* I believe I have never yet told you, that the Publick papers have sent the Prince of Whales to sup with us, about 2 Months since.[30] And it was believed by many People, some who were acquainted in this family really supposed it. It was I suppose a pareigraph to answer their own Ends. And Mrs Right[31] who was not much pleased at it tho She really belived it till we told her the truth, says that the Princes servants did not deny it, and he said himself in Princely Language—Dam it—it is time to go—and be friends—this is entree Nous.

1. "THE DEATH OF GENERAL WARREN AT THE BATTLE OF BUNKER'S HILL, 17 JUNE 1775," BY JOHN TRUMBULL, 1786

See page ix

Saturday 28th.

To day your Pappa dined at a Mr Wilmots, one of the Commisioners, to judge of the Claims of the American Refugees.[32] Mr Humphryes and Mr Smith dined at Mr Binghams so Mamma and myself were alone, till Even.

Sunday 29th.

We went to Church, and herd an Excellent sermon from Dr Price, upon the chain of Universal being. He tells us, that we all have, good and bad Angells, Gaurding over us, and that all our actions are under their influence and [. . .]. His system is that that this chain of being also exists from animate matter in gradation up to Man (and which many suppose there stops) goes still further and that Man is only one link, which is persued, to infinite perfection. And I recollect in one of his sermons he has given this sentiment that we have existed before, our present state and that when we make our exit from hence we shall asscend by gradual stages, and become more and more perflect provied we are good and virtuous. These cannot be speculative opinions from him whith which he only amuses, the Minds and pleases the imagination. They must be his real sentiments, or he would not deliver them from the Pulpit.

After we returnd from Church I left a Card with Miss H. Mr Bridgen[33] called upon Pappa, and Mr R R Randall Brother to the Gentleman you know.[34] As we had engaged a company of Americans to dine to day Pappa askd him to stay which he did. He is not so agreeable as his Brother. Mr Anstly calld this Morn, to take leave of Pappa he expected to have gone before. My former opinion was confirmed of him as much as it could be. Our Company to dine were, Mr Forrest an American Merchant settled here. He was formerly an officer in the Army, where he lost his Leg, but he has got into business and seems to be a worthy Man.[35] Dr Bancroft you know. There were four Gentlemen from Carolina, Mr Heyward, Mr Gibbs, Mr Shewbreck and Mr Readhead.[36] Mr Murry was invited with Mr Forrest but he has lately been extremely ill and has not recoverd enought to go into Company. The Death of his father has distressed him very much and his Mother is in a Maloncholy state of Mind.[37] The former event renders it absolutely necessey for him to go out in the spring. He is now recovering his Health. Did you receive a Letter from him which was enclosed by Charles Storer to my Uncle Tufts or Cranch? It went by a ship, which saild about a week before Lyde. As you have inclosed no letter for him I fear it has missd you.[38] Most all the Americans, who are here seem to be going in the spring. Mr and Mrs Bingham Mr and Mrs Rucker[39] Miss Ransey[40] Mr and Miss Hamilton Mr Chew, and indeed most that I am acquainted with, will make theier exit. Some I shall very much regret, and others I shall not think of, at all. There seems to be but little Communication at present between Ouer state and this Country, and Politicians say there will be still less, that the Trade of America is stopd to this Country never to begin again, that France will receive more and more every day. You will hear perhaps, that Mr Boylston has sold his Oil in Paris at a very great advantage 30 per cent clear gain, and that Mr Barret has made a Contract to send so much Oil, and to receive French Goods.[41] The Marquis, has his influence and it has had its affect. The Person who has the lighting of the 30 Citties, prefers our Oil to ⟨*ether Dutch or*⟩ Any other.[42] These are things with which your Father is pleased.

Monday 30th.

This afternoon I received your letter by Young, but I was not a little surprised to find it no later than the 7th of september, and can only account for it by supposing there must be another in Capt Youngs Care.

Tuesday 31st.

Pappa went at three o clock this Morn to ⟨*the House of*⟩ Parliament. Mr Wilmot with whom he dined a saturday and who is a member of P— introduced him. He had spoken to Mr Pit and some other Gentlemen, and they were very sivil. The Person on whose particular department it is to admit Gentlemen, said, that sometimes Member of P— introduced Counts and Barons, under the title of Foreign Ministers, which makes him allways carefull, to know who he admited but we all know Mr Adams, and I shall be happy to see him whenever he chooses to come. But the House ajournd, and Pappa got home before four much pleased with the marks of civility shown him. He walkd home with Mr Penn, who is very polite and told Pappa that if we wanted to go to the Play at any time Mrs Pen, would accommodate us, with places, for by some means or other She has so much influence with the Box keepers as to have a Box whenever she pleases. We have been trying for some time to get a Box, but it is impossible unless you bribe the Box keepers, and we have never yet done that. But there are Ladies who go so far as to give twenty Gueaneas a years, as a present to the Box keepers, for which they have places whenever they apply. ⟨*it is not so in F*⟩ They manage this matter better in France said yorick[43]—upon some other occasion. A Gentleman may Generally get accommodated with seats. Pappa ges often with Mr Humphries. This Evening he went to Covent Garden to see the Distressd Mother,[44] in which Miss Brunton playd. She is a very promising Actress, a little more than seventeen, and for her age really surprizing. I saw her in juliet of Shakespear, and was much pleased, she plays with the greatest judgment.[45] I thought She was deficient in sensibility but I am told that She does not in other Characters. ⟨*She hasnt such a countenance as Mrs siddons but in time she may approach*⟩ There have appeard several new peices, lately one calld the Heiress, which is said to be written by Genl Burgoine, and Mr Smith says, He has not seen so delicate a Comedy since he has been in England.[46] I have not seen it yet.

Wedensday Februry the 1st. 1786.

Mr and Mrs Bingham askd Pappa to present them at Court on the Birth day, but as this is contrary to etiquette, they must be presented this week or stay till the Week after the Birth day. This was not a little disappointment. Last Eve Pappa received a Card from Mr B. telling him that Mrs B. would defer her presentation *but that his anxiety was so great to pay his respects to the King that he begd he might be presented to day at the levee insted* of Thursday at the drawing room. These were his own words and this Morning by Pappas appointment he called at half past twelve, accompanied by his Dear friend Mr Crawford, with whom they returnd from Paris. When they got to the levee your Pappa says, he teized him till he got him to introduce him to Lord Carmarthen, and in this way it is that he forces himself upon People—ridiculous being.

We dined to day at Mr Copelys, the Company were only Pappa Mamma myself Mr Smith Mr Humphryes Mr and Mrs Roggers. I passd an agreeable day. Mr and Mrs C— look as if [bowed?] down under affliction they lost two Lovely Chrildren, about, two Months since with the inflamatory soar throat.[47] No one can wonder at their dejection they seeem to exert themselvs to appear chearfull. We came away at Nine oclock.

Thursday Feb 2d.

Pappa and Mr Smith went to the Drawing room. Mr B. was presented to her Majesty. Mr Crawford went with Mr Bingham and

NOT ACTED THIS SEASON.

BY HIS MAJESTY'S COMPANY,

At the Theatre Royal in Drury-Lane,

This preſent SATURDAY, October 20, 1787,

The HEIRESS.

Sir Clement Flint by Mr. KING,
Lord Gayville by Mr. KEMBLE,
Alſcrip by Mr. PARSONS,
Chignon by Mr. BADDELEY,
Mr. Blandiſh by Mr. BANNISTER, Jun.
Mr. Rightly by Mr. AICKIN,
Prompt by Mr. R. PALMER,
Chairman by Mr. CHAPLIN, William by Mr. WILSON,
And Clifford by Mr. SMITH.
Miſs Alſcrip by Miſs POPE,
Miſs Alton by Mrs. CROUCH,
Mrs. Blandiſh by Mrs. WILSON,
Mrs. Sagely by Mrs. BOOTH, Tiffany by Miſs TIDSWELL.
And Lady Emily by Miſs FARREN.
In Act II. a Song in Character by Mrs. CROUCH.

To which will be added the Maſque of

COMUS.

Comus by Mr. WROUGHTON,
Firſt Bacchanal by Mr. KELLY,
Second Bacchanal by Mr. DIGNUM,
Spirit by Mr. BARRYMORE,
Elder Brother by Mr. WHITFIELD,
Younger Brother by Mr. BENSON,
The Lady by Mrs. BRERETON,
Paſtoral Nymph by Mrs. FORSTER,
Sabrina by Miſs ROMANZINI,
Bacchants by Miſs COLLETT, Miſs STAGELDOIR, &c.
And Euphroſyne by Mrs. CROUCH,
With the Song of 'Sweet Echo,' accompaied by Mr PARKE

On Monday, (1ſt Time this Seaſon) She wo'd and She wou'd not,
With the Pantomime of Harlequin's Invaſion.

2. PLAYBILL FOR GEN. JOHN BURGOYNE'S *THE HEIRESS*

See page x

Pappa yesterday to the levee, from here in our Carriage, and to day, the papers say Mr Crawford was presented by your Pappa to the King tho he was presented a forghtmight since. The Foreign Ministers were rallying your father about it to day. Mr Eden, is appointed to make Commercial arangments and Treaty with France.[48] It is said he is going to Paris soon. The Papers have been full of this matter for this Month, but tis thought that he will meet no better success than Mr C[raufurd].[49] Tis said he has the sallary of an Ambassador. The Duke of Dorset has returnd to Paris, and tis said that Conpt D'adamah [*d'Adhémar*], is on his rout to London.[50]

Fryday 3d.

Mamma and myself went down and passd the day with Mrs Roggers. Pappa was going to Parliament and the Gentlemen dined from home.

Saturday 4th.

We were at home all day. We rode in the Park in the Morning the weather was very fine indeed. In the Evening Mr Voss a Virginian[51] and Mr Trumble called upon us.

sunday 5.

Pappa and Mamma went to Meeting. I stayd at home to write to you. The Gentlemen dined with us. Mr Brown called in the Evening. Mr Humphryes went to Mrs Paradises. The Baron de Lynden and Mr Duker called upon us. The Baron to invite us to dine on Wedensday with Madame Bingham.

Monday 6th.

We were out in the Morning. Mr S and H dined in the City. In the Evening Mrs and Miss Paradise called upon us, and appeard more ridiculous than ever. The Chavalier Dolombieu, a Knight of the order of Molta who has been here some time and was introduced to Pappa by Mr Jefferson, called and pasd an hour.[52] Mr Jefferson, gives him credit for being a sensible Man, but his manners which are all that one can judge from at first do not prejudice in his favour, tho there is nothing particuliarly disagreeable.

Tuesday 7th.

We had a party of Gentlemen and Ladies to dine. Mr and Mrs Pen, Mrs and Miss Masters Mr and Mrs Bingham, Mr Crawford Mr Wilmot Mr Chew. I have described to you already, those of this

Company who you are not acquainted with. They were singular and extraordinary Characters la tout.

Wedensday

Pappa presented Mr Hamilton and Mr Chew at Court to day. Now the ice is broken I suppose there will be no end—to presentations. We went to dine with the Baron de Lynden at 4 because Mr Hamilton has been so obliging as to offer us seats in a Box he had engaged at Covent Garden. Our Company at dinner were Pappa Mamma myself Mr Smith Mr and Mrs B. an oald German Baron Bowd down under the smiles of fortune, or with age, the Baron seckingdorf, Mons. Jeanneret de Luniac,[53] the Baron de Lynden and Mr Duker. The dinner was neat rather than elegant. There was no display of Luxury, except in a Large silver tereen which was very elegant. Madame B. shone away in all her splendor, her dress was that she wore last Winter black and Pink, and I have not seen so elegant a Woman, since I have been in England. A Gentlem[an] who sat next me at table Told me I was in Love with her. O it is true that I never see her without admiration in the highest degree. We being engaged to go to the Play were obliged to leave the Table, at the desert. I was not much gratified with the Play neither. It was the Comedy of the provoked Husband.[54] There were two celebrated Actresses apperd, but I was not char[*me*]d with them neither.[55] Pappa went to see Mrs siddons who made her firt appearance in Tragedy since her Confinement and in Jane Shore, two.[56] We could not get a Box, and therefore could not go. Mamma myself and Mr Smith, went to Mr Hamiltons Box, he was there with his Neice.

Dft (Adams Papers); begins on the back of the last page of AA2 to JQA, 5 Dec. 1785 (vol. 6:478; Microfilms, Reel No. 366).

[1] The final dateline of AA2's letter of 5 Dec. 1785, vol. 6:481.

[2] The profile, undoubtedly of WSS, has not been found.

[3] Former Pennsylvania lieutenant governor Richard Penn was elected a member of Parliament in 1784. In 1772, in Philadelphia, he married Mary Masters, daughter of William and Mary Lawrence Masters (*DAB*). From AA2's description of the party (below), Mary Lawrence Masters was living with the Penns in London.

[4] Sarah Masters was roughly 28 years old at the time. She would later marry Turner Camac, an Irishman whom she met on another tour of the British Isles in 1795. They eventually settled in Philadelphia (*PMHB*, 8:293, 297–299 [Oct. 1884]; Howard M. Jenkins, *The Family of William Penn Founder of Pennsylvania*, Phila., 1899, p. 194).

[5] Prodicus of Ceos, *The Judgment of Hercules, a Poem*, transl. Robert Lowth, Glasgow, 1743, lines 42–44. The poem was reprinted by Robert Dodsley as "The Choice of Hercules" in *A Collection of Poems . . . by Several Hands*. There is an edition of Dodsley's *Collection*, 6 vols., London, 177–, with JQA's bookplate, at MQA.

[6] Ann Hamilton and her uncle William Hamilton of Pennsylvania were frequent visitors to the Adams household in London (JA, *D&A*, 3:184). AA2 first described her to JQA

in a letter of 4 July 1785 (vol. 6:208).

[7] Possibly the wife of Thomas Lamar, a friend of the artist Benjamin West (Robert C. Alberts, *Benjamin West, A Biography*, Boston, 1978, p. 65, 72).

[8] A card game with cards face-up on the table, where each player improves their hand by exchanging their cards with those on the table.

[9] Benjamin West and his wife Elizabeth Shewell (Alberts, *Benjamin West*, p. 64–65).

[10] Gaming and gambling were extremely popular among both men and women in London. Commerce and whist were fairly tame, but fortunes were won and lost playing other, more sophisticated games. The practice of paying for the deck of cards was common, but not universally accepted. Even newspapers were critical of the practice, and in 1794 the London *Times* called it an "imposition upon hospitality . . . that when one person invites another to partake of the conviviality of his house, he should not lay an impost upon him." A few years later they called the "extortion" of card money a "*shabby genteel* custom" that should be abolished (John Ashton, *The History of Gambling in England*, London, 1898, p. 76–82).

[11] JQA to AA2, 29 Aug. 1785 (vol. 6:317). The last dateline of the letter is actually 7 Sept. (see under "Monday 30th.").

[12] See under the next dateline, where AA2 picks up her daily journal-style narrative at 23 January.

[13] William, a Philadelphia banker, and his wife Anne saw the Adamses frequently while mixing business and pleasure during a 1784–1786 trip to England and the Continent. Anne Willing Bingham, a renowned beauty, was only a year older than AA2 (see vol. 5:336, 451; JA, *D&A*, 3:149, 167).

[14] Following JA's appointment as minister to Great Britain on 24 Feb. 1785, Congress selected William Livingston of New Jersey as his successor as minister to the Netherlands. Livingston declined the appointment as did Congress' next choice, John Rutledge of South Carolina. Congress took no further action, leaving JA as minister to both countries until he returned home in 1788 (*JCC*, 28:474, 481; 29:497, 654–655).

[15] Lucy Ludwell Paradise, her daughter Lucy, and her husband John frequently entertained the Adamses in their home in Cavendish Square (see vol. 6:208–209, 304–305, 470, 480).

[16] Maria Hadfield Cosway was the daughter of English parents who had settled in Italy. She married Richard Cosway, the famous English miniaturist, in 1781. A painter in her own right and a musician, she exhibited over thirty works at the Royal Academy. *The Deluge* and *Basilæas's Dream* were among the six she showed at the Academy's 1785 exhibition (*Jefferson Abroad*, ed. Douglas L. Wilson and Lucia Stanton, N.Y., 1999, p. xx; Algernon Graves, *The Royal Academy of Arts; a Complete Dictionary of Contributors and their Work from its Foundation in 1769 to 1904*, 8 vols., London, 1905–1906).

[17] Elizabeth Mayhew of Boston, of whom AA2 wrote, "She has a most strange facinating power over me—I cannot account for it. I only know by experience that it is most true, and, I lament it" (vol. 5:195; see also vol. 3:108, 223).

[18] Pascal Paoli (1725–1807), Corsican general and patriot, helped free the island from Genoese domination during his fourteen years as its ruler. Unable to resist a new Genoese effort to regain control of Corsica with the help of the French military, he sought refuge in England in 1769. JA included Paoli in a possible guest list of "the oddest Collections of Personages that were ever put together" (*DNB*; JA, *D&A*, 2:381).

[19] Benjamin West Jr. was thirteen years old; possibly AA2 means his older brother, Raphael Lamar West, nineteen (Alberts, *Benjamin West*, p. 112, 72).

[20] *The Death of General Warren at the Battle of Bunker's Hill, 17 June 1775* by John Trumbull was the first in his series of American historical paintings. See the Descriptive List of Illustrations, No. 1, above. *The Death of General Montgomery in the Attack on Quebec, 31 December 1775* was completed in June (Theodore Sizer, *The Works of Colonel John Trumbull*, rev. edn., New Haven, 1967, p. 95, 96, and fig. 145).

[21] Mary Hallowell (b. 1762) was the daughter of Benjamin and Mary Boylston Hallowell (see Elizabeth Storer Smith to AA, 3 Jan., note 3, above; Robert Hallowell Gardiner, *Early Recollections*, Hallowell, Maine, 1936, p. 4, 11).

[22] John Anstey was appointed by the Loyalist Claims Commissioners in London to gather additional evidence and investigate fraudulent and unsubstantiated claims in the United States. He traveled throughout the U.S. from 1786 to 1788 (Smith, *Letters of*

Delegates, 23:243–244). He was a barrister but not a member of Parliament although described as such by both AA2 and JA. JA's letter to the state governors is dated [18] Dec. 1785 (LbC, Adams Papers). JA also wrote on Anstey's behalf on 26 Jan. 1786 to Samuel Adams (NN:George Bancroft Coll.) and John Jay (PCC, No. 84, VI, f. 79–82).

[23] On 12 May 1785 JQA left his family in Paris to return home to continue his education (*Diary*, 1:266).

[24] David Humphreys' *A Poem on the Happiness of America; Addressed to the Citizens of the United States* was published in London (see vol. 6:219, 223). His previous poems included *A Poem, Addressed to the Armies of the United States of America*, 1780, and *The Glory of America; or, Peace Triumphant over War: A Poem*, 1783.

[25] AA2 may have heard about Barclay's slow progress from David Humphreys (Thomas Jefferson to Humphreys, 5 Jan., Jefferson, *Papers*, 9:152). Barclay left Paris for Spain and Morocco on 15 Jan. but did not reach Cadiz until 9 May, and Morocco on 19 June. He promptly negotiated a treaty of peace and friendship with the emperor and returned to Spain in September. Jefferson approved the treaty on 1 Jan. 1787 in Paris, JA approved it on 25 Jan. in London, and Congress ratified it on 18 July (Jefferson, *Papers*, 9:234, 539; 10:71, 141, 403; Miller, *Treaties*, 2:185–227).

[26] John Lamb and Paul R. Randall left Paris for Spain and Algiers in Nov. 1785, arrived in Spain in December, but did not sail for Algiers until March. Randall stayed there only a few days while Lamb remained about a month and had an audience with the dey on 3 April; however, he found the price for ransoming 21 Americans then held captive to be prohibitive and returned to Spain. The United States did not conclude a treaty with Algiers until 1795 (Jefferson, *Papers*, 9:14, 137, 526, 530, 549–550; Miller, *Treaties*, 2:275–317).

[27] On 22 Sept. 1784, the American Commissioners (JA, Benjamin Franklin, and Thomas Jefferson) wrote to the Conde de Aranda, Spanish ambassador to France, informing him of their commission to negotiate a treaty of amity and commerce with Spain. De Aranda responded on 27 Sept., explaining that it was the custom of the Spanish court for such discussions to take place inside the boundaries of one of the countries involved and inquiring whether any of the U.S. commissioners was prepared to travel to Madrid to undertake the negotiations. Because the commissioners expected that negotiations with other maritime powers would occur in Paris, they replied on 28 Oct. that it was impossible to know when any of them would be able make the journey. Perhaps AA2 had offered to accompany JA if he was needed in Madrid (*Dipl. Corr., 1783–1789*, 1:508, 513–515).

[28] William Smith of Clapham, longtime member of the House of Commons, and his wife Frances Coape Smith welcomed the Adamses into their social circle shortly after the family's arrival in London (see vol. 6:305, 311, 361, 381, 479).

[29] While Queen Charlotte was born on 19 May 1744, she traditionally celebrated her birthday on 18 January. The queen's youngest brother, Prince George Augustus of Mecklenburgh-Strelitz, died on 9 Nov. 1785. Her sister-in-law, Princess Charlotte Wilhelmine of Hesse-Darmstadt, wife of Prince Charles of Mecklenburgh-Strelitz, died on 12 Dec. 1785 (vol. 6:483; *London Chronicle*, 20–22, 27–29 Dec. 1785).

[30] The *London Chronicle* of 6–8 Dec. 1785 printed a false report that the Prince of Wales was "supping" with the Adamses on 6 Dec. (see vol. 6:496–497).

[31] Patience Wright was a frequent visitor at the Adamses' Grosvenor Square home (vol. 6:172, 218, 306, 384).

[32] In 1782 Lord Shelburne named John Wilmot, a member of the House of Commons, a commissioner to investigate the claims of the American loyalists (Namier and Brooke, *House of Commons*, 3:645–646).

[33] On Edward Bridgen's friendship with the Adams family, see vol. 5:333 and JA, *Papers*, 9:12.

[34] JQA was acquainted with Paul R. Randall in Paris in 1785 (vol. 6:144, 147, 148).

[35] Uriah Forrest of Maryland was serving with the 3d Maryland Regiment when he was wounded and lost a leg at Germantown, 4 Oct. 1777. He resigned from the army in Oct. 1781 (Heitman, *Register Continental Army*).

[36] James Heyward (b. 1764) of St. John, Berkeley Parish, traveled extensively in Britain and the rest of Europe after obtaining a large income from his father's estates (James Barnwell Heyward II, *Heyward*, n.p., 1931, p. 54). Henry Gibbes (b. 1764) of Charlestown was admitted to the Middle Temple in April

1785 (E. Alfred Jones, *American Members of the Inns of Court*, London, 1924, p. 86). The other two South Carolinians were possibly George Redhead (b. ca. 1749) of Berekeley County and Thomas Shubrick Jr. (b. 1756) (*The Papers of Henry Laurens*, ed. David R. Chesnutt and C. James Taylor, 16 vols., Columbia, S.C., 1968–2003, 11:297, 472).

[37] JQA's friend, William Vans Murray of Cambridge, Md., was the son of Dr. Henry and Rebecca Orrick Murray. He was studying law in London in 1785 when he received the news of the death of his father, from, he later recalled, a "cold hearted lawyer" from home. Murray left the next day to stay with a friend in the country where he "went to bed from which [he] never rose for six weeks." He returned to the United States in 1787 (Peter P. Hill, *William Vans Murray, Federalist Diplomat*, Syracuse, N.Y., 1971, p. 1, 3, 7 [where Henry Murray's death date is erroneously given as 1787]; to JQA, 9 Feb. 1801, Adams Papers).

[38] Murray to JQA, 2 Aug. 1785 (Adams Papers). No reply from JQA has been found, and his correspondence with Murray did not resume until 1797, when Murray succeeded JQA as minister to the Netherlands (JQA, *Memoirs*, 1:189).

[39] John and Jane Marshall Rucker met the Adamses in France. He was a partner of Robert Morris' New York company (JQA, *Diary*, 1:233 and note 2; M. M. Quaife, ed., "Detroit Biographies: Alexander Macomb," *Burton Historical Collection Leaflet*, 10:7 [Nov. 1931]; *Recollections of Samuel Breck*, ed. H. E. Scudder, Phila., 1877, p. 85, 87).

[40] Betsey Ramsay was the half-sister of Jane Marshall Rucker (*Recollections of Samuel Breck*, p. 87). She is misidentified in the index to vol. 6.

[41] Thomas Boylston traveled from London to France in 1785 to sell American whale oil. On his 30 percent profit JA wrote, "He is an admirable Patriot when thirty per Cent can be made by Serving his Country" (to Jefferson, 19 Jan. 1786, Jefferson, *Papers*, 9:183). Nathaniel Barrett, representing American merchants, agreed on a six-year contract to supply oil for 400,000 livres per year with Pierre Tourtille Sangrain, who himself had a contract to supply oil to thirty French cities for fifteen years (vol. 6:388, note 10, 431, 432; Lafayette to JA, 9 Jan., MiU-C:Sydney Papers; Jefferson, *Papers*, 8:144–145; see also JA to Richard Cranch, 20 March, note 3, below).

[42] In 1785 JA had enlisted the help of Lafayette to explore the possibilities of selling American whale oil in France. Lafayette used his influence with Sangrain to help both Boylston and Barrett. Barrett wrote that the "Marquis de la fayette has been indefatigable in this Business" (to JA, 29 Jan., Adams Papers; Jefferson, *Papers*, 8:144–145; 9:46).

[43] "They order, said I, this matter better in France," Parson Yorick's opening observation in Laurence Sterne's *A Sentimental Journey*.

[44] Ambrose Phillips' tragedy *The Distrest Mother* was an adaptation of Racine's *Andromaque* (Margaret Drabble, ed., *Oxford Companion to English Literature*, 5th edn., N.Y., 1985).

[45] Ann Brunton (b. 1768), eldest child of actor John Brunton, first performed at Covent Garden in 1785, and her first appearance there as Juliet was on 14 Nov. (Phyllis Hartnoll, ed., *The Oxford Companion to the Theater*, 2d edn., London, 1957; *London Stage, 1776–1800*, 2:842).

[46] Gen. John Burgoyne was the author of the newly published *The Heiress*. See the Descriptive List of Illustrations, No. 2, above. JQA read the play in July 1786 (*Diary*, 2:65).

[47] Nine-year-old Susanna Copley and her three-year-old brother Jonathan died on 24 Oct. and 3 Nov. 1785, respectively (Jules David Prown, *John Singleton Copley*, 2 vols., Cambridge, 1966, 2:317).

[48] William Eden served in 1778 as a member of the Carlisle Peace Commission. A member of Parliament, he was part of the opposition to William Pitt until he changed sides in Dec. 1785 and was promptly named special envoy to France to negotiate a commercial treaty, which was concluded in Sept. (Namier and Brooke, *House of Commons*; *DNB*).

[49] Eden's predecessor, George Craufurd, had received his instructions in Sept. 1784 to open negotiations for a commercial treaty with France (Jefferson, *Papers*, 8:363). AA2's sentiments about Eden's potential success closely parallel those expressed by JA in a letter to Jefferson of 19 Jan. (Jefferson, *Papers*, 9:183).

[50] John Frederick Sackville, 3d duke of Dorset, was British ambassador to France 1783–1789; Jean Balthazar, Comte d'Adhémar, was French ambassador to Great Britain 1783–1787 (*DNB*; *Repertorium*, 3:118).

[51] Otherwise unidentified, Mr. Voss was described by Lucy Ludwell Paradise as "a very amiable honest and good young gentleman and a native of Virginia." He provided JA with information on the Virginia economy during his time in London and later delivered letters to JA from Thomas Jefferson (Jefferson, *Papers*, 9:183–184; 10:256, 302).

[52] In Oct. 1785, Jefferson wrote JA a letter of introduction for Déodat Guy Sylvain Tancrède Gratet de Dolomieu, a former French Army officer in America (Jefferson, *Papers*, 8:585).

[53] AA2 may intend Jeannerat de Dunilar, secretary of the Prussian legation in London since 1772 (*Repertorium*, 3:329).

[54] *The Provoked Husband*, completed by Colley Cibber in 1728, had been started as *A Journey to London* by John Vanbrugh (d. 1726) (*DNB*).

[55] The two actresses were probably Elizabeth Bannister and Patty Ann Bates (*London Stage, 1776–1800*, 2:860).

[56] Nicholas Rowe's *The Tragedy of Jane Shore*, based on the life of the mistress of King Edward IV. See also vol. 6:378, 388, for AA2's earlier comment on Sarah Siddons' pregnancy.

Abigail Adams to Mary Smith Cranch

My Dear Sister | London Janry 26 1785 [*i.e. 1786*]

A mr Anstey who is appointed by the British Goverment to visit the different States; for the purpose of assertaining the claims of the Loyalists, is going out in the Newyork packet. He dinned here on twesday. His manners are much in his favour, he appears well bred sensible and modest, a real Gentleman in his appearence. He was so kind as to offer to take Letters for us. As mr Adams and col Smith have large packets to charge him with I must be modest in mine, and can only write you one Letter. Of this too I must be circumspect, as it is probable it must have a post conveyance from Newyork to Boston.

I know not of any other opportunity whereby I can transmit you a line, to acquaint you that we have past through the Gloomy months of November and December without falling a sacrifice either to the cord, or Bullet, that we have all enjoy'd a comfortable share of Health. For myself I have had fewer headaches and less of the Rheumatisem than last winter.

Your Letters by captain Cushing came safe to hand, but those by Fletcher were drownded, some scattering fragments were however sent us.[1] My Friends will wait the return of cushing for answers to their kind Letters. He talks of sailing next month.

The Court and indeed the whole city of London have been two Months in mourning for the Queens Brother and a sister in Law. Tho Cloathed in Sable my mind has not corresponded with my dress untill last week; when I read in a Boston paper an account of the death of my dear and amiable Aunt. From your last letters, I feared the event, but hoped that she would gragele through as winter approachd. The melancholy news afflicted me with that real sorrow which flows from tender affection; and Sympathetick feelings for those whom she has left to mourn an affectionate wife, a most tender parent; a kind Aunt, and a truly benevolent Friend. Every tie which heretofore endeard the place of my Nativity to me is broken, and I think I should feel more reluctance at visiting it, than any other spot upon the Globe.

> "When Heaven would kindly set us free
> And Earths enchantments end
> It takes the most effectual way
> And robs us of our Friends."[2]

Poor Lucy has again lost a Mother,[3] may she imitate her virtues, which will ever endear to me, her memory.

I fear my dear sister that you will think the time very long before you will get any Letters from us. No opportunity has offerd except by way of Newyork. I wrote one Letter by the last packet, but had my reasons for writing no more.

We have been looking for Capt Young untill we are quite anxious for his fate. I wisht him to arrive before I replied to your Letters. I expect to learn by him what has been said respecting the decision upon a certain affair:[4] I suppose it will be the cause of much Speculation and I know that no arguments will now convince the Gentleman that the conduct of the Lady with respect to him, originated and resulted from his neglect of her. The World too I expect will asscribe to her fickleness and perhaps infidility. I know that she does not deserve the censure. I find mr — is desirious of keeping the matter Secreet. In justice to her character it ought to be known that with respect to him she considers herself perfectly free. I could have wisht that a longer period of time might have elapsed, that the World might have had no shadow for censure. At any rate the Gentleman in America can have *no hope left*, and I should sincerely rejoice to hear that he was married or upon the point of being so, and let him not asscribe his dissapointment to you, to me, or to any person but himself. He has been too liberal in his censure, he is totally mistaken. You have been as tender as I know you ought to have been. I wish him no harm, but every happiness in his power to obtain. I value his good qualities, and I feel not a little for the Situation in which he has placed himself.

I know I leave you in a puzzel. I cannot be more explicit at present, but rest assured that I have papers in my possession which will convince all concernd, that no dishonorable conduct has been practised.

I hope long before this time mr Storer has reach'd his Friends in Boston. We learn by the Newspapers only of his arrival at Newyork. We wonder he did not write. We mist him much, and the more, because col Smith did not return from his Tour to Berlin Vienna and Paris, till some time in december. Col Humphries came with him from Paris and has been here ever since. Col Humphries is a Gentleman of Learning wit and Humour with a benevolent disposition and a good Heart, united with perhaps the best poetical Genious our Country can boast. I dare say you have seen his poem addrest to the American Army. He is now publishing an other poem here; one of which I will send you by the first opportunity. In short I do not know two Worthyer characters than the two Secretaries of Legation who are very intimate Friends, yet very different in their manners and accomplishments.

You wish to know how I pass my time, my acquaintance my amusements &c.

Those matters I must leave for more direct conveyances. I thank you my dear sister for all your kind attention to my children. I have no anxiety on their account, what I feel arises from a fear of burdening my Friends and not having it in my power to make them compensation. I fear I shall not be able to write only to you, so kindly remember me to all my dear Friends and believe me ever your affectionate Sister AA

RC (MWA:Abigail Adams Corr.).

[1] The *Ceres*, Capt. Fletcher, which sailed from Boston in late Oct. 1785, struck the sands near Boulogne, France, on 27 Nov. and was lost (vol. 6:474; *Massachusetts Centinel*, 1 Feb.).

[2] Edward Young, *Resignation in Two Parts, and a Postscript*, Part 1, lines 310–313.

[3] In addition to losing her aunt Lucy Quincy Tufts, Lucy Jones also had lost her mother, AA's cousin Anna Tufts Jones, who had died at age thirty in 1774 (*Vital Records of Salem, Massachusetts: to the End of the Year 1849*, 6 vols., Salem, Mass., 1916–1925, 5:364). Lucy's father, Peter Jones, had died in 1772 (same, p. 365).

[4] AA2's dismissal of Royall Tyler.

John Quincy Adams to William Cranch

My dear Friend Haverhill Feby: 6. 1786

Although I have been writing a long Letter to Charles,[1] I still must find something to say to you, as I believe, I am in your debt. I hope however you will not stand upon ceremonies, but write whenever you can. Your benevolence will induce you to take the will for the deed, if I am not quite so punctual, as I should wish to be. I have just this moment shook hands with one Mr. Xenophon, that put out a book once, *consarning* history. I have finished four books, and shall therefore have nothing more to do with him here.[2] I got through the first book of the Iliad, three or four days, after you left us, and shall attempt the second, to-morrow, I wish you would inform me exactly where you are, and where you suppose, you may be at the end of the ensuing Quarter. I think you said you had just begun the sixth book, do you think, you shall more than go through it? If not I hope to be up with you, by that time. But above all, be kind enough to remember, and enquire of Mr: Williams, whether he begins his Lecture, in March, or not till the end of the spring Vacancy.[3]

Sister Eliza came from Master White's last Thursday, and we shall now be favoured with her Company, during the remainder of her stay here; our friend Leonard, will carry you a letter from her.[4]

The nearer we approach to any thing we desire, the greater is our impatience, to obtain it. I think more and more every day of being with you, and am pleased to see the time continually shortening. I had almost said like a certain gentleman expert in similies, that to be with you is as necessary to my Nature as a ——.[5]

On Wednesday the 15th: day of February, of the current year 1786, do you William Cranch, between the hours of 8 and 10, in the Evening, write me a Letter, in which you will in a rational, Philosiphical, and Mathematical, (ay and a Logical) manner, prove that the green ends of asparagus, were designed by Nature, to be eat by man; and mind, upon what foundation your System shall stand, for as I mean to oppose it, with all the zeal, that the importance of the matter requires; I shall take every possible advantage, to support my plan: which is that the white ends were designed by nature for the food of man. However if you are of my opinion, I would not force you to maintain the Contrary; because I always stand up for Liberty of Conscience, and I exhort you, in the discussion of this Question, to be cool; because, violence never can do good to any System, upon a contested point. I might enlarge upon this subject, but will wait for your answer, first.

I intend to fill this page, before I close this Sentimental, poetical, and affecting Letter of mine, and I have been rubbing my skull to bring something out of it; but it tells me, it has nothing to say, and that I must e'en close the Letter, as I have carried it on, without the help of the brain.

You will write back by the first opportunity, and tell me how all the folks in Braintree &c do; and especially, that sweet gentleman, who expressed so much indignation, to think a youth who had made the tour of Europe, should study closely after returning.

Have you look'd into that piece of Poetry put out some time ago by one Cleanthes. If you have let us hear how he talks in English.[6]

Thy loving friend JQA

RC (privately owned, 1957); addressed: "Mr: William Cranch Cambridge. favd: by Mr: White."; endorsed: "JQA. Feby. 6. 1786 Haverhill."

[1] Not found.

[2] JQA began Xenophon's *Cyropaedia*, a historical novel in eight books, in Nov. 1785 (*Diary*, 1:363).

[3] Samuel Williams, Hollis Professor of Mathematics and Natural and Experimental Philosophy at Harvard College, offered a lecture course on experimental philosophy (physics) annually (same, 2:ix–x, 11).

[4] Elizabeth Cranch had been visiting Peggy White in Haverhill since Oct. 1785. Her brother Leonard White was a student at Harvard (vol. 5:209; 6:421).

[5] Thus in MS.

[6] The first entry in M/JQA/28 is "A Translation of Cleanthes, his hymn to Jupiter" completed by JQA on 1 Nov. 1784 (Adams Papers, Microfilms, Reel No. 223). See also vol. 6:448, 450, for JQA's previous correspondence with Cranch about the hymn.

Abigail Adams 2d to John Quincy Adams

N 12

Feb. 9th. [1786] Thursday

This my Brother is the day appropriated for the celebration of the Queens Birth day. It really comes in june but as the Kings is in that Month they defer its celebration to this season. Kings and Princess you know may do any thing which their power will permit with impunity. But to tell you—at 2 oclock we were dressd, Mamma in a sattin of the new fashiond Colour which is Called the spanish fly,[1] trimed with Crepe and Gold fringe. My dress was pink sattin trimmed with Crepe and silver fringe and some *Persons of taste* told me that tho they saw more expensive and more superb dresses at Court they did not see one, more elegant and neat than my Ladyships. Now who think you this was. *Why Mr Humphryes—and for all the World his taste is excellent*. At two oclock, Mamma and myself got into the Carriage, and proceeded, on our way to st James's. The Curiossity of People was so great having never seen any thing of the kind before. That the road from, Piccadilly to the Pallace was so obstructed by Carriages full of People to look at the Ladies who might pass on their Way, that there was no such thing as getting through. So we went through st James park and found no difficulty. Mr Humphryes attended us. Every thing is upon so independant a scale here that the attendance of a Gentleman is Considered almost unpolite. The Ladies, assume all the Roughness, and Assureance necessary to support them upon every occasion, and in General I think they look like Giant apes. But tho we found no difficulty till we got to the 2d room, here commenced such a scene as I was never, Witness to before. Their Majestys had gone in before we arrived. At the dore of the 2d room, I was, struck with the appearance of a figure which at first sight I took to be King Brant or Joseph Brant an Indian Cheif, who has, been here sometime from America.[2] He was engaged against us in the late War. It is a matter of speculation what can be his erand here at present. Some suppose it is to get payd for the scalps he took in the War, and to get Compensation for his services. He has been presented to the King and Queen and has appeard at the drawing Room, in the dress of his Nation with that *pretty plaything his Tommy Hawk* in his hand. The Ladies admired his figure, and saw in his Countenance something Good. He has indeed been noticed by some People of importance. There was a feast made for him by, some Persons of distinction at Which the Company all were drunk, except himself. He observed it would not do for him to Get drunk in this Country, tho it would in his own. But to adone with Joseph Brant after telling you one anecdote more which is that Colln Smith was upon an expedition against him during the Ware when Brant and Butler had like to have been taken.[3] He is celebratd for his Cruelty at Yomen.[4] And to return to the Personage whom I was presented with, it was no less than the Minister from Tripoli,[5] with two pages, dressd in the Habit of his Country a turban upon his Head and his [long?] baird, and his dress otherwise as singular and such a dirty set of creatures I never saw. I was absolutely frightened. He is an addition to the singularity of the Corps diplomatick. I hear the Foreign Ministers donot intend to have any intercourse with him—but more of him by and by. At the entrance of the door of the third appartment where the drawing Room is held, I thought for all the World that I should have been squeezed to death between the post of the door, and half a dozen great Hoops. Indeed you can have no idea at all of the croud. I am sure I never was in such a one before. This you must suppose excellent for the Ladies dresses. [We?] at last got into the room, and situated ourselvs, so that the King spoke to us very soon. He has askd me one question for these three Months—(*do you get out much this weather*) instructive, improving, indeed. After this ceremony was over we attempted to put ourselvs in the Way of the Queen, but the room was so croudd that was two Hours before we could find out in what part of it she was. Finally your Mamma was spoken to, and I made my escape as quick as I could. The King was very richly dressd the Queen very plain. The Prince of Waless cloaths were Coverd with silver. I dare not venture to say how much I heard they Cost, but I did not think them elegant. The Princesses[6] were not so elegant as many other Ladies, present. The dressing were very various there was no prevailing Colour or fashion, every-one seemd to have exerted their own fancy. But such was the crowd that the floor was covered with fragments of triming and lookd as if the Ladies had been paling Caps.[7] We got home at five, not a little fatigued but however as it was the first time we were told it was essential that we should go to the Ball, and as there were seats for the families of the Foreign Ministers and I had an inclination to see it we went. Pappa dined with Lord Carmarthen Mr Humphrys and Mr Smith with us. At half after seven we set off again, and arrived before the Ball Room was open, which was an advantage as we could get in before the croud. At the door of the Ball room we met the Master of the Cerimonies, Mr Cottril, who was very polite and seated us in the Foreign Box. There was no person in it except the Tripolian, who I described in the Morning, the singularity of Whose appearance attracted the eyes of all the Ladies. There was a Gentleman who was an interpreter to him, for he speaks not a Word of English. In describing the Ball room to you I shall easily find words to convey to you an idea of its elegance. Consert Hall is as much superior to it, as you can conceive, the room is as large again as Concert Hall. You know the palace was formerly an oald Abby and I suppose this was the Chapell. There is a galery above which is Called the Lord Chamberlins Box, where Persons are admitted as spectators. It is generally very crouded. As you enter the door upon the right hand is half a dozen rows of seats for the Lords and Ladies attending upon their Majesties. Upon the other side of the room, are the seats for the Foreign Ministers. At the Corner are seats for the Pearesseses. And upon the opposite side are seats for any Persons who may choose to go provided they wear a ball dress. For their is no distinction any body may go to the Ball—in bal dress—which is a singular arangment I think. These seats are all inclosed, by rails, and you are let in like a turnpike. Sir Clement Cottril Master of the Ceremonies, came and placed himself, next Mamma, as he said to keep the turnpike and to be sure it had the appearance, these rails, you see [faced?] also the inclosure. At the Head, there were placed two oald Chairs for their Majesties. Before the seats of the Foreign Ministers were seats for the Ladies attending upon the

Princesses, and before them were three seats, for the Prince of Wales and Princesses. Within this, were seats for the Ladies who were to dance. There were a Dozen I believe. In this way the Company were seated. A little before Nine the Prince came staggering in. I dont mean he was in Liquaur, but his manner was, careless drowliry. He chatted with the Ladies who were to dance. There is a good deel of good Humour in His Countenance and you [*know*] it is the fashion to think him the Criterion of perfection. At Nine their Majestys entered, with the 2 princesses. The Company all rose, the King and Queen went round the Circle and spoke to the Ladies who were to dance. When they Came to the seats of the Foreign Ministers, they spoke to the Spanish, who is a great favourite at Court as it is said, to the dutch and to the French.[8] I was seated next del Campo who is allways very polite, and the King came Laughing and grining and addressd him as Mrs Wright say What What What What in a breath. At last they sat down, and the Company also. The Prince opened the Ball with the Princess Royal, and danced a second minuet with the princess Augusta after which there were many minuets danced, till I was quite tired. Each Gentleman and Lady when they came up to dance, made a bow and Curstey first to their Majestys, and then danced ther minuets, and I am sure without prejudice I have seen better minuets in America. The Princesses do not dance so well as many other Ladies. When the minuets were finished six People stood up as for County dances, the Prince and Princess Royal, at the Head. There were three dances danced and the Prince askd the Quen, if He shold be permitted to dance another, but She nodding dissent, the Royal Family retird at Eleven. At the 3d dance the Prince some how, I dont know how, had a fall, and the first that we saw was he Laed flat on his back. But fore we could think he recoved himself and continued, his dance. And now I must repeat that I have seen Gentlemen and Ladies dance better in America. But it would be dreadfull to say so, nor shold I be beleived so Ill save my opinion for some other time. We came away immediately, and got home 20 minutes past Eleven, drank tea and retired. And here you have an accout of the Birth day Ball. I hope it will amuse you. I am quite sattisfied I assure you with seeing it once, and am sure that my own inclination will never carry me there again, tho every thing was as we could have wishd. Mr Smith took Care of us.

[*10–12 February*]

Fryday Saturday and sunday, we were alone, and at home.

Monday 13th of Feb.

Mr Humphryes breakfasted with us and soon after sett off for Paris. He proposes returning to America in April, the reason he gives is that he has written to Mr Jay that he should return early in the Spring if he did not hear from him. Pappa advises him to stay till the expiration of his Commision which is not till june, but He thinks the season will be too far advanced and I believe, his real intention is to return and spend some time with General Washington to Collect what materials he can for, the History of America. At least from a Letter of the Generals Which He shew a friend: wherein this wish was exprest, I am led to judge it, and He told the same friend that He would go home and shut himself up for six months to write prose.[9] He has risen much in our esteem, since this visit, and is a very worthy Good Man, not possessd of all the elegances of appearance, but has all the essentials of a Worthy character and is an amiable Man. We were much amused with his Wit and good Humour, and we shall miss him much. Mr Shot goes out with him to America. Mr Jefferson will be left alone.[10]

Mrs Bingham called upon us very early, to request Mamma to present her at Court on thursday, where I suppose she will make a figure. I went at twelve to visit, Call upon Mrs Roggers at Mrs Copelys, where she is setting for her picture.[11] And in the Evening we went to Drury Lane Theatre, we took a Box a week ago, and offerd Mrs Rucker seats. This Evening we went, there were Mamma Pappa myself Mr Smith Mr and Mrs Rucker Miss Ramsay. Mrs R. is much disappointed by Mr Ruckers concluding to continue here 18 Months longer. She had made ⟨*some*⟩ great dependance upon returning this spring. The peices given were the Strangers at home, and the Romp. In both Mrs Jordon a favourite Actress playd a principle part.[12] She is small, and pets the romp, in imitably. I never saw so much vivacity in any Countenance or in any action before. She received the greatest applause, and very deservedly. I think her stile of play is in Wild Characters, and She supports them better than any of the American *Ladies*, ⟨*who displease you so much*⟩ The romp represents a young West Indian sent to England for her Education. Her Gaurdian ⟨*prepares to Marry her to his*⟩ as an oald Miser who has a Nephew who is a Grocer, and a fool, his Name is Potty. He

3. ABIGAIL BROMFIELD ROGERS, BY JOHN SINGLETON COPLEY, 1786
See page x

makes Love to her and proposes going off with her. And she sees a young officer, who pleases her and she determines to run of with him. To affect this she proposed to go off with potty and to meet the Captain who is to take her from him and marry her himself, but in this she is detected and brought back to her Guardian. The Whole is very comick, and her Acting makes it very amusing. The Character as a West Indian is Well supported. She has a little Negro called Washeball, and her treatment of her is, quite, as a West I.

Tuesday 14th.

Agreeable to invitation we went to dine at Mr Blakes from Carolina. His family has been in this Country many years. He was in Boston about 18 Months since and would have purchased General Warens House at Milton but they differed in the Price. He is the first fortune in America. His income is fiteen thoussand, a year. Mrs Blake appears to be a worthy amiable Woman. She reminded me of aunt Smith in Person and manners. They have one Daughter about fifteen years oald. She is a pretty figure but not a handsome face, agreeable in her manners, plays vastly well, and draws very prettyly. They live very elegantly.[13] The Company was, Pappa Mamma myself Mr Smith a Mr Hayward and Mr Gibbs, from Carolina and Mr Bridgen. The dinner was elegant and every thing very cleaver. Miss Blake playd to us after dinner. We sat till Nine and came home. They are regular Folks. Mrs B. does not seem to be fond of the kind of Life in vogue here. And we had no Cards.

When we got home we found upon the table a budget of letters which kept us employd from Nine oclock to twelve in reading. You know the pleasure of such a feast. Yours No 9 10 11, gave me great pleasure.[14] I shall indeed be very loth to give up, so much gratification but however, I leave you to act as your time will permit knowing that nothing but necessity will induce you to omit this attention. In my turn I will indeavour to be as Constant in my diary as I have been, and shall omit no opportunity when it is avoidable, for you have appeald to a very interested principle for desicion. I can write to you, always, and never take my pen, not knowing what to say but to my other Correspondents I am often at a loss, and sometimes neglect to write for want of a subject, or rather from not knowing what will please them. Pappa asks to see your journal, and I cannot refuse him. He appears allways gratified with it, and told me that he can excuse your not writing to him, as your diary to me is so particular and entertaining. He is often pleased when you have mentioned his oald friends. Mamma, derives equal pleasure from it, and says, you must not discontinue it: she cannot allow it, that you must spare half an hour a day to it, and When you get to Cambridge, you will have time enough to continue it. To me you must know my Dear Brother that it is one of the greatest Gratifications I can receive. You have been very good hithertoo and, I know if it is possible you will continue. Your observations upon Characters is not only entertaining but improving, and my pleasure must be lessened when you curtail your observations. Your letters I submit also, to the perusal, of Mr Smith, who is equally pleasd. Donot tell me I am wrong—you must not think so. He is interested in what gives me pleasure, and you would not refuse an opportunity to return it. He says sometimes that he will write you, and I believe it will not be long before you receive a letter. Mamma I suppose will tell you in what relation this Gentleman is Considered in this family, and you my Brother know that your approbation is dear to me. I will now begin and Notice your letters reguliarly.

Wedensday, 15th.

Mr Barthlemy[15] and Mr and Mrs Bingham Called in the Evening they had dined with Lord Lansdown, and called to let us know it I suppose.

Thursday, 16th.

Mamma went to Court to present Madame Bingham—and Pappa presented Mr Chew.[16] Mrs B. is comeing quite into fashion here, and she is gretly admired. The Hair dresser who dresses us upon Court days, inquired of Mamma whether she knew the Lady so much talkd of here from America—Mrs Bingham. He had heard of her from a Lady who saw her at Lord Lucans,[17] where she was much admired. At last speaking of Miss Hamilton, he said, with a twurl of his Comb, Well it does not signify but the American Ladies to beat the English all to nothing. I did not attend her, for going to Court is not so agreeable to me. Perhaps, admiration might heigten the pleasure, but as it is what I never wishd nor have no pretentions to I shall not be mortified by silence: Mamma says, if admiration could make this Lady happy she must be so, for she never saw one so much stared at. There she goes cried one, what an elegant Woman, another as she passd. And some Gentlemen told mamma she had got to present one of the finest Women he ever saw. I dare say she is not void of vanity and if not must have been gratified. She is indeed a fine Woman.

Thursday Eve Pappa went out to make some visits, and Mamma myself and Mr Smith were soberly seated at a Game of Cards when Mr Crawford, came in, and soon after Lady Juliana Pen.[18] They passd, an hour and went of. But now to give you some account of a visit Pappa made this Evening. It was to no less a Personage than the Ambassador from Tripola. As the Foreign Ministers had many of them left Cards at his Excellencys door, Pappa thought proper to do so too, and as he was making a Number of visits in this Way, stopped at his door, intending only to leave a Card, but the servants announced his Turkship to be at home. So Pappa went in and by a little Italian and French with some Langua Franca, they got into Conversation, and understood each other wondrously. There were to pages present and a servant soon brought too long Pipes, one for Pappa and the other of Monsieur la Turke, with two cups of Coffe. Pappa took both and resting the bowl of the Pipe upon the floor, while the stem was in his mouth smoaked away, taking a sip of Coffe and a Whif at his pipe. The Abassador did the same. At last one of the secretaries cried out in ectacy, to Pappa—Monsieur vous etes un veritable Turk. When the pipe was out Pappa left him. We were much amused with this account of the visit.[19]

Sunday [*19 February*].

The Ambassador from tripola sent a mesage to Pappa that he wished to return his visit in the same friendly stile which he had made his, and begd him to appoint an hour. At twelve they came, I only saw them getting out of the Coach. The Ambassador, was dressed as usual, and his secretary both as described in the former part of my letter. He brought with him an interpreter of his own, not choosing the one appointed by this Court. He was attended by two servants in the habit of their Country there dress was a kind of orange Colour, loose, tied round the Waiste, with a kind of turban on their heads, and sandals on their feet. He was here two Hours, but Pappa could not offer him a long Pipe, so that was dispenced with. This must not be communicated in America, something favourable may arrise from these Conferences. But we are not at liberty to say, what. Thus much I may say to you, as sacred, that the Treaties with the 4 states Algiers Morrocco Tripoli and Tunis will cost two hundred thousand Guineas, at least. The Ambassador is known to many of the Foreign Ministers and they all agree that he is a very good Man. There were several Gentlemen dined with us to day. Capt Lyde Mr Jenks, and a Capt Beaudinoit from NY, Mr

Trumble and a Dr Lions, a virginian agreeable in his manners.[20] He reminded me of Mr Short. Now you will laugh, and say I am always, finding resemblances, where they donot exist. I think that I can observe a simularity in the looks and manners of all the Virginians. The rest of our Company you know. In the Evening Pappa and Mr Smith went to see Dr Jebb,[21] who has been confined for some time by indisposition and this Evening Poor Mrs Wright died. Her zeal I beleive for America, has ended her days.

Monday 20th.

Pappa and Mr Smith dined with Mr William Vaughan,[22] and made a third visit in the Evening to his Turkship.

Tuesday 21st.

Coll Smith set off for Paris to persuade Mr Jefferson to come over upon *matters of importance* but his real erand is not to be made known here—it is upon the subject of the *late Conferences*.[23] What arrangements they will produce I know not at present. The Baron de Linden called in the Evening. Did you ever see this Genious, he has strong traits of National Character, which are very appearant and he is profuse in nothing but Compliments which cost him nothing, not even a tax upon his sincerity, for they are not esteemed of more value by the receiver than the doner. He sat an hour, and drank tea parcque les belles mains du Mademoiselle le fait.

Wedensday [22 *February*].

In the Evening a Mr Peters from Philadelphia, who was formerly in the War office with your father and a friend of his, called upon us. He had just arrived, and this was the first visit he had made. His first appearance was not very promising, but he soon discovered the character which I had heard of him. He is rather rough in his manners, but he is sensible, and has a great del of Wit, which soon appeard, and made us very mery. It seems his erand to this Country is to see his father who has lived here many years, and he has one Brother who has been with him and has had influence enough over him in his oald age to induce him to make a Will so much in his favour, as to be very injurious to this Gentleman as well as all his other Chrildren and he has I think nine sisters. This Gentleman has been with him and dispairs of any alteration, which has made him very low spiritted, he says.[24] He does not regret it for himself, because he is one of those extraordinary Men who think they have enough but it is for others that he is interested. He has not neither heard from his family since he left them, which Oh, Dear, When shall I hear from my Wife, said he, taking a packet he had just received out of his pocket to search for a letter and finding a very long one from some friend after looking it over, oh, I had rather have one line from my Wife than the Whole of these pages. Pappa told him he had been seperated from Madame 4 or 5 years. Ah said he you are a Politician and I am a domestick man, who takes pleasure only in my family. He made many good observations upon this Country, and would not live in it for half the Kingdom. Said he was disappointed he had thought more highly of it than he found it deserved. Pittied Pappas situation and advised him to go home. Scolded at Congress, at the states &c. He left us at Eleven.

Thursday, 22d. [*i.e.* 23]

Pappa went to the drawing Room, and afterwards to dine with Lord Carmarthen. Mamma was very much indisposed, all day.

Fryday 23d. [*i.e.* 24]

I went out in the Morning and called on Mrs Roggers, passd two hours with her, and then made a visit to Mrs Rucker, at the Adelphi. Mr R has determined to spend another year here, and Mrs R is much disappointed in not going home this Spring. Miss Ramsay is quite Sick of England, since she came from Paris, and they seem to be much retired. Mr Peters dined with us, and Pappa proposed going to the Play with him. The Carriage was ordered, but they got engaged in Conversation till it was too late, for we dine so late here that one must Hurry to be in season.

Saturday 25th.

Mamma and miself went and drank tea with Mrs Roggers.

Sunday 26th.

To-Day we had three Gentlemen to dine. Mr John Boylstone from Bath you know, He is a [tired?] oald Bachelor, and was very sociable.[25] A Capt Biglow from Boston[26] and Mr Peters, who seems to be in a disagreeable situation of Mind, he calls it the Blue Devils. I never saw a Person so much agitated without any known cause. He told us after dinner that he felt much better for the Hermitage and Maderia, which he had drank. You ask in one of your letters about Pappas Wine.[27] That from the Hague came very well and secure.

But that from Paris got piladged at the Custom House and as much more as there was, above the quantity permitted to the Foregn Ministers we had to pay duties for, and it happend [*to*] the Wine ordinaire, which was intolerable. Pappa often recollects what you used to say, that when he got to England he wold think all his Wine good. Mr Boylstone inquired after, you. Pappa told him that you were gone home to go to Colledge. What said he as Professor of something I suppose. No, you was gone as a student to pass one year. Why he knows more than students Tutors, Governors and all. What he is gone to teach them then, and seemd very much surprizd and said you had begun at the wrong end first, and in his Way, payd your Honour these Compliments. He gave us some very pressing invitations to Come to Bath. Capt Biglow, I dont recollect having seen in Boston yet his Countenance was not that of a stranger.

Mr Bingham called this Morn. There Baggage is all on Board and they are only waiting for a fair Wend. He made a declaration this Morning that if he got safely to America, there was nothing in this World that should induce him to come again to Europe. He was heartily sick and tired of a wandering Life and longed to get home and settled in Business. But after all I guess there was a mental reservation in all this—What think you!—I have lately heard that he is connected with some Houses in America which owed large sums to this Country. But there is no danger but he will take Care of himself.

Monday, Feb 27th.

We have had the last Night and it continues to day, as severe a snow storm as, we have in america at this season. The weather has been as cold since last tuesday so we have it with us, and the Wind East and so high, that it has been impossible to pass from Dover to Calais. Colln Smith has been detained there ever since tuesday, and there is no prospect of its discontinueance. It now snows with all violence. The weather for a forghtnight before was, as uncommonly fine. Indeed too warm to be agreeable for the season, which renders this sudden change particuliarly disagreeable.

Dft (Adams Papers).

[1] Named for a bright green beetle native to southern Europe, often made into a powder and used medicinally.

[2] Mohawk chief Joseph Brant (Thayendanegea) was in London to expedite the settlement of Mohawk claims for losses incurred during the Revolutionary War. He also desired a definitive answer from the British government as to whether it would support the Indians during any future hostilities with the United States (Isabel Thompson Kelsay, *Joseph Brant, 1743–1807:*

Man of Two Worlds, Syracuse, N.Y., 1984, p. 380–392).

[3] In Aug. 1779, Maj. Gen. John Sullivan's troops, including WSS, routed a combined British and Indian force led by Maj. John Butler of the British Indian department and Joseph Brant at Newtown (now Elmira), N.Y. WSS commanded several detachments as Sullivan pursued the enemy and destroyed forty Indian villages in New York over the next two months (same, p. 258–267; John Sullivan, affidavit of WSS's military service, 13 Oct. 1779, MHi:De Windt Coll.).

[4] Probably a misspelled reference to the Wyoming massacre (July 1778), where Maj. John Butler's forces took over 200 scalps and caused great destruction. Brant, however, did not participate in the action though many people believed he did (Kelsay, *Joseph Brant*, p. 218–222).

[5] Ambassador Sidi Haggi 'Abd-ur-rahman Aga presented his credentials in January (*Repertorium*, 3:457–458). The London newspapers made much of the ambassador's presence in Great Britain and at the ball. The *Morning Post and Daily Advertiser*, 10 Feb., noted that he came with two attendants, "all of them were dressed in the habits of their country, and appeared much delighted and astonished at the crowd of beauties that surrounded them; nor were they less objects of wonder to our fair countrywomen, who beheld with admiration; the venerable beard of this *great Plenipo*."

[6] George III's two eldest daughters, Charlotte and Augusta (*London Chronicle*, 9–11 Feb.).

[7] That is, decorating their caps with stripes (*OED*).

[8] Spanish ambassador Bernardo del Campo y Pérez de la Serna, Dutch minister Baron Dirk Wolter Lynden van Blitterswyck, and French ambassador Jean Balthazar, Comte d'Adhémar.

[9] On several occasions Humphreys suggested that George Washington write a history of the American Revolution, or, more specifically, an autobiographical account of the war. Unable to persuade Washington to undertake the project, Humphreys contemplated completing it himself, an idea the general enthusiastically endorsed in a letter dated 25 July 1785 (Washington, *Papers, Confederation Series*, 2:269, 3:148–151). Humphreys did not begin work on his "Life of General Washington" immediately but returned to the project in 1787 or 1788 while staying at Mount Vernon. He published portions of the material anonymously in 1789 but never finished it. For a complete history of the manuscript, as well as the text itself, see *David Humphreys' "Life of George Washington,"* ed. Rosemarie Zagarri, Athens, Ga., 1991.

[10] Humphreys sailed for America in April but William Short, Jefferson's private secretary, did not accompany him (vol. 6:9; Jefferson, *Papers*, 8:547, 9:449).

[11] For Copley's portrait of Abigail Bromfield Rogers, see the Descriptive List of Illustrations, No. 3, above.

[12] *The Strangers at Home*, a comic opera by James Cobb, music by Thomas Linley, was first performed at the Drury Lane Theatre on 8 Dec. 1785 and marked Dorothea Bland Jordan's debut as a singer on the London stage. T. A. Lloyd's *The Romp*, a farce, ca. 1780, was an abridgement of *Love in the City*, a comic opera by Isaac Bickerstaffe, 1767 (*Biographia Dramatica*, 2:388, 3:223, 303; *London Stage, 1776–1800*, 2:848).

[13] William and Anne Izard Blake and their daughter Anne, who lived to the 1860s and died unmarried (vol. 6:479, 482; JA, *D&A*, 3:182; Walter B. Edgar and N. Louise Bailey, *Biographical Directory of the South Carolina House of Representatives*, Columbia, 1977, 2:82–83; *South Carolina Historical and Genealogical Magazine*, 1:162 [1900]).

[14] JQA to AA2, 8 Sept., 19 Sept., and 1 Oct. 1785 (vol. 6:350–355, 369–377, 398–406).

[15] François Barthélemy, the French chargé d'affaires in London (vol. 6:303, 311).

[16] Benjamin Chew Jr. (1758–1844) studied at the College of Philadelphia and the Middle Temple. He returned to Philadelphia in 1786 and practiced law (Henry Simpson, *The Lives of Eminent Philadelphians, Now Deceased*, Phila., 1859, p. 203–204; vol. 6:388, note 4).

[17] Charles Bingham (1735–1799), Baron Lucan of Castlebar, later Earl of Lucan (*DNB*, Margaret Bingham).

[18] Lady Juliana Fermor Penn (1729–1801), a daughter of Thomas, 1st Earl of Pomfret, was the widow of Thomas Penn, a son and heir of Pennsylvania founder and proprietor William Penn. Her son John held the largest claim to the family's American estate (*DNB*; Lorett Treese, *The Storm Gathering: The Penn Family and the American Revolution*, University Park, Penna., 1992, p. 17, 195–200, 205).

[19] For a more detailed account of this visit, see JA to Thomas Jefferson, 17 Feb. (Jefferson, *Papers*, 9:285–287).

[20] Dr. James Lyons, College of William and Mary 1776, completed his medical degree at the University of Edinburgh in 1785 and was on his return trip to the United States (Jefferson, *Papers*, 9:259, 15:484; Washington, *Diaries*, 5:330).

[21] For Dr. John Jebb, a former cleric and physician, see 6:222, note 30.

[22] William Vaughan (1752–1850), a merchant and author, was a long-time supporter of the American cause (*DNB*; JQA, *Diary*, 1:198).

[23] In their recent conversations, the Tripolitan ambassador had presented JA with the chance to conclude a treaty of peace between their two nations. JA was convinced the United States must do so immediately or be drawn into "a universal and horrible War . . . which will continue for many Years." He impressed upon Jefferson that "There is nothing to be done in Europe, of half the Importance of this, and I dare not communicate to Congress what has passed without your Concurrence" (to Jefferson, 21 Feb., Jefferson, *Papers*, 9:295; see also JA to John Jay, 17 Feb., JA, *Works*, 8:372–373).

[24] Richard Peters (1744–1828) served on the Continental Board of War and Ordnance from 1776 to 1781 and was elected a delegate to Congress in 1782. He served in both the Pennsylvania house of representatives and senate before being appointed judge of the U.S. district court of Pennsylvania in 1792, an office he held until his death. He married Sarah Robinson in 1776. His father, William Peters, had been register of admiralty and judge of the court of common pleas in Philadelphia prior to returning to England sometime after 1771. Peters evidently resolved the situation with his father, as he eventually inherited his father's estate, Belmont, in Pennsylvania. While in England, Peters also worked to arrange for the ordination of episcopal bishops for the United States (*DAB*).

[25] For John Boylston, the cousin of JA's mother, see vol. 4:201. JA and JQA visited Boylston in Dec. 1783 when they made a brief visit to Bath, and AA would visit him during her trip to Bath in Dec. 1786 (JA, *D&A*, 3:151; AA to JA, 30 Dec., below).

[26] The *Two Brothers*, Capt. Biglow, arrived at Gravesend from New England, 11 Feb. (London *Daily Universal Register*, 14 Feb.).

[27] JQA to AA2, 29 Aug. 1785 (vol. 6:324–325).

Mary Smith Cranch to Abigail Adams

My dear Sister — Braintree February 9th 1786

The vacancy is up and our Sons are just return'd to their Studies at college. Were they Brothers they could not be fonder of each other than they now are. They have spent eight or Ten days at Haverhill, and have rov'd about visiting their Friends till they both long'd heartily for the methodical Life they left at Cambridge. I have promiss'd them a chamber and a Fire too themselves if they should live to see another winter vacancy In which they may study as much as they please. It is impossible they should do it amidst the business of a Family. We have had our Hands full ever since they came home, for notwithstanding we mend their Linnen and stockings [*e*]very week yet their other clothing wants abundance of repairing. Yesterday we loaded them away stores and all. Cousin charles says "Aunt I am sure you must hire a waggon, to convey us and our Baggage when we all get to college." I know you wish to hear how cousin charles behaves. As well I believe as a youth possible can. I can neither hear off nor see any thing that looks like extravagance in him.

He has the Love of his class and the approbation of his Tutors. He is exceedingly fond of mr James whos Freshman he is.[1] I keep a good look out upon the children, and I think I am not deceiv'd in any of them. As for Cousin John, He has not lost his studious disposition by coming to america. I was almost affraid to let our children visit Haverhill this vacancy least it should interrupt him as I knew he had little time enough to prepair for his admission, but Mr Shaw Said [*they*] must come to inform him of some things, which he had forgot or never knew. Billy sat with him several nights till one o clock. He never retires for sleep till this Hour. He must not do so long, if he does he will soon wear out both Body and mind. Sister speaking of him in a Letter to me says, "He esteems knowledge as a hidden Treasure and searches it out a choice Gold: as one who expects to stand before Princes[2]—Neither the Gaities of Life nor the most pressing invitations can allure him from the grand object he has in pursuit. He is as regular in his Division of time as a well regulated Clock. He has great strides to make in order to be receiv'd by the university as he wishes. For this purpose he woos the fair Goddess of Science with uncommon ardor, and never suffers himself to retire for rest till the clock strikes one. He has not I believe one vacan[t] moment, and his Zeal and diligence has been exceedingly benificial to His Brother Tommy. He finds that his Brother is highly esteem'd by all for the closeness of his application to things of the greatest importance and that he himself is daily reaping the advantage of it."[3] Judgeing you by my self my dear sister, I thought I could not more acceptably fill my Paper than by transcribing the above: If mr Williams begins his lectures in March Cousin will enter then if he does not he will omit it till April.

Betsy has not yet return'd from Haverhill she and all our Freinds were well last week. Mr and Mrs Allen were well also. She is as Happy I beleive as she expected to be and he much more so if I may judge by his recommending the state to those who have not yet enterd it.

Captain Leyde sail'd about twenty four days since. It is not likely he has reach'd London yet. I hear by mr Storer that mrs Palmer has written to my Niece upon the subject she wish'd no one to write to her upon. She ask mr Storer if the report was true, said that mr —— was terrible hurt but was intirly ignorant of the cause of her conduct and had written to her to know what had caus'd such a change in her mind. "That mr was as worthy a young Fellow as liv'd. That he had a great deal of business and was very attentive to it. That he had many enemies but did not know who they were. That Somebody had been writing against him, and had influens'd her to do as She had done."[4] He suspects me mr Storer told me. I am more thankful than ever that I have been so cautious in what I said about him. If you look over your Letters I think you will find that I have not written any thing with a design to lessen him in your Esteem. I have never willingly misrepresented any thing. As to his oddities I do not mind them I am too much us'd to them to care any thing about them but I should were I connected with him. I hear several piople have told him that they have heard that the connection is broke between him and a certain Lady. He denys it and says tis only a story rais'd by her D–sh relations. The letters nor any thing else are yet deliver'd up. I am told that neither Miss Gray nor miss Braadstreet could ever get their Letters from him.[5] He is now I am *told* erecting a very large wind-mill: tis to be set by the schoole House mr Prat is Fraiming it. I hear also that he is going to housekeeping in the spring, in his own House.[6] Mrs Vesey is to keep it. Servants he has already at mrs Veseys. Mrs church has hire'd mrs Veseys House. All this I hear abroad not a word of it have I heard from him. I wonder if he thinks he mortifies us by such an air of secrecy. He is most certainly mistaken we have not a wish to know his business any further than to be able to serve him. We are very civil to each other but nothing more. He eats his breakfast at home, and we seldom see him again till after Eleven at night.—Mrs C⟨*hurc*⟩h is an agreable woman, and keeps a very good Table.

I wish there was a Law against Grog Shops that was sufficient to prevent any being set up. They are sinks of scandle. If they would make people cautious they might do some good but if they do not they had better never exist. I do not know a Town where there are any of them in which a Gentleman can gallant a Lady and be *very particular* to her, if her Husband is absent or present, but what her character will be tore to peices in them.

I hope you will keep this Letter in your strong Box and I beg you would do the same by those I sent by Lyde,[7] for although I have not said any thing but what is true, yet if my Niece should change her mind she would always think I ought to have been silent: and had I thought she could have been anything like happy with one of his peculiar Temper I should have been. I have been as much if not more concern'd about you through the whole affair than her. I wrote to you once to beg you to let mr. Adams know his true character that if he should not be such as he expected to find him: that he might not blame you for decieving him but I burnt it. I was affraid to send it, and my dear Neice has sav'd us all by her prudent conduct and whether she perseveres or not she shall always find me an affectionate Friend. Next to my own children those of my sisters are dearest to me and as they increase in years I find my affection increase also.

A vessal has arriv'd from London she has had a Passage of twenty nine days only but not one Letter can I hear off for us. I am sadly dessapointed. I hope there is another not far behind which has a large Pacquet for us. I have been concern'd least this vessall should slip away without a line for you. I have been so busy I could not write before.

We all din'd with your Brother Adams last week your mother Hall looks very well for so aged a person. The Family were all well.

Weymouth have given Mr Evans a call. They are better united than I ever expected they, would be. He is a worthy sinsible man much of a gentleman and as spritly as our dear Father was and his composetion not unlike his. He is very Pathetick. His ruling Passion is benevolence. He has seen much of mankind being chaplain in the Army during the whole of the war has given him an opportunity of studying human nature.[8] He is a good Bell Letter Schooler and is exceeding fond of Sterns writings. I believe he can repeat every fine Sentiment in them. He brought Hulda Kent[9] here and was keept by a Storm from returning above three days. He is quite a Domestick man and we spent our time very agreably.

Mrs Alleyne has been here this afternoon.[10] She found me writing and desires me to give her Love to your Familly. Mrs Hunt[11] says pray give my kind Love to her and tell her I have seen her a Hundred times since she went away, "but I wish she was Bodyly in her own House," pray say something about her she is always asking if you have not.

Do you remember Hannah Nightingale who wanted a gown that look'd like a rainbow. She is Divorcd from her Husband. He has turn'd her almost naked and near lying in upon this town. He is a sad Fellow and she is not a good woman.[12]

I wish you would send a Peice or two of Linnen for your sons and some course enough for Drawers &c. They are very high here now, course Linnen is sold at vendue for twenty per cent above the sterling cost. How is cambrick with you? We cannot get any fit to wear under sixteen shillings or three Dollars a yard. We have taken the Piece of unglazed for your Sons. I hope we have done right.

Uncle Quincy has his Health much better this winter than the last. Our Germantown Friends are well as usual, their affairs yet in great uncertainty.

I design to write again by cap callahan. He will sail the last of this month. Yours affectionatly Mary Cranch

RC (Adams Papers); endorsed: "Mrs Cranch Febry 9th 1786."

[1] Eleazar James, Harvard 1778, the Latin tutor (*Harvard Quinquennial Cat.*; JQA, *Diary*, 2:1, 2).

[2] A rough paraphrase of Proverbs, 2:3–5, 22:29.

[3] Not found.

[4] No letter from Elizabeth Hunt Palmer has been found. Royall Tyler increasingly spent more time lodging with the Palmer family on Beacon Street in Boston than with the Cranches in Braintree (G. Thomas Tanselle, *Royall Tyler*, Cambridge, 1967, p. 19).

[5] Tyler routinely neglected to deliver letters from AA2 sent under cover to him (vol. 6:164, 454–455, 504). AA2's letters to Patty Gray and Miss Bradstreet have not been found. Patty Gray was probably Martha Hall Gray, who married Dr. Samuel Danforth (1740–1827) in Boston in Dec. 1788 (*Boston*, 30th report, p. 117; John Joseph May, *Danforth Genealogy*, Boston, 1902, p. 48).

[6] Tyler purchased the Vassall-Borland estate in Braintree in 1783 (vol. 5:286, 288).

[7] These were probably Mary Smith Cranch's letters to AA of 18 and 23 Dec. 1785 (vol. 6:493–495, 499–502).

[8] Israel Evans (1747–1807) of Tredyffin, Penna., Princeton 1772, served as chaplain of the 1st Regiment of the New York Line, the 1st and 2d New York Regiments, and the 3d New Hampshire Regiment. Following the battle of Yorktown, Evans delivered the celebratory sermon before the troops. He did not settle in Weymouth but accepted the call of the Old North Church in Concord, N.H., where he served as permanent minister from 1789 to 1797. The Evans professorship of oratory and belles lettres at Dartmouth is named in his honor (*Princetonians*, 1:209–214).

[9] Kent was related by marriage to AA. She was the granddaughter of Ebenezer Kent of Charlestown by his first marriage; he married a second time to Anna Smith, AA's aunt (Thomas Bellows Wyman, *The Genealogies and Estates of Charlestown, 1629–1818*, 2 vols., Boston, 1879, 2:571).

[10] Possibly the wife of Thomas(?) Alleyne of Braintree, for whom see vol. 6:45.

[11] Possibly Hannah Hunt, whom AA provided a subsidy for in 1784 (vol. 5:346; see also Mary Smith Cranch to AA, 26 Nov., below).

[12] Hannah Nightingall of Braintree married John Wales of Dorchester in 1781 (*Braintree Town Records*, p. 883).

Abigail Adams to Thomas Jefferson with a Memorandum of Purchases

London Grosvenor Square Febry 11 [*1786*]

Col. Humphries talks of leaving us on monday. It is with regret I assure you Sir that we part with him. His visit here has given us an opportunity of becomeing more acquainted with his real worth and merit, and our friendship for him has risen in proportion to our intimacy. The two American Secretaries of Legation would do honour to their Country placed in more distinguishd stations. Yet these missions abroad circumscribed as they are, in point of expences, place the ministers of the united States in the lowest point of view, of any

Envoy from any other Court, and in Europe every Being is estimated, and every country valued in proportion to their shew and splendor.

In a private Station I have not a wish for expensive living, but whatever my Fair Countrywomen may think, and I hear they envy my situation.[1] I will most joyfully exchange Europe for America, and my publick for a private Life. I am really surfeited with Europe, and most Heartily long for the rural cottage, the purer and honester manners of my native Land, where domestick happiness reigns unrivalled, and virtue and honor go hand in hand. I hope one season more will give us an opportunity of making our escape. At present we are in the situation of Sterns's starling.[2]

Congress have by the last dispatches informd this Court that they expect them to appoint a Minister. It is said (not officially), that mr Temple is coldly received, that not an Englishman has visited him, and the Americans are not very social with him.[3] But as Col Humphries will be able to give you every intelligence, there can be no occasion for my adding any thing further, than to acquaint you that I have endeavourd to execute your commission agreeable to your directions. Enclosed you will find the memorandom. I purchased a small trunk which I think you will find usefull to you, to put the shirts in as they will not be liable to get rubd on the journey.[4] If the balance should prove in my favour I will request you to send me 4 Ells of Cambrick at about 14 Liv. pr Ell, or 15, a pr of black Lace Lappets, these are what the Ladies wear at Court, and 12 Ells of black lace at 6 or 7 Liv. pr Ell. Some Gentleman comeing this way will be so kind as to put them in his pocket, and Mrs Barclay I dare say will take the trouble of purchaseing them for me. For troubling you with such trifling matters is a little like putting Hercules to the Distaff.

My Love to Miss Jefferson compliments to Mr Short. Mrs Siddons is actting again upon the stage and I hope col Humphries will prevail with you to cross the channel to see her. Be assured dear sir that nothing would give more pleasure to your Friends here than a visit from you and in that number I claim the honour of subscribing myself

A. Adams

4 pair of Shoes for Miss Adams by the person who made Mrs As, 2 pair of Sattin and 2 of Spring silk without straps and the most fashionable Colours.[5]

ENCLOSURE

	£	s	d
to 2 peices of Irish linen at 4s. pr. yd.	8	14	0
to making 12 Shirts at 3s. pr Shirt	1	16	0
to buttons thread silk	0	3	0
to Washing	0	3	6
a Trunk	1	1	0
	11	17	6

the Louis I parted with at 20 shillings

RC (NHi:Gilder Lehrman Coll., on deposit, GLC 5749); enclosure: Memorandum of Purchases in AA2's hand (MHi:Jefferson Papers, under 12 Oct. 1785).

[1] Possibly a response to a letter, which has not been found, from Mercy Otis Warren; see AA to Warren, 24 May, below.

[2] In "The Passport. The Hotel at Paris," a chapter of Laurence Sterne's *A Sentimental Journey through France and Italy*, a starling in a cage cries out to each passerby, "I can't get out," causing Yorick, who is unable to release her, to reflect on slavery's "bitter draught" and the blessings of liberty.

[3] For John Temple, first British consul general in the United States, see vol. 5:272, 6:81.

[4] In Nov. 1785, Jefferson requested that AA have a dozen shirts made for him (vol. 6:463).

[5] The postscript is in AA2's hand.

Charles Storer to Abigail Adams

Dear Madam Boston. 12th. February. 1786

Times without number have I been questioned on the history you communicated to me just before I left London, and which I touched upon in my last, by Capn: Lyde.[1] I find that all our friends are anxiously interested in the matter, and I must confess I find in my heart to join with them. Though we all highly applaud what has lately been done, [y]et many are fearfull of an accommodation. "The Gentleman talks of going to England, the Lady has been deceived by some ill-natured friend and prejudiced against him, she was once partially fond of him, may there not remain a tender sentiment that will plead in his behalf, he is artfull and insinuating, may she not swerve from her new resolution." Thus concludes almost every Conversation on the subject, and I know but one person (*a lady*) of all our acquaintance and I might say more too, who wishes it might so happen.[2] I have been at Haverhill since my last, where I was closeted by *Mrs: Shaw*. She was much pleased with the little information I was able to give her, and was willing to draw pleasing inferences from it. She in return, and also several other friends have let me into the history of the transactions on this side of the water:

so that I have now a pretty good idea of the affair. It appears to me altogether *a Farce*. I cannot call it anyway *a Tragedy*, however serious some, who are concerned, may think it, for I am sure the catastrophy will be no more than a Puff, at least on one side, and on neither side do I think there will be much harm done: on the contrary I am inclined to think there will be good.

Here now Charles, you will say, is a page and an half on a subject that you have no business with. Indeed, Madam, I have as mu[ch] as other friends, and the Communication you made to me in London [gives] a degree of right to say thus much. I would by no means abuse your Confidence, however; for I esteem it highly flattering. Pardon me therefore upon the principle that I meant no harm.

I mentioned having been at Haverhill, and have to add that I am extremely pleased with *Mrs: Shaw*. Her friendly reception was highly flattering, and so agreable to my own feelings, that, though the family were all strangers to me, I felt myself as much at home as I should in Grosvenor-Square. *John* I found as studious as an Hermit. Though he is not a very early riser, yet "he trims the midnight taper," and that's the only way to become a great man, as *Mr: Adams* told me once. He is to pass examination next April, and wishes it over, as also that he was already through College. *Charles* I saw a few days ago at Braintree for the first time since my return. He bids very fair. I hope he will call on us when he comes to town, at least I have invited him. But I should have mentioned *Son Thomas*, tho' I might easily overlook him, since I did not know him at Haverhill. He was some[whe]re in the room without my recognising him, for he h[as n]ot the least resemblance to any one of your family. Mr: Shaw speaks well of him and says he is a very good Boy. Thus you have the history of all the family. I might however among the number mention *Betsey Smith*, who is a clever, fine Girl.

Before I close I would mention to you that I have paid *the 5. Guis:*, you were kind enough to lend me, to Dr: Tufts, and also that he has received *the 12. Guis:* due from Dr: Crosby to Mr: Adams. I hope *Dr: T.* will write you respecting *his Commission* tho' I am sorry he has not better accounts to give you.[3] "At it again, Charles?" No, Madam, therefore pray do not be angry with Yrs: C. S.

RC (Adams Papers); addressed: "Mrs: A. Adams Grosvenor-Square London."; endorsed: "Charles Storer Febry 12: 1786." Some loss of text where the seal was removed.

[1] Storer to AA, 21 Dec. 1785 (vol. 6:497–499).

[2] Probably Elizabeth Hunt Palmer.

[3] Cotton Tufts was charged with recover-

ing a miniature of AA2, her letters, and JA's account books from Royall Tyler (vol. 6:285–286; Tufts to AA, 5 Jan., above; Tufts to AA, 15 Aug., below).

Abigail Adams 2d to Elizabeth Cranch

No 5

Grosvenor Square Feb 14th 1786

Mr Smith informed me last Evening of an opportunity of writing by Way of N York and as I know of no immediate Conveyance to Boston I shall accept it to acknowledge the receipt of your two last letters by Capts Cushing, and Lyde,[1] and to assure you that tho I have been negligent of writing, I have not been unmindfull of my friends. Indeed I have several times attempted writing you and have began several letters: but I could not please myself, nor produce any thing worth your perusal so I threw them aside, and have not writen for many Months. "Yorick says it is not every hour nor day of ones life that is a fit season for the duties of friendship, sentiment is not all ways at hand—and without sentiment what is friendship."[2]

Contentment and Happiness my Dear Eliza I begin to think more in our own power than we often suppose, and that they are immediately dependant upon the arangements of our own Minds. Surely it is best to look on the bright side of every subject, and there are none that will not admit of some Consolation, and if our happiness is often ascertained by Comparison with the situations of others, as is sometimes said, and I believe in some instances with truth, you and I my friend have but little cause to be otherwise. If we look into the circle of our own acquaintance we shall find but few who have less cause for unhappiness than we. Tis true that a benevolent heart is ever sensible to the sufferings of those around it, and when it is not in our power to releive those, we are in a degree unhappy. But it would be wrong, to embitter our own Lives by this want of power. If we do as much as our ability enables us, we must be Content with the reflection. We sometimes Complain of the unfeelingness of the World, but we may generally find, some trait in every character to admire. Why not please ourselvs with those, and pass over their foibles in silence. They are not injurious to us, but to themselvs. Happiness must result from Contentment and Contentment arrises from our sattisfaction with ourselvs. From this scource you must be happy, and I am sure you can never have cause to be otherwise, because the rectitude of your heart precludes the Possibility.

On your list of Marriages the precipitancy of Miss A—s was a little suprizing.[3] You ask what I think of sudden Matches; I am not fond of extremes of any kind and it appears to me that a delicate mind must revolt at the idea of forming a Connection in which its happiness is so greatly dependant, so very precipitately, and with a Gentleman who was a perfect stranger, not only to herself and family, but to her Country. Indeed to tell you the truth what excites my surprize more than any thing is that the Ladies of our Country should be so fond of Connecting themselvs with Foreigners. If the Gentleman had been an Americin whose Character was known and approved it would have been a very different case. But we sometimes see persons who on the other Hand Consider, and reconsider, and delay, till they are doubtfull what they would do. I join with you in wishing Mrs N happy; you justly say let us not pretend to determine what will make another so.

I have a Letter by Lyde from Mrs Russell[4] wherein she tells me that she is the Happiest of Mortals, and I am allways gratified to hear this acknowledgement from my friends in whatever degree they make it. I was glad to hear that your visit to Haverhill was so agreeable to you, a knowledge of Musick with so good a taste for it as you have, must be a scource of pleasure, and prove a great amusement. That you found a sattisfaction in the society of my Brother I can never doubt, I know him capable of contributing to the happiness of his friends, and I am sufficiently sensible of his worth to regret his absence, but it was for the best. The seperation of our Family has been the greatest, I may say *only cause* for anxiety that I ever knew, and I see no prospect that it is to be otherwise, *for any length of time in future*. My Brothers are now of an age when their education would prevent their being with us if we were in America. When they leave Colledge it is probable that their future persuits will engage most of their attention. But there would be times when we should meet and enjoy each others society, which we are now debared from. As to myself Eliza I am equally uncertain as to my future movements. How long I may be continued in Europe is impossible to say. I make no arangements beyond the present period, and shall take every thing as it arrises, and derive great sattisfaction from knowing my Conduct and my sentiments meet the approbation of my friends.

Were I to tell you how much I often wish for you, it would I am sure increase your desire of visitting us. A sister I was never blessd with and for near two years I have had no intimate, or Companion.

My happiness would have been greatly augmented by the society of a female friend, it would have sweetened many a lonely hour. Society here is not as with us. A large acquaintance is unavoidable but at the same time you meet with none of that friendly social intercource which sweetens Life. Forms, and ceremony are considered so essential that they have become universal, and you may make ten visits in a Morning every day in the week and I would venture to say, you would not find one Lady in a day at home. It is not that they would be out of their Houses, but they are never visible unless you are invited to dinner or to Evening visits, where you are set down to Cards as soon as possible, and it is unavoidable. There are several very amiable American Ladies here, who are not attached to the follies predominant. Mrs Roggers is a very amiable friendly Woman, her greatest pleasure seems to be in obliging her friends. There is, I find, from my observations, upon others, some thing strangely facinating in Europe, and I have seen but very few of either sex who do not quit it with regret. I think myself perfectly safe upon this subject and I can assure you that I am well convinced my happiness is not to be promoted by the amusements Conveniences or Gayeties of Europe. I should be gratified to pass a few years in visitting many parts of it, but I would not Consent upon any Conditions to settle here for Life, and I shall look forward with pleasure to the period when I may return. Tho I may form transient acquaintances who may be capable of amusing, and with whom I may be gratified, the ties of relationship, the friends of my earliest years, cannot be replaced. I feel an interestedness in whatever concerns them, that cannot be excited by those I may form at this distance. But do not suppose my Dear Eliza that there may not be some *one* individual that may interest my Mind, and whom my judgment and reason may approve—but this may prove an additional incitement to my return to America. But I shall Confess too much if I dont take care, least I should I subscribe myself yours affectionately, Amelia

RC (MHi:C. P. Cranch Papers); endorsed: "Miss A Adams"; docketed: "Letter from Miss A Adams to Miss Eliz: Cranch. London Feb 14. 1786."

[1] Not found.

[2] Laurence Sterne, *Letters of the Late Rev. Mr. Laurence Sterne*, Dublin, 1776, 3 vols., 2:117. The full quotation reads, "It is not every hour, or day, or week of a man's life that is a fit season for the duties of friendship—sentiment is not always at hand—pride and folly, and what is called business, oftentimes keep it at a distance—and without sentiment, what is friendship?—a name, a shadow!"

[3] Lucy Ann Apthorp married Lt. Richard Nash of the British Navy on 24 Sept. 1785 after an acquaintance of three months (JQA, *Diary*, 1:329–330).

[4] The letter from Sarah Sever Russell has not been found.

Elizabeth Smith Shaw to Abigail Adams 2d

Haverhill February 14th 1786

Yours My Dear Niece, of October 2d came safe to hand,[1] and as I read, I could not but admire the justness of Thought, and the propriety and Elegance of Expression. My Heart assented to the truth of every Sentiment, but if you make the frequent writing to you, the *Scale* by which you judge of the love and affection of your Friends, I fear I shall be *found wanting*, through a multiplicity of Cares and the opinion I entertain of my own Letters being incapable of affording any entertainment, or pleasure, *only* what arises from the Idea, that they were dictated by a sincere, faithful, and affectionate Heart. This is not a fit of Humility, which has this moment siezed me, but is what very sensibly affects me whenever I peruse the Letters of my Friends, more espicially those of my sister and my Nieces. Often while I have been impressing the Seal, the thought of its little worth, the triffling and insignificant Matter it contained, has forced out an humble Sigh, and called up a conscious blush. And if it were not for some encouraeging candid, kind expression of regard from my Correspondents as if they some how were gratified, I veirily believe I should not venture to do any thing more than copy after, an Original, that sometime since fell into my Hands. Dear Friend These few Lines come hoping, you are well, and all in good Health, as I am at this present writing. Send me word of all the good news, such as Deaths and marriages, &cc. So I remain your loving Friend till Death. AB.[2]

Now this short Letter gave the person it was written to as much real satisfaction, as if it had been in the sweet and elegant stile of King.[3] So I conclude the pleasure is derived[4] from the good, and kind Intentions, of the Writer, more than from any other Cause. ⟨*and From their being kindly interested in every thing that befalls us, from their often talking and thinking of us, and in Idea fondly accompanying us in our Amusements, Entertainments, in* [. . . .][5] *the domestick and more retired walk of Life*⟩ And will therefore without further hesitation proceed to tell you in my own way that Mr and Mrs Allen made us a visit yesterday, that he said he was forced to come with her, for she would not rest without seeing us. He told us, he was loth to recount the Tears that she had shed last Friday and Saturday because he could not accompany her over. This was all said in perfect good humour, nor did I love her the less, you may be sure, for this tender Evidence of her affection for us. Indeed I was more pleased with his Behaviour to her yesterday than I have ever been before. Though there was nothing really censurerable, in his Conduct, yet there was a great deal wanting. There was not that polite attention, that complacency which so much delights me and is ever the result of Hearts meeting heart recreprocally kind. The formal phelegmatic Lover, and the cold, indiferent Husband, are equally the Objects of my aversion. Not that I wish to see one, like the "rapt Seraph, that adores and burns,"[6] For Such a Flame must soon decay, such an enthusiastic Fire must of consequence soon be extinguished and meet with an early check, for a Life of rapture, is not the Life of Man. If Virtue, good sense, Benevolence, and the kindest affections will ensure me but peaceful, tranquil Days, kind Heaven, I ask, no more.

Eliza Cranch left Mr Whites' hospitable and amiable Family the 5th of February, and came to tarry with us, but upon finding Mrs Allen very desirous of her going home with her, the gentle creature has taken her flight last evening from us, and perchd upon the other side of the River, where she stands this moment, I suppose, in a kind of triumph, looking at our Candle, for she, like your Brother, is a Bird of Night, as well as Wisdom. Your Uncle, Brother, nor I, did not like to have her leave us, and we could not help frowning upon her, for it, but at last concluding it was wrong to be so selfish, we gave our Consent, provided she would come back again next monday.

It is with greif that I find the time so nearly approached, that your Brother JQA, must leave our Family. The 21st of March Mr Williams begins his phylosophical Lectures. Mr Shaw has written to Dr Williams upon the Subject, and he thinks it is of importance that he should be there upon the first opening of them. We have really been happy in his company this winter, but his close application to his studies, has not given us an Opportunity of enjoying it so much as we otherways should. His Candle goeth not out by Night, I really fear he will ruin his Eyes. Upon my word, I never was half so afraid of any young Man[7] in my Life. These Journal of [*h*]is are a continual Spy, upon our Action and your Brother is exceedingly severe upon the Foibles of Mankind. He has no *patience* to see people, degrading, and debasing themselves beneath the Rank, which the God of Nature assigned them, in the Scale of Being. And as to *our Sex*, but little Mercy is shown them. "Thanks to our Faults, for such a fruitful Theme,"[8] that have furnished him with so many wise and witty observations. The other Day I very candidly mentioned to him those Lines of Prior, "Be to their Virtues very kind, be to their Faults a little blind," and do you believe it, he had the politeness to place them in his Journal,[9] in a most satyrical point of view. And if any one says to him, Mr Adams you are too satyrical—Not more severe than Just, I have never disapproved or censured Things lovly and amiable—My Aunt thinks as I do, and assents to what I say. So he finds a fine shelter for himself, under my Wing.

Indeed my Dear Neice, it mortifies me to look around and see how few Ladies there are, who are capable of making agreeable, or fit Companions to Gentlemen of Education, and Literature. Some I have seen who could neither join in Conversation, and who were not possessed with sufficient discernment, to know when to be silent, but would interrupt by the most triffling question, Affairs of the greatest Concern. Ladies who have Leisure, and Opportunities should endeavour to furnish themselves, with something more than what is merely Ornamenttal. They should study to render themselves agreeable *Companions*, ever keeping this one thing in view, that it is of little importance to *engage* unless they have qualities to *preserve* affection.

I hear a Vessel has been Shipwrecked near France, I fear there were Letters in her for you.[10] But that is nothing, when we think of the poor Souls, lost in her. Cousin Billy, and Charles spent a week with us this winter Vacation. I think Charles grows more, and more agreeable. He sustains a good Character in Colledge, and is greatly beloved. Thomas is A fine Lad, and does not run so often to look of his Doves in studying Hours, since Mr Adams has been here. Mr Shaw, and my Children are well. Your Brother relates every thing in so much better manner than I can, that it not worth while for me to say any thing more than that I am, your ever affectionate Aunt

E Shaw

Dft (DLC:Shaw Family Papers; at DLC, separated into two parts); addressed: "To Miss A: Adams London."

[1] Not found.

[2] Possibly Abigail Tufts Bishop, sister of Cotton Tufts.

[3] Possibly poet William King (1663–1712) (*DNB*).

[4] Shaw wrote "is derived" above "arises."

[5] Four words unreadable.

[6] Alexander Pope, *Essay on Man*, Epistle I, line 278.

[7] Shaw wrote "young Man" above "person."

[8] Edward Young, *The Universal Passion. Satire V. On Women*, Dublin, 1728, line 10.

[9] Matthew Prior, "An English Padlock," lines 78–79. See JQA, *Diary*, 1:387.

[10] Probably the *Ceres*; see AA to Mary Smith Cranch, 26 Jan., note 1, above.

Abigail Adams to Charles Adams

Dear Charles [*ca. 16 February 1786*][1]

Your Letters of october 23 and your last by capt Lyde[2] gave me great pleasure, and the account your uncle Aunt and other Friends give me of your conduct and behaviour makes me very happy. A perceverence in the same steady course will continue to you the regard and Esteem of every worthy character and what is of infinate more importance your own peace of mind and the Approbation of your Maker. I am very glad you have engaged in the reading of History. You recollect I dare Say how often I have recommended to you an acquaintance with the most important events both of ancient and modern times. You have begun properly by attending to that of your own Country first. It would not be amiss if you was to read Hubbards history of the Indian Wars and Neals history of ⟨*America*⟩ Massa. Those with Hutchinsons[3] will give you a just Idea of the first Settlement of America and the dangers perils and hardships which our Ancestors encounterd in order to establish civil and Religious Liberty. As there was no settlement on any part of the continent Northward of Maryland except in Massachusets for more than fifty years after the landing of our ancesters at Plimouth. That state may be considerd as the parent of all the other new England states, altho the first setlers fled to obtain liberty of conscience. They appear to have carried with them much superstition and bigotary, which may be attributed in some measure to the Spirit of the times in which they lived and the percecution they had sufferd, which always tends to narrow the mind and to make it more tenacious of its principals. At the same time they possessd that zeal for religion and that Strickt Piety together with the principals of civil Liberty which enabled them to brave every hardship and to build them up as a people, and laid the foundation for that Noble Structure which the present generation have founded, and which Ranks us as an Nation and which if we depart not from the first principals of our ancestors will in a course of years render us the admiration of future ages. Tho as individuals each may think himself too unimportant to effect so desirable an event, yet every one is accountable for his conduct and none so insignificient as not to have some influence. Ever keep in mind my Dear Son that virtue is the dignity of Humane nature. As you peruse history, remark the characters their views persuits, and the concequence of thir actions. See what an influence justice honour integrity and Reverence for the deity had upon the Nations and kingdoms when ever they predominated either in the Rulers or the people. Behold the Havock and devastation of Rapine cruelty Luxery avarice and ambition; there is an other course of reading which I would recommend to your attention. I mean moral Philosophy. There are a number of valuable Books upon this subject, Grove Butler Smith. Dr Watts upon the improvement of the Mind[4] is particularly calculated to assist a Young Studient. This Book I advise you to an immediate attention to. I think you must find them all in the library.

By the time this reaches you your Brother will also become a student at Colledge. He will advise you with judgment. I hope you will preserve the Strickest Friendship for each other. If you can get time to pay Some attention to your handwriting it will be an advantage to you. This part of Your Education has been too much neglected ⟨*in your Perigrinations*⟩ oweing to Your commencing traveller too Young.

I am very happy to find that you have a studious youth for your companion. The enlargment of knowledge should be the constant view and design of every studient, reflection and observation must form the judgment. We must compare past event with the present in order to form a just estimate of Truth never taking any thing merely from the opinion of others, but weigh and judge for ourselves.

Your sister will write to you I suppose. She is well and so is your Pappa. Your uncles and Aunts are so kind to you that they releive me from any apprehension of Your being any ways neglected. I have sent a peice of Linnen which your Aunt will apply to those of you who stand most in need of it, and I have seald you a Small present in the corner of the Letter. Remember me to Mrs Dana and family and to your cousin Cranch and believe me your most affectionate Mother

AA

Dft (Adams Papers); filmed at [*1786?*], Adams Papers, Microfilms, Reel No. 367.

[1] The date is assigned from AA to JQA, 16 Feb., below, which was probably written about the same time as this letter.

[2] Not found.

[3] William Hubbard, *A Narrative of the Troubles with the Indians in New-England: from the First Planting Thereof in the Year 1607. to This Present Year 1677*, Boston, 1677; Daniel Neal, *The History of New-England, Containing an Impartial Account of the Civil and Ecclesiastical Affairs of the Country, to . . . 1700*, London, 1720; Thomas Hutchinson, *The History of the Colony of Massachusets-Bay*, Boston, 1764–1767.

[4] Henry Grove, *A System of Moral Philosophy*, London, 1749; Joseph Butler, *The Analogy of Religion, Natural and Revealed, to the Constitution and Course of Nature*, London, 1785; Adam Smith, *The Theory of Moral Sentiments*; and Isaac Watts, *The Improvement of the Mind; or, A Supplement to the Art of Logick*. The first two are listed in the *Catalogue of JA's Library*.

Abigail Adams to John Quincy Adams

My Dear Son London Febry 16 1786

Captain Lyde is arrived to our no small joy and brought us a charming parcel of Letters, amongst which I found one from each of my Dear Sons.[1] You know how happy a circumstance of this kind always makes me. Two days before we had heard of his arrival in the River, and waited every hour with impatience for the Letters, for those by Young have not yet come to hand, he is still at Plimouth repairing his Ship.

Yesterday we went to dine with a mr and mrs Blake, who came formerly from Carolina, but who have many years been setled in this Country. Mr Blake is said to be the richest citizen belonging to the Southern State of carolina. I am loth to mention that he owns 15 hundred Negroes upon one plantation; as I cannot avoid considering it disgracefull to Humanity. His anual income is said to amount to 15 hundred sterling, which is very handsome for any Country.[2] He lives in a stile of great elegance. Soon after my arrival in this Country his Lady visited me at the Bath hotel, he was then in carolina. Upon his return, he immediately paid his respects, after which we invited him and his Lady to dine; he came but the Lady decline'd, knowing that the compliment ought first to pass from them to us. A short time after: we received the invitation of yesterday. They appear a very amiable family. It is not the fashion in this Country to dine large parties, few rooms are calculated for it. There were no Ladies present except myself, your sister, mrs Blake, and daughter mr Bridgen whom you know; two young Carolinians, who have lately arrived and dinned with us some time before;[3] your Pappa and col. Smith made the company. We past our time very agreably but still the Letters kept running in my Head. About nine oclock we returnd home, and John Brisler[4] who you know is never so happy as when he has any good News for me, opend the Carriage Door with a smiling countanance, and an 'O Mam'! There are a thousand Letters come. This quickned my pace you may be sure. Well says your Pappa as he was getting out, now I shall see your Eyes Glisten, nobody ever enjoy'd a Letter more than you. During this discourse Miss was fled, and had mounted the stairs before I could get into the House, nor could the col. keep pace with the nimble footed Daphne. From that moment untill half past twelve we were all employd in reading our Letters. Even the Watchmans Cry, of "half past ten oclock" which upon other nights puts your pappa in motion for bed, past unheeded by.

Mr S. amused himself, or tried too, with reading the News papers, yet I saw he watchd my countanance at every Letter. A little before 12 the servant informed him that his carriage was at the Door, he rose and comeing to me placed himself in a pensive attitude, then askd me if I would write by a vessel going this week to Newyork? I replied yes I will to my son. Will you said he, with an expression which I easily read from his Heart, will you remember me . . . to him—I promised him I would. Know then my dear Son that this Gentleman is like to become your Brother. I dare say you frequently heard honorable mention of him whilst you was in Newyork. His Character is not only fair and unblemishd, but in high reputation wherever he is known. At the early age of 21 he commanded a regiment and through the whole war conducted with prudence Bravery and intrepidity, when armd against the foe, but when Conquerer, he never forgot the Man in the Soldier. True Courage is always humane and from many accounts, which his Friend col Humphries has given me, with justice may be applied to him those lines of Douglas in the Tragidy—

> "His Eyes were like the Eagle's yet sometimes
> Liker the Dove's, and as he pleasd he won
> All hearts with Softness, or with Spirit aw'd."[5]

Delicacy of sentiment and honour are the striking traits of his Character. Perhaps col Humphries might be a little poetic, when speaking of him, he said "it would take more proofs and arguments to convince him that col S. could be guilty of a dishonorable action, than any other Man he ever knew in his Life." What a contrast some will say? but comparisons are odious—let the memory of former attachments, since the recollection of them can only be attended with pain, sleep in oblivion. As they proved not to be founded upon a durable superstructure, they have properly vanishd like the baseless fabrick of a vision, nor do I think even a wreck is left behind[6]—you will say, is not this Sudden?

Rouchfoucault says, and shakspear makes the same observation that a Heart agitated with the remains of a former passion is most susceptable of a new one.[7] But sitting this aside, you know the pensive sedateness which had long hung upon the brow of your Sister. This was not mitigated amidst all the hurry and bustle of the scenes which surrounded us when we first came to this Country. Loth very loth was she to believe and still more so to confess it, but at last fully convincd from the neglect with which she was treated, (and the account of some Friend I know not whom) of the unsteadiness and dissipation of a certain Gentleman, that he was unworthy her regard. She wrote him a letter very soon after we arrived here, expressive of her mind, tho she did not at that time make it known to her Friends. But she afterward produced a copy of the Letter as a full proof that her conduct was the result of proper conviction and mature deliberation. The final dismission and the last Letter she ever wrote him was in concequence of my expressing a doubt of his strickt honour.[8] It was then as I think I before related to you, that she disclosed her mind fully upon the subject, and askt advise of your pappa, upon which he told her if she had sufficient reason to doubt both his honour and veracity, he had rather follow her to the Grave than see her united with him.

I will not disguise to you that we had not been long removed to this House, before I saw that the Gentleman who made a part of the family was happier in sitting down and reading to the Ladies, in walking riding or attending us to the Theaters, than of any other company or amusement. I began to feel very anxious because I knew he was a stranger to your sisters Situation. Yet nothing could be said, as I really believe he was not him self conscious of his Situation, till I thought it my duty to hint to him carelessly her being under engagements in America. This led him to know himself, and to request an explanation from her; Which She gave him with the utmost frankness. Upon which he immediately ask'd leave of absence, and went to the Prussian Review determined never more to think upon the Subject, for upon his return, he took an early opportunity to assure me that nothing should ever pass from him, inconsistant with the strickest Honour, and the laws of hospitality, that his attentions in future should only be general, and askt my excuse if upon some occasions he should even appear neglegent. I commended his resolutions, and approved his plan, without the most distant hint to him, of the connections being dissolved. Accordingly he did not make one at any of our Parties, he dined with us and then immediately retired. Thus we went on for several weeks at a perfect distance, and you will easily judge of my reasons for wishing to keep from him a real state of facts. But the Little Deity tho represented blind, has a wonderfull nack at making discoveries. Perhaps it was assureances similar to those made to me, which might draw from her an explanation. This is a matter that I shall not be very likely to learn, but I perceived all at once upon a Day, a Dejection dispell'd, a Brightness of countanance, and a lightness of Heart and in the Evening the Gentleman ask'd permission to attend us to the Theatre where we were going with col Humphries; when we returned it was late, and Pappa was gone to bed: as the Gentleman was going: he ask'd a moments audience of me' upon which he put into my Hand with much emotion a Bundle of papers and a letter,[9] which he requested me to read, and communicate to your Pappa; the Papers were votes of congress and commissions, with the amplest testimonies from the Generals under whom he had served of his Brave and good conduct. The letter informd me, "that as the connection which appear'd an insurmountable obstacle to the accomplishment of the wishes nearest his Heart, existed no longer—and from the opinion he had of the Lady, he was persuaded that nothing dishonourable on her part could have occasiond its dissolution. He hoped that Mrs Adams would not be surprised at his early anxiety to gain the confidence of her Daughter, and to lay a proper foundation for a future Connection, provided it should meet with the approbation of her Parents and Friends." There were many other matters in the Letter which were: mention of his family situation &c. I according to request communicated to your Pappa the Papers and Letters. As it appeard to him that this Gentleman possesst all those qualifications necessary to make a faithfull and agreeable companion, he left it wholy to your Sister to determine for herself. I begd her to satisfy herself that She had no prepossession left in her mind and Heart, and she assured me She never could be more determind. I think she must feel a calmness and serenity in her present connextion; which she never before experienced. I am sure it has releived my mind from a Weight which has hung heavy upon it, for more than two years; I rejoice that her conduct meets the approbation of her Friends. I doubt not but her present choise will do so equally. I think she will herself communicate the matter to you.

Coll Humphries has made us a visit of two Months. He has publishd an other Poem much longer than the former, its poetick merit is fully equal to the first. By the first vessel which sails for your port, I will send you one. A more intimate acquaintance; discovers him to be a Man possesst of much more learning, judgment and genuine wit, than I had any Idea of. His visit has raisd him greatly in all our estimations, and we parted with him last monday with much regret.

Your sister I suppose has acquainted you with the Death of poor

Williamos. He tarried in paris untill he could not leave it, for debt; and he had borrowd of every American there; untill he could get no further credit. His Death was perhaps fortunate both for him self and others. During his Sickness he must have sufferd, but for the kindness of mr Jefferson, who tho he had found it necessary to check mr W. and had urged him so much to go out to America that he had quitted mr J–n, he supplied him with necessaries during all his sickness. Thus ended the Days of this curious adventurer, who possesst Benevolence, without conduct, and learning without Sense.[10]

Mr and Mrs Bingham arrived here about 3 weeks ago with a full determination to go out to America in March, but having as usual Spaired no pains to get introduced to the families of my Lord Landsdown and my Lady Lucans, they are so *supreemly blest*, that poor America looks like a bugbear to them. "O! now I know mr Bingham you wont go out this Spring. Give me but ten Years, and take all the rest of my Life." Who can withstand flattery and admiration? What female mind young beautifull rich–must she not be more than woman if vanity was not the predominate passion? I accompanied her last thursday to Court and presented her both to the King and Queen, and I own I felt not a little proud of her. St James's did not, and could not produce an other so fine woman. Yet it was the most crouded drawing Room I ever attended, except the late Birth Day. You know this Ladies taste in dress is truly elegant. She had prepaird herself in France for this occasion, and being more fleshy than I have seen her before, she is concequently handsomer than ever.

"She Shone a Goddess, and She moved a Queen."[11]

The various whispers which I heard round me, and the pressing of the Ladies to get a sight of her, was really curious, and must have added an *attom* to the old *score*, for she could not but see how attractive She was. Is she an American, is she an American, I heard frequently repeated? And even the *Ladies* were *obliged to confess* that she was truly an elegant woman. You have, said an English Lord to me, but whose name I knew not, one of the finest Ladies to present, that I ever saw. The Emperers Ambassador[12] Whisperd your Pappa, sir your Country produces exceeding fine women. Aya replied your Pappa bowing and Men too, presenting to him at the same time a mr Chew of Philadelphia, a very likely Youth who with several others have been lately presented by your Pappa to their

Majesties. There is a Young Lady here a Miss Hamilton one of the lovelyest Girls in the World, whom I expect next to present. She has a finer face than Mrs Bingham, her person well proportiond. She does not equal Mrs Bingham in stature, but person and mind!! I have thought it was fortunate for you that you went to America, for she is a good deal intimate with your Sister, and it is impossible not to be charmd with her sweet modest affible deportment, animated with the Sparkling Eye of sensibility. Her uncle is doatingly fond of her, never said he, to me one day did Girl possess more discretion. I could always leave her to direct herself, and I never had occasion to say, Ann why do you so? He is wisely going to carry her to America this summer. She is not yet 18. She is the adopted heir of this rich uncle.

The Royal family appeard much out of spirits yesterday, the prince of Wales like Benidict the married Man.[13] The Nation are all in a ferment, tho they hardly dare speak loud. It seems this amourus Prince has been for two years voilently in Love, with a widow Lady near 40 years of age. As she is said to be a Lady of a virtuous Character she avoided him, but he percecuted her so that she was obliged to flee to Paris. After having resided there for a year and half, she returnd in hopes that absence and other objects had banishd her from his remembrance. He however renew'd his attacks, and finding that he could not bring her to his terms, he swore that as he never expected to be king of England for his Father would out live him, he would please himself. And it is said and universally believed that he has married the Lady, Setled 6 thousand pr An upon her, for which the Duke of Queensburry is responsible, and she now appears with him at the opera, rides in his carriage with her servants behind it. He is 3 times a day at her House. The Clergyman who married them is absconded, as it is Death to him. In the Eye of Heaven the marriage may be valid, but the law of the land annuls it. She can never be Queen, or the children ligitimate. Such a step in the British heir Apparant you may well suppose, gives an allarm. They say his toast is, fat fair and forty, what a taste. This is the Ladies 3 marriage.[14]

Having given you so many Domestick occurrences, I shall not write you a word of politicks. Your Friend Murry has been very sick, looks almost like a Ghost.

I shall write you again by captain Lyde. If there is any thing in particular which you want let me know. Would that my ability was equal to my inclination, but here we stand at the old Standerd, tho our expences are a Quarter part more. You go beyond the mark methinks I hear you say. We do, but let C—ss Blush that they continue to degrade themselves in the Eyes of Europe as well as England.[15] This time twelve months, and unless different measures are persued, from what there is now any prospect of, I quit this kingdom for my native Land. I quit it without one regreet, but with a firm belief that it is Devoted to destruction. Like the Swine, they know not the value of the Jewel, once placed in the Bourben scale, poor old England will kick the Beam.[16]

Begone politicks I hate you, did not I say I would not speak of you.

I do not know how to consent that you should give up your diary, it is the kind of Letters which I love best of any.[17] Your sister has been very closely writing ever since she received your Letters. I am rejoiced to find that you are no ways dissapointed in the reception I promisd you from your Friends. Your sister Eliza as you justly term her is very dear to me, as you well know, and that my own children only, are dearer to me than those of my sisters. Never was there a stronger affection than that which binds in a threefold cord your Mamma and her dear sisters. Heaven preserve us to each other for many Years to come.

Your Pappa has a vast deal of writing to do, and he sometimes groans and says but little comes of it. Yet do I know much essential service results from it, and much more might, were our Country wise as they ought to be.

I presume it will not be long before I hear from you at Cambridge. Watch over your Brother, gain his confidence be his Friend as well as Brother. Reverence yourself, and you will not go asstray. Your Friends give me most flattering accounts of you and I give a ready credit to their word, may your honour your integrity and virtue always prove your safe gaurd.

I fear mr King will think I intrude upon him by requesting him to frank this bulky Letter.[18] By captain Lyde I shall write to all my Friends. Let your Aunt know I have received her kind Letters. O but I must mention to you a Gentleman who designs to visit Cambridge in the course of the summer, whom you will notice tho he has no Letter to you, a mr Anstey who is appointed to go to America by this Government to assertain the claims of the Loyallists. Lord Carmarthan introduced him to your Pappa, and askd Letters from him to the different Governours which your Pappa gave him. He dinned with us and appears a sensible modest Gentleman, he saild in the last packet.

4 "WIFE & NO WIFE — OR — A TRIP TO THE CONTINENT," BY JAMES GILLRAY, 1786

See page xi

Remember me to all my Haverhill Friends and cross the River present my congratulations.[19] Love to my Thommy and be assured you are all equally dear to your ever affectionate Mother

AA

RC (Adams Papers); endorsed: "Mamma. Feby: 16th: 1786."; docketed: "Mrs: Adams. Feby: 16. 1786."; "My Mother. 16. Feby: 1786."; and "Mrs: A. Adams Feby: 16th. 1786."

[1] Probably JQA to AA, 28 Dec. 1785 (vol. 6:503–506). Letters from CA and TBA have not been found.

[2] AA is almost certainly mistaken, possibly meaning to write that William Blake owned 150 slaves on one of his plantations. According to the 1790 federal census, Blake held 695 slaves (*Heads of Families at the First Census of the United States Taken in the Year 1790. South Carolina*, Washington, D.C., 1908, p. 35). Also, AA2 puts the Blakes' annual income at £15,000 per year (to JQA, 9 Feb. 1786, above).

[3] For Heyward and Gibbes, see AA2 to JQA, 22 Jan., note 36, above.

[4] For John Briesler, the Adams family's servant, see AA to JA, 11 Feb. 1784, and note 4 (vol. 5:302–305).

[5] John Home, *Douglas, A Tragedy*, Act IV, lines 208–210.

[6] "These our actors, / As I foretold you, were all spirits and / Are melted into air, into thin air; / And, like the baseless fabric of this vision, / The cloud-capp'd towers, the gorgeous palaces, / The solemn temples, the great globe itself, / Yea, all which it inherit, shall dissolve; / And, like this insubstantial pageant faded, / Leave not a rack behind" (*The Tempest*, Act IV, scene i, lines 148–156).

[7] A paraphrase of Maxim No. 10 from François, Duc de La Rochefoucauld, *Moral Reflections and Maxims*, London, 1746, p. 28, which reads, "There is in the Heart of Man a perpetual Succession of Passions, insomuch, that the Ruin of one is almost always the Rise of another." In Shakespeare's *Two Gentlemen of Verona*, Act II, scene iv, lines 192–195, Proteus says, "Even as one heat another heat expels, / Or as one nail by strength drives out another, / So the remembrance of my former love / Is by a newer object quite forgotten."

[8] AA2 may have written to Royall Tyler about the future of their engagement in June or July 1785, but the letter has not been found. For her dismissal of Tyler as a suitor, see AA2 to Tyler, [*ca. 11 Aug. 1785*]; AA to Mary Smith Cranch, 15 Aug. 1785; and AA to Cotton Tufts, 18 Aug. 1785 (vol. 6:262, 276–280, 283–287).

[9] WSS to AA, 29 Dec. 1785 (vol. 6:508–509), which AA paraphrases in the next sentence. For the testimonials from Gens. John Sullivan and George Washington that accompanied the letter, see AA to Cotton Tufts, 10 Jan., note 6, above.

[10] Charles Williamos, an intimate friend of Jefferson and the Adamses in Paris in 1784–1785, died in early Nov. 1785 (vol. 6:463, 478). Jefferson assisted Williamos financially during his illness, even though he had broken off all contact with the latter in July 1785 upon learning that Williamos was suspected of being a British spy (Jefferson, *Papers*, 8:269–273).

[11] "She moves a goddess, and she looks a queen" (Alexander Pope, *The Iliad of Homer*, Book III, line 208).

[12] Friedrich Graf von Kageneck, envoy extraordinary and minister plenipotentiary from the German Empire to Great Britain, 1782–1786 (*Repertorium*, 3:76).

[13] Benedick of Shakespeare's *Much Ado about Nothing*.

[14] For the marriage of Maria Anne Fitzherbert to the Prince of Wales, see the Descriptive List of Illustrations, No. 4, above.

[15] Congress reduced the annual salaries of its ministers by 19 percent in May 1784. See AA to Mary Smith Cranch, [*5 Sept. 1784*], and notes 4 and 6 (vol. 5:439–445).

[16] An allusion to Proverbs, 11:22, "As a jewel of gold in a swine's snout, so is a fair woman which is without discretion."

[17] JQA had apologized for the infrequency of his letters, explaining that he devoted ten hours a day to studying, which left him little time for writing or other activities (JQA to AA, 28 Dec. 1785, vol. 6:503–504).

[18] Rufus King was a Massachusetts delegate to Congress, then meeting in New York City.

[19] Rev. Jonathan and Elizabeth Kent Allen lived in Bradford, Mass., across the Merrimac River from AA's sister Elizabeth Shaw and her family.

Abigail Adams to Cotton Tufts

My Dear sir London Febry 21 1786

Captain Lyde arrived a week ago, and yesterday, he and mr Jenks dinned with us. By the latter we received your kind favour of December and Janry.[1] I had just closed a Letter to you, which I have sent by way of Newyork, and requested mr King to Frank for you; the comunication directly to Boston is like to become much less frequent, than formerly, and the more it lessens, the better it will be for our Country. For the mines of Spanish America exist not in our northern climate, yet every vessel brings such quantities of specie, as is sufficient to allarm all those who wish well to our Nation, as there is not the least present appearence of a more liberal System being adopted towards us. It is time to shake of the strong propensity we have, of loveing our enemies better than our Friends, which is going a step further than Christianity itself enjoyns. It appears to be the object of this Country; or rather the ministry to keep us, as much as possible out of Sight; and whenever they are obliged to look at us, to view us as surrounded with clouds and Darkness, enveloped with fogs, which the Glorious sun of our independance can neither dispell, or shine through. But they will find e'er long that the Cloud by day, may prove a pillar of fire by night, and lead us from a worse than Egyptian Bondage, that of becomeing devoted to their Luxeries, their venality and profligacy. Our intercourse with any other Country cannot for a long time have so great a tendency to injure our morals and manners, as this, for speaking the same language, descended from the same ancesstors, professing the same Religion, with all our habits and prejudices in favour of it, its very vices, like those of our near kindred, we wish to cover and extenuate.

By the paper inclosed you will see what the sentiments of Mr Jenkingson are, "that we cannot unite in our measures, and that at any rate they are sure of our commerce."[2] The Americans are so much secreetly feard, but openly hated, that no man dares risk his popularity, which is the Deity all in Power worship, by avowing any liberality of sentiment towards them. A little longer time will more fully devellope their system. *The Posts* have been *demanded*.[3] Some replie must be the result.

Mr Barrets success in France will give a spring I hope to our Whale fishery, and there is a good prospect of a speedy conclusion of the treaty with Portugal as the minister here has lately received full powers to setle it with Mr A.[4] I wish I could say as much with respect to the Barbery powers but Congress have done in regard to them, as they have with most of there other foreign affairs, delay'd and neglected them, till common danger has forced them into action.

The sending out such a —— as Lamb is represented to be, not only from America, but from those who saw him in France, is truly astonishing. Mr Jefferson was distresst and so was Mr Adams, but neither of them thought themselves at Liberty to prevent his going, as he was sent by Congress expressly for that purpose. A whole year has elapsed since his appointment and he has got no further than Madrid yet. All that could be done here was to find some American of learning and prudence to appoint as Secretary to him. Mr A, accordingly prevaild upon a mr Randle[5] who was here from New York to undertake the office, which he did without seeing his associate. But when he arrived in France, and saw his principal, he was throughly sick of his engagement. Yet the less capacity one possesst, the more necessity there was for the other. What Idea must these Barbarians entertain of the American Character, when a greater one than themselves is sent to treat with them. Besides the Algerines are said to be the most difficult power to treat with, and all the money which Congress have assigned to treat with the different states, will be found insufficient for one. What then can be done? If we war with them: the expence and horrours are inconceiveable, and after all we must make a peace at a Greater expence than it is probable it will cost us now. The more captives they take and the more property they acquire, the greater will the difficulty be. Yet will our Country be astonishd at the sums which must be given. There is at this Court a minister lately arrived from Tripoli. I have seen him twice at Court. He is of a copper coulour and was drest in the stile of his own Country, with a Turban upon his Head sandles upon his feet and a Mantle with a Beard of no small length. He was attended by two secretaries, who were permitted to wear only whiskers. They do not keep a minister stationd at any Court, but he travells from Court to Court, leveying his contributions upon the powers he visits. By his interpretor he appears a sensible candid well disposed Man. I am not at liberty to say more respecting him at present. Tripoli is one of the largest of the Barbery states, and has great influence with the rest, but the Money, the Money, where can it be had.

Whilst too many of our Countrymen are dancing, and playing, they think not of the perplexityes in which there publick ministers are involved, nor how many sleepless nights it costs them to plan for them, nor of the reproaches to which they expose them; by neglecting to take measures for the fullfillment of their engagements, but they can cavill at a minister even in C—ss, if through hurry or inattention, he happens to be *inelegant* in his *stile*.[6] It lies wholy with our Country to determine whether they will be a respected or a despiced Nation—thus having given you a political dish, not a very palatable one I fear, I must turn my thoughts to domestick affairs. The Books and papers you speak of, you will call for whenever you may think it proper. I found the same Dilatory disposition which you complain of and a disposition to keep the knowledge of my affairs wholy from me. So that I was sometimes obliged to demand explanations, and on that account I had all my notes &c registerd in the Book which I gave you. I would have taken them all away, if I had not been particularly situated when I left America.

The Letters which were so long detained, I have not a doubt, were all copied before they were deliverd to you; but as no improper Ideas I dare say were ever communicated, and such Sentiments of Regard only exprest as a modest young Lady need not blush to avow where the object is really worthy. He must retain them to his own shame and confusion, and as She is now like to become the wife of an other Gentleman, I should think he would not wish to recollect what he has lost.

I have had an Idea that he will sell his place at Braintree, nothing likelier from the instability of the Man. If he should, Mr A would wish to purchase it. I question whether it has all been paid for. This you will not hint to any one. If he should not design it, it might look indelicate to mention the Idea, and if he should, it would be better for some other person to negotiate the buisness. Mr Adams says you may draw upon him for a hundred pounds whenever you think proper. Bills upon him ought to sell better than those which are doubtfull, as there is no danger of a protest and there is always prompt payment. Mr Rogers told me that his Brother Mr Bromfeild[7] gave 7 pr cent by the last vessels. If you should find that an other hundred would be advantageous laid out in certificates you will draw again; but never for more than a hundred at a time. I hope our state will not be so distracted as ever to make paper money again. The note you will take up Immediately. Inclosed is Doans account, not a copper of which was ever paid to my certain knowledgd. I never would have it tenderd to mr Doan during the paper currency as I knew it to be a good Debt. The Portsmouth buisness was setlled one Day at our door in Braintree without mr Doans getting of his Horse. So no charge was made of that.

With regard to mr Pratt; mr Adams request you would make him such an allowance as in like circumstances you would do for yourself; at the same time be so good as to let him know that he must let Pheby have some manure for her Garden, but you will limit her to a certain quantity, and what She wants more abdee must collect from the Street.[8] There are some Records for the state which Mr Adams has procured here, for which he has paid 15 Guineys. He has forwarded them to mr King, Leiut. Govenour cushing wrote for them. Mr A has desird that the money may be paid to you.[9]

I shall send some linnen by captain Lyde, but if linnen is to be had at Milton Hill I wish it may be taken there, as it is an article always usefull. I thought I left that account with you, but if I did not, Mrs Warren has one which I gave her a few Days before I Saild.[10] The Gentleman you inquire after, visits us frequently, and is a very great hypocrite if he Loves the English any better than his Neighbours. He has danced a very faithfull attendance upon the great, without yet being able to get any answer from them. Be sure he is a little elated when a Lord sends him a card, or a great man notices him, but in this he only resembles some other of our Countrymen who are here. He says but little when in mixd company upon politicks, because he does not wish to offend those with whom his buisness lies. But I never saw any thing which gave me any reason to doubt his attachment to His Country, or its interests, and I do not think he would interest himself to serve this, in the Whale buisness.

Your Nephew I have made inquiries about and do not find that he is in England. I own I was sorry to see the Senate more strenuous than the House with Regard to the return of the Refugees.[11] It is impossible to describe how happy many of them were; with the prospect, and it was considerd here as a master stroke of policy, many of them would be our fast Friends, and gratefull to us forever. They have seen and felt the difference between the two Countries. They would be glad to take the property given them here, and lay it out with us. Those at Shelburne are wretched, what greater injury can they do with us than from us? The worst Spirits will never return, but hundreds who fled through fear and folly are repentant sinners, and would become good citizens. I hope the Senate will be both magnanimous and generous with respect to them.

Mr Adams's best Regards attend you, he says I write so much that

I leave him nothing to say. My daughter joins me in Love to Mr Tufts[12] and a remembrance to all our Friends. I shall write to mrs Cranch if not by this vessel, by the next packet. I am dear sir with the sincerest Regard Your affectionate Neice. AA

RC (Adams Papers); endorsed: "Mrs. Adams Feby 21. 1786 Via New York Fav of R. King recd May. 19."

[1] Probably Tufts to JA, 21 Dec. 1785 (Adams Papers) and to AA, 12 Jan., above.

[2] Charles Jenkinson (1727–1808), former British secretary at war and later Lord Liverpool, became in 1786 president of the reconstituted Council for Trade and Plantations. He had recently published *A Collection of All the Treaties of Peace, Alliance and Commerce between Great-Britain and Other Powers . . . To Which Is Prefixed a Discourse on the Conduct of the Government of Great-Britain in Respect to Neutral Nations* (London, 1785) and played a principal role in framing the proposed commercial treaty between Great Britain and the United States (*DNB*). On 15 Feb., he had introduced a bill in the House of Commons that would continue Britain's regulations on trade with the United States for an additional year; it passed unanimously on 17 Feb. His speech in favor of the bill on 17 Feb. was widely reported in the London newspapers (London *Morning Post and Daily Advertiser*, 16, 18 Feb.; *London Chronicle*, 16–18 Feb.; London *General Evening Post*, 16–18 Feb.).

[3] In a memorial dated 30 Nov. 1785 that he presented to Lord Carmarthen on 8 Dec., JA demanded that the British ministry immediately withdraw all troops from U.S. territory, especially the western posts, as agreed upon in the Preliminary and Definitive Treaties of Peace. JA admitted to John Jay that he did not expect an answer until "next Summer" (Memorial to the British Ministry, 30 Nov. 1785, PRO:F.O. 4, vol. 3; JA to John Jay, 9 Dec. 1785, PCC, No. 84, VI, f. 13–16).

[4] Luiz Pinto de Balsamão, Portuguese minister and envoy extraordinary to Great Britain 1774–1789 (*Repertorium*, 3:317).

[5] Paul R. Randall, a New York lawyer, visited often with the Adamses in Paris in May 1785. He was in London in October to visit his fiancée when JA and Col. David S. Franks prevailed upon him to accompany Lamb to Algiers (John Jay to JA, 8 March 1785, Benjamin Franklin to JA, 2 May 1785, both Adams Papers; vol. 6:406, 433, 436).

[6] Perhaps a reference to debate in Congress surrounding the appointment of JA as minister to Great Britain. One of the objections raised by JA's detractors was that his vanity would inhibit his attention to duty. They cited a passage from JA's "Peace Journal" in which he relayed to Congress a compliment comparing him to George Washington. Elbridge Gerry cautioned JA in Feb. and Nov. 1785 to be less detailed in his reports to Congress to deflect any additional criticism (Smith, *Letters of Delegates*, 22:215–216, 23:8–11; JA to Gerry, 26 Aug. 1785, MHi:Gerry-Knight Coll.). For more on JA's controversial "Peace Journal," see JA, *D&A*, 3:41–43, 50–51.

[7] Henry Bromfield (1751–1837), Daniel Rogers' brother-in-law, was a Boston merchant. In 1787 Bromfield settled in London (*NEHGR*, 26:42, 141 [Jan., April 1872]).

[8] Phoebe and William Abdee were living in and caring for the Adams home in Braintree. Phoebe, a slave of AA's father, was given her freedom at his death in 1783 (vol. 5:247, 303).

[9] On behalf of the agents appointed by the General Court to prosecute Massachusetts claims to lands in western New York, Thomas Cushing had requested that JA obtain authenticated copies of the 1620 Charter of New England issued by James I and the Massachusetts Charter of 1629 (Cushing to JA, 9 May 1785, Adams Papers). JA employed a Mr. Maltby to search for the documents; Maltby succeeded in finding the first item requested (Maltby to JA, 3 Jan., Copy, MH-H:bMS Am 1582 [2]). JA enclosed a copy of the 1620 Charter and a bill for expenses in his letter to Rufus King, 4 Jan. (NHi:King Papers, 1785–1787, #67). For more on Massachusetts' boundary disputes, see vol. 5:485, note 4.

At around the same time, James Duane, as agent for New York, asked WSS to procure the same documents to support New York's claims to the land (*Law Practice of Alexander Hamilton*, ed. Julius Goebel, N.Y., 1964, 1:571).

[10] Mary Cranch had informed AA of an offer by Mercy Otis Warren to settle a debt in linen instead of money. AA was instructed to notify Cotton Tufts if this was acceptable (vol. 6:273–274).

[11] In Nov. 1785 the Massachusetts House of Representatives overwhelmingly approved a bill repealing all legislation restricting loyalists from returning to or settling in the state. The Senate, however, failed to pass the bill (Rufus King to JA, 10 Dec. 1785, Smith, *Letters of Delegates*, 23:56; Van Beck Hall, *Politics without Parties: Massachusetts, 1780–1791*, Pittsburgh, 1972, p. 142; *Massachusetts Centinel*, 19, 26 Nov. 1785).

[12] Probably Cotton Tufts Jr.

Abigail Adams to William Stephens Smith

Dear sir Febry 25 [*1786*]

Last evening col Forrest sent a servant with a Letter addrest to me, but upon opening it, I found I was honourd only with the cover. The inclosed I deliverd the Lady who sat next me but as I could not prevail with her to communicate a word more than "that the cake was good" I threatned her with opening the next unless I should find something in the cover to appease me. But I did not keep my word, for I deliverd two others which came this day.[1] I foretold at Breakfast, every morning since your departure, that you could not cross.[2] I therefore commissirated your situation, and wished you back again; mr Peters arrived the day you set of. He has spent two evenings with us, and I enterd into the mans character from one single circumstance. There were several letters here for him, which when I gave them to him he rose and went to the lights unseald them, then threw them upon the table, and with an honest bluntness broke out—not one line from my wife. I have lost two letters from her. The d—l, I had rather have found two lines from her, than ten folios from any one else, you know the man.

I forgot to desire you to present my compliments to mr Jefferson and desire him to bring Patty with him and let her tarry with me whilst he is London.[3] I designd to have askd you to have got me a certain article in France. I had the memorandum, and money in my hand, but first tried you with respect to yourself, and you lookd so solemn, and hesitated so much to serve yourself, that I put my money again into my pocket, and threw the memo into the fire. Adieu, yours &c &c AA

⟨*compliments to all good folks*⟩

Dft (MB:Rare Books Dept., Ms.CH.A.4.46).

[1] None of the letters from WSS to AA2 have been found.

[2] JA dispatched WSS to Paris to personally apprise Thomas Jefferson of his recent conversations with the Tripolitan ambassador. WSS was to persuade Jefferson to return with him to London, where the two ministers could open negotiations with Sidi Haggi

'Abd-ur-rahman Aga and also finalize the details of the commercial treaty with Portugal (JA to Jefferson, 21 Feb., Jefferson, *Papers*, 9:295). WSS left London on 21 Feb. and reached Paris by the 27th, suggesting he was only delayed in crossing the English Channel for a day or two at most, despite AA's concerns. He and Jefferson left Paris together on 6 or 7 March and reached London by the 12th (AA to JQA, 9 Feb., above; Jefferson, *Papers*, 9:307, 318, 325).

[4] Martha (Patsy) Jefferson accompanied her father to Europe in 1784; see vol. 6:76, note 4. She did not travel to London in 1786 (Jefferson, *Papers*, 9:318).

Abigail Adams to Mary Smith Cranch

My dear sister London Grosvenor Square Febry 26 1786

To you I am largely indebted for domestick intelligence and many valuable Letters. I have not found a single opportunity of writing to you since captain Callihan saild, except by way of Newyork which I have improved but once least I should put you to expence. Col Smith wrote a few lines in my Name to Mr Cranch with a bundle of Newspapers which he said should go by a private hand. I did not know of the opportunity till he was making up dispatches, and then I lamented that I had not time to write, he said he would counterfeit a letter for me, and afterwards told me that he had written.[1] Your Letters by Young will indeed be old, for I have not yet received them, his ship was much injured and he put into Plimouth to refit and has not yet got up to London. But your Letters by mr Jenks I received in one month from their date which seemd to shorten the distance between us.[2]

From the account you give as well as others of my Friends of the conduct of a certain Gentleman, I am rejoiced that it can no longer give me the uneasiness it has done in time past. I am not very apprehensive of his taking a voyage.[3] I am sure he will not, when he learns that the Lady is already engaged to a Gentleman much Worthyer of her than himself, a Gentleman whom you will be proud to take by the Hand, and own as a Nephew. I cannot pass a higher encomium upon him, than to Say that there is something in his manners; which often reminds me of my dear Brother Cranch. With regard to his person, he is tall Slender and a good figure, a complextion naturally dark, but made still more so, by seven or 8 years service in the Field, where he reaped laurels more durable than the tincture of a skin.

He appears a Gentleman in every thought, word and action, domestick in his attachments, fond in his affections, quick as lightning in his feelings, but softned in an instant. His Character is that of a dutifull son and a most affectionate Brother. If you wish to know more of him Major Rice and mr Tudor are both acquainted with him as well as mr Gerry, and a parson Evans who I hear is courting miss Kent. With him he trod the uncultivated wilds through the Indian Country and commanded a Regiment under General Sullivan.[4] As an officer his Character is highly meritorious, as a citizen he appears all that a Man ought to be, who loves his Country, and is willing to devote his talants to the Service of it.

"Her voice in Counsel, in the fight her sword."[5]

Let not the world say, that Pecuniary motives have prompted to this connection. I do not know that the prospects of the one are superiour to the others, only that Col S. has repeatedly been honourd with the confidence of his Country and stands fair for future promotion, and that he is an honourable Man. I have been more explicit upon this Subject, because I do not know but a speedier connection may be thought proper, than I could wish for, on account of the political situation of affairs. Things appear in such a state upon this Side the Water and we receive such accounts from your Side, that I cannot say what will be the result. Col S. is now gone to Paris upon buisness of great concequence, Mr J—n is to return here with him. The mutual conference may produce measures which may perhaps bring you and I together sooner than we are at present aware of. This is communicated in confidence. Let it not pass any further than to Mr C— and Dr T. Should that be the case Col S. will be left here, and I know he will not consent to be left alone. The concequence is easily foreseen. The Book of futurity is wisely closed from our Eyes. If our prospects are built upon a virtuous foundation, it is all we can do towards ensureing their success. My own lot in Life has been attended with so many circumstances, that at my first Sitting out, I could have formd no Idea of, that I did not think it worth my while to object to the present connection of your Neice, because it was probable that She would be seperated from me, and that I could not see what her future destination in life might be. It will feel very hard however to me to part with her, but then, I have not an anxiety with respect to the Man.

Braintree is much alterd from what it was a few years ago. The circumstances of our Friends and acquaintance are so much changed for the worse that I feel a degree of melancholy when I reflect upon them. Weymouth is lost to me, and I can only think of it as the Tomb of my Ancestors. Whilst there dust sleeps there, I shall feel a respect and veneration for the spot, but the pleasureable

Ideas that used once to dilate my Heart when I thought of the Parental smile, and Joy which always welcomed me to the Hospitable mansion—are fled—whither are they fled? With my Friends to that Mansion where I humbly hope to join them in some future period without the painfull alloy of a Seperation.

I cannot thank you enough my dear sister for all your kind care and attention to my Children. Having Friends; who I know tenderly Love me and who take pleasure in manifesting their regard to my Children, I have no anxiety in my absence, but the fear of being troublesome to them. As to your care of my things I know and am fully satisfied with it, do what ever you think best. I did not know I had left an oz of sugar in the House, the Spice I remember. There is an old great coat I wish you would give it to abdee and as to my other Cloaths do with them as you think best. I shall send a trunk by Lyde with some Cloaths which are useless here, but which may serve the children. I shall execute your order, but I felt sorry it did not reach you before I read it in the letter,[6] as I had determined upon it before I heard from you. I wish you would be so good as to give each of my Neices B and L Gauze the best I have, enough for Aprons, and to Miss Polly and B Palmer[7] Tammy enough for skirts, if you think it will be acceptable.

If you can get linen at Milton take it. I am very sorry you did not before, you know it is an article which will not injure, and is always wanted. Mrs Quincy has written to me for a black Padusoy.[8] I cannot find such a silk as we used to call such, I believe they have quite done making them. I find what we used to call ducapes very good 3 quarters wide at 10 shilling sterling and half a Guiney, but I am totally at a loss to know what to do. You know there is a drawback upon the exportation of Silk by whole sale, which enables the Merchant to sell them as low in America as they can be purchased here. If mrs Quincy could send me word in a baloon I would execute her orders with pleasure. As it is I believe I Shall venture upon sending out the Silk. Yet I should be greatly mortified if it did not Suit. All I can say is that I will do my best, my best respects to her. I shall write you again by Lyde and to the rest of my Friends, to whom you will present my Love and affection. Mr Adams sends his regards—he is much perplexed and much to do—to no purpose—he says, which is not very pleasent you know to one who always wishes to be doing good. But if he cannot make a treaty with this country, I hope he will be able to Effect what our country may find of more importance to them.

Adieu my Dear sister and believe me as ever your affectionate Sister
AA

You will keep this letter much to yourself.[9]

RC (MWA:Abigail Adams Corr.).

[1] AA to Richard Cranch, 23 Dec. 1785, not found. Cranch acknowledges its receipt in his letter to AA of 13 April, below.

[2] Mary Smith Cranch to AA, 18 and 23 Dec. 1785 (vol. 6:493–495, 499–502).

[3] Mary Smith Cranch mentioned Tyler's intention to visit England in her letter of 23 Dec. 1785 (vol. 6:501). He never made the trip.

[4] For Nathan Rice (1754–1834) and William Tudor (1750–1819), both of whom studied law with JA, see vol. 1:142, 146. Rice and WSS were both encamped at Valley Forge in early 1778 (William Walton, ed., *The Army and the Navy of the United States*, 2 vols., Boston, 1889, 2, suppl.:15–17). Elbridge Gerry had originally put WSS's name forward in the Continental Congress for the position of secretary to the London legation and recommended him highly to JA (Gerry to JA, 5 March 1785, Smith, *Letters of Delegates*, 22:246–247). WSS served with Rev. Israel Evans in Maj. Gen. John Sullivan's Indian campaign of May–Nov. 1779 (*Journals of the Military Expedition of Major General John Sullivan against the Six Nations of Indians in 1779*, ed. Frederick Cook, Auburn, N.Y., 1887, p. 318, 321). For Evans' marriage to Huldah Kent, see Mary Smith Cranch to AA, 7 May, below.

[5] Prodicus of Ceos, *The Judgment of Hercules, a Poem*, transl. Robert Lowth, Glasgow, 1743, line 128. See also AA2 to JQA, 22 Jan., note 5, above.

[6] Mary Cranch had requested that AA purchase lustring (a plain, strong, lustrous silk) and muslin for her (vol. 6:494–495).

[7] Mary (Polly) and Elizabeth Palmer, daughters of Gen. Joseph and Mary Palmer, were nieces of the Cranches.

[8] No letter from Ann Marsh Quincy, the third wife of Col. Josiah Quincy, has been found. Mary Cranch previously mentioned the request for paduasoy, a rich, heavy silk with a corded effect (vol. 6:494, 495).

[9] Written in right-hand margin of the last page of the letter.

Abigail Adams to Elizabeth Smith Shaw

My Dear Sister
London March 4 1786

I seldom feel a sufficient stimulous for writing untill I hear that a vessel is just about to sail, and then I find my self so deep in debt, that I know not where to begin to discharge the account. But it is time for me to be a little more provident for upon looking into my list I find I have no less than 18 correspondents who have demands upon me. One need to have a more fruitfull fund than I am possessed of, to pay half these in Sterling Bullion. I fear many will find too great a Quantity of alloy to be pleased with the traffic.

I think in one of my letters to you last fall I promised to give you some account of the celebrated actress Mrs Siddons, who I was then going to see;[1] you may well suppose my expectations were very high, but her circumstances were such then as prevented her from exerting that force of passion, and that energy of action, which have renderd her so justly celebrated. ⟨*She was* [. . .] *in the* [. . .] *of her pregnancy. You [will?] suppose that she ought not to have appeard [at?] [. . .] upon appeard at all upon the stage; I [should?] have thought so too if I had not [seen?] her. [. . .] contrived her dress in such a manner as wholy to [disguise?] her situation and [have?] only those tragedies where little exertion was necessary.*〉[2] The first peice I saw her in was Shakspears Othelo. She was interesting beyond any actress I had ever seen: but I lost much of the pleasure of the play, from the Sooty appearence of the Moor. Perhaps it may be early prejudice, but I could not Seperate the affrican coulour from the man, nor prevent that disgust and horrour which filld my mind every time I saw him touch the Gentle Desdemona, nor did I wonder that Brabantio thought some Love portion or some witchcraft had been practised, to make his Daughter "fall in Love with what she scarcly dared to look upon."[3] I have been more pleasd with her since in several other characters particularly in Matilda in the Carmilite, a play which I send you for your amusement.[4] Much of Shakspears language is so uncooth that it sounds very harsh. He has beauties which are not equald, but I should suppose they might be renderd much more agreeable for the Stage by alterations. I saw Mrs Siddons a few Evenings ago, in Macbeth a play you recollect, full of horrour. She supported her part with great propriety, but She is too great to be put in so detestable a Character. I have not yet seen her in her most pathetick Characters, which are Jane Shore, Belvedera in venice preservd and Isabela in the fatal marriage,[5] for you must make as much interest here, to get a Box when she plays, as to get a place at Court, and they are usually obtaind in the same Way. It would be very difficult to find the thing in this Country which money will not purchase, provided you can bribe high enough.

What adds much to the merit of Mrs Siddons, is her virtuous Character, Slander itself never having slurd it. She is married to a Man who bears a good character, but his Name and importance is wholy swallowd up in her Fame. She is the Mother of five children, but from her looks you would not imagine her more than 25 years old. She is happy in having a Brother who is one of the best tragick actors upon the Stage, and always plays the capital parts with her, so that both her Husband, and the virtuous part of the audience can see them in the tenderest scenes without once fearing for their reputation.[6] I scrible to you upon these subjects, yet fear they do not give you the pleasure I wish to communicate for it is with the Stage, as with Yoricks Sentimental journey, no person can have an equal realish for it, with those who have been in the very place described. I can however inform you of something which will be more interesting to you because it is the work of one of our own Countrymen, and of one of the most important events of the late War. Mr Trumble has made a painting of the battle at Charstown and the Death of Generall Warren. To speak of its merit, I can only say; that in looking at it, my whole frame contracted, my Blood Shiverd and I felt a faintness at my Heart. He is the first painter who has undertaking to immortalize by his Pencil those great actions; that gave Birth to our Nation. By this means he will not only secure his own fame, but transmit to Posterity Characters and actions which will command the admiration of future ages and prevent the period which gave birth to them from ever passing away into the dark abiss of time whilst he teaches, mankind, that it is not rank, or titles, but Character alone which interest Posterity. Yet notwithstanding the Pencil of a Trumble, and the Historick Pen of a Gorden and others, many of the componant parts of the great whole, will finally be lost. Instances of Patience perseverence fortitude magninimity courage humanity and tenderness, which would have graced the Roman Character, are known only to those who were themselves the actors, and whose modesty will not suffer them to blazon abroad their own fame. These however will be engraven by Yoricks recording Angle[7] upon unfadeing tablets; in that repositary where a just estimate will be made both of principals and actions.

Your Letters of Sepbr 7 and Jan'ry,[8] I have received with much pleasure and am happy to find that the partiality of a Parent, with regard to a very dear son, had not lessned him in the Eyes of his Friends, for praises are often so many inquisitors and always a tax where they are lavishd. I think I may with justice say, that a due sense of moral obligation integrity and Honour are the predominant traits of his Character, and these are good foundations upon which one may reasonably build hopes of future usefullness. The longer I live in the world, and the more I see of mankind, the more deeply I am impressd with the importance and necessity of good principals and virtuous examples being placed before youth; in the most amiable and engageing manner whilst the mind is uncontaminated and open to impressions. Yet precept without example is of little avail, for habits of the mind are produced by the exertion of inward practical principals. "The Souls calm Sunshine"[9] can result only from the practise of virtue, which is conjenial to our natures. If happiness is not the immediate concequence of virtue, as some devotees to pleasure affirm, Yet they will find that virtue is the indispensible condition of happiness, and as the Poet expresses it,

> "Peace o virtue! Peace is all thy own."[10]

But I will quit this Subject least my good Brother should think I have invaded his province.

I was much gratified by the account you gave me of the marriage of my Loved Friend and companion of many of my solatary hours.[11] What ever can increase her happiness will augment mine, for I loved her as my Friend as well as Relation. I always found her Sincere in her professions, constant in her attachments, benevolent in her disposition, and disposed to do all the Good in her power. Such Characters deserve well of mankind tho they may be deficient in less essential qualifications. I hope she will meet with every attention and tenderness in her connection which I know her to be deserving of. I think She is calculated for the station and relation in which she is placed, and I dare say it will not be her fault if she does not fill it, with reputation to herself and Friends. My Love to her and my best wishes attend her. I know she will rejoice with me in the dissolution of a Connextion the circumstances of which She has been more acquainted with, than any other of my Friends. Her sentiments and opinions were well founded, and she never kept from me a truth however dissagreeable that she thought it of importance to communicate, tho she knew and experienced the displeasure of one, whom time and her own experience; has taught, who were her disinterested Friends. Your Neice has always been more communicative to you, than to any other of her Friends. Your gentle soul taught her confidence. She will perhaps inform you that she has partialities better founded than those she has escaped from: may she have occasion to bless the day, that a sense of duty and fillial affection, overpowerd every other consideration; Sanctiond now by the voice of reason judgment and her Parents. She can look forward with happier prospects.

I must hasten to a close, as the watch which ticks upon the table points to two oclock, and I am not yet drest. I will however first inquire whether you ever received a peice of calico which I sent my little neice by mr Gardner for a slip, or whether he kept it as mr Remington did the shoes two months after he got home.[12] People are sometimes very ready to offer their service, but think no more of the matter afterwards.

I have purchased of the best Italian lutestring I could find, sufficient for a Gown for my sister which I request her acceptance of. The coulour is quite new and perfectly the mode but it does not follow from thence that it is very handsome; I think however it will look well when made up.

We have had for this fortnight past, the severest weather we have known for the whole winter, and the most snow. It frezes hard in the House, the wind constant at east, many vessels for Newyork that were to have gone out 15 days ago, are yet detaind. I frown on account of it because I wrote by them to Dr Tufts my son John and mrs Cranch. Cushing will be ready to sail as soon as any of them. The Young Man by the Name of Wilson[13] I sent to inquire for and should have askd him to have dined with us, when captain Cushing did but he staid only one day in London.

You will be so good as to remember me to good old Madam Marsh and family, to judge Sergants and to mr Whites. Tell mrs White I have a gratefull sense of her kindness to all my sons, they express to me her maternal regard to them. I am rejoiced to hear of miss Pegys recovery.[14]

Mr Adams desires his Love to mr Shaw to you and yours. Adieu my dear sister and believe me at all times Your affectionate Sister,

AA

I hope my youngest son has out grown the Rheumatisim. This cold weather has stird up mine, but I am better now than I have been.

RC (DLC:Shaw Family Papers).

[1] AA to Elizabeth Smith Shaw, 15 Sept. 1785 (vol. 6:361–363).

[2] AA crossed out over five lines of text.

[3] Act I, scene iii, line 98: " . . . to fall in love with what she fear'd to look on!"

[4] *The Carmelite*, a tragedy by Richard Cumberland, 1784 (*Biographia Dramatica*, 2:85).

[5] The three tragedies are *Jane Shore* by Nicholas Rowe, 1713; *Venice Preserved; or, A Plot Discovered* by Thomas Otway, 1682; and *Isabella; or, The Fatal Marriage* by David Garrick, 1758, reworked from Thomas Southerne's *The Fatal Marriage; or, The Innocent Adultery*, 1694 (same, 2:229–230, 340; 3:377).

[6] Sarah and William Siddons, also an actor, married in 1773. Her brother, John Philip Kemble, joined the Drury Lane company in 1783 (*DNB*).

[7] "The accusing spirit, which flew up to heaven's chancery with the oath, blush'd as he gave it in;—and the recording angel as he wrote it down dropp'd a tear upon the word and blotted it out for ever" (Laurence Sterne, *Tristram Shandy*, Book 6, ch. 8).

[8] 7 Sept. 1785 (vol. 6:347–350) and 2 Jan., above.

[9] "The soul's calm sunshine and the heartfelt joy," Alexander Pope, *Essay on Man*, Epistle IV, line 168.

[10] Same, Epistle IV, line 82.

[11] Elizabeth Kent Allen. See Elizabeth Smith Shaw to AA, 2 Jan., above.

[12] Shaw acknowledged receipt of the cloth on 6 Nov. 1785 (vol. 6:453), but see also Elizabeth Smith Shaw to AA, 18 June 1786, below. Mr. Gardner was probably either

Samuel or William Gardiner, both of whom arrived in Boston on the *Boston Packet*, Capt. Lyde, in Oct. 1785 (*Massachusetts Centinel*, 22 Oct.). John Remington was a retail trader who had served several terms as a town selectman for Watertown (Henry Bond, *Genealogies of the Familes and Descendants of the Early Settlers of Watertown, Massachusetts*, 2 vols. in 1, Boston, 1855, p. 410, 912; vol. 6:207).

[13] James Wilson carried letters to AA for Elizabeth Smith Shaw (vol. 6:349, 421, 422).

[14] Peggy White, daughter of John and Sarah White, had suffered from "melancholy" during the winter of 1784–1785 (vol. 5:469; JQA, *Diary*, 1:377). For Haverhill residents Mary Marsh and Nathaniel Peaslee Sargeant, see vol. 3:319, 5:408.

John Adams to Richard Cranch

My dear Brother — Grosvenor Square March 11. 1786

I am very much obliged to you, for your Friend Ship to my Brother Adams, and hope that his Conduct in his new office, will do no dishonour to his Appointment but he will stand in need sometimes of your Advice.[1]

Inclosed with this is a Book of my Friend Jefferson, which, you will entrust to none but faith full Friends. It is not yet to be published.[2]

We are at War with Morocco, Algiers, Tunis and Tripoli. By the Laws of those Nations all Nations are at War, who have no Treaties with them. It is of vast importance to us to make Peace with them. But Congress uninformed of the sums necessary to be given, have limited us to 80,000 Dollars, which is not one quarter Part of what will be found indispensible.

The English are so happy, in our Indolence and Simplicity which yeilds up to them with so much patient good Nature the entire Markett of Italy, Portugal and Spain, which tamely throws into their Hands the Fisheries of Cod and Whales, and all our own carrying Trade and Navigation, that they have nothing to do but laugh at us. To treat with us, would be an affront to their understandings, as they think. What! give us our own carrying trade, when We are willing to give it to them? It would be an Affront to us too, not to accept of our Generosity.

But my Countrymen will not always be so lazy and so Silly. If they are they will deserve!. . . . We are so good as to fill their Coffers, give them surpluses of Revenue, Ballances of Exchange, let them build Men of War, multiply sailors—all to be poured in Vengeance upon us, ten or twelve years hence! But Mass., N.H. and R. Island have more sense. Let them persevere and convert the rest.

We must and will rival the English in the Cod and Whale Fisheries; in the carrying Trade of Italy, in the East India Trade—in the Affrican Trade, and in all other Trades. Since they will consider and treat us as Rivals, Rivals we will be; and in naval Power too. Navigation Acts will make Us Rivals to some Purpose.—Twenty Years will show this Nation if it pursues its present Course, its own Nothingness, and the mighty Power of America.

But We must not be afraid of two hundred Thousand Pounds to procure Treaties with the Barbary Powers which will be worth two Millions. We must not be afraid of laying Twenty Pounds Bounty upon oil, if necessary, nor of laying round Duties upon British Articles. We must encourage Merit. The publick Mind must be generous, not mean and niggardly. Such a Disposition Stints the Growth and Damps the ardour of Genius and Enterprize. If there is meanness of soul enough, to wear fine Cloaths, keep Country seats, and ride in Carriages, upon Money borrowed of English Merchants and Manufacturers, We must be content to be poor and vain and despised. I will not say proud, one grain of Pride would scorn the Base situation.

What is become of the 300 Pieces of brass Coin, which were found in Medford? Will the Accademy, publish an Account of them? They are pronounced here not to be Phoenician but Moorish.[3]

What is become of the Art of making salt Water fresh? Will the Discoveror, communicate his secret to the state or to Congress? I hope he will not dishonour his Country so much as to come here, to sell his Art.[4]

My Love to sister and the Children, to my ever honoured Mother, to my Brother and his Family, to Uncle Quincy, Mr Wibirt and all Frids. Your affectionate Brother John Adams

RC (privately owned, 1962); endorsed: "Lettr: from His Exy. J. Adams Esqr Mar 11th 1786."

[1] Peter Boylston Adams was appointed justice of the peace in 1785 (vol. 6:458–459).

[2] In May 1785, Thomas Jefferson had 200 copies of *Notes on the State of Virginia* printed in Paris for private distribution. He gave a copy to JA just prior to the Adamses' departure for England (Jefferson, *Papers*, 8:147–148, 160).

[3] In Oct. 1785, Royall Tyler sent JA one of the coins found in Mystic, Conn. Through JA the coin was presented to the Society of Antiquaries in London, who concluded that the writing was not Punic but closer to Arabic or Turkish. No account by the American Academy of Arts and Sciences regarding the coins has been found (vol. 6:430, 492, 493).

[4] Cotton Tufts apprised JA in Dec. 1785 of the claims of a Mr. Allen of Martha's Vineyard to extract fresh from salt water by filtering it through sand. Allen apparently attempted to persuade the American Academy of Arts and Sciences to pay him for the secret of his system. By February the scheme—which had been hailed as "The Most Useful Discovery of this Age of Discoveries" by the *Massachusetts Centinel*—was revealed as a hoax. Unknown to observers, Allen wet the sand with fresh water before beginning the demonstration; the fresh water

would filter out, and Allen would close the spout before the salt water was released (Cotton Tufts to JA, 21 Dec. 1785, Adams Papers; *Massachusetts Centinel*, 17 Dec. 1785; *The Belknap Papers*, Part III, MHS, *Colls.*, 6th ser., 4 [1891]:308–309).

John Adams to Cotton Tufts

Dear Sir Grosvenor Square March 11. 1786

Your kind Favours of Nov 12.[1] and 24. and Decr 21 are before me. I Sympathize with you, under the Loss of your amiable Mrs Tufts, who was Innocence and Charity itself and Innocence and Charity can never put off the Flesh but for an happier state.

It gives me great Satisfaction to be informed that my Sons Behaviour is approved, by you. As they must labour for their Lives, I hope they will acquire early habits of Application to study, which is an excellent Preservative against the Dissipation which is so fatal to Youth, as well as a foundation for Usefulness in more advanced Years.

I hope to Send the Books you desire by this Vessell. I have employed a Book seller to look for them, upon the best Terms, and hope he will find them in Season.[2]

I received from Dr Holyoke, the President of the Medical Society, a polite and obliging Letter, inclosing a Vote of Thanks from the society, very honourable to me: but as the subject did not seem to require any further Attention on my Part, I never answered it. I know nothing of the Answer to the Royal society at Paris. The original Vote of the society, copy of which I transmitted is somewhere among my Papers: but I have so often removed that my Papers are packed up in Trunks, and I know not how to come at it, at present.[3]

The Sentiments in yours of Decr 21.[4] have great Weight, and from all that appears, in this Country, your Maxims will have full opportunity to come into Fashion: for there is no Disposition to a Treaty, and certainly never will be as long as our states will Suffer this Kingdom to monopolize the Navigation of both Countries. They now think us simple enough to let them be carriers for us as well as themselves, and they love us so well as to take Pleasure in obliging us in this Way.

My Correspondent Mathew Robinson Esqr, Author of a Pamphlet in 1774 intituled Considerations on the Measures carrying on &c has published lately the inclosed Address which contains the first honest View of the State of this Nation that has appeared since the Peace. This is an honest and Sensible Old Man of Fortune, and formerly Member of Parliament.[5] The Minister upon reading the Pamphlet said "if John Adams had given the author five hundred Pounds for writing it, he could not have laid out his Money to more Advantage." But that "if the state were true, it was a d—d wicked thing to publish it."

Alass poor John Adams has no Money to lay out, in hiring Englishmen to save themselves from Destruction, and if he had any it would be his Duty to give it to the Algerines, first. My Love to Mr Quincy, Your son and all Friends John Adams

RC (Adams Papers); endorsed: "Mr Adams Letter of March. 11. 1786 Recd May. 22. 1786."

[1] Not found.

[2] Tufts' request has not been found.

[3] Edward Augustus Holyoke wrote to JA on 6 Nov. 1783 (Adams Papers) to thank him for arranging a correspondence between the Massachusetts Medical Society and the Société Royale de Médecine at Paris (see JA to AA, [9 *June 1783*], vol. 5:168–170). In his letter of 24 Nov. 1785 (Adams Papers), Tufts desired to know whether Holyoke's letters to JA and to the Société Royale had arrived.

JA acknowledged Holyoke's letter in April and enclosed the original letters from the officers of the Société Royale and its vote acknowledging its Massachusetts counterpart (JA to Holyoke, 3 April 1786, MSaE: Holyoke Family Coll.).

[4] Tufts argues in his letter that Great Britain's continuing refusal to establish a commercial treaty with the United States might actually benefit American trade and commerce. Earlier widespread availability of British credit "has ever discouraged every Attempt to Independance in Trade and the Establishment of our Manufacturies. The Restrictions of Great Britain and the Refusal of further Credit are however happily calculated to remove these Difficulties: And can We but continue a few years in a State of Exclusion from her Commerce, Our Debts will be paid and our Independance of Mind established" (Cotton Tufts to JA, 21 Dec. 1785, Adams Papers).

[5] JA opened a correspondence with Matthew Robinson-Morris, later 2d baron Rokeby, in February, through the offices of Dr. Price. Robinson-Morris authored several pamphlets sympathetic to America in the 1770s, including *Considerations on the Measures Carrying on with Respect to the British Colonies in North America*, London, 1774, for which see 1:xvi, 202–203. His recent publication was *An Address to the Landed, Trading and Funded Interest of England on the Present State of Public Affairs*, London, 1786 (published as *The Dangerous Situation of England* in the 2d edn.). See JA to Robinson-Morris, 21 Feb. (LbC, Adams Papers).

Robinson-Morris represented Canterbury in the House of Commons from 1747 to 1761 (Namier and Brooke, *House of Commons*, 3:367).

Abigail Adams to Mary Smith Cranch

My dear Sister London March 15 1786

Mrs Hay[1] call'd upon me a sunday whilst I was gone to meeting to let me know that She expected to Sail in a few days for Newyork. When I saw her before she determined to go out in captain Lyde who will not go till the middle of April, but Captain Cooper is a British Bottom, and on board of him they will not have algerines to fear.[2] I cannot but think She is right. I freely own I should be loth to risk myself, as American vessels are unsecured. I shall call upon her in a day or two, and get her to take in her trunk a peice of silk which I have procured for you, and Mrs Shaw, and which I had determined to send by Cushing. You requested that it might be dark, the coulour is new and fashionable, I think dark enough. I never had any great affection for dark coulours but the observation of Pope Gangenella, that the Lady who talkd Scandle was in an ill humour, or Pevish against mankind, was commonly drest in a brown habit,[3] has put me quite out of conceit of Dark Cloaths. Besides I am of opinion that they do not suit Dark complexions. I have sent my Mother silk for a Gown which you will present her with my duty, and some waistcoat patterns for our sons upon commencment day whom I have directed to drink my Health upon the occasion. These things my dear Friends will do me the favour to accept of, as a small token of my regard for them. I have made a peice of linen up for my older Son having his measure here, and I have bought an other peice both of which I shall send by cushing or Lyde and Mrs Quincys silk too, but I dare not encumber mrs Hay with any thing more. Since I began writing have received a card from mrs Hay informing me that she expects to sail on saturday.

I have written to you by way of Newyork and requested mr King to forward the Letters to you. I shall write again by Lyde, what Letters I have by me I shall commit to Mrs Hay. I will write to my neices and other Friends soon. I have received the chocolate by Lyde and give you a thousand thanks for it.[4]

I have nothing of importance to inform you of at present, I have written largely to you so lately. My best regards Love &c attend you all from your affectionate

Sister A A

There is a peice of calico for Louissa sent to your care. I have not written to her but shall soon.

RC (MWA:Abigail Adams Corr.); addressed by AA2: "Mrs. Mary Cranch Braintree Massachusetts."

[1] Katherine Farnham of Newburyport, Mass., married Capt. John Hay in 1774. The Adamses frequently saw her in London and Paris (John J. Currier, *History of Newburyport, Mass., 1764–1909*, 2 vols., Newburyport, 1909, 2:258).

[2] On 26 May, the *Edward*, Capt. Cooper (or Coupar), arrived in New York after a 35-day voyage from London (*New York Packet*, 29 May).

[3] AA is closely paraphrasing a letter from Giovanni Vincenzo Antonio Ganganelli, Pope Clement XIV (1705–1774, served 1769–1774), who writes, "True devotion, Madam, neither consistes in a careless air, nor in a brown habit. . . . Observe, moreover, that the lady who talks scandal in an assembly, or appears peevish, or in an ill humour against mankind, is most frequently dressed in brown" ("To Madam ***," *Interesting Letters of Pope Clement XIV. (Ganganelli.)*, London, 1777, Letter X).

[4] At AA's request, the Cranches sent her a dozen pounds of chocolate (vol. 6:279, 502, 507).

John Quincy Adams to Abigail Adams 2d

Cambridge, March 15th, 1786

What shall I say to justify the date of this letter, after so many fair promises to be punctual, and so many obligations to be so, from your being so exact? To skip nearly four months without writing a line. Indeed, my only plea is, that which I have already offered—a want of time. I have been, indeed, very much hurried since I came to Haverhill, and of late more than ever. At the beginning of the year I was informed, that of the short time I expected to be at Haverhill, six weeks were to be curtailed, and that instead of entering at the last of April, I must come by the middle of March, in order to attend two courses of experimental philosophy. I might have waited till next commencement, and then entered as senior; and in that case I should have had time enough to write to my friends, but I should have missed one course of lectures. Besides, I had undertaken last fall, to be ready to enter before the class began upon natural philosophy. When I found my time shortened, I determined to lay aside every thing else, and attend only to my present business; supposing you would prefer to have me qualified in every respect for the place I was to enter in this University, to hearing from me often. And to enter here, it is not necessary to know any thing but what is found in a certain set of books, and I have heard it asserted, that some of the best scholars, after having taken their degrees, would not be received if they offered as freshmen, because they commonly forget those parts of learning which are required in a freshman. Since the first of January, I have not, upon an average, been four hours in a week (Sundays excepted) out of Mr. Shaw's house. And now, I thank heaven, I have got through this business, and shall have time to write you more often.

Yesterday I came here from Haverhill, and this day passed examination before the president, professors and tutors.[1] After they had done with me, and laid their wise heads together to consult whether I was worthy of entering this University, the president came marching as the heroes on the French stage do, and with sufficient pomposity said: "Adams, you are admitted." I have already come to the resolution of showing all the respect and deference to every member of the government of the College that they can possibly claim, but to you, I can venture to give my real sentiments, such as arise spontaneously in my mind, and that I cannot restrain.

It is necessary, after having gone through the ceremony of examination, to pass a number of others before you can be considered as a member of the University.[2] When I went the last time to the President, said he, "Adams, both Mr. Shaw and Dr. Tufts have informed me that you wish to live within the walls of the college, and when you return here you may come to me." He did not tell me where I was to live; but I found out it is to be with a Mr. Ware, who took his degree last commencement, and is now keeping the town-school here.[3] He is very much esteemed and respected in college, and has an excellent chamber; this was a very fortunate circumstance, as it will be both more agreeable and less expensive to live in college, than it would have been to board in town. I strolled about with Charles Storer, heard the debates in the House of Representatives, and some pleadings at the Supreme Court, which is now sitting.[4]

Cambridge, 22d.

I dined at Boston, and came here on foot. I went to the President, as he had commanded me. Said he, "Adams, you may live with Sir Ware, a Bachelor of Arts," with an emphasis upon every syllable. The reputation of the President is that of a man of great learning, without partiality in favor of any scholars in particular, and turning all his views towards promoting the honor and interest of the University, but he has very little knowledge of mankind, and is consequently exceedingly stiff and pedantic, and has made himself ridiculous at times, by reproving gentlemen who did not belong to college for calling a student Mr. in his presence; so sure as any one says Mr. to a scholar, so sure the President will inform him that there are no Misters among under-graduates; for three years after they take their degree he calls them Sir. Whenever George Storer goes to see him, he is addressed "Sir Storer," and he would lose his place before he would call any person in this University Mr., before he had taken his second degree. There are many other instances of his carrying this pomposity to an extreme, and although he has two students that board in his house, yet he thinks it beneath his dignity even to speak to them. Notwithstanding all this, he is much better liked as a president than he was as a tutor; and although he is often laughed at for affecting so much importance, yet he is esteemed and respected for his learning, and the good qualities that I have already mentioned.

We have had one of the most extraordinary northern lights that I ever saw. It is now ten o'clock, no moon, yet I can read a common print in the street.

Friday, 24th.

I have already begun with the studies with the class. They recited this week to Mr. James, the Latin tutor.[5] This afternoon I declaimed. Every afternoon two scholars, either senior or junior sophisters, speak pieces from some English author. They speak in their turn alphabetically, and to-day it came to me. I took my piece from Shakspeare's "As you like it." All the world is a stage. At the description of the justice in fair round belly, with good capon lined,[6] every person present, the president excepted, burst into a loud laugh. I was sensible it was at my expense, but I expected it, and was not disconcerted.

28th.

We recite this week to Mr. Read, tutor in mathematics and natural philosophy.[7] We are now in the fourth book of Euclid, which we are to finish this week, and then we are to go upon Gravesande's Experimental Philosophy.[8]

Mr. Williams gave us this forenoon the first lecture upon experimental philosophy. The course consists of twenty-four. We are to have three in a week till he gets through. This will employ a large portion of my time, as I intend to write down as much as I can recollect of the lectures after I come out. I find great advantage in having the French work upon that subject which I brought with me from Anteuil.

My duty to my dear and honored parents. Compliments where you please. Yours, J. Q. Adams

MS not found. Printed from AA2, *Jour. and Corr.*, 3:93–99.

[1] JQA was examined in Latin, Greek, logic, geography, and mathematics by president Joseph Willard and other members of the faculty (*Diary*, 2:1–2).

[2] JQA refers to the various steps in obtaining and filing a bond (to be forfeited if quarterly bills were not paid) and certificate of admission with the proper college authorities (same, 2:1–3).

[3] Henry Ware of Sherburne, Mass., would become minister of the First Church in Hingham in 1787. He returned to Harvard in 1805 to serve as Hollis Professor of Divinity, a position he held until 1840 (Sprague, *Annals Amer. Pulpit*, 8:199–202; *Harvard Quinquennial Cat.*).

[4] JQA heard the debates and pleadings in Boston on 18 March. In the evening he rode to Braintree, where he stayed until 22 March (*Diary*, 2:3–5).

[5] Eleazar James, Harvard 1778, served as tutor 1781–1789 (*Harvard Quinquennial Cat.*).

[6] *As You Like It*, Act II, scene vii, lines 139, 154.

[7] Nathan Read, Harvard 1781, was a tutor

at the college 1783–1787. He became an inventor, designed many innovations to improve and utilize the steam engine, and received several patents. In 1795 Read settled in Danvers and was agent for the Salem Iron Factory from 1796 until he moved to Belfast, Maine, in 1807. He served as a Massachusetts Representative in Congress 1800–1803 (*Harvard Quinquennial Cat.*; *NEHGR*, 50:430 [Oct. 1896]).

[8] Euclid, *Elements of Geometry*; Willem Jacob van Gravesande, *Mathematical Elements of Natural Philosophy, Confirmed by Experiments; or, An Introduction to Sir Isaac Newton's Philosophy*, transl. John Theophilus Desaguliers, 2 vols., London, 1720–1721.

Elizabeth Smith Shaw to Abigail Adams

Haverhill March 18th 1786

Should I my Dear Sister, too much alarm the Heart of an affectionate Mother, solicitous for the welfare of her Children if I were to say plainly, that I wish Mr JQA had never left Europe. That he had never come into our Family. Then we should not have known him. Then we should not have been so grieved. Then we should not have this ocasion of Sorrow.

His leaving it.—Indeed my Sister, our House looks gloomy now he has left it. Mr Shaw and I feel the loss of him more than of any Pupil that has ever lived with us. He used to read to me in the Evening in his leisure Moments, which always gave me pleasure, for his manner of reading was a good comment upon the Subject, and did honour to his Author. He had imbibed some curious Notions, and was rather peculiar in some of his Opinions, and a little to decisive, and tenacious of them. Mr Thomas said to him one Day, "I think Brother you seem to differ most always from every one else in company." And I used to tell him that I had seen People, while they thought they were possessed of, and adopting the most liberal Sentiments grow contracted and illiberal. And that though I was willing to allow him every *advantage*, which I *knew* he was *possessed* of above his cotemporaries, yet there was more than a probability that he would think differently, at different periods of Life. Most young People of his Age, are apt to think they are certainly *right*. It is a Fault which at the early period of eighteen, (if I may be allowed the expression) that generally arives at its *greatest perfection*. But it is what good-sense, Time, and Experience will naturally expell.

In company Mr JQA was always agreeable, pleasing, modest, and polite, and it was only in private Conversation, that those imperfections of Youth, were perceivable,[1] and I should not have mentioned them now, if I had not have supposed you would wish to know every thing about him.

His Father is *his* ⟨*Delphic*⟩ Oracle. There never was a Son who had a greater veneration for a Father, and none (perhaps) who have more reason than yours.

I think my sisters very happy in their Children for they *all* appear to be blessed with Talentes, superior to what we commonly meet with in those of their Age. It is our wish that they may improve them to their honour, their own real good, and to their Countries Service.

In Mr JQA, I see an high sense of honor, great Abilities well cultivated, and improved by critical Observation, and close attention to the Tempers, and dispositions of People, the Laws, the Customs, and the Manners of those Countries where he has travelled.

In him I see the wise Politician, the good statesman, and the Patriot in Embrio.

In Charles I behold those Qualities that form the engaging, the well accomplished Gentleman, the Friend of Science, the favorite of the *Muses*, and the *Graces*, as well as of the Ladies.

In Thomas B A, I discern a more martial, and intrepid Spirit. A fine natural Capacity, a love of Buisiness, and an excellent faculty in dispatching it. Indefatiguable in every-thing that shall render him a useful member of Society, and independant of the World.

And as to my Dear, dear lovely Niece, I consider *her*, as a mere Phœnix, as exhibiting to the world greatness, and strength of Mind, and coolness of Judgment which has few examples. Possessed with those Sentiments, with which she left America, her *Conflict* must have been great.

Mr Atkinson, Mr Storer, and Mr Smith kept Sabbath here, this winter,[2] and brought with them your Letter dated October 2d. which you sent by Callihan,[3] accompanied with a kind present of a pair of Shoes, which are full large, and fit me very well. I receive every Token of Love, from my Sister, to me, or mine, with more than a grateful Heart.

I wrote Mr Storer a Billet upon his arrival, begging the favour of a Visit from him. I wanted to ask questions, to hear him talk about you and yours. He was so good as to gratify me, and I think him a fine agreeable, sociable, modest Man.

Your Son Charles, and Cousin William Cranch made us a Visit in the Winter Vacation. They both are studious, behave well, and have the approbation of their Tutors, and the love of their Classmates.

I assure you it made us happy to see your Children. They chose to lodge together in our great Bed, though there was another in the

Chamber. I went up after they were abed to see if they were warm, and comfortable as I told them, but *really* to enjoy the satisfaction of seeing the three Brothers embracing each other in Love, Innocence, Health, and Peace. All my Sister rose within me—Joy—Love—Gratitude, and maternal Tenderness sparkled in my Eye.

"What said I, would your Mother give to look upon you all, and see you happy as I do."

Would she were here.

I know that you can have no greater pleasure, than to hear that your "Children walk in the Truth."[4]

Mr JQA was accepted by the Proffessors without the lest dificulty, and Mr Shaw procured him a Chamber in the University with a Graduate, with whom he is to live till after Commencment. Mr Thomas B A, the Dr says, must enter the University next July. He has been with us so long that it hurts me to think of parting with him. But his advantage must be consulted more than my pleasure.[5]

Both my Children always ask me, whether I am writing to their Aunt Adams, and beg I would give their *Love* to you, for they have no Idea of any-thing better.

Mr Shaw best, kindest wishes attend you. He feels not a little proud of his Pupils I assure you.

Thomas presents his Duty, has nothing new to tell you, and so omits writing.

Betsy Smith wishes she may have a few Lines from her cousin Nabby, and begs her Duty and Love may be accepted.

My Dear Sister, believe me most affectionately yours.

Eliza Shaw

This Letter I intended to have sent by the first Opportunity this Spring, but was not apprized of Callihans sailing soon enough for the purpose.

I will send it to Mr Smith however, to go by the first Vessel, hoping it will be accepted, because I know it was dictated by the greatest Love, and Affection of Your Sister Eliza Shaw

I am impatient to hear from you.

RC (Adams Papers). Dft (DLC:Shaw Family Papers).

[1] In the Dft Shaw concludes this paragraph: " . . . and I know not whether I have done right in mentioning it now—only as I thought you would wish to know our opinion of him." For JQA's perspective on this subject see his *Diary*, 1:398.

[2] John Atkinson, Charles Storer, and William Smith visited Haverhill in January. Atkinson married Elizabeth Storer, the half-sister of Charles, in 1773 (JQA, *Diary*, 1:387–388; *Sibley's Harvard Graduates*, 12:213).

[3] Not found.

[4] A reference to 3 John, 1:4: "I have no greater joy than to hear that my children walk in truth."

[5] TBA began his studies with Rev. John Shaw in April 1783 (vol. 5:105–107, 118).

John Adams to John Quincy Adams

My dear son — Grosvenor Square March 19. 1786

This Letter, I presume, will find you at the University, where I hope you will pass your time both pleasantly and profitably. Let Us know how you find Things, and take care of your health. You have in your Travels had so much Exercise, that it is not Safe to discontinue it, and indulge your self too much in a Sedentary Life. Never fail to walk an hour or two every day.

I have read the Conquest of Canaan and Vision of Columbus, two Poems which would do honour to any Country and any Age. Read them, and you will be of my mind.[1] Excepting Paradise lost, I know of nothing Superiour in any modern Language. What Success they will have in England is uncertain, at least for some years.

I will Say thus much in favour of our Country that in Poets and Painters, She is not at present outdone by any nation in Europe.

Your Letters to your sister are a great Refreshment to Us. Continue the Correspondence as often as you can without interfereing with your Studies.

I am my dear son, with the tenderest Affection your Father

John Adams

RC (Adams Papers).

[1] Timothy Dwight, *The Conquest of Canäan*, Hartford, 1785; Joel Barlow, *The Vision of Columbus*, Hartford, 1787. For further commentary on how JA had access to these works and on his involvement with attempts to publish them in London, see JA, *D&A*, 3:189.

Abigail Adams to John Quincy Adams

My Dear Son — March 20th 1786 London

Altho I have written you a very long Letter by way of Newyork,[1] yet should one vessel go to Boston without a few lines from me, I flatter myself you would be dissapointed.

Captain Cushing and Lyde both dined here yesterday. Each of them expect to sail in all this month, but Cushing in the course of the present week. By him I send you a set of shirts, as we had your measure I supposed it was as well to send them made up, as to trouble our Friends to do it for you. I have also sent a peice of linen which mr Jenks has engaged to pack up with some things which he is sending to mr Tufts, and which is to be deliverd to your Aunt Cranch for the use of your Brothers. By mrs Hay I have sent several little bundles to my Friends (She is gone in a British bottom by way of Newyork,) amongst which is silk for a waistcoat for you and your Brother Charles, which you are to have made for commencment day. The Books you requested are also sent by Captain Cushing. If there is any thing more you wish, write me word and I will procure it for you, because I know you will circumcribe your wish to my ability. If that was more ample, many should I rejoice to benefit by it. But if we are not the favorites of fortune, let us be; what is of much more importance to us, the Votaries of Virtue, and consider that being denied the former we are secured from many temptations that always attend upon that fickle Dame. The Prayer of Augur, was that of a wise Man, who was aware that Poverty might expose him to acts of injustice towards his fellow creatures, and riches, to ingratitude towards his Maker. He therefore desird that middle state which would secure him from the temptation of the first, and Gaurd him from the impiety of the latter.[2] And in that middle State, I believe the largest portion of Humane happiness is to be found. Riches always create Luxery, and Luxery always leads to Idleness Indolence and effeminacy which stiffels every noble purpose, and withers the blossom of genious which fall useless to the ground, unproductive of fruit.

Your Sister has written you so many pages that I suppose she has not left me any thing material to write to you but as I am very rarely honourd with a sight of any of them I shall venture, tho I repeat what has already been written, to inform you that mr Jefferson is here from Paris, and that the treaty with portugal will be compleated in a few days.[3] Conferences have been held with the Tripoline minister who is here. The subject terms of Treaty &c been all transmitted to Congress,[4] and it is for them to decide whether they will purchase a Peace, or whether they will submit to a War which will cost them 3 times as much as a peace, provided they had Ships for the purpose, and after all, will be obliged to make a peace, redeem their prisoners, and pay a still larger tribute than is at present demanded, tho that is very great, or will they take an other whole year to decide upon the subject. This month compleats *one*, since the appointment of Lamb, who is not yet got to Algiers and when he does, get there, by all accounts, he will not find a greater Barbarian than himself. Is this for the Honour of our Country to send such characters as a specimin of our Nation!

Do the united States wish to become the Scorn of Europe and the laughing Stock of Nations, by withholding from Congress those powers which would enable them to act in concert, and give vigor and strength to their proceedings. The states dishearten many able Men from joining in their counsels, whose years and experience teach wisdom, and send their beardless Boys to cavil at words, with all the pedantick and shallow Pierian draughts which intoxicate the Brain, who know perhaps how to place their comas and points, but to the weighty matters of the State are quite incompetent, who know no more of the nature of Goverment, or possess any clearer Ideas of the politicks of nations than the Member of Parliament understood of the Geography of America when he talkd of the Island of Virginia.[5]

Heaven forgive me if I form too unfavourable an opinion of them, but many of the states do not certainly attend sufficiently to the experience and abilities of those to whom they commit, not only their own most important Interests, but those of generations yet to come. Nor are the states fully represented, seven are not competant to Money Matters. Nor do they chuse to transact any buisness of importance. By this means their affairs lag on from Month to Month, even when their is the greatest call for desicion. To those who love their Country and wish to serve her, this conduct becomes burdensome and puts them out of all Patience. But why should I preach, it will do no good. As to this Country—

> "Full soon, full soon their envious minds shall know
> our Growth their ruin, and our Peace their woe"[6]

and thus I take my leave of them.

With respect to the conference with the Tripoline, you will mention that circumstance cautiously. Write me as often as possible & believe me ever Your affectionate Mother AA

PS. inclosed is a triffle.[7]

RC (Adams Papers); addressed by AA2: "Mr John Quincy Adams Cambridge"; endorsed: "Mamma. March 20th: 1786."; docketed: "My Mother. 20. March 1786."; and "Mrs: A. Adams. March 20th: 1786."

[1] Probably that of 16 Feb., above.

[2] A paraphrase of Proverbs, 30:8–9: "Give me neither poverty nor riches; feed me with food convenient for me: lest I be full, and deny thee, and say, Who is the Lord? or lest I be poor, and steal, and take the name of my

God in vain."

[3] The treaty was not signed until 25 April. See AA2 to JQA, 25 April, below.

[4] American commissioners to John Jay, 28 March (Jefferson, *Papers*, 9:357–359).

[5] AA may have been referring to a comment by John Fothergill in his "An English Freeholder's Address to His Countrymen" in which he writes, "*The* Island *of Virginia* has been spoken of in a Court of Judicature, by a *learned* pleader; and similar instances of a general ignorance, a criminal one, of this vast region, pervaded the Country, the Universities, the Courts of Law, the Legislature in too general a manner, and even Administration itself" (John Coakley Lettsom, *The Works of John Fothergill, M.D. . . . with Some Account of His Life*, London, 1784, p. 478).

[6] Timothy Dwight, *The Conquest of Canäan*, Book 1, lines 621–622.

[7] Not found.

John Adams to Richard Cranch

Sir — Grosvenor Square March 20. 1786

In a Letter to R. R. Livingston, Secretary of state for foreign Affairs, dated The Hague July 23. 1783, I gave him an account of Conversations with Mr. Van Berckel and others, in which I learn'd that there were in holland a great Number of Refineries of Sugar; "that all their own Sugars were not half enough to employ their Sugar Houses, and that at least one half of the sugars refined in Holland were the Production of the French West India Islands. That these Sugars were purchased chiefly in the Ports of France. That France, not having sugar-Houses, for the refinement of her own sugars, but permitting them to be carried to Amsterdam, and Rotterdam, for Manufacture She might be willing that they should be carried to Boston New York and Philadelphia, from her own Ports in Europe in American Bottoms."[1]

That the Sugars which America might purchase, would be paid for in Articles more advantageous to France, than the Pay which is made by the Dutch. That if any Sugars refined in Holland are afterwards sold in France, it would be less against her Interest to have them refined in America, because the Price, would be laid out in french Produce and Manufactures. That there is a difference between us and the Dutch and all other nations, as We Spend in Europe all the Profits We make and more. The others do not. That if French Sugars refined in Holland, are afterwards Sold in other Parts of Europe (as they are in Petersbourg and all round the Baltic in Germany and Italy) We have Sugar Houses as well as the Dutch and it would be as Well that We should sell them, because our sugarhouses ought not to be more obnoxious to french Policy or Commerce, than theirs. That as there is in America a great Consumption of sugar, it is not the Interest of any Nation who have sugars to sell, to lessen the Consumption, but on the contrary they should favour it, in order to multiply Purchasers and quicken the Competition by which the Price is raised. None.

That if the worst Should happen, and all the nations who have Sugar Islands, should forbid Sugars to be carried to America, in any other, than their own Bottoms, We might depend upon having enough of this Article at the Freeports, to be brought away in our own ships, if We should lay a Prohibition or a Duty on it, in foreign ships. To do either, the States must be united, which the English think cannot be. Perhaps the French think so too, and in time they may perswade the Dutch to be of the same Opinion. It is to be hoped We shall disappoint them, all in a Point so just and reasonable, When We are contending only for an equal Chance for the Carriage of our own Productions, and the Articles of our own Consumption: When We are willing to allow to all other Nations, even a free Competition with Us, in this Carriage, if We cannot Unite; it will discover an Imperfection and Weakness in our Constitution, which will deserve a serious Consideration.

March 24.

I had begun to write you upon this Subject, but concluding to write particularly to Govr Bowdoin, I beg leave to refer you to him.[2]

I have given him an History of Mr Boylstons Voyage to France, Sale of a Cargo of Oil and Purchase of sugars.[3] It is the first Attempt, or Experiment of the Plan which I mentioned frequently in my Letters to Mr Livingstone 3 years ago[4] But every Thing written to Congress is lost. Our Merchants have not discovered so much Industry and Ingenuity as was expected. The Idea of sending to Europe from America for Sugars is odd, but We must come to it and shall find our Account in it. J. A.

RC (MWA); endorsed: "Lettr from His Exy. John Adams Esqr Mar: 20th. 1786."

[1] JA to Livingston, 23–25 July 1783, PCC, No. 84, V, f. 17–25.

[2] JA to James Bowdoin, 24 March 1786 (MHi:Winthrop Papers).

[3] With the proceeds from the sale of whale oil in France, Thomas Boylston purchased raw sugar to ship to Boston for refining and exportation to Europe or Russia (JA to James Bowdoin, 24 March, MHi:Winthrop Papers). Boylston's effort was part of a larger plan on his part to establish a regular trade in American whale oil, French goods, and West Indian sugar. For the specifics of his plan see Jefferson, *Papers*, 9:29–31. His negotiations resulted in the lowering of duties on all whale oil imported by Americans into France on either French or U.S. vessels (same, 9:88).

[4] JA to Livingston, 23–25 July, 28 July, and 30 July 1783 (all PCC, No. 84, V, f. 17–25, 45–48, 57–62).

Abigail Adams to Mary Smith Cranch

My dear sister London March 21 1786

I have just returnd from a visit to Moor Place Moor feilds, Where I have been to take leave of my much esteemed Friends, mr and Mrs Rogers, who set out on wedensday for France, and from thence are to sail in the April Packet for Newyork. Mr Rogers thinks it most for his benifit, and those connected with him, to quit England, and endeavour to adjust his affairs himself in America. She communicated their design to me some time ago in confidence, only our own family and Mr Copleys are acquainted with their intention. I hope he will be able to settle his buisness to his own advantage, for he is a worthy Man, and she one of the best and most amiable of women. There is not an other family who could have left London that I should have so much mist, go and See her my sister when she arrives. You will find her one of those gentle Spirits in whom very little alteration is necessary to fit for the world of Spirits, and her Husband seems to be made on purpose for her.

Only two days ago did your Letter by captain Young reach me.[1] The contents of it more and more convince me of the propriety of your Neices conduct, and give me reason to rejoice that I crost the atlantick with her. But what Shall I do with my Young soldier, who is much too zealous to be married, and will hardly give me time to tell my Friends that such an event is like to take place. I have no Idea of such a hurry, and so I tell him. He presses the matter to me, but cannot get me to communicate it, because I know very well, that mr A. would have so much compassion for the Young folks, that he would consent directly. He remembers what a dance he led. Now tho I have no objection to the Gentleman, yet I think marriage ought not to be his immediate object. The Services he has renderd his Country, joined to the abilities he possessess will always ensure to him a distinguished Rank in her service. His Character is universally amiable, and I have the prospect of seeing my daughter united to a Man of Strict honour and probity. But I wish he would not be quite so much in a Hurry. I believe not one of our American acquaintance Suspect the Matter. Mrs Rogers excepted to whom I told it.

Mr T. I Suppose has received my Letter by way of Newyork,[2] after which I presume he will not be very solicitious for a voyage. Your

Neice has never noticed a line from him, since She closed the correspondence by way of Dr Tufts. She received two very long Letters from him, both of which I have seen, they were perfectly Characteristic of the Man.[3]

In one of them he reflected very severely upon you, and threw out insinuations respecting many other of her correspondents, who I know had never mentiond his Name. But I know he must be mortified, so I can pardon him, wish him well and forgive him, nay thank him for no longer wearing a disguise. ⟨*He*⟩ The Creature has many good qualities, but that first of virtues Sincerity. How small a portion has fallen to his share! I have written to you by mrs Hay and sent the Lutestring &c by her. Captain Lyde deliverd me the Chocolate safe, but Young, *half seas over*, let the customhouse Seize his, which could not have happend if he had put it into his Trunk. It would do you good if you was to see how Mr Adams rejoices over his Breakfast, for the stuff we get here is half bullocks Blood. Mr Rogers will be a good hand to Send any little matter, he knows how to manage. I will write to My Dear Neices by Lyde. It mortifies me that the length of my purse is so curtaild that I cannot notice them as I wish. What letters are not ready for Cushing expect in Lyde. Do not fail of writing by way of Newyork, only do not send any News papers or very large packets that way, because every vessel stops at some outport and sends her Letters up by Land.

Remember me affectionately to all my dear Friends, particularly to my honourd Mother to whom I have sent by mrs Hay Lutestring for a Gown. Mrs Quincys silk will send by Lyde.

It is 3 oclock, and I am not drest for dinner tho Esther warnd me that it was past dressing hour some time ago, but I would finish my Letter. A double rap at the door signifies a visit. Adieu I must run, affectionately Yours, Abigail Adams

RC (MWA: Abigail Adams Corr.); addressed by AA2: "Mrs: Mary Cranch Braintree near Boston."

1 Of 8 Nov. 1785 (vol. 6:454–457).

2 AA wrote to Royall Tyler in Dec. 1785 (not found); see AA to Mary Smith Cranch, 13 June, below.

3 Not found.

Mary Smith Cranch to Abigail Adams

My dear Sister Braintree March 22d 1786

Your Son JQA is become a son of Harvard. He was admited last wednesday, and we are now prepairing him for House-keeping. He has a chamber with one of the Masters till commencment, then He and his Brother charles will live together if they can. The young Gentleman finds the Bed and Linnen. I have taken the Furniture for the Chamber from your House a few things were to be purchased at Boston. Lucy went yesterday to procure them. A Tea Kettle and a Tea apparatus were wanting. I did not chuse to take your best Blue and White for him, cousin charles had the others. It is no matter what they are if but decent ones for it will not be six months before they will not have two alike. They lend them, and if they have there number return'd they think themselves well off. Cousin Thomas will I believe enter next July. I will be quite perfect in the business of fixing off my sons: If you was to see them all together it would give you great pleasure. Four more promising youth are Seldom Seen, may nothing happen to blast our hopes! I shall wish most heartily for you in their vacancy and Should we have life and health my pleasures will exceed yours, although sourounded by all the pomp of a drawing Room at St James's. I live over my youth again in these our children. Betsy is not yet return'd from Haverhill. Billy will go for her in the Spring vacancy.

Lucy and I have had another lonely winter, not so much as one Letter from you to vary the Scene. You told me you should write by the way of newyork but I have receiv'd none. I have had so many oppertunitys to write from Boston that I have had no occation to send that way. There is a vessel or two up for London. I mean to write at my leasure till they are ready to Sail.

I think I told you that Weymouth had given Mr Evans a call. He is to give his answer Soon, I believe He will accept. I hear he is prepairing to bee married, and I know a Parish is all he has been waiting for some time. He appears the most likely to fill my dear Parents place with Dignity and honour of any one candidate they have had. It is astonishing that the greatest part of the People who are so fond of him, Should Six months ago have been raving mad for a —— Fool compair'd to this Gentleman.[1] He is a gentleman in every Sense of the word. He is Humain and benevolent, kind and affectionate to every one: He is a great admirer of uncle Toby, consciquently of

Sterns writings.[2] You can easily discover this by his publick discoursses. He is 15 year older than miss Huldah, "old enough for her Father" said somebody the other day. "There are very few younger worth having" reply'd our arch Lucy. He is very plain. Sister Shaw writing to me about him says "His Face you know. The more you See it the more it Shines." He was upon a Journey and preach'd for mr Shaw. His Subject the Prodigal Son, a fine one for his Luxuriant Fancy.

Charles Warren my dear Sister is no more, he dy'd in about a month after he arriv'd in Spain.[3] The Family did not hear of it till last week. I have not seen any of them yet. It must be a shock to them tho it is what they expected. They have an affliction which swallows up this. Mr John Codman receiv'd directions from a Gentleman in Holland to get security or arrest the Person of Winslow Warren for a debt due from him. Mr Codman shew him the Letter and Power. Mr Warren told him he could not pay him immediately but would give him His note and his Father's. Mr Codman desir'd it might be done that day as he was writing to the Gentleman. He wish'd to let him know that the matter was settled. "He should not go to milton till Satturday and then he gave his word and honour it should be done." Mr codman relying upon it wrote that it was settled to his Satissfaction. Mr C waited above a week without hearing a word from mr. W–r–n, he then found that mr W–r–n Went out of Town the next day and set out for york. He went immideatly to his Father, told him the Story, and said that unless he would give him Security for the sum he should Send after his son and arrest him where ever he could find him. The General told him his Son would be back in a few days, that he had receiv'd a Letter from him desiring that he would not be answerable to any body for any debt of his contracting. Mr C. immediatly sent an officer after him and brought him back. He had return'd part of the way home. Mr W Warren was very angry, and the first time he Saw mr C upon change, he can'd him very severely. Mr C. has Sued him for an assault, laid the Damage at two thousand pound. This is mr Cs' Side of the story. This happend about three weeks ago. I design to see mrs Warren next week. I pity her. She must be greatly afflicted.[4]

25th

Mr Evans came here this morning. He tells me he has accepted the Call at Weymouth. I am heartely glad. Doctor Tufts has got his choice at last.

It has been so remarkably warm for two or three days that we cannot keep any fire in our Room. The Bushes are leaving and the Trees budding, our Grass plot is as green as in the month of may. Lucy is return'd from cambridge our Sons are well, were all got together in Billys chamber after the exercises of the Week.

Teusday 28th

The windmill is raising to day. Mr T has just Sent his compliments to *Judge C* and desir'd his company to see it rais'd. Tis the first time he has ever mention'd one word about it to any of us. A choculate mill and a Bolting mill are to be made to go with the wind. I wonder if the Law business is to go by wind also. With Such a variety of business it will be hard if he does not get a good Living. Mr Thayer is to move off his place immediatly. Mr T says he has got possession of it and is going to repair it directly. He has bought the House and Farm which was Doctor chaucys, whether for himself or any body else I know not. The Deed was given to him.[5] The canidia and vermont Tour was prevented by the Snows leaving us here before he was ready to set out. He caught a little Snow we had and went as far as conecticut, he and mr Vesey in his Sley, and was lucky enough to get back the very last day which a Sley could go.

Thursday 30th

The raising is over it took two days to compleat it. On the first mr T made an ellegant entertainment at mrs Veseys of meats and drinks a Dinner and Supper, not for the workmen, mr Prat found them, but for the large company invited to see the raising. You love you say to have me write to the moment as it makes you seem to be among us, or I should not mention Such matters.

Mr G. Thayer has [. . .] Germantown or will do it, he is about it.[6] Mr Palmers Family are greatly distress'd. The general, holds on yet "and will not quit" it. I am affraid, without he is absolutely drove off. He supposes that if he could Stay, he should yet be able from the Salt business to pay his debts and make an Estate. His Family wish him to give up the Idea, and leave the place. You know his Temper, they are affraid of opposeing him violently. He has apply'd for madam Apthorps House upon the Hill, and may have it, if he is oblig'd to move.[7] I wish he would give up all he has and thro himself upon the generosity of his crediters, I am Sure they would be happier than they now are. We have had Robert Cranch here all Winter. He came so bad with the Rhumatism occation'd by colds or intemperance I know not which that he cold not rise from his chair or turn in his Bed. He is now much better. Mr cranch has got a place for him to work at and as soon as we can get him a little decently cloath'd, we shall send him along. It is very hard that he should come so often to be cloath'd, we had to do the same for him about a year ago.[8]

We have lately heard from our unhappy connection.[9] He has been in poor health, but is better. We once heard that he was dead. It shock'd me more than I can express. While I know he is alive I shall hope for a reformation, and that the prayeres and efforts of his dying Parents will sooner or later have some effect. He was not found guilty upon trial, of forging those notes he pass'd. He took them in the State they were found upon him, of another man. He has lately written to mr Haartly a neighbour of Sisters to inquire about his Family, his children and sisters, but not a word about his wife. Since that he has written to her, desiring to know if his children are Supply'd with the necessarys of Life and what kind of education she is giving them. As soon as he is able he is going, he says to land a Store of english Goods, and again wishes to hear from his Sisters. Sister Smith Sent me a Letter upon hearing an account of his Sickness which I will send you.[10] I sent it to Sister Shaw for her to comment upon. I have made mine, and I wish to see if we do not all think alike about it. Mr cranch upon reading it Said, "Act the first, Scene the first." If we have all the necessarys and so many of the comforts and convenicys of Life as she has, it is not right to complain of feeling the "Iron hand of Poverty pressing hard upon us." Is it possible that she can look upon her Farm Stock, and well dress'd children and utter such a complant? Our dear Parent did not leave her in poverty, my Sister, and we have done much for her in addition to what he left her. We never complain'd that he did more for her than us, but it is true that he did.[11] ⟨[. . . .]⟩[12] Louissa has been at Judge Russels at charlestown and uncle Smiths the greatest part of the winter. Billy lives at Lancaster with a mr Wales from Braintree. He keeps a Store and has taken him till he is twenty one if it should be agreable to both upon trial. They board with the widdow of Levi Willard a kind good woman as lives I have heard.[13]

April 2d

Such a Snow Storm as we have had to day has not been seen in April since that about thirteen or 15 years ago when mr John Joy came as far as your house from fathers the night after, and could get no further for the Banks. Such a wind I never did know. It has lasted thirty six hours and does not yet look as if it was over. I have trembled for the poor creatures upon our coasts. It is Sunday but too bad to open the meeting house. Mr Cranch went as far as the Barn this morning and return'd declaring that he thought it impossible for any person to face the Storm and breath many minutes. The cold is as remarkable as the Storm a perfect contrast between this with last Sunday. It was then so warm that we sat with our win dows open. Mr T went as soon as breakfast was over to mrs veseys I suppose. We have not seen him since. He went out without Saying any thing. I hope he has not perish'd in a snow Bank. I would not have turn'd a Dog out in it.

If you should ask me where mr T boards, I should find it hard to tell you. He Lodgs and has his Linnin wash'd and mended here. He some times breakfast with us, but we seldom see any more of him till eleven at night and not always then for when we are tier'd with waiting, leave a candle for him and go to Bed. He still retains our office in his Hands although he makes very little use of it. It is very seldom open'd at all. He has I believe transacted all his business this winter in mrs veseys Parlour. One would scarcely have thought a Room in which a Family liv'd, and through which another Family of children and servants seven in number must pass to get into their Kitchen the most convenient place to make an office off—but there are People Who love to make, and live in a Bustle. I would not have you think that we have done any thing to offend him, or drive him from the House. I know of nothing. We are as civil as possible to each other. I suppose he will go to housekeeping soon. Mrs Church says he told her that he is going to europe this Spring. He will not own that he has had a dismission. He is exceeding apt to loose a Picture which he wears about his neck—to leave it in the Bed when he is upon a journey and lodges in a gentleman or Ladys Family. This when found and with the rapturs he express's and the kisses he bestows upon it, are certain evidences that he has not been dismiss'd. We have never said a word to each other about it. We never talk about any Letters we recieve. I cannot. I know he is mortified and I have not a wish, to hurt him.

April 6th

This morning as I was dressing my self, I saw a son of coll. Thayer ride up the yard and take a large Pacquit from his saddle Bags. From my sister thought I in a moment I found by the cover that they came from new york. They were Frank'd by mr King, but alass when it was open'd there was found only one for mr cranch. Two for General Warrens Family one for mr Gordon and one for Coffin Jones.[14] Not one for me or the Girls. Mr King writes that he had receiv'd a large bundle of news papers. That it was too big for the mail to bring, but that he would Send them by the first safe conveyence. I hope the Letters are amonge the Papers. Oh how impatient I feel! A little mortification is perhaps good for me. It is our anual Fast this day. A Letter from my dear Sister would have converted it into a Thanksgiving day if it had convey'd me the good tydings of the Life Health and happiness of herself and Family. As it is we have receiv'd great pleasure, for as mr Adams has not mention'd you we suppose you are well. My pen must be mended. Adieu.

7th

Last monday was the day for the choice of a Governer, &c can you believe it? Yes I know you can believe it, If I tell you, That mr Hancock after being chosen a member of congress, and by them President of Congress, has been making interest by himself, or his Friends to be chosen Governer. Is it not an insult to keep the united States waiting five or six months for an answer, only that he might have an oppertunity of elbowing a very worthy man out of his seat? Mr Bowdoin had almost every vote here, mr H-n k a few in Boston. Mr Bowdoin 765 mr H n k 13.[15]

Mr cranch and mr Tyler use'd all their interest to get mr S Adams chosen L Governer and he had 64 votes mr Cushing a few. The member for Braintree was very angry and said publickly, that the county in a Caucus had determin'd that mr Cushing, should be L Governer: and he was Sure that mr Bowdoin would not have a vote in Hampshire.[16] You will have the Papers, they will Show you Some truths and Some Lyes. They have represented the senators of this county as meeting and determining who shall be chosen Senators for the comeing year. There is not the least foundation for the report. I never Saw Doctor Tufts more angry. He is determin'd to make the printers tell their author.[17]

M T has acted as moderator at the Town meetings for the year past and makes a very good one mr Cranch says.[18] He keeps the people in good order. He has popolar Talents you know, and has great influence in our meetings. "Steady Friend, Steady" and your influence will increase.

General Warren made interest for L Govr but it raisd a Hornets nest about his ears, they have abused him shamefully. I believe I never wrote so much Pollticks in my life before. I have really felt interested in the choise of mr Bowdoin. He has fill'd his station with so much dignity and wisdom and given such proofs of his attention to the publick welfair that I could not bear to see him remov'd before he had time to execute his salutary Plans. No court Sycophant has fill'd the Papers with flattering Panegyrics upon his useful administration. His superior qualifications for the seat of goverment have been made publick only by the wisdom of his speeches and the usefulness of the Plans which he has lay'd before the court.

Lucy is writing to cousin Nabby,[19] Betsy would if she knew of this oppertunity. I hope my dear Niece has spent an agreable winter and that the conscieucness of having done what she thought was right, has yealded her more delight than the indulgence of any Passion which her reason would not approve could have done. I want to know how you have spent your time my dear sister, and how your health has been. Is cousin Nabby learning musick. If she has any tast for it I wish she would. Nancy Quincy has been learning this winter to play upon a Harpsicord. I am told She has a good ear.

Your mother Hall and Brother Adams's Family are well. Boylstone continues his studys but whether he will go to college this year or not I do not know.[20] Your Neighbours are well. Mrs Field has had her health very well this winter, mr John Feilds Family have mov'd beyond Luneeybourge.[21]

If there is any doubt in the British nation whether we populate fast or not, let them be inform'd that in the north Parish of Braintree only, there have been born within the last Week Seven children, and many more daily expected.

When I was writing a page or two back I told you that I thought g Palmers Family must move. They inform'd me yesterday that they had by means of another person taken Germantown another year. Another year they will have it to perplex them again. Doctor Simon Tufts is thought to be in a consumtion. Mrs Brooks is much better, and like to have her thirteenth child.[22]

Mr Wild has been upon the point of leaving his People for want of a support. They have had a counsel, and he stays upon a promise of a hundred a year paid quarterly. She lays in in June with her third child—a parsons blessing.[23]

April 9th

I have just heard that callahan will sail next Tousday. Mr Cranch will not have time to write by this vessel and I am affraid Doctor Tufts will not have his Letters ready and I know he wants to write largly. I am much dissapointed that I cannot get a Letter from you before I send away this. I think I must have some in the great Bundle mr King mentions.

There were several vessals cast away last sunday in the snow Storm. Several Dead Bodys have been taken up on the plymouth Shoar. It is not known where they came from, or who they were. I heard last week from sister Shaw and Family. They were all well. Cousin Thomas depends upon going to college next commencment. He will be fit I understand. I hope you will send me some Linnin for Your Sons. They want not a few Shirts among them all. We wash once a fortnight and tis sometimes a month before I can get, and have their Linnin return'd them. If cousin JQA and Charles should live together as they propose, there will be nothing wanting but a Bed &c which I shall send them. Cousin Thomas, will take his Brothers Furniture and his chum whoever he may be must find a Bed. I have a fine Barrel of cider to send our children as soon as the roads will let me. They are to Bottle it. It will Save abundance of wine. I have taken mr Adams Russet Gown for Cousin JQA, but the plad is laid up for Papa, and a crimson callamanco must supply its place. Young Folks do not love to be singular, and aunt is willing to indulge them in every thing that is reasonable. I wish to keep you inform'd of every thing I do with regard to them. I keep an account of every thing we take from your House for them. Next wednesday they are to come home for the Spring vacancy and to be fitted up for the summer, I have ingag'd miss Nabby Marsh to come to help me.

I write many things which appear to me not worthy your attention, but yet if you were not inform'd of them, you would loose all knowledge of your neighbourhood and acquaintance. Were I to copy what I write I should leave one half out. Tell me my Sister if I am too particular I will not trouble you again if you think so. I have receiv'd Letters from Betsy almost every week since She went to haverhill. She has had a gay winter of it excepting the former part of it. Mrs Duncans death[24] suspended for a little while their amusements.

There are some parts of this letter I must leave intirely to your prudence whether to cummunicate to any creature or not—I sometimes am sorry that I have written Some things which I have. There is a great difference between saying and writing a thing. I have often been at a ⟨*great*⟩ loss to know what I ought to do. Life is uncertain. I can never tell whose hands my Letters directed to you might fall into. I would not injure. I would not wound any body.

I have written by cushing Young Lyde and Davis since I have receiv'd any Letters to inform me of their arrival. I hope they are all safe. The ceres was cast away I hear. Somebody told that a *Gentleman* had Letters abourd for your Family. When a man writes so seldom he should send Duplicates.[25] Mr Cranch desires me to give his very particular Love to you, and tell you that he longs to talk Politicks with you again by our, and your Fire side. Oh my Sister when will these happy times return. Many has been the time this winter when We had after dinner brush'd our room and rekindled our fire that Lucy and I have said: "now let us look for aunt adams and Cousin" but alass alass, we look'd in vain. Yrs affectionately

M Cranch

RC (Adams Papers); endorsed: "Mrs Cranch March 22. 1786."

[1] The First Church of Weymouth had gone without a pastor since the death of William Smith in 1783. Over the years, various men had preached there temporarily, and the parish had called first Samuel Shuttlesworth of Dedham, then Asa Packard of Bridgewater, then Israel Evans to the position. All eventually declined the post. Finally, in April 1787, Jacob Norton accepted the call (Gilbert Nash, comp., *Historical Sketch of the Town of Weymouth*, Weymouth, 1885, p. 103–104). The "Fool" may have been Adoniram Judson, who was probably the Mr. Judson invited to preach at Weymouth in the summer of 1785 (MHi:First Church [Weymouth] Records; Spague, *Annals of the Amer. Pulpit*, 2:22–23).

[2] A character in Laurence Sterne's *Tristram Shandy*, known for his benevolence, courage, gallantry, grace, and modesty (E. Cobham Brewer, *The Reader's Handbook*, rev. edn., London, 1902).

[3] Charles Warren, who suffered from tuberculois, died near Cadiz, Spain, on 30 Nov. 1785 (Rosemarie Zagarri, *A Woman's Dilemma: Mercy Otis Warren and the American Revolution*, Wheeling, Ill., 1995, p. 114; *Massachusetts Centinel*, 25 March).

[4] John Codman Jr. (1755–1803) initially had a mercantile partnership with AA's cousin William Smith and later went into business with his brother Richard (Cora C. Wolcott, *The Codmans of Charlestown and Boston*, Brookline, Mass., 1930, p. 13–14, 20). Codman successfully pursued his suit against Winslow Warren and was awarded £100 damages by the court in 1787 (M-Ar: Supreme Judicial Court, Minute Books, Suffolk, Feb. term, 1787).

[5] Rev. Charles Chauncy, pastor of the First Church, Boston, owned a home west of the Vassall-Borland property on present-day Adams Street in Quincy (Pattee, *Old Braintree*, p. 237, 579).

[6] Gaius Thayer was a Braintree constable (*Braintree Town Records*, p. 560).

[7] Gen. Joseph Palmer became heavily indebted to John Hancock in 1778 when he invested in real estate in Pomfret, Conn., that had been mortgaged to Hancock. See Palmer to Robert Treat Paine, 14 Dec. 1781 and enclosures (MHi:Robert Treat Paine Papers).

Possibly Grizzell Apthorp (1709–1796), the widow of Boston merchant Charles Apthorp (1698–1758) and mother of James Apthorp of Braintree (Pattee, *Old Braintree*, p. 253, 623; John Wentworth, *The Wentworth Genealogy: English and American*, 3 vols., Boston, 1878, 1:519–520).

[8] Robert Garland Cranch, the nephew of Richard Cranch, emigrated from England in 1768 and opened a sadlery shop adjoining Richard Cranch's home and watchmaking shop on Hanover Street in Boston. R. G. Cranch left Boston when the British Army occupied the town, leaving behind and sub-

sequently losing the majority of his property. This loss combined with the death of his wife, Mary Clemmens, in Jan. 1779, evidently left Cranch mentally unstable. He was committed to the poor house in Nov. 1779, from which he ran away four months later, and his brother Joseph was temporarily made his guardian. Thereafter Cranch's employment and drinking habits were erratic. In March 1786, Richard Cranch arranged for Robert to work in Rehoboth, Mass., for the son of Ephraim Starkweather who was engaged in the chaise-making business. Starkweather ultimately was unable to employ Cranch, but in May the latter found a temporary position with John Sebring, a Providence, R.I., sadler. (Christopher Cranch to Richard Cranch, 23 May 1768, Richard Cranch to Mary Smith Cranch, 28 Jan. 1779, Joseph Cranch to Thomas Cushing, 9 June 1780, all MHi: Cranch Family Papers; *Boston Evening Post*, 27 March 1769; Boston, *30th Report*, p. 72; MHi:Boston Overseers of the Poor Records, 1733–1925; Starkweather to Richard Cranch, 13 March and 9 May, Richard Cranch to Ephraim Starkweather, 20 March, Robert Garland Cranch to Richard Cranch, 20 May, all MHi:C. P. Cranch Papers).

[9] William Smith Jr.

[10] Not found.

[11] For the last will and testament of Rev. William Smith and the value of his estate as divided among his heirs, see vol. 5:245–249, and note 3.

[12] A little more than three lines of text are heavily crossed out here.

[13] Louisa Catharine and William Smith were the children of AA's brother. Louisa had visited James Russell, a superior court justice prior to the Revolution and friend of Rev. William Smith. Russell lived for a time at his son's home in Lincoln, Mass., and had recently rebuilt his Charlestown, Mass., home which was destroyed during the Battle of Bunker Hill (vol. 5:227, 229; 6:446–447). Louisa's younger brother Billy, age eleven, lodged with Catherine Willard in Lancaster and probably worked for Joseph Wales, who served as town clerk of Lancaster (1791–1794) and married Elizabeth Willard in Jan. 1794 (Henry S. Nourse, ed., *The Birth, Marriage and Death Register, Church Records and Epitaphs of Lancaster Massachusetts. 1643–1850*, Lancaster, 1890, p. 6, 195, 333, 361, 373, 406, 443).

[14] These included JA's letters of 12 Dec. 1785 to Richard Cranch (LbC, Adams Papers), James Warren (MB), and Mercy Otis Warren (MHi:Warren-Adams Coll.). Letters from the Adamses to William Gordon and John Coffin Jones have not been identified.

[15] James Bowdoin received 6,001 of the 8,231 votes cast in the gubernatorial election. Braintree cast 41 votes for Bowdoin and none for any opponent. Mary Cranch reports the election results in Boston (Mass., *Acts and Laws*, Resolves of 1786, May sess., ante ch. 1; *Braintree Town Records*, p. 564; *Massachusetts Centinel*, 5 April 1786).

[16] Thomas Cushing was reelected lieutenant governor with 5,651 of 7,429 votes cast. In Braintree, Samuel Adams received 62 votes for lieutenant governor, Thomas Cushing 20, and James Warren 6 (Mass., *Acts and Laws*, Resolves of 1786, May sess., ante ch. 1; *Braintree Town Records*, p. 564). Bowdoin actually received 65 percent of the votes in Hampshire County (Van Beck Hall, *Politics without Parties: Massachusetts, 1780–1791*, Pittsburgh, 1972, p. 197).

[17] The *Massachusetts Centinel* reported "that *certain* members of the late *Senate* and *house*" had composed a list of the "*most proper persons*" to be senators of Suffolk County in the coming year. The group recommended John Lowell, William Phillips, Cotton Tufts, and Stephen Metcalf as certain, and William Heath, Jabez Fisher, and Richard Cranch as doubtful. The *Centinel* labeled the act an infringement on the freedom of elections (29 March 1786).

[18] Royall Tyler was first chosen to be moderator of the Braintree town meeting at its 19 Sept. 1785 session (*Braintree Town Records*, p. 558).

[19] Not found.

[20] Boylston Adams (1771–1829), the son of JA's brother Peter Boylston Adams, did not attend Harvard.

[21] Probably Lunenburg, Mass.

[22] Mercy Tufts Brooks of Medford, Cotton Tufts' sister and AA's cousin. Her son Edward was born 18 June (Henry Bond, *Genealogies of the Families and Descendants of the Early Settlers of Watertown, Massachusetts*, 2 vols. in 1, Boston, 1855, p. 725–726).

[23] Rev. Ezra Weld, Yale 1759, minister of Braintree's Second Parish since 1762 (Pattee, *Old Braintree*, p. 286). Weld married Abigail Greenleaf of Boston in 1779; it was the minister's third marriage (*Braintree Town Records*, p. 862, 879, 882).

[24] Elizabeth Leonard Duncan had shown evidence of mental instability for several months. On the evening of 9 Nov. 1785 she took her own life by drowning in the Merrimack River. Duncan was the aunt of Peggy White, Betsy Cranch's friend and host in Haverhill (JQA, *Diary*, 1:354).

[25] There is no evidence that Royall Tyler sent letters by the *Ceres* (see AA to Mary Smith Cranch 26 Jan., note 1, above).

Abigail Adams to Charles Storer

Dear Charles London March 23 1786

Your kind Letter of [1] came to hand by captain Lyde. I had chid you for not writing by way of Newyork, as you could not but suppose we were anxious for your safety. I constantly inquired what vessels were arrived, and Had the pleasure of hearing that Captain Stout was safe a month before your Letter came. I suppose you thought you would be very particular, yet mark, you never told me how the children behaved at sea, nor who was the best Nurse, nor how Mrs Atkinson stood the voyage,[2] nor whether your cold was troublesome, *and all that*. You were so rejoiced that you had got once more to dear Boston that what was past, was all vision. Well, well I excuse you, only next time do better, and tell me what you have been doing since your return. Are you studying divinity as you talkd? Or are you planning schemes for merchandize. The Youth of our Country must turn their minds to Agriculture, to Manufactories, and endeavour to benifit their Country in that way. There is vast scope for them. I am glad to learn from you that Luxery is in some measure retrenchd, necessity itself may carry virtue in its train, I want to come home and live amongst you, for with all your faults I love you better than any other people. Good Dr Price gave us a discourse last sunday upon the Jew and Samaratin, and with his usual Phylanthropy told us, that, all mankind were our Neighbours, and every Being who was in distress, of whatever Country, or Religion, was our Brother, and demanded from us our aid, and assistance. It is impossible to hear this good Man without having our Hearts and minds enlarged. It was virtue more than consanguinity that clamed our preferable regard. Now upon this principal I believe I ought to love my Countrymen best, as I really think them possest of a larger portion of virtue than any other Nation, I am acquainted with, and my wish is that they had still more, and wisdom enough added to it, to convince them of a necessity of a union of counsels and conduct with regard to their publick measures. In vain will they call for commercial Treaties, in vain will they look for respect in Europe, in vain will they hope for Peace with the

Barbery states, whilst their own citizens discover a jealousy of Congress and a reluctance at enlargeing their powers, a fear even to trust them with commercial arrangments.

Age and experience should teach wisdom and if the Beardless youths whom some of the states send to judge of elegant diction and well turnd periods, are only competant to *com'as* and *points*, why let them not be rob'd of their mite, but sent as *preceptors* to *instruct* the *rising generation* but let not the science of politicks, and the interest of Nations be quibled out of countanance by these Butterflies of yesterday. What but a pidling genious would think of quarrelling with words? Tell them I despise them—I have however given the hint to the person for whom it was designd, and in future he will endeavour to leave out the monosyllable *I* as much as possible. A parcel of Blockheads said he, let them send me a private Secretary then. You know the drugery too well, and have unrewarded done your share.[3] The writing which this negotiation takes up is incredible, altho nothing Scarcly appears to come of it. Amelia too, has her portion of private Letter-copying,[4] at which she scolds sometimes. Politicks you know she pretends to hate, but I do not find however that she dislikes the Gentleman in the politician.

As to the other confidential matter you communicated, I can only say that if the Gentleman is ungenerous enough, either to copy the letters, or to detain any of them, it can only be to his own mortification, when he reflects that through his own imprudence and missconduct, he has forfeited the Esteem of a family who were disposed to have owned him as a member of it, and the affection of a Lady who would have studied to have made him happy, but each of the Parties have much more agreeable prospects before them now. Let it not surprize you when I tell you that your Young Friend is under engagements, and to a Gentleman of unblemishd reputation, an amiable Character irreproachable honour and approved integrity. You will be at no loss to determine that col S. is the person described, and as the matter is agreed upon by all parties, I have no desire to keep it a secreet, more especially as I Suspect matrimony is very soon the object of the Gentleman. I think he is in full haste enough, and I tell him so, but he says in replie, what is there to hinder? Nay consider sir—it is but a few months since you made a declaration of this kind—"yes Madam thats true, but *you* were no stranger to the sentiments of my mind or the situation of my Heart, when I found it necessary for my own Peace—to ask leave of absence. The Situation of the Lady is different now, and what was formerly an impediment exists no longer, pray my good Madam, persuade yourself of the propriety of a speedy union." I believe a soldier is always more expeditious in his courtships than other Men, they know better how to Capture the citidal.

As to the Gentlemans asking no questions respecting the family, I do not wonder at that. He could not but feel dissagreeably, and could not have said any thing to you, who he had reason to think, knew all the circumstances. He will have too much pride to shew his dissapointment. I am rejoiced that his conduct can no longer give me the pain which it has done, for a long time. I will bid him adieu I wish him no evil.

The treaty with Portugal is just concluding, mr Jefferson is here and will sign it before he quits London. I wish I could say as much with respect to this Country. As to the Posts, they will be held till the states repeal those laws which prevent the course of Justice. And perhaps the states will say, that they will not repeal the Laws untill the posts are given up.[5] The Question then is, who shall first do right? Congress are made acquainted with all that has been done or said upon the Matter, tho I know not whether it has yet reachd them. There is an other matter before them, which demands wise Heads. I mean the terms upon which the Barbary powers will make peace. This knowledge has been obtaind through the Tripoline Minister who is now at this Court. He has full powers to make treaties, and is perpetual Ambassador, a good kind of Man. Mr A visited him, smoakd in his long pipe and took coffe with him. He had two Secretaries who were not permitted to set in his presence, and he is very cautious to keep from this Court any knowledge of conferences with the united States.

These two last matters you will be *Mum* upon; as it is best to be silent yet. My best regards to your Pappa Mamma sisters and Brothers, &c. &c. Be assured that the shortness of my paper curtails my pen and obliges me to subscribe my self your Friend AA

RC (Adams Papers); endorsed: "23d. March. 1786."

[1] Blank in MS; the letter is that of 21 Dec. 1785 (vol. 6:497–498).

[2] Charles Storer, his sister Elizabeth Storer Atkinson, and her family sailed from London in September and arrived in New York on 8 Nov. 1785 aboard the *Triumph*, Capt. Stout (vol. 6:208, 365, 369, 458; *New York Packet*, 10 Nov. 1785). English merchant John Atkinson, who married Elizabeth Storer in 1773, had sailed from Boston with his family of four in March 1776 (Boston, *30th Report*, p. 331; James H. Stark, *The Loyalists of Massachusetts and the Other Side of the American Revolution*, Boston, 1910, p. 133).

[3] Storer acted as JA's secretary in Aug. and Sept. 1785, following WSS's departure for Prussia to see the military review of Frederick the Great's troops (vol. 6:260, 343, 365).

[4] AA2 also aided JA with secretarial tasks during WSS's absence from Aug. to Dec.

1785 (vol. 6:407, 471).

[5] In response to JA's memorial of 30 Nov., Lord Carmarthen stated that Great Britain would not relinquish the frontier posts until U.S. states removed restrictions inhibiting British creditors from collecting American debts (Carmarthen to JA, 28 Feb., Adams Papers).

John Quincy Adams to Elizabeth Cranch

Cambridge March 23d: 1786

I came yesterday as far as Boston with Sister Lucy, who is employ'd in fixing me off: I came here in the afternoon finally to settle.[1] Your Brother goe to Boston this morning, and I have but a few minutes to write. All at Braintree are well, [Mr. Tyler's?] Windmill is to be raised this day. There's another thing, that you would never let me know. I have got a number of articles of impeachment, which you are to answer next Court. How do all the good folks at Haverhill? Present my best respects to Uncle and Aunt Shaw; I would write to Madam, but have not Time at present. Remember me to all friends, but especially to Mr: White's family, for whose many kindnesses to me, while I was at Haverhill, I shall ever retain the most grateful remembrance. Your's J. Q. Adams

RC (MHi:Jacob Norton Papers); addressed: "Miss Eliza Cranch. Haverhill." Some loss of text where the seal was removed.

[1] Lucy Cranch helped her cousin purchase furniture to outfit his room at Harvard (JQA, *Diary*, 2:5).

John Adams to Richard Cranch

My dear Brother Grosvenor Square March 24th. 1786

In yours of the 10th. of Novr.[1] you desire me to give you the Connection between the Premises and conclusion, when I said that the Navigation act would compell all the other states to imitate it.[2] If they do not the Massachusetts will soon get so much of their carrying Trade as will richly compensate her for any present Inconvenience.

I take it for granted that the United States will make peace with the States of Barbary altho' it may cost them two or three hundred thousand Pounds that the fears of our Sailors and Premiums of Insurance may not make a difference between our Navigation and European Navigations.

I take it for granted too, that the New England States, and such other as come into the same measure and even that New Hampshire and Massachusetts if they should be alone, will take care that their Laws shall not be eluded by carrying their Produce to other states to be exported in European Bottoms.

These postulates being premised, I am of opinion the Massachusetts can build Ships and carry the produce of the southern States to markett, cheaper than the English can do it, or french, or any other Nation.

I know it is the opinion of some, that the Britons especially from the Northern and Western Parts of their Island, can sail their ships as cheap as we can, but this opinion I think is ill founded, and will appear so more clearly now, than it did before the late War for two reasons, one is the increase of taxes in Britain the other, that they do not now purchase our ready built ships, but must build them at home at a much dearer rate. I may now add, it is impossible for the English to furnish ships for the exportation of the Southern States, who will be obliged to make navigation acts to encourage their own shipping, or to hire ours which will increase the Ballance against them too much in our favour.

Let it be considered further, that if we can purchase raw sugars in France with our Oil, refine them in Boston and then send them to Petersburgh to purchase Hemp and Duck, Navigation will support our oil trade and that our Navigation.

If any thing can prevent this conclusion it must be the want of Industry, and the Excess of luxury in our Merchants and others. But if Luxury and Idleness are more prevalent in the Massachusetts, than in England at present, they will not be so long, for the unbounded Credit which gave rise to it, is at an End. Yours

J. A.

LbC in WSS's hand (Adams Papers).

[1] Adams Papers.

[2] In an effort to stimulate the state and national economy, Massachusetts, on 23 June 1785, passed a navigation act prohibiting British vessels from carrying Massachusetts exports, levying higher duties on imports transported by foreign vessels than those on American ships, and restricting entry of foreign bottoms carrying imports to three Massachusetts ports—Boston, Falmouth (later Portland, Maine), and Dartmouth (Mass., *Acts and Laws*, Acts of 1785, May sess., ch. 8).

John Quincy Adams to Elizabeth Smith Shaw

Dear Madam Cambridge March 29th: 1786

I should, certainly have written before this, at least to show how gratefull a Sense, I retain, of the numerous obligations, I was under both to my Uncle, and Aunt, while I was at Haverhill. But what with going to Braintree, and what with having been since I [ca]me here, much more closely engaged, than I shall be for the future, my [in]tention till now has failed. About 10 this morning, the man got here with my Trunks,[1] very à propos, as I began, to be quite scanty for clean Linen. Every thing is as safe, and free from damage, as I could wish. I thank you, my dear Aunt, for your Congratulations.[2] It was a very fortunate Circumstance, that I obtained so good a Chamber, so near my friends, and with a Gentleman, whose Character is much esteemed and respected universally through College.

My articles of impeachment, will never I believe have any fatal Consequences. Indeed when I found what was going forward at Braintree, I was so highly diverted, that I almost wished I had known it before: but I never doubted but my Cousin, had very good Reasons, for not letting me know it. I do not know by what association of Ideas, I never can think of a Wind-mill, but what Don Quixote, comes into my mind. He used to fight Wind-mills, and if his Head, had not run so much upon fighting, perhaps he might have built them. There is no great difference, between the two projects.

The man, returns so soon, that I have not Time, to say, any more: by the next Post I intend to write to my Cousin, and shall be able to be more particular.

Your obliged Nephew, & very humble Servant.

J. Q. Adams

RC (ICN:Herbert R. Strauss Collection); addressed: "Mrs: E. Shaw. Haverhill"; docketed: "March 29 1786." Some loss of text at a tear.

[1] In JQA's Diary this arrival occurs on 30 March (*Diary*, 2:11).

[2] Letter not found.

John Quincy Adams to Abigail Adams 2d

Cambridge, April 1st, 1786

What shall I say to my sister? Indeed, I am quite at a loss. I spend much more time in thinking what I shall say to you than I do in writing. I find here continually the sameness which I complained of at Haverhill. To give an account of one day, would give one of a month. Monday, Tuesday, and Wednesday, every minute of our time is taken up. The rest of the week, any person that chooses may loiter away doing nothing. But a person fond of studying will never want for employment. Now, for the want of some thing better to say, you shall have a long detail of the distribution of our time at present. One week we recite to Mr. James, the Latin tutor. The next to Mr. Read, in Euclid. The third to Mr. Jennison, in Greek; and the fourth to Mr. Hale, in Locke.[1] Then begin again. Monday morning at six, bell for prayers; from thence reciting; half after seven, breakfast; at nine, go to Mr. Williams', upon practical geometry; at eleven, a lecture upon natural philosophy; half after twelve, dinner, and reciting again; five, prayers. Tuesday, instead of practical geometry, at nine, it is a lecture from the Hebrew professor; at two in the afternoon, a lecture from the professor of divinity.[2] Wednesday, at nine, another lecture upon divinity; at eleven, lecture on philosophy; two, afternoon, lecture on astronomy. Thursday, reciting in the morning. Friday, nothing but a lecture on philosophy. Saturday, reciting in the morning to Mr. Read, in Doddridge's Lectures on Divinity, a pretty silly book, which I wonder to find among the books studied here.[3] So we go on from day to day, and if there is once a week an episode, such as going to Boston, or dining out, this is the greatest show of variety that I can make. Now where, from this story, can I possibly find materials for letters? If I had the art of writing half-a-dozen pages upon nothing, at least I should be enabled to fulfil my engagements with you. But I scarcely know what to say when a continued variety of scenes was rising before me; much less can I now that, like a horse in a mill, I am going continually the same round.

4th.

We had a very uncommon month of March, fine weather almost all the month; but the first day of this, at about noon, it began to snow, and for twenty-six hours it stormed with great violence. In some places there was more than five feet of snow.

The senior class have had, this forenoon, a forensic disputation upon the question whether a democratical form of government was the best. It went through the class—one supporting that democracy was the best of all governments, and the next that it was the worst. This is one of the excellent institutions of this University, and is attended with many great advantages.

7th, Friday.

Yesterday was fast day. We had two sermons from the president, who bewailed a great many things. He labors a great deal in preaching, shows much good sense, but no eloquence.[4]

This forenoon, just as I was going to the lecture upon experimental philosophy, Mr. Storer gave me a letter, upon which I saw your superscription—it contained your account till the ninth of December.[5] But only think how I was tantalized. I was obliged, before I could read a line in your letter, to go in and listen for almost an hour and a half, to projectile motion and the central forces. At any other time Mr. Williams would have entertained me very much; but now I lost half the lecture, and was so impatient that every minute seemed ten. As soon as I came out I did not wait to get to my chamber, but walked there reading as I went. It was almost four months since I had received a line from you, and if ever expectation made the blessing dear, I had that to perfection. I have received all your letters except No. 2, which was the first you wrote me from England. Of that I never heard a word but what you wrote me.[6]

Saturday, 8th.

I dined this day at Mr. Tracy's. He has been here ever since he returned from Europe, but intends to go to Newbury in May.[7] Our company was Mr. Molyneux, Mr. Price, Mr. Moses [*Mores*], an Englishman, H. Otis, C. Storer, and Dr. Cutting.[8] Were you ever in company with two professed wits? I don't know that I was ever more diverted with such a circumstance, than this day. Dr. Cutting and Mr. Hughes were very smart upon each other, and let fly their bon-mots as fast as they could pass; and they appeared both to be as sensible of their wit as any body present. Mr. Price you remember. He proposes coming and settling in Boston. He, you know, is quite solid. Mr. Molyneux appears to be quite a gentleman. You know, from the first appearance of a gentleman, that nothing is perceived that can be taken notice of. I believe that every person has something in his character peculiar to himself. But as these peculiarities are, most commonly, disagreeable, the gentleman endeavors, as much as possible, to be free from them, and so far succeeds that an intimate acquaintance with him is necessary to perceive them.

Tuesday, 11th. *Braintree*.

The spring vacancy begins to-morrow. We had horses sent for us this day; and this afternoon we came. We had an exhibition this morning; there are three every year. You have doubtless heard of them, probably been present at one. We had an English, a Latin, a Greek and an Hebrew oration; a syllogistic and a forensic disputation; an English dialogue; and last of all, some vocal and instrumental music. There are none of the exhibitors that you know, except your cousin Cranch, who spoke the Greek oration.[9] We came home in company with Beale, one of my classmates, who belongs to Braintree. About thirty years since, your father taught navigation to his father.[10]

In the course of the next quarter, I shall attempt to give you my opinion of the different members of our government. I shall write as freely as I think, and if you should find me too saucy in speaking of my superiors, at least you will have my real sentiments, unterrified by authority, and unabridged by prejudice.

Saturday, 15th.

Yesterday we went down to Germantown and spent the day. The —— family[11] are pretty well, but their spirits are broken by adversity—their misfortunes seem to come upon them in a rapid succession. The first, the greatest of the general's misfortunes was a vast ambition, which deprived him of the substance by inducing him to grasp at the shadow. Mr. Cranch came home from Boston, and brought a large parcel of English newspapers, and a short note from mamma.[12] All are complaining here that you write no oftener, except myself. I have had such proofs of your punctuality, that although I was near four months without having a line from you, yet I did not suffer myself to doubt a minute of your exactness. Captain Cushing is expected hourly, and I hope to have another continuation of your journal. You ask me to find "fault with the length of your letters," indeed, my dear sister, there is not a line, in any of your letters, that I could spare, and if I complain at all it is that they are not as long again. I have been quite out of humor with your colonel on that account, as I supposed it took so much of your time to serve as secretary, that my letters were considerably shortened; but now he has returned, you will have much more leisure, and I hope I shall profit by it, (as the Dutchman says.)

18th.

This afternoon, in the midst of the rain, who should come in but Eliza,[13] who, in the beginning of October last, went to spend six weeks at Haverhill, which have been spun out to seven months. There was talking all together, the eyes of one glistened and the face of another looked bright, and all were happy—such scenes as these might cure the spleen of a misanthropist—the word is not English, but that is nothing to the purpose.

Mr. I. was married in the winter at New-York to Miss T. This is another victory of the ladies over the old bachelors.[14] Mr. R. was married three weeks ago to Miss A.[15] I have mentioned her in a former letter. I was surprised very much when I first heard this, but £20,000 sterling will cover almost as great a number of faults as charity.

I shall write to both our parents by this opportunity, and have therefore only to subscribe myself yours. J. Q. Adams

MS not found. Printed from AA2, *Jour. and Corr.*, 3:99–105.

[1] Timothy Lindall Jennison, Harvard 1782, Greek tutor 1785–1788, and John Hale, Harvard 1779, tutor of metaphysics 1781–1786 (*Harvard Quinquennial Cat.*; JQA, *Diary*, 2:1, 28).

[2] Eliphalet Pearson, Harvard's Hancock Professor of Hebrew and other Oriental Languages, 1786–1806, and Edward Wigglesworth, Hollis Professor of Divinity, 1765–1791 (*Harvard Quinquennial Cat.*).

[3] Philip Doddridge, *A Course of Lectures on the Principal Subjects in Pneumatology, Ethics and Divinity*, London, 1763.

[4] JQA comments at greater length on Joseph Willard's sermons and his delivery in his Diary (*Diary*, 2:14–15).

[5] That of 5[–9] Dec. 1785 (vol. 6:478–483).

[6] In addition, letters numbered 1, 3, and 4, written in May and June 1785, have not been found.

[7] Nathaniel Tracy, a Newburyport merchant and ship owner, owned the Vassall-Longfellow house in Cambridge. He lost that home in 1786 when he declared bankruptcy but retained residences in Newbury and Newburyport. (*Sibley's Harvard Graduates*, 17:249–250).

[8] Dr. John Brown Cutting (1755–1831) of New York was formerly the apothecary of the eastern and middle hospital departments of the Continental Army, 1777–1780. He first studied law with John Lowell in Boston in 1783, then continued his studies in London in 1786–1787. He became an important correspondent of both JA and Jefferson in the 1790s (Heitman, *Register Continental Army*; *Doc. Hist. Ratif. Const.*, 14:460).

[9] JQA describes the "exhibition" in greater detail in this day's Diary entry (*Diary*, 2:16).

[10] Benjamin Beale, Harvard 1787, was the son of Capt. Benjamin Beale, a Braintree merchant who married and resided for several years in England. Capt. Beale and his family moved from the Squantum district of Braintree in 1792 to a new home he constructed adjacent to the Adams Old House. The Beale estate was purchased by the National Park Service in the 1970s and forms part of the Adams National Historical Park (vol. 5:421–422, note 4; JQA, *Diary*, 2:166–167; *Boston Globe*, 26 April 2001, p. H1).

[11] Gen. Joseph and Mary Cranch Palmer.

[12] AA to Richard Cranch, 23 Dec. 1785, not found; see Cranch to AA, 13 April, below.

[13] Elizabeth Cranch.

[14] Undoubtedly a reference to Elbridge Gerry's marriage to Ann Thompson of New York on 12 January. Gerry was 41 years old and Thompson only 20 (*DAB*; Billias, *Elbridge Gerry*, p. 147).

[15] JQA may have intended to write "Mr. R. K." See Charles Storer to AA, 13 April, below.

Abigail Adams to Elizabeth Cranch

My dear Neice London April 2. 1786

I think my dear Betsy that some Letter of yours must have faild, as I have none of a later date, than that which you sent me from Haverhill by mr Wilson, by which I find that you are studying Musick with Miss White.[1] This is an accomplishment much in vogue in this Country, and I know of no other civilized Country which stands in so much need of harmonizing as this. That ancient Hospitality for which it was once so celebrated, seems to have degenerated into mere ceremony. They have exchanged their Humanity for ferocity and their civility, for, for; fill up the blank, you can not give it too rough a name.

I believe I once promised to give you an account of that Kind of visiting call'd "Ladies Route." There are two kinds, one where a Lady sets apart a particular day in the week to see Company, these are held only 5 months in the Year it being quite out of fashion to be seen in London during the summer. When a Lady returns from the Country she goes round and leaves a Card with all her acquaintance, and then sends them an invitation to attend her Routes during the season. The other kind are where a Lady sends to you for certain Evenings and their Cards are always addrest in their own names both to Gentlemen and Ladies. Their Rooms are all set open and card tables set in each Room. The Lady of the House receives her company at the door of the drawing Room, where a set number of Curtizes are given; and received, with as much order, as is necessary for a soldier who goes through the different Evolutions of his excercise. The visotor then proceeds into the Room without appearing to notice any other person and takes her Seat at the Card table.

"Nor can the Muse her aid impart
unskild in all the terms of art
Nor in harmonious Numbers put
the deal the shuffle and the cut
Go Tom and light the Ladies up
It must be one before we Sup."[2]

At these Parties it is usual for each Lady to play a rubber as it is termd, where you must lose or win a few Guineas; to give each a fair Chance, the Lady then rises and gives her seat to an other set. It is no unusual thing to have your Rooms so crouded that not more than half the company can sit at once, Yet this is calld *Society and Polite Life*. They treat their company with Coffe tea Lemonade orgee[3] and cake. I know of but one agreeable circumstance attending these parties which is that you may go away when you please without disturbing any body. I was early in the winter invited to Madam de Pintos the Portegeeze Ministers. I went accordingly, there were about 200 persons present. I knew not a single Lady but by sight, having met them at Court, and it is an establishd rule tho you was to meet as often as 3 Nights in the Week, never to speak together or know each other unless particularly introduced. I was however at no loss for conversation, Madam de Pinto being very polite, and the foreign ministers being the most of them present, who had dinned with us and to whom I had been early introduced. It being *Sunday* evening I declined playing at Cards. Indeed I always get excused when I can.

> "Heaven forbid, I should catch the manners living as
> they rise"[4]

Yet I must Submit to a Party or two of this kind. Having attended Several, I must return the compliment in the same way.

Yesterday we dinned at mr Paridices. I refer you to mr Storer for an account of this family. Mr Jefferson, col. Smith, the Prussian and Venitian Ministers were of the company, and several other persons who were strangers.[5] At 8 oclock we returnd home in order to dress ourselves for the Ball, at the French Ambassadors to which we had received an invitation a fortnight before.[6] He has been absent ever since our arrival here till 3 weeks ago. He has a levee every Sunday evening at which there are usually several hundred persons. The Hotel de France, is Beautifully situated, fronting St James park, one end of the House standing upon Hyde park. It is a most superb Building. About half past nine we went, and found some Company collected. Many very Brilliant Ladies of the first distinction were present. The Dancing commenced about 10, and the rooms soon filld. The Room which he had built for this purpose, is large enough for 5 or 6 hundred persons. It is most elegantly decorated, hung with a Gold tissue ornamented with 12 Brilliant cut Lustures, each containing 24 candles. At one end there are two large Arches, these were adornd with wreaths and bunches of Artificial flowers upon the walls; in the Alcoves were Cornicup loaded with oranges sweet meats &c coffe tea Lemonade orgee &c were taken here by every person who chose to go for it. There were coverd seats all round the room for those who did not chuse to dance. In the other Rooms card tables and a large Pharo table were Set. This is a New kind of game which is much practised here. Many of the company who did not dance retired here to amuse themselves. The whole Stile of the House and furniture is such as becomes the Ambassador from one of the first Monarchs in Europe. He had 20 thousand Guineas allowd him, in the first instance to furnish his House and an anual sallery of 10 thousand more. He has agreeably blended the magnificence and splendour of France with the neatness and elegance of England. Your cousin had unfortunately taken a cold a few days before and was very unfit to go out. She appeard so unwell that about *one* we retird without staying Supper, the sight of which only I regreeted, as it was in a stile no doubt superiour to any thing I have seen. The Prince of Wales came about eleven oclock. Mrs Fitzherbet was also present, but I could not distinguish her. But who is this Lady methinks I hear you say? She is a Lady to whom against the Laws of the Realm the Prince of Wales is privately married, as is universally believed. She appears with him in all publick parties, and he avows his marriage where ever he dares. They have been the topick of conversation in all companies for a long time, and it is now said that a young Gorge may be expected in the Course of the Summer. She was a widow of about 32 years of age whom he a long time percecuted in order to get her upon his own terms, but finding he could not succeed, he quieted her conscience by Matrimony, which however valid in the Eye of Heaven, is set asside by the Law of the Land which forbids a Prince of the Blood to marry a subject.

As to dresses I believe I must leave them to describe to your sister.[7] I am sorry I have nothing better to send you than a sash and a vandike ribbon, the narrow is to put round the Edge of a hat, or you may trim what ever you please with it. I have inclosed for you a Poem of col Humphriess. Some parts you will find perhaps, too high seasond. If I had observed it before publication, I know he would have alterd it.

When you write again tell me whether my fruit trees in the Garden bear fruit, and whether you raisd any flowers from the seed I sent you. O I long to be with you again, but my dear Girl, Your cousin, must I leave her behind me? Yes, it must be so, but then I leave her in Honorable Hands.

Adieu I have only room to Say Your affectionate

Aunt A A

RC (MHi:Jacob Norton Papers); endorsed: "Letter from Mrs A Adams to Miss Eliz Cranch, London Apl. 2 1786 (No. 9.)."

[1] Elizabeth Cranch to AA, 9 Oct. 1785 (vol. 6:421–422).

[2] Jonathan Swift, *The Journal of a Modern Lady. In a Letter to a Person of Quality*, London, 1729, lines 211–212, 219–222. AA reverses the order of lines from the original.

[3] Probably orgeat, a cold syrup or beverage made from barley, almonds, or orange-flower water (*OED*).

[4] Alexander Pope, *Essay on Man*, Epistle I, lines 13–16: "Eye Nature's walks, shoot folly as it flies, / And catch the manners living as

they rise; / Laugh where we must, be candid where we can, / But vindicate the ways of God to man."

[5] Graf Spiridion von Lusi, Prussian minister plenipotentiary since 1781, and Gasparo Soderini, who presented his credentials as Venetian resident in February (*Repertorium*, 3:329, 464).

[6] The invitation from Comte d'Adhémar to attend a supper dance on 30 March is at MQA.

[7] To Lucy Cranch, 2 April, below.

Abigail Adams to Lucy Cranch

London April 2. 1786 London[1]

Your kind Letter[2] my dear Neice was received with much pleasure, these tokens of Love and regard which I know flow from the Heart, always find their way to mine, and give me a satisfaction and pleasure, beyond any thing, which the ceremony and pomp of Courts and kingdoms can afford. The social affections are, and may be made the truest channels for our pleasures and comforts to flow through. Heaven form'd us, not for ourselves, but others; ["]and bade self Love and social be the Same."[3]

Prehaps there is no Country where there is a fuller excercise of those virtues than ours at present exhibits, which is in a great measure oweing to the equal distribution of Property, the Small Number of inhabitants in proportion to its teritory, the equal distribution of justice to the Poor as well as the rich, to a Government founded in justice, and excercised with impartiality, and to a Religion which teaches peace and good will to man, to knowledge and learning being so easily acquired and so universally distributed, and to that sense of Moral obligation which generally inclines our countrymen; to do to others as they would that others should do to them. Prehaps you will think that I allow to them more than they deserve, but you will consider that I am only speaking comparitively. Humane nature is much the same in all Countries, but it is the Government the Laws and Religion, which forms the Character of a Nation. Where ever Luxery abounds, there you will find corruption and degeneracy of manners. Wretches that we are thus to misuse the Bounties of Providence, to forget the hand that blesses us and even deny the source from whence we derived our being.

But I grow too serious, to amuse you then, my dear Neice I will give an account of the dress of the Ladies at the Ball of the Comte D'adhémar. As your cousin tells me that she sometime ago gave you a history of the Birth day and Ball at court,[4] this may serve as a counter part, tho should I attempt to Compare the Appartments; Saint James's would fall as much short of the French Ambassadors;

as the Court of his Britanick Majesty does; of the splendour and magnificence of his most Christian Majesty. I am Sure I never saw an assembly Room in America which did not exceed that at St James, in point of Elegance and decoration, and as to its fair visitors, not all their blaze of diamonds, Set of with Parissian Rouge, Can match the blooming Health, the Sparkling Eye and modest deportment of the dear Girls of my native land. As to the dancing the space they had to move in, gave them no opportunity to display the Grace of a minuet, and the full dress of long court trains and enormous hoops, you well know were not favourable for Country dances, so that I saw them at every disadvantage. Not so the other evening they were much more properly clad. Silk waists Gauze or White or painted tiffiny coats decorated with ribbon Beads or flowers as fancy directed, were Chiefly worn by the Young Ladies. Hats turnd up at the side with diamond loops and buttons, or steel, large bows of ribbons and wreaths of flowers display'd themselves to much advantage upon the Heads of some of the prettyest Girls England can boast. The light from the Lustures is more favourable to Beauty than day light and the coulour acquir'd by dancing more becomeing than Rouge. As fancy dresses are more favourable to Youth, than the formality of an uniform, there was as great a variety of pretty dresses borrowd wholy from France as I have ever seen, and amongst the rest some with Saphire blew Sattin waists spangled with Silver and laced down the back and Seams with silver stripes, white sattin peticoats trimd with black and blew velvet ribbon, an odd kind of Headdress which they term the Helmet of minirva. I did not observe the Bird of wisdom[5] however, nor do I know whether those who wore the dress, had suiteable pretensions to it. And pray say you how was my Aunt and cousin drest. If it will gratify you to know, you shall hear. Your Aunt then wore her full drest court cap, without the Lappets, in which was a wreath of white flowers and blew sheafs, 2 black and blew flat feathers (which cost her half a Guiney a peice but that you need not tell of) 3 pearl pins bought for Court and a pr of pearl Earings, the cost of them—no matter what—less than diamonds however.

A saphire blew demisaison with a Sattin stripe, Sack and peticoat, trimd with a broad black lace; Crape flounce &c leaves made of blew ribbon and trimd with white flose wreaths of black velvet ribbon Spotted with steel beads, which are much in fashion and brought to such perfection as to resemble diamonds, white ribbon also in the vandike stile made up the trimming which lookd very

Elegant, a full dress handkerchief and a Boquet of roses. Full Gay I think for my *Aunt*—thats true Lucy, but nobody is old in Europe. I was seated next to the Dutchess of Bedford[6] who had a Scarlet Sattin sack and coat, with a cushing full of Diamonds, for hair she has none and *is but* 76 neither. Well now for your cousin, a small white Leghorn Hat bound with pink Sattin ribbon a steel buckle and band which turnd up at the side and confined a large pink bow, large bow of the same kind of ribbon behind, a wreath of full blown roses round the Crown, and an other of buds and roses withinside the Hat which being placed at the back of the Hair brought the roses to the Edge. You see it clearly 1 red and black feather with 2 white ones compleated the Head dress. A Gown and coat of chamberry Gauze with a red sattin stripe, over a pink waist and coat, flounced with crape trimmed with broad point and pink ribbon, wreaths of roses across the coat Gauze Sleaves and ruffels. But the poor Girl was so Sick of a cold that she could not enjoy herself, and we retir'd about one oclock without Waiting supper by which you have lost half a sheet of paper I dare say. But I cannot close without describing to you Lady North and her daughter.[7] She is as large as Captain Clarks wife and much such a made woman, with a much fuller face, of the coulour and complexion of mrs cook who formerly lived with your uncle Palmer, and looks as if Porter and Beaf stood no chance before her. Add to this, that it is coverd with large red pimples over which to help the natural redness, a coat of *Rouge* is spread, and to assist her shape, she was drest in white sattin trimd with Scarlet ribbon. Miss North is not so large nor quite So red, but a very small Eye with the most impudent face you can possibly form an Idea of, joined to manners so Masculine that I was obliged frequently to recollect that line of Dr Youngs—

> "Believe her dress; shes not a Grenidier"[8]

to persuade myself that I was not mistaken.

Thus my dear Girl you have an account which prehaps may amuse you a little. You must excuse my not copying I fear now I shall not get near all my Letters ready—my pen very bad as you see—and I am engaged 3 days this week, to a *Route* at the Baroness de Nolkings the sweedish ministers;[9] to a Ball on thursday evening and to a dinner on saturday. Do not fear that your Aunt will become dissapated or in Love with European manners, but as opportunity offers, I wish to See this European World in all *its forms*, that I can with decency. I still moralize with Yorick or with one more experiencied, and say Vanity of vanities—all is vanity.[10] Adieu & believe me sincerely Yours A A

RC (MWA:Abigail Adams Corr.).

[1] The second "London" appears to have been written at a different time from the rest of the dateline, perhaps when AA finished the letter.

[2] Of 8 Dec. 1785 (vol. 6:484–485).

[3] Alexander Pope, *Essay on Man*, Epistle III, line 318.

[4] AA2 to Lucy Cranch, 20 Feb. (MWA: Abigail Adams Corr.).

[5] The owl is commonly associated with Minerva, the Roman goddess of wisdom.

[6] Gertrude Russell, dowager duchess of Bedford, whose late husband John Russell, 4th duke of Bedford, was lord president of the privy council from 1764 to 1765 (*DNB*).

[7] Lady Anne Speke North, wife of Frederick, Lord North, the former first lord of the treasury and prime minister. The Norths had three daughters: Catherine Anne (b. 1760), Anne (b. 1764), and Charlotte (b. 1770) (*DNB*).

[8] Edward Young, *Love of Fame, the Universal Passion. Satire V. On Women*, London, 1727, line 464.

[9] Gustaf Adam, Baron von Nolcken, the Swedish envoy (*Repertorium*, 3:409).

[10] Ecclesiastes, 1:2.

John Quincy Adams to John Adams

Honoured Sir Cambridge April 2d: 1786[1]

After having suffered so long an interval of Time to pass, since I wrote you last,[2] it is absolutely necessary, for my own justification, to give you, an account of my Studies, since my return home, and if it is not sufficient, to exculpate me intirely, I hope, at least it will induce you to forgive me. When I arrived here, I found, that I had far more to go through, than I had an Idea of before I left France. For such is the Institution of this College, that if a Person, has studied *certain books*, he may be admitted; but those, I had not studied, and although my Vanity might have lead me, to suppose, I was as well prepared as many of the Class into which I was to enter, yet as I had not acquired knowledge from the Same Sources, the Government of the College, could not admit me, untill I had in some degree become acquainted, with those particular Authors, which had been studied by the junior Sophister Class. I went to Haverhill the 30th: of last September. The Class had then gone through 4 books of Homers Iliad, 2 of Xenophon's Cyropaedia, the Greek Testament. In Latin they had gone thro' the Odes, and Satires of Horace, and were in the Epistles. In English, they had finished the Study of Geography, and that of Logic, and had entered, upon Locke on the understanding.[3] It so happened, that when I was examined, the only book, which, I was tried in, that I had studied, before, I came to America was Horace.[4]

Immediately upon going to Mr: Shaw's I began, upon the Greek Grammer, which I learnt through, by heart. I then undertook the Greek Testament, in which I went before, I came here, as far, as the Epistle to Titus. In this I was not so far as the Class. I went through 6 Books of the Iliad, and four of the Cyropaedia; 1 book in each further than the Class. I also finished Horace, and the Andria, of Terence. In Logic, I was equal with the Class and in Locke, about 70 Pages behind them. Guthrie's Geography I had also finished. On the 15th: of last Month, I was examined before, the President, 3 Professors, and four Tutors.[5] 3 Stanza's, in the Carmen, Saeculare, of Horace, 6 Lines in the 4th: Book of the Iliad, a number of Questions in Logic, and in Locke, and several in Geography, were given to me. After which, I had, the following Piece of English to turn into Latin. "There cannot certainly be an higher ridicule, than to give an air of Importance, to Amusements, if they are in themselves contemptible, and void, of taste. But if they are the object, and care of the judicious and polite, and really deserve that distinction, the conduct of them is, certainly of Consequence."[6]—I rendered it thus. "Nihil profectó, risu dignior potest esse, quam magni aestimare delectamenta; si per se, despicienda sunt atque sine sapore. At si res oblatae atque cura sunt sagacibus, et artibus excultis, et reverà hanc distinctionem merent, administratio eorum, haud dubié, utilitatis est." The President soon after informed me, that I was admitted; and, what I had not expected, that I might Live in the College, as there was one Vacant Place; the Chamber is one of the best in College, and is one of those that are reserved for the resident Batchelors. Johonnot, had left College, a few weeks before,[7] and I now Live with his Chum; Mr: Ware, who graduated last year, and was one of the best moral, and Literary Characters in his Class. He spoke the English Oration, when he took his Degree, and that is considered as the most honourable Part, that is given. I shall remain with him till Commencement, and next year, I believe; I shall Live, with my brother.—I went to Braintree, to get some furniture, and returned here the 22d: of last Month. On Tuesday last, the 28th: Mr: Williams, gave the 1st: Lecture of his Course of Experimental Philosophy. He did not begin Last Year till 6 weeks after this: and that has hurried me, at Haverhill more than any thing; for till within these 2 months I did not expect to enter till the Latter part of this Month.

Our Studies are, at present, one week in Latin to Mr James, Caesar, and Terence, the next to Mr: Read in Euclid; but we finish that this week, and go into Gravesande's Philosophy, the next Quarter. If you could make it Convenient to send me, the 8vo: Edition, of Desagulier's translation of Gravesande I should be happy, as I believe it is not in your Library at present, and there are none to be bought in Boston, there are two Volumes of it.[8] I should wish to have it by next August if Possible. The third week, we recite to Mr Jennison, in Homer, and the Greek Testament; and, the fourth to Mr: Hale, in Locke on the understanding. This is as particular an Account of our Studies, as I can give, and perhaps it will be, so much so, as to become tedious. There are many great advantages derived, from being a member of this Society; but I have already seen many, things which, I think might be altered for the better. One is, that there is not sufficient Communication between the Classes: they appear to form four distinct orders of beings, and seldom associate together. I have already become acquainted, with every one of my own Class; and I do not, know four Persons in any one of the other Classes. Another is, that the Tutors, are so very young, they are often chosen among batchelors, that have not been out of College, more than two years, so that their acquirements are not such, as an Instructor at this University ought to be possess'd of: another disadvantage of their being chosen so young; is that they were the fellow scholars of those they are placed over, and consequently do not command so much Respect, as they seem to demand. However take it all in all, I am strongly confirmed, in your Opinion, that this University is upon a much better plan, than any I have seen in Europe.[9]

I believe you have with you, four or five New Testaments in Greek and Latin.[10] Could you spare a couple of them? I wish to have one for the use of my brothers and myself, and to present another to Mr: Shaw who has none.

With my Duty to Mamma, and Love to Sister, I remain, your affectionate Son.

J.Q. Adams

RC (Adams Papers); endorsed: "J.Q. Adams. Ap. 2. Ansd. June. 3. 1786."

[1] This letter was probably completed on 9 April (JQA, *Diary*, 2:15–16).

[2] On 3 Aug. 1785 (vol. 6:248–250).

[3] These included William Guthrie, *A New Geographical, Historical, and Commercial Grammar; and Present State of the Several Kingdoms of the World*, London, 1770; Isaac Watts, *Logick; or, The Right Use of Reason in the Enquiry After Truth*, London, 1725; and John Locke, *Essay Concerning Human Understanding*, London, 1690.

[4] JQA first studied Horace in 1783 under the direction of C. W. F. Dumas at The Hague (*Diary*, 1:175).

[5] JQA describes the examination in more detail in his Diary (same, 2:1).

[6] Adam Fitz Adam, *The World*, No. 171.

[7] Samuel Cooper Johonnot, sent as a boy to study in Europe, was a fellow passenger with JA, JQA, and CA on their 1779 voyage to France aboard *La Sensible*. Johonnot was educated in Passy with the Adams boys and

later in Geneva. He returned to the United States in 1784 and earned an A.M. from Harvard in 1786, having been granted an A.B. in absentia in 1783. Johonnot studied law in Boston under James Sullivan and practiced in Portland, Maine, from 1789 to 1791 (JQA, *Diary*, 1:2–3; Charles W. Akers, *The Divine Politician: Samuel Cooper and the American Revolution in Boston*, Boston, 1982, p. 356, 426 note 34).

[8] JA's library at MB has the quarto sixth edition of Gravesande's *Mathematical Elements*, trans. J. T. Desaguliers, London, 1747.

[9] JA praised Harvard's attention to the "Morals and Studies of the Youth" compared to its European counterparts in a letter to Harvard president Joseph Willard dated 8 Sept. 1784 (MH-H:Corporation Papers).

[10] Among the Adamses' books are many copies of the Bible in either Latin or Greek published before 1786. JA's books at MB include *Selectæ è Veteri Testamento historiæ, ad usum eorum qui linguæ Latinæ rudimentis imbuuntur*, new edn., Paris, 2 vols. in 1, 1777, and *Novi Jesu Christi Testamenti Græco Latino Germanicæ*, 2 vols. in 1, Rostock, Germany, 1614 (*Catalogue of JA's Library*). The collections at MQA include *Vetus Testamentum Græcum ex versione Septuaginta interpretum*, Amsterdam, 1683; *Biblia Sacra Vulgatæ Editionis Sixti Quinti Pont*, Antwerp, 1628, with JQA's bookplate and the draft of a prayer, in JQA's hand, for the restoration of George III and for the regent, the Prince of Wales; *La Biblia, cum concordantus veteris et Novi Testamenti et sacrorum corronum*, [Nuremberg], [1521]; *Novum testamentum, cum versione Latina Aliae Montani* (Greek), Amsterdam, 1741, inscribed "Charles Amsterdam Adams. 1780" and "Charles Francis Adams from his father. August 5, 1832."; *Biblia polyglotta*, London, n.d., with the signature of CFA; and New Testament (Greek), 2 vols., n.p., n.d., with CFA's bookplate.

John Adams to Cotton Tufts

Dear sir | Grosvenor Square April 3. 1786

Inclosed with this is a Letter to Dr Holyoke and all the original Papers from the Royal Society of Medicine.[1]

You will be so good as to inclose and direct them to him.

I hope Mr. John is, or will soon be at Colledge. You may draw upon me for two hundred Pounds st. and invest it as before, to help you pay the Expences of my Boys. Yours John Adams

Inclosed is a Note from my Friend Count Sarsefield.[2] Will you be so good as to enquire and write me any Intelligence you can obtain of these Mac Auliffes, at Boston.

RC (MWA:N. Paine Coll.); endorsed: "Hond John Adams April 3. 1786 London Recd May 10. 1786."

[1] See JA to Cotton Tufts, 11 March, and note 3, above.

[2] The unidentified note was probably enclosed in Comte de Sarsfield to JA, 6 March (Adams Papers).

John Adams to Abigail Adams

My dear | Buckingham April 5. 1786

We have Seen Magnificence, Elegance and Taste enough to excite an Inclination to see more. We conclude to go to Birmingham, perhaps to the Leasowes, and in that Case shall not have the Pleasure to see you, till Sunday or Monday.[1]

Love to my dear Nabby, and to Coll Smith. He will be so good as to give this account of Us, if any Questions are asked. Yours forever

John Adams

RC (NhD).

[1] JA and Thomas Jefferson left London on 4 April on a tour of English gardens, country houses, and historic sites. Their stops included Alexander Pope's gardens at Twickenham and the landscaped estates of Woburn Farm, Caversham, Wotton, Stowe, The Leasowes, Hagley Hall, and Blenheim Palace. They also visited Stratford-upon-Avon to view the home and tomb of Shakespeare; Edgehill, site of the first great battle of the English civil war; a Birmingham paper factory; and Oxford before returning to London on 10 April. See also JA, *D&A*, 3:184–187, and Jefferson, *Papers*, 9:369–375.

Abigail Adams to Mary Smith Cranch

My dear sister London April 6 1786

Altho I was at a stupid Route at the sweedish ministers last Evening, I got home about 12 and rose early this morning to get a few thinks ready to send out by Lyde. When a Body has attended one of these parties; you know the whole of the entertainment. There were about 2 hundred persons present last evening, three large rooms full of card tables. The moment the ceremony of curtsying is past, the Lady of the House asks you pray what is your Game? Whist Cribbage or commerce, and then the next thing is to hunt round the Room for a set to make a party. And as the company are comeing and going from 8 till 2 in the morning, you may suppose that she has enough to employ her from room to room. And the Lady and her daughter, last night, were most fatigued to death, for they had been out the Night before till morning, and were toiling at pleasure for Seven hours, in which time they scarcly Set down. I went with a determination not to play, but could not get of, so I was Set down to a table with three perfect Strangers, and the Lady who was against me stated the Game at half a Guiney a peice. I told her I thought it full high, but I knew she designd to win, so I said no more, but expected to lose. It however happend otherways. I won four Games of her, I then paid for the cards which is the custom here, and left her, to attack others, which she did at 3 other tables where she amply made up her loss; in short she was and old experienced hand, and it was the luck of the cards rather than skill, tho I have usually been fortunate as it is termd. But I never play when I can possibly avoid it, for I have not conquerd the dissagreeable feeling of receiving money for play. But such a set of Gamblers as the Ladies here are!! and Such a Life as they lead, good Heavens were reasonable Beings made for this? I will come and shelter myself in America from this Scene of dissipation, and upbraid me whenever I introduce the like amongst you. Yet here you cannot live with any Character or concequence unless you give in some measure into the Ton.

I have sent by captain Lyde a trunk the key inclosed containing some Cloaths of mr Adams's which may serve for the children, and if you can find any thing usefull for cousin Cranch pray take it. I thought of the lappeld coat. By Jobe[1] I have sent my neices chintz for a Gown, tell them to be Silent, for reasons which I once before gave you.[2] Some Books you will find too.[3] Will you see that they are Sent as directed.

Mr Adams is gone to accompany mr Jefferson into the Country to some of the most celebrated Gardens. This is the first Tour he has made since I first came abroad, during which time we have lived longer unseperated, than we have ever done before since we were married. Cushing I hope will be arrived, and mrs Hay also before this reaches you. By both I sent some things and Letters.[4] Adieu a terible pen as you see obliges me to write no further than to add your affectionate Sister AA

RC (MWA:Abigail Adams Corr.); addressed: "To Mrs Mary Cranch Braintree."

[1] Job Field, a Braintree neighbor and crew member of the *Active* when AA and AA2 crossed to England (vol. 5:359, 383). For JA's financial aid to Field and other Braintree prisoners of war, see vol. 4:257, 259–261, and JA, *Papers*, vol. 11 and 12.

[2] AA requested that the family not make known publicly the items they received as gifts from the Adamses (vol. 6:359).

[3] Not identified.

[4] Katherine Hay carried AA's letter of 15 March, above. AA's letter of 21 March, above, was sent by Cushing.

John Quincy Adams to Elizabeth Cranch

Cambrige April 7th: 1786

My things, are yet pretty much in Confusion, and I do not expect to get well settled till the next Quarter. I find much more, to do here than I expected; it is true that every persons who chooses, may be idle 3 days in the 6; but every one may also, find full sufficient employment if he chooses. Mr: Williams's Philosophical Lectures, began, Tuesday the 28th: of last month; we have already, had four, and shall have another this day. This alone takes up, between 3 and 4 hours of my time, each day, that he gives us a Lecture. I am contented with my Situation, as indeed I almost always am, and if I was not obliged to lose so much of my time, in attending to the mere ceremonies here, I should be still more happy. I have computed that between 5 and 6 hours are taken up, every day, at Prayers and recitations; but we can't have all things to our will. So much for myself; now let me assume a better subject. We do not know yet whether your brother will go immediately to Haverhill, at the beginning of the Vacation, or wait till the week after;[1] to speak as an egoist, I say, the sooner the better; though others would doubtless have as good a right to say the contrary. I want very much to see Haverhill, but suppose I shall not till the Summer Vacation.[2]

In your Last[3] you promised, to raise a smile, and I have been expecting it ever since: but there was one part of your Letter which I could not understand: you talk about raising a frown, which you cannot do; and as I know you have too much Sense, to pretend to perform impossibilities, I suppose, that from some mistake, or absence of mind, you put that word instead of some other.

RC (MHi:Jacob Norton Papers); addressed: "Miss E Cranch. Haverhill."

[1] William Cranch went home to Braintree at the beginning of the college vacation (Richard Cranch to AA, 13 April, below).

[2] JQA went to Haverhill on 26 July and stayed until 5 Aug. (*Diary*, 2:71–75).

[3] Not found.

Abigail Adams to Isaac Smith Sr.

Dear sir London April 8th. 1786

The Barrel of Cramberries you was so kind as to send me in the fall never reachd me till this week, oweing to Captain Youngs long passage and being obliged to put into port to repair the ship, he did not get up to London till about a Week ago. The Cramberries I believe were very fine by the Appearance of the few which remain; and would have proved a most acceptable present if they had arrived in season. We are not however less obliged to you for them, but I would just mention to those who wish to send presents of this kind to their Friends, that Casks about as large as raison casks, made water tight, with just water sufficient to cover the cramberry, preserves them best. This I found by a cask of that kind which col Smiths Friends sent him, and which were as fine as if they had just been gatherd. Captain Lyde has a cask of Split peas on Board addrest to you. If you will be so good as to send Mrs Cranch a peck of them, and accept the remainder, you will do me a favour.

I wish Sir I could give you a pleasing account of affairs here, as they respect America but the reluctance which the States Shew to give Congress powers to regulate commerce, is to this nation a most agreeable event. They hold it up as a proof that a union of counsels is not to be expected, and treat with contempt the Authority and measures of the different States. There have been however some motions lately, within a few days past, and mr Pitt has requested that an other project of a Treaty might be offerd. It was agreed to, and is now before the Cabinet, but whether any thing is meant to be done, time only can unfold.[1] You will see by the publick papers that mr Pitt's Surpluss, is much doubted, and it is Said that the Mountain is in Labour, whilst the people are trembling through fear of new burdens.[2]

Letters have been received from Mr Randle at Madrid. He and his principal expected to arrive in Algiers some time in March.[3] From mr Barclay, no intelligence has yet come. The embassy of these Gentleman may serve this good purpose, the terms of each Barbery State may be learnt. Congress may then compare them, With those transmitted to them from hence. But the Sum required is so much beyond the Idea of our Countrymen that I fear they hazard a War rather than agree to pay it. They will I hope count the cost of a war first, and consider that afterwards they must pay them a larger Subsidy. Portugal is treating with them and they will soon be at Peace with all other powers and at Liberty to prey upon us. The Tropoline minister who is here, and with whom mr Adams has had several conferences, appears a Benevolent sedate Man. He declares his own abhorrence of the cruel custom of making Slaves of their prisoners. But he says, it is the law of their great Prophet that all christian Nations shall acknowledge their power, and as he cannot alter their Law, he wishes by a perpetual Peace with the Americans to prevent the opperation of it. He swore by his Beard that nothing was nearer his Heart, than a speedy settlement with America, which he considerd as a great Nation, and a people who had been much oppresst and that the terms which he had mentiond were by one half the lowest which had ever been tenderd to any nation. He could answer for Tunis also, and he believed for the other powers with whom the Tripolines had great interests. He said that Spain could not get a Peace with Algiers, untill, tripoli interposed, and he was willing and ready to do every thing in his power to promote a Peace. Every circumstance has been transmitted to Congress, and they must determine.

You will however Sir mention this only to particular Friends, as the Tropoline has been cautious to keep all his transactions from this People, would never have the english interpretor which is allowd by this Court, present.

Be so good as to present my Duty to my Aunt from whom I received a kind letter,[4] and to whom I design soon to write. Regards to the two mr Smiths. Love to cousin Betsy mrs Otis Mrs Welch, and all other Friends. I am dear Sir affectionately Yours

A Adams

My daughter thanks you for your kind mention of her in your Letter and presents her duty to you and her Aunt.

RC (MHi:Smith-Carter Papers).

[1] On 4 April, JA and Thomas Jefferson submitted a new draft of a treaty of commerce with Great Britain to Lord Carmarthen (PRO:F.O. 4, vol. 4). Carmarthen and William Pitt had requested the revised project after suggesting that earlier proposals had contained political items not appropriate to a commercial treaty. JA and Jefferson were attempting to expedite negotiations in advance of 12 May, when their commissions to negotiate the treaty would expire. For additional information on the submission of the commercial articles, see American Commissioners to John Jay, 25 April (Jefferson, *Papers*, 9:406–407).

[2] The London newspapers contained extensive coverage of Pitt's report on the budget, which purported a surplus for the year. Some in Parliament disbelieved Pitt's figures and speculated that "both the Minister and the Public would find themselves much mistaken in the calculation made, and that something different from a surplus will turn out to be the case at length" (*London Chronicle*, 25–28 March). Several also suggested that the proposed budget was irresponsible in its expenditures and that "the public were in a state of actual oppression" due to the government's profligate spending (London *General Evening Post*, 6–8 April).

[3] Paul Randall wrote JA on 17 and 25 Feb. (both Adams Papers) from Barcelona, where he and John Lamb would embark for Algiers. The pair arrived at Algiers on 25 March (John Lamb to William Carmichael, [26 *March*], FC, Adams Papers).

[4] From Elizabeth Storer Smith, 3 Jan., above.

Abigail Adams to Cotton Tufts

Dear sir April 8th 1786 London

Captain Lyde talks of leaving London tomorrow. I just write a line by him to inform you that we are all well. Mr Adams and mr Jefferson are gone a little, journey into the Country, and it is the only excursion mr Adams has ever made since he first came to Europe without having publick buisness to transact.

I have nothing particular to communicate, but what I have mentiond in a letter to uncle Smith which he will shew you.

The Last letters from Congress inform us, that not more than seven states were, or had been for some time represented;[1] concequently no buisness of any great importance could be transacted;

thus every wheel in the machine, is retarded both at Home and abroad.

Mrs Quincy will pay you Eight pounds, two shillings sterling on my account. This you will be so good as to add to the Sum I Sent by my son,[2] and dispose of it in the same way. Regards to all Friends from your affectionate Neice A Adams

RC (Adams Papers); addressed by WSS: "The Honourable Cotton Tufts Boston pr. Capt Lyde"; endorsed: "Mrs. Adams Lettr April 8th. recd May. 16 1786 Pr Capt Lyde"; notation by Tufts: "Mrs. Quincy to pay me £8.2.0 sterlg."

[1] Rufus King, currently in Congress, and Elbridge Gerry, who wrote from New York but had ended his service under the Articles of Confederation in Nov. 1785, both reported that no more than seven members had been present since the previous fall (Rufus King to JA, 1 Feb., and Elbridge Gerry to JA, 2 Feb., both Adams Papers; Smith, *Letters of Delegates*, 23:11).

[2] AA sent £50 of Massachusetts currency, which she had not used in Europe, back home with JQA (to Tufts, [26 *April*] 1785, vol. 6:108).

Richard Cranch to Abigail Adams

My dear Sister Boston April 13th 1786

Last Evening I received a few Lines from you dated the 23d of Decr.,[1] with Newspapers to the 4th. of January 1786. The shortest Note from a Friend, when it contains an Information with which our Happiness is intimately connected, must be highly esteemed. Yours informs me that you and your most amiable Daughter are well.

I have also, pr favour of Mr. King, received Bror. Adams's Letter of the 12th. of December,[2] for which I most sincerely thank him. I shall endeavour, as far as my small Sphere extends, to forward every Measure that tends to free us from that mercantile Dependance on G: Britain into which we have foolishly fallen. I think I can plainly see that the People at large in this State are convinced of their Error in suffering themselves to be led away by the finery and accidental Cheapness of English Goods, to the neglecting of their own more substantial Manufactures; which, under all the Disadvantage and Calamity of War, had been carried on with a Spirit and to a Degree scarcely to be credited by those who were not Eye-Witnesses of the Fact. With a View to the Enlargement of our home-Manufactures, Government in the last Session took up the Subject of encreasing by publick Encouragement the raising and keeping larger Flocks of Sheep.[3] A number of other Bills also, under the Auspices of our worthy Governor, are under Consideration for encouraging the raising of Hemp and Flax.[4] A Committee of the Academy has also been appointed for the special Purpose of promoting Improvements in Husbandry and Agriculture.[5] A Bill is also in contemplation for encouraging the Manufacture of Salt-Petre, by making it receivable instead of Money in a certain Proportion of the publick Taxes.[6] This will soon set our Powder Mills a going once more, which since the Peace have been stupidly neglected. We are also putting our Militia on a better footing by dividing the State into nine military Districts, each of which is to be under the immediate Care and Inspection of a Major-General. The Persons chosen to this high Office are Gentlemen who have born an important and active Part in the late War, and have proved themselves worthy of such important Trusts; such as Genl Lincoln for Suffolk, Genl Brooks for Middlesex, Genl. Cobb for Bristol &c.[7]

I must now pass to a little domestick Information. Our young Family at Colledge behave so as to make a most agreeable Part of our present Connexions. I visited them last Tuesday in a publick Capacity, as one of the Committee of the Board of Overseers, appointed to examine into the State of the University. We met in the Philosophy Room, and after Enquiery had been made of the President, Professors and Tutors, respecting the Behaviour of the Youth under their Care, and the Proficiency they had made in the several Branches of Science; the Committee, of which the Lt. Governor was Chairman,[8] proceeded to the Chapple of Harvard-Hall. On our Entrance we were entertained with a Concert of instrumental Musick, performed by the under-Graduates. The President, in his collegiate Uniform, being seated in the Pulpit, an ellegant latin Oration on the Advantages of Education enjoy'd by the Students of that University under the fostering Care of the Governors of it, was deliver'd by one of the junior Class; next an english Dialogue; then a Dialogue of the Dead between Julius Cesar and Scipio. Mr. Waldo's Son, of Bristol, who came from England to receive his Education at this University,[9] performed the Character of Julius Cesar in a manner that did him Honor as a Speaker and an Actor. After this a greek Oration was spoken by my Billy, and was said to be well performed.[10] Then followed an Oration in the hebrew Tongue; which preceded an English Oration. And last of all a well-sung Anthem finished the publick Exercises. After Dinner your truly worthy and amiable Sons John and Charles went to Braintree, your Sister Cranch having sent them Horses for that purpose; and Billy went there next Day. The Friendship that subsists between our Children will make the Vacancy run off pleasantly—they are to be at home a Fortnight. Your Sister Cranch writes you by this Ship (Capt. Callahan).

We are all as well as usual in the several Families of our Connexions, except Doctr. Simon Tufts, who is in a very declining State, and is not expected to continue long. Please to give my kindest Regards to Mr. Adams and my dear Niece; and believe me to be, with the warmest Sentiments of Esteem and Friendship, your affectionate Brother Richard Cranch

RC (Adams Papers); addressed: "to Mrs: Adams, Lady of His Excellency John Adams Esqr. Grosvenor Square Westminster"; endorsed: "Mr Cranch 13 April 1786"; notation by WSS: "Mrs. Wheeler Upper Brook street Thomas Johnstone Left her 5 months past."

[1] Not found.

[2] LbC, Adams Papers.

[3] Possibly a reference to the "Report of the Committee for Encouragement of Manufactures, &c. in this Commonwealth," which was submitted on 17 Nov. (Mass., *Acts and Laws*, Resolves of 1786, Sept. sess., ch. 132). "Resolve Granting a Bounty on Hemp Raised in This Commonwealth, and Laying an Impost Duty on All Imported Hemp" passed on 8 Nov. (same, Resolves of 1786, Sept. sess., ch. 83). On 20 Oct. the General Court altered a clause in "An Act, Regulating the Exportation of Flax Seed, Pot Ash, Pearl Ash, Beef, Pork, Barreled Fish, and Dried Fish" that supported the shipping and exportation of flax seed (same, Acts of 1786, Sept. sess., ch. 35).

[5] The Committee for Promoting Agriculture formed on 6 Nov. 1785 by the American Academy of Arts and Sciences was composed of 31 members from across the state including several of the Adamses' intimate friends: Richard Cranch, Francis Dana, Cotton Tufts, and James Warren. Benjamin Lincoln served as chairman. In April 1786 the committee advertised a subscription fund to support improvements in agriculture and proposed offering premiums to those persons whose crops produced the greatest yield (*Fleet's Pocket Almanack* 1787, p. 67–68; *Massachusetts Centinel*, 18 Feb., 5 April).

[6] On 21 Feb., Gov. James Bowdoin addressed the legislature on the importance of Massachusetts' having a steady supply of gunpowder and suggested instituting a tax on the state payable in the form of saltpeter to encourage the building of factories to produce it. On 8 July, the committee assigned to review the proposal recommended in favor of it, and on 17 Nov., the legislature resolved to allow residents to use saltpeter as a form of payment for taxes (Mass., *Acts and Laws*, Resolves of 1785, Feb. sess., ch. 27; Resolves of 1786, May sess., ch. 103; Resolves of 1786, Sept. sess., ch. 113).

[7] The commonwealth completely revamped the regulation and governance of its militia in March 1785. One provision of an amendment to the aforementioned act passed in Nov. 1785 was to form the militia into nine divisions based on the fourteen counties within the commonwealth: 1. Suffolk Co. (Benjamin Lincoln); 2. Essex Co. (Jonathan Titcomb); 3. Middlesex Co. (John Brooks); 4. Hampshire Co. (William Shepard); 5. Plymouth, Barnstable, Bristol, Dukes, and Nantucket Cos. (David Cobb); 6. York and Cumberland Cos. (Ichabod Goodwin); 7. Worcester Co. (Jonathan Warner); 8. Lincoln Co. (William Lithgow); 9. Berkshire Co. (John Paterson). The General Court specifically addressed the commissioning of major generals in a further amendment made on 20 March 1786 (Mass., *Acts and Laws*, Acts of 1784, Jan. sess., ch. 55; Acts of 1785, Oct. sess., ch. 36, and Feb. sess., ch. 73; *Fleet's Pocket Almanack* 1787, p. 81).

[8] Thomas Cushing.

[9] Boston merchant Joseph Waldo, Harvard 1741, removed to Bristol, England, about 1770. His son, John Jones Waldo, was admitted to the class of 1787 in 1784 (*Sibley's Harvard Graduates*, 11:91–94).

[10] Opposite this sentence, on the largely blank third page of the letter, appears "my Nephew," written by WSS.

Charles Storer to Abigail Adams

Dear Madam Boston. 13th. April. 1786

What in the name of wonder can you be doing on your side the Atlantic? We hear no more of you than if you were in the regions above the Moon. It is not to be long so I hope, for we are become very impatient now for news. Here, we seem to be almost at a stand, as it were; waiting for good tidings from afar. I fancy the case is much the same with you.

With this I send you some newspapers,[1] which will give you some little insight into matters and things here: But *Dr: Gordon* is going in the same vessell, and should you see him, he will be able to tell you more than I can write. Is it probable you will see him? I mentioned sending a pacquet for you. He told me if I would give it to him, he would take care that it should be forwarded to you by the Penny-Post. This looks as if he did not mean to see you. He has been writing the history of the Revolution and has had many squibs against him in our papers, which have vexed him not a little. 'Tis supposed he will state his grievances in England, publicly, in order to promote his subscriptions and the sale of his history.

Have you yet heard of Mr: Gerry's being married? I spent yesterday with him, his wife and her Sister at Mr: Tracey's at Cambridge. Mrs: G. was a Miss Thompson of New York, originally from Ireland, a delicate, pretty woman.[2] She has been at Mr: T. Russells since they arrived here, (about 3. weeks,) where she has been very ill. They are now at Mr: Tracey's, where I fancy her ill-health will detain her another week: from thence they are going to Marblehead. They talk of purchasing a seat at Cambridge.[3]

Mr: G. is neither the first nor the last Delegate in Congress that has been married in N York. *Mr: King* is lately married to a large fortune[4] and sev[eral] others have done the same. Congress have not much business on hand at present, as they are waiting to know if the States will all comply with their requisitions: this interim of business they improve in getting married. From this circumstance perhaps they will sooner settle the federal town, which is an object to be wished. However, this will not altogether compensate for the expence of their support.

I saw *John* and *Charles* a day or two ago at Cambridge, where there was an exhibition before a Committee of the Overseers of the College, after which they went off to Braintree for the vacation, which will be for a fortnight. John is very well settled, has a good room and every apparent convenience he can wish. He needs no stimulus or encouragement to attend to his studies, he pursues the method which will be effectually beneficial to him, he is exact in his attendance on the lectures, and particular in taking minutes of them afterwards. The only thing he complains of is that so much time should be wasted in prayers and recitations as there is. Were he to go on by himself he would proceed much faster. But you will hear from him by this opportunity and he will tell you more of himself and our friends at Braintree than I can, as I have not been there this long while.

We have been alarmed almost every day for the month past by fire; which has several times done mischief, but to the activity of our Firemen we are much indebted that it has done so little. A Barn *full of hay*, in our street has been lately burnt down, and tho' it was surrounded by old wooden houses, nay, joined to one or two, no further damage was done. Great part of *board-Alley*, near Trinity Church, was burnt down this last week.[5]

When you write me I hope you will mention a certain subject, which I wrote so largely of in my last. The story seems to have died away here. The Gentleman says all is now well.

I am, with much esteem, Madam, Yrs. C. S.

RC (Adams Papers); addressed: "Mrs: A. Adams, Grosvenor-Square, London"; endorsed: "Charles Storer April 13 1786." Some loss of text where the seal was removed.

[1] Not identified.

[2] Ann Thompson (1763–1849), daughter of James Thompson, a New York merchant, was considered "as distinguished by her beauty and personal worth as by her family and social connections" (Rufus Wilmot Griswold, *The Republican Court; or, American Society in the Days of Washington*, 2d edn., New York, 1856, p. 100; Billias, *Elbridge Gerry*, p. 377, note 29). The sister with her was either Catherine or Helen (JQA, *Diary*, 2:105).

[3] Gerry purchased Elmwood, the elegant mansion once owned by royal lieutenant governor Thomas Oliver, and moved permanently to Cambridge later in 1786 (Billias, *Elbridge Gerry*, p. 147–148).

[4] Rufus King married Mary, daughter of New York merchant John Alsop, on 30 March (*DAB*).

[5] A fire in a stable on Cambridge Street on 31 March was contained without damaging adjoining buildings. Eleven days later, a fire in a stable on Board Alley destroyed one home, a wheelwright's shop, a carpenter's shop, and two stables, and severely damaged another residence (*Massachusetts Centinel*, 1, 12 April).

Cotton Tufts to Abigail Adams

My Dear Cous. Boston April 13. 1786

In some of my former Letters I mentioned the Probability, that Belchers Place would shortly be on Sale. Mr. Morton Atty. to C. W.

Apthorp Esq has offered it to me but has not as yet set his Price.[1] As I conceive it to be Your Wish to purchase it—If it can be obtained at a reasonable Price, I shall secure it. I have frequent offers of Salt Marsh and other Lands, in Braintree, some of them adjoining to yours, that of the late Widow Veazies adjoyning to Belchers, will shortly be sold.[2] But as Lands bring in but very little Profit, It can not be adviseable to engage very far in the Purchase of them. The Scarcity of Specie and the Danger of being forced into a Paper Medium to supply the Want, together with the Weight of Taxes, Conduce greatly to lessen the Profits of real Estate. Payment of Rents dayly become more difficult and I find them to be slow. This will oblige me to depend on Draughts on Mr. Adams for defraying the Expences of Your Childrens Education. We propose to offer your Son Thomas for Admission in to our University at the next Commencment, unless you should direct otherwise. Mr John was admitted in March last into the Junior Class and is well seated in a Chamber with a Graduate. The Expences of your Three Sons cannot be estimated I apprehend at less than £50 sterlg each Pr. Ann.—supposing them to conduct with Oeconomy. And I have the Satisfaction to inform You, that there does not appear in them any Disposition to Extravagance. The parental Attention of Mr and Mrs Cranch to them, would do much to prevent it, were they inclined to excess; and their Attachment to their Cousin Wm. Cranch, who is an amiable Youth, of great Steadiness and Prudence makes their Station agreable to them and I flatter my self that they will form a little Circle distinguished for their good order and attention to their Studies.

Mr. T— I fear will give me much Trouble; for Twelve months past or more I have found it difficult to see him. His frequent Absence from his office, for a long Time, I imputed to necessary Calls and Business. And though I have of late made repeated Journeys to Braintree as well as wrote to him, in order to get an Account of Your Affairs and what Money he may have collected, yet nothing ensues but Messages that he will at such a Time or such a Time wait on me. Whether his Conduct has proceeded from a natural Versatility of Mind, his Fondness for Intrigue or more latterly from Resentment or a Wish to avoid a strict Compliance with the Demands of a former *Correspondent* or to a moveable Spirit caught from *his Windmill* lately erected—I do not pretend to determine—but I shall not long be content to feed on Uncertainties.

In my former Letter I requested you to let me know to what

Amount in the Course of the Year I might draw for, You will express your Mind on this and also let me know what may be said on Doane's Account. I mean with respect to its having been paid or not.

It is e[xpected], that Cap. Callihan will sail this Day or to morrow. I shall write further by him if Time will permit, but I must refer You to Bro Cranch for Politicks and Domestic Intelligence,[3] and I hope You will not refrain from giving me the Politics of the Country where You reside although I should in my Letters confine myself merely to Matters that relate to Your private Interest. The various Trusts with which I am charged, engross almost the whole of my Time during the Recesses of the General Court, that but very little is left for my own particular Concerns and does almost entirely prevent me from expatiating on Subjects other than those that have immediate Reference to Matters of Trust. My Compliments and Love &c to my Cous. Nabby. I shall shortly write her a Line—at present I can only tell her, that I have made no further Progress in my Embassy, than what she has already had information of. When will My Friend Mr. Adams his Lady and Daughter return to Braintree! Should the Answer be, Shortly it would give Pleasure to Your Affectionate Friend

Cotton Tufts

P.S. Since I wrote the above, I have drawn a Bill on Mr Adams for £50. sterlg in favour of Ebenr Storer Esq @ 7 Pr Ct. above par, which I found necessary, the produce of the last Bill having laid out (the greater part of it) in public Securities and expended a considerable Sum beyond what your Rents and other Means have produced, and no present Prospect of an adequate Supply for future Demands other by a Draught.

RC (Adams Papers); addressed: "Madam Abigail Adams Grovesner Square London"; endorsed: "Dr Tufts April 13th 1786." Some loss of text where the seal was removed.

[1] On JA's behalf, Tufts purchased the approximately 5 1/2 acre lot on Penn's Hill formerly owned by Moses Belcher Jr., and more recently occupied by his son Elijah Belcher, from James and Sarah Apthorp for £70 on 4 April 1787. The property included half a dwelling house, barn, and well; JA previously had purchased the other half of said structures and adjoining land from Joseph and Mary Palmer (James Apthorp *et ux.*, Deed to JA, 4 April 1787; Joseph and Mary Palmer to JA, 6 May 1771, both Adams Papers, Adams Office Files, folder 13). See also Cotton Tufts to AA, 14 Oct. 1785, vol. 6:425–426.

[2] Martha Vesey's land lay to the northeast of the lot in question; JA acquired it from William and Sarah Vesey in Feb. 1788 (James Apthorp *et ux.*, Deed to JA, 4 April 1787; William Vesey and Sarah Vesey, Deed to JA, 12 Feb. 1788; both Adams Papers, Adams Office Files, folder 13).

[3] To AA, 13 April, above.

John Adams to Richard Cranch

My dear Brother London April 15. 1786

Can you give me any Information concerning the Persons named in the inclosed Paper?[1]

Mr Jenkinson, I presume, has, by his late Motions in Parliament, all of which are carried without opposition, convinced the People of America, that they have nothing but a ruinous Commerce to expect with England.

Our Crisis is at hand, and if the states do not hang together, they might as well have been "hanged Seperate," according to Dick Penns bon Mot in 1784.[2] Your Brother John Adams

RC (NN:John Adams Papers); endorsed: "Letter from his Excelly. John Adams Esqr Apl 15th. 1786 Wth. Memo. about Enquirey for Messrs. MacAuliffs"; notation: "Mem: To Enquire of Mr. Bowers at Little Cambridge."

[1] Not found.

[2] JA's 1784 date for Richard Penn's response to this saying, commonly attributed to Benjamin Franklin at the signing of the Declaration of Independence, is either a mistake or its meaning to JA and Cranch is not evident.

Abigail Adams to John Quincy Adams

My Dear son London April 24 1786

Your Father and Col Smith are gone to Night to Covent Garden theatre to See the School for Scandle represented, it being a Benifit Night, no places for Ladies who would not lavish Guineys.[1] Now as I can See it at any other time at a common price I did not think it worth my while to gratify my curiosity at the expence of my purse, tho it is one of the best modern plays which has appeard upon the Stage. Scandle is the *fort* of this nation and a school in which they have arrived at great experience. That and lyeing make the greater part of their daily publications, as their numerous gazets fully testify.

I thank you for the entertainment afforded me in the perusal of your journal to your sister,[2] which is always pleasent till I get to the last page. There indeed I experience some regreet, from its finishing.

I presume from your Aunt Shaws Letter,[3] that this will find you at Cambridge. I hope you will not be obliged to such late and close application, as you have follow'd through the last six Months. Your Health may suffer by it.

You will receive some letters from me which give you a state of the Situation and prospects of your sister that will I hope occasion you less anxiety, than what you have heitherto experienced upon her account. I think however that they would be better off, if they were to postpone their union to an other Year, for as the Play Says, "marriage is chargable,"[4] and we cannot do for them what we should be glad too. Such is the continued Parsimony of . . . [5] I Sometimes think we should do better at Home, yet fear for my poor Lads whose education is very near my Heart, and who knowing the circumstances of their Parents will study economy in all their movements. I hope you will gaurd your Brother against that pernicious vice of gameing, too much practised at the university.

I would not let mr Jenks return without a few lines from me tho I have written You largly very lately. Your Friend Murry dined with us last week and always mentions you with regard. I think he is consumptive, he looks misirably. You must correct as you read, or be so intent upon the matter, as to neglect the manner. Col Humphries is returnd to America in the April Packet which was to sail on the 15th. Mr and Mrs Rogers are also on board the Same vessel. If you want any thing I can supply you with, let me know. I have Sent you some shirts by captain Cushing.

Your sister who is writing at the same table with me, is filling up page after page and I suppose tells you all the News of the day.[6] Mr Jefferson has made us a fine visit, but leaves us on wednesday. After the Birth day[7] we are to Set out upon some excursions into the Country; which will probably find us some entertainment. My Love to your Brother. I shall not have time to write him now, as tomorrow I am engaged with company, and it is now Eleven oclock. Your Letter to your Sister[8] came to day noon. We found it upon the table when we returnd from a ride which we had been taking. Not a line for Mamma! Yours AA

RC (Adams Papers).

[1] Richard Brinsley Sheridan's *The School for Scandal* was actually performed at Drury Lane, for the benefit of Anna Maria Crouch, the noted actress and singer (*Morning Chronicle and London Advertiser*, 24 April; *DNB*).

[2] The most recent JQA letter received by AA2 was that of 1 Oct. 1785 (vol. 6:398–406).

[3] Probably Elizabeth Smith Shaw to AA2, 14 Feb., above.

[4] Thomas Otway, *Venice Preserved*, Act II, scene ii.

[5] Thus in MS. AA certainly must mean Congress.

[6] AA2's letter No. 13 has not been found. See AA2 to JQA, 25 April, below.

[7] The celebration of George III's birthday took place on 5 June (*London Gazette*, 3–6 June).

[8] JQA to AA2, [26] Oct. 1785 (vol. 6:442–445).

Abigail Adams to Mary Smith Cranch

Grosvenor Square London
My dear sister April 24 1786

Captain Cushing is arrived. Mr Adams this day received Some letters by the post, and Nabby got one from her Aunt shaw and an other from her Brother.[1] This was a little mortifying I own, not that others were happy, but that I was dissapointed, but I do not give over, some passenger has them I Say or else the vessel saild, and has left my Letters behind. Why I am Sure my Sister Cranch has written to me if nobody else has, she has never faild me yet; so I comfort myself that they will be here in a day or two, but not soon enough I fear to replie to them by mr Jenks who leaves London tomorrow. He is hurried away by the sudden elopement of several american Merchants as they call'd themselves, some call them Swindlers. They are persons unknown to me, of whom I never heard till there failure. The odium brought upon the American Character by such conduct cannot be defended. It is really painfull living in this Country at this time, because there is but too much foundation for many of their reproaches against our Country. There does not appear any symptom of a political change in the sentiments of this people, or their Rulers, they say Congress has no power and that the States can not unite. They depend upon our continuing their dupes, and we appear [I] think quite enough disposed to be so.

I have written to you by way of New York, by mrs Hay and by captain Cushing and Lyde, all of which I hope will go safe and the little articles I sent you and my other Friends. I wish I could communicate to you and Mrs Shaw a little of that which Shylock was so determined to take from poor ⟨*Bassiano*⟩ Antonio; you should have it too from next my Heart, and having bestowed some pounds I should move nimbler and feel lighter. Tis true I enjoy good Health, but am larger than both my sisters compounded. Mr Adams too keeps pace with me, and if one Horse had to carry us, I should pitty the poor Beast, but your Neice is moulded into a shape as Slender as a *Grey hound*, and is not be sure more than half as large as she was when she first left America. The Spring is advancing and I begin to walk so that I hope excercise will be of service to me. I wish I could transport my dear cousins in a Baloon. Betsy should go to Stow with me and to Hagly and the Leasows, which I hope to see in the course of the summer, and Lucy should go to Devonshire with me.[2] I may feel lonely, tho in this great city; should col S. insist upon being married this Summer, and go to Housekeeping as he talks, but I advise him not to be hasty. They will find marriage very chargeable. I should not feel anxious for them in America with half his sallery, but it will require Economy here to live upon it. The servants that one is obliged to keep in Europe who live in publick Characters, are the greatest moths one can conceive of, and in spight of all your caution will run you in debt.

I want to hear how you all do, and what you are about. You would Smile if you was to See me questioning the Captains of vessels who come from America and particularly those who come from Boston. They are generally very intelligent Men. I learn how the bridge goes on,[3] what new houses are building, what the trade is to this place, and that, how the Trees flourish in the common, and whether you are growing more frugal or more Luxurious. I make it a rule when a vessel arrives from Boston to send a card to the Captain to come and dine with us, whether I know him or not. Some who are not acquainted feel a diffidence at comeing without an introduction or an invitation. Captain Young dined with us yesterday. Tis a feast to me when I can set them talking about the Country, and learn as I frequently do, pleasing things with respect to its husbandry and fishery; its trade is at present in a cloud, but I hope it will be dispelld in time to their advantage. When a people once become Luxurious nothing but dire necessity will ever bring them to their senses. I do not believe that ever any people made a greater Show, with less capitals than my dear mistaken countrymen have done. I thought them rich, I thought it was all their own, but how many now, not only upon your side the Water, but upon this, are eating the Bread of Sorrow, or what is worse, having none to eat, of any kind. Not a House here which has been connected with the American trade, but what are in the utmost distress. Our Countrymen *owe Millions* here. Can you believe it? Alass it is a miserable truth, and much of this debt has been contracted for mere gew-Gaws and triffels. I am sometimes apt to think that the more strictly this Country addheres to her present system, the better it will prove for ours in the end. You will easily discern that I cannot copy so excuse all inaccurices, and do not read any part of my letter to any one who may feel pained by the observations. Love to all friends from your ever affectionate

AA

RC (MWA:Abigail Adams Corr.); addressed by WSS: "Mrs. Mary Cranch Braintree Boston Hon'd by. Mr. Jenks."

[1] Elizabeth Smith Shaw to AA2, 14 Feb., above, and JQA to AA2, [26] Oct. 1785, vol. 6:442–445.

[2] JA and Jefferson visited Stowe, Hagley Hall, and The Leasowes on their garden tour in early April, see JA to AA, 5 April, and note 1, above. Devonshire was the home of Richard Cranch's family.

[3] The Charlestown, or Charles River, Bridge, the first bridge connecting Boston and Charlestown, opened on 17 June. See the Descriptive List of Illustrations, No. 6, above.

Abigail Adams to Elizabeth Smith Shaw

My dear sister London April 24th 1786

Mr jenks is suddenly obliged to return to America and I have only time to write you a few lines, to inform you of my Health. I yesterday heard that Captain Davis is arrived at Plimouth. By him I hope to hear again from all my Dear Friends. I have written you lately by mrs Hay who went to Newyork and by Captains Cushing and Lyde, all of whom I hope will arrive Safe.

In the political World Matters remain much as they were. I expect to spend this summer chiefly in making excursions into the Country, which will afford me an ample fund to entertain my Friends with. We went out last week to visit a Seat of the Duke of Northumberlands calld Sion House. It was formerly a Monastry, and was the first which was surpressed by Henry 8th.[1] As we had not tickets we could not see the House, but were admitted to the Gardens and pleasure grounds which are very extensive and beautifull. The pleasure Grounds in this Country contain from 2 hundred to a thousand acres and are ornamented and kept up at a vast expence. We askd the Gardner how many hands were employ'd in this Seat at Sion which is about 2 hundred acres. He told us 15. We have since received tickets and shall visit it again. Woods grottos meandering waters templs Statues are the ornaments of these places—one would almost think themselves in Fairy land. Mr Adams and mr Jefferson made an excursion of 3 hundred miles and visited Several of the most celebrated Seats. They returnd charmd with the beauties of them, and as soon as the spring is a little further advanced, I shall begin upon them. Amongst the places they visited was the house and Spot upon which Shakspear was born. They Sat in the chair in which he used to Study, and cut a relict from it.[2]

Is my son admitted colledge, I am anxious to know? My Tommy will be left quite alone. Mr Adams some times wishes him here, but I never can join him in that wish. I am more satisfied with his present situation, tho it would give me pleasure to have him here if I thought it for his benifit. The Young Gentleman here is so very Zealous to be married that I Suppose it will take place in the course of a few months, and they chuse to keep House. I Shall be much engaged very soon in preparations for this matter.

Mr Adams bought a few days ago at second Hand; dr Clarks Sermons,[3] which he desires me to present to mr shaw in his Name: and I have requested mr Jenks to take Charge of them for him. Remember me to all Friends & believe me Dear Sister most affectionatly Yours AA

RC (DLC:Shaw Papers); addressed by WSS: "Mrs. Eliza. Shaw Haverhill Boston Hon'd by Mr. Jenks"; endorsed: "April 24th. 1786 Received July 16th."

[1] The Adamses and Thomas Jefferson visited Sion (Syon) House in Brentford, about seven miles west of London, on 20 April. This monastery had been established by Henry V in 1415 as a convent for Bridgettines. It was one of the first to be suppressed, in 1539, by Henry VIII, who used it in 1541 as a prison for his fifth wife Catherine Howard just prior to her execution (JA, *D&A*, 3:190; George James Aungier, *The History and Antiquities of Syon Monastery*, London, 1840, p. 21, 83–85, 90–91).

[2] For JA and Jefferson's visit to Stratford-upon-Avon, see *D&A*, 3:185.

[3] Probably a volume by Samuel Clarke (1675–1729), rector of St. James', Westminster (*DNB*). There are several compilations of Clarke's sermons. JA's library at MB contains *A Discourse Concerning the Unchangeable Obligations of Natural Religion . . . Being Eight Sermons Preached in the Year 1705* (in Richard Watson, ed., *A Collection of Theological Tracts*, 5 vols., London, 1785, 4:109–295).

Abigail Adams 2d to John Quincy Adams

N 14

London April 25th 1786

Last night I Closed my Letter to you[1] and shall send it to Mr Jenks's care this Morning. I determine not to delay writing from day to day, till it becomes urkessome, but to finish my story and then go on regularly—theres a good resolution—I shall now begin by telling you a peice of News—Call all your fortitude to your aid before you proceed—*here pause a moment . . .*[2] do you think yourself sufficiently guarded—be sure of that—and then attend—Mr Bowdoin, the Gentleman you left in Paris,[3] proceeded from thence to Holland, where he has been till within a few weeks: when he returnd to this place, proposing to go from hence to America. He called to pay us his respects one Morning. We inquired after your friends at the Hague, and he told us that he had heard Miss Dumas was soon to be very well Married.[4] *I do not here ask any Confession of your Faith*. You will

I dare say be happy to hear so pleasing an account of a Lady for whom you have so much respect and Esteem.

I just mentiond the letter I received yesterday,[5] in my Letter last Eve, and shall now notice it particularly. Your Letters my Dear Brother afford me more pleasure than you can beleive. I expect them with impatience, and am allways, made happy at their arrival. Do not discontinue them. I am sure you will not. I do not wonder that your meeting with our Dear Brothers after so long a seperation, put you in such Spirits. Could our family meet in some such moment, I should consider it as a happy period. But I have, said enough upon this subject to convince you that it is one of the first wishes of my heart. But I dare not think how long it may be, before it arrives.

I think my Brother that you do not discover Candor enough for the foibles, of others especially the Ladies. The best dispositions are not Convinced by Severity, and austerity. Only reflect upon your own disposition, and I am sure you will be convinced of this. And remember that if a young Lady is Capable of inconsistencys if she is deficient in judgment prudence &c, that the fault is not half so much her own as, those who have had the Care of her education. We are like Clay in the Hands, of the Artist, and may be moulded to whatever form, they please. The more knowledge and judment they possess, the fewer faults will be found in their productions. I believe that the earliest impressions of the Mind are too generally neglected, and it is those which often have the greatest affect. You may if you attend to it, observe in many of your acquaintance, habits and fauts, which have from not being early enough attended to, Grown up, and proved so forcible as to resist all future attempts to Correct them. You may observe it in the most trifling circumstances and you may generally decide, by hearing a Person converse an hour, what has been their early education. You may judge from their Language, the very frases they use to express their ideas. And tho they may be sensible in some degree of those faults, I am inclined to beleive it is not in their power to correct them. A Gentleman who is severe against the Ladies, is also, upon every principle very impolitick. His Character is soon established, for a Morose severe ill Natured Fellow. And upon my word, I think it the most Convincing proof that he can give, that He feels their Power importance, and ⟨*equallity*⟩ Superiority. It is I assure you a want of Generosity, and I will challenge you to produce one instance of a Person of this disposition who did not at some period of his Life, acknowledge his dependance upon them. Persons who are conscious, of their superiority in any subject, are generally diffident in proclaiming their own merrit. They will prefer to prove it by their actions and Conduct, rather than discover their own knowledge of it. ⟨*I would never dispute with you, were you to assert that we were your inferiors incapable even of those improvements which you would the superiors*⟩

Miss Hamilton of whom I wrote you quits England in a few days, and not with out regret. She has got a little attached to the amusements and pleasures of this place, tho she behaves perfectly well upon the Subject. She is a sweet amiable Girl. I shall regret her more than any other Lady of my acquaintance.

Your account of Mrs Duncans Death is very melancholy. It must have been a great shock to her family. I have I think noticed most of your letter. I presented your respects to Mr S— and he desird me in return to say every thing to you for him which you could wish—he says he will write you and tell you that I dont keep, a strict journal.

I want much to hear from you from Cambridge, and to know how you like your new Situation. I hope now to receive later letters from you for do you know that five months have passd since the date of your last N 12,[6] which leads me to hope that I shall receive another by Davis.

Your friend Winslow Warren has returd, to Milton we hear. Pappa wrote him and forwarded to him letters from his father in December,[7] but they did not reach him, before his departure from thence, and have been since returnd, and forwarded to him at Boston. Pappa had promised him his interest as Consull to Lisbon. It was then supposed that Congress would have impowerd their Ministers to appoint Consulls, but they have not received any commission for it. Mr Gerry wrote Pappa that Congress had resolvd to appoint him Consull General to this County and Mr Jefferson in France, but they have heard nothing further of it.[8] I suppose they meant it to save any sallery with the Commission, but Pappa determines that it is not possible for him to Act in it. It would be a scene of trouble and vexation withot any reward. This how ever seems to be expected by Congress, that every Body in their service shold submit to. The March Packet has not yet arrived, and the 2 or thre last Months Packets have brought nothing New. There were but Seven states represented by the last accounts and Mr —— the Presidents Health did not permit him to attend.[9] The Commercial Commissions you know Expire in a few days. So that nothing more can be done with any Power, till it is either renewd or something done by Congress. Soon after Pappa arrived here he proposed the plan of a treaty to Mr Pitt.[10] It was taken no notice of. When Mr Jefferson arrived, they informd Lord Carmarthen of it and likewise that their Commissions would expire soon. His Lordship then desird another Plan, might be proposed, merely Commercil. The Gentlemen drew up, a Treaty in 5 articles, giveing equal Libertys rights &c, to the two Nations, since which not a word of answer has been receivd, and Mr J— Leavs London tomorrow, so that tis plain they will do nothing. They pretend to doubt the Powers of Congress, in short their Conduct appears Consistently ridiculous. What time will produce we know not. Pappa Complains and sometimes talks of going home, but I doubt it I Confess, till Congress recall him, which perhaps they will if there is no Minister appointed to them from hence. Before Bingham went away he told a friend, that the Cabbinet had now determined upon sending a Minister to America and *he* beleived it was in Consequence of a Conversation he had had a few days before with Mr Eden, and went off perhaps in the beleif. Hower his Mourtion [*Motion?*] has as yet prodouced nothing. If you see the English papers you will see that Mr Eden is sent to Paris to ⟨*form*⟩ a finish, Crawford Commercial arangements which perhaps were never began[11]—*but enough of Politicks.*

25th.

We had a Company to dine to day. Mrs Smith from Carolina Mr Ridley who goes to America in a few weeks, Dr Bancroft Colln Forrest Mr Brown the Painter, Mr Drake from Connecticut who brought a Letter of introduction from your friend Mr Brush, to Pappa, he does not appear to be any thing extra. Mr Barthelemy the Charge d'Affairs de France le Comt de Baigelin and le Compt de Gramond, 2 young French officers who brought Letters-of introduction from the Marquis de la Fayette.[12] Mr Jefferson and Pappa went after dinner to the Chevalier de Pintos to put their Names to the Treaty with Portugal.[13]

Wedensday 26th

Mr Jefferson left London, to our regret. He has dined with us whenever he has not been otherwise engaged, and made this House a kind of Home which you will know must have been very agreeable to us all.[14] He has given Mr Trumble an invitation to go to Paris and keep at His House, where he intends to have his pictures engraved.

He is acquiring great reputation by the subjects he has taken up.[15] In the Evening we went to one of the little Theatres here to see Tumbling Rope dancing and wondrous feats of various kinds performed some of Which were really astonishing—but cannot be described.[16]

Thursday 27th.

We went for the first time this season to the Opera, and I imagine it will be the last. The English Boast of this House as superior to any the French have. It may be larger, but for Elegance of artichetere there is no Comparison. It was the benefit of Md Mason, one of the principle dancers who fearing I suppose that the House would not be full went round and left Tickets, asking your attendance at her benefit. We accordingly went, the House was not full, the Company were highly dressd. The performance is all in Italian you know, and People never go to the Opera to understand what they hear. The Instrumental Musick was very good but there was no singing extraordinary. The Dancing was fine. Vestris is here this Winter, and Bacthell, who was last winter at the Duke of Dorsetts Hotell.[17] She is a good figure and Dances, as well as Vestris I think. After the Opera, the greatest Curiossity is to go into the Coffee Room, where the Whole Company resort to wait for their Carriages and take some refreshment if they Choose, for you know, the English have no amusement where eating and drinking, is not introduced. The Prince of Wales, the Duke d'Orleans and the Duke de Fitz James,[18] just made their appearance, for ten minutes I suppose, to sett the Whole House a staring and then went off. The Princes followers might all be distinguished by their dress, a blue frock with Gold frogs. There were several of them in his suit this Eve. They appeard all about the same size, and so delicate, eff[*em*]inate and Languid, just fit for Companions for[19] a Prince who professs to make pleasure is only pursuit.

Saturday 29th.

We have dined to day with an oald Bacheller, Mr Wm Vaughan. He had invited us to make a little excursion out of Town about Seven miles, to see a celebrated House and Garden belonging to Lord Tylney,[20] and we intended to have gone, but the weather for several days has been disagreeable and we deferd it to some other time. The Company were our family Mr B Vaughan and Lady, Dr Priestly who has been in Town a few weeks, upon a visit, Dr Price,

Dr Keppis, Dr Reives, and one or two other Gentlemen who I did not know.[21] 5 of the Company were dissenting Ministers and opsd Liberal Men, all of them are writers of Eminence. The two first you know by Character Dr Priestly is a little stiff trig Man, his Countenance as Calm and unruffled as a summers sea. He was the most silent Person in Company. ⟨*Mr B V— who has no objection to talking*⟩ Dr Price took a seat between Mrs Vaughan and myself, and Dr Keppis, upon the other side of Mrs Vau, and Mamma. Some person observed that those two Gentlemen were very happily situated. Dr P— said he had the best seat, Mr Wm V— told him that ought to have been his place, but the Dr refused to Change, and said Mr V. had told him before we came that he was to have a young Lady to dine with him to day. The Dr answered he did not know what young Lady would trust herself with him, but he said she had come with her Mother. Mr V. said the Dr after gave him some kind admonitions about Marrying, yet said Dr Price, I never think a young Man safe till he is Married. The Conversation was very sprightly among the oald Gentlemen who all Commended Dr P— galantry. Balloons, Messmarism Witchcraft &c &c, were the subjects of general Conversation, and I had like to have obserd that I thought that Foolish Folks could talk quite as well as Wise ones.

We came home about eight oclock, and Called upon Mrs Shipley the Wife of the Bishop of St Asaph, who's family has visitted us, but were not at home this Eve.[22]

Dft (Adams Papers).

[1] Letter No. 13, not found.

[2] To emphasize the pause, AA2 inserted an entire line of short dashes at this point.

[3] JQA met John Bowdoin, a Virginian, at Jefferson's home in Paris the week before his departure for the United States (*Diary*, 1:262).

[4] Anna Jacoba (Nancy) Dumas (b. 1766), the daughter of JQA's former tutor, married a Mr. Veerman (Jan Willem Schulte Nordholt, *The Dutch Republic and American Independence*, Chapel Hill, N.C., and London, 1979, p. 48; D/JQA/24, 11, 18 Aug. 1796, Adams Papers, Microfilms, Reel No. 27).

[5] JQA to AA2, [26] Oct. 1785 (vol. 6:442–445).

[6] JQA's letter No. 12 to AA2 was presumably that of [26] Oct. 1785 (vol. 6:442–445).

[7] 3 Dec. 1785 (LbC, Adams Papers).

[8] Elbridge Gerry to JA, 8 Nov. 1785 (Adams Papers). Congress resolved on 28 Nov. that their ministers plenipotentiary in Europe assume the duties of consul general for the countries in which they resided (*JCC*, 29:855).

[9] John Hancock was elected president of Congress on 23 Nov. 1785, but a severe attack of gout prevented him from traveling to New York to attend its sessions. He resigned the post on 6 June 1786 (Harlow Giles Unger, *John Hancock: Merchant King and American Patriot*, N.Y., 2000, p. 307–308).

[10] For JA's meeting with William Pitt on 24 Aug. 1785, see vol. 6:296, note 4, and references there.

[11] William Eden presented his credentials as special envoy to France on 4 April. The commercial treaty was signed on 26 Sept. (*Repertorium*, 3:162). For the terms of the treaty see *Cambridge Modern Hist.*, 8:284–285.

[12] Neither the letter of introduction from

Eliphalet Brush nor those from Lafayette have been found.

[13] The treaty with Portugal, although signed by Jefferson and possibly later by JA, was never ratified by either Portugal or the United States. For a complete discussion of the negotiations of the treaty, see Jefferson, *Papers*, 9:xxviii–xxix, 410–433.

[14] While in London Jefferson lodged at No. 14 Golden Square (*Jefferson's Memorandum Books*, 1:623).

[15] Trumbull accepted Jefferson's invitation, spending the month of August with him at the Hôtel de Langeac. In Paris, Trumbull met his publisher, Anthony Poggi, who would arrange for *The Battle of Bunker's Hill* to be engraved in Stuttgart. The artist departed Paris on 9 Sept., traveled the next two months in Germany, and returned to London in November (*Jefferson's Memorandum Books*, 1:635; Jefferson, *Papers*, 10:251; *The Autobiography of Colonel John Trumbull: Patriot-Artist, 1756–1843*, ed. Theodore Sizer, repr., N.Y., 1970, p. 91, 121–122, 146).

[16] The Adamses probably attended the performance at Sadler's Wells, which was known for its shows featuring tumbling, acrobatics, and rope dancing, as well as musical numbers and short plays (*Morning Chronicle and London Advertiser*, 26 April).

[17] This was a performance of Pasquale Anfossi's *I Viaggiatori Felici*, followed by the ballet *Le Premier Navigateur; or, La Force de l'Amour*, choreographed by Maximilien Gardel, at King's Theatre. The ballet featured Marie Auguste Vestris, one of the most celebrated dancers of his day; Giovanna Zanerini, whose stage name was Bacelli; and Mademoiselle Mozon. Zanerini was the mistress of the Duke of Dorset (Hoefer, *Nouv. biog. générale*; *Morning Chronicle and London Advertiser*, 25 April; Ivor Guest, *The Ballet of the Enlightenment: The Establishment of the Ballet d'Action in France, 1770–1793*, London, 1996, p. 205, 272).

[18] Louis Philippe Joseph (1747–1793) succeeded his father as Duc d'Orléans in 1785. He became a leader of the opposition in the Assembly of Notables in 1787, joined the Third Estate in 1789, and changed his name to Citizen Egalité in 1792. Egalité was guillotined during the Reign of Terror. His son became King Louis Philippe of France in 1830 (Hoefer, *Nouv. biog. générale*).

Jacques Charles, Duc de Fitz-James (1743–1805), was the grandson of Jacques Fitz-James, Duc de Berwick (1670–1734), the illegitimate son of James II (*London Chronicle*, 27–29 April; Christophe Levantal, *Ducs et pairs et duchés-pairies laïques à l'époque moderne (1519–1790)*, Paris, 1996, p. 446–448, 592–597).

[19] AA2 wrote "Companions for" above the words "attendants upon."

[20] William Vaughan to JA and AA, 21 April (Adams Papers). Wanstead House, Essex, was built for Richard Child, 1st earl Tylney, see AA to Elizabeth Cranch, 18 July, and note 4, below.

[21] Benjamin and Sarah Manning Vaughan were the elder brother and sister-in-law of William Vaughan. Benjamin (1751–1835), a London merchant, was a good friend of Benjamin Franklin and an American sympathizer. For his unofficial role as Lord Shelburne's confidant in the Paris peace negotiations, see JA, *D&A*, 3:53–54, 57–58, 72, 77–78, 100–101, 103–106. Vaughan's parliamentary career (1792–1794) was cut short when some of his papers containing critical remarks about Pitt's ministry were found in the possession of a French agent. He was examined before the Privy Council on 8 May 1794 and fled Britain later in the month. Vaughan spent the next three years in France and Switzerland before settling in Hallowell, Maine, with his family (*DNB*; Mary Vaughan Marvin, *Benjamin Vaughan, 1751–1835*, Hallowell, Maine, 1979, p. 30–55).

Joseph Priestley (1733–1804), dissenting clergyman and scientist, resided in Birmingham (*DNB*). For JA's relationship with Priestley see JA, *D&A*, 3:189.

Andrew Kippis (1725–1795), dissenting minister in Westminster. Among his many literary works, Kippis undertook the second edition of *Biographia Britannica*, publishing five volumes with a colleague before his death (*DNB*).

Abraham Rees (1743–1825), dissenting minister, pastor of the Old Jewry congregation in London, and encyclopedist. Rees issued the 45-volume *New Cyclopædia; or, Universal Dictionary of Arts and Sciences*, 1802–1820 (same).

[22] Jonathan Shipley (1714–1788), bishop of St. Asaph, was married to Anna Maria Mordaunt (d. 1803); they had five daughters (same). In June, the bishop officiated at the wedding of AA2 and WSS.

John Quincy Adams to Abigail Adams 2d

Braintree, April 15[1] [*i.e.* 25]th, 1786

This is the eighth day it has rained and stormed without intermission, the weather is worse than that of England commonly is.

The parson[2] has been here to-day. Smoked some pipes, was sometimes witty, and always ready to laugh at his own flashes. The vacancy expires to-morrow. The weather has been such that we could not stir out of doors. I have employed my time in reading, writing and taking lessons on the flute, for you must know we are all turning musicians. I never had before an opportunity of paying any steady attention to any musical instrument, now I am settled, in one place for fifteen months, vacancies excepted, and shall be glad for a relaxation from study, to amuse myself with a little music, which you know

> When the soul is press'd with cares
> Awakes it with enlivening airs.[3]

Cambridge, Saturday 29th.

Charles and I came up on Wednesday. I spent the eve on Wednesday at Mr. D.'s,[4] and was again there this afternoon. I saw there a gentleman and heard his name, but do not recollect it, who had a vast deal of small talk with Miss E.[5] upon matrimony and so forth. I think the conversation of this kind is still more ridiculous in this country than it is in Europe; there, the theatres furnish subjects, and there is an opportunity, now and then, of hearing some good critical remarks; but here, complete nonsense is a word not expressive enough of the insipidity and absurdity that reigns in our polite conversation.

The class to which I belong recite this week to the Greek tutor. His name is Jennison; a youth who was chosen tutor before he had been three years out of college; he is not more than twenty-four now: and is very far from being possessed of those qualities which I should suppose necessary for a tutor here. He is so ignorant in Greek, that he displays it sometimes in correcting a scholar that is right, and other times suffering the most absurd constructions to pass unnoticed. We had a capital instance of this no longer ago than this morning, but notwithstanding these circumstances, he is not so unpopular in college as some other characters are, because he is not fond of punishing; he has, upon many occasions, shown his lenity in this way.

My room is directly over his, and am obliged to take the greatest caution to make no noise, for fear of a message from him. The other day a person came into my chamber, and seeing my flute on the table, took it up, and played about a dozen notes. I had immediately a freshman, who came to me with orders to go to Mr. Jennison; he said he would inform me once for all, that he desired I would confine myself for my amusements, to the hours allotted for that purpose. To tell him I did not play would have been of no service, for here you are responsible, not only for what you do yourself, but for whatever is done in your chamber. I have not been used to such subjection, but I find I can submit to it with as good a grace as any body. If there was not such an awful distance between a tutor and a scholar, I should submit to them with equal pleasure and be much better satisfied, but a Turkish bashaw could not be more imperious than they are; nor will they, in any manner, mix with the students so as to give them information upon any subject.

Tuesday 9th.

We attend this week Mr. James, the Latin tutor. He is not very popular, and indeed it would be difficult to point out more than one person belonging to our government that is, that one is Professor Williams; but to return to Mr. Jones [*James*]; no one doubts of his literary qualifications, but he is accused of great partiality towards his own class in general,[6] and towards particular persons; and what makes this more disagreeable to the students is, that his partialities are not in favor of good characters, but are owing rather to interested views. But in this I am only the herald of public fame. Since I have been here, he has shown me no favor, nor any partiality against me. The tutors here, have a right to lay pecuniary punishment on the students for misbehaviour of any kind, and this is the greatest cause of their unpopularity. The tutors often show a fault in their judgment or their justice. If they have a pique against any particular scholar, they will gratify it by punishing him as often as they can possibly find opportunity, and sometimes without any valid reasons at all; but any one who is favored by a tutor, may do almost anything and it will pass by unnoticed; and when the students see one punished for a trifle, and another running into every excess with impunity, it is very natural they should dislike the tutor's conduct. But people out of college say Mr. James is much of a gentlemen, which we have no opportunity of discovering here; for it is entirely inconsistent for a tutor to treat a scholar like a gentleman. How do you think this sets upon your brother's stomach? My chum, who has already graduated, often has the tutors in the chamber. He always informs me of it a short time before, and I never fail of being absent at the time; for if I was to stay, I might be three hours in the room with them, without having a word said to me, or a look at me, unless one of a proud superiority. Such are these giants, who, like the Colossus, bestride the whole length of Harvard College. But you will think it does me good, as it will mortify my vanity and teach me a little humility. I wish it may have this good effect.

Saturday, 13th.

Nothing extraordinary has happened in the course of the week—the same scene continually repeated. My time is taken up much more than I expected it would be. I have adopted a system, which you will immediately see leaves no time: six hours of the day are employed in the public exercises of the college; six for study, six for sleep, and six for exercise and amusements; the principal of which now is my flute. I very seldom go into company out of college, and have been but once to Boston since I came here.

It is usual for every class, in the beginning of the senior year, to choose one of the class, to deliver a Latin valedictory or farewell oration, before the government of the college and the other classes, on the 21st of June next ensuing, the day when the seniors leave college, but this has been neglected by the present senior class till two days ago, when they appointed a youth by the name of Fowle to speak, not a Latin oration, but an English poem, he is quite young but a very pretty poet, I have heard some lines of his read which would do honor to any young man.[7]

Tuesday, 16th.

We recite this week to Mr. Hale, the metaphysical tutor; it would be difficult for me to name one student that loves this man; he is cordially hated even by his own class, which is not the case with the other tutors. Nobody accuses him of partialities in favor of any one; he is equally morose, surly and peevish to all; he has got the nickname of the cur. We this day experienced his ill nature, we had this morning to dispute upon a certain question that he gave out some time since; this is called a forensic. We began at 9 1/2, at 11 Mr. Williams had a philosophical lecture, when the bell rung two or three of those who had read their parts applied for leave to go out and attend Mr. Williams' lecture, and he refused them, so that we must infallibly, have lost a lecture, had not Mr. Williams been so kind as to wait near half an hour for us.

Remember me to all friends, and believe me yours.

J. Q. Adams

MS not found. Printed from AA2, *Jour. and Corr.*, 3:106–112.

[1] This is probably a copying error for "April 25," the correct date of the events of the opening paragraphs (JQA, *Diary*, 2:21).

[2] For Rev. Anthony Wibird, minister of the First Church in Braintree, see vol. 1:146.

[3] A paraphrase of Alexander Pope, *Ode for Music on St. Cecilia's Day*, lines 24–27: "If in the breast tumultuous joys arise, / Music her soft, assuasive voice applies; / Or when the soul is press'd with cares, / Exalts her in enlivening airs."

[4] Francis Dana, an associate justice of the Supreme Judicial Court since 1785, had served as JA's official secretary from 1779 to mid-1781. JQA accompanied Dana to St. Petersburg in 1781, when the latter took up his appointment as minister to Russia, and acted as his private secretary and translator for over a year (JQA, *Diary*, 1:ix–x; *DAB*).

[5] Almy Ellery of Newport, R.I., Dana's sister-in-law (*NEHGR*, 8:318 [Oct. 1854]).

[6] Perhaps a vestige of an archaic Harvard mode in which each tutor was responsible for administering all subjects in the curriculum as well as overseeing the general well-being of an entire class of undergraduates throughout their college career. In 1767 the system was revised and each tutor instructed all classes at the college in specific subject matter (Samuel Eliot Morison, *Harvard College in the Seventeenth Century*, Cambridge, 1936, p. 51–53; Samuel Eliot Morison, *Three Centuries of Harvard, 1636–1936*, Cambridge, 1936, p. 90).

[7] Robert Fowle (1766–1847), Harvard 1786, served as the Episcopal minister of Holderness, N.H., from his ordination in 1791 until his death (*Harvard Quinquennial Cat.*; Samuel Seabury, *A Discourse Delivered in St. John's Church . . . Conferring the Order of Priesthood on The Rev. Robert Fowle, A.M. of Holderness*, Boston, 1791, Evans, No. 23755).

Mary Smith Cranch to Abigail Adams

My Dear Sister Braintree May 7th 1786

Yes my dear Sister I have thought it very long since I have receiv'd a Letter from you and thought it very Strange that you should not write me one line by the January Pacquit when mr cranch receiv'd one from mr Adams.[1] You say you wrote but one Letter by it, but do not tell me who it was too none of your Friends here have receiv'd any, and mr King directed a number of other pioples to mr cranchs care. I have a suspician it was to mr T–l–r, but I have not heard a word about it.[2] Pray tell me who it was too? You Surely did not call the three Lines you inclos'd in the Bundle of news papers a Letter.[3] Your Letter by the Febry. Pacquit came last evening by the Post.[4] Mr King could not find a Private hand to send it by, and truly my Sister, it contains wonderful things. A few more dashes and marks under names would have render'd it more intiligible. I cannot help thinking that mr — has receiv'd its counterpart, for last evening he came home before nine, and went immidiately to Bed. He seldom comes home till after we are abed. I was Saying yesterday morning to Betsy, that nothing would afford me more pleasure than to hear that a cousin of hers was married to a worthy american who would come and settle among us. You have mention'd three in your Letter. If I am to guess among those, I Should Say that Colln H–m–s is the favor'd Man. Eliza says "no. He has been with you but a month!—what then." This is not their first acquaintance. She recolects a mr murray of whom you have given a fine character and whose Letters to Cousin JQA[5] She has seen and admir'd. I hope you do not design to keep us in this Suspence long. It is now very generally known that my Niece has dismiss'd mr T and what it is for, and such universal rejoicing I beleive there never was before upon such an occation. I have thought it my duty to let it be known that she was not influenc'd to do it by any of her Friends, but that his neglect of her had open'd her eyes and made her think with the rest of the World that he was not calculated to make her so happy as she once thought he was. I want to know what Letters were pick'd up from Fletchers wreck.[6] I thought I had not sent one by him. Young and he or cushing Sail'd So near together that I do not know whether some of my Letters might not be put aboard the ceres. Mr T writ by one of them. If you know what, I wish you would tell me. I know he was jealous of us at that time, but without a cause. He in general denys his being dismiss'd. Says there has been some little misunderstanding between them, that some Fiend or other on this side the water has occation'd it. That as soon as he gets his mills going and his Business into good order, he Shall visit you, and shall Settle the matter in half an hour. But what does He mean by keeping the things and Letters She desir'd him to deliver to Doctor Tufts?[7] Will he wish to keep and wear the Picture when the origanal is in the possession of another?

I have written you largly by capn. Calhahan and hope they will reach you Safe but we have many fears about him. His vessel was So crank when She went out that many have thought she would overset if She Should meet with a heavey storm. The *importance* of Doctor Gordons History may save it. He and his History are on board. His Lady[8] is with him also, and several other Ladies. Your Sons were well a few days ago. The two colegians spent an agreable vacancy here, for us it was so and I hope for themselves. They look'd very happy. I had miss N Marsh here all the time to help us. It is no small job to keep three Such Lads in repair. Eliza says she is sure she came home in the right time to make Gowns and wastcoats for them. Cousin charles must be equipt for the expiration of his Freshmanship. I have got him a Gown too. I was determin'd to please my Fancy if it could be done in Boston and I have done it. I hope he will think it as handsome as I do.

Mr Evans was married last thursday. He set out on monday for Philadelphia upon a visit to his Friends. His Lady goes with him. He will return to his charge in about two months.[9]

I hope you will not forget to send some linnen both course and fine for your sons. Charles Storer is going to Settle at the eastward there is nothing to be done at Boston to any purpose. We have not had a line from mr Perkins Since the Letter I mention'd to you last Fall.[10] Mr Storer had some thoughts of going to Kentucky some time past, but he has alter'd his plan. He is indeed a fine youth. I could have wisht to have keept him among us. I do not recollect the Poem address'd to our army which you mention but I will inquir for it.[11] Pray send me any thing that you approve of. We Want Something new. We go out but Seldom and want Something to vary our scene. Mr —— is nothing to us, he Sleeps here and that is all. My dear Niece need not fear that the world will charge her with fickleness or infidelity. Mrs P–l–r may and will I know.[12] She means well but is not always judicious. I wish cousin to be very cautious in writing to her.

I long to have cushing come in. We begin to be anxious about him. We are all well, your Mother Hall and Brothers Family also. Our children will write as soon as they recieve Letters. What is the reason that cousin Nabby has not written to any of us for so long a time. Tell Ester[13] her Freinds are in general Well. Ned Baxters wife has been sick but is better. Yours affectionatly M Cranch

RC (Adams Papers).

[1] Probably JA to Richard Cranch, 12 Dec. 1785 (LbC, Adams Papers).

[2] AA wrote to Royall Tyler in December (not found). See AA to Mary Smith Cranch, 13 June 1786, below.

[3] AA to Richard Cranch, 23 Dec. 1785 (not found). Cranch acknowledges its receipt in his letter to AA of 13 April 1786, above.

[4] Of 26 Jan., above.

[5] William Vans Murray to JQA, 2 Aug. 1785 (Adams Papers).

[6] JQA's letter to AA2 of 20–28 Aug. 1785 was rescued from the water (vol. 6:287–292).

[7] Cotton Tufts had been asked to collect a miniature of AA2 and the letters she sent to Royall Tyler (vol. 6:285, 287).

[8] Elizabeth Field Gordon, sister of London apothecary John Field (*DAB*, William Gordon).

[9] Rev. Israel Evans and Huldah Kent were married 2 May in Charlestown by Rev. Joseph Eckley of Boston's Old South Church (Boston, *30th Report*, p. 78; *Massachusetts Centinel*, 6 May; Sprague, *Annals Amer. Pulpit*, 2:137–140).

[10] Thomas Perkins of Bridgewater, Harvard 1779, tutored the Adams and Cranch children in the early 1780s. Perkins settled in western Virginia, now Kentucky, and prac-

ticed law (vol. 4:309). Perkins wrote to Elizabeth Cranch on 1 March 1785, a letter which was subsequently published anonymously in *The Boston Magazine*, Sept. 1785, p. 342–345 (Mary Smith Cranch to AA, 14 Aug. 1785, vol. 6:268–275).

[11] David Humphreys, *A Poem, Addressed to the Armies of the United States of America*. See AA to Mary Smith Cranch, 26 Jan., above.

[12] Elizabeth Hunt Palmer.

[13] Esther Field, AA's servant.

John Quincy Adams to Abigail Adams

My Dear Mamma — Cambridge May 15th 1786. Monday

Several months have again elapsed, since, I wrote you,[1] but I shall henceforth, be able to spare more Time, than I could since I went to Haverhill before this. There is now neither the Necessity, nor indeed the possibility, for me to keep as close, as I was in the Winter. I was obliged in the Course of 6 months, to go through the studies, which are perform'd here, in 2 years and 9 months. So different had my Studies been, from those, at this Place, that I had not before last October look'd into a book, that I was examined in except Horace. Had I arrived here 3 months earlier, it would have been easier to enter into the Class, which graduates next Commencement, than it has been to enter the one I am in. This would have advanced me, one year, but there are a number of public exercices here, that I should not have performed and which I think may be advantageous. Such is speaking in the Chapel, before all the Classes; which I shall have to do in my turn 4 or 5 times, before we leave College. Such also, are the forensic disputations, one of which we are to have to-morrow. A Question is given out by the Tutor in metaphysics, for the whole Class to dispute upon; they alternately affirm or deny the Question; and, write each, two or three pages, for or against it, which is read in the Chapel before the Tutor, who finally gives his opinion concerning the Question. We have two or three of these Questions every Quarter; that for to-morrow is, Whether the immortality of the human Soul is probable from natural Reason. It comes in Course, for me, to affirm; and in this Case, it makes the task much easier. But It so happens, that whatever the Question may be, I must support it; I shall send a Copy of my Piece, to my Father, although I doubt it will scarcely be worth reading.[2]

You will be perhaps desirous to know, how I am pleased with my Situation, how I like my fellow Students, and what acquaintances I have formed. I am very well pleased, as to the first matter. There are a few inconveniences, and some necessary loss of Time, that I must be subjected to; but I never was able any where to Study, more agreeably, and with so little interruption, (excepting the exercices of the College) as I am here. I cannot now attend so much to any particular branch, as I have done formerly. The languages, natural Philosophy, mathematics, and metaphysics; all together, will employ any one sufficiently, without making a rapid progress in either of them. We are now attending a Course of Lectures upon experimental Philosophy, by Mr. Williams. They will be finished by the 21st: of June, when the Senior Sophister Class, leave College; they will consist of 24 Lectures, 9 of which we have already had. As to the Students, I find, a confused medley of good, bad, and indifferent. There is but little intercourse, between the Classes. I am acquainted with very few of the other Classes. I know all, that belong to my own. I have endeavoured to find out those, that have the best Reputation, both, as Students, and moral Characters. Those will be my Companions; and fortunately I am left to my choice, for we are not obliged to associate with those, who are dissolute or negligent. These two Qualities I perceive most commonly go together: the instances, are very rare, where a person of a loose Character, makes any figure as a Scholar.

Friday. May 19th:[3]

I received your favour of March 20th: the day before yesterday, and I receiv'd a hint of a certain Circumstance, by a Letter from Aunt Cranch, to my Cousin, at the same Time. I do not know, that ever in my Life, I felt so much anxiety, and impatience, as I have, from that Time, till this Afternoon, when your's of Feby. 16th: was delivered into my hands, with my Sister's Diary to Feby. 15th: nor did I ever feel such strange Sensations, as at reading the first Page of my Sister's Letter, where in the most delicate, manner possible, she inform'd me of the Connection. I laid it down immediately, and for 5 minutes, I was in such a Confusion of thoughts, as berieved me of almost every feeling. It would be as impossible for me now to account for my Situation, as it was then to form an Idea. I could not read a word further there, and I took up your's, in which I found an ample account of the affair, and indeed, as you observed the Contrast was striking. Surely, if there is a providence, that directs the affairs of mankind, it prompted your Voyage to Europe. I intended in this Letter to have given you an account of the late Conduct of a certain person, but we may now throw a veil over the errors of a Man, whose folly, has deprived him, of the Advantages which Nature, with a liberal hand, had bestow'd upon him. The Gentleman, you mention, enjoys a Reputation, which has always commanded my Respect; I wish henceforth to esteem him as a friend, and cherish him as a brother: as Circumstances have prevented me, from enjoying a personal acquaintance with him, his connection, with a Sister, as dear to me as my Life, and the Opinion of my Parents, will stand in lieu of it. Will you be so kind, as to remember me affectionately to him? The Books I have not received, nor any Letter from my Sister, by Lyde, or Cushing, who both arrived, last Tuesday.

I believe you have Reason, to think it fortunate for me, that I did, not go to London. Your description of Miss Hamilton, and that of my Sister, who mentions her in almost every Letter I have received, since their first acquaintance, are almost enough, to raise a Romantic, Knight Errant flame; what then would have been the Consequence, had I seen her often; but what with a little Resolution, and some good luck, your young Hercules, has till now escaped, the darts of the blind Deity: and will be for 15 months very secure: there is now no Lady, with whom I am acquainted around here, that I consider, as dangerous; Study is my mistress, and my endeavours will be to

"Listen to no female, but the Muse."

By the bye, you know I am now and then addicted to the rage of rhyming. I shall enclose to my Sister a short speciman, of my loss of Time in that way. If your candour and indulgence, is such, as to think it worth crossing the Atlantic I shall be fully satisfied.[4]

But it is now midnight, and I must be up by 6. and this as well as my Paper bids me, come to the Conclusion of my Letter; my Duty to my Father. I fear I shall not get a Letter for him by this opportunity. Your dutiful Son. J. Q. Adams

RC (Adams Papers); endorsed: "J Q Adams May 15 1786."

[1] JQA to AA, 28 Dec. 1785 (vol. 6:503–506).

[2] JQA copied his essay into his Diary on the date of its presentation (*Diary*, 2:32–34). No other copy has been found, but this may have been the "Dialogue" for which JA thanked JQA in his letter on 10 Jan. 1787, below.

[3] JQA probably started the continuation of the letter on the 18th, because he received AA's letter of 20 March (above) on 16 May and both AA's letter of 16 Feb. (above) and AA2's letter No. 11 ending on 15 Feb. (not found) on the 18th (same, 2:35).

[4] Possibly "An Epistle to Delia," a poem by JQA, which he completed on 12 Dec. 1785 (M/JQA/28, Adams Papers, Microfilms, Reel No. 223). Delia was the name JQA gave to Anna (Nancy) Hazen, a young woman who lived with the Shaws for over a year, and for whom JQA briefly had formed an attachment (vol. 5:473, 476; JQA, *Diary*, 1:321, 400–401; 2:96). AA2 acknowledges seeing the verses to Delia in her letter of 22 July, below.

John Quincy Adams to Abigail Adams 2d

Cambridge, Friday, May 18, 1786[1]

I received this afternoon your No. 11 and I never received a letter which caused such a variety of sensations. I will only say, that I received the profile with pleasure, and the person for whom it was taken will for the future be very dear to me.

It is very disagreeable to be continually making apologies for having nothing to write; but it is really so, I am more than ever out of a situation to write anything that you can think worth reading. I have heretofore sometimes had recourse to giving you sketches of character, and sometimes to moralizing, but I am now deprived even of those sources. Pedants like most of the characters among the government of our college, and of boys, as a great part of the students are, could afford you but a pitiful entertainment, and you have given me such a rap on the knuckles with respect to proverbs and wise sayings, that I must take care how I show my gravity. I believe, upon the whole, that the philosophy of Democritus, who laughed at all the world, was preferable to that of Heraclitus, who was always weeping. The follies of the world made one very unhappy, while they rather increased the enjoyments of the other;[2] for my part, when I reflect upon all the plans and schemes, the ceremonious nothings, the pompous trifles which men are always employed about, it sometimes raises a smile, and sometimes a sigh, when I behold vices and follies which lessen the natural dignity of human nature and which injure society, then I cannot restrain my indignation; but when they are only such as the little greatness of a self-conceited coxcomb, or such as have their source in vanity, I can then indulge all the ludicrous ideas which naturally arise in my mind; these have sometimes assisted me to fill up a letter to you; but as to proverbs and wise sayings, I am not ambitious of producing any. I will endeavor henceforth to change my style, and follow your example, in employing satirical irony, and leave you to your own reflections.

Tuesday, 23d.

I have, in former letters, given you a short sketch of the characters of two or three members of this government. The next that comes in course is Mr. R., the tutor of my own class.[3] This man, too, like all the rest, is very much disliked by the scholars. He has a great deal of modesty, and this is a disadvantage to him here. He is passionate and vindictive; and those are qualities which do not fequently inspire love or esteem. In short, our four tutors present as ridiculous a group as I ever saw. They appear all to be in a greater necessity of going to school themselves than of giving instruction; and one of them, at least, is below par as to genius. He is, however, the best of the tutors. He possesses a sweet simplicity, which creates a great deal of mirth among the students; and as he has observed that the other tutors command respect by maintaining an awful distance between themselves and the students, he likewise assumes an air of dignity, which is quite becoming. You would suppose that this immense distance between tutors and scholars was impolitic; but in fact it is quite the contrary. Were these gentlemen to be frequently in company with some of the good scholars among the students, the comparison would be too much to their disadvantage not to be mortifying and humiliating.

We have been in somewhat of a bustle this day. The parts for next commencement were given out this morning. It is curious to observe how the passions of men are adapted to the situations in which they are placed. You must know that about two-thirds of every class have to read syllogisms when they take their degrees. Now, these syllogisms are held in abomination by the students, because the other parts are commonly given to the most distinguished scholars. A syllogism is considered as a diploma, conferring the degree of dunce to all to whom it is given.[4] All the senior sophisters have been waiting the giving out of the parts for three weeks, with as much impatience and anxiety as if their lives and fortunes depended upon it; and there are not, I suppose, now more than half-a-dozen in the class that are satisfied. This time twelve-months the case will be the same with the class to which I belong. But I must inform you, that the president, who distributes the parts, is by no means infallible; that he gives good parts sometimes to bad scholars, and syllogisms to good ones. So, you must not hastily conclude that I am a fool, or an ignoramus, in case I should have to read a syllogism; which, for two or three reasons, I think is probable enough. But it is not necessary to look so far before us.

Saturday, 27th.

I have been thinking, I believe a full hour what to say to you, and am now as much at a loss as when I first began.

I have been out of town but once this quarter,[5] and I see no company out of college. I have nothing to draw me from my studies, (but the college exercises,) and I keep as close to them as I can conveniently; but it is the same thing continually repeated, and can therefore furnish very little matter for a journal.

The next character, which follows in course among the governors of the college, is the librarian, Mr. W.[6] He is a man of genius and learning, but without one particle of softness, or of anything that can make a man amiable, in him. He is, I am told, severe in his remarks upon the ladies; and they are not commonly disposed to be more favorable with respect to him. It is observed that men are always apt to despise, what they are wholly ignorant of. And this is the reason, I take it, why so many men of genius and learning, that have lived retired and recluse lives, have been partial against the ladies. They have opportunity to observe only their follies and foibles, and therefore conclude that they have no virtues. Old bachelors too are very apt to talk of sour grapes; but if Mr. W. ever gets married, he will be more charitable towards the ladies, and I have no doubt but he will be more esteemed and beloved than he is now, he cannot be less.

Wednesday, 31st. Election day.

This, you know, is the only day in the year, which resembles what in France is called a jour de fête. Almost all the college went to Boston. I have no great curiosity to see such things and therefore remained at home. The elections have been in general the same with those of the last year, excepting that in Boston they have turned out Mr. Hitchborne from the House of Representatives, and Mr. Lowell from the Senate.[7] This is supposed to be in consequence of some writings which have appeared in the newspapers under the signature of Honestus, against the lawyers. They were written by Mr. Benjamin Austin, a merchant, and it is supposed will considerably injure the practice of the law. They are intended to rouse and inflame the passions of the people. His proposals are in general as extravagant and absurd as they can be, yet to a certain degree they have been successful, and they may be still more so.[8]

Saturday, June 10th.

This day Mr. Williams closes his course of lectures on Natural Philosophy. He has given us of late two or three lectures upon fire, containing a system of his own with respect to Northern Lights. This is a phenomenon which has never yet been well accounted for. This new system is specious and may lead to further discoveries on this subject. Mr. Williams is more generally esteemed by the students, I think, than any other member of this government. He is more affable and familiar with the students, and does not affect that ridiculous pomp which is so generally prevalent here. The only complaint that I have heard made against him was of his being too fond of his ease, and unwilling to make any great efforts for acquiring a perfect knowledge of the branch which he professes. I believe he is a very good man, but I must see more proofs of genius than I have yet observed before I shall think him a great man.

I am very glad his lectures are over. The weather is now so warm that to be shut up in a room with a hundred people, is enough to stifle one. At one of the lectures, two or three days since, Thompson, the most distinguished character in the senior class, fainted away, and has been ill ever since.[9]

As to news, I can only inform you of two marriages and one courtship. I have heard Mr. G. is humbly paying his addresses to your friend Miss Q. So, you see, I shall probably be supplanted, notwithstanding my prior claim, and he has great advantages over me, as it is against the law for me to look at a young lady till the 20th of July, 1787,[10] and then I suppose it will be too late. Indeed, I am almost determined to write one of your lamentable love songs, talk of flames, darts, perjured vows, death, and so on, according to custom. Death, you know, in romances and love-songs, is one of the most busy actors. When lovers are happy, they say death only can part them; when they are unsuccessful, death is always ready immediately to relieve them from pain. In short, death appears to be a jack-of-all-trades, but I have never been able to discover who or what he is. However, I don't see why I should not invoke him, upon occasion, as well as any body; for in poetry he is the most innocent being on earth.

Saturday, June 17th.

This day the bridge between Boston and Charlestown was completed. An entertainment was given upon the occasion by the proprietors, to six hundred people, on Bunker's Hill. It is the anniversary of the famous battle fought there. It is better, to be sure, that oxen, sheep, calves, and fowls be butchered than men; and it is better that wine should be spilled than blood; but I do not think this was a proper place for revelling and feasting. The idea of being seated upon the bones of a friend, I should think would have disgusted many. Such feelings may be called prejudices, but they are implanted by nature, and cannot, I think, be blamed.[11] You will see in the papers how the poets have been exerting their talents upon the occasion. I have seen five different sets of verses, not one of which has escaped the simile of the Phœnix rising from its own ashes, applied to Charlestown.

I have written to papa and mamma lately. You will present my duty to them.

Yours, J. Q. Adams

MS not found. Printed from AA2, *Jour. and Corr.*, 3:112–120.

[1] JQA probably began the letter on Thursday the 18th, the day he received AA2's letter No. 11, not found (*Diary*, 2:35).

[2] Greek philosophers Democritus and Heraclitus, known respectively as the laughing and weeping philosophers (Simon Hornblower and Anthony Spawforth, eds., *The Oxford Classical Dictionary*, 3d edn., 1996).

[3] Nathan Read.

[4] For JQA's additional comments on the disdain with which class members viewed the syllogistics, see *Diary*, 2:37–38.

[5] JQA and Leonard White went to Boston for the day on 4 May (same, 2:27).

[6] James Winthrop, Harvard 1769, was college librarian 1772–1787. Winthrop held numerous judicial appointments, ending his public career as chief justice of the Court of Common Pleas. He never married (*Sibley's Harvard Graduates*, 17:317–329).

[7] Benjamin Hichborn, Harvard 1768, a Boston lawyer and John Lowell, Harvard 1760, formerly of Newburyport, a justice of the U.S. Court of Appeals (same, 14:650–661, 17:36–44).

[8] Benjamin Austin Jr., a Boston merchant, published a series of articles in the *Independent Chronicle* between March and June under the name of Honestus that assailed the Commonwealth's legal system and demanded the abolition of the professional bar (*DAB*).

[9] Thomas W. Thompson of Boston was assigned the premier part, the English oration, at the upcoming commencement but because of illness was unable to attend the ceremony. Thompson studied law with JQA in Theophilus Parsons' Newburyport office, settled in New Hampshire, and served in that state's legislature as well as in the U.S. Senate (JQA, *Diary*, 2:37–38, 275; *Biographical Directory of the American Congress, 1774–1927*, Washington, 1928).

[10] The approximate date of JQA's graduation from Harvard.

[11] JQA viewed the Battle of Bunker Hill with AA from a vantage point atop Penn's Hill in Braintree in 1775. The brutality of the conflict and the death of family friend Dr. Joseph Warren deeply affected him. He repeated his distaste for the revels on the site of the battlefield in his Diary entry on this day and disapprovingly noted that "to crown the whole, The head of the table, was I hear placed on the very spot where the immortal Warren fell" (*Diary*, 2:50–51). For JQA's reminiscences of 17 June 1775 and his lifelong displeasure with celebrations connected to the day, see vol. 1:223–224.

Elizabeth Cranch to Abigail Adams

My dear Aunt Braintree May 20th 1786

We have sat off our English Friends[1] for Boston. Mama has accompanied them; Sister Lucy has gone to your deserted habitation, and taken our Boy with her to clean the closets, rub the furniture &c. The dampness for want of Fires being kept in the Rooms moulds the things very much, and makes the Paper peal off, and it requires considerable care, to keep them in tolerably good order. And here is your Eliza left entirely alone. I would recollect my thoughts and arrange them in some degree of order if possible, but they have been so confused for some time past that I fear tis impracticable; The arrival of my Cousins this week, the reception of Letters from you by Lyde and Cushing,[2] who came in this week also, together with the intelligence relative to my Cousin contain'd in yours, has quite turned my head, and I feel now as if I had just awoke from a dream.

You think some of *my* Letters must have miscaried as you have recd. none since that by Mr Wilson; Tis no wonder my Aunt should be loth to suppose her Neice capable of so great neglect, as she must prove herself to be, when she makes the mortifying confession, that She has not once written since that time! I will not attempt an apology: my future attention, must prove, my penitence and reformation.

I did not return from Haverhill, till the 17th of April, *only* a *Visit* of 7 months,! two of which I spent with my dear and amiable Aunt. I have pass'd the Winter *very happily*: Society and Amusements pleasing; Friends, attentive and sincere; *Health* my companion doubly pleasing, as long unenjoy'd; A heart (usually) at ease, and a mind perfectly disposed to relish and enjoy, all the good or pleasure which the bountiful hand of Heaven is pleased to spread before me; with all these blessings, why Should not I be happy? My Cousin JQA–s company afforded me much pleasure, he was very good to visit us often at Mr Whites. He is a great favourite with that family, I believe Mr W— (natturally indifferent) never paid so much attention to any Person before; or felt a greater esteem. And as for my Friend Peggy, if she had not have lost *her* heart before,[3] She would have stood no chance of securing it this winter. O! tis a *comfortable* thing to have ones heart secure, either in our own possession, or in the hands of one, who will *treat* and *value* it as their own.

You have puzzled us my dear Aunt most amazingly with respect to my Cousin; I want to write to her, but for my heart I dont know how to address her; whether as Mrs S—h Mrs H–p–s, or Miss A. I hope however, notwithstanding *all changes*, I may still call her *my* Friend, and be acknowledg'd as *hers*. Yesterday Mama recd. a small parcel from you containing a Crape Apron, and a peice of Ribbon wound upon a *visiting Card*. Curiosity induced some of us to read it. It was read and thrown by, I took it, and said instantly, it is my Cousins writing—what should *she* fill up a Card for Mr and Mrs Smith for?

and who are they? Upon the whole we concluded it must be, even herself and Husband, and that this ingenious scheme for informing us of her marriage was of my good Aunts inventing. To finish the matter, we put the Card up in our *post Office* (by the side of my picture you know) and placed it before a Letter directed to Mr ⟨*T.*⟩—which was deposited their till his return, supposing *He* could very *easily* discern if it was *her* writing—was it cruel? Compassion! tenderness! Generosity! all, all forgive us if it was! The temptation was irisistable: perhaps, he knew it all before, and perhaps *we* are mistaken, another person may write exactly like my Cousin.[4]

You enquire, how your fruit Trees flourish. Phoebe says the Peach trees are decaying, the others are in good condition. The Laylocks are just opening, and have grown very much.

The grass Plot before the house looks most delightfully green. I went and stood at the door the day before Yesterday, and could not help thinking, how often *you* had ocupied the same place and with how much satisfaction you used to observe the dayly increasing Verdure; Could you my dear Aunt look upon it *now* do you think, with the same pleasure you formally did? Your Cottage *then* had *charms* and its appearance was equal or superior, to any in the Village; Could you return to it now, and after comparing it with the splendor and elegance of your present habitation, still pronounce it pleasing, still find it the abode of contemtment, of rational enjoyment and domestick peace? O! if you could how happy should *We* be! I took some encouragment to hope from one expression in your last Letter to me, that you *did* think of returning. You say "how shall I *leave* your Cousin?" Unpleasing as the Idea is to me of her settling so far from us, your connecting it, with the truly pleasing one of *your* return, divested it of some of its dissagreableness and rendered it more surportable; but I must hope it will not be always. I cannot, cannot, consent to it! I am sure she cannot be so happy in Europe. Tho the possessing the sincere and affectionate attachment of one worthy Heart, may be to *her* the first of blessings, yet, how much more might enjoy *that* here, in the midst of friends interested for her and who would greatly encrease her happiness, by being the pleasd witnesses of it. She must indeed return.

You inquire about the flower seeds, you was so good as to send me. They came too late for planting last year; I sent for them to Haverhill this winter, to take out some for Mr Dalton, who has a beautiful Garden at Newbury.[5] The remainder I put up in my Trunk to bring home, but to my great dissapointment I cannot yet get it brought from H—. I am very much affraid they will be too old, I shall however try them in Pots, and distribute, some to my Friends who are curious in that way. Mr Apthorp[6] makes great dependance upon rearing some of them. He has had a very pretty Fence before his House since you went away, and made the enclosure look very neat and elegant.

I hope you will congratulate us upon the *probability* of a new Fence to *Our* Garden. Mr A— has long been ashamed of *ours*, for us, and indeed we have stood in need of one. It is to be like Genll. Warrens, the materials for it are gatherd togather in the Yard, as also for a new Barn, which is as far advanced as *framing*.

I am exceedingly obligd to you my dear Aunt, for your kind attention to me and my Sister, we shall ever retain a grateful remembrance of your goodness. Mama informs you of all the News. She writes so largely, that she leaves very little for me to say. I have read the Poem you was so good as to send me and am much pleasd with—but accidentally, I suppose, in the sewing, 4 Pages are wanting, just at the conclusion. I was very sorry as it leaves it quite unconnected.

I hope you will be so good as to continue to write to me. Your Letters in some measure compensate for, and fill up that dreadful Chasm which your absence makes, in our enjoyments and which would otherwise be quite insuportable. Please to offer my respectful and affectionate regards to my Uncle. I shall write my Cousin by the next Vessel, which will sail a few days, after this. I have not had but one Letter from her since her Brothers arrival—tis Strange!

I am my dear Aunt with the Sincerest Love & gratitude your obligd & Affectionate Neice
Eliza Cranch

RC (Adams Papers); endorsed: "Betsy Cranch May 20th 1786."

[1] See Richard Cranch to JA, 20 May, below.

[2] AA2 to Elizabeth Cranch, 14 Feb.; AA to Mary Smith Cranch, 21 March and 6 April; AA to Elizabeth Cranch, 2 April; and AA to Lucy Cranch, 2 April, all above.

[3] Peggy White lost her heart to Bailey Bartlett; the two married on 21 Nov. (*Vital Records of Haverhill Massachusetts to the End of Year 1849*, 2 vols., Topsfield, Mass., 1910–1911, 2:329).

[4] The visiting card was not an announcement of AA2's marriage. The William Smiths of Clapham left the card at Grosvenor Square. See AA to Mary Smith Cranch, 4 July, below.

[5] Elizabeth Cranch sent the flower seeds to Ruth Dalton, daughter of Tristram Dalton, a Newburyport merchant and one of JA's classmates at Harvard. Dalton served in the Massachusetts House of Representatives, 1782–1785, and Senate, 1786–1788, as well as the U.S. Senate, 1789–1791. At one time the wealthiest citizen of Newburyport, Dalton lost his fortune and ended his days as surveyor of the port of Boston.

Dalton's countryseat, Spring Hill, located on the Merrimack River, was admired by many for its terraced garden, fruit trees, hot house, dairy, and picturesque view of the surrounding countryside (Ruth Dalton to Elizabeth Cranch, 8 April, MHi:Jacob Norton Papers; *Sibley's Harvard Graduates*, 13:569–578; Eben F. Stone, "A Sketch of Tristram Dalton," Essex Inst., *Hist. Colls.*, 25:1–29 [Jan.–March 1888]; *Recollections of Samuel Breck with Passages from His Note-Books (1771–1862)*, ed. H. E. Scudder, Phila., 1877, p. 97–99).

[6] James Apthorp (1731–1799), the Cranch family's neighbor (John Wentworth, *The Wentworth Genealogy: English and American*, 3 vols., Boston, 1878, 1:519–520). For JQA's thoughts on Apthorp, see *Diary*, 1:329–331; 2:247, 267.

Richard Cranch to John Adams

Dear Bror Boston May 20th. 1786

We have received the Favour of your Letters and those from Sister Adams, by the Captains Cushing and Lyde. Cushing arrived on Sunday last and Lyde on Monday.

I thank you for the further explanation of your Sentiments respecting the probable Operation of our Navigation Act, and think they are well founded. I think what you mention about the Sugar Trade with France in return for our Oil, is a matter of vast Importance to the N England States, and may be prosecuted to great Advantage by our Merchants. The Vessell said to belong to Tom: B— is this week arrived at Boston with a Cargo of Sugars from France; and, it is reported, will make a fine Voyage. I have not time at present to write on publick Matters—a great Cry in some Parts of the State for Paper Money—great aversion to it in others—probably it will be warmly agitated in the lower House, perhaps carried there: But I think it will not pass the Senate. R: Island has just passed an Act for making an Emission of Paper Money, to be on landed Security, but it is greatly opposed and remonstrated against by their principal Towns.[1]

The Votes for Govr. and Lt. Govr. in this State are returned, and are said to be full in favour of Govr Bowdoin and Lt Govr Cushing. Senators are much the same thro' the State as last Year. In this County all but Mr. Lowell came in by the People. Mr Lowell and Mr. Ben: Austin (the Father of J: L: Austin) are the Candidates. In Worcester is one Vacancy, Mr Sprague the Lawyer did not come in by the People. He and Genl. Ward are the Candidates.[2] Our Friend Doctr. Tufts is unanimously chosen for Member for Weymouth, as well as Senator by the highest number of Votes in the County. Your Sons at the University, and Master Tom: at Haverhill are well. Cous: Charles was here this Week. They behave unblameably as far as I can learn, and follow their Studies with the greatest Attention. I have not heard a Complaint or Suggestion against either of them. They and Billy make an agreeable young Triumvirate, and are very happy together. My Kinsman Mr. Wm: Bond, who married Mrs. Elworthy's Sister, arrived here safe from Bristol with his Wife and two Children and her Sister Ebut, after a very agreeable Passage, on Saturday last.[3] The Ladies and Children went up to Braintree last Wednesday, where they are at present at our House. They expect to sail for Falmouth in Casco Bay the first fair Wind. You will please to let Cousn Elworthy know this. Your Hond. Mother and your Bror. and Family are all well, as are all the Circle of our near Connections.

May 22d.

Since writing the above we have received your favours by Mrs. Hay who is safe arrived at Boston. I thank you for the learned and very valuable account of Virginia by Govr. Jefferson, which you sent me, and shall follow your injunctions respecting it. I have diped into it in various places, and find his Natural History of that Country to be very curious, and his Observations on the Varieties among the Human Species, particularly with respect to the Indians and Blacks, to be ingenious and worthy of a Philosopher. His Argument drawn from Fact in favour of american Genious, would be greatly strengthened, if, to a Washington, a Franklin and a Rittenhouse,[4] we should add a Jefferson.[5]

Your favour of the 11th. of March contains Matters of vast moment to all the United States, but more especially to those concerned in the Cod-Fishery. I mean the american Commerce with Britain, and the War with the Moors. But as I am in hourly expectation that Capt. Barnard will sail for London, and fearing lest I should loose this Oportunity of acknowledging the receipt of your and Sister Adams's obliging Favours, I must postpone the Consideration of those important and interesting Matters for the present.

You ask what is become of the Art of making Saltwater fresh? I think it is come to nothing, and that our old Friend *Pater* West has been imposed on by a worthless Fellow, who is now said to be run off and left him in the lurch. Mr West like many other recluse Men, tho' very learned, is credulous and open to Imposition.[6] I hear he is greatly mortified.

The Coins, if they be so called, found at Mistick, have been a Subject of Speculation. They are extremely inelegant in their Form, and the [impre]ssions very few and clumsy. I rather think they are

[nei]ther of Phoenician nor Moorish Original; but that they were a kind of Substitute for the Indian Wampum, and used by our first Settlers in their Trade with the Natives while in their rude and most simple State. I will endeavour to send you some of them.

I herewith send you a Packett of Letters from our Family to yours, and shall only add my most affectionate Regards to your deservedly dear Partner, and most amiable Daughter; assuring you that I am with the highest Esteem your obliged Friend and Brother.

Richard Cranch

RC (Adams Papers); addressed: "To His Excellency John Adams Esqr: L. L. D. Minister from the United States of America at the Court of Great Britain. Grosvenor Square, Westminster"; stamped: "COWES SHIP LRES"; notation: "3/3½" and "5/11"; endorsed: "Mr Cranch. May. 20. Ansd. July. 4. 1786." Some loss of text where the seal was removed.

[1] In an effort to control the state's internal debt, the Rhode Island legislature passed an act to print 100,000 pounds in paper currency to issue as loans in return for mortgages on real estate. Additional legislation required creditors to accept the paper money or forfeit the amount of the loan and be subject to a fine. Every delegate from the towns of Providence, Newport, Bristol, Portsmouth, and Westerly opposed the initiative, which was enacted at the behest of Rhode Island farmers (Boston *Independent Ledger*, 15 May; Daniel P. Jones, *The Economic and Social Transformation of Rural Rhode Island, 1780–1850*, Boston, 1992, p. 30–31).

[2] John Sprague (1740–1800) had represented Lancaster, Worcester County, in the state House of Representatives from 1782 to 1785, and in the state Senate from 1785 to 1786; he was not reelected in 1786 (*Doc. Hist. Ratif. Const.*, 6:1187).

Gen. Artemas Ward (1727–1800), having served numerous positions in state government as well as representing Massachusetts in Congress, was reelected as the representative from Shrewsbury, Worcester County, and also chosen to serve as speaker of the house by a near unanimous vote (Mass., *Acts and Laws*, Resolves of 1786, ante May sess.; *Sibley's Harvard Graduates*, 12:326–348).

[3] William Bond of Kingsbridge, England, and his wife Hannah Cranch, the niece of Richard Cranch and sister of Elizabeth Cranch Elworthy, emigrated to Falmouth (now Portland, Maine). Hannah's younger sister Ebbett died in Falmouth in 1789. By 1796, Bond was established as a watchmaker in Boston (Extract from a Register of the Bond and Cranch Families, 1852, MHi: Cranch-Bond Papers; *Boston Directory*, 1796; "Richard Cranch and His Family," *NEHGR*, 27:41 [Jan. 1873]).

[4] Jefferson's *Notes on the State of Virginia* included his response to the Abbé Raynal's observation that America had not yet produced "a man of genius" in any of the arts or sciences (Jefferson, *Notes on the State of Virginia*, ed. William Peden, Chapel Hill, N.C., 1955, p. 64–65).

[5] Cranch emphasized the name "Jefferson" by writing it in oversized letters.

[6] Rev. Samuel West, Harvard 1754, minister of the First Congregational Society in Dartmouth, now New Bedford, was taken in by Mr. Allen's claims that he could desalinate seawater. West brought Allen's "discovery" to the attention of the American Academy of Arts and Sciences and had also "written a pompous account of this affair to the Ambassador of the Court of London" (*Sibley's Harvard Graduates*, 13:501–510; *Massachusetts Centinel*, 4 Feb.; John Eliot to Jeremy Belknap, 8 Feb., *The Belknap Papers*. Part III, MHS, *Colls.*, 6th ser., 4 [1891]:308–309). For Allen's scheme, see JA to Richard Cranch, 11 March, note 5, above.

Abigail Adams to Mary Smith Cranch

My Dear sister London May 21 1786

Your kind Letter of Feb'ry came safe to hand, and proved my assertion, that I was sure you had written to me tho it did not reach me by the post. As Letters are always Subject to inspection when put into the bag, it is not best to trust any thing improper for a News paper by that conveyance unless addrest to some merchant, which address prevents curiosity. In writing to you, I am not under that apprehension, my Letters going immediately to the place of their destination. I had as leaves trust them in the Bag as by a private hand.

I presume before this reaches you you will be fully satisfied with regard to the Subject you wrote me upon, and can have no apprehensions of Change of mind. It is not unlikly that when I write again to you, you may add another Nephew to the list of your Relatives.[1] A House is taken and I have been for the last week employd in buying linnen china Glass &c. In other respects the House is ready furnishd. I wish I had one of my Neices with me, whilst I remain in this Country, but it will not be long before I shall quit it. Not ten days ago I expected to have taken my passage in the july packet, in concequence of some intelligence which afterwards wore a different appearence; things are so fluctuating upon both Sides the water that it is really difficult to draw up conclusions. Prussia has treated; Portugal has treated; and the Emperours minister has just received Powers to treat also; but very unfortunatly the joint commissions of the American ministers expired this month So that nothing can be concluded till new powers arrive.[2] Whoever has any thing to do with Courts, must have Patience, for their first Second; and third requisites. I wish I was well out of the Way of all of them. My object is to return to America early next Spring, if nothing arises to oblige us to take this step Sooner. I cannot think of a fall passage, of this I shall be better informd in a few weeks. But there is no office more undesirable than Minister of the united States, under the present embarrasments, there is no reputation to be acquired, and there is much to lose.

Negotiations with other powers may be, and have been effected, but with England there is not the least probability of a treaty untill the States are united in their measures, and invest Congress with full powers for the regulation of commerce, and a minister here can be of very little service untill that event takes place. It is true he may be invested with other powers, and one more important than treating with this Country, is making peace with the Barbery States. But as mr A foretold so it has turnd out, Lamb is returning without being able to effect any thing, the dey would not even see him and the demand for the poor fellows who are in captivity is a thousand Dollars pr Man and there are 21 of them.[3] The sum allotted by Congress is so inadaquate to the thing, that we must look only for war upon us. Unless Congress endeavour to borrow the sum demanded, and treat immediately, their demands will increase in proportion to the Captures they make, but of all this they are regularly and fully informd. You will not however make these matters known till you hear them from some other quarter. These are droll subjects for one Lady to write to an other upon, but our Country is so much interested in these affairs that you must excuse me for troubleing you with them, and you can communicate with discretion.

I thank you most Sincerely for all your kindness to my dear sons and hope they will ever bear a gratefull remembrance of it. The account you give of their behaviour and conduct is such as I hope they merit.[4] The Idea that their success in Life depends upon their diligence and application to their studies, to a modest and virtuous deportment, cannot be too Strongly impresst upon their minds. The foolish Idea in which some of our Youth, are educated: of being born Gentleman is the most ridiculous in the world for a Country like our. It is the mind and manners which make the Gentleman and not the Estate. There is no Man with us, so rich as to breed up a family in Idleness with Ideas of Paternal inheritance, and far distant may that day be from our Land: he who is not in some way or other usefull to Society, is a drone in the Hive, and ought to be Hunted down accordingly. I have very different Ideas of the wealth of my Countrymen, to what I had when I left it. Much of that wealth has proved falacious and their debts exceed their property. Economy and industery may retrive their affairs. I know that the Country is capable of great exertions but in order to this, they must curtail their Ideas of Luxery and refinement, according to their ability. I do not believe any Country exceeds them in the article of dress.[5] In Houses in furniture in Gardens and pleasure Grounds and in equipage, the wealth of France and England is display'd to a high pitch of Grandeur and magnificence. But when I reflect upon the thousands who are Starving, and the millions who are loaded with taxes to support this pomp and shew, I look to my happier

Country with an enthusiastick warmth, and pray for the continuance of that equality of Rank and fortune which forms so large a portion of our happiness.[6]

I yesterday dinned at the Bishop of Saint Asaphs, in company with dr Preistly and Dr Price and some Strangers. The Bishops Character is well known and respected as a Friend to America, and justly does he deserve the Character of a liberal Man.[7] He is polite affable and concequently agreeable. He has a Lady and an unmarried daughter, both of whom are well bred according to my Ideas.[8] According to British Ideas good Breeding consist in an undaunted air, and a fearless, not to say, bold address and appearence. The old Lady is both sensible and learned, quite easy and social. The Young one is modest and attentive. This is a family, the friendship and acquaintance of which I should like to cultivate.[9]

Dr Priestly is a Gentleman of a pale complexion spair habit, placid thoughtfull Countanance, and very few words. I heard him preach for dr Price, his delivery is not equal to the matter of his discourses. I dinned twice in company with the Dr. and was mortified that I could not have more of his company at our own House, but he was engaged every moment of his time whilst in London.—I believe I have frequently mentiond Dr Price. He is a good and amiable Man, a little inclined to lowness of spirits, which partly arises from the melancholy state of Mrs Price who two years ago had a paralytick stroke, and has been helpless ever Since.

Captain Bigolew has promised to take this Letter From your ever affectionate Sister

AA

RC (MWA:Abigail Adams Corr.). Dft (Adams Papers); undated, filmed at [1786], Adams Papers, Microfilms, Reel No. 369.

[1] In the undated Dft, after this sentence, AA wrote the following in place of the remainder of this paragraph and the next: "Some affairs have turnd up which give us reason to think that Mr A must go to Holland. If so I shall accompany him and leave to the young folks the care of the House and family and they will be married previous to our going. In a week or ten days it will be known whether we must go, and the result of the business there will determine whether we em bark for America in the july packet, which I assure you I do not think improbable. This will be an unexpected Step, and will not be taken without sufficient reasons to justify it. Those reasons must be kept Secret at present nor would I have our apprehensions mentiond as it would lay open a wide feild for conjecture. As we are too short sighted beings to see far into futurity our only study should be to do our duty for those with whom we are connected, as far as we are capable of judging of it, and leave the event for time to devolope." JA's thought of returning to America arose from the shortage of U.S. funds in Europe. To avoid defaulting on interest payments to the Dutch loan, JA was asked to limit his own spending and the amounts drawn for negotiating with the Barbary powers. If these monies were indefinitely appropriated to pay the interest, JA predicted that Barclay and Lamb's missions would be "undone" and that he must either "starve or go home" (Board of Treasury to

JA, 7 March; Wilhem & Jan Willink and Nicolaas & Jacob van Staphorst to JA, 5 May, both Adams Papers; and JA to Willinks and van Staphorsts, 11 May, 19 May, and 21 May, all LbCs, Adams Papers).

[2] Florimund Claude, Comte Mercy d'Argenteau, ambassador from the Austrian emperor to France, informed Jefferson of his powers to negotiate upon the latter's return to Paris (Jefferson, *Papers*, 9:507). The commissions sent to JA, Jefferson, and Benjamin Franklin to negotiate commercial treaties expired on 12 May, two years from their date of issue (*JCC*, 27:372–374).

[3] The most recent reports received by JA predicted that Lamb's mission to free American prisoners and conclude a treaty of amity and peace with Algiers would end in failure (Lamb to Thomas Jefferson, 29 March; Thomas Barclay to the American Commissioners, 10 April, Jefferson, *Papers*, 9:364–365, 383–384). Lamb ultimately was granted three audiences with the dey of Algiers, but the sums demanded for the prisoners or for peace were so extraordinary that the commissioners suspended the mission and referred the matter back to Congress (John Lamb to the American Commissioners, 20 May; Jefferson to Lamb, 20 June, same, 9:549–554, 667).

[4] In the Dft, AA adds at this point: "I look upon a colledge Life as a sort of ordeal. If they pass unscorchd it is in some measure a security to them against future temptations."

[5] In the Dft, the previous three sentences read: "Economy and industery will retrieve their affairs and the Country is capable of great things. But their Ideas of Luxery and refinement have leapd a century to be sure. In the article of dress amongst the Ladies of our Country, diamonds excepted, I believe there is no nation exceeds them in extravagance."

[6] In the Dft, AA continued the paragraph with: "Where industery is sure of a reward, and each individual may become a landholder without being Subject to taxes amounting to 15 Shillings in the pound which is the case here. Inclosed is a print which may give you Some Idea of the taxes of this Nation. Yet notwithstanding all this the kings civil list is 200 thousand in debt and the prince of Wales 4 hundred thousand. What a picture added to their National debt?" The print, if enclosed with the RC, has not been found.

[7] In the Dft, this sentence reads: "He has the manners and appearence which I have always annexed to the Idea of a good Bishop. I need not say that he is liberal in his sentiments with respect to Religion and politicks."

[8] Two of Jonathan and Anna Shipley's daughters remained unmarried throughout their lives: Betsy (1754–1796) and Catherine (1759–1840) (*DNB*; Franklin, *Papers*, 18:199–202).

[9] The Dft concludes here with the following passage: "I have written you so frequently of late that I have nothing further to add than my affectionate Regards to every branch of your family. The ship you mention as arriving without letters put up for Nantucket I believe no other has arrived without."

John Quincy Adams to John Adams

Dear Sir Cambridge May 21st: 1786 Sunday

I am now much more at my disposal, with respect to my Time, than I was at Haverhill, and can devote more of it to writing, though, it is said, this Quarter, that is, the last of the Junior Sophister year, is most important, and busy, than any other in the four years. Mr: Williams's Lectures on natural Philosophy, render it so; his Course consists of 24 Lectures, 13 of which we have already had. I have hitherto, taken, minutes, while he was speaking, and written off, after I came out, as much as I could recollect of them. Some of my Class have told me, they were not worth the Time, and Pains I have spent upon, them; but I think they are, as they may serve to fix firmer in my Mind; the principles of an important branch of Science, which I never before have studied. In my last letter, to you, I requested Desagulier's Translation of S. Gravesande's, in 2 Volumes octavo, there is a 4to: Edition, but the other is that which is studied here. They are very scarce in this Country, as they can neither be bought, nor borrowed out of College. We begin to recite in them tomorrow, but I shall endeavour to borrow them of some Classmate, for the 2 weeks, we shall recite in them this Quarter; and I hope to receive one, before I shall have occasion for it again. This is the last Quarter, in which we recite in the Languages, the next year, we shall be confined to Mathematics, natural Philosophy, and Metaphysics; we shall finish Locke on the understanding, before the end of this year, and begin, in Reid on the Mind;[1] our progress here is very slow, but we have so many things to attend to at once, that it cannot well be other wise.

I received a few days since, your favour of March 19th: and at the same time, from my Sister Coll: Humphreys's Poem, which I think superior to the former, among its beauties is, a very happy imitation of a famous passage in Virgil, AEn: 6: 847. &c. It is in the 30th: page

> Let other Climes of other produce boast &c.[2]

I think it is, as Boileau, says of himself, même, en imitant, toujours original.[3]

America, appears to hasten towards, perfection, in the fine arts; and any Country, would, boast of a Belknap, as an historian, a Dwight, as a Poet,[4] and a West as a Painter. There, are in this University, one or two Students, (now Senior Sophister's) who promise fair to become very good Poets. One of them by the name of Fowle, was appointed a few days since, to deliver a valedictory Poem, on the 21st: of June, and it is said, has another assign'd him as a Part at Commencement. There is among the governors of the College, one, who for genius and learning, would make a figure in any part of Europe. I mean the Librarian, Mr: Winthrop. He has lately discovered, a method of trisecting an Angle, which, has so long been attempted, in Vain.[5] Mr: Sewall too the former Hebrew Professor, is now producing his talents. He was obliged to resign, because, it was said he was addicted to drinking. He most sacredly declared, at the Time, that the accusation was false; it has been said as an argument, to prove, he was subject to the Vice, that his mental faculties were impair'd: to show that this was not the fact, he has undertaken, to translate Young's Night Thoughts into Latin Verse. The first Night is to be published soon; the work may be considered as a curiosity, and I shall send one, as soon as they are printed.[6]

June 14th.

I have been so busy, since the date of the Former Part, of this Letter, that I have not been able to finish it. I have taken in writing extracts of all I remembered of the Lectures upon natural Philosophy. The Course finished last Saturday, and I have now the disposal of my Time, much more than I had before. The Performances at Commencement, are distributed, and are more numerous, than they ever have been before; it is a doubt, at present whether this is only a mark of favour, to the Class that is about to graduate, because it is said to be one of the best Classes taken collectively, for genius, and Learning, that has ever gone through College; or whether, it is the Intention of the Government for the future to increase the number of good Parts as they are called. Hitherto about two thirds of each Class, have had syllogistic disputes, to perform at Commencement, and as they are never attended to, they are held in detestation by the Scholars. And every one thinks it a reflection upon his Character as a genius and a student to have a Syllogistic; this opinion is the firmer, because the best Scholars almost always have other Parts; there are many disadvantages derived, from these Syllogisms, and I know only of one benifit, which is this. Many Scholars, would go through College without studying at all, but would idle away all their Time; who merely from the horrors of Syllogisms, begin to Study, acquire a fondness for it, and make a very pretty figure in College. And it is not uncommon to see young fellows the most idle, in a Class the two first years, have the Reputation of great Students, and good scholars the two Latter.

The next Commencement, there will be delivered, 2 English Poems, two English Orations, two Latin Orations, a greek Dialogue, 3 Forensic Disputes, and an English Dialogue between four. *Thompson*, a young gentleman from Newbury, has one of the English Orations. He is generally supposed to be the most distinguished Character in College. It is said by his Classmates, that he will outshine Harry Otis, who will deliver at the Same Time an Oration upon taking his second Degree, but it is now a doubt whether Thompson, will appear, as he is very unwell. He has injured his Health by hard study, and it is feared he has a slow Fever.

The Bridge, at Charlestown is very nearly compleated. Next Saturday, being the 17th: of June, there is to be a long Procession, over the bridge, and an Entertainment for 600 persons provided on Bunkers Hill. I know of no News, as I am here quite retired. It is now eight-weeks since this Quarter began. Near as we are to Boston, I have been there only once in that Time. A Person, who wishes to make any figure as a Scholar at this University, must not spend much Time, either in visiting or in being visited.

I Have one more request to add to those I have already made; it is for Blair's Lectures,[7] in Octavo, so that they may be in the same form with the Sermons, and because an Octavo is much more convenient than a Quarto.

Your dutiful Son, J. Q. Adams

RC (Adams Papers); endorsed by WSS: "21st. May 1786. J. Q. Adams."

[1] JQA's copy of Thomas Reid, *An Inquiry into the Human Mind, On the Principles of Common Sense*, 4th edn., corrected, London, 1785, is at MQA.

[2] The line JQA quotes from Humphreys, *A Poem, on the Happiness of America*, appears on p. 29 of the Hartford, Conn., 1786, reprint edition (Evans, No. 19723). Humphreys suggests that other nations will produce many fine items, "But men, Columbia, be thy fairer growth, / Men of firm nerves who spurn at fear and sloth, / Men of high courage like their sires of old, / In labour patient as in danger bold!" (lines 586–589). JQA is comparing this sentiment to Book Six of the *Aeneid*, in which Virgil extols the acts of various Romans but praises the development of Roman law and government above all else (lines 847–853).

[3] Even in imitation, always original (Nicolas Boileau-Despréaux, *Oeuvres Poëtiques*, London, 1730, Epigram 52).

[4] Rev. Jeremy Belknap of Dover, N.H., published the first volume of his *History of New Hampshire* in 1784; *The Conquest of Canäan*, an epic poem by Rev. Timothy Dwight of Greenfield Hill, Conn., and later the president of Yale College, appeared in 1785 (*DAB*).

[5] James Winthrop's findings were printed as "A Rule for Trisecting Angles Geometrically," *Memoirs of the American Academy of Arts and Sciences*, vol. 2: pt. 1, p. 14–17 (Evans, No. 25092).

[6] Stephen Sewall, Harvard 1761, first began teaching Hebrew at the college in 1761. He served as Hancock Professor of Hebrew and Oriental Languages from 1764 until his dismissal in 1785. Sewall's translation of Young's *Night Thoughts*, Night I, *Nocte cogitata, auctore, anglice scripta, Young, D.D. quæ lingua Latii donavit America*, was printed in Charlestown in 1786 (Evans, No. 20170; *Sibley's Harvard Graduates*, 15:107–114).

[7] Hugh Blair, *Lectures on Rhetoric and Belles Lettres*. Two copies of these lectures, both later editions but with JQA's bookplates, are located at MQA.

Mary Smith Cranch to Abigail Adams

My dear Sister Braintree May [21] 1786[1]

Is it possible that my dear Niece should really be married and the little visiting Card upon which a peice of Ribbon was wound be the only way in which my sister has thought proper to convey the pleasseing intellegence to her Friends?[2] It is an event which almost every one hop'd, and every one I know will approve. For my Self, I most heartily congratulate you all, not only upon your acquisition but upon your escape:—can he after this delude another Family, must another unsuspecting fair one fall a victim to his vanity. I have no pity to bestow upon him unless for his folly. He means to brave it I see. He puts on such an air of indifference and gaeity as plainly show's how much he is mortified. He is dressd out to day in his best attire even his head is comb'd. It is Sunday. I hope said he, there will be many strangers at meeting to day—for his comfort there has been mr and Mrs Story and Family.[3] We have not chang'd one Word with him upon the subject from the first of the affair to this day. I am rejoice'd that his Letters were not lost.[4] I knew he had abus'd me and charg'd me with things which were false. He wanted to impose upon me too and was angry that he could not and reveng'd himself by endeavouring to rob me of the affection of my dear Niece, for this I know not how to forgive him. It was quite accidental that I knew any thing about it—and now I only know in general. I hope she does not believe what he has alleg'd against me. I believe you think I have no curiosity. I have a reasonable share I assure you and wish to know much more than you have told me of the rise and progress of the sudden match in your Family. Do you know that you never mention'd the name of the Gentleman in one of your Letters to any of us nor any thing which could lead us to guess Who it was. The manner in which you spoke of coll. Humphries made us think that it was him rather than coll. Smith,—nor did we know other ways till we Saw Doctor Tufts Letter.[5]—But oh my Sister must you leave her in Europe when you return. I cannot bear the Idea. Shall I not be a witness to the Happiness I have so often wish'd her. I must hope I shall. How much more pleasure do you feel by introducing a man of such a universally good character into your Family than one exactly opposite to it. May you always have reason to rejoce. By an expression in your Letter to Betsy I cannot help hopeing that you may soon return. Esters Letter too to her mother speaks the same thing. She says you are to return by the way of Holland, is it so? The hope of its being really so has brought a tear of joy into my eye.

You say in one of your Letters that you have written largly to me. I have receiv'd one Letter by the January Pacquit at least it was dated January 26th Mr King sent it. One by mrs Hay one by cushing and one by Lyde as I suppose but they came in so near together that I cannot very well tell which the Letters came in. I have receiv'd the Key of the Trunk the latter is not come ashoar yet.[6] Mr and mrs Rogers are not arriv'd in Boston. I went yesterday to see. I hope she has Letters for me, for I am not half satisfied with what I have got. They will not all make one long Letter.

I am provok'd with young for his ill conduct about the chocalate. He promiss'd to put it into his chest. We dare not send much at one time. I am now very glad it was no more. I will send more when we can find a captain we can trust. I have no notion of giving a feast to the custom house Officers. I design to speak in Season for some nuts for you. Accep a Thousand thanks my dear Sister for your kind presents to me and my children but why my Sister have you not sent me a Bill of the Silk and apron. I feel my Self under obligations which I cannot repay. I am thankful that your sons stand in need of some of my care and attention, as it is the only way in which we can show our gratitude. They are good children and give us no unnecessary cares. I am sure I long for their vacancys to commence as much, and I believe more than they do. We have a bustling time tis true and have work enough to do to repair the damages of their late session and prepare them for the next, but the chearfulness they infuse is a full compensation for all that is done for them. Our young Folks improve fast in their musick. Two German Flutes, a violin and a harpsicord and two voices form a considerable concert.[7] Come my Sister come and hear it. It will give you more pleasure than those scenes of Dissapation which you decribe, you must I think be heartily tir'd of them. You do perfectly right to be a witness to as many of them as you can with propriety so long as you can detest them, but I cannot bear you should leave my Niece in the midst of them: She is young and habit may render them less odious to her. Why has She not written to any of us? Her amiable Partner must not ingross all her time. He must spare her a little to her Freinds, at least long enough to tell them how happy She is. I design to write to her as soon as I am properly inform'd how to address her.

RC (Adams Papers); endorsed: "Mrs Cranch May 7th 1786." The endorsement suggests that AA received this undated letter with Mary Smith Cranch to AA, 7 May, above.

[1] Mary Cranch comments in the course of the letter that she is writing on Sunday and that she visited Boston "yesterday," an event that Elizabeth Cranch places on the 20th (Elizabeth Cranch to AA, 20 May, above).

[2] For the visiting card from the William Smiths of Clapham that the Cranch family mistakenly believed was intended to annouce AA2's marriage, see Elizabeth Cranch to AA, 20 May, and note 4, above.

[3] Perhaps Ebenezer and Hannah Storer and his children George and Mary, whom Elizabeth Cranch saw at the home of Hannah's stepmother, Ann Marsh Quincy, on Monday the 22d (MHi:Jacob Norton Papers, Elizabeth Cranch Diary, 22 May 1786).

[4] The letters have not been found.

[5] AA to Cotton Tufts, 10 Jan., above, which Tufts received on 19 May.

[6] The trunk was sent with Capt. Lyde and AA's letter of 6 April.

[7] JQA's Diary entry for 17 July describes

the musical scene at the Cranches: "we play'd on the flute, on the harpsichord, and sung. There is always some fine music of one kind or another, going forward in this House. Betsey, and Miss Hiller finger the harpsichord Billy scrapes the Violin, Charles and myself blow the flute" (*Diary*, 2:66).

Abigail Adams to John Quincy Adams

My dear son London May 22 1786

I have time only to write you a line or two, not expecting captain Bigolow to Sail so Soon. I was yesterday informd that he would not go till the middle of the week, but this morning he has sent for the Letters. I thought your sister had letters, but she says they are not ready. She wrote you by mr Jenks 3 weeks ago.[1] I must refer you to your Friend Storer for further information as I have written to him more particularly. I send you a Book[2] which was presented us by the Author. Your Friend Murry dinned with us yesterday and wonders he does not hear from you. Tis probable you will meet with some curious annecdotes in the English papers respecting Lord Gorge Gorden, mr Simon Tufts and mr Lewis Gray, Who took it upon them to assert that your Pappa received his Sallery Quarterly from Count d A[*dhé*]mar the french Ambassador. I designd to have transmitted the whole correspondence to dr Tufts, but have not time to write him. The Publick advertizer is the paper which contains the matter, and in which they are challenged to produce their evidence. Not a Syllable has since appeard.[3] Adieu yours AA

RC (Adams Papers).

[1] AA2's No. 13 to JQA, not found, was carried by John Jenks (AA2 to JQA, 25 April, above).

[2] Possibly François Soulés, *Histoire des troubles de l'Amérique anglaise*, 2 vols., London, 1785, a set of which, with JQA's bookplate and JA's notes throughout volume two is now at MQA. Soulés was known to the Adamses and had borrowed money from JA (Soulés to JA, 9 June 1785, 3 Feb. 1786, both Adams Papers). JQA acknowledged the receipt of Soulés' volumes in his letter to AA, 30 Dec., below, but they were sent via Callahan, not Bigelow (*Diary*, 2:115–116).

[3] See AA to Cotton Tufts, 22 July, below.

Abigail Adams to Elizabeth and Lucy Cranch

Dear Girls May 22.1786

Excuse me I have time only to tell you that I designd to have written, but the captain sails sooner than I expected. I send you some magizines to amuse you, and will continue them to you. Give my Duty to my Honourd Mother and Love to my cousins, to the Germantown family[1] remember me. I have a letter too for milton Hill partly finishd.[2] See what procrastination does, but I wanted to have my letters late, and so I am dissapointed of sending any. I am much hurried just at present. Dont you pitty your cousin, not a female companion of her age. Miss Hamilton, the only one she has had in England, is saild for Philadelphia. I wish for you I am sure every day of my Life. Adieu dear Girls. Love me always as I do you, & believe me ever your affectionate Aunt AA

RC (MSaE:Abigail Adams Letters); addressed by WSS: "Miss Betsey Cranch Braintree"

[1] The Palmers.
[2] To Mercy Warren, 24 May, below.

Abigail Adams to Charles Storer

Dear Charles London May 22. 1786

It is a very pleasent morning Sir, and I have risen a little after five, that I might have the pleasure of writing you before Captain Bigolew Sails, so Sir I have seated myself at a desk near the window of the Chamber in which you used to lodge, from whence you know the square has a beautifull appearence, delightfully green it is, but the weather continues so cold that we still keep fires. As I have informd you of my present position, I will go on to relate that in which your letter found me, (know then, tis a fortnight since) that I was Sitting in the drawing room upon the Settee earnestly engaged in conversation with Miss Macauley, daughter to the celebrated Lady of that Name,[1] and a very fine young Lady She is, present Miss Hamilton of Philadelphia. O Charles it is fortunate that you did not know that young Lady. Since you left us she has been very intimate in the family. So modest so Sweet and amiable, affable and engageing, so Beautifull, and yet so unconscious of it, in short she is "all that Youthfull poets fancy when they Love."[2] She has an uncle whose adopted child she is, and he almost worships her. He was obliged to come abroad about 2 years ago, and brought her with him then only sixteen years old. He has carrid her into company publick and private, shewn her the world under his own Eye, and preserved her from growing giddy at the view. After having introduced her here, he requested my protection for her and accordingly I have frequently taken her with me to publick places. For this purpose she had come to drink tea with me and go to Ranaleigh. Col Smith Col Norten mr Trumble Dr Bancroft mr Ridley were all present, when mr Adams came into the room and presented me your Letter. I wishd to open it, but so much company present I could not, so I put in my pocket. The company staid till ten. The Carriages were then ready at the door and it was time to go to Rana [3] and will you believe it, mr A went with us for the first time. About eleven we got there, and expected to meet a party from Clapham.[4] They did not however come till 12. The room not being very full, and we old fashiond people, we retired at one, but your fashonable Friend mrs Paridice, staid a few Evenings since till four oclock. Altho I practised so much self denial, I did not go to bed till I had read your Letter, for which accept my thanks, tho you were very neglegent in it, not a word of Mrs Atkinson nor the children not a syllable of Mamma or Sister Polly.[5] It is true you were very good in giving me a minute account of my own Children, and your visit to Haverhill which gratified me much. You are a Young Gentleman of taste, so could not be otherways than pleasd with mrs Shaw. The three Sisters are all clever, I am really at a loss to know which is most so, something different in their manners be sure, but the same principals of Benevolence actuates them all.

You see I write you with the same freedom and confidence as if you was one of us. Let me then assure you that there cannot be any change of mind in the Lady for whom you have exprest an anxiety. She will soon be the wife of a Worthy Man, by her own free and unbiassed Choice; a House is engaged, and I am buisy in prepairing matters for an event not far distant. I understood by dr Tufts that he was in possession of the papers some months ago. I cannot Suppose the Gentleman would be so dishonorable as to wish to retain them, when all hopes of the Lady are annhialated. She has never written him a line since that Letter which past through the hands of Dr Tufts[6] and I presume never will again. I wish the Gentleman well. He has good qualities, indeed he has, but he ever was his own Enemy.

As to politicks my dear Charles, when a people have not ability to go to War, why they must be at Peace if they can. But there is not a less Hostile Spirit here against America than there was during the administration of Lord North. They Hate us and the French equally, and every effort to crush us, to breed ill will amongst us, to ruin our commerce, to destroy our navagation will be, and is studiously practised. The Laws of Nations require civility towards Publick Ministers. This we receive, but our Country is vilifye'd by every hireling scribler, and will be so untill the States invest Congress with Powers which shall convince them that we are *still united*. I can give you a very recent instance of the illiberal prejudice of those who call themselves Men of Science and abilities, and no doubt are such. It is customary for the Royal Society of Academicians to have an Annual dinner and to invite all the Foreign Ministers and Strangers of distinction. But this Year to shew their servility to crowned Heads and their hatred of Republicks, they voted to invite only the foreign ministers from crowned Heads, and by that means you see they could exclude the Minister from America, with three others to keep him company, so that the distinction should not amount to an open affront.[7] Yet these are the Men of Letters, Men of Science!!! O Britain Blush, that these are the degenerate Sons of thy Sydney, Hamden, Pym, and Russel.[8]

As to the Algerines, why mr *A—s* Prophesy is but too true, and Lamb is returning having effected—nothing. Mr Barclay I suppose will be in the same situation, and now what is to be done? You was long enough in the political line to see and feel perplexities of various kinds. You know how much they affect mr A. They surround him from all quarters, and sometimes it is palpable darkness, then a Gleam of light breaks out. There are many things you know, which cannot and must not be told. The honour of America requires silence. I wish all her Sons were as carefull of it. But I wish, what? that I was safe in my little rustick cottage at the foot of pens Hill. Do you hear, when you write again dont tell us one dismall Story. Let us have sun shine from some quarter, if it is only imaginary.

I cannot tell you any more about Lamb untill mr Randle arrives, who we daily expect. I do not know that any other person would have met with a more favourable reception, but he had not half money enough to procure him an audience. This is to ourselves do you mind. Let us keep it from the English as long as we can, tis enough that congress are informed of every thing—politicks adieu.

Remember me to all inquiring Friends, uncles Aunts & cousins, believe me ever your Friend xxxxxxx

PS If you will only put this letter into Your own hand writing, what an improvement it will be.

RC (Adams Papers); endorsed: "22d. May. 1786."

[1] Catherine Sophia Macaulay, the daughter of historian Catharine Macaulay Graham and Dr. George Macaulay (Bridget Hill, *The Republican Virago: The Life and Times of Catharine Macaulay, Historian*, Oxford, 1992, p. 16).

[2] Altamont speaks this in Nicholas Rowe, *The Fair Penitent*, Act III, scene i, line 246.

[3] Blank in MS.

[4] Probably William and Frances Coape Smith.

[5] AA inquires after Charles' elder sister,

Elizabeth Storer Atkinson, and her children, younger sister Mary (Polly), and his stepmother Hannah Quincy Lincoln Storer, AA's cousin.

[6] AA2's letter breaking off her engagement with Royall Tyler may have been sent in care of Cotton Tufts (AA2 to Tyler, [*ca. 11 Aug.* 1785]; AA to Tufts, 18 Aug. 1785, vol. 6:262, 283–287).

[7] The Royal Academy hosted their annual celebration on 29 April. Among the attendees were the ministers from Russia, Sweden, Denmark, Poland, Spain, Sicily, Portugal, and Sardinia. Missing from the festivities were the diplomatic representatives from Genoa, Venice, the Netherlands, and, of course, the United States (London *Daily Universal Register*, 2 May).

[8] Algernon Sidney, John Hampden, John Pym, and Lord William Russell, all seventeenth-century anti-Stuart figures who became heroes to both Britain's and America's eighteenth-century Commonwealthmen and republicans (*DNB*).

Mary Smith Cranch to Abigail Adams

My dear Sister Braintree May 22d 1786

I have been almost frighted out of my senses this afternoon. Your Mother Hall and Polly Adams came to spend the day with me, but had like to have been kill'd before they return'd. As they were geting into the chaise to go home, the Horse took a fright and although he was fastind to the hook in the Tree, he broke the Bridle and a way he went. Mr Wibird had just help'd in miss Polly and had turn'd round to help mrs Hall as he started. I saw the Horse run but as the gate was shut I suppos'd that would stop him, but I was mistaken he jump'd over it, but the chaise not being so nimble as he was it tore the gate all to peices. Polly had no command of him as she had not the reins. She jump'd out against the office without doing her self any harm except spraining her back a little. Nobody could Stop the Horse till he had got almost home. When they did and to the astonishment of every body the chaise was found not the least hurt. I was very thankful that mrs Hall was not in it. She was much frighted. The Horse is not fit for a woman to drive. This is the third time he has ran away. Sister Shaw her good man and Daughter are just arrived. Adieu I must run and welcome them.

23d

I went down and found my Friends well. They say your son[1] is so also. O! my Sister now we wish for you. Pleasures and pains will be mix'd in this world. What a painful visit shall we make to weymouth. I have not been there since I follow'd my dear Aunt to the Silent Grave. We are happier for receiving our Letters about this time. It adds greatly to our happiness when we can communicate it.

Satturday 26th [*i.e. 27th*]

Mr Shaw and Sister are gone to weymouth to keep Sabbath and uncle and aunt Smith are come to spend it with me but my Sister, I fear we shall soon be call'd to mourn the loss of this good Aunt. She appears to me not to have many months to Stay with us. Her countenance is bad and she is so weak and feeble that She can scarcly walk about the House. She is Sensible of her own decay and think she has not long to stay with us. A Lethergy is what I am aprehensive of. She falls asleep in her chair as she sets in company one arm is half of it turnd purple. She is going to princtown to an ordination. She is not able I am sure. She is not to go into so much company, but her heart is set upon it. I would have her come and stay with me instead of going into so much confution. She will she says after she returns.

June 24th

I have had so much to do and have been so unwell ever since I wrote the above that I have not had time nor health to continue my Journal of events as I intended. I have had a very bad cold and cough which has made me quite sick. I hope I am better but I am far from well. The Soreness upon my Lungs and a little cough still remains. If I could have had an oppertunity of sending you what I have already written you would have been in some measure prepair'd to have heard the sad news I have now to tell you. Doctor Tufts has just inform'd us that Aunt Smith was last night taken with convultion Fits and is now if living in that Lethargick State I have long expected she would sooner or later be in. This was the day that she was to have set out for her Journey to Princtown. She had got all her cloaths put up and went to beg [*bed*] as well as She had been for several days, by no means fit to go as the Doctors thought. About two a clock uncle was wak'd by the shaking of the Bed. He found her in a voilent convultion. The Docr. was soon there and bled her before she came out of it. She has had four and when the Doctor came away he thought her dying. The poor Family my Heart achs for them. She has no senses, but She was ready I have no doubt we that know her piety must think so. Such a loss my dear Sister, but the will of Heaven be done.

Teusday 28th [*i.e. 27th*]

Our dear Aunt is no more an inhabitant of this earth. She dy'd about three a clock this morning. Her Reason never return'd. They are a most affeected Family,[2] but they are not the only one I am call'd to mourn with. Uncle Thaxter has lost his youngest Daughter mrs Cushing. She has not been well for several years, but has been better sinc she was married. She was brought to Bed about Ten days since and liv'd but six and thirthy Hours. She left an infant Daughter to supply her place.[3] I have not heard any particulars. I did not hear of it till after she was bury'd and I have not had time to go thire since. It is a dreadful Shock to the Family I am sure. How one Friend drops after another. May we be ready our turn cannot be very far off.

June [*July*] 3d

I return'd last night from the House, the melancholy House of my dear uncle Smith. I found the Family in deep afflection, uncles sorrow of that kind which will not soon wear off. It is tender yet manly. I Staid with him two days after aunt was bury'd. He wish'd it and I could not deny hime. Betsy is very sorrowful but does not know her loss. Cousin Billy is Steady but afflictted, but the Gentle the amiable Preachers Heart is almost broken. He talks of his dear Parent till sobs interupt his speech. He is appointed chaplain at the castle with as good a Salary at least as any country minister and much more independant, but it is mortifying too see those who have not half his abilities prefer'd before him.[4]

Mrs Otis is no stranger to affection but she is oppress'd with Grief. Her circumstances in life makes the stroke doubly severe.[5] You can scarcly concieve how tender how attentive and how affectionate uncle appears to his children and Friends. Betsy wants a companion Lucy is going to spend a few days with her. I must not forget Nabby who is as much affected as if it had been her own mother. There never was a Family where the loss of the mistress of it would make so little alteration as in this, Nabbys faithfulness and faculty the cause of it all.

We have not heard from mr Perkins Sinc I wrote you last summer till about a fortnight since. He has written but his letters did not reach us. He is well and in good business as a Lawyer. He is determind not to see N England again without a Fortune sufficient to set him above want and tis not he says so easey a matter as some may think to gain a Fortune suddenly without sacrificing principles in which he has always liv'd and is determind to dye, whether he is poor or rich.

I was at cambridge mr cranch and Eliza with me last friday[6] our gone were well. Cousin JQA has not been in Boston but once untill he attended his Aunts Funireal since this term began. I think he does not use exercise enough. I told him he wanted his Papa to take him out. You will see by the Papers that the under graduates are all to have a uniform. Your Blue coats &c come in good time.[7] Lucy is gone with Betsy Apthorp this day to make a visit to her Brothers as She calls them.[8] Our children live sweetly, the most perfect harmony and Brotherly Love Subsists between them.

Not one word of Politicks have I written nor shall I have time to do it now. If I had I would tell you what wonderfull things the House are doing with the Lawyers the court of common Pleas &c but the news papers will do it for me.[9] I am thankful there is a senate as well as a House. [Wh]at has congress done? any thing to detain you [in] Europe. I love my country too well to wish you to return yet, much as I wisht to see you. I did design to write to my dear Niece by this vessel but fear I shall not have time. My sincere Love and good wishes attend her and hers. Tis very late good night my ever dear Sister and believe me, yours Affectionatly

M Cranch

RC (Adams Papers). Some loss of text where the seal was removed.

[1] TBA had lived with the Shaw family since April 1783 in order to prepare for college under the direction of Rev. John Shaw (vol. 5:118).

[2] Elizabeth Storer Smith (1726–1786) left her husband, Isaac Smith Sr., two sons, Rev. Isaac Jr. and William, and two daughters, Mary Smith Gray Otis and Elizabeth (Betsy).

[3] Lucy Thaxter (1760–1786), AA's cousin, married John Cushing in March 1785. She died on 22 June after giving birth to a daughter, Lucy (*History of the Town of Hingham, Massachusetts*, 3 vols. in 4, Hingham, 1893, 2:165).

[4] Castle William, the fortified post on Castle Island in Boston Harbor. The commonwealth established the office of chaplain on 21 March, to be appointed by the governor with the advice of the council. Smith began performing services there on 9 July (Mass., *Acts and Laws*, Resolves of 1785, Feb. sess., ch. 154; Boston *Independent Ledger*, 10 July).

[5] For the Aug. 1785 bankruptcy of Boston merchant Samuel Alleyne Otis, triggered by a lack of capital and an overextension of credit to export merchants, see John J. Waters Jr., *The Otis Family in Provincial and Revolutionary Massachusetts*, Chapel Hill, N.C., 1968, p. 199–201. See also vol. 6:271, 273, 275, 317, 337, 417–418.

[6] In addition, William Smith joined the Cranches in the visit to JQA (JQA, *Diary*, 2:58).

[7] At a 13 June meeting, the Harvard College Corporation decided to require a uniform, which included blue coats, waistcoats, and breeches (*Massachusetts Gazette*, 19 June).

[8] Elizabeth (1763–1845), daughter of Sarah Wentworth and James Apthorp (John Wentworth, *The Wentworth Genealogy: English and American*, 3 vols., Boston, 1878, 1:519, 524). See also JQA, *Diary*, 2:267, for his thoughts on Betsy Apthorp.

[9] For the recent attacks against the legal profession by Honestus, see JQA to AA2, 18 May, and note 8, above. In the wake of these attacks, the General Court established a committee to examine the practice of law in the Commonwealth, and eventually passed "An Act for Rendering the Decision of Civil Causes, as Speedy, and as Little Expensive as Possible" and "An Act for Rendering Processes in Law Less Expensive" (*Massachusetts Centinel*, 14 June; Mass., *Acts and Laws*, Acts of 1786, May sess., ch. 21, and Sept. sess., ch. 43).

Abigail Adams to Mercy Otis Warren

My dear Madam London May 24 1786

The affliction under which you are now labouring has been protracted to a much longer period, than I feard when I first left America.[1] It was then I Buried the Dear and amiable Youth, for whose loss your Maternal Bosom heaves the sad Sigh, and over whose urn, all who knew him must drop a tear of affectionate remembrance.

> "Long at his Couch Death took his patient stand
> And menanc'd oft and oft withheld the blow
> To give Reflection time with lenient art
> Each fond delusion from his soul to steal
> Teach him from folly peaceably to part
> And wean him from a World, he lov'd so well."[2]

Nor were the admonitions given in vain. The last visit which I made him, I saw in his languid countanance, the Smile of complacent resignation to the will of Heaven.

> What ever farce the Boastfull Hero plays
> Virtue alone has Majesty in death.[3]

Be this your consolation that tho young in Years, he was Mature in virtue, that he lived beloved and died lamented, and who that lives to riper Years can ensure more to themselves.

Let not the populor torrent which at present Sets against your Worthy Partner distress you, time will convince the World who are their approved and unshaken Friends, whatever mistaken judgments they at present form.[4] I foresaw this when I so earnestly pressd the general to accept his last appointment and attend Congress, if only for a few Months.[5]

All that is well intended is not well received, the consciousness of doing our duty is however a support, but the designing Jack daw will somtimes borrow the plumes of the Jay, and pass himself off to those who judge only by appearences.

You appear to think your Friend at the height of prosperity, and swallowd up by the Gayetyes of Europe, but the estimate is far from the truth. I am much less addicted to them than most of my Fair countrywomen whom I have left behind me. I do not feel myself at all captivated, either with the Manners or politicks of Europe. I think our own Country much the happiest spot upon the Globe, as much as it needs reforming and amending. I should think it still happier, if the inclination was more wanting than the ability, to vie with the Luxeries and extravagance of Europe.

Be so good my dear Madam as to present my best respects to your worthy Partner; and affectionate remembrance to Your Sons, and be assured I am at all times Your Friend Abigail Adams

RC (MHi:Warren-Adams Papers); endorsed: "Mrs Adams May 24th 1786 *No 16*."

[1] AA was replying to Warren's letter of 8 April to JA (Adams Papers) announcing the death of Charles Warren. See Mary Smith Cranch to AA, 22 March, note 3, above, and JA to Mercy Otis Warren, 24 May (InU: Signers Coll.)

[2] William Mason, "Elegy V. On the Death of a Lady," lines 47–52.

[3] Young, *Night Thoughts*, Night II, lines 648–649.

[4] On 1 April the *Massachusetts Centinel* published a letter signed Veritas criticizing James Warren's public spirit and accusing him of accepting or refusing public office based on rank, personal safety, and salary. Warren replied with a public statement defending himself (not found), which Mercy Warren sent to JA in a letter of 8 April (Adams Papers). See also Mary Smith Cranch to AA, 22 March, above.

[5] For AA's forthright views on James Warren's avoidance of public office, see AA to JA, 13 Nov. 1782, vol. 5:36–37, and AA to Mary Smith Cranch, 25 May (1st letter), below.

Thomas Welsh to Abigail Adams

Madam Boston May 24th 1786

I have wrote your Daughter[1] on the Head of common Intelligence. As to political I hardly know how to give a summary of that; as relates to this Commonwealth however I think that altho the Legislature of the last Year deliberated long they at last concluded like the Representatives of a wise People and have taxed smartly.[2] This will operate in a few Years to reduce their public Debt greatly.

The People have shewn their good sense in their Elections for the next Year. They have given 4 Votes in 5 for Mr Bowdoin through the Commonwealth. Many Towns have determined to send no Representatives upon the Plan of Oconomy. Others have set aside some of the most troublesome Members three or four have come to my knowledge. *Deacon Chamberlin, Mitchell of Bridgewater* and *Fessenden* of Rutland are all omitted[3] a saving this of 800 or 1000£ for the next year.

Britain too has done as much for us as we have for ourselves. She has drained us of our Cash the accursed Mean of Extravagance and Luxury henceforward from Necessity our Farms must be cultivated our Herds must be increased our Flocks which had been suffered astonishingly to diminish will be multiplied. These things will make Provisions and Labour low. Our Fishery supplied low will prove proffitable and the Merchant enabled to navigate his Ships at a more moderate Rate will be encouraged to enterprize which will call for large Supplies from the Farmer and both find themselves richer in the End by an Increase of their Assiduities.

It was not from a Want of Zeal in our Merchants that their Trade has not been more productive; it is true that they have been enterprizing in the Path which they and their Fathers had persued in the Routine of British Remittances, they have been to the West Indies for Freight for Europe and have almost ruined themselves.

Some of them however have made large Fortunes by other Persuits. Mr Thomas Russell particularly by the Russian Trade.

I understand by Mr Cranch that Mr Adams proposes that the americans should import raw Sugars from France and manufacture them. The owners of Sugar Houses in this Town have been very attentive this two or three Years past to repair their Works so that there is scarcely one in the Town but what is in better order than has been known these twenty Years. This is partly the Effect of great Duties on British Loaf Sugr. These Sugar Houses are owned by able and spirited young Men capable of making the most of any Project in the Line of their Business.

The Rope Walks are in great improvement and by the Supply of Materials would be able to furnish the whole Navy with Cordage.

The President of Congress has never gone on altho he has been wrote to in a public and private Way and has not deigned to make any reply, he was appointed if I remember right last Novr. Many Acts of Congress long unfinished waiting his Arrival.[4]

The Time of Mr Ramsay's Election having expired about the 15th. Mr Gorham was appointed Chairman in his Place.[5]

If you will be kind enough to procure for Mrs: Welsh 9 Yds: 1/4 of Black lace of a width of the inclosed and send the Cost thereof to Dr: Tufts I will pay him for it, and Mrs W. will feel herself once more obliged by you. She desires to be remembered to you and your's to whom please to present my Compts and accept the same from your's &—

Thomas Welsh

PS: I forgot to inform you that Mr I Smith is appointed Chaplin to the Castle.

RC (Adams Papers); endorsed: "Dr Welch May 24th 1786."

[1] Not found.

[2] On 23 March the General Court apportioned and assessed a tax of £300,439.1.3 on the individual towns throughout the commonwealth in order to comply with Congress' requisition of 27 Sept. 1785; to support

the state's civil government; to pay the interest on state-issued consolidated notes; to redeem army notes; and to replenish the state treasury for funds paid members of the House of Representatives for their attendance at the previous five sessions of the General Court. The sums appropriated to comply with Congress' requisition were to be paid on or before 1 Jan. 1787; those due the state were to be paid on or before 1 April 1787 (Mass., *Acts and Laws*, Acts of 1785, Feb. sess., ch. 74).

[3] The town of Chelmsford elected Ebenezer Bridge in place of Aaron Chamberlain; Nathan Mitchel and Capt. Elisha Mitchel, representatives of Bridgewater, were replaced by Daniel Howard; Rutland chose not to elect anyone in the place of John Fessenden (Mass., *Acts and Laws*, Resolves of 1785, May sess., ante ch. 1; Resolves of 1786, May sess., ante ch. 1).

[4] John Hancock's letter of resignation was read in Congress on 5 June (*JCC*, 30:328).

[5] David Ramsay of South Carolina was named chairman of Congress 23 Nov. 1785 until such time as Hancock arrived in New York to assume the presidency. Ramsay served until the expiration of his term in Congress, 12 May 1786. Nathaniel Gorham succeeded him as chairman and upon Hancock's resignation was elected president of Congress on 6 June (*JCC*, 29:883; 30:264, 330).

Abigail Adams to Mary Smith Cranch

My dear sister London May 2⟨4⟩5 1786[1]

Captain Callihan arrived yesterday at Portsmouth and to day your letter came *safe* to hand. A thousand thanks my dear sister for all your intelligence. No you have not been too particular, every thing however trivial on that Side the water interests me. Here—nothing. I go into the midst of thousands who I know not, and behold all the Boasted Beauty of London with a cold indifference. I sometimes attend the theaters or other places of publick amusement, and have by particular invitation attended several Routes, which of all Senseless things are the most Supreemly Stupid to me; to visit in a croud because it is the mode, to make play a science and follow it as a daily occupation is spending the most precious Gift of the Deity, to very bad purpose. How can a Nation of Gamblers be a respected Nation? I mean by the Nation, the Nobility and Gentry who are the leading Members of it, and direct its counsels. The Morals of Europe are depraved beyond conception, Love of Country and publick virtue, mere visions.

Can there be any pleasure in mixing in company where you care for no one, and nobody cares for you? This is a feeling I never experienced untill I came to Europe. I have derived more real pleasure from one afternoon with my Friend Mrs Rogers, than in all the ceremonious visits I have made in the Country. That was the only family I could visit in without reserve. Before this time, I hope they are, safe in America, as they saild early in April. Many hard things have been said of mr Rogers, since he left London, on account of his going away privattly, but he knew what he was doing, and meant it for the best as I wish it may prove, for nobody questions his integrity. I hope you will be intimatly acquainted with her. She is one of the most amiable of women. Mrs Hay is I hope safe, the account you give of the April storm, makes me apprehensive for her, By her I Sent several articles for my Friends, Cushing and Lyde each had a few also. My inclination would lead me to Send much more than I find my ability competant to, the expences of living in this Country are enourmous.

I am happy to hear by you, that your Nephew was admitted college in March. As yet no letter is come to hand from him. His sister complains, but I know his main object has been, the persuit of his Studies that he might enter colledge with reputation, which I hope he has accomplishd. I think Tommy full young but it will be a benefit to him, to have his Brothers care and advice. You will have your Hands full my sister to take charge of them all. May they all do credit to themselves and their connections. What a tasteless insipid life do I lead here in comparison with what I used to in Braintree, looking after my children and family—seeing my Friends in a Social way, loveing and being beloved by them. Beleive me I am not in the least alterd, except that I wear my Hair drest and powderd, and am two years older, and somewhat fatter which you may be sure is no addition to my looks. But the Heart and the mind are the Same.

Be still sir. Nabby dont talk. I am writing at the table and Col S. is sitting upon the Settee, and prating so fast that he disturbs me. I told him I would write about him. He is talking of his old Friend Evans, who he says is a good Soul. He is inquiring about the Lady mr Evans is going to Marry. Nabby is informing him. Pray Madam he says, write my respects to him.

The dissagreeable Situation of our Milton Friends, I have long feard, and much more since I came abroad than before, as I have learnt that several debts were contracted abroad. In short I am led to question the circumstances of almost every person in the Mercantile line. No judgment can be formed of their property by the appearence they have made and the difficulties which they labour under with respect to their commerce with this Country. Daily adds to their difficulties, and I See not the least prospect of releaf, for this Country had rather lose thousands, than we should gain hundreds.

The death of the amiable Charles was not unexpected to me. I think him happy in being releasd from Scenes which would have greatly distresst him.

Mrs Warren in her letter to mr Adams[2] complains that they have no political Friends in Braintree or Weymouth, and is quite at a loss to divine the reason of it. How different do some people estimate their motives and actions from what the world forms of them. Judge of the Supreem Court, Liut Govenour, and 3 times chosen Member of Congress, these are offices that ought not to be subject to repeated Refusal. And why should a people continue to chuse a Gentleman, and Subject themselves to constant refusals, untill it suited his conveniency to serve them. As to sacrifices, what honest Man who has been engaged in publick Services, in the perilious times through which we have past, is there, but what has made them, both of time and property? Had Genll W—n been appointed commissoner at the Court of France, instead of mr A—s would she, think you, have consented that he should have hazarded the Dangers of the sea in the midst of winter, and all the horrors of British Men of war to have served his Country, leaving her with a Young family, without even the means of giving them an Education, had any misfortune befallen him, at the same time relinquishing a profittable profession. If I may judge by what has taken place, I think she would not. Why then should the publick be deemed ungratefull? I believe no body has ever doubted his attachment to his Country, or his integrity in office and I wish the people would again chuse him, but not without an assureance from him that he would Serve.[3] I have ever considerd him as a Gentleman of a good Heart, estimateing himself however higher than the World are willing to allow, and his good Lady has as much family pride as the first dutchess in England. This is between ourselves. Poor Mrs Brown, who was Betsy Otis, had all her Grandfather left her, in the Hands of Mr Allen otis and Genll Warren. She has written several Letters to mr Adams upon the subject requesting his advice what to do. Her Father left her nothing. It is very hard she Should lose what her Grandfather left her.[4]

As to our Germantown Friends I am Grieved for them. There distresses are great. The age of some and the ill Health of others, puts it out of their power to extricate themselves.[5] Those who undertake great Scheems should have great abilities, and great funds. Blessed is a little and content therewith. I hope every one of my family will gaurd them selves against that ambition which leads people to relinquish their independance and subject themselves to the will of others, by living beyond their circumstances, as I know our own to be very moderate, for we are not able to lay up any thing here. I expect whenever we return, to have a hard struggle to get our Lads through their Education.

We expect to return in the Spring, for there is not the least prospect of doing for our Country what is expected. Mr Adams has represented every thing to congress, and his opinion with regard to every thing. Yet his Country look for a redress of Grivences from his exertions, which the conduct of the States have renderd it impossible to effect. He cannot lay these things open to the world, concequently many will censure him and clamour against him. I am prepaird to expect it.

Unstable as Water, said the old Patriarch to his son, thou shalt not excell.[6] Such an assemblage in one Character, as the Windmill builder exhibits, is seldom to be met with. The abilities of that Man applied to one point might have made him respected in it. He will triffel upon a thousand scheems, till like Icarus, his waxen wings melt, and he falls headlong to the ground. The Man who fears not debt, is not to be trusted. How is it, that he Still retains the picture? It was Demanded with the papers, and his own sent in lieu of it. I wrote him a letter by the packet which had the Newspapers you mention. I dare say he kept the contents of it a Secreet, but I did not write any other letter at that time. By the next packet I wrote to Dr Tufts and to you.[7] I hope you have got, and will soon have; many letters from me. What will be his conduct when he finds he has lost for ever the Girl he once pretended to doat on?

Alass my sister, I feel strong ties of affection for our unhappy connection, and hearing of his Sickness affected me much. Poor Man. I wonder what his circumstances are, whether he gets a comfortable support or whether he addicts himself to intemperance.

As to his wife we all know her, she has read too many Romances. Ambitions to excess—She did not think of the force of her expressions, and a well turnd period, had charms for her whether founded in fact or not. Her whole method of writing, is always in that Stile. There is always a necessity of saying, Stop, Stop, to her. She makes enchanted Castles, and would send all her children to live in them if she had *but the ability*. I am glad Louissa has been in the families you mention. I love the dear Girl who had a sweet temper. I hope she will not be spoilt. When ever I return she must be mine again. The Cloaths I sent her and what I left her, have made her decent I presume. If she wants a skirt and a winter gown, be so good as to get some red tammy from my trunks. I have sent her calico for one dress by mrs Hay and I shall send her an other and some linnen the first opportunity. Captain Biggolow sent me word on monday morning that my Letters must go that very morning, and I thought he was gone till last evening. When I returnd from a ride to Hamstead, I found a Gentleman by the name of Drake, who was introduced here not long ago and dinned with us, had calld in my absence, and left word that he should not go till tomorrow and that he would take any letters we had.

I was glad of this opportunity of replying so soon to your Letter of March and April. I think this Gentleman belongs to connecticut, he is to drink tea with us this afternoon.

Tell charles Storer, I have never been to Hamstead since he left it till yesterday, and then the coachman without any orders, stopt at the House Mrs Atkinson used to live in. We gave him orders to drive on, got out and walkd over the old Spot where we once rambled, talkd of him and wishd him with us; and mrs Atkinson in the old habitation that we might Breakfast with her again.

How have you been able to spair Cousin Betsy all winter So. Does the Parson[8] visit you often? My Regards to him, to uncle Quincy to mrs Quincy, Mrs Alleyn, and all my Neighbours. Tell Mrs Hunt I have not forgotton her, my Love to her. I shall not be able to write to Sister Shaw I fear, you will however communicate to her always if I do not write.

I will send more linnen by the first opportunity. Cambrick is as dear here as with you. I would not have you use my best peice of Cambrick, it is too good. Adieu my dear sister, always remember me kindly to mr Cranch & believe me ever your truly affectionate Sister

AA

RC (MWA:Abigail Adams Corr.).

[1] AA probably wrote most of the letter on the 24th. See her 2d letter to Cranch of the 25th, below.

[2] Of 8 April (Adams Papers).

[3] James Warren declined an appointment to the Massachusetts Superior Court in 1776, election to Congress in 1779, and the office of lieutenant governor in 1780. In 1782 he was elected to Congress but resigned in June 1783 without serving (vol. 1:403–405; 3:208; 4:20; 5:14). For additional public offices Warren either refused or resigned, see vol. 5:37.

[4] Elizabeth Otis Brown of Sleaford, Lincolnshire, daughter of James Otis Jr. and niece of Mercy Otis Warren, sought JA's advice in recovering money bequeathed to her by her grandfather Otis. The 1785 business failure of her uncles Joseph and Samuel Alleyne Otis, who were her grandfather's executors, necessitated that Brown, her husband, or a lawyer present themselves in Boston to secure her principal and interest. Elizabeth Otis married Lt. Leonard Brown of the British Army on 25 Feb. 1776 (Boston, *30th Report*, p. 70; *Sibley's Harvard Graduates*, 11:284). See Brown to JA, 8 Dec. 1785 (Adams Papers) and JA's response, 10 Dec. 1785 (LbC, Adams Papers).

[5] The Joseph Palmer family. The general, age 70, had been "confined by lameness" for several weeks in 1784; his wife Mary, age 66, lost her sight in one eye in 1782; the health of their eldest daughter, Mary, had suffered

since 1765 when she was severely frightened by the unexpected and close discharge of a gun (vol. 5:53, 464; Pattee, *Old Braintree*, p. 488, note 1).

[6] Jacob's words to Reuben, his eldest son (Genesis, 49:4).

[7] To Cotton Tufts, 10 Jan.; to Mary Smith Cranch, 26 Jan., both above.

[8] Rev. Anthony Wibird.

Abigail Adams to Mary Smith Cranch

My Dear Sister London May 25 1786

After I had closed my letter to you of yesterday I went into the city four mils distant I am from St Pauls, beyond which the New England coffe House is; where I usually Send to inquire for our Boston Captains. I found the vessel was not yet gone. I went to a shop where I buy almost every thing in the Linnen Draper way and purchased a peice of linnen for Tommy, and some calico, which is done up with it, and directed to mr Cranch. The calico of ten yd and half is to be divided between you and sister Shaw, the 5 yd is for Polly Adams and the 4 /2 for Louissa, which you will be so good as to dispose of accordingly. I also send some corded Dimity to make each of our sons a waistcoat, I consider cousin Billy in the Number. I know white increases washing, but nothing so cool and pretty for summer. You write for some cloth to make draws for them, this I will endeavour to procure for the next vessel.

I hope my dear Neices like'd the Gowns I Sent them by Jobe Field. Let me know if any thing in particular is wanted either for yourself or children and I will do my utmost to procure it for you.

How is mr otis's family, is he yet confined? She has been a doubly unfortunate Woman.

How is Mrs Welch and family, is She Still increasing it?[1] I am indebted to our Good Aunt Smith for a Letter,[2] but tis a sad thing to write to a person when you know not what to say to them; and are forced to bite your pen for a subject. What does cousin Isaac? A Parish I fear he must despair of obtaining, so much for . . . fear.

Is not Sister Shaw just making her anual visit to you? O how I envy you, believe me my dear sister, there is nothing can compensate for the vacancy of those Social feelings, or supply their pleasures, and every person who knows their value must feel alone tho in the midst of the world, a world where cold ceremony is in lieu of friendly Salutations and greetings.

Man was not made to be alone. There is more force in that expression than I once conceived there was, for I did not then suppose a person might be alone tho in a croud. Breakfast waits once more adieu with Love to cousins Lucy and Betsy, remember me also to mrs Hay and Mrs Rogers. I Saw mr and mrs copley yesterday who were both well. I am butsy I believe I told you before making linnen &c for House keeping. Nabby has written to her cousins by this opportunity[3] and presents her Duty both to her uncle and you. Pray how are my sable tennants.[4] You have not said a word about them for some time.

To one & all of my Neighbours remember me kindly & believe me as ever your affectionate Sister AA

I wrote you by mr Jenks who saild from France.

RC (MWA:Abigail Adams Corr.); addressed: "To Mrs Mary Cranch Braintree."

[1] Dr. Thomas and Abigail Kent Welsh had two sons, Thomas Jr., born in 1779, and William, born in 1784. Their family also included Harriet and Charlotte Welsh, the doctor's daughters by his first marriage (vol. 6:299; Mary Smith Cranch to AA, 14 July, below).

[2] Elizabeth Smith to AA, 3 Jan., above.

[3] Only AA2 to Lucy Cranch, 25 May, below, has been found.

[4] Phoebe and William Abdee.

Abigail Adams 2d to Lucy Cranch

Grosvenor Square May 25th 1786

Yesterday my Dear Lucy I received your kind favour of the 9th of April,[1] and it was the only Letter for me, in Pappas packett. However I hope there are others on Board. My Brother I am sure must have written. Indeed my Dear Cousin I feel under great obligations to you for your repeated attentions to me, and only lament that it is not in my Power to make you more frequent returns. I have really so many Correspondents that I find it impossible to be so particular to any of them as I wish. You my Cousin are in the first Class of my Esteem and Love and it gives me pleasure whenever you favour me with your Letters. If I should not answer them so punctually as I ought you will not attribute it to any want of affection, but necessity. I wrote you a long Letter by Mrs Hay[2] which I hope you have received er'e this. She sailed from hence in March, and we hope has had a good passage.

Mrs Warren, must, have been greatly afflicted by her sons Death, and tho not unexpected, yet his being absent must have added, to her Grief. We cannot but lament that the most amiable and Worthyest Characters are thus early removed from this Theatre. But so little do we know, that even to lament may be wrong.

Can you tell me my Dear Lucy what has become of my friend

Polly Otis Mrs Lincoln that now is.[3] I have not heard a word from her since I left America. I wrote to her soon after my arrival here, from America, and I heard through Mrs Dana,[4] that she had received my Letter but not a line from herself have I ever been favourd with. I will not however Condemn her, for she may have written, and even now may think I neglect her. But If she has, I have not received her Letter.

Next Saturday compleats a year since our arrival in this City[5] time has flown strangely, I can scarce realize it I assure you. We have been very much confined to this place, and have not made but one or two excursions of a day at a time. I wish much to go into the Country and enjoy its beauties after having been shut up, in this Noisy smoky Town for so long a time. We propose Leaving Town for a few weeks soon after the Birth day, which will be celebrated next Monday week. We talk of going to Devonshire, or to Lincolnshire, if to the former I shall it is probable be able to give you some account of your friends there, which will give me great pleasure.

We went a few days ago, about Nine Miles out, to Aysterly to see the seat of Mrs Child,[6] which, exceeded any ideas I had formd of Beauty Elegance neatness, and taste. If I had time I would attempt a particular decription of it, for your amusement. To day it is not in my power, as I have several Letters to get ready for a Gentleman who is to Call this Evening for them, and who perhaps my Cousin may see when he arrives in Boston. All I know of him is that his name is *Drake*, that he is an American, and has dined with us twice, and has now offered to take our Letters to Boston as he is going in Biglow.

We were very happy to hear that my Brother J Q A, had entered the University. The account you give of our Brothers is very pleasing. That they may Continue to merit the approbation of their friends, is my ardent and Constant wish.

Be so good my Cousin, as to remember me to all our friends, your Uncle Palmers family, Miss Paine, from whom I received a Letter[7] that I have not yet answerd, but intend to soon, to Uncle Thaxters family, to all our Cousins particularly, they are most of them Married I suppose. I find if I were to attempt to particularize every one, I should fail, therefore must request you to remember me to *all*. Adieu my Dear Cousin, write me as often as you can and continue to Love yours very sincerely A Adams

RC (MWA:Abigail Adams Corr.); addressed: "Miss Lucy Cranch Braintree."

[1] Not found.

[2] Possibly that of 20 Feb. (MWA).

[3] Mary (Polly) Otis, daughter of James Otis Jr. and Ruth Cunningham, married Benjamin Lincoln, Harvard 1777, son of Gen. Benjamin Lincoln of Hingham, on 1 Feb. 1785 (*History of the Town of Hingham, Massachusetts*, 3 vols. in 4, Hingham, 1893, 3:9, 10; Horatio N. Otis, "Genealogical and Historical Memoir of the Otis Family," *NEHGR*, 2:289, 295, 296 [July 1848]).

[4] No letters to Mary Otis or from Elizabeth Ellery Dana have been found.

[5] 27 May. For the Adamses arrival in London on 26 May, see vol. 6:169–170, 173, note 3.

[6] Osterley Park, Heston, Middlesex, the home of Lady Sarah Jodrell and Robert Child (d. 1782), heir of the London banking family. The Adamses and Jefferson visited Osterley on 20 April. See JA's description of the estate in his Diary (Namier and Brooke, *House of Commons*, 2:212; JA, *D&A*, 3:189–190).

[7] Not found.

John Adams to John Quincy Adams

My dear son London May 26. 1786

Give me leave to congratulate you on your Admission into the Seat of the Muses, our dear Alma Mater, where I hope you will find a Pleasure and Improvements equal to your Expectations. You are now among Magistrates and Ministers, Legislators and Heroes, Ambassadors and Generals, I mean among Persons who will live to Act in all these Characters. If you pursue your Studies and preserve your Health you will have as good a Chance as most of them, and I hope you will take Care to do nothing now which you will in any future Period have reason to recollect with shame or Pain.

I dont expect you to Spend much of your time in Writing to me: Yet a short Letter, now and then will be indispensable, to let me know how you do, what you want and how you like. If your Brother Thomas is fitted, I hope he will enter, this Summer: because, he will have an Advantage in being one Year with you. My love to Charles. I hope he loves his Book. I have great dependence on you to advise your younger Brothers, and assist them in their Studies. You talk french I hope, with Charles, and give him a taste for french Poetry: not however to the neglect of Greek and Roman, nor yet of English. Your Letters to your Sister have been very entertaining to Us, and I hope you will continue them, as much as you can without neglecting Things of more Consequence. My Respects to the President, Professors and Tutors, if any of them should enquire after me. You are breathing now in the Atmosphere of Science and Litterature, the floating Particles of which will mix with your whole Mass of Blood and Juices. Every Visit you make to the Chamber or study of a schollar, you learn something.

Inform yourself of the Books possessed by private Schollars and of the Studies they pursue. This you will find a valuable source of Knowledge. But I must Subscribe myself, your affectionate Father

John Adams

RC (Adams Papers); addressed: "Mr John Quincy Adams Student at the University of Cambridge near Boston"; endorsed: "Mr: Adams. May 26. 1786." and "My Father 26. May 1786."

John Adams to Cotton Tufts

My dear Friend London May 26. 1786

There is a Subject So closely connected, with the Business of my Mission to this Court, that I can no longer be Silent upon it, with Honour. The most insuperable Bar, to all their Negotiations here, has been laid by those States which have made Laws against the Treaty. The Massachusetts is one of them. The Law for Suspending Execution for British Debts, however coloured or disguised, I make no Scruple to say to You is a direct Breach of the Treaty.[1] Did my ever dear honoured and beloved Massachusetts, mean to break her public faith? I cannot believe it of her. Let her then repeal the Law without delay.

I cannot conceive the Reason, why the senate did not concur with the House, in repealing the Laws excluding the Tories. Why should a Silly Warfare be kept up at so great an Expence against those Wretches?

It is our Persecution alone, that makes their Enmity powerful and important. Are We afraid they will be popular and persuade our People to come under the British Yoke again? We have one infallible Security against that, I assure you. This Government and this Nation would Spurn Us, if We were to offer them, the Sovereignty of Us. The Reason is plain, they know it would be the certain and final Ruin of the Nation to accept it, because We could throw them again into a War, not only against Us, but France Spain and Holland, and emancipate ourselves again whenever We should please.

Are the Merchants afraid, the Tories will get their Commerce? What is this to the Country? Their Capitals will assist Us in Paying our Debts and in opening a Trade every Way. Are our Politicians afraid of their Places? In Freedoms Name let our Countrymen have their own Choice, and if they please to choose Jonathan Sewal[2] for their Ambassador at st James's, I will return to Pens Hill with Pleasure.

I long to see my Countrymen Acting as if they felt their own great Souls, with Dignity Generosity and Spirit, not as if they were guided by little Prejudices and Passions, and partial private Interests.

On the one hand I would repeal every Law that has the least Appearance of clashing with the Treaty of Peace, on the other I would prohibit or burthen with Duties, every Importation from Britain, and would demand in a Tone that would not be resisted, the punctual fullfillment of every Iota of the Treaty on the Part of Britain. Nay I would carry it so far, that if the Posts were not immediately evacuated I would not go and Attack them but declare War directly and march one Army to Quebec and another to Nova Scotia.

This is decisive Language you will say. True. But no great Thing was every done in this World but by decisive Understandings and Tempers, unless by Accident.

Our Countrymen have too long trifled with public and private Faith, public and private Credit, and I will venture to say that nothing but Remorse and Disgrace, Poverty and Misery will be their Portion untill these are held sacred.

I am my dear Friend ever yours John Adams

RC (Adams Papers); endorsed: "recd. July 10th Capt. Bigelow."

[1] The "Resolve Directing the Common Law Courts to Suspend Rendering Judgment for Interest on Actions brought by Real *British* Subjects, or Absentees, to Third Wednesday of the Next Session," which violated Art. 4 of the Anglo-Amer. peace treaty, passed on 10 Nov. 1784. It was renewed on 7 Feb. 1785 (Mass., *Acts and Laws*, Resolves of 1784, Oct. sess., ch. 77; Jan. sess., ch. 38; Miller, *Treaties*, 2:98).

[2] Jonathan Sewall, Harvard, 1748, former attorney general of Massachusetts, and one of JA's closest friends until the Revolution drove them apart. During the 1760s the two men debated the merits of James Otis Jr. and Govs. Bernard and Hutchinson in the Boston newspapers. (For JA's contributions, see *Papers*, 1:58–94, 174–211.) Sewall and his family left Boston in 1775 and were living in Bristol (*Sibley's Harvard Graduates*, 12:306–325). For JA's parting with Sewall in 1774 and reunion in 1787, see vol. 1:135–137, note 5.

Abigail Adams to Isaac Smith Sr.

Dear sir London May 27 1786

Dr Gordon call'd upon us this morning and deliverd me a letter from mr Storer. The dr is very mild, looks as if he had not recoverd quite from the Mortification under which he labourd in Boston. I know not what Success his History will meet with here, but this I can tell him, neither Americans or their writings are much in fashion here, and the Dr cannot boast the Honour of being born an American. I fancy there will be found as forcible objections against him.[1]

Mr Ramseys History which is written in a cool dispassionate Stile and is chiefly a detail of facts, cannot find a Bookseller here who dares openly to vend the ready printed coppies which are sent him.[2]

A Gentleman by the Name of Drake will hand you this, he is from conneticut. Any civilities you may shew him will oblige him, as he is a Stranger in Boston. My best Regards to all Friends. I am calld of to wait upon Dr Price who is come to make a morning visit. Yours

A A

RC (MHi:Smith-Carter Papers); endorsed: "London 27 May 86 Mrs. Adams."

[1] Rev. William and Elizabeth Gordon had sailed for London on 16 April, intending to spend the remainder of their days in England. Their return to their native land and the reverend's decision to have his history printed in Great Britain rather than the United States provoked criticism and suspicion that his work would have a British bias (Boston *Independent Chronicle*, 9 Feb., 20 April; Samuel Williams to JA, 9 April, Samuel Adams to JA, 13 April, both Adams Papers).

[2] David Ramsay, *The History of the Revolution of South Carolina from a British Province to an Independent State*, 2 vols., was published in Trenton, N.J., in 1785 and in London in 1787 (Arthur H. Shaffer, *To Be an American: David Ramsay and the Making of the American Consciousness*, Columbia, S.C., 1991, p. 303).

John Adams to Charles Adams

My dear Charles London June 2. 1786

I thank you for your Kind Letter of the 9th. of April,[1] and congratulate you on the admission of your Brother, which must add much to your happiness. Thomas I suppose will join you in the fall, my Heart will be often with my treasure, at the University. My friends in their Letters give me favourable accounts of all my sons and of my Nephew Mr. Cranch, Your Characters are fair take care to keep them so. I may be near you, sooner then you imagine—the sooner the better, but this is all uncertain.

What Profession, Charles do you thing of? You need not decide irrevocably, but it is not amiss to turn the subject in your thoughts. The Youth who looks forward and plans his future Life with judicious foresight, commonly succeeds best and is most happy—trust the Classics for History—they contain all that is worth reading. Mathematicks and Natural Philosophy you should attend to with earnestness.

Tell your Brother John, that I think it is worth while for him and you, to take your Lessons in Hebrew—it will require an hour of a few mornings—and the Letters &c are worth knowing so far, that you may be able in future Life by the help of a dictionary and

Grammar to Know the true meaning of a word or a sentence, I leave it however to your Inclinations.

You have in your nature a sociability, Charles, which is amiable, but may mislead you, a schollar is always made alone. Studies can only be pursued to good purpose, by yourself—dont let your Companions then, nor your Amusements take up too much of your time.

Read all the Books that are commonly read by the Schollars with patience and attention, but I must not enlarge. Your tender father

J. A.

LbC in WSS's hand (Adams Papers).

[1] Not found.

John Adams to John Thaxter Jr.

Dear Sir London June 2d. 1786

Yours of 22. Jan.[1] reached me, but yesterday. You would have entertained and obliged me, by an account of Grumblections and Prognostications, one wants them sometimes. They are of use, They sometimes enlighten and often fortify.

Give yourself no anxious moments about me nor my Mission, confine your anxiety wholly at home. My Mission will never be worth a groat to my Country unless it should be by persuading her to do her Duty, by fullfilling the treaty of Peace and preserving her faith. Much is well said, lately in favour of keeping faith with public Creditors abroad and at home, but nothing or very Little has appeared to excite a regard to the sacred faith of treaties solemnly sworn before the holy trinity. Britain it is true is as culpable, but this is no excuse for us.

As to me personally you know that success does me no more good than no success, I get nothing by it but abuse and I could get no more than abuse by ill success or no success. This will not abate however my Industry or Zeal to do all in my power.

I will stake all my Credit on this, that Britain will never fulfill the treaty, on her part unless we fulfill it on ours, nor open her Colonies in the W. Indies or the Continent to our Commerce, untill we shew that we have sense and spirit enough and are a Nation. The Burthen of Proof all now lies upon my Countrymen, the Labouring oar is in their Hands, and there is nothing that I can do but wait patiently and obey orders.

The Measures taking in America to promote and improve agriculture and Manufactures, do honor to the Understandings of the People and will have lasting good effect.

Let us for mercy sake be independent of the world for ships and Arms.

Let us discover too the important Mathematical Demonstration, that it is a saving to pay two hundred thousand pounds sterling, for a perpetual Peace with the five Nations of Turks, rather than to pay two hundred thousand pounds a Year, to more cruel Turks at Loyds Coffee House for insurance. Let us learn too that our trade with spain and Portugul and up the straights is worth something to add to the tribute at Loyds. When are you to be married? Do you get money fast enough. Yours J. A.

LbC in WSS's hand (Adams Papers).

[1] Adams Papers.

John Adams to Cotton Tufts

Dear sir London June 2. 1786

I am proud to learn by your Letter of 13. April[1] that I am so rich at the University. If Thomas gets in, I shall be still happier. The Expence will be considerable, and your Draughts shall be honoured for the necessary.

A Year will soon be about, and what are We to do then with John? What Lawyer shall We desire to take him, in Town or Country? and what Sum must be given with him? and what will his Board and Cloathing cost? and where shall We get Money to pay all these Expences. Shall I come home and take all my Boys into my own office? I was once thought to have a tolerable Knack at making Lawyers, and now could Save a large sum by it. I am afraid I shall not get it done so cheap as I used to do it.

I dont see, why I should stay here, unless there should be a Change in the sentiments and Conduct of my fellow Citizens. There are however some Appearances of an approaching Change.[2]

Dr Gordons Language is decent and friendly as far as I have heard. I believe the Suspicion of him that appears to have taken Place in America is needless. What Profit he will make of his History I know not. It is a story that nobody here loves to read. Indeed, neither History nor Poetry, or any Thing but Painting and Musick, Balls and Spectacles, are in vogue. Reading is out of Fashion, and Philosophy itself has become a Fop gambolling in a Balloon, "idling in the wanton summers Air," like the Gossamour, so light is Vanity.[3] Herschell indeed with his new Glass, has discovered the most magnificent Spectacle that ever was seen or imagined, and I suppose it is chiefly as a Spectacle that his Discovery is admired. If all those Single double, tripple quadruple Worlds are peopled as fully as every leaf and drop is in this, what a merry Company there is of Us, in the Universe?[4] All fellow Creatures Insects Animalcules and all. Why are We keept so unacquainted with each other? I fancy We shall know each other better, and shall see that even Cards and Routs, dancing Dogs, learned Piggs,[5] scientific Birds &c are not so despicable Things as We in our wonderful Wisdom sometimes think them.

The Bishop of Landaff, has made the Trees, not walk, but feel and think, and why should We not at once settle it that every Attom, thinks and feels?[6] An universe tremblingly alive all over.

The more We pursue these Speculations the higher Sense We shall have of the Father, and Master of all, and the firmer Expectation that all which now Appears irregular will be found to be Design. But where have I rambled? Your Fnd John Adams

RC (PHi:Society Collection).

[1] To AA, above.

[2] JA had received reports that New York, the only remaining state to approve the Continental impost, was considering its adoption, and that an interstate commercial convention was planned for Annapolis in September (from Charles Storer, 7 April; from Elbridge Gerry, 12 April; both Adams Papers).

[3] Shakespeare, *Romeo and Juliet*, Act II, scene vi, lines 18–19: "A lover may bestride the gossamer / That idles in the wanton summer air."

[4] Astronomer Sir William Herschel (1738–1822), who developed and built increasingly larger telescopes (up to forty feet in length), discovered the planet Uranus in 1781 and recently had completed *Catalogue of Double Stars, Catalogue of One Thousand New Nebulæ and Clusters of Stars*, and *On the Construction of the Heavens*, which contained the first approximately accurate model of the Milky Way (*DNB*).

[5] For AA2's reference to performing dogs, "the Learned Pig," and other animal acts presented in London, see vol. 6:220.

[6] Richard Watson (1737–1816), bishop of Llandaff since 1782, was formerly professor of chemistry at Cambridge. JA's library includes Watson's *Chemical Essays*, 3d edn., 4 vols. of 5, London, 1784–1786, and *A Collection of Theological Tracts*, Cambridge, 1785 (*DNB*; *Catalogue of JA's Library*). Watson's *Chemical Essays* was one of the first "popular" chemistry texts, selling over 2,000 copies in five years. His work discussed at length how flora and fauna respond to their environment, thus inspiring JA's comments that trees might "feel and think" (4:preface).

John Adams to John Quincy Adams

My dear son London April 2. [*i.e.* 3 *June*][1] 1786

Dr Gordon brought me your Letter of the 2d. of April, which gave me, great Pleasure. In order to get acquainted with the other

Classes enquire who are the most remarkable Scholars in each, and drop in upon them frankly, make them a visit in a Leisure hour at their Chambers, and fall into Conversation. Ask them about their Tutors manner of teaching. Observe what Books lie upon their Tables, ask Questions about the Towns they were born in, the Schools they were fitted in. Ask them about the late War, what good officers belonged to their Town. Who is the Minister and who the Representative and who the Justices or Judges that live there. What Brigade or Regiment of Militia it is in? &c Or fall into Questions of Literature, Science, or what you will.[2]

Dr Williams writes me, handsomely of You.[3] Minute down Questions to ask him, modestly. He has Sent a Volume of the Transactions of the society of Arts and sciences to sir Joseph Banks,[4] but not one of my Friends has thought of sending me one. I long for one.

One should always be a Year or two beforehand with ones affairs, if possible. Pray, do you think of any Place, or office in which to study Law? A Year will soon be round. Or shall I come home and take you into my office? Or are you so disgusted with our Greek Breakfasts at the Hague, and our Euclid suppers at Auteuil as to prefer another Praeceptor?

Take care of your Health. The smell of a Midnight lamp is very unwholesome. Never defraud yourself of your sleep, nor of your Walk. You need not now be in a hurry.

Your Books shall be sent you as soon as possible, but the Trade is so little with Boston and the less the better, that it will be I fear Several Months before I can send them. Love to Charles and Thomas. Your affectionate Father John Adams

RC (Adams Papers); endorsed: "Mr: Adams. April 2. 1786" and "My Father: About June 1786."

[1] An obvious inadvertence. JA's endorsement on the letter from JQA of 2 April, above, says that he replied on 3 June.

[2] During his senior year at Harvard, JQA intermittently entered in his Diary brief biographical accounts and assessments of his classmates. See *Diary*, 2:index, JQA–Writings and Personal Papers, for the location of each sketch.

[3] "It gives us much pleasure to have two of your Sons in this University. Both of them [*JQA and CA*] are young Gentlemen from whom their friends have the most encouraging hopes and prospects. . . . The eldest has been with us but a short time; and appears to engage with ardor in mathematical and philosophical studies. He cannot do me a greater pleasure than to put it into my power to be of any service to him in this way" (Samuel Williams to JA, 9 April, Adams Papers).

[4] *Memoirs of the American Academy of Arts and Sciences*, 1st series, vol. 1, Boston, 1785. Sir Joseph Banks (1743–1820), a botanist, was president of the Royal Society, 1778–1820 (*DNB*).

Elizabeth Smith Shaw to Abigail Adams 2d

Haverhill ⟨*May*⟩ June 4th 1786[1]

Pray Madam, are you married? Nay then the wonder ceases. No matter now how loose your affections are towards every other Object. No matter now if every former friend, lies neglected, and forgot. But is *Love really* a *narrower* of the *Heart*?[2] Does it as, Mr JQA asserts, "diminish general *benevolence*, and *particular* Friendships"? Does it like a Vortex draw all into one point, and absorb every stream of social Affection? If so—Why then I have been a long while mistaken—For I have ever considered it as an Emmanation from the almighty Mind. Though like a variety of other Passions, it may operate differently, upon different Characters. Yet when this divine Spark, is lighted up in a virtuous Bosom, and directed to a worthy Object, how is it productive of every generous, and noble Deed. How does it enlarge the Heart, give elegance to Thought, and refine the Taste, and from believing *one* Object deserving of our best affections, find ourselves drawn out in universal benevolence, and Complaceny towards the whole human Race.

Here is the opinion of your Aunt, and your Brother upon the same Subject, you see how opposite they are. I assure you, we did not always differ so much in our judgment. But in this matter we were always opposed. I would never allow, it was so *base, and sordid, a Passion* as *he* thought it. I told him however wise he was in other things, yet he was but a novice in this—that he was no judge and that in a few years, I should hear quite another Language from him.

I have a recent instance of the change of Persons with Time, and Circumstance in Mr Thaxter. Who ever spurned more at the Idea of being *in Love* than he—yes, I will say, *in Love*.[3] And where can we *now* find a greater Votary. Where can we see a more tender, attentive, fond Lover than in him. Who ever *looked his Soul* away more than *he*.

So that I have great hopes of your Brother. His time is not yet come. Minerva will I hope for a *while* shield him from the fascinating Charms of Calipso a Eucharis, or any of the *wood* Nymphs.[4] His Business now is quite of another nature. To woo fair Science, in her secret Walks, he must now hardly indulge the Idea of anything else, or view it only, as a beautiful Landscape, whose original he may one day, probably reach.

Miss Hazen after whom you enquire, left our Family last February. The frequent Assemblys occasioned her being out at so late hours as made it very inconvenient. You may possibly recollect that *in America*, late Hours were considered as greatly prejudicial to Health, and as incompatible with the Peace, and good Order of Families. And any deviation from those good and wholsome Rules, would be viewed as more criminal in our Family than in Others. This with some other things made me feel very desirious, that she should remove her lodgings.

Nature has indeed been very bountiful to this young Lady, and lavished her Favours (I had almost said) with too liberal a Hand. She appears at the first Acquaintance "Made to engage all Hearts, and charm all Eyes." I wish I could proceed with my Lord Littleton.[5] It is with grief that I find myself necessitated to forbear. At the first interviews my Neice would have thought her a precious Vine, that would have yielded the choicest Fruit, under the kind, fostering hand of Education. Unhappy girl! She lost a Parent in Infancy, feign would I, have endeavoured to supply the place—but alas! Her opinions were formed and her Mind had received a Bias, intirely inconsistent with my Ideas of a wife, amicable Woman, before she came into Haverhill. Gay company Scenes of dissapation, and the adulation payed by the other Sex, had called of her attention from things of real importance, and every worthy pursuit; and two years at A boarding School had induced her to think that to dress, to dance, to Sing, to roll the Eye, and to troll the Tongue were the only essential, and the highest Qualifications of a Lady. She has quik Wit, a fine flow of Spirits, and good humour, a lively imagination and an excellent natural Capacity. Too lovely and too charming to be given up, and lost. Yet with all these Endowments I found it utterly impossible to establish those Sentiments of Sincerity, Delicacy, and Dignity of manners, which I consider as so essential to the female Character. As she was a Lady of leisure I wished her to appropriate certain portions of time, to paticular Employments. To read with attention and methodically—but you might as easily have turned the Course of Merimac from East to West, as perswaded her to have wrote, read, or worked only as her volatile Spirit, and inclination prompted her. Words which would turn a double Construction, a double entendre, that subtle and base corruptor of the human Heart she was no ways averse to. She did not fully consider that an ungaurded look, or gesture would excite familiarities from the Libertine, and in the Eyes of a sensible, delicate Youth, forever tarnish her Reputation. Accustomed to the voic of adulation, the Language of sober Truth, was too bitter an ingredient for her to relish, and was never received without many Tears, which always grieved me, for it is much more agreeable to my feelings to commend, than to reprove.[6]

And now, my dear niece, I will plainly tell you that I feel hurt that so many vessels have arrived without one line to your aunt Shaw, who loves you so tenderly, and feels as interested in every thing that befalls, or can happen to my dear friend, as any one in America. I am sorry if you want assurances of this. I wrote to you twice in the course of the winter. One was a particular answer to yours of October the 2d, and August 3d.[7] As they have not been noticed I fear they are lost. I cannot believe my niece so wholly devoted to scenes of dissipation as to forget her friend; nor will I believe that her new connection has engrossed all her time and attention. If I thought this to really be the case, I would petition Colonel Smith to permit you to appropriate a certain portion of your time to write and to think of me. I assure you your descriptions, your sentiments, your reflections, constituted a great part of my pleasure and happiness. And as I would wish you, for your own comfort, to be a most obliging wife, I would tell him that it was really an act of benevolence to write to your aunt; that the mind gained strength by exercise; that every benevolent act sweetened the temper, gave smiles and complacency to the countenance, and rendered you more fit and disposed for the kind and tender offices of that new relation which, I presume, ere this you have entered into.

But in whatever relation, situation, or circumstances of life this may find you, Mr. Shaw joins me in wishing you "health, long life, long youth, long pleasure, and a friend,"[8] to heighten joy and soften the sorrows of this uncertain state.

Adieu! my ever dear niece, and believe me most sincerely and affectionately Your Aunt, Eliza Shaw

Dft (DLC:Shaw Family Papers); printed in AA2, *Jour. & Corr.*, 2:45–49. The editors chose in this case to print the draft copy of the letter because it is probably closer to the text of the recipient's copy than the version published and edited by AA2's daughter, Caroline Amelia Smith de Windt.

[1] In the published volume, the letter is dated 12 June.

[2] At this point in the Dft, there is an "X." There are two sentences added here in the printed copy: "Is it to this cause that I must ascribe the long silence of my niece? That not one friend has been favoured with one line since October, that I can hear of, except her brother. '*Reserve will wound.*'" The quotation is from Young, *Night Thoughts*, Night II, line 560.

[3] John Thaxter's love and future wife was Elizabeth Duncan of Haverhill (see vol. 6:351, 354, 422).

[4] A reference to François de Salignac de La Mothe-Fénelon's *Les aventures de Télé-*

maque, 1699, which, modelled on Homer's *Odyssey*, recounts the adventures of Odysseus' son Telemachus, including his shipwreck on the island of the sea nymphs Calypso and Eucharis. His journey is guided by the goddess Minerva, in the guise of Mentor (J. Lewis May, *Fénelon: A Study*, London, 1938, p. 71–73, 79).

[5] George, Lord Lyttelton (1709–1773), served as an influential member of the British government for over forty years in a variety of capacities, as well as being a noted author. The quote comes from an epitaph and inscription Lyttleton prepared for a monument to his first wife, Lucy Fortescue, who died in 1747 at the age of 29. Lyttelton continues in his description, "Tho' meek, magnanimous; tho' witty, wise; / Polite, as all her life in courts had been; / Yet good, as she the world had never seen; / The noble fire of an exalted mind, / With gentle female tenderness combin'd" (*DNB*; George, Lord Lyttelton, *The Works of George Lord Lyttelton*, London, 1774, p. 639).

[6] The text of the Dft copy ends here.

[7] Shaw wrote to AA2 on 19 Nov. 1785 (vol. 6:459–462) and 14 Feb., above. AA2's letters have not been found.

[8] Alexander Pope, "To a Lady, on her Birth-day, 1723," *Letters of the Late Alexander Pope, Esq. to a Lady*, London, 1769, p. 31.

Abigail Adams to John Quincy Adams

Grosvenour Square London June 13 1786

And so my Dear son your sister is really and Bona fida married, as fast as the Bishop and a Clerk could tie them, in the ceremony too of the Church of England with all its absurdities about it, and that through necessity, for you know that Such is the liberality of this enlightned Country that the disenting Clergy are not permitted to Marry. To your Aunt Cranchs Letter[1] I must refer you for particulars.

When I used to visit your Chamber at Autieul, and converse with you, and mutually express our anxiety with respect to future events, neither of us Dreemt of what has now taken place. You was then frequently witness to a regard and attachment, which repeated proofs of neglect, happily I presume for her, finally dissolved. Instability of conduct first produced doubt and apprehension which in silence she Sufferd. Time and reflection dispelld the mist and illusion and has united her to a Gentleman of a very different character, possessing both honour and probity, without duplicity either of mind or manners, esteemed and beloved both in his publick and private Character, and sufficiently domestick to make a worthy woman happy.

Your sister was much dissapointed that she did not receive a line from you by dr Gorden and the more so as mr Storer wrote her, that you had received hers by way of Newyork. The Letter to your Pappa gave us great pleasure.[2] We are constantly Solicitious to hear from you, and your Brothers to whom present my Love.

We are anxious to hear whether Newyork can have been so unjust and stupid as to rise without passing the impost. Such is the rumour here.[3] If she has, adieu to publick faith. How is the forfeit to be avoided. I should think Congress would do well to recall all their publick ministers and dissolve themselves immediately. It is too much to be so conspicuously ridiculous. As to this Nation, it regards neither its own interest or that of any other people.

This Letter will go by way of Newyork, or first to Baltimore. Lamb and Randle are upon their return! Alass! Affectionately yours.

AA

RC (Adams Papers).

[1] See AA to Mary Smith Cranch, 13 June, below.

[2] Storer's letter to AA2 has not been found; AA2's letter to JQA may be that of 5 Dec. 1785 (vol. 6:478–483), which JQA records receiving on 7 April (*Diary*, 2:15); JQA's letter to JA is that of 2 April, above.

[3] On 4 May, the New York legislature approved the 5 percent Continental impost but attached so many provisions to it that Congress found the New York act unacceptable. In August Congress urged Gov. George Clinton of New York to convene a special session of the legislature to reconsider approving the impost in accordance with the federal guidelines. Clinton refused their requests and the attempt to implement a general impost failed (E. Wilder Spaulding, *New York in the Critical Period 1783–1789*, New York, 1932, p. 176–178).

Abigail Adams to Mary Smith Cranch

four oclock morg

My Dear Sister Grosvenour Square London june 13. 1786

Any agitation of mind, either painfull or pleasureable always drives slumber from my Eyes. Such was my Situation last Night; when I gave my only daughter, and your Neice to *the man* of *her choice*, a Gentleman esteemed by all who know him, and equally beloved by his[1] Friends and acquaintance. A Man of strict honour, unblemish'd reputation and Morals, Brave modest and delicate, and whose study through life will be I doubt not, to make her whom he has chosen for his companion happy. Yet Satisfied as I am with the person, the event is too Solemn and important not to feel an agitation upon the occasion, equal to what I experienced for myself, when my own lot was cast. God bless them, and make them as happy through Life as their Parents have heitherto been.

When I wrote you last I informd you that the marriage would be in the course of a Month or two,[2] but it was hastned on account of the Bishop of St Asaph going into the Country, and the ceremony can be performd but in two ways in this Country, either by regular publication, or a licence Speicial from the arch Bishop of Canteburry. A Licence from him dispences with going to Church, but they are only granted to Members of Parliament, and the Nobility. When col Smith applied, the arch Bishop said it was a new case, (for you know we are considerd as foreigners) and he wisht to ask advice upon it. The next Day he wrote a very polite Letter and said that considering mr Adams's Station, he had thought proper to grant the Licence,[3] and mentiond in a friendly stile the forms which it was necessary for col Smith to go through previous to it. And as the Lady was not 21 a Notary publick must wait upon mr Adams for an attestation of his consent. All forms being compleated, the Bishop of Saint Asaph, and the Clerk of St Gorges Parish in which we live; yesterday afternoon being sunday, performd the ceremony in presence of mr, mrs and Miss Copley, mr Parker of Watertown whom you know, and Col Forest, two intimate Friends of col Smiths.[4] It was the wish and desire of both mr Smith and your Neice, to have as few persons present as with any decency could be. I really felt for her because upon this occasion, however affectionate a Parent may feel a companion of their own Sex and age must be preferable. Miss Hamilton the only Young Lady with Whom she was intimate, was gone to America, and next to her the amiable Mrs Rogers, but both were gone. Mr and Mrs Copley were the next persons with whom we were intimate, each of them of delicate manners, and worthy good people. The ceremony has some things which would be better left out; and the Bishop was so liberal as to omit the grosest, for which we thankd him in our Hearts.

In what a World do we live, and how Strange are the visisitudes? Who that had told your Neice two years ago, that an English Bishop should marry her, and that to a Gentleman whom she had then never seen; who of us would have credited it? Had Such an Idea been Started, she would never have consented to have come abroad, but the Book of futurity is wisely closed from our Eyes. When the ceremony was over, the good Bishop came to me and told me that he had never married a couple with more pleasure in his life, for he was pleas'd to add, that from the knowledge he had of the Parties, he never saw a better prospect of happiness. Heaven grant that his words may be prophetick. Think of Dr Bartlets Character, and you will know the Bishops. He is a fine portly looking Man, mild in his manners and Speach, with a Grace and dignity becomeing his Character. The arch Bishop is a still finer looking Man.

I feel a pleasure in thinking that the person who has now become one of our family, is one whom all my Friends will receive a Satisfaction in owning and being acquainted with. Tell my cousins Betsy

5. COL. WILLIAM STEPHENS SMITH, BY MATHER BROWN, 1786

See page xii

and Lucy, that they would Love him for that manly tenderness, that *real* and *unaffected* delicacy both of Mind and Manners which his every sentiment and action discovers.

On Saturday night Some evil Spright sent mr T. to visit me in a dreem. I have felt for him I own, and if he *really had any regard* for the person whom he *profest* so *much*,[5] he must be chagrined. Sure I am that his conduct in neglecting to write to her as he did for months and Months together, was no evidence of regard or attachment. Yet I have repeatedly heard her tell him, that she would erase from her Heart and mind every sentiment of affection how Strong so ever, if she was conscious that it was not returnd and that She was incapable of loveing the Man, who did not Love her. And Such has been the conduct of mr T. Since her absence, that I hope every step she has taken with respect to him, will justify her conduct both in the Sight of God and Man.[6]

Much and many Months did she suffer before She brought herself to renounce him for ever, but having finally done it, she has never put pen to paper since. When she received a Letter from him this last fall,[7] it was before she had given any incouragement to col S. and during his absence, she laid the Letter before her Father and beggd him to advise her, if upon perusing it he considerd it as a satisfactory justification, she would receive it as such. May he never know or feel, half the Misiry She sufferd for many days. Upon perusing the Letter mr A. was much affected. I read it—but I knew the Hyena too well, I knew his *cant* and *grimace*, I had been too often the dupe of it myself. I then thought it my duty to lay before mr A. Some letters from you, which he had never seen and he returnd the Letter of mr T's to your Neice and told her the Man was unworthy of her, and advised her not to write him a line. At the same time he thought it proper that I should write to him. I did so by the same conveyance which carried some letters and News papers in December.[8] Since which not a line has come from him, and I hope never will again.

I wish I Could send a Balloon for one of my Neices. I shall want a female companion Sadly. My desires will daily increase to return to Braintree. We shall take a journey soon and then the young folks go to Housekeeping in wimpole Street.[9] I have made them agree to Dine every day with us, so that only occasionally will they be obliged to keep a table by themselves.[10] Adieu my dear Sister there are parts of this Letter which you will keep to yourself. There is one ceremony which they have got to go through at Court, which is a presentation to their Majesties upon their marriage. This is always practised.

Mr and Mrs Smith present their regards to all their Friends and mine. We hope for an arrival from Boston daily, this Letter col Smith Sends for me by way of Newyork. I hope all the vessels which have saild from hence have arrived safe, if So you will find that I have not been unmindfull of you. Ever yours AA

RC (MWA: Abigail Adams Corr.). Dft (Adams Papers).

[1] In the Dft AA wrote "her."

[2] AA's last letter to Cranch was on 25 May (2d letter), above. She last mentioned AA2's marriage in her letter of 21 May, above.

[3] In the Dft AA further explained that "considering the Station of a foreign minister who takes Rank of all the Bishops in the Kingdom, he very politely granted the licence." John Moore (1730–1805) was archbishop of Canterbury from 1783 to 1805 (*DNB*).

[4] AA2 and WSS were married on Sunday, 11 June, Jonathan Shipley, the bishop of St. Asaph, officiating. The entry in the marriage register reads: "William Stephens Smith, Esqr., B[*atchelor*], and Abigail Adams, S[*pinster*], a minor. By Sp[*ecial*] Lic[*ense*] Abp. Canty. in the dwelling-house of her father his Excellency John Adams in Grosvenor Sq. by 'J. St. Asaph.'" The witnesses were John Adams, Uriah Forrest, Daniel Parker, and John Singleton Copley (John H. Chapman, ed., *The Register Book of Marriages belonging to the Parish of St. George, Hanover Square, in the County of Middlesex*, 4 vols., London, 1886–1897, 1:389).

Daniel Parker of Watertown, Mass., was a merchant and former army contractor, currently living in Europe (*Doc. Hist. Ratif. Const.*, 7:1591).

[5] In the Dft AA wrote "professt to Love."

[6] In the Dft AA included the observation that AA2 had "the free consent of her parents and an approving world upon her conduct, than their reluctant apprehensive disapproving assent."

[7] Not found.

[8] Not found.

[9] Between 20 and 24 June the Adamses traveled to Portsmouth, viewing Painshill, the estate of Charles Hamilton, deceased, near Cobham in Surrey on the 21st, and Windsor as they returned (JA, *D&A*, 3:191). See AA's comments on these sites in her letters to Elizabeth and Lucy Cranch, 18 and 20 July, respectively, both below. AA2 and WSS left Grosvenor Square for Wimpole Street on 30 June (same, 3:191).

[10] In the Dft AA noted that Wimpole Street was "not far from Grosvenor Square," and conceded that "I know it is most for the happiness of families to live by themselves. I have not therefore opposed their remove."

Elizabeth Smith Shaw to Abigail Adams

My Dear Sister Haverhill June 18th. 1786

Your Letter March 24th.[1] by Capt Cushing, with the Apron, came safe to Hand 2 Days after his Arrival at Boston. Lyde, and Cushing got in the same Day. Mrs Hays Baggage could not be broke till she came from Newyork, so that I did not get that Token, and Expression of your Love, and kindness, till a fortnight after.[2]

I cannot think what is become of a Letter I sent you last November,[3] giving you an account of my Fall Visitation.—Of my Dear Aunts Tufts's Sickness, and of her christian Resignation, and Death.—I sent it to Boston, and cannot tell you what Capt. it went by, accompanied with one for my Neice.[4] If you had received it, you would not have enquired whether the things you sent me were safe. For in that I acknowledged the Receipt, and presented my Childrens thanks to their good Aunt; for they think you are *very* good indeed to remember them.

My dear Sister your kindness oppresses me, I know that not any thing *new* is purchased for your Sons, and I cannot bear to think you should do it for me, perhaps there may sometimes be things that with you are out of Date, which if they are not in too high a Stile, may be of great service to me, and will not be valued the less by your Sister, for there dear Owner's sake. Mr Isaac Smith supplies the Pulpit at Weymouth, for Mr Evans, who married our Cousin Hulda Kent upon a Thursday and the next monday, they set of upon a Tour to new York, Philadelphia, &cc. Mr Smith purposed an exchange with Mr Shaw the last Sabbath in May, which was very agreeable, as we wished to visit our Friends. Accordingly we took Betsy Quincy,[5] and journed on till we came to Cambridge. At the University we stoped, and spent an agreeable hour with our *foster Sons*. There was a Paragraph in your Letter by Capt Cushing that I received a week before, that surprised me, or *rather* excited my Curiosity. I thought of a Mr Murry, Col. Smith, and Col. Humphries. Did you think we should not want to know the Name of this favoured youth? or did you think we were high priests this year, and could divine? I did not know but you sent me that Phamplet of Col. Humphries, to anounce, and deleniate the Man. But of Mr JQA, I demanded *immediate Satisfaction* which was readily complied with by puting your Letter into my Hands, which informed him of the *Rise* and *progress* of this late Attachment. Love founded in virtue, and approved by Reason, must rise, or fall in proportion as the Object is deserving.[6] However she may be represented to the World, in my view she stands free from the charge of Fickleness, and Inconstancy. For what affection can withstand the force of continued, studied neglect.

I consider the human Mind something like a musical Instrument, where if any of the Notes are silent, or out of tune, it produces a vacuum, a discord, which interrupts the harmony of the whole Machine. So the Mind when once touched by the tender Passion of Love, and set to a certain number of Ideas, will never after be in Unison, unless it find some Object capable of vibrating those delicate Keys. And experience informs us, that it does not require so great an Artist to put an Instrument in Tune, as it did at first to form one.

We pursued our Course from Cambridge, to Milton where we stoped, and drank Tea, with General Warren and, Lady. It was here, that I was first Informed of my Neices Marriage.[7] And as I had but just heard of the Choice, it rather hurried my Spirits, and I could not but consider the News as premature, and without sufficient foundation, to announce a matter of so much Importance, as it must really be to Mr T–. I found the Story was spread far, and wide, and I could see no person, but what would accost me–"Your Neice is married then, what will Mr. T– do, and say." *You*, who know Mankind, and particular Persons so well, can easily imagine what each one will say. I heard but one person say they were sorry, and they gave this reason, "that now he would direct his distructive Course, and disturb some other peaceful Family." I could not but recollect that Line in Young,

> "*Poor* is the *friendless* Master of the World."[8]

Yet the Man has a Capacity that would ensure him buisiness, and Talents, which if Virtue was their Basis, would endear him to the whole World.

I felt–I cannot tell you how for him. He came home late, and rose by day light–and avoided us, as he would a Pestilence.[9] Mr Shaw sought for him at Mrs Vesseys, at Mr Thayers, at the wind-mill, but all in vain. I cannot bear to see a person unhappy, even though I know it is the inevitable Consequence of evil, and wrong Conduct. I never could triumph over a dissappointed Person, but whether *he* is really so, I cannot tell. But some tenderness is always due, to those who have ever expressed regard, and have been esteemed by us. The least said, I verrily believe is best. I know my Neice must feel happy in her Choice, as she has now the sanction of both Parents. I have enquired, and his Character is good here. William Smith is a Name, which from my earliest Infancy, I have been taught to revere, and love. It is the Name of my only Son. Your Daughter now ties my affections, with *more* than a threefold Cord. May they for Days, and years to come dwell together as "the pleasant Roe and as the loving Hind."[10] But when–O when shall I see you all again. Your Son Thomas is in good health, grows tall and thin. I hardly think he will enter the University this year. I have taken for him the light silk Camblet Coat, and have provided a Taylor in the house, I can have greater prudence used, and the things done to suit me better, than if I put them out.

Adieu–ever yours E S

Write often, and *scrible* you always please your Sister. You will excuse my not coppying. I hope you will be able to read.

RC (Adams Papers); docketed in an unidentified hand: "Mrs Shaw June 18. 1786."

[1] Possibly an error for AA's letter of 4 March, above.

[2] Katherine Hay carried a piece of silk from AA for Elizabeth Shaw (AA to Mary Smith Cranch, 15 March, above).

[3] Of 6 Nov. 1785 (vol. 6:451–454).

[4] To AA2, 19 Nov. (vol. 6:459–462).

[5] Elizabeth Shaw's daughter.

[6] AA to JQA, 16 Feb., above.

[7] The news probably came from the Cranch family, who misunderstood a visiting card from the William Smiths of Clapham, which was enclosed in a package from AA. See Elizabeth Cranch to AA, 20 May, and note 4, above.

[8] Young, *Night Thoughts*, Night II, line 571.

[9] The Shaws were visiting the Cranches, where Royall Tyler had been boarding.

[10] An allusion to Proverbs, 5:19.

John Adams to Isaac Smith Sr.

Sir　　　　Grosvenor Square June 20. 1786

Yesterday I received yours of Ap. 18.[1] Via Leverpool. Money may be sent to the East, to purchase Tea and other Commodities for which We now send it to London, and pay double Price. Besides Tobacco Peltries and Ginzeng, may be procured.

Our Oil might easily find a Market in almost any great Town in Europe. Nothing is wanting but to make known the superiour Qualities of our Sperma Cæti Oil, by Samples and Experiments. This Method Boylston took and Succeeded. But Indolence always sees a Lion in the Way.

If there is a third less of real Property now, in Boston than there was in 1775, what is become of it?

Some of it is banished, I suppose with the Tories, and would return if that Banishment were taken off. Some of it has been spent in a more elegant and convenient mode of living perhaps, and some say that much of it has been consumed in sloth and Idleness. If this is true Industry and Frugality may restore it.

In all Events, I am convinced, that We shall find no kind of Relief from this Country, untill We repeal all the Laws that bear hard upon the Treaty of Peace, nor Shall We then find an effectual Relief, but in Measures calculated to encourage, our own navigation Agriculture and Manufactures, the Commerce of the states with one another, and transferring our foreign Commerce from Great Britain to other Countries.

On Sunday the 11th. of this Month, Miss Adams was married to Mr William S. Smith, a Name forever to be respected in this

Family. My Regards to all our Friends. With great Respect your most obedient John Adams

RC (MHi:Smith-Carter Papers); addressed by WSS: "Isaac Smith Esquire Boston"; note in an unknown hand: "America Atkin's"; note in another hand "Recd & forwarded by Your Mt Obdt Carneau & Marlin"; endorsed: "London June 86 J Adams."

[1] Not found.

Lucy Cranch to Abigail Adams

Braintree June 24. 1786

How good you are my dear Aunt, to favour me so often with your charming Letters, you cannot think how proud I am of them. I read them very often. I hope I shall even be the better for the instructions contained in them, and catch some of that warm regard for honour and virtue which shows itself in every sentence.

What an idea do you give us of high life in Europe. Is it possible that beings who call themseves reasonable, can so far relinquish every mental pleasure, and wast their lives in a continual round of dissapation, and dignify it with the name of happines, of enjoyment: what a perversion of terms! Well may our Country dread every step to luxury, every step we advance towards it, we are farther from the path of happiness. Yet their are many who sigh for the dissapations of foreign courts, for routs, and draws. A number of families in Boston are indeavouring to bring them into fashion. We must be obliged to fortunes fickle wheel, for preventing them.

You my Aunt have given me an account of a Ball: I will endeavour to give you a discription of the parade at the opening of Charlestown Bridge.[1] If I had your discriptive pen: I might give pleasure. I am sure you would have felt as much interested in it as you do at a Birth night Ball.

It was: on the 17th. of June, the aniversary of the day which beheld Charlestown in flames. Sister and I went to town to *see*. The proprietors, of the Bridge, invited each branch of the legislature, the Governors of the College, the Clergy the Lawyers, and a large number of Gentlemen besides, to an entertainment on Bunker hill on the very spot where the memorable battle was, fought and where the military glory of our country began.

6. "VIEW OF THE BRIDGE OVER CHARLES RIVER," 1789
See page xiii

We went to Charlestown in the morning that we might have a full view of the procession. It went frome the state house in Boston. The appearence the most pleasing to me was that of the artificers who had been employed on the Bridge. They walked derectly after the artillery, each of them carring one of the instruments they had ussed, in forming that stupendious work.

What a striking contrast to that day eleven years when every mecanick threw down the harmless instruments of industry, and caught hold of the sword, and rushed impetuous to the fight. After the artificers followed the proprietors then the Govenor Leunt Govenor, Councel, Senate, representitives, &c. &c. &c: to near a thousand Gentlemen who dined upon the Hill. When the procession came to the draw, which was then first passed, the Cannon were fired and the Bells rang. After, diner 13 toasts were drank a ussial, and a number of patriotick songs were sang accompanied by a band of music: the one composed on the occation I, will, enclose you.[2] I never saw such a vast crowd of people in my life, they poured in from every part of the country. The Bridge looks beautifully in the evening, there are 40 lamps on it.

Cousin Charles and my Brother were with us. Mr. J.Q.A is too much of the philosopher, and student to be at such a *frolick*, it could not draw his steadiness aside.[3] We sometimes fear that he will injure his health by his very great attention to his studies. He is determined to be *great* in *every particular*.

Our good Aunt Smith has been declining fast all this summer. She is now very ill her life is dispaired of even for a day. Her truely pious life gives us assurence the change for her must be for the better. She will leave an afflicted family. Mrs Cushing she that was Lucy Thaxter, is numbered with the silent dead. She has been married but littel more than a year. She lived but a day and a half after the birth of her child. She died last week. We did not know of it till to day. It must have been a great shock to the family. It is by these afflictive strokes, that heaven weans from a world we Love too well, and by taking from us our friends, bids us be also ready.

Where is my dear Cousin Nabby, what can be the reason that her pen has been so long silent. It is almost a year since her last Letter to me was wrote.[4] I have wrote to her four of five times since.[5] I will not write again 'till I am certain by what name to address her. I hope to find the same friend in Mrs S—th that I ever have in my Cousin Nabby. Remember me most affectionatly to her. She has my sincer wishes for her happiness. Since I wrote last we have had the pleasure of seeing some of our English friends, and relations.[6] We are much pleased with them, I wishe they could have settled in Braintree. They would in some measure have supplied the place of your dear family.

Mr Evans is married to Huldah Kent, they are to live in our house at Weymouth. We shall yet have one inducement to visit it.

Be pleased my dear Madam to make my respects acceptable to my Honoured Uncle; and receive yourself, the sincerest Love and respect of your ever obliged— Neice Lucy, *Cranch*

Sunday July 2.

We have lost the paper that had the song in, which I intended to have enclosed you, Papa will send the Papers you will see it in them. I have just made these ugly blots. I am asshamed to send such a slovenly Letter. I have not time to coppy it as papa must take it to town tomorrow. I must beg your condour. I am made obbliged for my Gown and ribbon. It will never be in my power to return your goodness to me.

RC (Adams Papers); endorsed: "Lucy Cranch july 24th 1786."

[1] For the Charlestown Bridge, see the Descriptive List of Illustrations, No. 6, above.

[2] Not found.

[3] See JQA to AA2, 18 May, and note 11 for JQA's reasons for not attending the celebration.

[4] Of 23 June 1785 (vol. 6:183–186). AA2's letter of 20 Feb. (MWA) had not yet reached Braintree.

[5] None of these letters has been found.

[6] See Richard Cranch to JA, 20 May, and note 3, above.

Elizabeth Cranch to Abigail Adams

My dear Aunt Boston July 1st. 1786

I have this moment heard that Cushing will sail for London in 3 days, It mortifies me to let one oppertunty pass unimprovd that might convey to my Aunt the assurances of my grateful affection, and earnest wishes for her happiness; Time nor absence have abated that (may I not call it) *filial regard* which your tender kindness, early inspired my heart; the recollection of inumerable instances of it call forth, many a time the trickling tear; when I am fondly indulging myself in contemplating the *pleasing past*! and cherishing the chearful hope that those days of happiness, repose and friendship may soon return; In the future plan of happiness which fancy has portray'd, *your return* makes so essential a part, that it would be quite incomplete without it. But, the melancholy occasion that has brought me to town, warns me to beware of placing too strong an attachment on any future Scheme, nothing can be more uncertain; The sudden death of *our* Aunt Smith is an afflictive stroke to us all. You will have accounts probably before this reaches you. The day before Yesterday, I followd her to the silent Tomb!

> "The sweet remembrance of the *just*
> Shall flourish when they Sleep in dust."[1]

Sure then *this* good Woman will live forever in the hearts of her Friends; her unaffected piety, threw a continual serenity and chearfulness over her whole Life, and disrobed Death of all its Terrors! Another, a more striking proof of deaths power to "cull his Victims from the fairest Fold,"[2] we have in the sudden exit of *Mrs Cushing* (Lucy Thaxter). This day week she was buried, and left a little infant, one day old! What changes *have been made* in the Circle of your friends since your absence by this all powerful conqueror! And ah! I tremble at what *may* be!

Yesterday, PM, being very pleasant, induced Papa, Mama, Cousin Wm: Smith, and myself, to take a ride over *the Bridge* to Charleston and Cambridge, to drink Tea, with my Brother, Your two Sons, and Leonard White; they always appear so happy to see us, that I know not any Visits that I recive so much pleasure from.

We could not help regretting, that you and my dear Cousin, should lose so much satisfaction. Before Thomas, leaves, Colledge, tho, we thougth, we hoped, we might all assemble *yet*, at *his* Chamber.—I could not help laughing at Cousin john, for the *learned dirt*, (not to say *rust*) he had *about* and *around* him. I almost scolded, however we seized his gown and Jackett and had a clean one put on. I took my Scissars and put his *Nails* into a decent form, and recommended strongly a *Comb* and *hair-string* to him. He invited me to come once a *Quarter*, and perform the like good services [for] him again.—Charles was a contrast, but [not?] *too* strikingly so, he is naturally and habitually neat. But they are *all good*—as yet. I feel proud of my *Brothers*, they are *beloved* and *respected*.

Tis dinner time and I am engaged to dine at my Uncles.[3] My dear Cousin, I long to write to, but feel so awkward, at addressing, *I know not whom*, that I shall only ask her *acceptance* and *belief* of my sincerest Love, of my real joy, at the prospect of her happy Connexion, and my constant wishes, that each day may encrease her enjoyment, that she may ever feel the self-approbation, of a steady uniform perseverence in the path of consious rectitude.[4]

Please to present my Uncle with my most respetful and affectionate regards, and accept the Dutiful and grateful affection of your

E C

Sister Lucy is at home and has been writing you.

RC (Adams Papers); addressed: "Mrs Adams. *Grosvenor Square*"; endorsed: "Betsy Cranch july 1 1786." Some loss of text where the seal was removed.

[1] A common paraphrase of Psalms, 112:6.
[2] Young, *Night Thoughts*, Night V, line 918.
[3] Probably Isaac Smith Sr.
[4] The remainder of the text is written lengthwise in the margin.

John Quincy Adams to Thomas Boylston Adams

My Dear Brother — Cambrige July 2d: 1786

I have not written to you before, since I left you,[1] because my Studies and European Letters have engrossed all my Time. But as you will probably soon enter this University, I wish to give you a few hints which you may improve as you please. You will consider them, not as the commands or instructions of a Preceptor, but as the advice of a friend, and a Brother.

Your intimate acquaintances will probably be in your own Class, at least alm[ost all] of them; and let me strongly recommend to you great caution, and Prudence in [the?] choice of them for on this in a great measure depends your reputation in College and even all through Life. If the Class which you will belong to is numerous, you will undoubtedly, find in it a great variety of Characters. Some will be virtuous and studious. These two Qualities are most commonly united, as are also their opposites, vileness and vice. It is not necessary to tell you that those of the first sort [. . .] will be proper Companions for you, and such as you may always call your friends without a blush. It is probable you will perceive that those, who are the most officious, the most complaisant, and perhaps the most agreeable, on a short acquaintance, will after some time prove unworthy of your friendship. Like paintings in crayons, which look very well at a distance, but if brought close to the eye, are harsh and unpleasing, the most amiable characters are often the most reserved, as wisdom, and prudence require, that we should establish an intimacy, with those only whose characters we have had opportunities to study, and who have given us proofs, of their attachment to honour, morality and religion. I could wish you to be upon good terms with all your Classmates, but intimate with few, endeavour to have no Enemies, and you can have but few real friends. Never be induced by ridicule or by flattery to depart from the Rule of right which your own Conscience will prescribe to you. There are [some] persons, who make it a practice to laugh at others whose principle is to [. . . .], of Virtue, but you may be persuaded, that whatever such fellows may pretend they will always esteem you, for behaving well. Vice will sometimes condescend to beg for respect, but Virtue commands it, and is always sure to obtain it.

Next to the Ambition of supporting, an unblemished moral Reputation, that of excelling as a Scholar, should be nearest your heart. These two Qualities are not frequently united: four or five is as great a number as a Class [can] generally boast of. But you will find, that they, are always the favourites of the Class, and never fail meeting with [esteem?], not only from their fellow Students, but likewise from the Government of the University. I have heard one of the most respectable Characters in the Class, which is now about to graduate, say, that he has made it a Rule, ever since he entered College, to study upon an average six hours in a day. If you feel yourself capable of this I would recommend it to you as an example. There is no difficulty in it, and I am persuaded that after a short Time it would be more agreeable to you than to be idle, and it would be a determination which you would remember, all the remainder of your Life with Pleasure; and you would soon, very soon perceive the advantages deriving from it. But if you would put such a resolution into execution, you should determine, not to content yourself merely with studying for recitations, and you will never be at a loss what to Study. In short that both your moral and your Literary character, be set as an example for your own Classmates and the succeeding classes to imitate, is the sincere, and [express] wish of your ever affectionate friend & brother J.Q. Adams

P.S. Present my best respects to [our] Uncle and Aunt and to Mr: Thaxter, my Compliments wherever you please.

N.B. I have requested of Dr: Jennison, that he would take you for his freshman, he did not give a positive answer, but you will not enter into any engagement contrary to it.[2]

RC (Private owner); addressed: "Mr: Thomas B. Adams. at the Revd: Mr: Shaw's *Haverhill* Honoured by Leonardus White Esqr." Some loss of text where the seal was removed and the manuscript was stained.

[1] On 14 March, when JQA left the Shaw family in Haverhill to enter Harvard (JQA, *Diary*, 1:415).

[2] This paragraph is written on the address page of the letter.

Mary Smith Cranch to Abigail Adams

My dear Sister Braintree July 2d 1786

I did not receive your last Letter by the way of new york[1] till after the vessail had Sail'd with my Letters. I was much diverted to think the few Lines coll: smith wrote in your name should have produce'd you So long a Letter from Mr Cranch. The coll really counterfitted your hand writing very well. Betsy said as soon as she saw it, that it did not look just like aunts hand. If it was hers She had mended it greatly.

I rejoice, I greatly rejoice with you in your agreable connection. I hear a very good character of him from every Person who has any knowledge of him, a perfect contrast to the other, but why my sister did you not tell us when and where they were married. Some of her Friends wish it had not been so sudden, but it is best, I believe as it is. Mr T would have given her not a little uneasiness while she remain'd single, but whether from Love or vanity I shall not pretend to say. I hear he says he is sure it is not her own doings, her Friends have been the wicked instruments. He was so sure of her that he thought he might treat her as he pleass'd. I want much to know what you have written him. I hope you have clear'd me and her other corrospondents from being the cause of his dissapointment. I have not said one word to him my self upon the Subject. He does not now live with us. He had not for above two months eat with us, excepting that he Breakfasted and din'd with us, a Sundays. He would come in after we were abed, and go out before we were up. I did not like such kind of Boarding, and last May I told him one morning, "that as he did not eat here, I thought it would be more convinient for him to sleep where he eat, and that I should want the chamber for my Nephews." He made me no answer but never has been in the House Since till yesterday morning before we were up. He came and took some of his Cloaths. He has not only forsook our House, but the publick worship also he has not been in the meeting house since he left us although he boards almost next to it. I believe he has not been out of Braintree Since. His mill and his Farm keep him fully imploy'd. He is finishing his office and repairing his House. He is *dismally* mortified, but I am sure he ought not to blame any body but himself. I cannot help pitying him a little *although* he has told so many Fibs about me.[2]

3d

I have just heard he is gone to see his mother, went yesterday morning. Will you believe it sister, His Sister is dead and bury'd and I am told he neither visited her in her sickness nor attended her Funeral, altho he was Sent for to do both. The poor woman dy'd of a broken heart. Her Husband has spent her fortune at the Tavern and Gameing Table, and is become quite a Sot I hear. Her poor Mother will now have two more little ones to take care off. She has Johns three and himself into the bargain.[3] How unhappy that poor woman is, not to have one child in whome she can take much comfort. How much of the comforts of our Lives may be distroy'd by the ill conduct of our near connections.

I have not yet been to Hingham. I design it, in a day or two, they must be very melancholy. I have not yet heard the perticulars of my Cousins Illness.[4] Uncle Quincy[5] has not been off his Farm since December. He fancys he cannot ride, and we cannot perswaid him to try. He walks about his Farm and is well excepting that he has the Rhumatism in one Leg sometimes, but not so bad but I found him one morning walking at five o clock after his sheep which had got into the Town land. I would have had him get into the chaise and rid home or took a littel ride, but I could not prvail with him to do it. I am affraid he will be as whimsical as our dear Aunts have been. Aunt Thaxter[6] has not been in the meeting house for above four years. So many Breaths she thinks would Stiffle her. What a pity she does not live in Braintree. She never would have that difficulty here.

Our good Parson thinks that variety is as hurtful to the heads as the Stomacks of his Audience and therefore continues to feed us with the same simple ⟨*Fish*⟩ Food you have so often partook off. He never fails making inquierys about you when he comes here, and his visits are not less frequent for your Family being absent I assure you.

Madam Quincy and Daughter as well. Mrs Q is well pleass'd with her Silk and desires me to present your Love and many thanks for your [care?] about it. As for me my dear Sister I want words to express my gratitude to you for your kindness to me and my children. Indeed my sister I fear you will do too much for us we cannot return the obligation. Billy is greatly oblig'd for his coat and wastcoat. They are made and look very handsome. The coat is rather Short for him he is I believe as tall as his Papa. The wastcoat is not to be put on till commencment when your Healths and that of the colln. and his Ladys will be drank.

I wonder if any body has told you that Bill Bracket dy'd last Summer and that his wife has left her Husband Vesey, and he has been in Jail three or four times for some of his mischeif.[7] Your mother Hall was well yesterday. She has her Silk you sent made, and it looks beautifully. Your Brother Adams and Family are well. Our Haverhill Friends are well. Cousin Thomas, will not go to college this commencment, he will be fitted, but his Brothers think he had better stay till one year is added to his age, and that his Studys with his uncle will be of greatter Service to him than going So young would be. I shall write again by the next vessel.

Yours affectionatly M C

RC (Adams Papers); endorsed: "Mrs Cranch july 2d 1786."

[1] Of 26 Feb., above.

[2] Cranch added "*although* he has told so many Fibs about me" when she continued writing the letter on the 3d.

[3] Royall Tyler's elder sister, Jane, married David Cook of Dunstable in 1780 and had two children, Horace and Mary. She died 22 June after a short illness and her funeral took place on the 26th from the Cooks' home in Boston, which Jane Tyler evidently inherited from her father. Royall Tyler Sr.'s estate had been divided equally among his three surviving children (*Grandmother Tyler's Book*, p. 331; *Boston Gazette*, 26 June; Thwing Catalogue, MHi).

John Steele Tyler, Royall's brother, married Sarah Whitwell, his stepsister, in 1775. Following Sarah's death on 19 Dec. 1785 in Billerica, Tyler and his three young children (John, Royall, and Sally Whitwell) moved to Jamaica Plain to live with his mother, Mary Steele Tyler Whitwell, a widow since 1775 (G. Thomas Tanselle, *Royall Tyler*, Cambridge, 1967, p. 6, 19; Boston *Independent Ledger*, 26 Dec. 1785; *NEHGR*, 96:191 [April 1942]; *Vital Records of Billerica Massachusetts to the Year 1850*, Boston, 1908, p. 194).

[4] Lucy Thaxter Cushing.

[5] Norton Quincy.

[6] Anna Quincy Thaxter, AA's aunt, wife of John Thaxter Sr. and mother of Lucy Thaxter Cushing.

[7] William Brackett (b. 1747) of Braintree served in several different companies and regiments during the Revolutionary War and died while stationed at the fort at West Point in either 1784 or 1785. He was married to Mercy Brackett on 6 Nov. 1773; they had three children (Herbert I. Brackett, *Brackett Genealogy*, Washington, D.C., 1907, p. 538; *Braintree Town Records*, p. 878).

Abigail Adams to Mary Smith Cranch

My Dear sister London july 4 1786

Your two Letters of May 7th and 15th[1] reachd me yesterday, and I was puzzeld a long time to find out what you could mean by the card, till your Neice, now really Mrs Smith, said that She recollected winding the ribbon upon a card of invitation which happend to lie by her, from Mrs Smith of Clapham, a Lady I have mentiond formerly to you, whose Husband is a Member of Parliament. You was however only a few Months too soon in Your conjecture, for on Sunday the 12 of june, was Married (by the Bishop of St Asaph), at his [*our*] house in Grosvenour square, Miss Adams the only Daughter of his Excellency John Adams esqr minister Plenipotentiary from the united States of America, to Col William S. Smith Secretary of Legation, as the News papers will inform you, if they do not publish this from them, on the 13th of june I wrote both to you, and my Son J Q A, by a Gentleman, col Forrest who was present upon the occasion and who saild for New York a few days after. The Young folks were terrible affraid of a Bustle upon the occasion, they were as timid as partrideges, and would gladly have had only the Bishop present, but two more witnessess were necessary to render it valid. Col Forest and mr Parker whom you know, were the Gentleman mr Smith chose, and I thought proper to ask Mr Mrs and Miss Copely to drink tea with me, tho they did not know the occasion untill the Bishop came. These with the Clerk of the Parish who was a necessary in the Buisness composed the whole company, and tho the ceremony was quite Novel to us all, Your Neice past through it with a good deal of presence of Mind, even repeating after the Bishop, I "Abigail take the William" &c which is rather more embarrassing than the curtzy of assent in the dissenting form.[2] The feelings of a Parent upon an event of this kind can only be known by experience, even where the most favourable prospect of happiness appears, to give a way a Child is a Solem peice of Buisness.

Upon the first of this Month they commenced House keepers in Wimpole Street, but tho they dine with us every day, it feels very Lonesome I assure you. On fryday evening they agreed to go to Renalegh with a Party and from thence go to their own House, but I was unwell and could not accompany them, and would have had them deferd going to house keeping till Monday, but as all their things had gone that afternoon they resolved upon going. The company who were of the party, were to drink tea with us but I found before the hour came that your Neice wisht to stay at home. She endeavourd to Suppress and conceal the Idea that had taken possession of her mind too strongly for her to enjoy any of the amusements of the Evening, that of quitting a Fathers House, feelings which I dare say you recollect to have experienced yourself. I known not how to express it better than an Idea of putting ourselves out of the protection of our parents to Set up for ourselves. This together with the apprehension that her Parents would be very Lonesome affected her more than I was aware of alltogether made her a very unhappy Night. The Soothing tenderness of a kind Partner who felt almost as much affected as She was, and the Chearfulness which her parents assumed dispelld the next day in some measure the cloud. I Say assumed for I really felt as great an inclination to cry as she did. Do not laugh at us my dear sister, may you never know what it is to be in the midst of the World, and yet feel alone. Here are we four, and no more. Do you know that company is widely different from Society? No I cannot leave her in this Country. New York is too far distant. The family with which she is connected is numerous and amiable, from their Characters will receive her I doubt not with Friendship and regard. Col Smith has received from his Mother[3] a very affectionate Letter in replie to one he wrote her requesting her consent to the Match. If we live to meet upon the other side the atlantick I promise my self with happy days yet.

The morning after they went to housekeeping Mr Adams went into his Libriary after Breakfast, and I into my chamber where I usually spend my forenoons. Mr A commonly takes his daily walk about one oclock, but by eleven he came into my room with his Hat and cane, "and a Well I have been to See them: what said I could not you stay till your usual Hour, no I could not he replied, I wanted to go before Breakfast."

You observe in your Letter that I had never mentiond the Name of the Gentleman, who is now your Nephew, in any of my letters to my Friends. You may easily conceive the reason why I did not. When we first came here the mind of your Neice was much agitated with mr T. conduct towards her. She was led to think that her Friends had reason for their opposition. She considerd herself as bound, and was fearfull of committing an act of injustice. She was greatly perplext, but silent, her little pocket Book would sometimes discover her Sentiments. She had coppied from Shakespear which she was then reading: the four following lines

> "I am sorry I must never trust thee more
> But Count the World a stranger for thy sake
> The private wound is deepest; oh time most curst
> Mongst all foes, that a friend should be the worst."[4]

It was natural for a Gentleman who was much in the family, to notice this uncommon Sedateness and to perceive that Something was amiss, tho he knew not what the cause was. He set himself to amuse and to divert. I believe it is Richardson who says, that the Grieved mind loves the Soother.[5] I soon perceived that the inclination for being alone lessned, and that the attentions of this Gentleman were not unpleasing besides she heard all mouths speaking in his praise. But in him I saw a growing attachment which distresst me. What to do I knew not. To him I could not say any thing, for I did not presume he had made any declaration. But it brought on a conversation which I related to you in a former Letter,[6] tho I avoided telling you then who the Gentleman was that her Question related to. When she upon my hinting to her that I had observed a partiality in col S towards her, askd, do you not think him a Man of honour? to which I replied yes, of strickt honour, and I wish I could say as much for all your acquaintance. I added further, but I do not think col S knows your Situation. Her replie was that he did. Then said I you must have very lately informd him. I went on to say, if you was disengaged not only I but every Friend you have would rejoice, for it is my opinion that mr T. has acted a dishonorable part by you. If he had really felt the regard for you which he professd, he could not so grossly have neglected you. If he meant to try your affections for him by such ungenerous methods they were unbecomeing a Man of Honour, and it my duty to say to you without any view to any future connextion that the accounts I have had of him, give me no reason to be satisfied with his conduct since I left America. But if you was really disengaged I do not think you ought to give any encouragement to col S. upon an acquaintance of so short duration. Tis true that he has a universally good Character, and is much respected and I have reason to think would Scorn to Supplant any person. Here ended our conversation and she retired in Silence, but an hour after sent me a note with the coppy of a letter which she wrote mr T. from the Bath hotel,[7] in which She had very plainly told him her mind, tho it did not contain an absolute dismission. A coppy of a card also to col S written the day before, and upon the first opening she had to inform him that she could consider him in no other light than as a friend.[8] The Letter to mr T. was written in May, and this note in August. I mention this to shew that her conduct was not the result of fickelness. With these papers, she requested me to lay before her Pappa, all the letters I had received from America with regard to mr T. and to beg his advice what to do, that his opinion should be the guide of hers. This produced a conversation between her and her Father which I related to you formerly. She said what I really believe she thought at that time, that she had no partiality for any other person. In this State of things col S. desired leave of absence, that he might go to the Prussian Review for a Month or two. He went and did not return till the begining of december: he was a stranger to what had taken place in his absence. A little before his return, she received a letter from mr T.[9] which distresst her beyond measure. He had touchd every string which was possible could affect her. In short it was the most artfull letter I ever read, pathetick and tender in the extreem. I could not read it without tears, yet I saw the consumate art of it. She gave it to her pappa and requested to know of him, if he thought it an exculpation of his conduct, and whether she ought to answer it. Mr Adams was not much less affected with it than I was, and not personally knowing the Man did not see all his art. But it was his judgment that it was not a justification and that I, instead of Your Neice Should answer it. This I did in December, and it was to him the Letter I mentiond by the newyork packet was written, a coppy of it I enclose to you.[10] I am sorry to find him disgracing himself, tho it so amply justifies her. Mr Trumble in congratulateing me upon a late event, and a happy escape added, nobody ever Yet knew T. without both Loveing and despicing him, and this I believe is a good picture of him.

Upon the return of col S. he was treated with more reserve than formerly. This piqued him, and he said to me a few weeks after his return: that he felt him self unhappy, that he was incapable of acting a dishonorable part. He wisht to treat the Lady as a sister, her conduct towards him had been generous, and she should find that his should be equally so. As I did not chuse to undeceive him, I told him I thought he had not been sufficiently gaurded and that supposing as he did that she was disengaged, he could not justi[f]y sudden attachments, and he must be sensible her greater reserve was in concequence of it. It was in some of these Brotherly and Sisterly conversations I suppose that the veil dropt—the little deity who had been watching for this moment, blind as he is said to be, felt his way to the Heart, and finding all obstacles removed, inclosed them both in one net, draw'd it close, and then marchd of in triumph. The Gentleman immediately made his Sentiments known to her Friends,[11] obtaind their sanction, and has given me but little rest till I consented to their Marriage, which would not however have been quite so soon, if the Bishop had not been leaving London for the Summer. Thus you have a History of this matter. You will not expose it, it would be ridiculous to relate it, to any but a particular Friend, and then only to justify her conduct.

I have nothing to regreet in this Matter but the Idea that she will be seperated too far from me. But to think her happy however distant; is less painfull than I fear it would have been to have had her near me.

You complain of the shortness of my Letters, but do you recollect, how many Friends I have to write to, who are pleasd to value my correspondence so highly, as to appear dissapointed when I do not write them. I own this is very flattering to me, but I feel myself exhausted in concequence of it.

I am glad to find the things I sent pleasd you, hope Biggolow has also arrived safe.

You will have a Buisy time this Month with all the Lads about you. I seem as if I was living here to no purpose, I ought to be at home looking after my Boys.

Mr and Mrs Graham lately returnd from France dinned with us this week and her daughter Miss Macauley and mr Copelys family, a Mrs Ann Quincy who lives in Northamtonshire, a maiden Lady, and a Relation to the Quincy family. I am pleasd with mrs Graham, whose manners are much more feminine than I expected to find them. Why why did she tarnish her lawrels by so Youthfull a connection. The Gentleman looks rather young to have been the Husband of her daughter, who is an amiable agreeable young Lady, but discovers very sensible mortification I presume at her Mothers Marriage. Mrs Graham expresses herself much satisfied with her reception in Boston, and indeed throughout America. She would have found more respect I conceive if she had visited it as Mrs Macauley.[12] But there must be frailty in all humane characters, and it should teach us in judging of the actions of others, to remember the weakness of Humane Nature and to examine the tenor of our own minds as well as the Strength of our own virtue, before we pass a rigid sentance upon their conduct.

Tis probable I Shall write you again before the vessel sails. I will not ask excuse for the contents of this letter, it is designd only for the perusal of an affectionate Sister who kindly interest herself in the welfare and happiness and in all the concerns of her affectionate Sister Abigail Adams

july 23.

I have been so constanly employd in writing for Several days that I cannot add any more to you than to tell you I am going on monday out of Town for a week,[13] and that those Friends to whom I Quit writing now will receive Letters by Bairnard. Callihan Sails on monday.

RC (MWA:Abigail Adams Corr.).

[1] Cranch's second May letter to AA was actually undated, and is printed above under [*21*] May.

[2] Puritans and other dissenters did not use holy vows in their marriage ceremonies but rather required a simple one-word agreement to the marriage (David Hackett Fischer, *Albion's Seed: Four British Folkways in America*, N.Y., 1989, p. 81).

[3] Margaret Stephens Smith of Jamaica, N.Y., widow of New York merchant John Smith (JQA, *Diary*, 1:296).

[4] Shakespeare, *Two Gentlemen of Verona*, Act V, scene iv, lines 69–72.

[5] Samuel Richardson, *Clarissa; or, The History of a Young Lady*, 7 vols., London, 1748, 3:letter LIX, "Mr. Lovelace, to John Belford, Esq., Tuesday, April 25": "The grieved mind looks round it, silently implores consolations, and loves the soother."

[6] To Mary Smith Cranch, 15 Aug. 1785 (vol. 6:276).

[7] Letter not found. The Adamses stayed at the Bath Hotel in London from 26 May to 2 July 1785 (vol. 6:172).

[8] Note not found. AA2 probably wrote it before WSS's request to JA of 4 Aug. 1785 to take leave to visit Prussia (Adams Papers).

[9] Not found.

[10] Neither AA's letter to Tyler nor the copy sent to Mary Cranch has been found.

[11] That is, AA and JA. See WSS to AA, 29 Dec. 1785 (vol. 6:508–509).

[12] In Nov. 1778, at the age of 47, Catharine Macaulay married 21-year-old William Graham, a surgeon's mate on an East India ship. She had previously been married to George Macaulay from 1760 until his death in 1766. Their daughter, Catherine Sophia, was in her mid-twenties in 1786. The Grahams toured the United States from July 1784 to July 1785, spending the first ten months almost exclusively in Boston and visiting Piscataqua in the District of Maine, Newport, New York, Philadelphia, and Mount Vernon (Bridget Hill, *The Republican Virago: The Life and Times of Catharine Macaulay, Historian*, Oxford, 1992, p. 16, 105, 108, 126; *DNB*). JA opened a correspondence with Macaulay on 9 Aug. 1770 after learning that she had been favorably impressed by his "Dissertation on the Canon and the Feudal Law" (see JA, *D&A*, 1:360–361, 2:75–76; JA, *Papers*, 1:250, 352–353; 2:164–165). Additional letters from JA to Macaulay are in the Gilder Lehrman Coll. on deposit at NHi.

[13] For the Adamses visit with Thomas Brand Hollis, see AA2 to JQA, 27 July, below.

John Adams to Richard Cranch

My dear Brother London July. 4. 1786

I have recd your Favour of 20 May. The Southern States will be forced to co operate with the Middle and northern ones, in measures for encouraging Navigation, because otherwise they will not be able to obtain ships for the Exportation of their Produce. The English have not and cannot obtain Ships, at a rate cheap enough for the purpose. The Ships taken from the Dutch, French Spaniards and Americans, during the War, which are now employed will Soon be worn out, and English oaks will not be found inexhaustible, and in all Cases the Freight in European ships will be too dear.

I have been Scribbling four years to Congress on the subject of Raw Sugars, but never was attended to. All the Sugar Houses you have and as many more might be employed, and the sugars sent to the Cape of good Hope as well as Rum for what I know, sold to Italians when they come for Fish or sent to the Baltic.

The Cry for Paper Money is downright Wickedness and Dishonesty. Every Man must see that it is the worst Engine of Knavery that ever was invented. There never will be commerce nor Confidence, while Such Systems of Villany are countenanced.

I see by the Cases of Lowell and Sprague, there is a Pique against Lawyers. A delusion, which will hurt our Country. Other Orders of Man, who are introducing Luxury, and Corruption, disgracing Us in the Eyes of foreign nations and destroying all Confidence at home, leading Us to innumerable Breaches of public Faith, and destroying in the Minds of the People the Sacred Regard to honour, are popular. This will not wear well.

Jefferson might have added to his Catalogue of American Genius's, Copley West, stuart, Trumbull, and Brown as Painters, Trumbull Dwight and Barlow as Poets, and many others. A Pack of Coxcomical Philosophers in Europe have made themselves ridiculous by doubting and disputing a Point that is as clear as day light. Jefferson has treated them with too much Ceremony. He should have treated their Insolence with scorn.

I have given my Daughter to New York. The Ceremony was performed by My Friend the Bishop of St Asaph, by a Special Licence from the Archbishop of Canterbury. Dissenting Ministers have not authority to marry. All Denominations of Dissenters are married here by the Clergy of the Chh of England, and without the Licence the Rite must have been performed in a Church, by Virtue of the Licence the Ceremony was performed in my House.

Colonel Smith is a Man of Sense and Spirit, Taste and Honour. I am very well satisfied with his Character Conduct, Circumstances and Connections: but my only Daughter must probably be soon seperated from me, for Life, as she will return to N. York and I to Braintree. This is an unpleasant Thought but it is the only one, and I ought to rejoice that there is no other. My Love to all our Friends. Your affectionate Brother John Adams

RC (MWA:Abigail Adams Corr.); endorsed: "Letter from His Excy. J: Adams Esqr July 4th. 1786."

John Adams to Cotton Tufts

Dear sir London July 4. 1786

I have accepted your Bill in favour of Storer, of 50£. and paid that in favour of Mr Elworthy of 40£.

I wish you to buy that Bit of an House and Land, which you mention, but am afraid they will make you give more for it than it is worth, it lies so to me that I must have it. The Pieces of Marsh adjoining to mine, I wish you to buy likewise. Draw upon me for the Money to pay for them. Let Thomas enter Colledge if you think him fit.[1]

As to Politicks, all that can be said is Summarily comprehended in a few Words. Our Country is grown, or at least has been dishonest. She has broke her Faith with Nations, and with her own Citizens. And Parties are all about for continuing this dishonourable Course. She must become Strictly honest and punctual to all the World before she can recover the Confidence of any body at home or abroad.

The Duty of all good Men is to join, in making this Doctrine popular, and in discountenancing every Attempt against it. This Censure is too harsh I suppose, for common Ears, but the Essence of these Sentiments must be adopted throughout America, before We can prosper. Have our People forgotten every Principle of Public and Private Credit? Do We trust a Man in private Life, who is not punctual to his Word? Who easily makes Promisses, and is negligent to perform them? especially if he makes Promisses knowing that he cannot perform them; or deliberately designing not to perform them? Yours John Adams

RC (Adams Papers).

[1] JA is responding to questions Tufts raised in his 13 April letter to AA, above, regarding the purchase of the Belcher property and Martha Vesey's marshland, as well as TBA's education.

Richard Cranch to Abigail Adams

My dear Sister Boston July 5th: 1786

Capt. Cushing having informed me that he shall sail tomorrow, I have requested him to take the Charge of a small Packquett containing a few Letters and News-Papers, which he has promised to deliver with his own Hands. You will see in the Papers an Account of the surprizing progress of Art, and effect of Industry, exhibited in the Completion of the Bridge across Charlestown Ferry, which was opened on the 17th. of June. I have enclosed a particular account of the Dimentions of this cellebrated Structure.[1] This Bridge renders our communication with Cambridge much easier than formerly, and gives us the Happiness of more frequent Visits to our dear Boys at the University. Your Sister Cranch and I went over the Bridge to see them a few Days ago, and my Lucy visited them yesterday. Your Son

John and my Billy live in Hollis-Hall, and have very pleasant Chambers, up two pair of Stairs, in the Entry next to Harvard-Hall. Master John's Chamber is on the south side of the Entry next to Harvard, and commands a fine Prospect of Charlestown and Boston and the extensive Fields between. Master Billy's Chamber is on the other side of the Entry fronting the Common and has a fine View of the Country towards Watertown. Master Charles has the corner Room next to Holden-Chapple on the lower Floor of the same Colledge.[2] This little Fraternity with their Chums (who are also very clever) live in the greatest Harmony, and behave so as to do honour to the Families from whome they sprung. I have never heard of a single Blemish on either of their Characters since they entered the University. I wish you could look in upon them: I assure you they live with great "decency and regularity"; not *Sharp* and his *Master* more so.[3]

I saw your Hond: Mother Hall and your Bror. Adams and Children last Sunday, who are all well. Uncle Quincy is often affected with rhumatick Pains so that he seldom goes abroad. Uncle Smith is left a sincere Mourner for the Loss of our worthy Aunt, who died a few Days ago as you will see by the Papers. Cousin Isaac is appointed Chaplain to the Castle, which will give him a decent Living while he continues a Batchelor. Colonel Thaxter's Family have lately met with a great Affliction in the Death of his Daughter Cushing who died in Child-bed about 48 Hours after the birth of her first Child. The Child is living.

I am uncertain in what manner to present my Regards to your most amiable Daughter, whether to congratulate her as a Bride or not. If that happy Relation has taken place, I send her my warmest Congratulations, and best Wishes that every Blessing may be attendant on her and the worthy Partner of her Life. Please to give my kindest Respects to Brother Adams, and excuse this merely domestick Letter from your ever obliged and affectionate Brother

Richard Cranch

Cousin Tommy, and our Friends at Haverhill, were well a Day [or] two ago, when I heard from them.

M[y] dear Partner you will hear from by the inclos[ed] Letters. We are all as well as usual.

July 6th:

Capt. Cushing not gone yet. I have enclosed a very good Election Sermon.[4]

RC (Adams Papers); some loss of text due to wear at the fold.

[1] Enclosure not found. Both the Boston *Independent Chronicle*, 22 June, and the *Boston Gazette*, 26 June, contained detailed descriptions of the Charlestown Bridge, for which see the Descriptive List of Illustrations, No. 6, above.

[2] Hollis Hall, named for Thomas Hollis, was built and possibly designed by Thomas Dawes in 1763 to relieve overcrowding at Harvard. It contains 32 room-suites and has been used continuously as a dormitory (Hamilton Vaughan Bail, *Views of Harvard: A Pictorial Record to 1860*, Cambridge, 1949, p. 52–55; www.harvard.edu).

[3] Probably a reference to David Garrick, *The Lying Valet*, in which valet Timothy Sharp endeavors to make his impoverished master pass for a man of affluence (E. Cobham Brewer, *The Reader's Handbook*, rev. edn., London, 1902).

[4] Samuel West, *A Sermon, Preached . . . May 31, 1786: Being the Day of General Election*, Boston, [1786]. A copy with Richard Cranch's autograph is among JA's books at MB (*Catalogue of JA's Library*).

Cotton Tufts to Abigail Adams

My Dear Cousin Boston July 6. 1786

I recd. yours of Jan. 10. Feby 21 and April the 8th And am obliged to you for your affectionate Letter of Condolance and also for the Intelligence conveyed in the several Letters.

The State of our Country is uncomfortable, if not hazardous. The Scarcity (real I rather think [*than*] artificial) of Gold and Silver prompts People to seek a Remedy in Paper Money, already has Rhode Island issued Paper, New York also and Newhampshire has made specific Articles a Tender. The Fear of a paper Currency in this State, prevents those who have Specie from parting with it. And the Distresses of People are undoubtedly great for want of a sufficient Quantity of circulating Cash. Attempts have been made in the Genl Court the present Session[1] to introduce a paper Medium, Many of the Representatives came instructed for that Purpose and for three Weeks it was agitated at Times and it was difficult to guess how the Question would turn in the House. An Act making Property both real and personal a tender for the Satisfaction of Executions was also for a long while in Debate, but at Length on a Decision there appeared 100. and upwards against it, immediately the Question on the former was put this faild also—the Number for it not exceeding 20. At present our Fears are in some Degree removed, but in the next Sitting of the Court I expect the Attempt will be renewed and unless before that Period (which will not be untill January next)[2] something favourable should turn up, I suspect that Paper Money or an Act for making Property a tender, will be carried. New York is now the only State that has not made some Provision for a general Impost. What will be the Issue of our Delays and Inattention to our National Faith and Honor God only knows. Where the Money is to be obtained for satisfying the lawless Demands of Algerines, is not in my Power to guess. It will not come from the Treasury of the United States, for there is not sufficient there (I suspect) to answer dayly Exigencies.

In former Letters I hinted to you the Probability of my meeting with Difficulties from Mr. Tylers Delay in accounting with me for Business done &c. I have not been deceived. I have frequently made Journeys to Braintree, repeatedly wrote to Him and although He has for a long while had Moneys in his Hand, I cannot get him to settle. What shall I do—must I break with Him and have recourse to Law. If Mr. Adams should think Proper, I wish He would specially order the Delivery of all Books Papers &c into my Hands, such an order to be used as Prudence may direct.

As I have not Time to write to Cousin A— I would just mention that I have received no Direction from Her, relative to the Trunk of Letters which Mr. T—r delivered to me as those Letters referred to in Hers to me which accompanied her Packet conditionally to be delivered to him—the Miniature Picture and morrocco Pocket Book I have not as yet received.

Is your Daughter married? a little Circumstance led your Friends at Braintree to suppose that the Connection was closed before your last Letter of April. Among the Letters sent was found a Card from a Mr. and Mrs. Smith to Mr and Mrs. Adams requesting their Company at Dinner, whether our Young Ladies have construed it right or not, Youll give us Information in your next.

Mrs. Quincy has discharged the order on her, but I have not heard a Word from the Lt. Governor relative to the Monies advanced by Mr. Adams for certain Copies mentioned in yours.[3] Would it not be best to send me a particular Account of the Disbursement. I find it exceeding difficult to get any Money from your Debtors and am obliged to depend principally on my Draughts on Mr. Adams for supplying your Children and defraying their Expences. Newhall has not paid any Thing for 3/4 of a Year—in case he neglects much longer, I must remove him.[4] I have not settled with Doane as Tyler keeps the Papers in his Hands and tho repeated application has been made for the Account, I cannot get it.

On the 13th. of April last I drew a Bill on Mr Adams in favour of Mr Storer for £50 on which I recd. 7 Ct. discount and have since drawn an order in favour of Mr Elworthy on my own Acctt. for £40—May the 17th.—of which I have given You an Acctt. Mr. Morton has several Times urged me to buy Belchers Place but I find his Expectations of Price do not conform to my Ideas. He has offered to leave to Three Men such as we may chuse the Determination of the Price, but I have not as yet complied with the Proposal. That Side of the House in which Belcher lives is out of Repair, the Roof near one half of it gone and lays open to the Heavens—the Land is much worn. However it would be a convenient Addition to your Estate could it be purchased at a reasonable Price. I wish You to write to me on this Matter. In last Thursdays Paper a Billet from Ld. Gordon to the Marquiss of Carmathaen was published, informing the Latter from what Quarter Mr. Adams received his Quarterly pay, and as receiving his Intelligence from a Mr. Tufts. What Was the Design of Lord Gordon in giving the Intelligence and what Mr. Tufts was it that he refers to?[5]

Our Friends like Leaves in Autumn drop off one after another. Our good Aunt Smith not long since compleated the Journey of Life and has reached as I trust, the Regions of Bliss and Immortality. With our kindred Spirits who have reached the Goal before us, May We one Day join, receive their Welcome and be secured in their Friendship and in the Joys of that better World. Adieu My Dear Friend and believe me to be with sincere Affection Your H Sert

C. Tufts

RC (Adams Papers); addressed: "Mrs: Abigail Adams London Grovesnor Square"; endorsed: "Dr Tufts Letter july 6 1786."

[1] The General Court met from 31 May to 8 July.

[2] Although not scheduled to meet again until Jan. 1787, the General Court was summoned by Gov. Bowdoin to convene on 27 Sept. to respond to the civil unrest of Shays' Rebellion (Boston *Independent Chronicle*, 13 July; James Bowdoin, *Proclamation* [to convene the General Court on 27 Sept.], Boston, 13 Sept., Evans, No. 19788).

[3] See AA to Cotton Tufts, 21 Feb., and note 9, above.

[4] Andrew Newell rented the Adamses' house on South Queen Street, now Court Street, in Boston (Cotton Tufts to AA, 2 Jan. 1787, below; JA, *D&A*, 2:63–64; vol. 6:258–260).

[5] See AA to Cotton Tufts, 22 July, below.

Isaac Smith Jr. to Abigail Adams

Dear Mrs Adams — Boston July 8. 1786

Tho' it is probable you will hear of it from some other of your friends, yet as I know the interest my dear Mother had in your affections, and that you will not fail of sympathizing with us, I Could not avoid the opportunity by Mr Gardner of acquainting you with the loss of her, and am sorry that the first occasion I should have of writing you since your residence in England should be of such a nature. She had been for some time apparently on the decline, but was not thought to be so near the period of her earthly Cares and sufferings, and had prepared for a journey as far as Princeton in hopes of its Contributing to her health, but such is the uncertainty of life, on the morning of the 24., the day she meant to have set out, she was seized with a fit of the apoplectic kind, which was followed by others, and threw her into a lethargy, in which she remained insensible of her situation, 'till the night of the 27., when she expired. I need not tell you how much the feelings of her family were excited by her Removal from us in such a way, or what an affliction it must be to my father; he is supported under it however, as well as my sisters, to a degree beyond what I expected. I have lost Connections, whom I loved, esteemed and valued, but this stroke comes nearer to my heart, than any I had felt before, and I feel thankful that I was not Called to bear it in a different situation, tho' we o't I own always to cultivate the temper of Resignation, since we know not where or when we may have need of the exercise of it.

You will hear from Braintree it is probable of a distressing event in your Uncle Thaxter's family at Hingham, and Dr Tufts I suppose will inform you of the critical situation of his brother at Medford.

It gives me pleasure to hear of the new and agreable Connection lately formed in your family, and hope it will long afford you the same degree of comfort and satisfaction, as at present.

I presume it will be some time before we may expect the pleasure of seeing you here again with Mr Adams. But as you have more frequent opportunities of hearing from your family and your friends on this side, than I Could have during the Course of the war, it renders I imagine your absence from home less unpleasant than mine was.

I beg My Respects to Mr Adams, Mrs Smith, (the name I suppose Miss A. wears by this time) [. . .] accept my best wishes. With the great[est estee]m, I am, my dear Mrs A., Your's sincerely

I Smith jr.

RC (Adams Papers); addressed: "Mrs Adams Grosvenor Square London favr'd by Mr Gardner"; endorsed: "I Smiths Letter july 8th 1786." Some loss of text where the seal was removed.

Mary Smith Cranch to Abigail Adams

My dear Sister Braintree July 10th 1786

I have within this Hour receiv'd your Letters by captain Bigelow and have also heard that cushing is not sail'd. He has one Letter on board for you already[1] but tis not so long a one as I have generally sent you. The Subject was So melancholy that I could not mix any thing with it. I expected every hour that Cushing would sail and had not time to write more.

11th

I began to write you last night but my eyes were so poor that I could not continue it. I am now risen with the sun to thank you for the charming Budget you have Sent me. Such frequent communications shortens the Idea of distants by many miles. I believe there have been Letters constantly upon the water for each other ever since you lefts us. The Idea of your returning soon to your dear Freinds here would be a much more joyfull one if this country would suffer you first to do all the good your inclinations lead you too, and what they really wish you to do tho they put it out of your Power to do it. I hope they will come to their Sensces before winter. The court is adjournd to next January. The House have been disputing half this Session whether we should have Paper money, any Lawyers or any Court of Common Pleas. They voted finally, against Paper money, Sent up to the senate a curious Bill with regards to Lawyers and the Infiriour Court. A committee of five of from the Senate have it to consider of till next term. Mr cranch is one of them.[2] Thus do they spend their time in curtailing Tea Tables while they are suffering thousand to be wrested from them for want of giving ampler Powers to Congress. It is dreadful to those who See the necessity of different measures to stand by and see such pursue'd as they fear will ruin their Country. Ask no excuse my dear Sister for writing Politicks. It would be such a want of publick Spirit not to feel interested in the welfair of our country as the wives of ministers and Senaters ought to be asham'd off. Let no one say that the Ladies are of no importance in the affairs of the nation. Perswaide them to renounce all their Luxirys and it would be found that they are, and beleive me there is not a more affectual way to do it, than to make them acquainted with the causes of the distresses of thier country. We do not want spirit. We only want to have it properly directed.

I have been long convinc'd of the Jealous disposion of [our] Milton Freinds. What would they have us do? Mr Cranch [has] tried every method in his Power to get the G–n–l into office. As to the chief Seat he will always use his influence for those Whome he thinks the best quallefied for it. The g–n–l has so often refuse'd what has been repeatedly offer'd him that think as he pleases it is impossible now to get him into anything. There was a counseler wanted lately. Mr cranch use'd his utmost influence to procure the Seat. He call'd out members from every county and talk'd with them seperatly. Mr C' had the G–n–l put up two more were put up. At the first voting he had votes within six or seven of enough, as many however, as the others, and all of mr C–hs procuring, upon the secound voting he lost it and so there was no thanks due to mr C–h nor any influence ascrib'd to him.[3] There is nothing harder to remove from the mind than Jealousy, and the most ambitious are the most apt to be tormented with it.

By my last letters you will See your were right in your conjecture that Sister Shaws was with me and we were also right in ours, for we thought that you would suppose it and we took a peculiar pleasure in supposing that we were at one time all thinking of the same thing. I had a Letter last week from Sister they were all well. She is prepairing Thomas to make his appearince at commencment, and is very anxious least she should not make him appear as smart as his Brothers. It is concluded I think that he should Stay another year with his uncle. Cousin JQA as well as his other Freinds think it will be best, and Thomas himself I hear thinks so too. The summer vacancy begins the day after to morrow. Miss Nabby Marsh is bespoke. A uniform must be prepair'd. The Blue cloths you sent will answer the purpose if the young Gentleman will think So. Your Sons are all well, their behavior unexceptionable. Oh! how happy we are thus far in our children. What has become of my dear Nieces Pen. Why Still So long? Her Happiness is near my Heart and I rejoice in the prospect of it. Introduce me my dear Sister to Colln. Smith. His character is such as intitles him to my utmost esteem.

I shall write again soon I have not half done and mr cranch calls and Says he cannot wait one moment for my Letter. So adieue yours most affectionately

Mary Cranch

Love to mr Adams.

Thanks a Thousand thanks for my callaco—oh my sister what

shall I do with you—or for you—I cannot lay under the weight of so many obligations.

RC (Adams Papers); addressed by Richard Cranch: "To Mrs: Adams, Lady of his Excellency John Adams Esqr. Grosvenor Square Westminster"; endorsed: "Mrs Cranch july 11 1786." Some loss of text where the seal was removed.

[1] Probably Mary Smith Cranch to AA, 2 July, above.

[2] See Mary Smith Cranch to AA, 22 May, note 9, above.

[3] The legislature chose Samuel Holten, John Bliss, and Benjamin Austin to fill vacancies on the Council (Boston *Independent Chronicle*, 8, 15 June).

Mary Smith Cranch to Abigail Adams

My dear Sister Braintree July 14th 1786

Capt Folger is slipt a way without one line from me. I did not design it should have been so, but it is vacancy, and I have been very unwell. Miss Nabby Marsh has been so sick that I could not have her but one day just to cut out work for us. I have been oblig'd to put out cousin charles's Red coat to turn and the Blue coat you sent to make for him. He will look quite Parsonish with his Black Frogs and Buttons. The wastcoats Gowns &c, we have made ourselves.[1] Betsy and Lucy are become quite expert at the business. They were reckning up this day foreteen wastcoats which they had made this season for the three colleagians, and a proportionable number of small cloaths. They cannot wear wash-cloath with out having five or six a peice of a sort. It makes our washes very large in summer, although we wash once a week. I cannot bear they should go dirty. We have made their silk, and white wascoats, and they look very handsome. Billy sends his Duty and is greatly oblig'd for his. Thomas is here upon a visit and they may now have a chance of drinking your Health altogether. Mr cranch could not help observing last evening as they were all siting in a row before our chimney board in the little Parlour drinking Tea, "What a fine String of young Fellows they were, and how much pleasure you would have taken in beholding them,["] and us their substituted Parents with our own dear Girls and Betsy Shaw who has been with us ever since her mama made her spring visit. Here was a circle every one of Whome love you tenderly, and are I know belov'd by you. Here you would have felt a pleasure which you never experienc'd in a drawing Room at St James. It is a high feast to mr cranch to have cousin John here. French Dutch and english in their turn is talk'd. To vary our Scene musick is often call'd for—Betsy my dear a Tune upon your Harpsicord, "young Gentleman Join your Flutes." My Son take yours or your violene and sing the Bass and then my sister how do I Wish for you. No one ever injoyd the pleasures of young People more than you use'd too. The Indian Philosopher by Doctor Watts is set to musick, tis a beautiful Tune.[2] The children play it. Mr cranch says he feels twenty years younger whenever he hears it.

Cousin Tommy will not enter college I believe till next year. Mr Shaw thinks another years study with him will be of more advantage to him, and he will have in cousin Charles a very sober, well behav'd Brother to guide and guard him if he conduct as well as he has done.

A year seems in this changable world a long time to look forward, but if our children should live till the next commencment, we must think of some little intertainment for them. Bacon and allamode Beef Seems to be the custom of providing for dinner, excepting those who chuse to lay out a thousand dollars for an intertainment which nobody is the better for. Some add a few cold roast chickings Punch wine and cider with it. Tea and cake in the afternoon. If you should not come home before I should wish to know your mind about it. Legs for Bacan must be procur'd in the fall. I have been thinking that as their Friends and acquaintance will be the same, that the same chamber will do for both of them, and we can divide the expence between us. I think if what I have mention'd will be Sufficient for cousin Such a Plan will be less trouble and a less expence.

I have receiv'd the callaco for my self and your Freinds. Most sincerly do I thank you for mine, tis a beautiful figure and colour. Polly Adams returns many thanks for hers. Your Mother Hall is well, and is to dine here this week with her Grand Sons.

26th

Mrs Hall dind with us yesterday. She looks well for such an aged woman. She talk'd much about you, and longs she says for your return, offers you many thanks for your kindness to her, and the children sends her Love to her son and Daughter, and her best wishes for the happiness of her Grandaughter. Your sons are set out this morning upon a visit to thier uncle and Aunt Shaw. Upon cousin Toms coming there has been a counsel of all the Freinds calld, upon the expediency of his entering college this year, and upon the whole it is concluded that he should return immediatly to his uncles and prepair himself to be offer'd at the end of the vacancy. Cousin John says he would have ventur'd to have done it at commencment, but as mr Shaw had givin up the Idea of it this year, he had some fears about him. I fear we shall not be able to get him a chamber in college this year. Mr John and charles will live together this. They will want nothing more but a Bed which I shall take for them, there will then be furniture enough for Tom. Whoever liv's with him must find a Bed.

The light colour'd cloth coat which cousin Charles had when you went away, Tom has now, and the old Silkish coat you sent last. The next he has must be mix'd Blue and white, or dark Blue with Black Frogs.

We had bought a peice of Linnen for Tom before that which you sent him ariv'd, as it is not so fine as yours we Shall make it up for winter shirts for him and Charles. You know our hard frosts cuts out fine linnen quick. You must not send any more silk cloathing for your children at college. They will not be allow'd to wear them. Some Strong cotton Stocking would be very useful and what they want more than any thing. Mending Stockings is my steady imployment. They are all fine hands for wearing holes in them. If when you are purchasing stocking for your sons you would be so kind as to add six pair more for a Freind of mine[3] who is very tall and not very slight, you will oblige both him and me. Send the price the suppos'd one will be immediatly accounted for with Doctor Tufts. Cousin Johns purple coat has no cape and he does not chuse to wear it without one. I think I have hunted every store and shop almost in Boston to get a piece any way near the colour, but have not been able to get it. He will put a Black one on for the present. I will send a scrap for a pattern and peice of the lead colour'd coat also, that coat wants a cape.

Mr Standfast Smith is come from the west Indias with a Power to Sell the Estate we live upon so that we must either buy this House or leave it.[4] He has not yet set the price I hope it will not be higher than we shall be able to give. I am very loth to leave it. Mr Evans will hire our House at weymouth, he does not chuse to buy at present. I had rather it should be sold. It sinks in Value every day Such an old House is forever out of repair.[5] Mr Evans has been gone a Journey ever since he was married and is not yet return'd. I shall deliver Colln. Smiths Respects whenever I see him.

Mr James Brackit has lost his Wife. She dy'd of a consumction about a fortnight since.[6]

I must now bid you adieue and begin another sheet.

It has been my luck to receive almost all your latest Letters first. Sometimes you refer to things in your former Letter, which Letter not having receiv'd I cannot possibly understand what you mean. This was the case with yours of the 24 of May. You there refer'd to a Letter by mr Jenks, and I did not recieve that till three weeks after I had reciev'd the others. I did not recieve your second Letter by the Way of newyork, till After I had reciev'd your Letters by Lyde and Cushing, and had sent away answers to them.

What a mistake your card from Mr and Mrs William Smith led us into. The writing was so exactly like my Nieces that we thought it must be hers. We got several of her Letters and compair'd it with them, and could almost have Sworn it was hers, and yet, we wonder'd that you should not have mention'd her being married to any of us, but we had such proof by that cards being her hand, that we could not doubt it. All her acquaintance suppos'd she was really so. Cousin Nabbys Letters to Betsy and Lucy by mrs Hay did not reach them, till last week.[7] They were inclos'd to charles Storer and he being gone to settle at Parsemiquodde, I believe. I am sure I donot know how to spell it, his Pacquit was Sent to him unopen'd. He is now return'd upon a visit and has brought them with him. He will himself write you an account of his adventures and prospects. There is no chance for a young Fellow in Boston. They must all turn adventerers, better do so than make a great show for a time upon other peoples property and then break all to peices. Billy Foster fail'd last week and tis a wonder if many other falurs are not involved in his.[8] Mr otis is still keept shut up. It is very foolish in his creditors. He is now living upon them as he cannot do any business in his present situation. He has offer'd to deliver up every thing. He looks very much worried. She bears her troubles with patience and fortitude. Mrs Welsh is well, nurses Billy yet. Mrs Allen is well, I hear of no prospect of increase.

Our Hingham Freinds are very melancholy, I have been to see them. The child is living and a very fine Girl she is. Quincy is to be married this Fall he is building an end to his Fathers House. Nancy will be married also this fall.[9] Mrs Quincy and Nancy are well and send a great deal of Love. Uncle Quincy has turn'd Hermit, he cannot be got out. I go as often as I can to see him. Your Nieghbours are all well. Esters Sister Fenno is at her mothers.[10] She has got into a poor nervous way but the Doctor Says will get better he thinks soon.

Abdy and Pheby do very well Live very comfortably. They were a little distress'd for wood last winter but it was because People who ow'd them would not pay them as the ought to have done. You would Smile to see her rig'd out in her French night cap. It is Gauze I assure you. She has bought that larg'd figure'd callaco Gown of mrs Hannah Hunt, and was most gaily dressd in it last sunday.

You mention cousin Isaac Smith. I think I told you he was fix'd at present at the castle as Chaplain. He will stand a very good Chance for Hingham as soon as mr Gay is remov'd. They admire him there uncle Thaxter thinks he will be the first person, they will invite.[11]

As to mr Tufts he is not yet married, but I am told *Stays* with Girls sometimes. Billy says he introduce'd Cousin JQA to him on Commencment day for the first time since he arriv'd. Oh how unlike his Father, or his dear Mother. I wish he was married. I know he would be more agreable.[12]

The windmill goes, but not so well as the Builder expected. He would take nobodys advise and must reap the conseiquencs. He does not come here. We have sent him an invitation twice to dine, and drink Tea but he takes not the least notice of any. I shall not court him, if he does not chuse to come. It is very foolish of him, he might have been upon visiting terms with us, if he was not connected in the Family. Not a single paper, or account-Book, or a coppar of money has The Doctor get [*yet*] been able to get from him. He speaks him fair but gives him nothing but words. What he has done with the Pictures I cannot think. The wearing the mineture can no longer decieve any body. The Letters are I suppose here, the Cabinett and Trunk are, but have not been deliver'd up, and I shall have notright to detain them if he should send for them. He certainly has no right to the Letters of her correspondenc whatever he may have to those Cousin has sent him. While he liv'd here, he would often bring the Trunk into the Parlour, and spread the Letters upon the Table and divert himself with reading them. I have seen Betsy so angry that if she could have got at her own Bundle she would have put them all in the fire. Had they been left in the hands of a man of strict honour he would not have turnd the Key upon them. How the Doctor will ever get them from him I cannot think. He has dancd attendence upon him and written to him above twenty times.

I fear my dear sister you will think the Cloathing and other expences for your sons have been greater than you expected. The Doctor thinks I need not indulge them in so many wash cloaths, but how can they be clean without as light as they are? They spend not a copper extravagantly that I can find out, and Sometimes I really think they do not have what they ought to.

Charles says Sometimes, "Aunt what shall I do uncle Tufts has not given me any money, and I do not love to ask him again.["] "Here my dear take what I have, I Will see that you have more. Your uncle is not unwilling you should have it, he may have forgot it, or finds a difficulty in collecting it. But he does not think how Small a young Fellow feels without any money in his Pocket." The Doctor never had such a parcel of young Fellows to provide for before, one only Son and no Daughters. The difference is very great, and aunt us'd to Say that his Father never knew all she did for him more than he allow'd him.[13] If I could have possible *now* had all the work for them done in the House I should, but miss Nabbys indisposition has oblig'd me to put out some of it. I think they will want but little more done for them in the Tailoring way till next spring.

Lucy is at haverhill upon a visit till the Fall. Both Betsy and she will write soon to their cousin.

You say I must not read your observations upon the debts due from this country to england to any one who may feel hurt by it, but really my sister you know better than we who those may be. No one ceases to role in Luxery, because he is in debt, and we seldom suspect it till they shut up. It has taught me not to feel small although I cannot make such a shew of riches as many others. I hope by our manner of Life not to injure any one. I have taken a few yards of Linnin for linings &c of mrs Warren and that is all. We never could get at any Irish Linnin and what was fine was too high for the goodness of it.

Has mr Tufts been to make any excuse for himself for abuseing mr Adams character. I know he was in a sad nettle when it was made publick. His poor Father is just gone in a consumtion. His grandmother will never dye of any thing but old age.[14] Yours affectionatly

RC (Adams Papers); endorsed: "Mrs Cranch july 14th 1786."

[1] These were some of the requirements of Harvard's new dress code. See Mary Smith Cranch to AA, 22 May, note 7, above.

[2] A 1705 poem by Isaac Watts. It appears in various American songbooks, the earliest dated ca. 1785 (*The American Musical Miscellany*, Northampton, Mass., 1798, p. 241–244, Evans, No. 33294; Sally Pickman, musical copybook, MSaE:Early Music Collection, Box 1, item A-1).

[3] Undoubtedly her son, William Cranch.

[4] Prior to the revolution James George Verchild of St. Kitts owned the house in which the Cranches lived. In 1784, Richard Cranch had attempted to locate Verchild's heirs in England to negotiate a purchase price. The Cranches apparently never purchased the land, however, but continued to rent until their deaths in 1811 (William Cranch to Richard Cranch, 26 April 1806, MHi:Cranch Family Papers; vol. 5:356–357; Pattee, *Old Braintree*, p. 491). Standfast Smith was a Boston merchant operating out of Green's Wharf (*Massachusetts Centinel*, 9 July 1785).

[5] For the history of the Weymouth par-

sonage, which Mary Cranch inherited from her father in 1783, see vol. 1:ix–x.

[6] Mary Brackett, wife of Braintree tavern operator James Brackett, died 10 July (Pattee, *Old Braintree*, p. 123, 168–169).

[7] Probably AA2 to Elizabeth Cranch, 14 Feb., above, and AA2 to Lucy Cranch, 20 Feb. (MWA).

[8] Possibly Boston merchant William Foster, brother and partner of Joseph Foster, a fellow passenger with AA and AA2 on their voyage to Europe in 1784 (JA, *D&A*, 3:156, note 2; JQA, *Diary*, 1:318). Contrary to what is stated in vol. 6:275, note 28, and JQA, *Diary*, 1:318, note 2, Richard Cranch lodged with James, not William, Foster on Cornhill Street when he was in Boston, and this is where the Cranches arranged for the Adams boys to dine whenever necessary when they were in town (Richard Cranch to Jacob Davis, 12 May, MHi:C. P. Cranch Papers).

[9] For the marriages of AA's cousins, Anna (Nancy) and Quincy Thaxter, children of John Sr. and Anna Quincy Thaxter of Hingham, see Mary Smith Cranch to AA, 28 Sept., and note 5, below.

[10] Esther Field was the daughter of Abigail Newcomb and Joseph Field. Esther's sister is probably Elizabeth, who posted an intention to marry William Fenno on 29 Oct. 1778 (Waldo Chamberlain Sprague, comp., *Genealogies of the Families of Braintree, Massachusetts, 1640–1850*, Boston, 1983, p. 829, 1661; Boston, *30th Report*, p. 442).

[11] Ebenezer Gay, Harvard 1714, was pastor of the First Parish Church in Hingham from 1718 until his death in 1787. He was succeeded by Henry Ware (*Sibley's Harvard Graduates*, 6:59–66; JQA, *Diary*, 2:viii).

[12] Cotton Tufts Jr. married Mercy Brooks in 1788.

[13] That is, Lucy Quincy Tufts discussing her husband and son, Cotton Tufts Sr. and Jr.

[14] On the problem with Simon Tufts Jr., see AA to Cotton Tufts, 22 July, below. His grandmother, Abigail Smith Tufts, was AA's aunt.

Abigail Adams to Elizabeth Cranch

London july 18th 1786

I thank you my dear Neice for your last kind Letter. There are no days in the whole year so agreable to me nor any amusements this Country can boast so gratifying to my Heart and mind as those days which bring me Letters from my Dear Friends. In them I always find the law of kindness written, and they solace my mind in the seperation.

Could I, you ask, return to my (Rustick) cottage, and view it with the same pleasure and Satisfaction I once enjoy'd in it? I answer I think I could, provided I have the same kind Friends and dear Relatives to enhance its value to me. It is not the superb and magnificient House nor the rich and Costly furniture that can ensure either pleasure or happiness to the possessor. [A] convenient abode Suteable to the station of the possessor, is no doubt desirable, and to those who can afford them, Parks, Gardens, or what in this Country is call'd an ornamented Farm, appears to me an Innocent and desirable object. They are Beautifull to the Eye, pleasing to the fancy, and improveing to the Imagination, but then as Pope observes,

> "Tis use alone that sanctifies Expence,
> And Splendor borrows all her rays from Sense."[1]

I have lately visited several of the celebrated Seats within 20 Miles of this City, Sion place, Tilney House, and park, osterley, and Pains Hill.[2] The last place is about 12 Miles distant from London. I must describe it to you in the words of the Poet.

> "Here Wealth enthron'd in Natures pride
> With taste and Beauty by her side
> And holding plenty's Horn
> Sends Labour to persue the toil
> Art to improve the happy soil
> And beauty to adorn."

My dear Neice will feel loth to believe that the owner of this Beautifull spot, (a particular account of which she will find in the Book I send her,) neither lives here or scarcly looks upon it; once a Year. The former proprieter enjoyd it as the work of his own hands: 38 years ago he planted out all the Trees which are now one of its chief, and principal ornaments. But dyeing about 3 years ago left it, to a tasteless Heir. The Book I send you is written by a mr Whately, he has treated the Subject of Gardning scientifically.[3] I should have overlookd many of the ornaments and Beauties of the places I have seen if I had not first perused this writer. Mr Apthorp I imagine would be pleased in reading this Book, and I wish you may derive as much entertainment from the perusal of it as it afforded me.

I dare say your imagination will present you with many places in Braintree capable of makeing with much less expence than is expended here, ornamented Farms. The late Col Quincys, Uncle Quincys, Germantown,[4] all of them, Nature has been more liberal to, than most of the places here: which have cost the labour of successive Generations, and many of them half a Million of Money. Improvement in agriculture is the very science for our Country, and many times ornament and Beauty may be happily made subservient to utility, but then to Quote Pope again,

> "Something there is more needfull than Expence
> And Something previous ev'n to Taste—'tis Sense."[5]

When you have read Whateley, read Popes fourth essay addresst to the Earl of Burlington, and I think you will see Beauties in it unobserved before.

You might suspect me of partiality if I was to say that nature shews herself in a stile of greater magnificence and sublimity in America than in any part of Europe which I have yet seen. Every thing is upon a Grandeur scale, our Summers heats and Winters colds, form a contrast of great Beauty. Nature arising from a temporary death, and bursting into Life with a sudden vegatation yealding a delicious fragrance and verdure which exhilirates the spirits and exalts the imagination, much more than the gradual and slow advance of Spring in the more temperate climates, and where the whole summer has not heat sufficient to sweeten the fruit, as is the case of this, climate. Even our Storms and tempests our thunder and lightning, are horibly Grand. Here nothing appears to leap the Bounds of Mediocrity. Nothing ferocious but Man.

But to return to your Letter, you have found that you was too early in your conjectures respecting your cousins marriage. She will write you herself, and inform you that she has commenced housekeeper, very soon after her Marriage. It would add greatly to her happiness, judging her by myself, if she could welcome her American friends often within her Mansion. Persons in the early stages of Life may form Friendships; but age grows more Wary, more circumspect and a commerce with the World does not increase ones estimation of its inhabitants. There is no durable basis, for friendship, but Virtue, disinterestedness, Benevolence and Frankness.

This is the Season of the Year in which London is a desert, even fashion languishes. I however inclose you a Print of the Bosom Friends.[6] When an object is to be ridiculed, tis generally exagerated. The print however does not greatly exceed some of the most fashionable Dames.

Pray does the fashion of Merry *thoughts*, *Bustles* and *protuberances* prevail with you. I really think the English more ridiculous than the French in this respect. They import their fashions from them; but in order to give them the mode Anglois, they divest them both of taste and Elegance. Our fair Country women would do well to establish fashions of their own; let Modesty be the first, ingredient, neatness the second and Economy the third. Then they cannot fail of being Lovely without the aid of olympian dew, or Parissian Rouge.

We have sent your cousins Some Books, amongst which is Rosseau upon Botanny,[7] if you Borrow it of them, it will entertain you, and the World of flowers of which you are now so fond, will appear to you a world of pleasing knowledge. There is also Dr Preistly upon air and Bishop Watson upon Chimistery[8] all of which are well worth the perusal of minds eager for knowledge and scientif[ik] like my Elizas and Lucy's. If they are not the amusements which females in general are fond of: it is because triffels are held up to them in a more important light, and no pains taken to initiate them in more rational amusements. Your Pappa who is blesst with a most happy talant of communicating knowledge will find a pleasure in assisting you to comprehend whatever you may wish explaind. A course of experiments would do more, but from thise our sex are almost wholy excluded.

Remember me affectionately to Your Brother and to all my Neighbours. Inclosed is a Book upon Church Musick which be so good as to present to Mr Wibird with my compliments. It was publishd here in concequence of an application of Dr Chancys Church for an organ, of mr Brand Hollis.[9]

Adieu my Dear Neice and Believe me affectionately Yours

A Adams

RC (MSaE:Abigail Adams Letters); notation in the upper left corner of the first page: "Letter from Mrs. A Adams to Miss Eliz Cranch July 18th. 1786 (No: 10.)." Some loss of text due to wear at the fold.

[1] *Moral Essays*, Epistle IV, lines 179–180.

[2] "Tilney House" was Wanstead House, Essex, a Palladian mansion designed by architect Colen Campbell and built ca. 1715–1720 for Richard Child, 1st earl Tylney (1680–1750). The Tylney estates were inherited by Sir James Long (afterwards Tylney Long) (1737?–1794), 7th baronet, in 1784 (Howard E. Stutchbury, *The Architecture of Colen Campbell*, Cambridge, 1967, p. 27–30; Namier and Brooke, *House of Commons*, 3:52–53, 570–571).

[3] Thomas Whately (ca. 1728–1772), best known to Americans in the late 1760s and early 1770s as an architect of George Grenville's American policy, had by the 1780s become celebrated for his *Observations on Modern Gardening, Illustrated by Descriptions* (London, 1770, with many subsequent editions). Jefferson highly praised this work and carried it with him when he made his tour of English gardens with JA in early April (Namier and Brooke, *House of Commons*, 3:627–628; *DNB*; Jefferson, *Papers*, 9:369–375; JA to AA, 5 April, above). JA's copy (4th edn., 1777) is at MB (*Catalogue of JA's Library*). The quotation AA cites above, which is otherwise unidentified, appears on the title page of Whately's book; his discussion of Painshill appears on p. 184–194.

[4] The home of the late Col. Josiah Quincy in the northern part of Braintree (whose 1770 house still stands); that of Norton Quincy on Mt. Wollaston; and probably that of Gen. Joseph Palmer in Germantown.

[5] *Moral Essays*, Epistle IV, lines 41–42.

[6] For the Bosom Friends, a satirical print, see the Descriptive List of Illustrations, No. 7, above.

[7] Jean Jacques Rousseau, *Letters on the Elements of Botany, Addressed to a Lady. Translated into English, with Notes, and Twenty-four Additional Letters, Fully Explaining the System of Linnaeus, by Thomas Martyn*, London, 1785.

[8] JA's books at MB include Joseph Priestley, *Experiments and Observations on Different Kinds of Air*, 3 vols., London, 1775–1779, and Richard Watson's *Chemical Essays* (*Catalogue of JA's Library*). A 1781 edition of Priestley, in six volumes, with JQA's bookplate, is at MQA.

[9] James Peirce, *A Tractate on Church Music; Being an Extract from the Reverend and Learned Mr. Peirce's Vindication of the Dissenters*, London, 1786. Thomas Brand Hollis refused requests by the First Church in Boston to provide funds for the purchase of an organ and instead arranged for the publication of this tract, dedicated to the ministers and members of the "First Congregational Dissenting Church in Boston in America," that argued against including instrumental music in church services (Arthur B. Ellis, *History of the First Church in Boston, 1630–1880*, Boston, 1881, p. 216–217).

7. "THE BOSOM FRIENDS," 1786

See page xiv

Abigail Adams Smith to Elizabeth Cranch

Wimpole Street London July 18th 1786

In your Letter to Mamma my Dear Eliza of — May[1] you are strangely puzled to know in what manner to address your Cousin. Your suppositions at that time were rather premature, and the Card on which they were founded was from a family by the Name of Smith who have been vastly civil to us since our residence in this Country. But at this period, a Letter addressd to your friend under the title of M[rs] Smith would not be improper, for in truth Eliza, Poor Abby Adams is no more—her friends took Leave of her on the 11th of June—about eight oclock in the Evening, and "twas such a solemn scene of Joy"—&c. She is at this moment settled in Wimpole Street, whare could you look in upon her, you would find her perfectly Contented, and would add to her happiness, which the additional society of a friend will ever do.

If your friend has any cause for anxiety, it arrises, from being obliged to Leave her Parents to whom she finds herself every day more attached, and more and more sollicitious to promote their Happiness. The seperation has but enlarged the scene to them, for we meet every day either with them, or with us, and Harmony and affection preside over our Circle; yet I wish Mamma could call in some one of her young American friends as a Constant Companion; but it is so uncertain how long we may *all* stay in this Country or how soon *we* may return to our own, that it is not possible to make any arangements for the future—all we can do is to wait patiently till the decissions of others mark out our future destination. In the mean time let us my Dear Eliza eleviate the disagreeables arrising from this seperation, by a Continueance of this friendly epistolary intercourse. Mrs Hay Carried proofs of my not having forgotten my friends, and you my Eliza was amongst the first in my remembrance. I am fearfull as my Letters were all under Cover to Mr Charles Storer that his absence may occassion thier delay for which I shall be very sorry.

My Letters from my Brother inform me that he is Learning to Play upon the flute which has given me much anxiety, do my Dear Eliza dissuade him from the practice. It is certainly very prejudicial to Health, and tho it may amuse him for the Present, I fear the Consequences. I hope Charles willnot attempt it. It would be more dangerous for him than for my Brother John. We have seen its affects upon the Warrens and I thought your Mamma was so well Convinced of the danger arrising from it as to prevent your Brother from the use of it, and I hope She will have an equal degree of influence upon mine.

Remember me to all who inquire after me. Do write me as often as you can find it Convenient and beleive me as sincerely your friend
A. Smith

RC (MHi:C. P. Cranch Papers); addressed: "Miss Eliza Cranch Braintree near Boston. Massachusetts"; endorsed: "Mrs Abigl Smith" and "Letter from Mrs. A: Smith: London July 18th. 1786 Here is mentioned her Marriage." Some loss of text where the seal was removed.

[1] Of 20 May, above.

Cotton Tufts to John Adams

Dear Sr.
Boston July. 18. 1786

Mrs. Cranch last Evening informed me, That a Mr. Standfast Smith of this Town is empowered to sell Verchilds Lands. Would it not be agreable to You to purchase those belonging to His Heirs which you have improved for some Years past?

Sometime past I sued Sloane and recovered judgment against Him. He has given a Release to the Lands mortgaged and I think it would be best to sell them as they can be no Profit to You. Should You be of that Opinion, Youll be pleased to write to me on the Subject. Will the Authority I now have be sufficient or must I have a particular Power for the Purpose.[1]

Rhode Island is suffering great Distress from their Paper Emission—and the State is in great Confusion—Trade stagnated Markets shut up—and the People begin to break open Stores seize Grain and sell it for Paper Money.

We have been in some doubt of the Utility of entering Mast. Thomas this present Year and as we had not heard from You, We had concluded to defer it. Last Week Mast. John showd me your Letter,[2] in which I discoverd Your Expectations of his entering this Commencement. I expect to see Mr Shaw on this our Anniversary[3] who I understand will bring Thomas with him to Cambridge; We shall consult upon the Matter and conduct agreable to what we suppose would be Your Mind were You present. If he enters the present Year I apprehend it will be best to have his Examination postpon[ed] to the End of the Vacation, as he does not expect to pass the Try[al] the present Week. Be pleased to present my Affectiona[te] Regards to Mrs. Adams & yr. Daughter. I am Your Affectionate Friend & H Ser Cotton Tufts

RC (Adams Papers); addressed: "His Excellency John Adams Esqr Minister from the United States of America at the Court of Great Brittain. Grosvenorsquare London"; endorsed: "Dr Tufts July 18. 1786." Some loss of text where the seal was removed.

[1] JA's power of attorney to Cotton Tufts, [6 *Sept.*] 1784 (vol. 5:455–456).

[2] JA to JQA, 26 May, above.

[3] The 150th anniversary of the founding of Harvard College. The Boston *Independent Ledger*, 24 July, described the exercises at Harvard's 19 July commencement. The paper noted the "anniversary of Commencement" but made no mention of the number of years or any special celebration.

Abigail Adams to Elizabeth Smith Shaw

My dear sister London july 19th 1786

Accept my thanks for your kind Letter of March 18th and for the pleasing favourable account you have given of your Nephews. May they ever continue to deserve the approbation of their Friends.

From an Eye so disserning as my sisters, I did not suppose that the fault which too easily besets a Young Gentleman, would long lie conceald. He might have informd You that his Pappa was often correcting him for it, and his Mamma gently reminding that young Men should never be possitive.

There are few persons upon a candid inquiry, who will not recollect and find that upon many occasions they have been faulty in this respect, yet must condemn it; in most instances, as a Breach of good Manners and politeness. Nor is a person let; his Learning be ever so extensive and his abilities ever so splendid; capable of rendering himself so usefull to Mankind: if at the same time, he discovers an overbearing and dogmatical disposition.[1] The late Dr Johnson, Author of the Ramblers and compiler of the dictionary was a very striking proof of this assertion, and he plainly discovers his sentiments in an observation which he makes in his Lives of the Poets, "Whoever is apt to hope good from others is diligent to please them, but he who believes his powers strong enough to force their own Way, commonly tries only to please himself."[2] Pope has juster Ideas upon this Subject and discovers a Greater knowledge of Mankind, which will be best convey'd to you in his own words.

"Tis not enough your counsel should be true
Blunt Truths more Mischief than nice falshoods do

Men must be taught as if you taught them not
And things unknown, propos'd as things forgot
Without good Breeding truth is disapprov'd
That only makes superiour sense beloved."[3]

Three of as Learned Men, as ever I had the honour of knowing, are three of the modestest Dr Priestly, Dr Price, and mr Jefferson, in neither of whom a self importance appears or a wish to force their sentiments and opinions upon Mankind. Whoever thinks too highly of himself will discover it, and just in proportion as he overvalues his abilities, will mankind endeavour to mortify and lessen them nor will they suffer him to take that as a right, which they claim the privelege of bestowing as a reward.

I hope however that your Nephew will strive to correct this disposition, and that he will never want a kind Friend like his Aunt, to reason with him from regard and affection, which have the surest effect upon generous minds and I feel no small satisfaction when I say to you, that I do not know an other fault which he has. Perhaps I discover the blind Partiality of a Parent.

Your Neice will write to you I presume under the signature of a Name once very familiar to you, and with it she has acquired a Man of Honour, Virtue and integrity for her Partner and companion. Sensible delicate and affectionate just the Character you would have chosen for your Neice, whose prospect (in this New connection), for happiness appear to be rationally founded. May Heaven Smile upon and bless their union is a petition in which I know you will join me. The only unpleasing Idea which attends it, is, that we must in all probability live in different states, perhaps in different Countries. But how small is this consideration, when compared with others? I gave her to him with all my Heart, he was worthy of her.

I want to return Home, and bring them with me, we should all be happier in America. There we should find sentiments and opinions more agreeable to us, society and Friends which the European World knows not of. It is all lost in ceremony and Parade, in venality and corruption, in Gameing and debauchery, amongst those who stile themselves polite People, the fashonable World. I would not check the Benevolence of my Country Men, but I would have them grow more cautious where; and upon whom they bestow it. This Nation surely has no claim to be considerd as the most favourd.[4] I wish a general Spirit of Liberality may prevail towards all Mankind. Let them be considerd as one Nation equally intitled to our regard as Breathren of the same universal Parent. Let Learning personal Merit and virtue create the only distinctions,[5] and as we have taken the Lead of all other Nations with respect to Religious toleration, let us shew ourselves equally Liberal in all other respects. Than will our Nation be a Phenomenon indeed, and I am Sure the more we cultivate peace and good will to Man, the happier we shall be.

Pray how does my Friend Mrs Allen? is the family like to increase?[6] I do not wonder as I formerly used to, that persons who have no children substitute cats dogs and Birds in their stead.

I design to write to mr Thaxter if I have time. I suppose I may congratulate him upon his Nuptials, or shall I say to him in the Words of Shakspear, "here is Benidict the Married Man."[7] I believe I ought to rally him a little, but all my Authorities are in America filed in the Letters he used to write me. I never believed his vows of celibacy of insensibility &c.[8] Young people are fond of Boasting sometimes not considering how great they make the merrit of the conquerer: Good Dr Price told us last sunday that Marriage was a Natural state, an honorable State, and that no man could be so happy out of it, as he might be in it, that those who by lose connections unfitted themselves for that state, perverted the order of Nature and would suffer a punishment concequent upon it. He also pointed out those virtues and qualifications necessary to a happy union, and the Duties resulting from that union. The Dr has been giving us a number of discourses upon Relative duties. You may judge of our value for his Sermons when we go six miles every Sunday to hear him.[9] He preaches only once a day.

Captain Callihan will sail next week. My Letters must all be ready this, and I have more than a dozen to write yet; provided I fullfill all my engagements. Next Monday I go into the Country to spend a week with mr Hollis at his Country Seat. Mr and Mrs Smith accompany us. Remember me to mr Shaw I hope the Books reachd him.[10] Be so good as to send one of the Phamplets to mr Allen with my compliments. Love to Billy and Betsys from your Ever affectionate Sister AA

RC (DLC:Shaw Family Papers). Dft (Adams Papers), dated 14 July.

[1] In the Dft, AA wrote this sentence without any internal punctuation. If the punctuation in the RC is changed, a possible, clearer reading is: "Nor is a person, let his Learning be ever so extensive and his abilities ever so splendid, capable of rendering himself so usefull to Mankind, if at the same time, he discovers an overbearing and dogmatical disposition."

[2] Samuel Johnson published *The Rambler* twice a week from 20 March 1750 to 14 March 1752 and *A Dictionary, with a Grammar and History, of the English Language* in 1755. *Prefaces, Biographical and Critical, to*

the Works of the Most Eminent English Poets first appeared in 1781 and later was published under the title of *Lives of the English Poets* ("A Chronological Catalogue of the Prose Works of Samuel Johnson, LL.D." in James Boswell, *The Life of Samuel Johnson, LL.D.*, 4 vols., Oxford, 1826, 1:xvii, xx–xxi). AA quotes from Johnson's essay on poet John Gay (*Lives of the English Poets*, 2 vols., 2:64–65, in *The Works of Samuel Johnson, LL.D.*, 9 vols., Oxford, 1825).

[3] Alexander Pope, *An Essay on Criticism*, Part III, lines 13–18. In line 13, Pope wrote, ". . . your counsel still be true."

[4] In the Dft, AA wrote the following instead of the previous sentence: "Let not the English be the most favourd Nation amongst us, unless personal merit intitles a man to respect, the country at large do not deserve that respect which was once shewn it."

[5] In the Dft, AA concluded this paragraph, "but perhaps this is wishing for more than mankind are capable of attaining till the mellinium, or the thousand years in which we are told the just only shall reign upon earth but I must still think that the more we cultivate this temper and disposition the happier we shall be."

[6] At this point in the Dft, AA added the following: "I wish I had my little Neice here I should find an amusement which I really want, I have a miss with me for a week or ten day during part of the School Hollydays a daughter of Dr Jeffries's of about 7 years old, a sprightly sensible child."

[7] Similar phrases appear in *Much Ado about Nothing*, Act I, scene i, lines 269–270; Act V, scene i, lines 185–186; and Act V, scene iv, line 99.

[8] Thaxter often wrote to AA during 1782–1785 about his intention to remain single. See, for example, his letter of 10 Nov. 1782 (vol. 5:34).

[9] Price preached regularly at a church in Hackney, in the northeast portion of London, several miles from the Adamses' home in Grosvenor Square (vol. 6:197).

[10] See AA to Elizabeth Smith Shaw, 24 April, and note 3, above.

Abigail Adams to Lucy Cranch

My Dear Neice London july 20th 1786

My fourth Letter I begin to you.[1] I dare not reckon the Number I have to write; least I should feel discouraged in the attempt. I must circumscribe myself to half a sheet of Paper. Raree Shows are so much the taste of this Country that they make one even of the corpse of great people, and the other Day a Gentleman presented me with a Card to go and see the corpse of the Duke of Northumberland, who died at his House in the Country but was brought here to be laid in state. It is said he, a senseless peice of Pagentry, but as such, I would advise you to see it. It is practised only with crownd Heads and some of the most ancient families of Dukes. The Late Duke was Father to Lord Peircy, whom the Americans well remember. His Lordship (who lives a few doors from us), being the elder son inherits the title and estate, and is now duke of Northumberland.[2]

Northumberland House is in the city, a great immence pile of Building to which one enters through massy Iron Gates.[3] At this Gate stood four porters clad in Black, the court up to the house was hung in Black and divided by a temporary railing that the spectators might pass in, upon one side and out upon the other. From the Court we enterd a long Suit of rooms, 5 in Number through rows of servants on each side of us; all Sabled as well as the rooms. I never before understood that line of Pope's

> "When Hopkins dies a thousand Lights attend."[4]

I believe there were two thousand here, for Day light was totally excluded. Upon the walls were as many Eschutcheon as candles, these are formd so as to place a light in each. These plates are all washd with Silver, being put up upon the black Cloth and lighted in this manner gave the rooms a Tomb like appearence, for in this manner are the Tombs of the Dead enlightned in Catholick Countries, and it is not uncommon for the great to leave a large Sum of Money for lights to be kept constantly burning. Through these rooms we moved with a slow pace and a Solom Silence into that which containd the corps. Here upon a superb Bed of State, surrounded with 24 wax Lights upon enormous silver candle Sticks, lay the remains of his Grace, as I presume, but so buried amidst Stars and Garters, and the various insignias of the different offices he sustaind, that he might as well have been at Sion House;[5] for all that one could see of him, for these ornaments are display'd like flags

> The George and Garter dangling from the bed
> Where Gaudy Yellow strove with flameing red[6]

Upon the Bolster lay the Ducal coronet, and round the bed stood a dozen Men in black whom they call Mutes. It was said that the Corps was cloathd in a white satin tunick and cap richly trimd with Blond lace, but for this I cannot vouch, tho I do not think it more ridiculous than the other parts of the parade which I saw: and this farce was kept up [ten?] Days. The Body was then deposited in westminster abbe, with as much Parade and shew as possible; but being out of Town, I did not see it.[7] We made an excursion as far as Portsmouth, which lies about 75 miles from London. I was much dissapointed in the appearence of the Country, great part of it being only barren Heath. Within 18 mils of the Town it appears fruitfull and highly cultivated. We spent only one Day at Portsmouth, but returnd an other road which brought us back through windsor. Here we stoped a day and half, and I was Charmd and delighted with it, the most Luxurient fancy cannot exceed the Beauties of this place. I do not wonder that Pope Stiled it, the Seat of the Muses. Read his

Windsor Forrest,[8] and give full credit to his most poetic flights. The road by which we enterd the Town was from the Top of a very steep Hill. From this hill a lawn presents itself on each side, before you a broad straight road 3 miles in length, upon each side a double plantation of lofty Elms lift their Majestick Heads, which is exceeded only by a view of the still Grandeur Forest at a distance which is 30 miles in circumference. From this Hill you have a view of the castle and the Town. This place as in former Days, is the retreat of the monarck. The Royal family reside here nine Months of the Year, not in the Castle, as that would require the attendance of Ministers &c. The present Queen has a neat Lodge here close to the Castle and there is an other a few rods distant for the princessess. His Majesty is a visitor to the Queen and the family reside here with as little parade as that of a private Gentlemans. It is the Etiquette that none of his Majesties Ministers approach him upon buisness here, dispatches are sent by Messengers, and answers returnd in the same way. He holds his Levies twice a week in Town. The Castle is one of the strongest places in Europe as it is said, and a safe retreat for the family in case any more Revolutions should shake this kingdom. It was first built by Edward the 3d, Charles the 2d kept his Court here during the Summer Months, and spaird no expence to render it Worthy the Royal residence. He furnishd it richly and decorated it with paintings by the first Masters.[9] It is situated upon a high Hill which rises by a gentle assent and enjoys a most delightfull prospect round it. In the front [is a wide and extensive][10] vale, adornd with feilds and Medows, with Groves on either side, and the calm smooth water of the Thames running through them. Behind it are Hills coverd with fine Forests, as if designd by nature for Hunting. The Terrace round the Castle is a noble walk; coverd with fine Gravel it is raised on a steep declivity of a hill, and over looks the whole Town. Here the King and Royal family walk on sunday afternoons in order to shew themselves to those of their Subjects, who chuse to repair to windsor for that purpose. In fine weather the terrace is generally throngd. From the Top of this tower on the castle they shewd us 3 different Counties.[11] To describe to you the appartments the Paintings and Decorations within this castle would require a volm instead of a Letter. I shall mention only two rooms and the first is that calld the Queens bed chamber, where upon the Top of the cealing is painted the Story of Diana and Endymion.[12] The Bed of state was put up by her Majesty, the inside and counterpain are of white sattin the curtains of pea Green richly embrodered by a Mrs Wright embroderer to her Majesty There is a full length Picture of the Queen with her 14 children in minature in the same peice, taken by mr West. It is a very handsome likeness of her.[13] The next room is calld the room of Beauties, so named for the Portraits of the most celebrated Beauties in the Reign of Charles the 2d, they are 14 in Number. There is also Charles Queen a very handsome woman. The dress of many of them, is in the Stile of the present Day.[14] Here is also Queen Carolinies China closet, filled with a great variety of curious china elegantly disposed.[15]

I have come now to the bottom of the last page. If I have amused my dear Neice it will give great pleasure to her affectionate

[A. Adams][16]

PS I send you the *fashionable* Magizine.[17]

RC (MHi:Misc. Bound Coll.). Printed in AA, *Letters*, ed. CFA, 1840, p. 338–343.

[1] AA's previous letters to Lucy Cranch written from London are dated 27 Aug. 1785 (vol. 6:312–314), 2 April, and 22 May (addressed to both Elizabeth and Lucy Cranch), both above.

[2] Hugh Percy, né Smithson, Duke of Northumberland, died 6 June. He was succeeded by his eldest son, Hugh, Earl Percy, who, as an officer in the 5th Regiment of Fusiliers, commanded the British camp at Boston and covered the British retreat from Lexington and Concord. The elder duke is again linked to the Adams family history, when in the 1830s and 1840s, JQA spearheaded the congressional effort to accept a $500,000 bequest from the duke's illegitimate son, James Smithson, and establish the Smithsonian Institution (*DNB*; *The Great Design: Two Lectures on the Smithson Bequest by John Quincy Adams*, ed. Wilcomb E. Washburn, Washington, D.C., 1965, p. 13–14).

[3] Northumberland House, Charing Cross, was built in the early seventeenth century in the shape of a "U," the opening of which led out to the gardens and river and was later enclosed. Additions in the mid-eighteenth century included an art gallery and a statue of the Percy lion above the arched entrance along the Strand. The house was demolished in 1874 (*London Past and Present*, 2:603–605; *London Encyclopædia*).

[4] Alexander Pope, *Moral Essays*, Epistle III, line 291.

[5] For AA's visit to the Duke of Northumberland's country seat, Sion House, see AA to Elizabeth Smith Shaw, 24 April, above.

[6] A paraphrase of Pope, *Moral Essays*, Epistle III, lines 303–304.

[7] The remains of the Duke of Northumberland were brought to London on 8 June for embalming. His funeral took place on the 21st (London *Daily Universal Register*, 9, 22 June).

[8] Line 2 of Pope's poem describes Windsor as "At once the Monarch's and the Muse's seats" (Pope, *The Complete Poetical Works of Alexander Pope*, N.Y., 1903, p. 28–34). He praises the rural delights of the town near which he grew up for nearly 300 lines.

[9] William the Conqueror was the first to build on the site of Windsor Castle, which occupies a naturally defensive position along the Thames, and his successors made many improvements and additions. Between 1359 and 1368, Edward III reconstructed and added to the castle to house both the private apartments of the king and queen and the state apartments used for official and ceremonial business. The palace was looted during the English Civil War and allowed to fall into disrepair. Upon the restoration of the monarchy in 1660, Charles II commissioned architect Hugh May to rebuild and restore the grandeur of Windsor Castle (Robin Mackworth-Young, *The History and Treasures of Windsor Castle*, N.Y., 1982, p. 6–7, 16–19, 33–45).

[10] The text in brackets is supplied from AA, *Letters*, ed. CFA, 1840, p. 341. For its subsequent loss, see note 16.

[11] While three counties may have been

pointed out to AA, twelve were visible from Windsor Castle's Round Tower: Bedfordshire, Berkshire, Buckinghamshire, Essex, Hampshire, Hertfordshire, Middlesex, Oxfordshire, Surrey, Sussex, and Wiltshire (W. H. Pyne, *The History of the Royal Residences of Windsor Castle, St. James's Palace, Carlton House, Kensington Palace, Hampton Court, Buckingham House, and Frogmore*, 3 vols., London, 1819, 1:187–188).

[12] Italian-born artist Antonio Verrio was commissioned by Charles II to decorate the ceilings and walls of the royal apartments at Windsor Castle with scenes illustrating classical mythology and glorifying the monarchy. Verrio's materials proved fragile, and paintings in the queen's bedchamber and other rooms deteriorated and were removed in later renovations. Three rooms by Verrio survive (Mackworth-Young, *The History and Treasures of Windsor Castle*, p. 40–42).

[13] The Benjamin West painting of Queen Charlotte was completed in 1779. It required several revisions to incorporate additional children as they were born. In the end, it showed the queen full-length with thirteen children around her and was considered to be the king's favorite royal portrait (Robert C. Alberts, *Benjamin West: A Biography*, Boston, 1978, p. 131).

[14] Sir Peter Lely painted ten of the portraits of the ladies of the court of Charles II, William Wissing three, and Jacob Huysman one. Another of Lely's portraits was of Catherine of Braganza, consort of Charles II (Pyne, *History of the Royal Residences of Windsor Castle*, 1:116–117, 154).

[15] Queen Caroline, wife of George II and a noted supporter of the arts, owned a substantial quantity of Japanese ware that had originally been a gift from the East India Company (John Van der Kiste, *King George II and Queen Caroline*, Stroud, Gloucestershire, 1997, p. 123).

[16] Supplied from AA, *Letters*, ed. CFA, 1840, p. 343. The signature, which was probably "A. Adams," has been neatly cut out of the RC resulting in the loss of five words on the reverse. In 1839, when CFA began gathering together his grandmother's letters for publication, Lucy Cranch, who married John Greenleaf in 1795, let him copy AA's letters to both her and her mother, Mary Cranch (CFA, *Diary*, 8:278, 297).

[17] *The Fashionable Magazine; or, Lady's and Gentleman's Monthly Recorder of New Fashions, etc.*, vol. 1, London, 1786.

Elizabeth Smith Shaw to Abigail Adams

The Day after Commencment—Noon

My Dear Sister Haverhill July 20 1786

Here I am, all alone for a great rarity. There is nothing more agreeable to me for a *little while*, than what the *world* calls Solatude. I have but one Servant maid in the House, and one Scholar in the Study. So that we are quite still. I hear nothing but the busy hum of Flies, and the warbling of a Wren, and spring-Bird in the Orchard, that set and swell their little throats as if the kind things knew how much I am delighted with their melody.

Cousin Sally Tufts (who has been here this fortnight) Polly Harrod,[1] Betsy Smith, are gone early this PM. to see Mrs Allen, and William S Shaw to wait upon them, as their happy Gallant. William reads, and speaks very plain, and begins to write cleverly. Seperating my Children the Summer you left us, was of very eminent Service to them both.[2] In three Months time you would have been surprized to have heard them. I thought William gained in plainess of speech, rather more than his Sister. But I have not the least fear of either of them now. Betsy Quincy had an Abcess formed just below her Bowells, upon the right side last September, and I think, though she is not in the lest lame, that she has never been so well in health nor so fat since. She has more Spirits now than strength, grows very tall, and is full of talk, and good humour. She is so livly, that I think sometimes she will fly off in air. I carried her the last week in May to Braintree, for the benefit of the change of Air, and Sister would not let me bring her back. I expect Mr Shaw and Thomas will bring her this Week or next home. They both went in a Chaise a Tuesday for Commencement. Mr Shaw thinks upon the whole, not to offer Thomas this year. He is full young, and not so well fitted in Greek as yet, as either of his Brothers. Mr Thaxter says, it would rather be a damage to him. Mr Shaw would not have thought of his going till the next year, only on account of his Brother JQA being there with him, but the freshman and the Seignor Class have but little connection with each other, and perhaps when he has himself, *received* the honours of the University, he will be better qualified to recommend, and advise his Brother how to acquire and preserve them, than he would now.

Last week he sent his Brother a kind, affectionate parental Letter.[3] It was worthy his Father, I am sure you would have been charmed with it.

I expect cousin Lucy Cranch to tarry with me, and all my *Children*, next week.

Mr Nathaniel Sparhawk of whom you have formerly heard me speak, called here, to take his leave of me, he is to embark for Europe in about a week. He has kindly offered to take a Letter for you. He wishes to be introduced to Mr and Mrs Adams. What his views in the mercantile way may be, I cannot tell. He has met with the same misfortune which few of our Merchants have escaped. Madam Hayly comeing to America, has sunk the *Spirits* of Many, as well as their Purses.[4]

Mr Sparhawk resided in Haverhill when I first came into the Town, and during his first wives Life, I was treated by them with the greatest politeness, and affection, and there was no place in the town where I was happier. Our Souls were in Unison. She was a Woman of reading, and sentiment, and those seldom fail of pleasing.[5] Such are the Salt of the World. How soon must Society grow insipid, and conversation wearisome unless it is enlivened by a Taste for Literature.

You will not fail my Sister of noticing this Gentleman—as an American.

I must go—adieu for the present my charming Sister—you must have more by and by. Last Week I received two Letters from you, dated 24th of April, and 25th of May.[6] Mr Shaw has received Dr Clarks Sermons, and begs his kindest Regards may be presented to Dr Adams, and his warmest Thanks. I think the Dimity you sent B Quincy is the nicest I ever saw. I hope the little creature will live to see you, and thank you herself. She is really a comical child. I said to her one Day, "B Q be very careful of your Cloaths, you must not hurt them, I shall not make any more for you if you do."—"No matter Mamma if you don't, Aunt Adams will send me enough."

The Callico you mention, I have not seen, I suppose it is with sister. My Lutestring has been much admired. I had it made, and honoured Mr and Mrs Porter with it upon the Celebration of thier Marriage. They are now gone upon a visit to Bridgewater, and next Week they are to go to Rye, and She to take her Residence for Life.[7] Rye is a Town 5 miles from Portsmouth, pleasantly situated they say. People here give me the credit of making the Match, but be that as it may, I heartily wish them happiness. They are both worthy. I have not heard that Mr and Mrs Evans have as yet returned from their Southern Journey. I know not how these 2 social sensible Creatures, will be able to content themselves in the—*town of Weymouth*.

It is to *Me*, like a Tree, stripped of its Fruit, and herbage.

Alas! (my Sister) we have many links in our Chain of Relationship, broken off, since you left us. I have met with another very great Loss, even as to my temporal Interest in our dear Aunt Smith. As I hear Cushing did not sail, till a week after my Aunts Burial, I suppose you will by him have had particular accounts, of the melancholly Scene. Her Death you may well think, is universally lamented. Such a Wife, Mother, Mistress and Friend, grow not every Tree. And such a Loss is not easily repaired. This my good Uncle and Cousins; especially Isaac, deeply feel.

You *knew* a part of her Virtues, and I need not expaciate. May they live in our Memory, and in our Lives.

When I was at Boston she had scurvy spots upon her Arms, as you and I have seen upon our selves, and her blood seemed in a lethargick, poor state, and had lost a great deal of her Flesh. But my uncle and she came to Braintree, upon a Saturday, and over to Weymouth a Monday, with our Brother Cranch, and Sister. It was the first Time that any of us had been there since my Aunts Tufts Burial. It was painful you may sure. *There* was her easy Chair—But *no* kind Aunt to sweetly smile, and bid me welcome. A Tear would steal across my Cheek, in spite of all my Resolution, and care to suppress, and *twinkle* it away. The good Dr behaved excellently, he acts from the best of Principles, and by his kindness and attention endeavoured to make us feel as little as possible the want of our amiable Aunt. My Uncle and Aunt returned with us to Boston, and she seemed much better, which encouraged her, and she told me that riding did her so much good that she should keep on visiting her Friends and would come and spend some time with me, after she had attended an Ordination at Prince-Town, where my Uncle was going as Delagate. But the Night before she was to set out, she was taken in Convulsions and never seemed to have her senses more than a moment or two after-wards. And instead of joining any longer here below in the Society of Mortals, she has taken a sweeter Journey to the heavenly Canan.

I have many things more to say, but Mr Sparhawk is now waiting.

Believe me my Dear Sister, with the deepest sense of Gratitude for your kindness, your truly affectionate Sister Eliza Shaw

RC (Adams Papers); endorsed: "Mrs Shaw july 20 1786."

[1] Sally Tufts, age fourteen, was the daughter of AA's cousin Samuel Tufts, a Newburyport merchant, and Sarah Moody (*NEHGR*, 51:303 [July 1897]; *Vital Records of Newburyport Massachusetts to the End of the Year 1849*, 2 vols., Salem, Mass., 1911, 1:399). Mary (Polly) Harrod of Haverhill, age fifteen, was the elder sister of Ann Harrod, whom TBA married in 1805 (Boston, *24th Report*, p. 322; CFA, *Diary*, 5:82–83).

[2] Elizabeth Quincy Shaw spent the summer of 1784 with the Cranch family (vol. 5:337, 352–353, 424, 475).

[3] Probably JQA to TBA, 2 July, above.

[4] Mary Wilkes Storke Hayley, the sister of English politician and American sympathizer John Wilkes, came to Boston in 1784 to collect the debts owed her late husband, George Hayley, a London merchant and alderman, a sum totaling nearly £80,000 (Thwing Catalogue, MHi; *Boston Gazette*, 31 May 1784; Katharine A. Kellock, "London Merchants and the pre-1776 American Debts," *Guildhall Studies in London History*, 1:129 [Oct. 1974]).

[5] Nathaniel Sparhawk Jr., Harvard 1765, a Salem merchant, married Catherine Sparhawk, his cousin, in Kittery, Mass. (now Maine), in 1766; she died in 1778. Sparhawk's second wife was Elizabeth Bartlett of Haverhill, whom he married in 1780. Following Elizabeth's death in 1782, Sparhawk married a third time, in 1783, to Deborah Adams of Portsmouth, N.H., but the couple soon separated (*Sibley's Harvard Graduates*, 16:235–237).

[6] AA's letter of 25 May has not been found.

[7] Rev. Huntington Porter, minister of the Congregational church in Rye, N.H., and Susannah Sargeant of Haverhill married on 28 June (*Vital Records of Haverhill Massachusetts to the End of the Year 1849*, 2 vols., Topsfield, Mass., 1910–1911, 2:261; Langdon B. Parsons, *History of the Town of Rye, New Hampshire, from Its Discovery and Settlement to December 31, 1903*, Concord, N.H., 1905, p. 149–150, 156–157).

Abigail Adams to John Quincy Adams

My Dear Son july 21 1786 London

Altho afflicted to day with one of my bad headaches; I must write you, least the vessel should Sail in my absence with out a Letter from me. A few weeks ago we Breakfasted with mr Bridgen whom you know. He collected several gentlemen of literature, and amongst them mr Hollis, who has often dinned with us. He is a Worthy good Man, and so well known at the university that I need give no further account of him. He was going in a day or two to his Country seat for the Summer and he made us promise that we would come out to Hyde and Spend a week with him. His invitation savourd so much of that Hospitality which this country was once celebrated for, that we did not hesitate to comply, and next week is the time appointed.

He told us that there was but one place in his House, but what was common to all his Friends, and that was his Liberary. They must be great favorites to be admitted there; for he could not bear to have his Books misplaced. This will give you an Idea of his neatness and regularity. Mr Bridgen col S and your sister are of the party.

By Captain Callihan we send the Books you wrote for, and a valuable little parcel your Pappa has added to them, for the benefit of you and your Brothers.[1] They cost 8 Guineys so be carefull of them.

I thank you for your Letter, it gave me great pleasure, and I am happy to find you so well situated. The attention you have always given to your studies, and the fondness You have for Literature, precludes any other injunctions to you than that of taking care of your Health. I believe I ought to except one other–which is a watchfulness over yourself; that the knowledge you have acquired does not make you assumeing, and too tenacious of your own opinions. Pope says, "those best can bear reproof, who merit praise." It is upon this principal that I would gaurd you against the only error that I am conscious you possess. I cannot advise you better upon this subject than in the words of Pope, and as you love poetry fix the following lines in your memory

Tis not enough taste judgement Learning join;
In all you speak, let Truth and candour shine
That not alone, what to your sense is due.
All may allow, *but seek your Friendship too*

Be silent always when you doubt your Sense
And speak; tho sure with *Seeming diffidence*
Some possitive persisting Fops we know
Who if once wrong will needs be always so.
But you with pleasure own your Errors past
And make *each day* a critic *on the last*.[2]

I inclose to you an Epitaph upon Dr Johnson written by as great a curiosity as himself. It was given me by Miss Shipley daughter to the Bishop of Saint Asaph. I have met with many persons here, who were personally acquainted with the dr. They have a great respect for his memory, but they all agree that he was an unpleasent companion who would never bear the least contradiction. Your sister Sent you Mrs Pioggi anecdotes of him. Boswells are too contemptable to be worth reading.[3] Your Friend Murry first lent me Mrs Pioggis and from it I coppy the following lines written by him in the blank page

"Like those bright sparks which comets leave behind
Appear the effusions of great Johnsons mind
Had its vast orb unclouded pour'd its rays.
The glorious flood had blinded by its blaize
But clouds of weakness thickly round it fly
And save the envy of the weakest eye."

Pray inform us from whence arises the illeberal Spirit which appears in the Boston Gazzets against the Law? or rather the professors of it. I am sorry any of our Countrymen should disgrace themselves by holding up such sentiments as Honestus, who ever he is, has publishd to the world. I suspect one may apply to him, the observation which Pope Gangenella made upon Voltair, that he attackd Religion because it was troublesome to him.[4] He had better adopt Johnsons opinion, "that the Law is the last result of Humane wisdom, acting upon humane experience for the benifit of the publick."[5]

If some of the professors are a disgrace to it, they would have been equally so as merchants Physicians or divines. Where is the profession composed only of Honest Men? annihilate the profession of the Law, and the Liberties of the Country would soon share the same fate. If they wish to suppress the influence of the Bar, Let them practise justice, and consider the Maxim, "that can never be politically right, which is morally wrong."

As to politicks Parliament is up[6] and a dead Calm ensues. With respect to America, things remain much in the same state as when I wrote you last, all the movements here, will depend upon the Measures of Congress. Untill some regular System is adopted, the less communication our Country has with this, the better. Lamb has orders to repair to Congress, and lay before them the result of his negotiations.

Col Smith has promised to write to you, and your sister will tell you all about herself.[7] I wrote you by Col Forrest on the 13th of june, who saild for newyork. I suppose you are very happy by this time to have enterd upon your last year, and your Brother Charles to have finishd his Freshmanship. If your Brother Tommy enters, be very attentive to him, and always give him the advise of judgment and reflection, rather than what may result from the feelings of the moment. And whatever your own sentiments may be with regard to the abilities and qualifications of your Preceptors, you should always endeavour to treat them with the respect due to their Station, and enjoin the same conduct upon your Brothers. It is not in your power to remedy the evils you complain of. Whilst the Salleries are so small it cannot be expected that Gentlemen of the first abilities will devote their lives to the preceptorship. The concequence will be, that young Men will fill those places, and the changes will be frequent. Get all the good you can, and beware that you do no ill to others. You must be conscious of how great importance it is to youth, that they should respect their teachers. Therefore whatever tends to lessen them, is an injury to the whole Society, besides there is nothing which a person will not sooner forgive, than contempt. If you are conscious to yourself that you possess more knowledge upon some subjects than others of your standing, reflect that you have had greater opportunites of seeing the world, and obtaining a knowledge of Mankind than any of your cotemporarys, that you have never wanted a Book, but it has been supplied you, that your whole time has been spent in the company of Men of Literature and Science. How unpardonable would it have been in you, to have been a Blockhead. My paper will allow me room only to add, my blessing to you & Your Brothers from your ever affectionate

A Adams

RC (Adams Papers); endorsed: "My Mother 21. July 1786"; docketed: "Mrs: Adams. July 21st: 1786."

[1] JQA had requested Gravesande's *Mathematical Elements* and a Greek and Latin New Testament (see JQA to AA2, 15 March, note 8, and JQA to JA, 2 April, and notes

8, 10, both above). The package contained many books "mostly upon philosophical subjects" and a French history of the American Revolution (JQA, *Diary*, 2:118; JQA to AA, 30 Dec., and note 3, below). JA's special gift has not been identified.

[2] Both quotations are from Pope, *An Essay on Criticism*, Part III, lines 3–12, 24. Here, and in the letter's last paragraph, AA seeks to correct the intellectual arrogance that Elizabeth Shaw saw in JQA (Shaw to AA, 18 March, above).

[3] Hester Lynch Salusbury Thrale Piozzi, *Anecdotes of the Late Samuel Johnson, LL.D., during the Last Twenty Years of His Life*, London, 1786. JQA received this work from AA2 on 14 July (*Diary*, 2:65). James Boswell's first work on Johnson, his *Journal of a Tour to the Hebrides with Samuel Johnson, LL.D.*, appeared in the spring of 1786 (*DNB*). The "Epitaph" has not been identified.

[4] On AA's reading the letters of Giovanni Ganganelli, Pope Clement XIV, in 1783, see vol. 5:268, 269. The quote regarding Voltaire appears in *Interesting Letters of Pope Clement XIV. (Ganganelli.)*, 2 vols., London, 1777, 1:xxxiii.

[5] Piozzi, *Anecdotes*, p. 58

[6] Parliament adjourned on 11 July and would reconvene on 23 Jan. 1787 (Namier and Brooke, *House of Commons*, 1:536).

[7] AA2 to JQA, 22 July, below; no letter from WSS to JQA has been found.

Charles Storer to Abigail Adams

Boston. 21st. July. 1786

And a good story you shall have, Madam, as you desire. Know then that your friends both at Haverhill and Braintree are well. But I had forgot. One sad stroke has caused us much trouble, *Aunt Smith is dead.* She died about a month since. She was first seized with a lethargic fit, was lost to every thing, but apparently had recovered from her disorder and was preparing to take a journey as far as Princetown, when she was suddenly seized, the evening preceeding her setting out, with convulsion fits, which in a day or two put a period to her existence. This account you have had from others perhaps already.

I have to thank you for yours of the 22d. of May. It found me in a place you little dream of. I was in Passamaquoddy Bay at the Eastward, where I was on speculation, and which is to be the place of my residence a few years to come, perhaps for life. You recommend Agriculture. It is an idea to me more pleasing than that of any other kind of life. 'Tis most natural and therefore, to a mind uncorrupted in the world, must be most happy. You must know that Genl: Lincoln, Mr: Thos: Russell and Mr: Lowell have lately bought two Townships in Passamaquoddy Bay which they mean to settle assoon as possible.[1] I went down with the General about two months ago, and am but just returned. The General's son[2] is one of the two and twenty settlers that went down with us, and your humble servant is another. There is a little trade carried on there, but believe me this is by no means my object, at least no further than to ennable me to clear and improve a good landed estate. This has ever been a wish of mine. More now than ever, and I feel happy in the idea that I am acting from the very principle on which you recommend Agriculture to me in a late letter: an additional motive is that here it is impossible for me establish. So that you see in part I am *obliged* to do right this time. I therefore fully depend on my resolution. But the ultimate of my plan, as mentioned above, you will not mention to any of our friends on this side of the Atlantick. They are a good many of them averse to my going at all, most of them against my establishing myself there. So I do not let anyone in the secret. See, Madam, how you can keep it. I know I shall have your approbation, because I am sensible I act from every principle of duty.

I have heard of Gentlemen's falling in love with pictures, but I am caught with your description of the amiable Miss Hamilton. Fortunate it may be, or unfortunate, that I staid not a little longer with you. Every thing is right. I frequently, in *a reflective* moment, have painted to myself a connection with beauty and virtue. This is but Romance however, yet I must say your description and my ideas in this instance perfectly correspond. I think you will laugh at me by this time for my *Quixotism* in thus admiring an unknown *del Tobosa*,[3] but I am not going to commence Knight Errant, so please to remember this is *entre nous*.

Be kind eno: to thank Amelia for her two favors No: 3. and 4,[4] both of May. I will duly answer them, but by this opportunity she will excuse me. My best wishes ever attend her. May she be happy in this new and every other Connection. To Mr: Adams my best respects. I wish to write to him on business, and will if time will allow.[5] My Compts: to Colo: Smith if you please.

Our family desire to be duly remembered to you and yours. They wish you every good and pleasant thing. We are preparing *to see folks*, today, and you know the poor help we have in this Country and will therefore excuse not hearing more from us.

When you return I shall happy to have the honor of your Company at Passamaquoddy to pass the Summer, & am Madam, with all respect & esteem Yr: much obliged friend & humble servt:

C. S.

RC (Adams Papers); addressed: "Mrs: A. Adams. Grosvenor Square London"; endorsed: "Charles Storer july 21 1786."

[1] In March, Benjamin Lincoln, Thomas Russell, and probably John Lowell purchased Townships Nos. 1 and 2, over 50,000 acres of land, at Passamaquoddy, with the condition that sixty families would settle there within six years. The adjacent townships, in what is

now Washington Co., Maine, were bordered by the Cobscook River to the west and Passamaquoddy Bay to the east. In 1818, they were incorporated as the towns of Perry and Dennysville (*Report of the Committee for the Sale of Eastern Lands: Containing their Accounts from the 28th of October, 1783, to the 16th of June, 1795*, Boston, 1795, accounts 1 and 3; Henry Jackson to Henry Knox, 12 March, MHi:Henry Knox Papers Microfilms; William D. Williamson, *The History of the State of Maine*, 2 vols., Hallowell, Maine, 1832, repr. ed. Freeport, Maine, [1966], 2:668; Osgood Carleton, "A Map of the District of Maine," engraved by Amos Doolittle, in James Sullivan, *History of the District of Maine*, Boston, 1795).

[2] Theodore Lincoln (1763–1852), the general's second son and a 1785 graduate of Harvard, settled in what was later Dennysville (*History of the Town of Hingham, Massachusetts*, 3 vols. in 4, Hingham, 1893, 3:10; *Harvard Quinquennial Cat.*).

[3] Dulcinea del Toboso, the heroine of *Don Quixote*.

[4] Neither letter has been found.

[5] Storer wrote to JA on 21 July (Adams Papers) to inquire about discussions during the 1783 peace negotiations with Britain, which established the boundary line between the United States and Canada and informed him of current disputes between the two parties. See also AA to Cotton Tufts, 10 Oct., and note 7, below.

Abigail Adams to Cotton Tufts

My Dear sir London july 22 1786

I inclose to you the papers which contain the correspondence between Lord George Gordon and mr Tufts.[1] As I suppose it will be matter of some specculation, and may tend to injure your Nephew. I will relate to you some circumstances attending it. Upon the Letter you wrote me some time ago,[2] I had made inquiries after mr Tufts, but could hear nothing of him, till mr Jenks just before he saild, wrote me a card[3] one Day that he had found him; and that from his conversation he beleived he sincerely wishd to return to his Friends in America. I immediatly wrote mr Tufts a friendly card and invited him to dine with me on the Sunday following. I received his answer of thanks and an acceptance of the invitation.[4] Accordingly he came, and was received with the cordiality of an old acquaintance. We talkd of our Friends and were very Sociable, and I assured him that I believed he might return and live unmollessted provided he would be prudent. He tarried till near eleven oclock, and we parted in perfect good Humour. You may judge of our surprize when the twesday following there appeard in the papers Lord Georges Letter quoteing mr Tufts as his Authority.

On wednesday morning mr Tufts came up to see us, not a little mortified you may be sure and said that mr Lewis Gray was his Authority, that he had no Idea of the conversations ever being publishd, and that it took place a fortnight before without his having any Idea of the use intended to be made of it. Mr Adams told mr Tufts that the assertion was totally without foundation, that neither directly or indirectly had he ever received a single sou through any such channel, but even Supposing it had been true, of what importance was it who were his Bankers, the united States only were answerable for his Sallery. But being false it behoved him to contradict it. He did not wish to injure him or mr Gray or mr Grant, but they must be sensible they had all exposed themselves, and that if he was disposed he could give them trouble enough. This frightned mr Tufts, and I believe he Heartily wishd, that he had never got into the Scrape. Some of the Foreign ministers thought Lord George ought to be procecuted, and all condemnd the answer given by Lord Car–then. Mr Adams refused doing any thing more than after a few Days waiting to hear what would be said, he publishd a Paragraph of May 9. After which Lord George publishd a few lines which paper I have lost, the purport of it was, to get himself out as well as he could, that hearing the report, and not crediting it himself, he publishd it to give the American Minister or his Friends an opportunity to contradict it. Thus ended this foolish affair.[5] Lord Georges views may easily be Seen through, and he made others the dupes of them. If the Letters should get into our papers, as I suspect they will, you will See that the Paragraph of May 9th is publishd also.[6] Do not let it give mr Tufts Friends any uneasiness. It was an imprudence in him but I do not imagine he meant any injury. I should have acquainted him with his Fathers illness, but I was affraid he would think that I wanted benevolence in the communication and I presumed he would receive an account of it from some of his Friends. I have not seen him since this affair.

Dr Welch will pay you 3£. 9s. 6d. on my account which together with 25 Guineys that you may draw on mr Elworthy for, and which I will pay to him upon Your inclosing the Bill to me. I wish you to add to the little sum you have purchased already for me, disposing of it in the same way by the purchase of notes. I think they must rise, and I have advised mr Adams to request you to lay out a hunderd pound in them if you are of the same mind, but you can judge best being upon the Spot.

With regard to Books and papers you will feel less embarressed now than formerly. Your Neice is I believe very happily married. I hope that time will confirm my present opinion.

As to politicks, they must come from your side the water to do any good here. Lamb will return to congress to give an account of his negotiation of which he thinks very differently from what he did when he left it. He has written an intelligent Letter[7] and did all that would have been in any bodyes power to do with the resources which he had. My affectionate Regards to all Friends From your affectionate A Adams

RC (Adams Papers).

[1] Not found. See note 5, below.

[2] Cotton Tufts to AA, 12 Jan., above.

[3] Not found.

[4] Neither the invitation nor the acceptance has been found.

[5] On 3 May the London *Public Advertiser* printed a letter from Lord George Gordon informing the Marquis of Carmarthen that JA's salary was paid quarterly by the Comte d'Adhémar and citing "undeniable intelligence" possessed by Simon Tufts as his authority. Over the next week Tufts and Gordon submitted a series of letters, including a sworn affidavit by Gordon, to the *Public Advertiser* and *London Chronicle* seeking to clarify their positions. Tufts insisted that he told Gordon only that he had heard from a third party, Lewis Gray, how Adams received his salary and repeatedly insisted that Gordon had no authorization to publish the account. According to Gordon, he first heard that JA was paid by the French court from a Mr. Grant of the Southern Indian Department. Grant introduced Gordon to Tufts, who allowed Grant to write down the facts as known to him and then authenticated the transcript in Gordon's presence (London *Public Advertiser*, 3, 5, 6, 9, 10 May 1786; *London Chronicle*, 2–4, 6–9, 9–11 May 1786). For AA's earlier opinions on Gordon, see vol. 6:172, 173–174, 442.

[6] JA published an anonymous rebuttal in the London *Public Advertiser* on 9 May; it was summarized in the *Boston Gazette* on 17 July and reprinted in full in the Boston *American Herald*, 4 September.

[7] JA received copies of Lamb's letters of 20 May and 5 June via Thomas Jefferson on 5 July. See Jefferson, *Papers*, 9:549–554, 610.

Abigail Adams to Thomas Welsh

Dear sir july 22d 1786

I have to thank you for your very inteligent Letter of May 4,[1] and am glad to find one writer who is not in the dismalls. Shades answer very well as a contrast to the light parts of a picture, but when it is all darkness one is apt to suppose that the painture is no artist, that he must be deficient in blending his coulours or too neglegent to procure proper material for them.

That our Country is prest with a heavey debt I am very sensible, and that she must excercise wisdom prudence and occonomy and industery to liberate herself from it, is equally true. But who that sees her future happiness can lament her restoration from extravagance and folly to the practise of those virtues which can and will save her? When a people become Luxurious, is there any thing that will reclaim them but dire necessity? Amidst the general cry of distress, are there any amongst us naked, or perishing with hunger? Are not our flocks fruitfull, do not our lands yeald an increase. Yes truly we have more than we can expend, but cannot find a Market sufficiently profitable for the overpluss. Nor that unbounded credit which we want, aya theirs the rub, but there are those who think the less credit we can obtain the better it will in the end prove for our Countrymen. This Country will do nothing towards a treaty of commerce or relinquishing the Posts untill the States repeal the Laws respecting British credittors. They do not deny our right to them by treaty, but say it is equally binding upon both parties. The reluctance in the different States to grant the impost has done us great injury not only here but in France and Holland. I have hopes that the present year will produce some Regular and wise System which will raise the credit of the united States and place ⟨*it*⟩ them upon a more reputable foundation than they have yet stood upon. The more harmony and peace is cultivated amongst ourselves the Stronger we link ourselves together and discountanance every little internal bickering and jealousy. The more formidable we shall become to our enemies and better able to defend ourselves against them. I am sorry to see our publick Papers so nearly allied to those of Britain. Liberty ought not to become licentiousness. Here are hireling who earn their daily Bread by vilifying Characters and countries. Heaven forbid our country should harbour Such virmin, who but Such could be the Authors of some publications which have appeard amongst you.[2]

Dft (Adams Papers). The text is written on a sheet of paper on which AA had begun a letter to JQA, probably in Dec. 1785 (see vol. 6:471, 473).

[1] 24 May, above.

[2] AA may be referring in part to the Boston newspaper essays by Benjamin Austin (Honestus) attacking lawyers (see JQA to AA2, 18 May, above).

Abigail Adams Smith to John Quincy Adams

July 22d 1786—Wimpole Street London

I have also to sollicit your Pardon my Dear Brother for haveing so long delayd writing you. I know that you will overlook it and forgive me. You are not at this time uninformd of the change which has taken place in our family, tho ⟨*I have till now been silent*⟩ my pen has lain unemploy'd from the 29th of April to this day.[1] At present your Sister is settled in Wimpole Street about half a mile from Grosvenor Square. I suppose Mamma will inform you of every particular that you may wish to be informd of, and I will indeavour for the future to take up, the thread of my discourse from the 22d of july, and continue to forward to you the subject of my reflections.

My friend will write you by this Conveyance,[2] and you must continue to favour me with your daily journal with as much freedom as ever, for your sister is not alterd, only in Name. She feels if possible an additionl attachment to her family, and more sollicitous to promote the pleasure and happiness of each individual of it, and more interested in what may concern them. I have to acknowledge the receipt of your N 13 14 15[3] by ⟨*Clallihan*⟩, and to assure you that they gave me great pleasure.

We were very glad to hear that you had entered Colledge, and I can easily excuse you for not writing when you had so important a work to accomplish. Persevereance with judgment with affect what ever you wish, that lies within your own ability. Yours will I hope be directed to important and usefull objects to those which will render persevereence Loudable. Many of the Customs at the University must undoubtedly appear to you ridiculous, and the manners of the Governors, unnecessary. It is a misfortune that People so often mistake the means, of promoting their importance and dignity but it is the case in almost every class of Men. They attend to triffles, more than to greater objects and often by such mistaken means destroy every particle of that, which they are so anxiously sollicitous to Support. I have ever thought that dignity exists in the mind and where it is not implanted by nature I am inclined to beleive all the forms and rigid formalities that can be invented by Pride and folly can never be mistaken by the least discerning for that, divine principle, possessd by a few. I have seen, an affectation of dignity very often, but I have never seen but very few, who possessd the real principle. You will I hope persevere in your resolution to pay all proper respect to every Govenor of the University, and tho to me you write with all possible Liberty you should be upon your guard, to others, especially in Colledge where your example would ⟨*have weight*⟩, be injurious to others were You to fail. I do not at all wonder at your observations.

The Death of Charles Warren must have been very distressing to Mrs W— particularly. I think he was the flower of the family. I am sorry for their misfortunes in every way. W[*inslow's*] Conduct must be the greatest affliction to them. Charles Storer has I think addopted the most eligable plan he could and his friend must approve him, but I doubt whether he is active and determined enough to overcome the Hardships and inconveniences to which he must be subjected.[4] But I hope he will, for he is a very worthy Youth.

Before I proceed further I must notice that part of your letter when you tell me you are learning the flute. This my Brothers gave me great uneasiness, and permit me to intreat of you not to continue the use of it. You may be assurd that it is extremely injurius to healhts. The first Complaints of Chareles W arrose from playing upon the flute. I must beg of you to lay it aside and to persuade your Brothers should they be so unwise as to use it to do so likewise. Charles would be more certain to receive injury than you or Thomas, but I hope you will all be persuaded to desist. It will be too Late when you feel the ill affects of it as you most certainly will, ere long.

I thank you for the vrces inclosed pray who is Delia a real or, feignd, Character.[5] The verse is smooth and the sentiments just. I shall be pleased whenever you favour me with your productions. I think it is a pleasing amusement and I dont see any disadvantages arrising from it, provided you do not spend to much time or steal a little from more important studies which I dare say *you* will not.

July 22d.

Mr Randall arrived last Saturday nigt. He left Mr Lamb at Madrid. They went to Algiers but the Dey would not see them. After spending 6 days there they Left it and returnd. Congress have not appropriated money enough for the purpose of Buying a peace. Mr R— is for Building ships and makeing War on them. Mr Barclay, the last account were from Macadore, about an hundred miles from Fez the seat of the Emperior of Morroco, from whom Mr B had received Mules and a Guard to Conduct him to Fez. The E— is represented as a very benevolent Good Man. Mr B, is much pleased with his excurssion. Tis a pitty his motions were not a little quicker.

Mr R, will I suppose be married and go soon to N Y.[6]

I have mentiond to you the ⟨*Turkish*⟩ Tripoline Ambassador.[7] He made me a vissit the other day, he is very oald, and seems to be honnest and good, in his Way. By Dr Gordon I was surprized not to hear from you. He has been to see us twice and looks as meek, as Moses. I think he is really to be pittyd, for really I dont see but his prospect is nothing less than wretchedness. In leaving America he has shewn great want of judgment, for he finds that he cannot print his History here without beeng Liable to procecution, and I suppose he placed all his dependance upon that prospect of Publishing it. He has already I heard from Dr Price been abused and insulted by one of his own Brotherhood, in a Coffe House where the dissenting Ministers meet every Tuesday.

Indeed I think his situation must be distressing. Mr Ramseys History of the Revolution in south Carollina, which is thought to be an impartial and well written Book, does not sell, here, and the Bookseller dare not offer it for sale. In short nothing respecting america nor any body or any thing from America, is esteemd or respected in this Country excepting by a few very few individuals. I think the sooner we get out of the Country the Better and I am very sure the sooner we return to America the happier for our family, but Congress are so slow in their motions and somany months and years, employd without affecting any thing, that tis enough to tire our patience. Ship after Ship arrives, and no letters nor no news. Pappa has written I am sure quires of Paper to Congress since his residence here, and, all he has yet got in answer is an acknowledgement from Mr J— of the receipt of letters of Such and such dates. We are expecting the June packet every day but whether it will bring any thing worth knowing is very uncertain. This has you know been the Case ever since Pappa has been in Europe, and so I suppose it will continue, this is *entree nous*. You have doubtless heard of Mr Humphriess arrival, and of Mr and Mrs Roggerss.

23d

Pappa has bought the Books you desird for and sends them by this Conveyance. Mr Appleton is going home. I beleive I shall give him my Letters. He is to dine to day with us in Grosvenor Square, with several other persons, amongst the No, is one singular Character, a Major Langbornn from Virginia, who has, spent these two years in walking over Europe, and in making his observations upon, every Class of Men, their Manners Customs &c—from le Roy sur le throne, to the lowest of his subjects.[8] He appears to be a sensible Man, and from his appearance and Conversation you would not suspect him of such an eccentricity of Character. He has been here about a week, and has dined with us, several times at Grosvenor Square, where we are almost every day.

Tomorrow we are going 25. miles out of Townn to visit Mr Brant Hollis, Nephew to the Gentleman so well known in your Universsity. He is an agreeable pleasant oald Bachelor, and we promise ourselves much pleasure from the excursion. The partty Consists of Pappa and Mamma Mr Bridgen Mr S, and your sister. While I am there or upon my return I will give an account of it.

I requested you some time since in one of my letters to send me a lock of your Hair.[9] I now repeat it and desire you to add to it a lock of each of my Brothers, dont neglet it, but by the 1st opportunity after the receipt of this, inclose them to me done up like yourself in three seperate papers—and remember it is the first request made You by your sister A S

Dft (Adams Papers).

[1] The last internal dateline of AA2 to JQA, 25 April, above.

[2] No letter from WSS to JQA has been found.

[3] JQA's letters of 15 March, 1 April, and 25 April, all above.

[4] To settle in northern Maine.

[5] For "An Epistle to Delia," see JQA to AA, 15 May, note 4, above.

[6] Randall previously had been engaged to a Miss White in Philadelphia prior to undertaking the Algerian assignment but in the end apparently married a French woman, Marie Anne Pertois (AA2, *Jour. and Corr.*, 3:187–189, 191; *NEHGR*, 110:128 [April 1956]).

[7] Sidi Haggi 'Abd-ur-rahman Aga.

[8] William Langborn (1756–1814), a cousin of Martha Washington and former aide-de-camp to Lafayette. Langborn spent twelve years walking the British Isles and Europe (Washington, *Papers, Confederation Series*, 3:547; Curtis Carroll Davis, "The Curious Colonel Langborn: Wanderer and Enigma from the Revolutionary Period," *Virginia Magazine of History and Biography* 64:402–432 [Oct. 1956]).

While traveling, Langborn kept a written record of some of his adventures. Many years later, in 1818, this material came into the hands of Richard Rush, son of Dr. Benjamin Rush. In a letter of Rush's to JA, 2 May 1818, he quoted Langborn's comments on this dinner and another Langborn attended with the Adamses a few days later. Langborn wrote, "Saturday—Did myself the pleasure, agreeably to yesterdays invitation, of dining with Mr Adams and his family. We had but one stranger, he remarkable for his American attachments. Our dinner was plain, neat, and good. Mrs Adams's accomplishments and agreeableness would have apologized for any thing otherwise. . . . Thursday the 23. Dined again with Mr Adams. Mr Trumball, a student of Mr Wests was there. The English custom although bad still exists; we set to our bottle; I not for wine, but for the conversation of the Minister, which was very interesting, honest and instructive. . . . I must not forget Mr Adams's requisites to make citizens, like those republicans of New England; they were, that we should form ourselves into townships, encourage instruction by establishing in each public schools, and thirdly to elevate as much the common people by example and advice to a principle of virtue and religion" (Adams Papers).

[9] See AA2's letter of 26 Aug. 1785 (vol. 6:310).

Abigail Adams to Elizabeth and Lucy Cranch

My Dear Girls London, 23 July, 1786

I bought me a blue sarcenet[1] coat not long since; after making it up I found it was hardly wide enough to wear over a straw coat, but I thought it was no matter; I could send it to one of my nieces. When I went to put it up, I thought, I wished I had another. "It is easily got, said I. Ned, bring the carriage to the door and drive me to Thornton's, the petticoat shop."[2] "Here, Madam, is a very nice pink coat, made too of the widest sarcenet." "Well, put it up." So back I drove, and now, my dear girls, there is a coat for each of you. Settle between yourselves which shall have the blue and which the red, pay no regard to the direction, only when you put them on, remember your aunt wishes they were better for your sakes.

Mr. Appleton and a Dr. Spooner[3] go with the Callaghan; they both dine here to-day, and I shall request one of them to put them in his trunk, and some black lace which I have bought for Mrs. Welsh.

Remember me to my dear and aged mother. You will make her caps for her, I know, but if you will cut and send me a pattern, I will make some here and send her. She will be better pleased with them, I know. If there is any thing in particular which you want, tell me. I have not written above half the letters I want to, yet I have done little else for a whole week. By Captain Barnard I design writing to Miss B. Palmer[4] and others, which I shall not have time to do now, because to-morrow morning I set out on my journey. If you and cousin Lucy will send me a shoe for a pattern I will get you a pair of new-fashioned morocco. I have not written a line yet, either to son Charles or Johnny.[5] I have been to Hackney to hear Dr. Price to-day, upon the duties of children to parents; it was an excellent discourse; but you, my dear girls, so perfectly practise what he preached, that there is no occasion of repeating it to you.

Adieu, and believe, your own parents excepted, nobody loves you better than your ever Affectionate aunt, A.A.

MS not found. Printed from AA, *Letters*, ed. CFA, 1848, p. 299–300.

[1] Also "sarsenet," a fine soft silk cloth (*OED*).

[2] Possibly Peter Thornton, linen-draper, 98 Cheapside (*Kent's Directory. For the Year 1781*, London, 1781).

[3] Dr. William Spooner (1760–1836) of Boston, Harvard 1778, received his M.D. from Edinburgh in 1785 (Henry Bond, *Genealogies of the Families and Descendants of the Early Settlers of Watertown, Massachusetts*, 2 vols. in 1, Boston, 1855, p. 905).

[4] No letter has been found.

[5] AA probably intended to write "Charles or Tommy."

Abigail Adams to Thomas Jefferson

Dear Sir London july 23. 1786

Mr Trumble will have the honour of [d]elivering this to you,[1] the knowledge you have of him, and his own merit will ensure him a favourable reception. He has requested a Letter from me, and I would not refuse him, as it gives me an opportunity of paying my respects to a Gentleman for whom I entertain the highest esteem, and whose Portrait[2] dignifies a part of [this] room, tho it is but a poor substitue for those pleasures which we enjoy'd some months past.

We console ourselves however b[y] the reflection which tends to mollify our Grief for our [depart]ed Friends; that they are gone to a better Country, an[d to a] Society more congenial to the benevolence of their minds.[3]

I supposed sir that Col Smith was your constant correspondent, and that his attention, left me nothing to inform you of.[4] This Country produced nothing agreeable and our own appears to be taking a Nap, as severals vessels have lately arrived without a Scrip, from any creature. By one of the papers we learn that col Humphries was safely arrived.

Perhaps neither of the Gentleman may think to acquaint you, that the Lords of the admiralty have orderd home Captain Stanhopes ship, and calld upon him for a justification of his conduct to Govenour Bowdoin. That having received what he offerd as such, they voted it not only unsatisfactory, but his conduct highly reprehensible. As such they have represented it to his Majesty, and Captain Stanhope will not be permitted to return to that station again. Thus far we must give them credit.[5]

I suppose you must have heard the report respecting col Smith—that he has taken my daughter from me, a contrivance between him and the Bishop of St Asaph. It is true he tenderd me a Son as an equivilent and it was no bad offer, but I had three Sons before, and but one Daughter.[6] Now I have been thinking of an exchange with you sir, suppose you give me Miss Jefferson, and in some [fu]ture day take a Son in lieu of her. I am for Strengt[hen]ing [the?] federal Union.

Will you be so good as to let Petite apply to my shoe maker for 4 pr of silk Shoes for me. I would have them made with Straps, 3 pr of summer-Silk and one pr blew Sattin. Col Trumble will deliver you a Guiney for them. Whenever I can be of service to you here, pray do not hessitate to commission me, be assured you confer a favour upon your Humble Servant A Adams

RC (DLC:Jefferson Papers). Dft (Adams Papers). Some loss of text where the seal was removed.

[1] Col. John Trumbull delivered this letter on 1 Aug. (Jefferson, *Papers*, 10:162).

[2] During his spring visit to London, Jefferson sat for American artist Mather Brown, paying the latter £10 on 25 April for his work. On 12 May, JA paid Brown six guineas for a portrait of Jefferson. Only the portrait received by JA, which remained in the possession of the Adams family until 1999, when it was bequeathed to the National Portrait Gallery in Washington, has survived. Brown did not ship his portrait of Jefferson to the sitter until the fall of 1788. Although Jefferson acknowledged its safe arrival in Paris, no record of its whereabouts is known since that time.

Scholars have long debated whether JA received Brown's first portrait of Jefferson or a replica. Because he paid a lesser amount, it has been argued that JA was given a copy. Conversely, Col. John Trumbull's correspondence with Jefferson implies that Brown was still working on a portrait of Jefferson in the spring of 1788, two years after JA had possession of one. Also, Trumbull reported from London on 23 May 1788, at which point JA and AA had already sailed for the United States with their portrait in hand, "I believe what He [*Brown*] means to send you of yourself to be the copy, and that Mr. Adams thus the original." Adams family tradition is that their portrait is the original.

Brown also painted two portraits of JA. The first in 1785, when AA and AA2 also sat for the artist; the second in 1788, commissioned by Jefferson, who as early as 22 Oct. 1786 desired WSS to persuade JA to sit again for Brown so that he might have a portrait of his colleague done from life and not a copy. The 1785 portrait of JA is believed to have been lost. Jefferson's 1788 portrait of JA was sold after his death and ultimately bequeathed to the Boston Athenæum in 1908 (Dorinda Evans, *Mather Brown, Early American Artist in England*, Middletown, Conn., 1982, p. 53–54, 62–65; Andrew Oliver, *Portraits of John and Abigail Adams*, Cambridge, 1967, p. 46–53; Smithsonian Institution, National Portrait Gallery). For Brown's portraits of AA and AA2, see vol. 6:xiii–xiv.

[3] These first two paragraphs do not appear in the Dft; rather, the Dft opens with the following: "As it appears to be doubly as long since I had the honour of a line from you, as the time you have stated to have received one from me, I am at a loss to know whether we shall understand the language of each other, nothing but the space being wholly lost to me, could justify my omitting to inform mr Jefferson how much we regreeted the loss of his company. But we reflect upon it with that consideration which tends to molify our grief for the loss of departed Friends, that they are gone to a better Country, and to a society more congenial to the benevolence of their minds."

[4] For WSS's correspondence with Jefferson, since the latter's departure from London in April, see Jefferson, *Papers*, vols. 9 and 10.

[5] For the Aug. 1785 confrontation in Boston between Capt. Henry Stanhope of the H.M.S. *Mercury* and two American seamen formerly impressed into service under his command and Stanhope's subsequent complaints to Gov. James Bowdoin, see vol. 6:435–440, 496, 497.

[6] The Dft concludes at this point with the following: "Now suppose Sir you should give me Miss Jefferson, at least till I return to America. Some future day, perhaps I might tender you a son in exchange for her. I am lonely in concequence of this, Theft I had almost said. I should think myself very happy to have miss Jefferson come and Spend the Summer and winter with me. Next Spring I hope to return to America."

Elizabeth Smith Shaw to Abigail Adams

My Dear Sister — Haverhill July 23d. *1786*

Mr Sparhawk called for my Letter Just as I was giving you an account of my Aunt Smith's Death. I was going to tell you that Mr Thaxter had lost his youngest Sister, Mrs Cushing, who had been married about 15 months died in Child-bed. Upon finding herself ill, they sent for Dr Barker, but before he got there, she was seized with Convulsion Fits, from which she never reccovered. She has a fine Daughter, though she did not notice it, nor live to clasp the dear Babe to her fond Bosom. I hear they have got an exceeding good Nurse for it.

There is hardly any Circumstance in which a Person can be taken from their Family, that excites my Pity, and Compassion more than this. At one fatal stroke the fair Prospects of a Family are cut down, and the weeping Husband stands but half blest—beholding the little help less Infant, extending its feeble Arms, and crying for that, (which alas!) Providence had thought fit to deny. For deaf were those Ears that with delight would have listened to thy Call—closed were those Eyes, that with pleasure would have dwelt upon thy growing Charms, and cold were those Arms that with delight would have folded thee, to her maternal Breast. But "thus runs Death's dread Commission—Strike—but so as most to alarm the living, by the Dead."[1] The Young, the Gay, the healthy, the beautiful, the rich, the wise, the good, the beloved—*all*, all alike must submit to the inevitable Stroke. "Dust we are, and unto Dust we must return," but *he* who has brought Life, and immortality to light, has assured us, by the Apostle, "that this *Mortal*, shall put on Immortality." And, that unless a "Corn of Wheat fall into the ground, and die, it cannot bring forth much Fruit."[2]

Mr Smith got here last Night, and makes an exchange with Mr Shaw. Mr Smith has lately fixed down at the Castle, and will have an handsome maintenance there. But poor Man, is deprived of what he supposed would afford him, the greatest pleasure, the frequent Visits of his Mother. He has a fine Temper, and I believe a very good Heart. You know our early Intimacy, and cannot wonder that I most tenderly sympathize with him, under his late Bereavment.[3]

25th.

Mr Shaw got home to day about Noon, and brought Cousin Lucy, and my Betsy Quincy. The little Creature came claping her hands, and rejoicing up the Hill, "there's Mamma—there's Brother—there's Cousin Betsy, ⟨*and Thommy*⟩.["] "Are you not glad I have got home Mamma? have you not been ansious about me since I have been gone." And her Tongue run as if her Stomack had gain'd considerable strength by the Braintree Air. I assure you she is no ways deficient in the *female Talent*.

27th

My worthy Nephews got here last Night, we do love them. Mr Shaw, and I, would have been quite disconsolate if they had not come. Mr Professor Williams told me, that my eldest Nephew had exactly hit it, (that was his expression) with the Scholars. By his studious, and affable Behaviour, he had gained the love of all his Classmates. *We* were affraid of him (said he) because S–C–J. had made the Tour,[4] and gave us so much trouble. By affecting a superiority, he gained the dislike of the Governors, and the contempt of the whole Colledge. It is at last concluded upon by Dr Tufts, Mr Cranch &cc, that Mr Shaw should offer Thomas at the end of this Vacation. I wish it may be for the best. But if he was my own Child I should rather he should be a year older. At this age, one year, makes a very material alteration in the Judgment. He has a good genius, and an excellent Temper, but not one of those forward Youths, whose genious *very early* comes to maturity. The fairest, and soundest Fruit seldom ripens the soonest, but requires Time to bring it to Perfection. Youth seldom know the advantages they are under, or (if they really wish to make a Figure in Life,) the great importance of the most diligent application, and the closest attention to their studies. What Milton says of a delicate, virtuous Woman, may be appliyed to Leterature. She "must be *wooed*, and not *unsought*, be won."[5]

If Mr Thomas's Abilities should entittle him to speak an Oration four years hence, I know his voice cannot be so pleasing, neither will he be able to command the attention of the audience so well, as if he was older. He is now innocently playful. I hope he will not learn to do Evil, but still be preserved in the Path of Virtue. You would be surprized to see how Thomas has grown, since you left us he is almost as tall as Charles, but I must speak intelligibly, wants about a head of being as tall as your eldest Son. I tell him I will let him go by measure, and not by weight. For he is rather thin, and I feel sometimes affronted because he does not credit his keeping. Poor "Child, I say, you are too much like Aunt Shaw." He retains his fine shape yet, and if he lives, will be a very tall Man, and I hope a very good One. I feel a greater tenderness for him I suppose, because he was the youngest, and seemed to come more under my Care. He has enjoyed exceeding good Health, and been very little troubled with the Rheumatism. He has been poisoned several times, but has met with no accident excepting, as he was runing upon the Snow last winter, he turned his Foot, and displaced three Bones. He told me he was lame, I bathed his foot, did it up in Bane, and put him to Bed. In the Morning I found it was more swelled, and we thought it best to send for the Doctor. He soon came, and set three Bones. After this he found but little Inconvinience, excepting that his Uncle thought it prudent and necessary, that he should be debarred the pleasure of skaiting for three Weeks, a week for a Bone.

July 29th.

I have spent this Week in the Society of my dear Friends, and Relations. To me who came so far from the midst of my Kindred, (though *you* will think it nothing) a *Nephew*, and a *Cousin* have an endearing, and an enchanting Sound. I have had a large Circle this Week, in one Day my Family increased from Six to twenty-seven, and this you will say is nothing too, I suppose, to what you have every Day. It is true I cannot say, Count, such an one, and my Lord, and Lady A. B. and C. but I feel that glow of generous Love, and Friend-ship, which those who always move in the higher Walks of Life, are too often a stranger to.

Mr, Mrs Austin, Mrs Allen, and Mrs Welsh, and Charlotte—Mr Smith, Mr Thaxter, Cousin Sally Tufts together with my own Household, formed such a Circle as would have made you smile with *more* than your usual Complacency, could you have presided at the frugal, but sufficient Board.

Yesterday my Sister, we formed one of the most agreeable Parties, that I ever saw. Mr White, and Capt Willis, gave a Turtle,[6] which was dressed elegantly, and carried to a litle beautiful Island in Merimac, which formerly belonged to Judge Saltonstall.[7]

There was a fine Booth erected, formed into Arches in the stile of Festoons, which afforded the most refreshing Shade. The Stakes which supported it were so artfully covered with grape Vines, and large Clusters of Grapes interwove with Wreaths of Flowers, which looked so fresh, that One would have supposed them placed there, rather by the hand of Nature, than of Art.

Return, to America for one moment, my Sister, and fancy yourself most conveniently seated in this Bower, your Sons, Neices, and particular Freinds noticed, by the most polite attention—sweet Merimac gently gliding beneath your feet—Health—Peace, and Plenty smiling around you—Good-humour—without ribaldry—Ease—Complacency—every Necessary, and Convenience, all conspiring to make you happy. Here a lofty Oak—and there a branching Elm—and little Thickets of Wood, which looked as if they were, "for whispering Lovers made."[8] Each One taking the Lass he preferred, and leading her to the Lawn, or the Wood, as fancy bent their way.

A little before Sunset we all embarked in our new Boat, with a sail spread over the Top, the School Benches answered for seats, and we were about three quarters of an Hour going down, and an hour and half returning. The Doors, Windows, and Banks of the

River, all thronged with People, who were drawn thither by the Musick. The Mr Adams's the Mr Osgoods, and Leonard White &cc &cc singing all the way, most beautifully. The few happy Matches, the Indian Warrior, &cc, &cc.

Upon the whole, I think it is allowed by the Visitors in Town, that it was one of the happiest, and most agreeable Parties, that they ever knew. I was delighted at the Time, and I cannot think of it since, without Rapture.

Here, I have given you a little account of the simple Efforts of Nature, while you are (I suppose) making Excursions this Summer, into the Country and surveying the Work of Time, and the labours of Art—the elegant Gardens the superb Palace, and the stately Dome. Those will fill your Mind with grand, and noble Ideas, which really must be *vastly* pleasing, and even in the decline of Life, be a Source of Entertainment to yourself, and Friends. But whether in all your Travels, you will find a happier Circle, than I have described, I something doubt.

The Laws, the Customs, the Education of this Nation all serve to render them pleased with each other, and happy in the Enjoyment of the sweets of Society. No haughty Lord *here*, to demand the hard earnings of the honest, and industrious Husband Man. But all share, almost equally in the rich Treasures and Bounties of Nature.

I really long sometimes to look in upon you, to see whether you are all mightily altered—"Much for the better, to be sure." Polite company gives an ease to the Manners—a Grace—a Charm yet good, (I hope) as you the "World had never seen." I should admire to visit with you, the Seats, and the remains of those whose Works have immortalised their Name. I believe I should be particularly charmed with Shenstones Garden,[9] from the descriptions, I have seen.

I wonder how Mr Adams felt when he was cuting a Relict from Shakespears Chair. In walking over those hallowed Grounds, I fancy Ones feelings, and thoughts must be *very peculiar*. I wish they had presented Mr Adams with a Box, (as they did Mr Garrick,) made out of a mulberry Tree, which Shakespear planted with his own hands.[10]

Now let me answer your enquiries about Mr and Mrs A–l–n. They have got a fine enclosure for a Garden, the soil looks strong, and fertile, and every thing appears well, and in good order, though it was rather late before he planted.

The House too, is as neat as wax, and she has five Cows, and is become a fine Dairy Woman. She thinks *me* but a Novice, when compared to her. I am content. *I* never will contend with her, about superiority. She has been over four or five times and spent the Day with me, but *he* is such an Oeconimist, and is so busy about his Hay, that he hardly ever could come for her, even at Night. But you say, all this does not answer my question. Why let me tell you, Complexion will not do alone. There must be some corresponding Qualities, alas, alas! I fear your Belcher will prove a true Prophet, for I cannot discern the least prolific *Sign*.

I beg You and Cousin Nabby would write to Mrs Warren. Friendship cannot bear a supposed slight. Her feelings are keen, she is a Woman of great sensibility. Her good Mind is corroded by Dissappointments of various kinds. By Mr Thaxters Influence, the General was chosen here Leiu. Govenor, this year. I think he had 2 *Votes* in Boston. This was mortifying I am sure, but when he might, he would not. He affronted the People, by refusing their Suffrages. I will be Ceasar, or nothing will not do for the Massachusetts.

I am perswaded no publick measure, will ever be properly adjusted, till *he* is in Office. If she does not have a Letter before Fall, I shall absolutely be afraid to see her. Dearly as I love your Letters, I will dispense with *one* the less, if you have not time, to write to us both. For my part, I think you must be a very extraordinary Oeconimist of your Time, to attend (as Mrs Hay says you do) to ceremony, and every Punctilio, and yet not neglect the weightier Matters, and get so much time to write, and gratify your Friends.

Mr Duncan, is a going to be married very soon to a Newbury Lady, Miss Greenleaf. Lovelace would say, she was in the *Tabby Order*.[11] Mr Duncan has seen her, but three times and was published last week. After the first marriage, Love, (I believe), has but little to do in the nuptial Bonds. Convinience is all.

Mr T. (I believe) is very silent as to a certain Affair, which does him credit, at least, in my Eyes. Mrs Quincy, and her Son, and Deacon Storer, and Lady[12] have both made me a visit. And if any-thing material had been said by him, it is likely they would have been informed of it. Mr T. has left Sister Cranch's House, but keeps the Office yet, and has not removed all his Things.

Mr Thaxter was exceedingly overcome at the News of his Sisters Death. It was the first near Relation he ever buried. You know his Nerves are very tender. He heard of it suddenly. Mr Duncan had just come from Boston, and mentioned to him supposing he had received a Letter from his Father. I was in possession of that Letter.

But knowing he was at Judge Seargeants by Invitation, and that we were all just going out to the Wedding of Mr Porter, and Miss Sukey, I thought it best to deffer giving it to him, and so desired he would come and see me early the next Morning, thinking that no one else would tell him of it. But calling in to present a piece of Plumb Cake to Miss Betsy,[13] he was shocked at the Account. It was too sudden a Transition, from Joy, to Grief. The poor Creature with his Heart most broke, came trembling up to me. I endeavoured all in my power to sooth his Mind. But it is *Time* alone, which only mollifies our Sorrow. He went home, but kept his Chamber, and his Bed chiefly for two or three Days.

I do not think he will be married these Twelve months. It is very difficult getting a House here, and more difficult to get money. But it is the universal Voice. No money, no Cash—I am sure I am tired of it.

Much as I want to see you, I think I ought not to wish Mr Adam's return till he has accomplished the important Buisness he went upon. I wish he had More power, and we were a wiser, and better People.

August, 20th.

I have known of no Vessel by which I could send this Letter. It has laid by me, and I fear you will think it is got already to an intolerable Length. I will venture however, to add a little more, about family Matters. When I was in Boston I took of Deacon Storer a Peice of Linnen to make for Thomas, because I had found they wore very strong. I left a part to be made for Charles, but as he is to go to Colledge your peice for him came in season, he will want many more than he would here. Cousin Lucy, and my two Betsy's have made him up five, and I have sent for some of the Cloth which you designed for him. What I got for him was yd wide, and a good penny-worth at four shillings pr yd, but he was so good as to let me have it at 3s. 6d. pr yd.

Next year he must wear blue Coat, and be in a Uniform, but this year, I am thankful it is not necessary, for it would make you a great deal of expence. I have gained a point with him, and have perswaded him to have drawers instead of linings to his small Cloaths, and have made him 2 of linnen, 2 of Cotton, and linnen, and one of Lamb Skins for winter. I have done everything I possibly could, even his winter Cloaths. I cannot think he can want any-thing new, till towards Spring. I wish to lighten Sister Cranch as much as possible, for she is not very well. She has the Reumatism, or something that worries her Stomack very much.

We have had a remarkable cool Summer. It is not half the time that I can bear the windows open. Yet the Corn, and things never looked more flourishing. Your Sons went from here the 5th of August, which was almost, the only hot Day we have had.

To-morrow Mr Shaw carries, and presents your Son to the University—Dear Lad—a Blessing be upon him.[14]

I think you discover the elegance of your Taste, by the choice of the Things you send Your Friends. Adieu My Dear, kind, Sister. My Love to Mr Adams, present in the most respectful manner, I hope to hear from my Neice that *her* affectionate Aunt, and your Sister may know how to direct a Letter. Ever yours E Shaw

RC (Adams Papers); endorsed: "Mrs Shaw 22 july 1786."

[1] Young, *Night Thoughts*, Night V, lines 807–808.

[2] The scripture is from Genesis, 3:19 ("Dust we are . . ."); 1 Corinthians, 15:53 ("that this Mortal . . ."); and John, 12:24 ("Corn of Wheat . . .").

[3] Isaac Smith Jr. courted Elizabeth Smith Shaw in the 1770s (*Sibley's Harvard Graduates*, 16:529; vol. 1:65).

[4] Samuel Cooper Johonnot.

[5] *Paradise Lost*, Book VIII, line 503.

[6] John White Sr. and Capt. Benjamin Willis Sr. were the party's hosts. See JQA's account of the day, *Diary*, 2:71–72.

[7] Richard Saltonstall (1703–1756), Harvard 1722, was associate justice of the Superior Court of Judicature from 1736 until his death. His estate in Haverhill, Buttonwoods, bordered the Merrimack River (*Sibley's Harvard Graduates*, 7:117–121; William T. Davis, *History of the Judiciary of Massachusetts*, Boston, 1900, p. 96).

[8] "The hawthorn bush, with seats beneath the shade, For talking age and whisp'ring lovers made" (Oliver Goldsmith, *The Deserted Village*, line 13).

[9] JA described the gardens at poet William Shenstone's (1714–1763) estate, The Leasowes, in Shropshire, as "the simplest and plainest, but the most rural of all. I saw no Spot so small, that exhibited such a Variety of Beauties" (*D&A*, 3:186).

[10] David Garrick, the noted actor, received a number of gifts crafted from the mulberry tree supposedly planted by Shakespeare. This is probably a reference to a box showing scenes from Shakespeare, carved by a T. Davis of Birmingham, which the Stratford Corporation of Stratford-upon-Avon presented to Garrick on the occasion of a Shakespeare jubilee attended by Garrick in Sept. 1769 (George Winchester Stone Jr. and George M. Kahrl, *David Garrick: A Critical Biography*, Carbondale, Ill., 1979, p. 453–454).

[11] James Duncan, twice a widower, and Hannah Greenleaf of Newburyport married on 5 September. Greenleaf was 57 years old, hence the reference to her being an old maid, or tabby, a phrase used by the character Lovelace in Samuel Richardson's *Clarissa* (*Vital Records of Newburyport, Massachusetts, to the End of the Year 1849*, 2 vols., Salem, Mass., 1911, 2:199; *Vital Records of Newbury, Massachusetts, to the End of the Year 1849*, 2 vols., Salem, Mass., 1911, 1:196).

[12] Abigail Phillips Quincy, widow of Josiah Quincy Jr., "The Patriot," and their son Josiah Quincy III, the future mayor of Boston (1823–1828) and president of Harvard (1829–1845). Abigail Quincy and Hannah Quincy Storer were sisters-in-law.

[13] Elizabeth Duncan, daughter of James Duncan and his first wife, Elizabeth Bell. She and Thaxter would marry in Nov. 1787 (JQA, *Diary*, 1:321, entry for 8 Sept. 1785, note 1).

[14] TBA was admitted to Harvard on 22 Aug. (same, 2:81).

Abigail Adams Smith to John Quincy Adams

N 15

july 27th 1786

When I closed my last to you on Sundey last I promised to give you an account of the excursion we proposed setting off upon the next day, either upon my return or during my visit. A Leasur hour presents itself, this morning and I embrace it to fullfill my engagements. On Monday Morning at Seven oclock, we were in the Carriage, Mr S and my self, at our door in Wimpole Street, from whence we proceeded to Rumford 12 miles from London where we allighted at ten oclock precisely, and orderd breakfast for 5 persons, as Pappa Mamma and Mr Bridgen were to meet us there. We waited till Eleven and then feeling a propensity to sattisfy our appetites we sat down, but before we had proceeded far, they came in. At twelve we were in the Carriage again. Pappa went to Thornton about 2 mills from Rumfd. to see the House of Lord Petres,[1] which is said to be worthy the observation of Strangers. Viewing the Houses and Gardens of Noblemen, constitutes one of the principle Summer amusements of this Country, Natives as well as strangers, and the Gardens of all the Nobility are open to the Latter. When Mr J—n was here, at some one of the Gardens which he visitted the Gardener told him he had orders from his Master not to admit Englishmen—but I am not an English man answerd Mr J.—Oh Sir then they are open to you—but What is the reason of your Masters prohibiting Englishmen, from his Gardens?—because Sir he cannot trust them, they will take something with them. The Houses are generally seen only by Tickets from the Owner, which is a mere matter of Form for any person may procure them who will take the Trouble to send for them. I thought as the day was very warm and it was exceedingly dusty that we had better proceed to Mr H—s, which we did, and at 2 oclock, arrived at Mr Thomas Brand Hollis's House at the Hyde in the Town of Torrington in the County of Essex. Mr H received us with politeness civillity and attention, and soon introduced to us Miss Brand his Sister a Single Lady about forty, who keeps his House, which stands, half a mile from the Road, upon a plain. At some distance it seems to be sarrounded with hills, Coverd with wood. The plain before the House consists of feilds, surrouded with hedges, trees in Groves Calfs, &c, scattered over it Cattle and sheep, feeding, and all together forms a pleasing view. At the back of the House is the Garden, filled with a variety of Trees shrubs, plants flowers, and, amongst which are many american productions such as furs, of various kinds. It is in a rude wild, but agreeable manner. At the end of the Garden is a Temple on which is this motto, ill repose. A little further amongst the Trees, is a Hermitage, which is rather ancient than elegant. It is dedicated to St [2] of whom I told Mr H I had never before heard. Just before it is a pond, with Gold fishes in it, and at a little distance, the kitchen Garden with in a large high Wall, for Fruit it contains every thing usefull and proper, for a Garden of this kind. Before the House are three other ponds, which have fish of various kinds in them, the ponds are not large, but have an agreeable affect.

The House is very oald but has been repaird. This Gentleman, has, a taste for antiquity, and I suppose he is attached to this House for the reason, of its being, some ages advanced. We must not talk of years in this House, every part of it is a perfect⟨*ly nice and*⟩ Cabinet every room, is filld with Some antiquitities, pictures Statues busts Vases, and a variety of other things. You enter at a large Hall, in which are the Busts of several persons, and many other antuiquities on the left to the dining room, which is also ornamented on the Chimney with figures in Bronze, which Mr H shews us, and add, this is two three or more hundred years old. On the right is the drawing Room which Contains several Curiossities. The furnitere is also ancient of yellow damask. There is a Cabinet of Ebony inclos'd with brass, which is *Called elegant*. This Contains Mr Bridgen tells us, Mr Hollis's hearts Treasure, which I shall tell you of by and by. There is a picture of one of reubens wives, and several other Curious ones, several oramets upon the Chimney of Bronze, Vases &c. Mr H says there is nothing made so beautifull in the present day, but I Confess I have not his taste. In a litle room adjoining called the Boudoier are many more curiossities but I cannot pretend to describe them. Amongs the Number, are pictures of all the Orders of Monks and Nuns in France, each singly in a small [Frem?]. At the bottom is an account of their manner of Life. This was a Collection made by Mr Bridgen, who, gave them to Mr Hollis. In the next room, is Mr H—s Librey, but here nobody ever enters. He told us that he never addmitted any body to his Librey, before we came, and he is particular and Carefull in all his Curiossities.

Pappa and [3] came a little before 4. We dined and after tea took a Walk in the Garden. ⟨*I think I Love the Country better every day*⟩.

Tuesday [25 *July*].

We took a ride about 8 mills to Chemsford to see an House which belongs to Lady a descendent of Lord Moilerds.[4] Mr H admires the artichecture of this House. I Convess it did not strike my fancy so much as many I have seen, the fernitere was ancient and not in so good order as is generally the Case in such large Houses. We re-turd to dine. The Weather is very warm, at present and almost re-minds us of an American season. After dinner we walkd-out as Mr S. amused himself with attempting to take Fish.

Wedensday 26th

In the Morning we took a Walk abut a mile, to see the Gardens and Gronds and House of a Mr Atlen who was a Wine Merchant, in London, by which I suppose he made a great Fortune and has Built him a House and Garden, in a sweet spot.[5] Mr Hollis being ac-quainted with the family sent in to desire to see the Grounds Gar-dens &c. The Gentleman came out to us and invited us to the House. We went in. Every thing is new, and the House furnitere &c are in a very ellegant Stile. The Lady came to us and was very civil. We walkd to the Garden which is filld with Trees plants Shrubs, flowers, and Fruit. There were two Green Houses, full of Fruit also, peaches Apricots Grapes, and a variety of others. And after rambling Some time in the Gardens we returnd home, through a gravel Walk, of half a mile in extent, on each Side of Which are trees whose Branches meet at the Top, and make an fine shade. At the end of the Walk is a pond with fish, from which is an ascent on either side. In front upon a litle rising there is a temple, which is very pretty. The Whole is indeed a sweet spot. This walk led us into Mr Holliss Ground, and we soon returnd to his House pleased with our excur-sion, dressd and at 4 dined. After dinner, we went to visit Mr H—s Gardner, whose House is a few yards from Mr H—s. He is very curi-ous in Bees, shew us several Hives, and gave us a Lecture upon their form of Government Laws, &c. He has allways been a great friend to the Americans, and was vastly Happy to see us in his Cot-tage. In short every person belonging to this family Seem to have imbibed a degree of the Masters Taste. An oald Faithfull domestick[6] who reminded me of the Character of le [Banq?] invited us to see his Garden. It was in the same stile. He had also, a Collection of antiquities and Curiossities in his Way, which were Curious and amuseing.

Thursday 27.

Pappa having a great curiossity to see Braintree which lies only 18 Mills from this, set of this Morning with Mamma to visit it. We amused ourselvs in the Morning with fishing, and walking, but could ceatch no fish large enough to eat, so they were only removed from one pond to another still enjoying their Lives Liberty. At 2 Pappa and Mamma returnd not much pleased with the appearance of the Town they had been to visit. Mr H told us it was a Poer dirty miserable village and such they found it.

After dinner Mr Hollis gave Pappa a Lecture upon antuiquitys, and Curiossities to which we were silent spectators and Listeners. The Ebony Cabinet was Opened, of Which I promised you an account. On the middle shelfe, in the Center was containd in a brass Case the Bust of Milton, which was surrounded on each side by 4 or five of the first additions of his own works. ⟨*he was an acquaintance friend of Mr Hollis's for whom he has great respect.*⟩ When he had finishd his Lecture upon the Contents of this Cabinet he opend another and shew us several curiossities Medalls, and figeures, of varias kinds several Boks, as oald as the Pales to Use a Common expression.[7] Amongst the rest was a Cook Book, &c, Henry Sixth.

Fryday, 28th.

At Nine in the Morning we left Mr H. House, much pleased with our visit, and proceeded on our way to Grosvenor Square, where we arrived at 3 oclock, and found a Packet or two from Mr J— Containing news Papers, and promises of writing by the next Ship.[8]

I like such excursions as these into the County. But to go, mere, because it is the fashion, to ride all day, and to dine and Lodge at some dirty village, where you can neither eat drink or sleep with any degree of sattisfaction, is not my Taste yet this is practiced by many, others who, dare not be so unfashionable as to stay in London, go to Brighthamstone[9] and only quit one scene of dissipation for another but it is the fashion, and, all must follow.

By the Packet which Pappa found upon his return, Containd the ratification of the Prusian Treaty, and as it was a good oppertunity for Mamma to visit Holland they set off, the Thursday following, 3d of August for the Hague.

Wedensday Pappa went to the Levee to take Leave of the King previous to his going to H. which is a point of Etiqueette not to be dispenced with.

8. "MARGARET NICHOLSON ATTEMPTING TO ASSASSINATE HIS MAJESTY KING GEORGE III," 1786

See page xv

A strange affair happened to day at St Jamess as the King was getting out of his Carriage at the Doer of the Pallace a Woman, apperd with a Paper in her hand which she said was a Petition to the King, which she requested of the Gauards she might be permitted to deliver. And when the Carrige came up, as the King was steping out She presented the Petition which the King took, and discover'd a knife which she was, advanceing towards him but being perceived by the Guards She was immediately taken. His Majesty tis said desired she might not be Hurt as he was not injurd. This request prevented her being torn in peices by the Guards and she was taken into Custody and is said to be Insane. Her name is Margaret Nicolson. She has since been examined, and is to be tried in a few days. It is Supposd She will be Confind in a priests Mad House for Life.[10]

August 18th.

We have heard from Pappa and Mamma twice since they left London, once since their arrival at the Hague. Mamma complains of the Passage. She was also disappointed on her arrival at finding Madam and Mademoiselle Dumas absent, at their Country House in Guilderland. Mamma paid a visit to the Lady of Sir James Haris who is the Minister from this Court to that Country and the only one who has a Lady.[11] In a few Hours, she retur̄d Mammas visit and they were invited to dine with them the next day. I have observed that Gentlemen in publick Characters from this Country, are more civil and polite in a Foreign Country than in their owns. The Duke of D— was You know, very civil to Pappa in France,[12] but the last Summer when he was here and also this, he does not even return a visit made him.

In short America and Americans are so out of Fashion at present, *at the fountain Head*, that no one dare be so excentrick as to cultivate or even make any kind of advances towards civility. Foreigners ask—do these people, ask their King, whom they shall be acquainted with. I see so little Liberallity of Sentiment So little Good manners, or even common civillity that I am quite sick of the Country. Or rather of the People, and it is not confined to the Natives of this Land alone, but appears to me that every Creature who comes to reside in the County, ⟨*gets in thre weeks*⟩ imbibes with the Air they breathe the illiberallity which exists, in the atmosphere.

The Conversation of the Day, and indeed since I wrote you, has been upon His Majestys *Wonderfull* marevolous and *happy* excape, yet It does not seem to have been made so serious an affair of as might have been expected. It has been observed in the Papers, that Mr Adams left the Kingdom the very day after the attempt was made upon his Majestys Life. These people are below contempt. If you see the English Papers you will find much said upon the Princes late change, upon the Kings refusing any augmentation to his income. He took the resolution to appropriate 30 thosand a year to the payment of his Debts, and to Live upon 20. Some suggest that Mrs F— has had this influence over him. The King and Prince are very generally applauded the former for his refusal, and the Latter for his firmness, in not only submitting to the Will of the sovereign, but in useing these means to pay his debts. His household has been dismissd and his Horses all sold. He is now at Brighthamstone. It is said that his going to Windsor to Congratulate the King upon his excape, that the king would not see him. Some suggest that serias consequences may ensue from the Kings displeasure towards him. Misteries which must explain themselves are not worth the time that it would take to unravell them.

Dr Cutting and Mr Shipping from Philadelphia arrived here about a forghtnight since. They propose passing some time in Studying in the Temple.[13] The Dr has improved much I think he does not Laugh above once in a visit. Mr S, I had seen in Boston some years agone. He is a modest young Man, a Son of Dr Shippens of Philadelphia. I inquird about Madame B—m. Poor Lady, she is showing away, and without a single Competitor. How extremely mortifying for in this Situation you know there will be no inducement to go a Step higher. She says that in the Circle of her own family she shall be happy, but out of that she expects no pleasure in America.

Finisd August 22d 86.

Dft (Adams Papers).

[1] For JA's description of Thorndon Hall, the seat of Robert Edward Petre, 9th baron Petre, see *D&A*, 3:196.

[2] Blank in MS.

[3] Blank in MS.

[4] Lady Anne Hervey Mildmay, widow of Sir William Mildmay, of Moulsham Hall (JA, *D&A*, 3:197; Enid Robbie, *The Forgotten Commissioner: Sir William Mildmay and the Anglo-French Commission of 1750–1755*, East Lansing, Mich., 2003, p. 221, 242, note 18).

[5] In his Diary, JA identifies the property as "Mill Green, or Mill Hill," the home of Mr. Allen, a London banker (3:199).

[6] John, the coachman (AA to JQA, 27 Sept., below).

[7] Possibly "old as Pauls," a reference to the steeple of Old St. Paul's Cathedral in London. This phrase was commonly used in response to someone who pretended that something common or out-of-date was unique (*Oxford Dictionary of English Proverbs*, comp. William George Smith, 2d edn., Oxford, 1948).

[8] John Jay to JA, 6 June (Adams Papers).

[9] Brighthelmstone, or Brighton (*The Edinburgh Gazetteer*, 6 vols., Edinburgh, 1822).

[10] For Margaret Nicholson's attack on George III, see the Descriptive List of Illustrations, No. 8, above.

[11] Sir James Harris (1746–1820), Earl of Malmesbury, served Great Britain in a succession of diplomatic posts, as ambassador to Spain, Prussia, Russia, and the Netherlands, and as a member of Parliament. He married Harriet Mary Amyand in 1777; she was the daughter of the late London merchant and banker Sir George Amyand and Anna Maria Corteen (*DNB*; Namier and Brooke, *House of Commons*, 2:20–21, 589–590).

[12] For the Adamses' acquaintance with John Sackville, Duke of Dorset, while in France, see vol. 6:41, 84, 106, 108, 151–152.

[13] Thomas Lee Shippen was the only son of Dr. William Jr. and Alice Lee Shippen of Philadelphia (William Shippen Jr. to JA, 26 July, Adams Papers; *DAB*). Cutting was charged with delivering a letter from Alice Shippen to AA in Aug. 1781 (vol. 4:204, 205).

Abigail Adams to Abigail Bromfield Rogers

My dear Madam London july 30th [*1786*]

When I returnd yesterday from a litle excursion which we had made for a week into the Country of Essex to the seat of mr Brand Hollis, *an excelent Englishman* I had the pleasure of finding your obliging favour of june 4th.[1] Mrs Copley had informd me a fortnight before of your safe arrival. I must congratulate you upon setting your foot again upon American ground. To Say that I love it above all other countries is only imitating the passion common to all Nations, each of which has something to endear it to its Natives, something which he prizes beyond what he can find elsewhere. Such are the friendships We form and the habits we contract in early youth. We do not easily part with what we look to as our solace and comfort, even tho we suffer a partial Seperation.

I am Sorry to find that you met with any thing to give pain when you ought to have received commendation and satisfaction. The first impressions here upon mr Rogers's departure were not favourable to him or to the character of Americans. Many censured him who had nothing to do in the matter. Mr Adams uniformly justified him, and your Friend always advocated for his conduct. A very little time however silenced those who were the first to complain and the remittances which arrived soon after mr Rogers's departure turnd the tables, and each one was wondering why he went away, and wishing he had staid. Such was the conversation I frequently heard repeated, so that I do not think but mr Rogers's credit here is in as high estimation as it was in the most Prosperous time of commerce.

I miss you much I assure you and shall always esteem those hours Spent with you as some of the pleasentest I have known in England. I hope your Health will not be injured by your voyage, and that you will find mrs L [2] for whom I have been much concernd, recoverd from her illness. My Regards to her whenever you meet. I do not Say compliments my esteem for her deserves a name more expressive.

Your Young Friend writes you by a New Name.[3] Mrs Copley can tell you that she was witness to the change. May it prove, as it at present appears productive of happiness.

I Shall always rejoice to hear from you. My Regards to mr Rogers, who I believe was formd on purpose for you and was more fortunate than the Souls which dr Watts tells us who lost their fellows on the road and never join their hands.[4] Mr Adams joins in wishes for your Health and happiness with Your Friend A A

Dft (Adams Papers).

[1] Not found.

[2] Blank in MS.

[3] No letter from AA2 to Abigail Bromfield Rogers has been found.

[4] Isaac Watts, "The Indian Philosopher," lines 35–39: "Then down he sent the souls he made, / To seek them bodies here: / But parting from their warm abode / They lost their fellows on the road, / And never join'd their hands."

Abigail Adams to Isaac Smith Sr.

My dear Sir London july 31 1786

This moment my cousin W. S. Letter of june 28th[1] is come to hand containing the melancholy tidings of the death of my dear Aunt, which has greatly afflicted me, and renderd me unfit to offer to you that consolation which I need at this moment myself. That I am a most Sincere Sympathizer with you, and all your family in this afflictive dispensation no one can doubt who knew her as I knew her, and who loved her as I loved her. She was to me a second Parent, and the Law of kindness and Hospitality was written upon her Heart. Nor was her benevolence confined to her kindred and Relatives, but she Streched out her bountifull hand to the poor and the needy. When the Eye saw her it blessed her and the ear gave witness to her.[2] By a Life of piety towards God and good will to her fellow Creatures she laid up for herself a sure reward which she is now gone to receive. I know not a better Character than hers. As Such I shall ever revere her memory.

To you my dear and honourd uncle I wish every consolation which Religion can afford, for that is the only fountain to which we can repair when bowed down with distress. My Love to all my afflicted cousins for whom I feel more than I can express. I will write them when my mind feels more composed.

I am Dear Sir most Affectionately Yours A Adams

RC (MHi:Smith-Carter Papers); addressed by WSS: "Isaac Smith Esquire Boston Pr Capt. Callihan"; endorsed: "London. July. 1786 A Adams."

[1] No letter from William Smith of this date has been found.

[2] An adaptation of Job, 29:11: "When the ear heard me, then it blessed me; and when the eye saw me, it gave witness to me."

Abigail Adams to Cotton Tufts

My dear Sir London August 1 1786

Mr Adams receivd yesterday your obliging favour of june 28th[1] by way of Liverpool. His Eyes which I sometimes fear will fail him, have a weakness oweing to too intense application, which is very troublesome to him, and this being now the case, he will not be able to write his Friends as he wishes. I have to thank you for him, the intelligence which your Letter contains ought to make our Countrymen wise. I think they were so in refusing the offers made them and they may serve to convince them of the importance which the Whale fishery is considerd in Europe.

The French as a Nation do not wish our Prosperity more than the English, only as they have sense enough to See that every indulgence stipulated to us, is a thorn in the Side of the English.

The Parliament is up, and every body is fled from the city into the Country to reemit their Strength and Spirits, exhausted by pleasure and buisness. We shall hear very little of politicks till next winter, and by that time I hope congress will have establishd a system which will render them more respected abroad. And I would add an other wish; which is that they would adjourn, and when they do meet take care to be fully represented. They would go to buisness with more spirit. Through the neglect of the States a Treaty with Prussia which was received by them last october was never ratified till june and arrived here only within a few Days of the times expiring for the exchange. Prussia having no minister either here or in France, obliges mr Adams to go imediately to the Hague to prevent the whole treaty's falling through.[2] As this presents a good opportunity for Seeing the Country, I Shall accompany him there. We expect to be absent a Month. Col Smith we leave charge des affairs in our absence.

I am afflicted at the loss of an other dear relative and affectionate Aunt. When we reach the Meridian of Life, if not before one Dear Friend or other is droping of, till we lose all that makes life desirable. She was a most valuable woman, I loved her like a Parent. I have frequently recollected what my uncle Said to me the morning I left his House. You will never I fear said he see your Aunt again. And I had the same apprehensions as I have lookd upon her Health in a very precarious Situation for several Years. That we may not neglect the main object of Life, a preparation for death is the constant wish of your ever affectionate Neice AA

RC (Adams Papers).

[1] Not found.

[2] JA and Jefferson enclosed the Prussian-American treaty of amity and commerce to John Jay, the secretary for foreign affairs, in a letter dated 2 and 11 Oct. 1785. Jay submitted it to Congress on 9 Feb., and it was ratified on 17 May. By Art. 27 of the treaty, the Prussian and American ratifications had to be exchanged within one year of the treaty's signing, which had been completed on 10 Sept. 1785. JA traveled to the Netherlands to exchange the ratifications with Baron Friedrich Wilhelm von Thulemeyer, Prussian minister to The Hague, with whom he had also negotiated the original treaty in 1784–1785 (Jefferson, *Papers*, 8:606; *JCC*, 30:61, note 1; Miller, *Treaties*, 2:162, 182–184).

John and Abigail Adams to William Stephens Smith

Three Cup's Harwich August. 5. 1786. Saturday

Dear Sir

After a very pleasant Journey, here We are. We came very leisurely, dined the first day at Ingatestone and Slept at Witham, dined Yesterday at Mistley (Mr Rigbys Seat very near) and Slept where We now are, in full View of the Land Guard Fortification, with a fair Sun and fine Breeze. Our Carriage is on Board. As Fortune will have it, Hearn is the Captain. It is my third Passage with him. The two first were tedious,[1] this I hope will be otherwise. The Agent for the Packetts called upon Us last night, in Consequence of Mr Frasers Letter.[2] Ld Walthams Seat,[3] and Mr Rigbys, We wished to ramble in. Rigbys looks at a fine Cove of Salt Water. As this Farm has been watered and manured with the Effluvia of an hundred Millions of Money, being the Nerves of the American War, it might have been more magnificent. It is a fine Seat.[4] My Love to my dear Mrs Smith. Mamma sends her Love to you both.

We passed a pretty Seat, of the Family of Hoar, perhaps the Same with that of President Hoar, once of Harvard Colledge.[5]

At the Sign of the 3 cups, a tolerable House where a better is not to be had, with a fine view of the water from 3 windows, and a memento mori from the fourth, viz a burying Ground and church with in half a rod of us. We are now Setting at the Breakfast table. Pappa having told you where we stopd dined Slept &c has left nothing for me to say excepting that he twic mounted Johns Horse and rode 7 miles twice, which you See by computation makes 14 ms. In concequence of a Letter from the Secretary of states office the captain is obliged to give us the great cabin to ourselves for which we must make him a compliment of 10 Guineys and 7 for the Carriage. We concluded as there were 10 other passengers one being a Lady, that if any of them were very sick we could not (doing as we would be done by), refuse them admittance. So it was as well not to retain it, as the captain promisd me a small room by myself. The Country from London to Harwich is very delightfull, we were not much incomoded with dust. We found a card at woods, from mr Hollis requesting us to call on him and take a dinner or Bed &c. We reachd woods about 2 oclock orderd our dinner and walkd to the Hide. Mr Hollis received us with great Hospitality, and miss Brands countanance shone. She treated us with some cake, we Sat an hour took our leave and dined at Woods. Esther sighd this morning as she was dressing me and said, how strange it seems not to have Mrs Smith with us. I had felt it strange through the whole journey—one must be weaned by degrees. I hope you are very happy, you cannot be otherways whilst you continue to have the disposition to be so. Look in if you please once a week at our House, and let me know that it continues to Stand in Grosvenour Square adieu. Your affectionately

AA

RC (MHi:De Windt Collection); addressed by JA: "To William S Smith Esqr Charge des Affaires of the United States of America Wimpole Street No. 16. London"; endorsed: "Harwich August 5th. 1786 Jno. Adams Ansd. 8th."; stamped: "7 AU" and "[H]ARWICH."

[1] JA and JQA sailed from Harwich to Hellevoetsluis in Jan. 1784. In August of the same year JA made the opposite voyage, alone, to join AA, AA2, and JQA, who had preceded him, in London (JA, *D&A*, 3:152, 170).

[2] William Fraser (Frazier) was undersecretary of state for foreign affairs in Lord Carmarthen's office (Jefferson, *Papers*, 8:302). The letter has not been identified.

[3] New Hall, the seat of Drigue Billers Olmius (1746–1787), 2d baron Waltham in the Irish peerage, was located in Boreham, Essex (Namier and Brooke, *House of Commons*, 3:225).

[4] Mistley Hall, on the River Stour, was owned by Richard Rigby (1722–1788). As paymaster general of the forces, 1768–1782, Rigby controlled vast sums of public funds. The office was reformed in 1782 and Rigby accused of personally profiting from the monies under his control. Although he agreed to repay the outstanding balances, the public was still owed £156,000 three years after his death (Namier and Brooke, *House of Commons*, 3:354–360).

[5] To this point, the letter is written by JA. The remainder is written by AA. Rev. Leonard Hoar (ca. 1630–1675), third president of Harvard College (1672–1675), was born in Gloucestershire, England. He came to Massachusetts as a child with his family, gradu-

ated at Harvard in 1650, returned to England in 1653, and preached at Wanstead, Essex, until 1662. In 1672, he accepted an invitation to preach at the Old South Church and returned to Boston. Soon thereafter he was named president of Harvard (*Sibley's Harvard Graduates*, 1:228–252; *DNB*).

William Stephens Smith to John and Abigail Adams

My dear Sir London Tuesday 8th. of August 1786

We were pleased by the receipt of yours of the 5th. inst. from Harwich, to find that your jaunt to that period and place had proved so agreable, you have our earnest wishes for its continuance. But we have been apprehensive since, that the fine Sun and fair Brieze which invited you on board in the morning, forsook you before, you had crossed the Channel. At this place, the after part of the day lowered, and it closed with light gusts and some rain, which continued thro, the night and part of Sunday, from this we were prevented from going to Church as usual, but our Prayers for your safety were equally fervent and as for Sermons, we had enough agreable to former allowance to last us a month, for we seated ourselves like sober people in the drawing room and read 4. Inclosed I send you a Letter from Mr. Rutledge of Charlestown South Carolina, introducing Doctor Moyes.[1] He dined with us yesterday in Company with Dr. Price, Mr. Hartley and Major Langborne. The Day passed very agreable the two Philosophers were much pleased with each other and their conversation entertaining and instructive. They left us between 9 and ten. Very shortly after I was beat at a game of Chess—by the dear Lady you desire your Love to, she returns it with all the warmth of an honest heart. There has nothing new transpired since your departure. Margaret Nicholson is still in confinement and furnishes Paragraphs and Prints. His Majesty is highly applauded for his presence of mind and humanity on the occasion, and the Prince of whales is said to have discovered great filial affection, in the expedition with which he flew to congratulate his Royal Father, on his escape. This shews his goodness of heart, and must encrease (if possible) that public admiration which has been exccited by his other virtues. A Card in the general advertiser of this Morning after Stating the general joy which pervades all ranks of People and the numberless addresses which are preparing to be presented, say's, let us add our mite to the general Joy. We rejoice that his Majesty's Life has been preserved *amidst a host of enemies, both open and secret*. May his future reign enable him to forget the national calamities of *late* years in the full enjoyment of peace and happiness and every Comfort, that a good Citizen can wish a good King.

So my good madam you were seated in a tolerable good House—with 3 Cups—at the breakfast table, with water in abundance—&c &c—but why did you bring in the *memento mori*—the burying ground and Church. I recollect when I was at that same house, I walk'd in that burying Ground and visited that Church, but thought more of you and your Dear Daughter than of either. But it has come to a happy period and I am contented and pleased. I sometimes wish for her sake, more Company and amusement. For myself, I wish for no other while I can please and amuse her. She is every thing I can wish in a Companion. If she was a little fonder of talking She would exceed the rest of her sex too much perhaps. We miss you and Papa very much and count the hours untill you return. You astonish us, thwice 7 Miles you say he appeard on the Back of Johns Horse, and did he Live? Well there is no Knowing what a body can do, before they try. On your return if the experiment should extend to twice 14, we'll both get hobby horses and Canter to Pain's Hill while you two Lady's are diverting yourselves in the Chariot with our bouncing &c. &c. Poor Esther sigh'd, and repeated the first verse in the Chapter of Lamentation.[2] It was in unison with your feelings, and No. 16 Wimpole Street about the same moment echoed something we could not tell what. But we must not indulge it, for this greif according to Sr. John Falstaff . . .[3] and is a terrible thing—adieu heaven bless you. My dear Abbey joins me in Love to you and Pappa. I am yours jointly and seperately I have made such a jumble of this that I can scarcely with any grace bring in the name of

W. S. Smith

RC (Adams Papers); endorsed by AA: "Col Smith August 8th 1786."

[1] Dr. Henry Moyes, a blind Scotsman, traveled the eastern seaboard of the United States, 1784–1786, delivering a series of lectures on the philosophy of chemistry and natural history. He lectured in Charleston in April and May before sailing for Britain (Brooke Hindle, *The Pursuit of Science in Revolutionary America, 1735–1789*, Chapel Hill, N.C., 1956, p. 284–286; Jefferson, *Papers*, 8:51; *Massachusetts Centinel*, 20 May; Boston *Independent Ledger*, 5 June). The letter of introduction, from either Edward or John Rutledge, has not been found.

[2] Lamentations, 1:1: "How doth the city sit solitary, that was full of people! how is she become as a widow! she that was great among the nations, and princess among the provinces, how is she become tributary!"

[3] Thus in MS. According to Sir John Falstaff, "A plague of sighing and grief! It blows a man up like a bladder" (*Henry IV, Part 1*, Act II, scene iv, lines 365–366).

Charles Storer to Abigail Adams Smith

Boston, August 8th, 1786

You know, Amelia, I am never backward in writing my friends: therefore, when I tell you that I have four of your favours by me unanswered,[1] I trust you will not lay the blame on my good will. Some of them were received where I could neither acknowledge them myself, nor had I one to do it for me, and the others came at an inconvenient time. Be persuaded, however, that the will is good, (as, indeed, it ever is in respect to you,) and no evil thought will rise up against your friend. * * * * *[2]

I am perfectly of your mind, Amelia, in regard to Europe. There certainly is something like fascination attending our acquaintance with it, and for my own part I must confess that a ten year's ramble through it would hardly satisfy me. There is that constant variety which must amuse, for we poor mortals have a deal of curiosity, one and all of us, however we may pretend to deny it. Some are diverted one way, some another; yet, though the means be directly opposed, the one to the other, the principle remains the same. I have no doubt but you would be highly gratified in a tour upon the continent, and I wish you may; it would be a source of very pleasing reflection ever after. But hush upon this subject, or I shall raise desires I may not be able to comply with.

My hints respecting what was said of you at New-York[3] were not mal apropôs it seems, though I must confess I had no idea of their being applicable to you at the time. I understand you, when you say "you may perhaps make us a visit here sometime within two or three years," though it is not speaking so plainly as you might have done. You have my best wishes, however, for every happiness.

The slippers you sent to Maria please her exactly. You will therefore accept her thanks, with mine, for them. You need not be concerned about the paying for them, I shall take due care of that.

You speak of Mr. Jefferson's being with you in March. *Entre nous*—did he ever mention receiving the books I sent him just before I left London, by your papa's advice? I ask because I am much disappointed in not having any acknowledgement of them from him, which I pleased myself with having.[4] The velvet dress you speak of I received but a few weeks ago, via L'Orient. Though plain and simple, 'tis, I think, beautiful, as are most of the French dresses; our opinions correspond in this I believe.

I wish, Amelia, it had been in my power to have met you at Stamford the day you mentioned to have rode out. How surprised you would have been to have seen me on the terrace. But, alas! those days are all over, past and gone! and I am going to enter on another line of life, altogether new and strange.

I saw your brother Charles yesterday in town. I asked him to dine. He was going to Cambridge. I spent the evening out, and when I returned home I was told that he was there and was gone to bed. This was acting on the friendly principle which pleases me much, I assure you. You have written to him on this subject, I fancy, else I shall be better pleased, it being his own choice. He staid with us most of the forenoon, and I hope he was not dissatisfied with his visit.

Your aunt Shaw I have not seen since last winter, though I have your uncle, who was at commencement. All our friends at Braintree are in usual health, as are those in town. Every thing here wears but a gloomy appearance at present, though there are many who try their utmost to be gay. There are many who are flirting about in silk and satin, but who have a sorrowful, aching heart, I am very sure. As for me, I am going to retire from this society while I can do it with a good grace. If success attends me, it will fully compensate for the sacrifice; if not, there will ever be a satisfaction in having acted as I thought right.

Write to me, and be assured it will afford particular pleasure, in his retirement, to

Eugenio

MS not found. Printed from AA2, *Jour. and Corr.*, 2:50–53.

[1] Letters not found. They probably included AA2's letters "No: 3 and 4, both of May" acknowledged by Storer in his letter to AA of 21 July, above.

[2] Thus in MS.

[3] For Storer's comments on how the ladies of New York envied AA2's social opportunities in England, see vol. 6:465.

[4] No record of Jefferson's receipt of books from Storer appears in Jefferson, *Papers*.

Thomas Jefferson to Abigail Adams

Dear Madam

Paris Aug. 9. 1786

It is an age since I have had the honor of a letter from you, and an age and a half since I presumed to address one to you. I think my last was dated in the reign of king Amri, but under which of his successors you wrote, I cannot recollect. Ochosias, Joachaz, Manahem or some such hard name.[1] At length it is resumed: I am honoured with your favor of July 23. and I am at this moment writing an answer to it, and first we will dispatch business. The shoes you ordered, will be ready this day and will accompany the present letter. But why send money for them? you know the balance of trade was always against me. You will observe by the inclosed account that it is I who am to export cash always, tho' the sum has been lessened by the bad bargains I have made for you and the good ones you have made for me. This is a gaining trade, and therefore I shall continue it, begging you will send no more money here. Be so good as to correct the inclosed that the errors of that may not add to your losses in this commerce. You were right in conjecturing that both the gentlemen might forget to communicate to me the intelligence about captn. Stanhope. Mr Adams's head was full of whale oil, and Colo. Smith's of German politics,[2] (—but don't tell them this—) so they left it to you to give me the news. De tout mon coeur, I had rather receive it from you than them. This proposition about the exchange of a son for my daughter puzzles me. I should be very glad to have your son, but I cannot part with my daughter. Thus you see I have such a habit of gaining in trade with you that I always expect it. We have a blind story here of somebody attempting to assassinate your king. No man upon earth has my prayers for his continuance in life more sincerely than him. He is truly the American Messias, the most precious life that ever god gave, and may god continue it. Twenty long years has he been labouring to drive us to our good, and he labours and will labour still for it if he can be spared. We shall have need of him for twenty more. The Prince of Wales on the throne, Lansdowne and Fox in the ministry, and we are undone! We become chained by our habits to the tails of those who hate and despise us. I repeat it then that my anxieties are all alive for the health and long life of the king. He has not a friend on earth who would lament his loss so much and so long as I should. Here we have singing, dauncing, laugh, and merriment. No assassinations, no treasons, rebellions nor other dark deeds. When our king goes out, they fall down and kiss the earth where he has trodden: and then they go to kissing one another, and this is the truest wisdom. They have as much happiness in one year as an Englishman in ten. The presence of the queen's sister enlivens the court. Still more the birth of the princess.[3] There are some little bickerings between the king and his parliament, but they end with a sic volo, sic jubeo.[4] The bottom of my page tells me it is time for me to end with assurances of the affectionate esteem with which I have the honor to be, dear Madam, your most obedient & most humble servant

Th: Jefferson

ENCLOSURE

Mrs. Adams to Th: J.

Dr.

			₶	s	d
1785. June 2.	To paid Petit		173.	8	
Aug. 17.	To pd mr Garvey's bill		96.	16.	6
Nov.	To cash by Colo. Smith.		768.	0.	0
1786. Jan. 5.	To pd Barin for Suortout de dessert & figures &c		264.	17.	6
Feb.27.	To pd for shoes for miss Adams		24.		
Mar. 5.	To pd for sundries viz.	₶			
	12. aunes de dentelle	96			
	une paire de barbes	36.			
	4. aunes of cambric	92.			
	4. do.	60	284.	0.	0
			1611.	2.	0

		£	s	d
(reckoning 24. livres at 20/sterl.)	being	67.	2.	7 sterl.
Mar. [*April*] 9. To balance of expences of journey between mr Adams & myself		8.	9.	4 1/2
		75	11.	11 1/2

Cr.

				£	s	d
1785. Oct. 12.	By pd insurance on Houdon's life			32.	11.	0
1786. Jan. 10.	By damask table cloth & napkins			7.	0.	0
	2. pr nut crackers				4.	0
		£	s			
	2. peices Irish linen @ 4/.	8.	14			
	making 12. shirts	1.	16			
	buttons, thread, silk		3			
	washing		3.6			
	a trunk	1.	1	11.	17.	6

Apr. 9.	By pd for 9. yards of muslin @ 11/		4. 19. 0
12.	By do. for 21. yds Chintz @ 5/6		5. 15. 6
	By pd for 25. yds linen @ 4/ £5.		
	for making 7. shirts 1. 6. 6	for mr Short	
			6. 6. 6
	By pd for altering 12. shirts		6. 6
	Balance		6. 11. 11 1/2
			75. 11. 11 1/2

RC (Adams Papers); endorsed: "Mr Jefferson August 9th 1786." Enclosure (Adams Papers); notation by Jefferson: "Mrs. Adams."

[1] Omri, Ochosias, Joachaz, and Menahem, kings of Israel in the 10th–8th centuries B.C.

[2] See JA to Jefferson, 16 July, and WSS to Jefferson, 18 July (Jefferson, *Papers*, 10:140–141, 152–155).

[3] Sophie Hélène Béatrix, the fourth and last child of Marie Antoinette, was born in July; she died in 1787 (Dorothy Moulton Mayer, *Marie Antoinette, The Tragic Queen*, N.Y., 1969, p. 158, 161).

[4] So I wish it, so I command.

Abigail Adams to Abigail Adams Smith

My dear Hague 8th. [*i.e. 11*] August 1786[1]

Your papa and I wrote you from Harwich the morning we embarked for Helvoet, the wind was very fair, and we went on board at 3 o clock, a vessel very commodious for passengers, clean, and the least offensive of any that I was ever in. But the passage is a most disagreeable one, and after being on board 18 or 20, hours one might as well proceed on a voyage to America, for I do not think I suffered more from Sea sickness, then than now, yet I layed myself down the moment I went on board, and never rose till eight o clock the next morning. It is a hundred and twenty miles across, the vessel went before the wind, and the sea was very heavy and rough, there were 17 passengers, most of whom were sick. In short I dread the return, and we are not without some thoughts of going round to Calais. The House on this side is very bad, as I slept none and had suffered much I could have wished to have gone to bed, but I saw no temptation to it. I thought the pleasure ought to be great in viewing the Country to compensate for the pain and fatigue. We determined to proceed to Rotterdam, and sent to procure horses and postillions for the purpose, after some delay came the horses with ropes[2] tied to their tails, and two great heavy clumsy whiffing Dutch men, who took their own way in spite of us. They have no saddles to their horses, so that we were obliged to take John into the carriage; my band-box the coach-man insisted he would set upon, as a drivers seat, nor could all our entreaties, prevent him, the other mounted the leading horse without any saddle, thus equipped we set of. After proceeding a slow jog of about three miles an hour the fellow, who was on the fore horse overtook a companion, who was going to visit a friend about six miles distant, he jumped down and ordered the band-box coach man to drive on, and he and his companion took a seat behind the carriage jabbering and smoking all the way, stopping at every village to take a glass of gin. I felt very wroth, but your Papa assured me there was no remedy but patience, we had only 24 miles to go in order to reach Rotterdam, this took up the whole day, the roads being bad. The whole Country is a meadow and has a very singular appearance, what are called the dykes are roads raised above the canals, upon each side of which are planted rows of Willow Trees. I inquired frequently, for the great road supposing we were travelling some bye path, but found the whole Country the same till we reached Rotterdam. The Villages are scattered through the Country, and the meanest Cottage has a neatness which indicates good husbandry, the people appear well clothed, well fed, and well smoked; I do not mean that their complexions are unusually dark, I think them rather fair, but whether riding, or walking, rowing or otherwise employed, a long or a short pipe occupies them all. We reached Rotterdam about eight o clock, and put up for the night, at a tolerable Inn near the market, in which is a Statue, in Bronze of Erasmus who was a native of that place. The Country every where appears fertile. On Tuesday morning we set out for this place, which we reached about twelve o clock. We stopped at an Inn to get Lodgings, but were told that the whole house was taken up for Prince Ferdinand, brother to the Emperor,[3] who was expected hourly; We then proceeded to the next best Inn, called the Marshal Turenne, where we now are. After adjusting our affairs, your Papa went in search of Mr Dumas, whom he soon found, but Alas, how unfortunate, Madam and Mademoiselle were gone to their Country house in Guilderland. I depended much on Miss Dumas, but fear I shall not see her. On Wednesday your Papa made his visits, and I made mine, to Lady Harris. The only minister who has a Lady here is the English, she returned my visit in a few hours, and we were invited to dine with them the next day, which was yesterday, accordingly we went. Sir James appears a friendly, social man, his Lady, who is about twenty five, is handsome, sociable, gay, she has fine eyes, and a delicate complexion. She asked me about Mrs B—g,[4] said Sir James had told her that she was very handsome. She has three fine children here, and one in England, she was married at seventeen. On Saturday we are to sup with the French Ambassador,[5] and dine with him on Sunday. Your Papa dines with the Prussian minister on Saturday, and on Monday we propose going to Leyden where we shall spend a day or two, and proceed to Amsterdam, to pass the remainder of the week, the beginning of the week after we shall set our faces homeward. The Hague is quite desolate, the Court being all absent with the Prince. I forgot to mention to you the honour we received at Helvoet, viz, the ringing of the bells, and a military guard to wait upon us. We went one day to Delft to see the church, in which is a monument, and marble Statue of William the 1st. Prince of Orange, which is executed in a masterly style. On one hand is justice, on the other liberty, religion, and prudence, behind him stands Fame with her trumpet reaching forward, and balancing herself upon one toe. The figure is very expressive and cost as I was informed twelve thousand Ducat's. At the foot of William lies the marble statue of the dog who died for grief at the tomb of his master. Here is also a fine monument and Statue of Grotius, but I shall leave nothing to tell you when I return if I spin out my letter much longer, you see by its rough dress that I have neither pens or patience to Copy. We are going to the play and the necessary article of tea, obliges me to close. I hope to hear from you soon, direct under cover to Mr Dumas, as I know not where we shall be, it will be sufficient if you read this to the Col. I feel too proud to let him see it. I want to get back, yet have some curiosity to see all that this Country offers first. Your Papa says he ought to write to Billy as well as I to Nabby. Adieu Papa calls to tea again, and you know, that I must hasten. Love to you all and a Kiss for *Billy*. Yours

A. A.

Tr in ABA's hand (Adams Papers); notation in CFA's hand: "A. A to her daughter. Mrs W. S. Smith." CFA made some minor corrections in ABA's transcription. Printed in AA2, *Jour. & Corr.*, 2:60–64. The Tr is preferred because it includes several brief passages omitted in the printed text. The sole case where the printed text contains words not in the Tr is noted.

[1] The Adamses arrived at The Hague from Rotterdam on Tuesday the 8th. AA makes it clear later in the letter that she wrote it on the 11th, the day after she and JA dined with Sir James and Lady Harris.

[2] The printed text has "reins and ropes."

[3] Ferdinand, Archduke of Austria and Duke of Modena (1754–1806).

[4] Anne Willing Bingham.

[5] Charles Olivier de Saint Georges, Marquis de Verac, French ambassador to the Netherlands from 1785 to 1787 (*Repertorium*, 3:126). See also AA to JQA, 27 Sept., below.

Elizabeth Otis Brown to Abigail Adams

Madam — Sleaford August 11th. 86

As I have been in Daily expectations of seeing London, I have defered answering your Letter,[1] meaning to pay my respects in person. But seeing by the Papers Mr: Adams is just on the eve of his departure for *Spain*[2] I have taken up my pen to request the favour of you to inform me whether you have heard from Mr: or Mrs: Warren since you wrote last, I still remain in the same situation I was then in, not having heard since last August. Mr: Brown proposes being in London in the course of a Month when I mean to accompany him and if you are then in Town I will do myself the pleasure to call on you. My Compt: and best wishes attend you Mr: A. and Your Daughter and I am Madam Yr: Humbl: Servt — Eliz Brown

RC (Adams Papers).

[1] Not found.

[2] On 4 Aug., the London *Morning Post and Daily Advertiser* mistakenly reported that the Adamses had left for Spain, purportedly to pursue a commercial treaty with Algiers. The London *General Evening Post*, 8–10 Aug., corrected the error and offered the real reason for the Adamses' trip, but the rumor of a trip connected to an alliance with Algiers persisted (see, for instance, London *Daily Universal Register*, 19 Aug.).

Abigail Adams to Abigail Adams Smith

Leyden 15th. August 1786

Yours of August the 7th.[1] and Col. Smith's of the 8th. reached us on the 14th. at this place. We left the Hague on Monday, I wrote you an account of our excursion, till Thursday Evening, when I was going to the play. The house is small and ordinary, the Actors as good as one commonly finds them in England. It was the birth day of the Princess of Orange, it was not distinguished that I know of in any other manner, than that both the French and English ministers Box was drest upon the occasion. The peices which were acted were in French, one of them was Fanfan and Colas.[2] The house though small was not half full, the Court being all absent. I have visited the Princes house in the Woods, where he resides, and holds his court during the summer, also his cabinet of Paintings which is small but well chosen, his cabinet of Natural History &c. I have also been to see the collection here, and the Botanical garden, in each I find something new, but in general they are the same species, of Birds,

Beast, minerals, and plant, fishes, and reptiles which we find in greater order and perfection in the Museum of Sir Ashton Lever.[3]

We went to see the Gardens &c, of Secretary Fagel,[4] and here I was led a jaunt of three miles, through a sand like Weymouth Hill. I puffed and blowed, sat down whenever I could find a seat, and thought the view, not worth the fatigue, it being very warm, and faint weather, especially after having seen Pains Hill, and other places much superior.

A Saturday Evening we went to the French Ambassadors, here were all the Foreign Ministers, some Officers, and Gentlemen of the Town, Lady Harris, and three other English ladies whom I dined with at Sir James's, two Danish, and two Dutch ladies made the company, in all about sixty persons. Cards, were the object till about eleven oclock, when the supper bell rang, and his Excellency escorted me into an elegant room, and a superb supper, about one we returned to our Lodgings. Sunday I regretted that I could not go to church, to hear Dr Mac Lean,[5] who was gone into the Country. Your papa dined abroad; it was very rainy, I tarried at home and read Plutarch's Lives, but I am determined if it should ever fall to my lot to travel into a foreign Country again I will make Don Quixote my companion. What with reading the Lives of these Roman Emperors, most of which exhibit tyranny, cruelty, devastation and horrour, and visiting the churches, here whose walls exhibit the gloomy Escutcheons of the silent inhabitants, dark and dreary cells, I have been haunted every night with some of their troubled Ghosts, and though seldom low spirited, I have here felt the influence of climate, and the objects I have beheld, there is a silence and a dead calm which attends travelling through this Country, the objects which present themselves are meadows, Trees, and Canals, Canals Trees, and meadows, such a want of my *dear variety*, that I really believe an English Robber would have animated me. The roads from the Hague to Harlem are one continued sand, so that one has not even the pleasure of hearing the wheels of the carriage. Leyden is the cleanest City I ever saw, the streets are wide, the Houses brick, all neat even to the meanest building. The River Rhine runs through the City. We tarried at Leyden till Thursday morning, and then set off for Harlem, at which place we dined. A curious circumstance took place after dinner. We sent John on before in the Boat, and he had very carefully locked the carriage, and taken the key with him, what was to be done? We sent for a Smith to force the lock, but that could not be effected, after much deliberation upon what was to be done I proposed getting in at the window, oh that was impossible! however a ladder was brought, and the difficulty was surmounted! true I assure you. When we got about half way, here, who should we meet, but poor John upon the full trot, with the key in his hand, looking so mortified that one had not the heart to blame him.

And here let me advise you never to travel the road when a great man is in motion, for when we got here, we were obliged to go to five different houses, before we could get any apartments even to sleep in for one night. Prince Ferdinand had taken the whole house called the Arms of Amsterdam, and company returning from Spa, had filled every other, we were obliged for last night to shift as they say, and take such as we could get. To day we are much better off. As to Amsterdam I can say nothing about it yet. I was disappointed in finding Mr Parker gone to London when we arrived. We have had some visits to day, and are engaged to dine at Harlem tomorrow with Mr Willink, at his Country House,[6] on Monday we are also engaged, and Wednesday. I fancy we shall make out our month, without *going to Madrid*. Let me hear from you and yours, if an opportunity offers to send Blair to America before our return, Col Smith will be so good as to purchase it.[7] Adieu my dear, I should be loth to tell you how often I have wished myself in London since I left it, till this day I cannot say I have felt well since I crost the water. Dinner comes, so I lay by my pen. The post goes at ten. You see that this letter was written part at Leyden, and part at Amsterdam, begun the 15th. and finished the 18th. I wrote you at the Hague.[8]

Tr in ABA's hand (Adams Papers); notation in CFA's hand: "A. A to her daughter Mrs W.S.S in London"; with two minor corrections, probably by CFA. Printed in AA2, *Jour. & Corr.*, 2:53–57. See the descriptive note to AA to AA2, [*11*] Aug., above.

[1] Not found.

[2] *Fanfan et Colas*, a comedy by Beaunoir (Alexandre Louis Bertrand Robineau).

[3] For Sir Ashton Lever's museum in London, see vol. 5:323, 324.

[4] For Hendrik Fagel (1706–1790), griffier (secretary) of the States General, see JA, *Papers*, 7:168–169. Fagel's home was within walking distance of The Hague. JQA wrote in his Diary, 27 May 1797, "Went out on the Ryswick [*Rijswijk*] road through the Oost Indisch weg; came out near the House in the wood [*Huis ten Bosch, or Royal Palace*]: from thence went round the grounds of Mr. Fagel, and returned by the road from Scheveling [*Scheveningen*]. Long and pleasant tour."

[5] Archibald Maclaine (1722–1804), pastor of the English church at The Hague (*DNB*).

[6] Both Wilhem and Jan Willink, two of the Amsterdam bankers with whom JA negotiated loans for America in 1782 and 1784, owned country houses in Haarlem (JQA, Diary, 2 May 1795; JA, *Papers*, 12:460–461, 472).

[7] JQA requested Hugh Blair's *Lectures on Rhetoric and Belles Lettres* in his letter to JA of 21 May 1786, above.

[8] AA2, *Jour. & Corr.*, closes with "Yours, A. A."

Charles Storer to Abigail Adams

Boston. 15th. August. 1786

Pray, Madam, be carefull how you send Cards to your friends on this side the water another time. It seems that since you have mentioned Amelia's intended Connection, you have sent a Card, with something wound round it, on which was written an invitation to you and Mr: A— to dinner from *Mr: and Mrs. Wm. Smith*. This was taken for a certain Information of Amelia's having entered the marriage state, particularly, as on comparing it with her hand writing it was determined universally to be hers. *Mrs: C.* to whom this Card came enclosed shew it to every and all her friends, but it was generally wondered why you should send the intelligence in that way. I was not here when it arrived, but on my return it was talked of every where that Miss Adams was married, and this story of the Card was always alluded to as the proof. This same Card occasioned a good anecdote, which perhaps you may not have heard. Mrs: C. on receiving this Card put it upon the Clock, as you know is customary here. *Mr: T:* observing it, took it down and read it. He put it again in its place and turning to *Miss Lucy*, who was alone in the room, and meaning to apply to the weather which was then very unsettled, said "'tis a very changeable time Miss L—" "Yes *Mr: T.* she replied, these are changeable times indeed." Without an other word he walked away. And apropos of this said Gentleman, your quondam favorite, You mention that *Dr: T—* has recovered every thing from him, belon[ging] to Amelia, but I am assured from the best authority that it is [missing?] a thing. I have mentioned it to the *Dr*: once or twice, but he always evades my enquiries. This *entre nous*, if you please.

You bid me tell you good news, Madam; but I am sorry it is not in my power so to do. We have just heard of the death of *Prentiss Cushing* in the W: Indies.[1] He was taken ill one day and died the next. This acco't came but yesterday, so I suppose he is but lately dead.

From the political world neither can I give you any agreable intelligence. The devil I am afraid has got in among us, and I dread his soon throwing us into a state of anarchy and confusion. County Conventions and associations have been frequent of late, to point out modes of redress for grievances that the Constitution does not provide against. Handbills and Covenants are passing in several Counties, which are signed by many to league and defend each other against the operation of law and justice, and to shut up the Courts of Common Pleas. Some cry out for Paper money; tho' since the emission of a medium of this kind in Rhode-Island state we have [had] repeated accounts of robberies, quarrells and even of pitched battles with [. . .]. If we are to come to this, the sooner the better, that we may know how it is to terminate. Our Sea Ports and the Country are at variance. The first shall be taxed and the latter go free. Be it so and may our docks be turned into fields. I believe too that, as a Country, we should do better. Then when we are all *Country* we shall all fare alike and each contribute in just proportion to the common support. Come what will, it must be right in the end.

I am, Madam, with much esteem Yrs: as ever, C. S.

RC (Adams Papers); addressed: "Mrs: A. Adams, Grosvenor-Square. London."; endorsed: "Charles Storer August 15 1786." Some loss of text where the seal was removed.

[1] Prentice Cushing (1758–1786), the son of Rev. Jacob and Anna Williams Cushing of Waltham, died at Demarara on 5 or 6 July. In a diary entry for 25 Aug., Elizabeth Cranch wrote that he "once lived with us—a most amiable Youth; he made a Voyage to Demarara and there died; I mourn the early exit of such Virtue, but he is I trust happy—for he was truly good" (*Massachusetts Centinel*, 26 Aug.; *Sibley's Harvard Graduates*, 12:252; Lemuel Cushing, *The Genealogy of the Cushing Family*, Montreal, 1877, p. 45; Elizabeth Cranch Norton Diaries, MHi:Jacob Norton Papers).

Cotton Tufts to Abigail Adams

Dear Cousin Aug. 15. 1786

In my Acctt. sent Mr. Adams[1] you will not find any large sums Credited for Your Farm. The Farm Acct. with Pratt I settled in April last, the whole Produce of Your half amounted (for the Year preceding) to £37. 5.11. This is accounted for in part in my last Acctt. part in this and the Remainder is discharged by Pratts Acct for Work, Rates and Sunds. debited Tho Pratt and J. Marsh. The Losses sustained in the Stock and the low Price of Produce greatly lessened your Income. As there is a large Tax the present Year and produce low I cannot expect it will be greater. You will find in my Acct Charges of Cash to Mrs Cranch, wherever You find them they are for Cloathing payment of Taylors and necessaries for the Children.

I have at Length by Patience and Perseverance brot Matters almost to a Close with Mr Tyler, he has voluntarily given me (and without a Request) the Acct Books Notes of Hand and some other Papers, his Acct for Business done I expect to have in a few Days.

On examining the Accounts and Notes I find that a greater Part of them will be lost, some are dead—their Estates, others gone out of the Government and many of them unknown to me or any Body that I can meet with.[2]

Newhall on whom I depended for Quartetly Payments is now £51. in Arrears. He must shortly quit the House and some one take it that will pay the Cash. Your Children are well. Thomas is to be examined Next Monday, his Examination was delayed at Commencement, waiting for Your Directions which were not recd timely for that purpose and we had concluded to postpone it to another. I had forgot that I had wrote in such a Manner, as that you would take it for granted that, he would be offered unless we heard to the Contrary. A few Days past I turnd my Eye upon a rough Copy of my Letter, and discoverd my Error. Tell Cousin Nabby I have fully executed her Commission and am in Possession of a dear little Creature which I look upon with Pleasure.[3] I should except the Two Morroco Pockt Books, which I believe he has disposed of. Accept of Love & Regards to all Yrs.

Cotton Tufts

RC (Adams Papers); addressed: "Madam. Abigail Adams London Grovesnor Square"; endorsed: "August 15 1786 Dr Tufts."

[1] Not found.

[2] JA's former clients who had "gone out of the Government" were probably loyalist emigrees living in Britain, Canada, or the West Indies.

[3] The miniature of AA2.

John Quincy Adams to William Cranch

Sir

Cambridge Augt: 20th. 1786

You are, though living in a garret
No more a Poet, than a Parrot
At first you take a doggrel verse,
And, alexandrine then rehearse.
You hobble on, or wrong or right
With sometimes ten and sometimes eight.
By your own syllogistic rule
You must confess yourself a fool.
and if Bob Longer lacks of wit
He that is shorter must have it.
Besides I see you've chang'd your name
Because the first brought you to shame

And must certainly be wrong
Who now is short, and now is long.

R. S.[1]

RC (Privately owned); addressed: "Mr: Bob Longer. In the paradise of fools."

[1] Probably an abbreviation for "Robert Shorter" (that is, Bob Shorter), a comment on JQA's and Cranch's relative heights.

Abigail Adams to Abigail Adams Smith

My dear Amsterdam 23d. August 1786

Mr S. and Mr Blount set off tomorrow for London and have engaged to call this Evening for Letters. We have not received a line from you except what these gentlemen brought us, this is the fourth time I have written to you.

If politeness and attention could render a place agreeable, I have had more reason to be pleased with this Country, than any other, that I have visited, and when I get across the water again, I shall not regret the visit I have made here.

These people appear to think of the past, the present, and the future, whilst they do honour to their former Heroes, and patriots, by paintings, sculpture, and monuments, they are establishing wise institutions, and forming the minds and manners of their youth, that they may transmit to posterity, those rights, and liberties, which they are sensible have suffered infringments, but which they appear determined to regain, and are uniting in spirited and vigorous measures, for that purpose. The death of his Prussian Majesty of which there appears at present no doubt, will diminish the influence of the Court party in this country, already in the wane, as the politicians say.[1] But of this enough. I was at the play the night before last, the Grand Duke and Dutchess,[2] with their Retinue were present, the Dutchess is a fine looking woman. The house is small, but neat well lighted, and I think handsomer than any of the Theatres in England, the actors pretty good. The ladies of this country have finer complexions than the English, and have not spoilt them by cosmeticks. Rouge is confined to the stage here. There is the greatest distinction in point of dress, between the peasantry of the Country and people of distinction, that I have seen in any Country, yet they dress rich and fine in their own way. I went yesterday with a party, to Sardam, by Water about two hours sail. It is a very neat village and famous, for being the place where Czar, Peter the great worked as a Ship Carpenter. It was their annual Fair, at which there was a great collection of people, so that I had an opportunity of seeing the various dresses of different provinces. Mr Willink, told us, that there were several peasants who belonged to Sardam, who owned, a hundred thousand pounds property.

To day we dine with the elder Mr Willink, whose lady speaks English very well, and is a very agreeable woman. And this evening we go with them to a different Theatre. They have three play houses in this place. We are undetermined as yet whether to go to Utrecht on Saturday, or set off for the Hague. We should have gone there to day, but the Grand-duke, had taken the boat, and all the publick houses, there fit to go into, so that we did not wish to fall into his corteg[3] again, if he continues there longer than Saturday we shall return without visiting that province. We shall make no longer stay at the Hague, than to take leave, as I suppose all will be sable there, we are not prepared to go into company. We have determined to return by Helvot, I suppose in Saturday weeks packet, so that I hope to see you by Monday night, or Tuesday at furthest. I have done what you desired, but to very little more advantage than in London.

Adieu you cannot want more to see us, than we do to return again to you. Love to both of you. I hope my family in Grosvenor Square, has not increased in my absence. I was not aware of a young cook till the morning I left home. I was then thrown into an astonishment in which I should be glad to be mistaken, but am very sure I am not.[4] Yours affectionately A. A.

Tr in ABA's hand (Adams Papers); notation by CFA: "AA to her daughter in London. Mrs W S. S." Printed in AA2, *Jour. & Corr.*, 2:57–59.

[1] Frederick the Great died on 17 August. Provoked by the arrest of his sister, Wilhelmina, Princess of Orange, Frederick's successor and nephew, Frederick William II, invaded the Netherlands in Sept. 1787, crushed the Patriot forces, and restored the full powers of his brother-in-law Stadholder William V (Simon Schama, *Patriots and Liberators: Revolution in the Netherlands 1780–1813*, N.Y., 1977, p. 106–107, 123–132).

[2] Ferdinand and Maria Beatrice d'Este, Archduke and Archduchess of Austria.

[3] "Vortex" in the printed version.

[4] Presumably a reference to one of the Adamses' servants who was pregnant.

John Quincy Adams to John Adams

Dear Sir Cambrige August 30th: 1786

I received a few days agone, your favour of June 2d:[1] you mention an Affair, concerning which I had determined to write in the beginning of this Quarter. I have thought much of an Office in which to Study the Law. Should you return home next Spring, and be yourself at Leisure to instruct me, I should certainly prefer that to studying any where else. But if you are still detained in Europe, I should wish to Live in some place, where there might be Society sufficient for relaxation at Times, but not enough to encourage dissipation. Boston I should for several Reasons, wish to avoid. The Principal ones are, that it is unfavorable to Study, and that it would be almost doubly expensive. Mr: Parsons of Newbury, has been mentioned, and I should be very glad to study with him. However it is not perhaps a matter of much consequen[ce] whose office I am in, if my Time is well spent in it. I look forward with ming[led] Pain and Pleasure, to the Time when, I shall finish the Collegiate Term. I have made it my endeavour to be intimate, only with the best Characters in my Class, and there are several, with whom I enjoy many social half hours: as our pursuits are confined here, meerly to Literature, it is necessary to be a very Close Student, in order to acquire a respectable Character. Out of an hundred and sixty Students, that are here, there is undoubtedly every gradation, from the most amiable disposition to the worst; from the smallest genius to the greatest, and from the compleat ignoramus to the youth of learning. There are some who do not study twelve hours in the course of a twelve month, and some who study as much almost everyday, and it always happens that their Reputation, is in an exact Ratio to the attention they pay to studying. The good scholar is esteemed, even by the idle; but the bad one, is despised as much by those who are like him, as he is by the judicious. This is the common Course; but in these peaceful mansions there is the same Spirit of intrigue, and party, and as much inclination to Cabal, as may be discovered at Courts. It has not the same Opportunities to show itself, and remains for the most part concealed. But there are certain Circumstances and Situations in which it breaks forth [with] great vehemence. This has lately been the Case with my Class. It is customary early in the first Quarter of the Senior Year, for Each Class, to meet, and choose by ballot, one of its members to deliver a Valedictory Oration on the ensuing 21st: of June; and four others, [to] collect the Theses which are published by the Class when they take their degr[ees. We] have lately gone through this business. There were different parties for three Persons, as Orator, and there was a great deal of intriguing carried on. One only could be successful, and *Little* of Newbury Port, was finally chosen. A Person who to an excellent genius, unites an amiable disposition, and an unblemished moral character.[2] The Class did me the honour to choose me among the Theses collectors; and for the mathematical Part. Little did I think, when you gave me those Lessons at Auteuil, which you call our suppers, that they would have been productive of this effect. It is a laborious task, and will confine my studies for the ensuing year, much more to the mathematics, than, I should have done if I had been left at my own disposal.

My Brother Tommy was admitted about ten days ago, and as there were no vacant Chambers in College, he boards at Mr: Sewall's. He may next year live with Charles, and by that means obtain a very good chamber. He is very young to be left so much to himself as all scholars are here. But his disposition is so good and his inclination for studying such, that I dare say he will behave very well. Charles is attentive to his Studies, and much esteemed both by h[is] Classmates, and by the other Students.

I write this without knowing of any opportunity to send it by. I hope soon to write to my Mamma, and Sister; but I am very much hurried yet for want of Time. And if I fail writing, I hope [they wi]ll not attribute it to neglect, or any diminution in my filial and fraternal [Senti]ments; but to the little Time that I can possibly spare. I should wish for Ferguson's Astronomy, 1 Vol 8 vo.[3] We shall begin to study it I believe in December, and shall be happy, to receive it by that Time. My Brothers and Cousin desire to be remember'd.

Your dutiful Son J. Q. Adams

RC (Adams Papers); addressed: "His Excellency John Adams Esqr: Minister Plenipotentiary, from the United States of America, to the Court of Great Britain London."; stamped: "24 NO." Some loss of text where the seal was removed and at tears in the paper.

[1] Of [3 *June*], above.

[2] JQA's class chose Moses Little as their valedictory orator on 28 August. His chief rivals were Nathaniel Freeman and John Jones Waldo (JQA, *Diary*, 2:82–84). For JQA's sketch of Little see *Diary*, 2:218.

[3] JQA's copy of James Ferguson, *Astronomy Explained upon Sir Isaac Newton's Principles, and Made Easy to Those Who Have Not Studied Mathematics*, 7th edn., London, 1785, is at MQA.

Abigail Adams Smith to John Quincy Adams

No 17.[1]

London September 1st 86

At length after long expectation your No 16[2] has arrived. Capt Cushing Called yesterday upon us, and delivered the Letters for Pappa, and amongst them I found one from yourself which was the only Letter I received except 2 from Dr Welsh.[3] I have been rather unfortunate respecting Letters, mine being so long delayd by being under Cover to Mr Storer that my friends one and all have taken up a resolution to write me no more. However, "tis an ill wind that blows nobody any good." I have not the trouble to answer their Letters. I am determined to find some Consolation. Mr Austin[4] Called upon us, a few days since he says that he Saw you at Commencement, and that you told him you had not time to write, by him. I will not Complain, because I know you will never omit an opportunity of writing with out some sufficient reason. Your Letters afford us all so much pleasure that it is a real disappointment when a ship arrives without any from you. Where is your Brothers Letters? is the question from Pappa, Mamma, my friend, and your Brother, I had rather read his than any of the rest follows—and to me my Dear Brother they are inestimable—every Letter strengthens that friendship which has subsisted ever since we have known each other and which I hope can never cease.

It gives me great pleasure to find that you Continue your attention to your Studies and that your Conduct is not marked with any of those youthfull follies, which would subject you to the observation of even the rigidly Wise. It might be Politick in you not to prejudice, the Heads of the University against you, by being satricical upon their foibles, and I could even wish for your own sake, that you could by an attention gain their esteem. But I know how Dificult it is to pay a *proper* attention to People, whom we can neither respect nor esteem the Mind revolts at the idea. I have often been impolitick myself upon this Subject, but I could never bring my Countenance or my actions, to oppose, the Sentiments which I possessd. I have allmost envyd some persons, that innocent and necessessary *art* which could conceal under the veil of politeness, the oppinions they possessd. I am inclined to beleive that it is in some implanted by the hand of Nature and that it is not to be acquired.

At least your disposition nor mine, are not of that accomodating kind, to spend much time in the Study.

But I really think that from your own account you stand a great chance to read a Syllogism at your exit from Colledge, and I dont know a Person in the World who would be more mortified at it than yourself. Therefore my advice is for you to take care, and if possible to get the blind side of the—so the saying is.

Sept 3d. sunday.

Pappa and Mamma have not yet returnd from Holland but we expect them to morrow or a Tuesday.[5] Mamma writes me word that she is not pleased with the Country, *there is such a want of her Dear Variety*. She however says that if politeness and attention could render any place agreeable She should certainly be more pleased with Holland than any Country She has yet visitted. And after She has Crossed the Channell again she shall be very glad that She has made the Excursion. She will have a fine feast of Letters on her return which will I hope give her pleasure.

I have nothing important or interesting to tell you of at Present and yet I would not appear to be less attentive to my friends, and to you in particular than formerly. I believe you never travelled, much in this Country, except upon the roads from Dover and Hardwich, to London. There are certainly some of the finest scenes, and situations which appear to be formed for the Cultivation of the Muses. We lately made a little excursion of about 20 miles, to Salt Hill and Stainss, a few miles from Windsor.[6] The Houses at which we put up, were finely situated upon the Borders of the Thames. They were beautifull by Nature, and there was very little appearance of Art. We sailed upon the river about 2 or 3 miles, and had the Prospect of some of the most rural romantick Scenes, that I ever beheld. The Gentlemen amused themselvs with fishing, and sometimes caught before ten oclock in the Morning 16 Dozen, of small Fish. Mr and Mrs Rucker Miss Ramsey Mr S. and myself were the party.

We went out on Fryday and returnd on Monday last, much pleased with our excursion at Stains. The river runs so near the House that we fishd from the Windows, the prospects arround them are perfectly romantick. Had you been with us, you might have indulged your passion for ryming. I am sure you would have been delighted with the visit—and we wishd much for a Gallant for Miss R—.

You have now, but a little time before you quit the University, at Least the time will soon fly. You are I Suppose fixed in your own mind what path to pursue, when you make your exit from thence. Mr Honestus will not frighten you from the Study you have allways appeard attachd to, I suppose. But have you formd any decissions with whom to Study. Is it not allmost time to propose the matter to your Father and to Communicate to your Sister the result of your determinations. I am greatly interested in every step which you may take, and I look forward, to that Period, when you shall have gone through the Couse of Study which is Customary to pursue and have in some degre established a Character as a Man of Business and knowledge. I have no fears respecting your Prudence, yet perhaps the most critical period has not yet arrived. But I hope from Natureall Disposition and long Habits you will be in no danger from the Dissipation of those who will allways indeavour to influence a young Mans Conduct and bring every one to their own Levell.

I fear that you do not pay attention enough to your Health. Remember if you once Loose this inestimable Good you may spend your future days in an indeavour to retreive it withing [*without*] affecting it. Exercise and some relaxation is absolutely, necessary. And tho you have no taste to see Strange sights, Yet as they may unbend the mind for a proper time from Study and, promote your Health I think it would be best to enter into some of those scence, which some embrace with avidity. However I must Commend your Taste in avoiding such unmeaning Crouded scenes as the one you mention. Where Pearsons can enjoy them they had better enter into them. I never had a taste for them myself and can easily account for your want Disposition to enjoy them.

With respect to myself it is not yet in my Power to decide my future destination whether I am to return to my own home or live in N Y—is not determined. As I have never seen that Country I dont know that I shall not like it Better than my own and my friend not haveing veiwed the Massachusetts with any prospect of Settling there can not determine, till we return to America and visit them together. I beleive it would be in my Power to determine him in favour of the Latter but I have my doubts whether it would be right. I think a Man who quits his own State for another, Should be only a Man of Leasure and pleasure, that any Business or employment shold not be thought of, for if a Gentlemans Character is ever so well esteemd by those who know him there will allways exist certain prejudices and objections in the minds of those to whom he is a Stranger, which it must take time to remove and perhaps they can never be intirely oblitered. There will exist littl jealoussies, that he may be sill more attached to the part of the Country or place which he has left than the one he now inhabits. Rather than Subject a friend to any Such inconveniences, I prefer giving up, what ever pleasure I migh derive from renewing the acquaintanc and friendships of those, with whom my earliest attachments were formd. I know that I can be happy in any part of america, and I am Sure I shall find a family of friends, in his relations. At Present I am for Living at N Y,—and then you see it would be so cleaver to return and Settle there and have you one of these Days come as a Member from the Massachusetts to Congress. We should be quite at home again. But alas this is looking too far forward, yet why shd we not indulge in, such a fancy if it can afford us Pleasure. There is a Gentleman here, Mr B, who is pleasing himself with the hope, of our going to my home.[7]

Sunday September 24th.

Since I wrote you on the first our Parents have returnd from Holland. After a terible Passage of 4 days they Landed. Such a storm has not been known a long time 2 Vessells, that were nearer the Shore than the Packet were lost and but 2 persons saved from them. Mamma, is quite Sattisfied with this excursion and never wishes to see Holland again. She has been much sattisfied at the attention and politeness she has received from those Persons who were acquainted with Pappa. Madame and Mademoisell Dumas arrived only the evening before they left the Hague, which was a great Loss, you know. Madame D. was also in great affliction for the Loss of her Daughter in Law,[8] who died a few weeks ago.

Since the return of our Friends we have been with them every day and much amused with Mammas account of Holland. I suppose she will give you an accout of her excursion.

Fletcher has arrived, but we have not yet received any Letters by him. I hope to find one.

October 12.

I hear of an opportunity for Boston on Saturday, and have taken my pen to Conclude my Letter, which has laid by so long. Altho I have not heard from you since the Month of june, I will not hesitate in writing. The day before yesterday being Tuesday the 10th, we dined at G S, in Company with, Mrs and Miss Smith from S— C—a[9] and Mr G S, who has but lately returnd from France. Mr Harrison who has been in some public Character from America to

Spain,[10] and who has arrived here with in a few days he brought Mamma a Letter from C Warren, written about a forghtnight before he died,[11] in which he express his hopes of recovering his Health, and that mentiones the attention and kindness this Mr Harrison has Shewn to him, with gratitude. I have heard that he has left an excelent Character in Spain, he appears to be near forty years old, and a sedate Man. I was prejudiced in his favour from Mr W— Letter.

He was accompanied by a Coll. Eustace[12] of whom I can only say, that he is a very handsome Man, a few marks of dissipation excepted. Mesrs Shippin Cutting and your friend Murry compleated the Company. I am sorry to say that Mr M— appears to me to have irretreavibly injured his Health by, dissipation you would Scarcely know him. He is thin, and instd of that degree of vivacity which used to animate him. There is a kind of Langour taken its place. He talks of going to America soon and I beleive nothing else will save him nor even that unless temperance and regularity are persued by him. Mr Cutting and himself made themselvs *very agreeable*. The former you know, is called Witty, and your friend is not deficient in Smartness, so that we were quite entertained with thier repartees. Mr Cutting is too sensible of his own tallents and takes too often opportunitys to discover them to be perfectly pleasing. He talks too much and to Loud. The observation General Lee made upon him was I think perfectly just—that he was the Happiest Man in the World—for he was perfecty in Love with himself and had not a rival in the World. Mr Shippin you do not know, he is Modest Sensible and agreeable, and I think appears to more advantage from being in some degree a Contrast to his Companion. They dine at G S, every Sunday.

We are going this Eve, to Covent Garden Thatre to see an old Man of Ninty years-old play the part of the Jew in the Merchant of Venice.[13] Mrs Siddons plays also this Eveng Isobela but we have engaged a Box, at Covent Garden, and so are obliged to go.

My paper scarce leaves me room to desire you to send me a lock of your Hair, by the first opportunity. Yours affectionately

A Smith

Dft (Adams Papers), written on sixteen small folded and numbered sheets.

[1] AA2 first wrote "16," perhaps because she was responding to JQA's No. 16, and then altered it to read "17." AA2's No. 16, presumably written in late August, has not been found.

[2] Of 18 May, above.

[3] Not found.

[4] Boston merchant Benjamin Austin Jr. (Samuel Adams to JA, 21 July, Adams Papers).

[5] The travelers arrived in London on Wednesday, 6 Sept. (Jefferson, *Papers*, 10:348).

[6] Salt Hill, Buckinghamshire, one mile west of Slough, was known for its views of Eton College and Windsor Castle. Staines, Middlesex, is about seven miles southeast, on the Thames (Samuel Leigh, *Leigh's New Pocket Road-Book of England, Wales, and Part of Scotland*, 2d edn., London, 1826, p. 37, 73, 74).

[7] Perhaps Charles Bulfinch of Boston, recently returned to London after a tour of the Continent, who brought with him a letter and goods from Thomas Jefferson for WSS and AA2 (vol. 6:163; Jefferson, *Papers*, 10:211, 393).

[8] Probably the wife of one of Maria Dumas' two sons by her first marriage to a Mr. Loder (Jan Willem Schulte Nordholt, *The Dutch Republic and American Independence*, Chapel Hill, N.C., and London, 1979, p. 48).

[9] Mary Rutledge Smith and, probably, her eldest daughter Sarah Rutledge Smith (vol. 6:385, 389; N. Louise Bailey, Mary L. Morgan, and Carolyn R. Taylor, eds., *Biographical Directory of the South Carolina Senate, 1776–1985*, 3 vols., 1986).

[10] Richard Harrison (1750–1841) of Maryland, a merchant at Cadiz, acted as U.S. consul at that port, 1780–1786, but was never formally appointed by Congress. He later served as first auditor of the U.S. Treasury, 1791–1836 (Smith, *Letters of Delegates*, 4:130).

[11] Not found.

[12] John Skey Eustace (1760–1805) of New York, William and Mary 1776, served as aide to Gens. Charles Lee, John Sullivan, and George Washington during the Revolution. After the war, he spent time in Venezuela, Spain, England, and France, where he served in the French Revolutionary Army. He was possibly in Spain in 1786 to register a complaint regarding his treatment by colonial officials while previously in Venezuela (*Appletons' Cyclo. Amer. Biog.*; John Skey Eustace, *Official and Private Correspondence of Major-General J.S. Eustace*, Paris, 1796; *The Papers of George Washington, Presidential Series*, ed. W. W. Abbott et al., 9 vols., Charlottesville, Va., 1983–1985, 3:67).

[13] Charles Macklin (1697?–1797), an Irish actor, was particularly known for his portrayal of Shylock (*London Stage, 1776–1800*, 2:926; *DNB*).

Abigail Adams to Mary Smith Cranch

My Dear Sister — London Sepbr 12th 1786

I am again safe arrived in this city after an absence of five weeks. By the last vessels I wrote Some of my Friends that I was going to visit Holland. That I had a desire to see that Country you will not wonder at, as one of those Theatres upon which my Partner and fellow traveller had exhibited some of his most important actions, and renderd to his country lasting Blessing. It has been the policy of some of our Allies, to keep as much as possible those events out of Sight and of some of our Countrymen to lessen their value in the Eyes of mankind. I have seen two Histories of the American War written in French, and one lately publishd in English by a mr Andrews.[1] In one of them no notice is taken, or mention made of our Alliance with Holland, and the two others mention it, as slightly as possible, and our own Countrymen set them the example. France be sure was the first to acknowledge our independance, and to aid us with Men and money, and ought always to be first-rank'd amongst our Friends. But Holland surely ought not to be totally neglected.

From whence have we drawn our supplies for this five years past, even to pay to France the interest upon her loan, and where else could we now look in case of a pressing emergincy? Yet have I observed in Sermons upon publick occasions in orations &c France is always mentiond with great esteem. Holland totally neglected. This is neither policy or justice. I have been led to a more particular reflection upon this subject from my late visit to that Country. The respect, attention civility and politeness which we received from that people, where ever we went, was a striking proof not only of their personal esteem, but of the Ideas they entertain with respect to the Revolution which gave birth to their connection with us, and laid as they say, the foundation for their Restoration to priviledges which had been wrested from them and which they are now exerting themselves to recover. The Spirit of Liberty appears, to be all alive in them, but whether they will be able to accomplish their views, without a scene of Blood and carnage, is very doubtfull.

As to the Country, I do not wonder that Swift gave it the name of Nick Frog,[2] tho I do not carry the Idea so far as some, who insist that the people resemble the frog in the shape of their faces and form of their Bodies. They appear to be a well fed, well Cloathed contented happy people, very few objects of wretchedness present themselves to your view, even amidst the immence Concourse of people in the city of Amsterdam. They have many publick institutions which do honour to Humanity and to the particular directors of them. The Money allotted to benevolent purposes, is applied Solely to the benifit of the Charities, instead of being wasted and expended in publick dinners to the Gaurdians of them which is said to be the case too much in this Country. The civil government or police of that Country must be well Regulated, since rapine Murder nor Robery are but very seldom found amongst them.

The exchange of Amsterdam is a great curiosity, as such they carried me to see it. I was with mr van Staphorst, and tho the croud of people was immence, I met with no difficulty in passing through, every person opening a passage for me. The exchange is a large Square surrounded with piazza. Here from 12 till two oclock, all and every person who has buisness of any kind to transact meet here, sure of finding the person he wants, and it is not unusal to see ten thousand persons collected at once. I was in a Chamber above the exchange, the Buz from below was like the Swarming of Bees.[3]

The most important places which I visited were Roterdam, Delpt the Hague Leyden Harlem Amsterdam and utrech. I was through many other villages and Towns, the Names I do not recollect. I was 8 days at the Hague and visited every village round it, amongst which is Seaven, a place famous for the Embarkation of king Charles. From Utrech I visited Zest, a small Town belonging wholy to the Moravians, who mantain the same doctrines with the Moravians at Bethelem in Pensilvana, but which are not the best calculated for fulling the great command of replenishing the earth.[4] I visited Gouda and saw the most celebrated paintings upon Glass which are to be found. These were immence window reaching from the Top to the bottom of a very high Church and containd Scripture History. Neither the faces or attitudes, had any thing striking, but the coulours which had stood for near two hundred years were beautiful beyond imagination.[5] From Amsterdam we made a party one day to Sardam a few hours Sail only, it was their anual Fair, and I had an opportunity of seeing the people in their Holly day Suits. This place is famous for being the abode of the Czar Peter whose ship Carpenter shop they Still Shew. At every place of Note, I visited the Cabinets of paintings Natural History and all the publick buildings of distinction, as well as the Seats of several private gentlemen, and the Princ of oranges House at the Hague where he holds his Court during the Summer Months, but the difference which subsists between him and the States, occasiond his retreat to Loo,[6] concequently I had no opportunity of being presented to that Court. We were invited to dine one Day at Sir James Harris's the British Minister at that Court, who appears a very sensible agreeable Man. Lady Harris who is about 24 years old may be ranked with the first of English Beauties. She was married at seventeen and has four fine Children, but tho very pretty, her Ladyship has no dignity in her manners or solidity in her deportment. She rather Seems of the good humourd gigling class, a mere trifler, at least I saw nothing to the contrary. I supped at the Marquiss de Verac the French Ambassadors with about 50 gentlemen and Ladies. His own Lady is dead, he has a Daughter in Law who usually lives with him, but was now absent in France. Upon the whole I was much gratified with my excursion to a Country which cannot Shew its like again. The whole appearence of it is that of a Medow, what are calld the dykes, are the roads which being raised, Seperate the canals, upon these you ride, through Rows of Willow Trees upon each side, not a Hill to bee seen. It is all a continued plain, so that Trees medows and canals, Canals trees and medows are the unvaried Scene. The Houses are all Brick and their streets are paved with Brick. It is very unusual to see a Single Square of glass broken; or a brick out of place even in the meanest House. They paint every peice of wood within, and without their houses, and what I thought not so wholsome, their milk pails are painted within and without, and So are their Horse carts, but it is upon a principal of economy. The Country is exceeding fruitfull and every house has a Garden Spot, plentifully stored with vegetables. The dress of all the Country people is precisely the same that it was two Hundred years ago, and has been handed down from generation to Generation unimpaird. You recollect the Short peticoats and long short Gowns, round [ear'd?] caps[7] with Strait borders and large Straw Hats which the german woman wore when they first Setled at Germantown. Such is now the dress of all the lower class of people who do not even attempt to imitate the Gentry. I was pleas'd with the trig neatness of the women, many of them wear black tammy Aprons, thick quilted coats or russel[8] Skirts, and Small hoops, but only figure to yourself a child of 3 or four drest in the Same way. They cut a figure I assure you. Gold earrings are universally worn by them and Bracelets upon Holly days. The dress of the Men is full as old fashiond, but the Court and Geenteel people dress part English and part French. They generally Speak both the languages, but French most. Since their intercourse with America, the English Language is considerd as an essential part of education. I would not omit to mention that I visited the Church at Leyden in which our forefathers worshipd when they fled from hierarchical tyranny and percecution.[9] I felt a respect and veneration upon entering the Doors, like what the ancients paid to their Druids.

Upon my return home I found that Captain Cushing had arrived in my absence, and a noble packet was handed me by your Neice soon after I arrived, but as we had not seen each other for 5 weeks, we had much to say. And in addition to that I had not closed my Eyes for two days and nights, having had a Stormy Boisterous passage of 3 days attended with no small danger, and as I had rode seventy five miles that day, they all voted against my opening my Letters that Night. Mortifying as it was I submitted, being almost light headed with want of rest, and fatigue. But I rose early the Next morning, and read them all before Breakfast. And here let me thank my dear sister for the entertainment hers afforded me, but like most of the Scenes of Life, the pleasure was mixed with pain. The account of the Death of our Dear and Worthy Aunt, reach'd me in a Letter from Cousin W. Smith[10] the week before I went my journey.

9. THE AMSTERDAM EXCHANGE, BY HERMANUS PETRUS SCHOUTEN, 1783

See page xv

Altho I took a final leave of her when I quitted America, yet I have been willing to flatter myself with the hope that I might be mistaken, and that her Life would be prolonged beyond my expectations. How often has her Image appeard to me in the Same Form that she addrest me when I left her House. You know how susceptable her Heart was to every tender impression. She saw how much I was distresst, and strove herself for a magninimity that gave to her whole appearence a placid Solemnity which spoke more forcibly than words. There was a Something undecribable, but which to me seemd Angelick in her whole manner and appearence that most powerfully impressd my mind; and I could not refrain when I arrived here mentioning it, to mr Smith who I dare say will recollect it. Like the Angle she then appeard, she now really is, fitted by a Life of piety and benevolence to join her kindred Spirits, she has left us her example and the Memory of her Many virtues to Comfort our afflicted Hearts—Beloved, Regreated and Lamented! She was like a Parent to me, and my full Heart has paid the tributary Tears to her Memory.

Cut of in early Life, and under circumstances peculiarly distressing is the young Branch of a family who never before experienced an affliction of this kind. The Tree fell whilst the Branch survived to keep alive the source from whence their Sorrows Spring.[11] When you see the family, remember me affectionately to them. My Heart feels for all their sorrows. Nor am I without a Share of Sympathy for the family distresses of a Gentleman who not withstanding his follies I cannot but feel for. I know there is in his disposition a strange mixture, there is benevolence and kindness without judgment, good Sense without prudence and learning without conduct. Early in Life that man might have been moulded into a valuable vessel, in the hands of a steady and Skilfull Master. Let all remembrance of his connection with this family cease, by a total Silence upon the Subject. I would not, add to his mortification, or be the means of giving him a moments further pain. My Friends will do me a kindness by stricktly adhering to this request. I wish him well and happy.

Adieu my dear Sister I Shall write you soon, more fully upon the subjects of your Letters. Remember me affectionately to my dear and aged Parent for whom I have purchased a tabinet. It is more costly than a silk, but I thought more suteable for her years. I shall send it by the first opportunity. Should any offer sooner than Cushing I shall forward this Letter.

I know not to whom we are indebted for the Chocolate, by captain cushings prudence in taking it out and getting it on shore a few pounds at a time we Saved it, tho he poor Man has had his vessel seizd and been put to much difficulty and trouble. The Chocolate came very opportunely. Mr Adams was just mourning over his last pound. You see I have only room to add Yours AA

RC (MWA:Abigail Adams Corr.). Printed in AA, *Letters*, ed. CFA, 1840, p. 343–350.

[1] John Andrews, *History of the War with America, France, Spain, and Holland, Commencing in 1775 and Ending in 1783*, 4 vols., London, 1785–1786.

[2] John Arbuthnot personified the country of Holland as Nicholas Frog in his pamphlet *Law Is a Bottomless Pit; or, the History of John Bull*, London, 1712. The work also has been attributed to Jonathan Swift.

[3] The Amsterdam Exchange, or Bourse, had become increasingly overcrowded by the late eighteenth century, to the point that scuffles occasionally occurred as traders fought for space, and many transactions had to take place at nearby cafes (Joost Jonker, *Merchants, Bankers, Middlemen: The Amsterdam Money Market during the First Half of the 19th Century*, Amsterdam, 1996, p. 37, 145–147). See also the Descriptive List of Illustrations, No. 9, above.

[4] For JA's comments on the Moravian community at Bethlehem, Penna., including the arranged marriages of its members, see vol. 2:154–156.

[5] The sixteenth-century stained-glass windows of the Sint Janskerk (Church of St. John) were created by Wouter and Dirk Crabeth and their pupils (*Nagel's Holland Travel Guide*, Paris, 1951, p. 224).

[6] Although the stadholder was required to be in residence wherever the States General and the Council of State met, William V had withdrawn to the palace of Het Loo in Apeldoorn during his power struggle with the governing bodies of the United Provinces (Herbert H. Rowen, *The Princes of Orange: The Stadholders in the Dutch Republic*, Cambridge, 1988, p. 221–223).

[7] AA, *Letters*, ed. CFA, 1840, reads "long short-gowns, round-eared caps."

[8] "Russet" in AA, *Letters*, ed. CFA, 1840.

[9] AA undoubtedly visited the Pieterskerk (Church of St. Peter's). For the long-standing confusion over where the English Separatists, or Pilgrim Fathers, worshiped while in Leyden, see vol. 4:40–41, note 3.

[10] Of 28 June, not found.

[11] A reference to the death of Lucy Thaxter Cushing in childbirth.

Charles Storer to Abigail Adams

Dear Madam Boston. 12th. September. 1786

So I see by the papers that Amelia has become *Mrs: Smith*, and this the 12th. of June. The news came by the way of Philadelphia, and the first intelligence I had was from our News-Papers.[1] By Callahan, who is expected here every day from London, I hope it will be announced to us officially. Joy to her and to you all! May it be attended with every blessing and pleasure the sanguine wish can paint. When you write, please to give me the particulars, and where she lives; that I may go and see her. I can find her out in almost any part of London or Westminster, the Burrough or St: George's fields.

In my last I find I was a little too hasty in a peice of intelligence I forwarded to you, in regard to a certain discarded Gentleman. From the same authority that I received the former information, I have since received the contrary; agreable to the Communication you made to me in your last. I congratulate both you and Amelia on the occasion.

In a day or two I shall leave this place for my new settlement, where from many Circumstances I am anxious to get myself established. Though few join me in my expectations, yet I promise myself much satisfaction and happiness. If viewed in any point of light I think I shall change my situation for the better. On the score of tranquillity, peace[2] and independance, I gain infinitely more at Passamaquoddy than here. On the idea of Agriculture, I am persuaded that he who tills an Acre of ground at this time does more real service to the Commonwealth, than he who imports a thousand Pounds worth of Gewgaws. And as to the quitting Society, in truth what do I lose? The sight of many a fine and showy outside, where I am sure is contained the cruellest heartacke and distraction. Therefore I only part with folly and extravagance, and tell me shall I be a loser, go where I will? Many times has the Question been put to me, what will you do down in that wilderness without society, you, that have passed thro' so many gayer scenes? In good truth Madam, and this is the answer I constantly make, when a person has a good object in view, and is persuaded that he is pursuing the line of his duty, I think he may be happy anywhere—be it in the City or in the wilderness. Do you approve the Sentiment, Madam? I feel as if you did.

I am happy to inform you that your family enjoy their usual health, and also all our other friends. To Mr: Adams I refer you for public news, to whom I shall write on the subject.[3] I could wish to talk with him; for such news have we at present as is most alarming. Heaven defend us from Anarchy and Confusion!!

Mr: Martin, who will deliver you this is a Kinsman of our family. He is fm Portsmo. We esteem him a worthy man, and as such I beg your notice of him, which will equally gratify him and oblige Yr: assured friend & humle: servt: Chas: Storer

RC (Adams Papers); addressed: "Mrs: A. Adams Grosvenor-Square. London. Pr. favr: of *Thos: Martin Esqr.*"; endorsed: "Charles Storer Sepbr 12 1786."

[1] AA2's marriage to WSS was announced in the *Boston Gazette*, 4 Sept., but had previously been reported in the *Pennsylvania Packet*, 23 Aug., and several other Philadelphia newspapers.

[2] In the margin, keyed to an "x" at this point in the MS, is the sentence: "You little suspect the Govr: has given me a Commissn: for the Peace—but so it is."

[3] Storer wrote to JA on 16 and 26 Sept. (both Adams Papers). His letter of 16 Sept. contains an urgent appeal to JA to return to Massachusetts to help quell the "anarchy and confusion" spread by "Mobs, Riots and armed associations" disrupting the Commonwealth.

Mary Smith Cranch to Abigail Adams

My dear sister Braintree September 24th 1786

In my last I told you I suppos'd your Son Thomas would enter college at the end of the vacancy. He did so, and enter'd with honour. He could not have a chamber in college this year, but he has a very good one at mr Sewalls, and boards with the Family. It is not so well as boarding in college, but it was the best thing we could do. We have furnish'd his chamber with Cousin Charles Furniture. It was no easy thing to get him—(Cousin Tom) into a place we lik'd. One ask'd too much and another had Boarders we did not like he should be connected with—and others were full already. The Doctor and I spent two days in Cambridge before we could get a place to our minds. I went with Betsy last week to see mrs Fuller, and Coll Hull and Lady, and I return'd through Cambridge, our sons were well. Cousin JQA had been unwell, a bad Swiming in his head attended With a sick stomack occation'd I believe by want of exercise and too close application to his studies. His cousin and Brothers complain that they cannot get him out. I talk'd to him of the necessaty of walking and some relaxation. I Shall see him again this week and shall give him a puke if he has a return of it. Judge Fuller and Lady were well. Mrs Fuller desir'd me to tell you that she sent her most affectionate regards to you and hop'd to see you again in your own country. She was with her Daughter who is in a poor State of health her lungs are dissorder'd. She has three children two Daughters and a son, but the poor little Fellow was very sick. He is a Beautiful Boy about six months old. The colln. has a fine countinance and is a fine Figure. They appear to be very happy. She has an excellent temper and inherites her mamas benevolence. They live near Watertown Bridge, have a very hansome house, and tis very well furnish'd. She is much improv'd by her camp life. Coll. Hull is acquainted with Coll Smith and told me more about him than any body I have seen. He was brought up with Coll Humphries and expects him in a few days upon a visit and has promis'd to bring him to see us.[1]

As I was siting in my chamber the other day mr wibird came into the House, in a few minutes I heard him tell Betsy that Her Cousin Nabby was married, that oaks Angier was dead, and that mrs P–l–r was brought to Bed. I Was rejoic'd at the first, felt solemn at the Second, and was astonish'd at the last peice of news. Accept my congratulations my dear sister. I hope the dear girl will be happy, but I cannot bear the Idea of your leaving her in Europe. I have not yet been call'd to part with any of my children, but I think it must be very hard to do it. I am impatient to recieve Letters from you. If the disunited State of america will forward your return, you will be here soon. We are all in confusion and what will be the conseiquence I know not. Anarchy I fear. The excess of Liberty which the constituton gave the People has ruin'd them. There is not the least energy in goverment. You will see by the Publick Prints in what manner the Mob have stop'd the courts, and open'd Jails and what their list of grievences are. There must be more Power Some where or we are ruin'd, but how to acquire it is the question.

The People will not pay their Tax, nor their debts of any kind, and who shall make them? These things affect us most severly. Mr Cranch has been labouring for the Publick for three or four years without receiving Scarcly any pay. The Treasury has been So empty that he could not get it, and now my Sister there is not a penay in it. The Publick owe us three Hundred pound and we cannot get a Shilling of it, and if the People will not pay their Tax how Shall we ever get it. An attendenc upon the court of common pleas was the only thing that has produc'd any cash for above two year:[2] part of this always went to pay Billys quarter Bills. If we had not liv'd with great caution we must have been in debt, a thing I dread more than the most extream Poverty. Mr Cranch is very dull, says he must come home and go to watch mending and Farming and leave the publick business to be transacted by those who can afford to do it without pay. What will be the end of these things I am not Polititian enough to say, they have a most gloomy appearence.

I believe I told you in a former Letter that mr Angier was in a consumtion. He did not Suppose himself dangirious till three days before he dy'd.[3] He then Sent for mr Reed his minister and wish'd to have his children Baptis'd, but did not live to have it done. This is all I have heard about him.

We live in an age of discovery. One of our acquaintance has discover'd that a full grown, fine child may be produc'd in less than five months as well as in nine, provided the mother should meet with a small fright a few hours before its Birth. You may laugh: but it is true. The Ladys Husband is so well satisfied of it that he does not seem to have the least suspicion of its being otherways, but how can it be? for he left this part of the country the beginning of september last, and did not return till the Sixth of April, and his wife brought him this fine Girl the first day of the present Month.[4] Now the only difficulty Seems to be, whether it is the product of a year, or twenty weeks. She affirms it is the Latter, but the learned in the obstretick Art Say that it is not possible. The child is perfect large and Strong. I have seen it my sister: it was better than a week old tis true, but a finer Baby I never Saw. It was the largest she ever had her Mother says. I thought So myself, but I could not say it. It was a matter of So much Speculatin that I was determin'd to see it. I went with trembling Steps, and could not tell whether I should have courage enough to see it till I had Knock'd at the Door. I was ask'd to walk up, by, and was follow'd by her Husband. The Lady was seting by the side of the Bed suckling her Infant and not far from her —— with one sliper off, and one foot just step'd into the other. I had not seen him since last May. He look'd, I cannot tell you how. He did not rise from his seat, prehaps he could not. I spoke to him and he answer'd me, but hobble'd off as quick as he could without saying any thing more to me. There appear'd the most perfect harmony between all three. She was making a cap and observ'd that She had nothing ready to put her child in as she did not expect to want them so Soon. I made no reply—I could not. I make no remarks. Your own mind will furnish you with sufficient matter for Sorrow and joy, and many other sensations, or I am mistaken.

Adieu yours affectionately

RC (Adams Papers); endorsed: "Mrs Cranch Sepbr 24 1786."

[1] The Cranches visited the home of Col. William and Sarah Fuller Hull in Newton on 20–21 September. Col. Hull, a native of Derby, Conn., graduated from Yale in 1772 and served with distinction in the 8th and 3d Massachusetts and Jackson's Continental Regiments, among others, during the Revolution. After the war he practiced law in Newton. Hull later served as governor of the Michigan Territory (1805–1812) until he was appointed brigadier-general in command of the Northwestern Army. Hull surrendered his army and the post of Detroit to the British in Aug. 1812, resulting in his court martial for treason, cowardice, and neglect of duty. President Madison remanded the execution of the death sentence and Hull retired to Newton.

The Hulls' three children were all under the age of four: Sarah (b. 1783), Elizabeth (b. 1784), and Abraham Fuller (b. March 1786). Mrs. Hull was the daughter of Hon. Abraham and Sarah Dyer Fuller of Newton. Her father represented Newton in the General Court; her mother was a native of Weymouth (MHi:Jacob Norton Papers, Elizabeth Cranch Norton Diary, 20–21 Sept.; Heitman, *Register Continental Army*; *DAB*; *Catalogue of the Officers and Graduates of Yale University in New Haven, Connecticut, 1701–1898*, New Haven, 1898; *Vital Records of Newton, Massachusetts, to the Year 1850*, Boston, 1905, p. 313, 104, 74, 284; Priscilla R. Ritter, *Newton, Massachusetts, 1679–1779: A Biographical Directory*, Boston, 1982).

[2] By serving as a judge on Suffolk County's Court of Common Pleas, Richard Cranch earned small fees for each case heard.

[3] For Oakes Angier of West Bridgewater, JA's former law clerk (ca. 1766–1768), see vol. 1:84. Angier died on 1 Sept. (JA, *Legal Papers*, 1:xcvi; *Sibley's Harvard Graduates*, 16:7).

[4] Elizabeth Hunt Palmer, who was married to Joseph Pearse Palmer, gave birth to a daughter, Sophia, on 2 Sept., allegedly fathered by Royall Tyler. In 1794 Tyler married Sophia's half-sister Mary, the Palmer's eldest daughter, and about 1798, Sophia went to live with the Tylers in Vermont. Sophia's paternity was never openly acknowledged by either the Palmers or Tylers, but it was known to later generations of the Cranch and Palmer families (*Grandmother Tyler's Book*, p. 47, 268–269, 283–284, 287–288, 291, 296–297; MHi:Caroline Wells Healey Dall Papers, Diary, 7 Oct. 1842; Bruce Ronda, *Elizabeth Palmer Peabody: A Reformer on Her Own Terms*, Cambridge, 1999, p. 17–29).

Abigail Adams to John Quincy Adams

My Dear son London Sepbr 27. 1786

Since I wrote you last I have made two excursions one to Holland, and one of a Week to the Hyde the seat of mr Brand Hollis. Here I was both entertaind and delighted. In the first place I must describe mr Hollis to you. He is a Neat, nice Batchelor of about 50 years old a learned Sensible Antiquarian. The late mr Hollis whose Name he bears could not have chosen a better Representitive to have bestowed his Mantle upon, for with it, has descended that Same Love of Liberty, Benevolence and phylanthropy which distinguishd his Worthy Benefactor.[1] At the entrance of the Hall you discover the prevaling taste. There are a Number of Ancient Busts, amongst which is one of Marcus Aurelias who is a great favorite of mr Hollis's. He told us that all the great Painters who had drawn Jesus Christ, had taken the Busts of Marcus Aurelias as a modle. There is a fine white Marble Bust of the late mr Hollis in this collection. This Hall is large and Spacious and has been added to the House by mr Brand Hollis since the Death of his Father,[2] who left it to him. The Chamber where we lodged was hung round with portraits of his family. It is at one end of the House, and from two windows in front and one at the end, we had a Beautifull view of Lawns and glades, clumps of Trees and stately Groves, and a peice of Water full of fish. The borders of the walks in the pleasure grounds, are full of rare Shrubs and trees, to which America has contributed her full proportion. To give you Some Idea of the Singularity in which this good man discovers his taste, near the walk from his door to the road, he has a large and beautifull Furr, which he calls Dr Jebb. Having pailed this Tree in with a neat ornament, he has consecrated it to the memory of that excellent Man, with whom I had only the pleasure of a short acquaintance before he was call'd to the Regions of immortality. He possess'd an excellnt understanding an unshaken integrity, and a universal benevolence and was one of the few firm and steady Friends to America. Cut of in middle age, he left a companion endowed with an understanding Superiour to most of her Sex, always in delicate Health but now a prey to the most peircing Grief which will shortly close the Scene with her.[3] They had no chil dren and being wholy a domestick woman, the pleasures of the world have no realish for her. Her Friends have at length prevaild with her to go into the Country for a few weeks.

But to return to mr Hollis's curiosities in his Garden he has a tall Cypress which he calls General Washington, and an other by its side which he has named for col Smith, as his aid du Camp. This Gentleman possesses a taste for all the fine Arts. In architecture Palladio is his oracle, amongst his paintings, are several of the first masters, over his Chimny in his cabinet are four small Portraits which he told me were his Hero his General his Phylosopher and his writer. Marcus Aurelias was his General, His Hero—pardon me I have forgotton him, Plato was his writer, and Hutchinson his Phylosopher, who was also his preceptor.[4] Mr Hollis speaks of him with great veneration and affection. In the dinning room is a Luxurient picture for a Batchelor, a venus and adonis by Rembrant, and two views of a Modern date; of the estate in dorsetshire which the late mr Hollis gave him. As there is only a Farm House upon it he never resides there. There are three pastures belonging to it, which are call'd Hollis, Mede, and Brand. In Hollis Pasture are the remains of its late owner, who left it as an order which was faithfully execcuted, to be buried there and ten feet deep, the ground to be ploughd up over his Grave that not a Monument, or stone should tell where he lay. This was whimsical and Singular be sure; but Singularity was his Characteristick, as many of his Works shew.

Between mr Hollis's drawing room and his Library is a small cabinet, which he calls the Boudoir which is full of curiosities, amongst them a dagger made of the Sword which kill'd Sir Edmundburry Godfrey and an inscription—Memento Godfrey, proto Martyr, pro Religione protestantium.[5] In every part of the House you see mr Holliss owl Cap of Liberty and dagger. In this cabinet is a Silver cup with a cover in the Shape of an owl with two rubies for Eyes. This peice of Antiquity was dug up at Canterbury from ten feet depth; and is considerd as a Monkish conceit. Amongst the curiosities in this room is a collection of Duodcimo prints to the Number of 45 of all the orders of Nuns, which mr Bridgen purchased Some Years ago in the Austerion Netherlands and presented to mr Hollis. Mr Bridgen has lately Composed some verses which are placed by the Side of them. The Idea is that banish'd from Germany by the Emperor, they have taken an assylum at the Hyde, in Sight of the Druids, the Portico of Athens, and the venerable remains of Egyptian Greek and Roman Antiquities.[6] I would not omit the mention of a curious Medallion on which is wrought a Feast of all the Heathen Gods and Goddesses Sitting round a table. Jupiter throws down upon the middle of it, one of his thunder bolts flaming at each end with Lightning. He lights his own pipe at it, and all the rest follow his example venus Minerva and diana are whiffing away. This is the first time I ever conceived tobaco an ingredient in the Feast of the Celestials. It must have been the invention of Some dutch Man. As select and highly honourd Friends we were admitted into the Library, and to a view of the Miltonian Cabinet. In this he has the original edition of Miltons works; and every other to the present day. His Library his pictures Busts Medals coins, Greek Roman Carthaginian and Egyptian, are really a selection, as well as a collection, of most rare and valuable curiosities. In the early part of his Life, he visited Rome Itally, and many other Countries. His fortune is easy, and as he has lived a Batchelor his time is occupied wholy by the Sciences. He has a Maiden sister of 45 I should judge; who lives with him when he is in the Country. They each of them own a House in Town and live seperatt during the Winter. Miss Brand is curious in China, and in Birds. She has a peice of all the different manufacters of porcelane made in this kingdom, either a cup or bowl a Mug or a Jar. She has also a variety of Singing Birds. But what I esteem her much more for, is that she has taken from the Streets half a dozen poor children cloathed them and put them to school. This is doing good not only to the present but, future generations. Tis really curious to See how the taste of the Master, has pervaded all the family. John the Coachman, has a small garden spot which he invited me to see. Here were a collection of curious flowers and a little grotto filld with fosils and shells. The Gardner whose House stands within a few rods of the Mansion House, is Bee Mad. He has a Great number of Glass Hives in which you may see the Bees at work, and he shew me the Queens cell. He handles the bees as one would flies, they never sting him. He insists that they know him, and will, with great fluency read you a lecture of an Hour upon their Laws and Government. He has an invention of excluding the drones who are larger Bees than the rest, and when once out of the Hive they cannot return.[7]

It would require a whole volm to enumerate to you all that was Worthy attention, and had you been one of the visitors I dare say you would collected a larger stock of improvement, and been much more minute than I have been in my account of curiosities, but I could not remember amidst Such a variety. I inclose you a drawing of the House[8] which mr Hollis gave me.

My visit to Holland was agreeable but to your Aunt Cranch I must refer you for particulars. Madam Dumar and Miss were absent upon her estate untill the evening before I came away. I call'd to pay them a visit, and had a very cordial reception; Mr dumas speaks of you with great affection, as well as Madam, and Miss Dumas look'd kind. The Marquis de Verac, inquired after you with great politeness; said you was interpretor for him and mr Dana, when you was at Petersburgh, and that if I was drest in your Cloaths, he should have taken me for you. Years excepted, he should have added, but that was a Mental reservation. He is Ambassador at the Hague.

October 2d. 1786

Captain Fletcher is arrived since I began this letter, and by the last Letters from my Friends I find that they had concluded upon your Brother Tommy's examination. If he is fit, I am not sorry that he has enterd. We might find it more difficult to carry you all through colledge if your Pappa was totally out of employ. How soon that may be I know not. Whatever additional expence we have been at here, has never been considerd, nor will be whilst so many demands are pressing from all quarters upon Congress. Neither Your Father or I wish to have you or your Brothers pinched in any reasonable expenditure. Your Friends Speak of you both as prudent and circumspect. Such I hope you will continue. I will send you from hence any article you want within my power, when ever you let me know what it is. Books have been heitherto your only object, and all have been Sent that you requested. Your sister will write you by Captain Cushing who will Sail this Month. I heard of the present opportunity but a day or two ago, and I have no other letters ready. I have been Sick ever since I returnd from Holland with the fall Disorder, hope I have got the better of it now as the Fever has left me.

Remember me affectionately to Your Brothers, and to all other Friends and believe me most tenderly your ever affectionate Mother

AA

October 14.

Inclosed you will find a medal of his present Majesty,[9] as you have no great affection for him you may exchange it for any property you like better.

RC (Adams Papers); endorsed: "Mrs: Adams. Septr: 27. 1786"; docketed: "My Mother. 27. Septr: 1786."

[1] Thomas Hollis (1720–1774), antiquary, editor of seventeenth-century republican and Commonwealth political works, and benefactor of Harvard College, was a year younger than his friend and heir, Thomas Brand (1719–1804), who took the name Hollis upon Hollis' death (*DNB*).

[2] Timothy Brand (d. 1735), a London mercer, bought the Hyde in 1718 (Caroline Robbins, "Thomas Brand Hollis (1719–1804), English Admirer of Franklin and Intimate of John Adams," Amer. Phil. Soc., *Procs.*, 97 [1953]:239–247; Namier and Brooke, *House of Commons*, 2:113).

[3] For Ann Torkington Jebb (1735–1812), see vol. 6:222.

[4] Francis Hutcheson (1694–1746), professor of moral philosophy at Glasgow University, where Brand Hollis studied in the late 1730s (*DNB*; Robbins, "Thomas Brand Hollis," Amer. Phil. Soc., *Procs.*, 97 [1953]: 240; Namier and Brooke, *House of Commons*, 2:113).

[5] Sir Edmund Berry Godfrey (1621–1678), justice of the peace for Westminster, is remembered as a Protestant martyr. Godfrey took the depositions alleging the Popish Plot of 1678 and presented them to the privy council. Soon thereafter he was murdered. Roman Catholics were immediately suspected, and two were convicted and executed, based on testimony that later proved to be false (*DNB*).

[6] A broadside of Edward Bridgen's verses, "On sending some Pictures of Nuns and Fryers to Thomas Brand Hollis, Esq. at the Hyde in Essex, supposed to be Real Personages turned out of the Convents and Monasteries in Flanders by the Emperor," without author's name, imprint, or date, is in the Adams Papers, filmed under the assigned date of ante 27 Sept. 1786.

[7] JA, *D&A*, 3:197–198, explains the gardener's invention in some detail.

[8] Not found. Several views of the house and grounds appear in John Disney, *Memoirs of Thomas Brand-Hollis, Esq.*, London, 1808.

[9] Not found. This was possibly a medal struck in 1785 by L. Pingo in recogntion of American independence, which showed a silhouette of George III on one side and a representation of Liberty on the other. Historians have speculated that this medal may have been issued to mark the first meeting between JA and George III on 1 June 1785 (Laurence Brown, *A Catalogue of British Historical Medals, 1760–1960*, 3 vols., London, 1980, 1:63).

Mary Smith Cranch to Abigail Adams

My dear Sister Braintree Sep 28th 1786

In the begining of this month I made a visit to Haverhill found them all well. Mr Duncan married to a maiden Lady about sixty years old a sister of Judge Greenliefs of Newburry port. We made the Weding Visit. It is the easiest thing in the world for Some people to Bury wives and get new ones. If you hear of any of your acquaintance losing a wife you may expect in the next letter, at least to hear that they are looking out for another. Our good uncle Tufts—but hush—he is not yet fix'd—a sure sign that they think the mariage State the happiest. In my next I expect to tell you something of uncle Smith. He and Cousin Betsy went with us to haverhill. We return'd through Newbury and Salem. Dolly Tufts is soon to be married to a mr oddion of Marvelhead,[1] but the most extraordinary of all is that miss Nabby Bishop is certainly soon to be married to Doctor Putman of Danvers. He liv'd with his uncle at Salem when we liv'd there.[2] He is a Bachelor of about forty has a fine estate, and is a Man of Sense—in some things. "Keeps a *matter* of twenty head of cattle milk tweilve Cows, chirns thirtty pound of Butter a week, but *you see* I shall have nothing to do with the Dairy *as it were*. The Doctor has an old woman to take the care of that. I shall be married directly, and if I do not like to live in the country, the Doctor says *as how* he has interest money enough to maintain us in the *most genteelist* manner in town."—These are the things which I am to suppose have captivated her. She brought him to see us last week, not a word did I hear of his Person or his abilities. She talk'd of those things only, of which she could judge. He is a comely man, and has a good understanding I assure you, is very affable and very Polite, but why, oh! why? when a man has so hansome an Estate will he be so solicitus to add acre to acre, rather than seek for a wife who opens her mouth with Wisdom and in whose heart is the law of kindness?[3] For her mothers sake I rejoice.

There was last Teusday a Publick Exibition at Cambridge.[4] JQA and W— C figur'd a way in a Forensick disputation. The Question was "whither inequality among the citizens is necessary for the preservation of the Liberty of the whole." JQA afirm'd that it was and gave his reasons. W— C deny'd it and gave his. Your son reply'd and ours clos'd it. They did not either of them, speak loud enough, otherways they perform'd well. There composition was good. There was also a Latin oration and an English one a Dialogue, a Syllogistick-disputation and a piece of Greek and Hebrew Spoken by two young Gentlemen. It was almost, equal to the performances of a commencment day. There were near four hundred persons Gentlemen and Ladies, present. Betsy and I were there, but We felt too much for our young Friends to be there again when any of them are to bear a part. Your Sons were well Cousin JQA has quite got well of his dissorder. Lucy is still at Haverhill. I made mrs Allen a visit when I was there. She looks very well and very happy, has a fine number of good looking Cheeses upon her Shelves and lives well and is much lik'd in the Parish.

Uncle Quincy has not yet been off his Farm. I do not now expect he will this winter. It is a Strange whim, he can walk about upon it as well as ever he could, his hip has never been intirely well, but it would be better if he would ride. Quincy Thaxter and Nancy are married.[5]

Your Brother Adams and mother Hall spent this afternoon with me in company, with mrs Thayer Deacon Adams wife and Daughter and mr Adams eldest Daughter of Luningbourge.[6] She is a very pretty Girl, comily and polish'd, and has a very sprightly Sensible countenance.

We desir'd captain Cushing to take a Dozen of chocolatt for you, but he Said he could not. I have heard from mr William White in Whose imploy he goes that he order'd the capt: to present mr Adams with part of a Box in his name. So that I hope you have not wanted it.

My Health is much better than it was, but I am very thin riding is of great Service to me.

Doctor Simon Tufts is just gone in a consumtion. Aunt Tufts cannot hold out much longer. She is very aged and very infirm. Mrs Tufts has a Severe trial her Father and one of her Brothers are sick and cannot continue long. Her youngest Son is with mr Shaw, but is dangerously sick with a Lung Fever, has not been out of his Bed for twelve days.[7] Poor Lucy has had a Sad time for her visit. Billy and the two Betsys have been sick also, but they are much better.

All the papers Pictures &c, are at last deliver'd up, all but the Pockit Books. I told the Doctor that I thought he had better not mention these, as I knew *he* had made cousin charles a present of one of them. I think he was very lucky to get the other things. You would be surpriz'd to hear how much he owes to labourers in this Town above two hundred pound I am told. Besides this, your Brother[8] said this day, that his Farm is mortgaged for six hundred more. If this is true he cannot hold out long at the rate he lives. When I was at a certain house in Boston[9] the other day I was attack'd upon the Subject of my Niece's conduct. Many Slighty things were said of the coll; her Brother and Sister pretend to know him. I felt angry and spoke my mind very plainly. I have not a doubt but it was communicated. I wish'd it might be: I hope you can read this I do not wish any Body else too.

RC (Adams Papers); endorsed: "Mrs Cranch 28 Sepbr 86."

[1] Dolly Tufts, daughter of AA's cousin Samuel Tufts of Newburyport, married George Odiorne of Exeter, N.H., on 4 Oct. 1787 (*Vital Records of Newburyport, Massachusetts, to the End of the Year 1849*, 2 vols., Salem, Mass., 1911, 1:399; 2:348, 488).

[2] Abigail Bishop, daughter of John and Abigail Tufts Bishop of Medford, married Dr.

Archelaus Putnam, Harvard 1763, on 12 November. The bride's mother was AA's cousin (*Sibley's Harvard Graduates*, 15:476). Richard and Mary Cranch lived in Salem 1766–1767 (vol. 1:53).

[3] A reference to Proverbs, 31:26.

[4] Harvard's fall exhibition occurred on 26 September. See JQA's account of the preparations and the proceedings in *Diary*, 2:93, 99–104.

[5] Quincy Thaxter married Elizabeth Cushing of Hingham on 27 August. His sister Anna married their cousin Thomas Thaxter, also of Hingham, the same day (*History of the Town of Hingham, Massachusetts*, 3 vols. in 4, Hingham, 1893, 3:235, 236).

[6] This group of Adams relatives was composed of Deacon Ebenezer Adams (1737–1791) of Braintree, a double first cousin of JA, his wife Mehitable Spear (1737–1814), and probably their daughter Alice (b. 1770); the Deacon's sister, Ann Adams Savil Thayer (1731–1794) of Braintree; and the Deacon's niece, Elizabeth Adams (1766–1852), eldest daughter of Rev. Zabdiel Adams (1739–1801) and Elizabeth Stearns (1742–1800) of Lunenburg (Adams, *Geneal. History of Henry Adams*, p. 401, 410, 411).

[7] Mary Cranch reports on the health of the family of AA's cousin Dr. Simon Tufts and his second wife, Elizabeth Hall, including the doctor's mother and AA's aunt, Abigail Smith Tufts (1701–1790); his father-in-law, Stephen Hall, who died on 1 Dec.; and their son Hall (1755–1801). Elizabeth Hall Tufts had four brothers alive in 1786. The first to expire, Aaron Hall (b. 1737), died 19 March 1787 from dropsy (*Vital Records of Medford, Massachusetts, to the Year 1850*, Boston, 1907, p. 382, 387; Charles Brooks and James M. Usher, *History of the Town of Medford, Middlesex County, Massachusetts*, rev. edn., Boston, 1886, p. 540–541, 544, 562, 563).

[8] That is, JA's brother, Peter Boylston Adams.

[9] The home of Joseph Pearse and Elizabeth Hunt Palmer.

Elizabeth Smith Shaw to Abigail Adams

My Dear Sister Haverhill October 1st. 1786

This Day is the Aniversary of Eleven Years since our dear Mother left *us* poor Pilgrims, to sojourn here a little longer upon Earth, while *she* (as we trust)[1] went to spend an eternal Sabbath in the blissful regions of immortality. The anual return of those Days, upon which some beloved Friend has been taken from me, I devote more particularly to the recollection of their amiable Qualities, and their many Virtues. I bedew their Ashes with a grateful, reverential, tender, silent Tear.—And while my Memory lasts,

> "*she* shall a while repair,
> To dwell a weeping Hermit there."[2]

I closed my last-Letter telling you, that your and our Thomas B. A. would leave us the next morning. I now have the pleasure of informing you that he acquited himself honorably, and was received without any dificulty. Mr Shaw carried him to Braintree, and left him there. It was not possible for love, nor money to get a Chamber in Colledge, and Doctor Tufts has put him to board with Mr Sewall. I hope the dear Lad will continue to deserve the Love of every one.

Mr Shaw was exceeding fond of him, and I tell him, really pines after his Nephew.

My Uncle Smith, and Cousin Betsy, Brother and Sister Cranch have made me a visit. It really grieved me to see my Uncle so dejected. His Voice had that mournful Cadence, and was upon that key, which bespeaks our solicitude, and pity. He appeared to have a bad cold, and I observed to him, that I feared he had not eat a sufficient quantity of food to support him. "Yes Child I have, (said he) but my food, nor my Sleep does not seem to do the good it used to—Nothing appears to me as it did once." Indeed, my Cousin Betsy, and he, both are deeply affected by their late Bereavment. My Uncle is not one of those passionate Mourners who easily throw of their Weeds, and dry up their Tears in the Bosom of another Love. But he is a good man, and behaves with dignity, and discovers proper magnimity, and Resignation of Mind, to the sovereign Disposer of Events.

Mr Allens Family all dined here, on a Saturday and we returned the compliment the next Monday. As her Freinds, and Relations are nearly the same with mine, I think they can make an agreeable division of their Time between us. Uncle, and his Daughter, Brother and Sister went home through Newbury, and I hear Sisters health is much better for her Journey.

I wish my Brother, and Sister Adams could as easily make me a Visit. Thy Sister would indeed, with pleasure "greet thy entering voice."—But ah me! mountains rise, and Oceans roll between us. You are *doing good*:—that is my Consolation—and that, is what I heard Betsy Quincy tell her Brother, God sent him into the world for, and all the rest of the Folks. I often tell my little Daughter, I wish she would do half so well herself, as she teaches, or pretends to teach Others.

When I closed my last letter to you, I had many more things to say, and I then intended to have begun another immediately, but since that time we have had somebody sick in the Family, though none with a settled Fever till about three weeks ago a Scholar of Mr Shaws, the Son of Dr Simon Tufts was seized with a Cold, which threw him into a fever upon his Lungs. He never set up, and had his Cloaths on for fiveteen Days, and what rendered it peculiarly distressing to me, was that his Father was in the last stages of a Consumption and it was not posible for his Parents to see him. His Mother was so overcome with the news of her Sons illness, that she almost fainted away. Poor Woman her Situation was indeed distressing. Every little while the Dr bloods extreamly, and every turn they fear will be the Last. So that she could not leave him, unless we had been very desirous of her coming. But Hall Tufts was very good to take medicine, and was very easy with my Care, which was some releif to my Mind. I have endeavoured that he should not suffer for the want of maternal tenderness, and he is now recovering as fast as any one could expect. How pleasureable it is, to tend upon a person, when we can smile, and say, "they are much better." I hear that Quincy Thaxter, and his sister Nancy were married at Mr Gays house. QT to a Miss Cushing, and N.T. to her Cousin.

The young widower Cushing, they say is courting his Sister Betsy Thaxter, but I can hardly believe it.[3]

Miss Nabby Bishop is published, *do you see*, and is going to be married to Dr Archelaus Putman, a Nephew of Dr Putmans of Salem a Gentleman of independant Fortune.

Mr Shaw talks of going to Bridgwater in about a week or fortnight, and we shall hear more as we pass through the Town. Perhaps I may pick up some anecdotes that may amuse you. At present my thoughts are not very bright, they have of late been so contracted, and absorbed in a dark, Chamber, arround a sick bed, that I believe I need some relaxation, and diversion to call up my Spirits.

Mr Thaxter and Miss Betsy are going to Boston next week. We have chosen him one of the Commitee, to answer an address of the Select men of Boston. I think he has drawn one that will do him honour.[4]

At present our States are in a dissagreeable Situation. The time is now come, for all to know, what manner of Spirits we are of, and whether we will support Government or not. The Court meet at Newbury the[5]

RC (Adams Papers).

[1] Closing parenthesis editorially supplied.

[2] William Collins, "Ode Written in the Beginning of the Year 1746," lines 11–12.

[3] John Cushing and Elizabeth Thaxter, the elder sister of the first Mrs. Cushing, did not marry. In Dec. 1787, Cushing wed Christiana Thaxter, the cousin of his first wife (*History of the Town of Hingham, Massachusetts*, 3 vols. in 4, Hingham, 1893, 2:165, 3:233).

[4] On 11 Sept., the town of Boston adopted a circular letter censuring those fomenting Shays' Rebellion and endorsing the governor's efforts to preserve state government. On 3 Oct., the town of Haverhill voted to approve Boston's address and appoint a committee to draft a reply. Haverhill's response, dated 10 Oct., concludes: "This town has borne its full share of all the burdens, losses and expences of the late war, and its subsequent proportion of public expences since the peace.—The present form of government we deliberately adopted and wish not to see it sacrificed—We are ready therefore, to join you in a firm and vigorous support of our Constitution, in the redress of grievances, and in promoting industry, œconomy, and every other virtue which can exalt and render a nation respectable." For the full printed

text of Boston's circular letter see *Massachusetts Centinel*, 13 Sept.; for Haverhill's response, see Boston *Independent Ledger*, 16 October.

[5] At this point, the text ends at the bottom of the fourth MS page of the letter; any continuation is missing.

Mary Smith Cranch to Abigail Adams

Dear Sister Braintree october 8th 1786

I last evening receiv'd your kind Letter by the Way of new york and most heartily congratulate you upon the marriage of your only Daughter. It is a very desirable thing to see our children happily Settled in the world. Your anxietys for my dear Niece for several years have been very many and great. They are I hope now all at an end, at least of such a kind. No state is exempt from troubles, and those which our children suffer are keenly felt by a tender Parent. The character you have given of coll. Smith Seems to insure her from any but what are unavoidable in the happiest marriages. They have my warmest wishes for their Happiness and prosperity. I do not wonder you felt agitated at giving your Daughter away. I think I Should tremble at such an event as much as I did when I gave myself away. My dear neice must have discover'd the difference between a real and feign'd attachment, though her good nature and delicacy may have prevented her making the comparison, but if I am to believe a Lady where —— Boarded last Fall his was real also. His mortification and rage were real I believe. I never doubted it. ⟨"⟩She veryly thought he would have gone distracted." "He put no Such airs on here, he too well knew we were not to be deceiv'd.⟨"⟩[1] We were us'd to call things by their right names. The violent Passion which he put himself into, the day you left us, excited no emotion in the beholders, but contempt. It procur'd him no pity, no *gentle* soothings from the girls. They knew not how to adminster comfort to a Person Who could thro himself upon the Floor—upon the couch—and upon the chairs, and bawl like a great Boy who had misbehav'd and was oblig'd to go to school without his dinner. Never did I see JQA laugh in such a manner as when he was told of this scene. Meeting with Such unfeeling companions then, he had no incouragment to seek consolations from them again. Both your and our Family are represented as treating him very ill. "If he was to blame for neglecting her so long he wrote her a long letter in vindication of himself," and at my expence as well as that of others of her correspondence who never mention'd his name said I." "Why he thought somebody must have been enjuring him so She never would have treated him in such a manner only for not writing to her." That was not all, and he knows it." "Well he has Suffer'd for it I am sure, poor creature. He had nobody but me to open his mind too," and happy had it been for *you* and *yours* if he had not open'd so much of it to you unhappy woman I could have said. "She has not better'd herself by what I can hear: my Brother and Sister know him, and say he is a man of no abilities and is of no profession and in any thing will not bear a comparison with." "I hope not in good truth, was what I thought." I said I knew him not, but I had receiv'd a good character of him from every one I had inquir'd of, who did, that he had been long enough in your Family for mr Adams to form an opinion of him and I believ'd he Was as capable of forming a Judgment of his character and his abilities as any one She had receiv'd her inteligence from: and that you were Satisfied as to both. How could She talk thus to me about Persons one of Whom I have reason to think, She had better never Seen.[2] I hope the coll will come and give them the lie. When you lay all three of my Letters together you will think of the Pupil of Pleasure, of Philip Sedley[3] and be thankful. Is it not astonishing that he should be continu'd in the Family and no notice taken? Some think it is not because, tis not severly felt, but that *he* is so unhappily circumstanced that he cannot resent it, and some say they have made a bargain.[4] I could give you some curious annecdotes of last Winters gallantry in this Town: I did hint it then I was affraid to do more. A Friend interposed and in some measure Sav'd her character.

I long my dear sister to have you return, but where we shall be I know not. This House is upon Sale and whether we shall purchase it or not is uncertain. We cannot unless we can get what is due to us from the publick, or Sell our estate at weymouth. Mr Evans has alter'd his mind and will not settle at Weymouth. After accepting their call he told them he must go to Phylidelphia to get a certificate of his ordination and a dismission from the Presbitiary. When he return'd he said he could not be sittled so Soon as he expected, as the body would not sit till october. They look'd upon him notwithstanding as their minister, and expected he would Stay with them at least part of his time. Instead of which he never has above three or four days excepting Sundays and above half his time has sent other persons in his room. He would not even stay to visit the sick when they had notis nor attend a funereal. They complain'd he resented it, and has ask'd leave to withdraw his consent which they will grant. I have thought ever since he return'd that he wish'd to be disingag'd and was trying to find some pretence to ask for a dismission. I know not what he has in view, but this I am Sure of, that he will hurt his character by it. He desir'd to have our House ready for him by July. Mr Hagglet[5] who was a very good Tenant left it and now we cannot find any body to take it. I wish it was in Braintree—Poor Weymouth has again to seek a Pastor, but it is not their fault.

Captain Barnard is arriv'd and brought us Some magazines for which I thank you, but no letters. Callahan is not yet arriv'd. I hope for some by him. You have sent an April magazine twice and no July one except one of the Fashens, which we did not need: for would you believe it if I were to tell you the Fashions had arriv'd before it? To what a Pitch of Folly have we arriv'd, they are study'd as a Science. Your Mother Hall and Brothers Family are well. Madam Quincy and daughter and all your Nieghbours also. Uncle Quincy cannot be perswaid'd out. Mr wibird is well and Still lives in the Worst House in Braintree. Betsy is at Bridgwater Plymouth &c upon a visit. Lucy is at newbury Port. I wish you had one of them with you, or rather I wish you would come home and let us be all together here. Our dear Sons are an honour to us, they are well, but what shall we do with them when they come out of college? We have each of us one which we must think of Something for. The Law was what they both thought of, but unless we have more peace among us they had better take their axe and clear new Land. They are good Lads and I hope will never want Bread.

RC (Adams Papers); endorsed: "Mrs Cranch 8 ocbr 1786."

[1] While trying to clarify her meaning here, Cranch may have neglected to cross out two of the quotation marks. Her use of quotation marks throughout the remainder of the paragraph is irregular.

[2] This extended passage of quoted dialogue conveys the heated exchange between Cranch and Elizabeth Hunt Palmer that took place at Mrs. Palmer's Boston home about 9 September. See Mary Smith Cranch to AA, 24 and 28 Sept., both above.

[3] Philip Sedley, the title character of Samuel Jackson Pratt's *The Pupil of Pleasure*, 1778, employs dissimulation, hypocrisy, and a pleasing façade to increase his personal profit and pleasure, the consequences of which introduce greater sorrow and vice into the community.

[4] A reference to Joseph Pearse Palmer's poor financial situation and Royall Tyler's status as a boarder in his home.

[5] For Rev. William Hazlitt, see vol. 5:480–481.

Mary Smith Cranch to Abigail Adams

My dear Sister Braintree october 9th 1786

As I was seting quite alone this evening somebody came in from Boston with a Hankerchief full of Letters from you my dear, dear

Sister. The Girls are neither of them at home, but I have ventur'd to open their Pacquits also, and a hearty laugh I have had at the extravagant Figures you have sent. Yes my sister our Ladies are foolish enough to deserve some of the ridicule. Those unnatural protuberences are daily encreasing and it was but last evening that mr Cranch was Saying to me that they had the appearence of deformity and always gave him pain.

I have no language that will express half what I feel for your generous kindness to me and my dear Girls. We have it not in our power to return it in kind, but I have a heartfelt satisfaction in thinking that we have one way left to express our gratitude more substantially than by mear words. I feel a pleasure in thinking that if you could look in upon your sons you would not think that a mamas or sisters care was wanting in any one instance. I cannot always command cash to do for them just as I would, this is all my difficulty. I always long to have you with us when we are all together in their vacancy's you have no Idea how pleasent it, is. There commons are good but the variety is small, you would laugh to see them attacking a large whartleberry Pudding and a good Family Apple Pye. I have prepar'd half a Bussel of dry'd whartleberrys against their winter vacancy. In a former Letter I mention'd the Exibition in which our sons bore a part, but I forgot to tell you that your son charles exhibite'd the Handsomest Face in the chapple without appearing in the least conscious of it. He is really too handsome. He will Soon steal the heart of every Girl Who sees him. He is as Soft and amiable in his manners as he is beautiful in his Person.

The children will want some Bandino Hankerchefs soon. I have taken all yours except the three best. I wish you would let me know at what price you can have them, they are so high here 8 shillings a peice that I cannot get them.

I thank you my dear sister for giving me so circumstantial an account, of the change of my Nieces affairs. I took perticular notice at the time of your writing it, of the Question she ask you "whither you thought a certain Gentleman of her acquaintanc was a man of honour." We talk'd about it, and suppos'd that something of the kind had taken place, which really had. I never supposs'd but what she had acted properly, but the world knowing so little of the matter as they have, had it been any other person but mr T would have censur'd her greatly, but he is daily making her conduct appear diferent and there is now no way left for revenge but to represent the coll. as a man greatly his inferior.

No no my sister, I have no inclination to laugh at you for being greatly affected at parting or being parted from: had I been with you, I should have only mingled a few Tears with yours. I have not forgot the many I shed in private before I got a thorough weaning, and yet you well know, no one could have a more tender or affectionate companion than your Sisters.

Your Letter to this disturber of the peace of Familys is just what I could have wish'd. Oh my sister you do not half know him yet, he will not long have any thing to do with Braintree I believe. I should not wonder if he should pack up and go to new york. I hope he will pay us first.

What should you think if you should pick up a Letter from a married Lady, whose Husband is absent, directed to a gentleman, with such sentences as these in it, "I am distress'd, distress'd by many causes, what can we do. I know you would help me if you could. Come to me immediately."—"Oh think of me, and think of your Self."[1]—It alarm'd me. It *was* misterious, but is no longer so—what will or can be done I know not. I was yesterday at Germantown. They seem all of them to be very Sensible of the Injury that has been done, the Family. It is a serious affair to break up such a large one, besides the disgrace which will forever attend even the Innocent ones of it. A man looks very Silly with a pair of horns stuck in his Front—and yet to suffer the enemy of ones peace to be under the same roof and to See—dividing her leering (I will not say tender) looks between himself and her Paramour is too much for Human nature to bear.

Both Barnard and Callahan have had very long Passages, 60 days each. You must have receiuv'd Several Letters from me since they sail'd. I wrote in July and in think in August but as I take no copys I cannot tell exactly. Whenever there is a vessal going I always feel as if I must keep writing till the last moment.

Why my dear sister will you make the tokens of your Love to us so expencive to you. There must be some things which in your station will be useless to you, which would appear very handsome upon us, and would never be the less acceptable for haveing been worn by a sister or Aunt. I wish you could See my Satten Quilt. Betsy drew it, and we quilted it our selves and a Beautiful piece of work it is. It is often affront'd by being pronounc'd as handsome as any English one. I wish your Petticoat merchant had offer'd you a Blue mode in stead of a pink because your Nieces quilted each of them a Pink mode the Fall you left us, but this you did not know.

They will try to Change it for a Blue. We are going this morning to your House to see that all is safe. We have had some difficulty to keep Pheby from admiting Stragling Negroe lodging and staying in the House sometimes three or four days together. I have forbid her doing it, and the Doctor did so also, but there have been poor objects who have work'd upon her compassion sometimes. Mr Ts negro who I told you was like to have a child, was put there (and wood and provision promiss'd if She would keep her), by mr v–s–y. Mr T did not chuse to appear in it himself. She was not a good Girl, and I did not think, your things safe. Pheby told them that we had forbid her sleeping again in the House, "keep her conceal'd was the answer." This rais'd me, and I talk to mr T about sending such creatures thire, for this was not the first he had sent. He deny'd it, but look'd guilty enough. She went of att last, and poor Pheby got nothing for all her trouble.

I wish I could step into your carriag this affernoon and make mr and mrs Smith a visit. Pray give my love to them, and tell them that nothing but the distance has prevented me. May this distance soon be shortend prays your ever affectionate Sister, M C

RC (Adams Papers); endorsed: "Mrs Cranch ocbr 9 1786."

[1] Cranch evidently quotes from a letter that Elizabeth Hunt Palmer sent to Royall Tyler.

Abigail Adams to Cotton Tufts

Dear Sir London october 10th 1786

Your Letters of july 6th and August 15th were duly received. The accounts containd in Yours of july 6th respecting publick affairs is not be sure so agreeable as the Lovers of peace and good order would wish. Our Countrymen have of late been so much accustomed to turbulent times, and stormy weather, that I cannot but hope that we have skillfull pilots enough to stear the Ship safe. Mutinous passengers will no doubt add to the Danger. More particularly so when encouraged and abetted by the crews of seditious and artfull Neighbours.

Your publick papers are full of Speculations, some of them be sure quite wild and ridiculous, others repleat with wisdom judgment and prudence. Such was the address to the General court, publishd in Adams & Nourses paper june 29th. which I conceive to be the production of mr Gerry,[1] and as he has there pointed out those Virtues which are essential to the union and good Government of the

State, by which it may render itself happy at home, and respected abroad. I will still hope that there is wisdom and integrity sufficient in the Mass of the people to bring them into practise. It is most earnestly to be wished, that the abilities of our literary Countrymen, would turn into some different channals from what seems lately to have occupied them and instead of abuseing and crying down one of the liberal professions, endeavour by decent measures to rectify the abuses which may have crept into it. It is not by enflaming the passion of Mankind that any benifit can result to a community at large. "The raging of the Sea, and the Madness of the people are put together in holy writ, and it is God alone who can say to either, hitherto shalt thou pass and no further, says a political writer."[2] The meetings of the people in different Towns of our state, can never terminate in any good, and every sensible Man will discourage them, and employ their pens in convincing their Citizens that, Whilst they have a free uncorrupted House of Assembly they cannot possibly be justified in the pursuit of Measures subversive of good order. Dean Swift observes that a usurping populace is always its own dupe, a mere under worker, and a purchaser in trust for some Single Tyrant whose state and power they advance to their own Ruin with as blind an instinct, as those worms who die with weaving Magnificent Habits for Beings of a Superiour Nature to their own.[3]

But when I consider what an influence the counsel of one wise Man possessd of integrity and publick spirit has had in all free countries over the passions of Men, I can never despair whilst I have reason to think, every little Town and Village possesses more than one; perhaps 5 of that description. Let not Him whom I address, and others like him, in whose Hands our publick affairs rest, be Disheartned or Dismayed, for publick virtue, sooner or later will meet with Glory and Success: the encouragement of Agriculture and manufactories will tend to lessen that rage for Luxery which has produced many of the evils under which our people are now groaning. Idleness is the parent of contention and disobedience.[4] The industerous Hollander wears his Coat in the same fashion which it descended to him from his Ancestors, and possessing a capital which in a Country I could name, would rear a splendid building, spread a Sumptuous table and harness an elegant equipage, the Hollander neat in his Cloathing, decent in his House frugal at his table employs his capital in the advancement of commerce, in the acquirement of future credit, in the Regular discharge of his obligations, and in the support of the Government, tho at present disturbed by internal commotions, and the usurpations of the Statdholder. If the meddlesome Genius of Neighbouring Princes does not intefere, they will Recover their ancient privileges. This disposition seems to prevail as strongly there, as the determination to shake of Tyranny ever did in the united States, from whence they acknowledge to have caught their present Spirit.[5]

You have seen no doubt Lord Carmarthens answer to mr Adams's Memorial. It was first communicated to the World in an American Paper Publishd at Baltimore. Upon its arrival here the Ministry publishd it from their own records, together with an extract from the Memorial; Can our Country expect any thing from this, untill the Treaty is complied with upon our part by the Removal of every legal impediment to the recovery of British Debts.[6] If the decisions of an American jury should be against allowing interest during the War, they will determine it so, and the British creditor ought to Set down satisfied. It is the opinion of those whom I have heard converse upon the Subject, that there would be more lenity on the part of the Creditor and less distress attending the debtor, if the Laws were repealed and justice had its fair course.

The papers received lately from Governour Bowdoin, respecting the encroachments made at Passamaquode have been laid before Lord Carmarthan on a private capacity. As mr Adams has not yet received them offically from congress, he could not deliver them in his publick Character. His Lordship said he was sorry to see disputes of that kind arising, but he hoped that Lord Dorchester, (Sir Guy Carlton) would Settle them *all* as he had Authority to do.[7]

Mr Barclay has made a Treaty with the Emperor of Moroco, but as it has not yet come to Hand can say nothing respecting it.[8] You will see by the papers how elated this people appear at their Treaty with France, which some persons say however will only end, in accelerating a War between the Nations. But War I imagine is far from the wish of the present Ministry even with America, tho they may press her as far as she will bear without turning, depending upon her inability. It is the opinion of some persons that France has deeper views in this late Maneuvre than at present appear to the world. Our own Country would do well to imitate the watchfull Argus instead of the Sleeping dragon, least the Gardens of Hesperides be rob'd of all their Golden Apples. Neither Country wishes our growth or prosperity. No dependance is to be placed upon them. Our Navy they fear the Growth of, and every measure will be concerted to keep it under.[9]

I Sent you sir by one of the last vessels the papers respecting the ridiculous publications of Lord George Gordon, with mr Tufts lame replies. Tho the Character of Lord Gorge Gordon is at present well known here, it is not so in America; where only these publications can do mischief, and as the Letters have only been partially publishd in America, I am well satisfied that they will infuse into the minds of the people there, that mr Adams is a pensioner of France, tho Lord Gorges assertion was that he received his Sallery from thence.[10] I am the more convinced of the injury this may do, by an extract of a Letter which I have cut from Your centinal and inclose to you.[11] Some such circumstances as these and with as little coulour of Truth, frequently descend to posterity, are related in history for facts and fix a lasting Stigma upon innocent Characters. Algernon Sydney and Lord Russel in Dalrimple papers are publishd to the World as receiving Bribes from France. Men who I dare say would have spurnd the Idea.[12] Mr Tufts I believe was ungaurdedly taken in, by a Man who would stick at no measures to do mischief, and whose medlesome disposition leads him to torment in some way or other every foreign Minister here. What I have to request of you Sir, is that the Letters may all be publishd together in one paper, and the denial of the assertion as you find it in the Daily, or Publick Advertizer I forget which, with a request to the printers who have made partial publication, to print the whole. If some little Stricture was added, that as no person every appeard; tho thus publickly challengd to produce any evidence upon the Subject, the whole ought to be considerd as the vagary of a distracted Brain, like Margrate Nicolsons attack upon the Life of the King.

I was much pleasd with my late visit to Holland, where we received every politeness and attention from the people which I could wish. I believe I have sufferd in my Health in concequence of the Climate, but Still I do not regret having once Seen a Country every way singular. I was witness too, to a Grand scene, the Triumph of Liberty, which having deposed a Number of their old Majestrates Elected 15 New ones, and in the most Solemn Manner in a large Square upon an elevated platform, amidst a Multitude of ten thousand persons assembled on the occasion, the chief Seecratary Administerd the oaths to them and all the people said Amen! in other words gave three huzzas. The free Choirs as they are calld or rather Militia; to the amount of 3 thousand were all under arms during the ceremony. The Magistrates were then conducted two and two to their Carriages, and the troops together with the Multitude retired in perfect good order. We were at the Window of a House in a room provided for us, from whence we had a perfect view of the ceremony. And in the Evening the Secretary who administerd the oath, came in the Name of the Citizens to make their compliments to mr Adams with their thanks for the honour he had done them, and wishes for the prosperity of himself family and Country.[13]

Thus sir I have given you a detail upon several subjects, which I should have omitted if I could have drawn mr A. from his present subject to Letter writing. But between ourselves, he is as much engaged upon the Subject of Government as Plato was when he wrote his Laws and Republick.[14]

From Congress no official Dispatches have arrived for three Months.[15] We hope they are deliberating to some purpose.

As to Domestick affairs you will draw for what you find necessary for the support of the Children and your Bills will be immediatly honourd. We feel Sir under obligations to you for your kind care and attention to all our domestick affairs. Mr Adams desires me to tell you that he would buy the two peices of Land, Belchers and verchilds, tho he thinks them of no great value. I am glad you are not like to have any further trouble with mr T. The least said upon a former subject the best. Wound not the Striken dear.

Both mr Adams and I request that mr Cranch should be paid the Board of our children during the vacancies and that mrs Cranch should charge washing mending &c. We cannot consent that our Children should be burdensome to our Friends. It is unreasonable.

I inclose the account of the Books purchased for .[16] The Bill of the papers procured here by mr Cushings request was inclosed to mr King with the papers and amounted to 15 pounds Sterling which mr Adams desired mr Cushing to pay to you. If it is not done, we will get a New Bill made out and Signd by the Gentleman and will inclose it to you.

Will you be so good sir as to accept a trifle, a new kind of Manufactory for Summer wear, which is used here for waist coats and Breeches. It is in a small trunk with some things I have sent to my children and the bundle addrest to you. My paper curtails me to two[17] AA

RC (NNMus:J. Clarence Davies Collection, 34.100.596); endorsed: "Mrs Ab Adams. octob. 10. 1786." Dft (Adams Papers), filmed at [1786], Adams Papers, Microfilms, Reel No. 369.

[1] AA refers to a speech delivered in the Massachusetts House during debate over whether state loan certificates should be called in at their current (depreciated)

value. Elbridge Gerry represented Marblehead (Boston *Independent Chronicle*, 29 June).

[2] Jonathan Swift, *A Discourse of the Contests and Dissensions between the Nobles and the Commons in Athens and Rome*, London, 1701, p. 52–53.

[3] Same, p. 47. JA included this passage in his *Defence of the Const.*, 1:104.

[4] The first two paragraphs of the Dft correspond to the RC up to this point but vary so considerably that the editors print them here in their entirety:

"Your Letters of july 6th and August 15 were duly received. The accounts contained in yours of july 6 as well as those to mr Adams of our publick affairs is not be sure so agreeable as the Lovers of peace and good order would wish, but we have been so used to turbelant times and stormy weather that I cannot but hope we have skillfull poilots enough to Stear the Ship Safe. Mutinous ⟨*hands*⟩ passengers will no doubt add to the danger, more particularly so when they are encouraged and abetted by the crews of Dangerous and powerfull Neighbours. There is a constant succession of Prosperity and adversity in all Humane affairs. Man is a wrestless Being and must be employd ⟨*either*⟩ for the benifit ⟨*or mischief*⟩ of his fellow creatures or he will sink into Idleness which produces contention disobedience to the Laws Ruin and confusion, and from this Source I imagine great part of the evils under which our Country is now groaning will be found to proceed. During the war money tho of small value was easily procured and the small estimation in which it was held, introduced Luxery and extravagance of every Specie. The lower cass of people who can least bear wealth grew indolent and overbearing. They could live easier upon less labour and in reality they felt little of the publick burden. Now they are obliged to labour more Gain less and pay more. They are exclaming on all hands and foolishly think that the fault lies with their rulers. But a Still greater evil results from the distress into which the mercantile part of the States have brought themselves by the Debts contracted to this Country. The difficulty of remittances and the calls of their Iritated creditors obliges them to shut their Doors and exposes them to the sudden attacks of all their credittors at once. British factors will swarm amongst us and pick up our remaining pence. The Guineys are already I presume nearly exported. But after some time these evils will be remided. We Shall emerge from our present State of depression made wiser by experience, and the little jealousys which Subsist between different States will be swallowd up in the one Idea of uniting for common Defence. Perhaps you will Say the remedy is worse than the disease. What ever it may be, a little time will oblige us to the experiment I fear.

"When I consider what an influence the counsels of one wise man possest of integrity and publick Spirit, has upon the mass of the people, I can never despair whilst I have reason to think ⟨*some*⟩ every little Town and village possesses more than one or even 5 of that description. Let not those in whose hands our publick affairs rest be disheartned or dismayed for publick virtue is always attended with Glory and Success. Your publick papers are full of Speculations, some of them be sure quite wild and riduculous others repleat with wisdom judgment and prudence. Such was the address to the General Court publishd in Adams & Nourse paper june 29th which I conceive to be the production of mr Gerry, as he has there pointed out those virtues which are essential to the union and good government of the State, by which it may render itself happy at home and esteemed abroad. I will still hope that there is wisdom and integrity Sufficient in the Mass of the people to bring them into practise. These meetings of the people in the different Towns of the State ought to be Discouraged and Discountananced by informing them that there can be no possible occasion for such measures whilst they have a free uncorrupted representation in the General assembly. The Craft of ⟨*some*⟩ a desiging knave is Sufficient only for a time to Dupe the Multitude. I have always observed in my countrymen a disposition to hear truth, as soon as their passions have subsided. Swift observes in some of his political observations that a usurping populace is its own Dupe, a mere underworker and a purchaser in trust for some Single tyrant, whose State and power they advance to their own ruin with as blind an instinct as those worms that die with weaving magnificent Habits for beings of a superiour Nature to their own."

[5] This very month JA published a series of letters he wrote to Hendrik Calkoen, an Amsterdam lawyer, in Oct. 1780 analyzing

Dutch and American society and comparing the Low Countries' revolt against Spain to the American Revolution. For JA's *Twenty-six Letters, upon Interesting Subjects, Respecting the Revolution of America* and the circumstances leading to their composition, see *Papers*, 10:196–252.

[6] For JA's memorial of 30 Nov. 1785, see AA to Cotton Tufts, 21 Feb., note 3, above. Carmarthen replied on 28 Feb., citing obstacles in violation of Art. 4 of the peace treaty that British creditors had encountered attempting to collect American debts; he concluded by stating that Britain would fulfill every article of the treaty when the United States had demonstrated its readiness to do the same. JA sent the response to John Jay on 4 March and it was presented to Congress in early May (*JCC*, 31:781–797; Smith, *Letters of Delegates*, 23:287).

The Baltimore *Maryland Journal* published Carmarthen's response on 4 July. AA probably saw the piece reprinted under that dateline in the London *Daily Universal Register*, 5 September.

[7] James Bowdoin's letter of 11 July (PRO: F.O. 4, vol. 4, f. 487–489) concerned a boundary dispute between Massachusetts and New Brunswick. On 26 June, New Brunswick officials seized two Massachusetts vessels anchored on the western side of Passamaquoddy Bay, claiming that their jurisdiction extended to its western shore. If true, New Brunswick could prohibit U.S. navigation into the bay, making several Massachusetts townships virtually inaccessible. Also at stake was the status of several islands in the bay (Mass., *Acts and Laws*, Resolves of 1786, May sess., ch. 92; Charles Storer to JA, 21 July, Adams Papers).

Included among the eight enclosures Bowdoin sent JA (not found) were Bowdoin's message to the General Court notifying them of the seizure, 7 July; the Court's resolve concerning the matter, 8 July (Mass., *Acts and Laws*, Resolves of 1786, May sess., ch. 92 and 127); the Council's advice; and various letters and depositions from residents at Passamaquoddy, including Massachusetts excise officers James Avery and Samuel Tuttle.

Guy Carleton, 1st Lord Dorchester, was reappointed governor of Canada in April and arrived in Quebec in Oct. (*DNB*).

[8] Thomas Barclay concluded negotiations with Morocco for a Treaty of Peace and Friendship and an additional article on 28 June and 15 July. Col. David Franks carried the treaty from Cadiz to Paris, where it was signed by Jefferson on 1 Jan. 1787, and then to London, where JA added his signature on 25 Jan. (Miller, *Treaties*, 2:185; Jefferson, *Papers*, 10:418, 618).

[9] In her Dft, AA does not mention Barclay and the Moroccan treaty but adds the following paragraph concerning the Anglo-French commercial treaty negotiated by William Eden and Pierre Samuel Dupont de Nemours in September: "Treatys of commerce you will See by the publick Papers are comeing so much into vogue that a very extrodanary one has lately been Signd by the Count de Vergenes and mr Eden. The papers are by degrees feeling the pulse of the Nation and giving out the articles by peace meal. The papers begin already to clamour and by the time Parliament meets ⟨I⟩ it is imagined there will be a warm contest. It is thought France has deeper views in it than is at present discoverd. ⟨*It is an event which*⟩ Our Country are interested in watching and attending to this Manuver with Argus Eyes."

[10] This controversy regarding JA's salary, for which see AA to Tufts, 22 July, above, was first reported in the Boston *Independent Chronicle*, 6 July. JA's rebuttal, originally published anonymously in the London *Public Advertiser*, 9 May, was summarized in the *Boston Gazette*, 17 July, and reprinted in full in the Boston *American Herald*, 4 September.

[11] Not found.

[12] Sir John Dalrymple (1726–1810) made the allegations against Algernon Sidney and Lord William Russell in his *Memoirs of Great Britain and Ireland. From the Dissolution of the Last Parliament of Charles II, until the Sea-Battle off La Hogue*, 1771, Part 1, book 1 (*DNB*).

[13] AA and JA attended the swearing-in ceremony for several Patriot magistrates who had been elected at Utrecht in early August. This event represented the triumph of the Patriot Party in its attempt to introduce at least limited democracy into the Council of Utrecht (JA to Thomas Jefferson, 11 Sept. 1786, Jefferson, *Papers*, 10:348–349; Simon Schama, *Patriots and Liberators: Revolution in the Netherlands 1780–1813*, N.Y., 1977, p. 88–91, 97–100).

[14] This is the first reference to the beginning of JA's work on what would become his

three-volume *A Defence of the Constitutions of Government of the United States of America*. JA began writing what was ostensibly a series of letters to his son-in-law WSS in Sept. 1786 and would conclude the first book by the end of the year. It was published in Jan. 1787 in London. Subsequent volumes appeared in London in Aug. 1787 and Jan. 1788, respectively. During that time, JA's other letter writing—especially personal letters—was substantially reduced and only picked up again in late December when the bulk of the first volume had been completed.

JA began the *Defence* as a response to a letter written by Baron Anne-Robert Turgot in 1778 and published by Richard Price in 1784, which attacked American state constitutions for their bicameralism. JA feared that too many Americans had come to agree with Turgot and sought to refute his ideas, arguing for the importance of a balanced government and separation of powers among the democratic, aristocratic, and monarchic elements of the state. Using material from a wide array of sources including historians, philosophers, and political theorists (some attributed, some silently quoted), JA examined various earlier republics and attempted to demonstrate that lack of balance in government led to civil war. The reports of growing unrest in Massachusetts, culminating in Shays' Rebellion, reinforced JA's concerns and provided a backdrop to the work.

The *Defence* received widespread distribution throughout the United States. The books first reached Boston in mid-April 1787, and Cotton Tufts arranged for their dissemination to various individuals as well as a Boston bookseller. By the summer, American editions of the first volume had been printed in New York and Philadelphia, and portions had been reprinted in various newspapers throughout the states. Despite this, it is not clear that the *Defence* had any significant influence on the Constitutional Convention then meeting in Philadelphia. While some praised the work for its commitment to a balanced government, others expressed concern about JA's admiration of the British constitution and feared that he was advocating a return to a monarchy.

For more extensive discussions of the work's ideas and influence on American political thought, see C. Bradley Thompson, "John Adams and the Science of Politics," *John Adams and the Founding of the Republic*, ed. Richard Alan Ryerson, Boston, 2001, p. 237–265; and "John Adams: A Defence of the Constitutions," *Doc. Hist. Ratif. Const.*, 13:81–90.

JA's literary notes for the volume, which include copies of lengthy excerpts from various sources quoted in the books and drafts of the preface and some letters, are filmed at M/JA/9, Adams Papers, Microfilms, Reel No. 188. The volumes themselves were reprinted by Da Capo Press in 1971.

[15] In the Dft this sentence concludes: "the Treaty with Prussia excepted which he hastned and exchanged a few Days before the Death of the King." The final paragraph in the Dft begins: "As we cannot know the determinations of Congress I cannot state what they may determine to do with their Minister here." The remainder of the paragraph thanks Tufts for his care of the Adams boys and directs him to pay the Cranches for boarding them during college vacations. The other topics appearing at the end of the RC are not in the Dft.

[16] Blank in MS; probably Rev. Manasseh Cutler (1742–1823), Yale 1765, an Ipswich, Mass., minister and later a director of the Ohio Company (Cotton Tufts to AA, 2 Jan. 1787, below; *Sibley's Harvard Graduates*, 16:138–154).

[17] AA probably refers to the fact that she only has space to sign her initials.

Abigail Adams to Mary Smith Cranch

My Dear Sister — London october 12th 1786

I wrote you some days ago, and mr Gardner comeing in just as I had closed my Letter I inquired of him, if he knew of any opportunity of sending to Boston, he replied, that a vessel belonging to Newyork had taken freight for Boston and would Sail that day. I gave him the Letter to you, the only one I had written which he promised to put into the bag; and which I hope has reachd you. I expected Captain Cushing would Sail this Month, and by him designd a large pacquet to my Friends, but his vessel has been seazd; and as it is not yet determined whether she will be condemnd, he knows not when he shall get out.[1] Captain Folger is the only vessel like to sail from here, and it was but yesterday that I learnt he was to sail this week, so that Several of my Friends I shall not have time to write to. The week I returnd from Holland I was taken sick and continued near 3 weeks very ill, and unable to Set up, but my disorder has now happily left me. You complain of ill Health my dear sister, I fear the addition to your family cares is too fatiguing for you. I know your sisterly kindness leads you to exert yourself for the service of your Nephews, but the washing and Ironing for 3 Lads is too heavy a load for your family, and if you would only get done under your inspection, it is all that I wish for. But if still done in your family I insist that you Charge it to me, together with their Board during the vacancy, neither mr Adams or I are easy on account of it. Your complaint is Rheumatic I am persuaded and you will find releif from Burgundy pitch[2] in your neck. I was long loth to apply this remedy to myself, but I never used it but with success. Ironing is very bad for you. You will Smile and Say you cannot bear them, but make you some fine flannel Bodices and wear them next your skin. You will find them an excellent Gaurd against the colds you are so subject to in winter. So much for Quackery.

With regard to commencment and the necessaries for it, both mr Adams and myself approve your plan as the best method, and one which will be attended with the least trouble to you. We submit wholy to your opinion and judgment whatever is proper and request you to draw upon Dr Tufts for the money necessary. We neither wish on the one hand to be lavish nor on the other Parsimonious, and with Regard to pocket money for them, whilst they shew no disposition to extravagance if you think a little larger allowance necessary, Supply them and I will repay you. I know it is critical and too much is apt to do more harm than too little.

I have put up in a small Trunk which I shall commit to the care of captain Folger a suit of half worn Cloaths, which I thought might be turnd for my Eldest Son if he has occasion for them. Here we cannot do such a thing, and they are of no service to lay by. I have got the ratteen patternd very near, the Cloth not so well, but if he has a waistcoat a peice can be taken from the back of that, and the Cloth I send may supply its place.

You desired me to send some strong cotton Stockings. I have purchased some, and you will find that I have attended more to Strength than fineness. The half dozen at 4s. 3 pences pr pair I bought for cousin Cranch. I did not buy any for my son John, as I did not know whether he wanted, but if he does, you will let me know and I must get a larger Size. You will find 5 yds of superfine blew Broad Cloth, for which I gave twenty Shillings Sterling pr yd. This I Send for my two younger Sons and Some Buff thick set for waistcoats and winter Breeches. Nankeen will be best for summer wear, that can be better bought with you than here. The Buff will wash very well provided too hot water is not used. The Silk handkerchiefs and waist coat pattern round them you will distribute to that son which stands most in need of them or divide between them. The Brown Tabinet you will be so good as to present to my Mother, with my duty and that of her son, Grandson[3] and Grand daughter. The calico is for my Neices Nancy and Suky Adams, the Linnen for Louissa. A small bundle addresst to Dr Tufts to be deliverd to him and some silk for my dear Betsy and Lucy a commencment Gown. I wish there was as much again but, the Spirit is willing, they will therefore accept the will for the Deed. A pound of best Hyson tea I think for my dear Sister Cranch closes the list. To mr Cranch the Trunk will be addrest. I presume they will not oblige the duty to be paid upon these things, as they are not merchandize to make a profit upon, and articles for the use of my children. I have always heitherto got the captains to put the things into their own Trunks, but now they are rather too numerous, and I am very little acquainted with captain Folger.

I wish you would send me the Measure of my two Eldest sons necks and wrists. We could then make their linnen here, as I am sometimes really put to it, for want of employ both for myself and Esther.

You never mentiond receiving the Shirts we made for JQA, nor a peice of linnen sent to Charles at the same time. I rely upon you from time to time to make known their wants to me.

I know not whether we are to continue here longer than the Spring. Till then I am determined not to move, it is now so far advanced in the year. Probably by the next opportunity, I shall be better able to say whether we may hope to meet Next year or not. Tis three Months Since mr Adams received any dispatches from Congress. I was very glad to hear from mr Perkins, and wish him success and prosperity but not my Neice. She must never go into a wildeness amongst Savages, tho she might make a paridice of one and Humanize the other. The Still Sequesterd walks of Life are more consonant to her disposition. I Scarcly know the Man who is sufficiently *civilizd* to make her happy yet I need not wish her a more affectionately tender partner than appears to have fallen to the lot of her happy cousin. I hope some day to have the pleasure of introducing him to my dear Friends in America.

You drew so lovely a picture of our children dwelling together in unity, around your Hospitable Board; that I am Sure no amusement here ever gave me such heartfelt satisfaction as I received from your description only. God Bless them all and make them wise and virtuous. Our Good uncle Quincy become a recluise; he wants Children and Grandchildren arround him to enliven his declining years. O how my Heart Bounds towards you all, when I cast a retrospective look on times past, believe me I have never known the pleasures of society Since I left my native shoar.

> "What is the World to me, its pomp its pleasures and
> its Nonsence all?"[4]

Compared to the cordial Friendship and endearing ties of Country kindred and Friends?

> "Source of every Social tie
> united wish; and Mutual joy."[5]

But whether am I wandering. We have here an agreeable addition to our American Party by the arrival of mr Shiping, the Young Gentleman who accompanied General Lincoln to Boston a few years ago. Dr cutting too is his companion, him you know; he laughs less I think than formerly, which is an amendment, he is very Sensible and really appears a promising young Man. I am much more pleasd with him than I expected to be. Mr Shipping from his family and connexions would be intitled to our civilities, but from his personal merit, he is deserving of Friendship. They are students in the temple.

Mr Bulfinch is about returning to Boston. From all that I have seen of him, I think him a modest deserving young Gentleman, without one Macaroni air. He has made a pretty large Tour and I dare say is one of those who will be benifitted by his travels.[6] As to what is call'd polishd, I am so prejudiced in favour of my countrymen; that those who have had a good Education at home and been accustomed to company, stand in no need of any outward accomplishments which Europe has to bestow.

You will find in some bundle a remnant of cambrick which I sent to know if it is better bought here than in Boston. I gave ten shillings sterling pr yd for it. I have a few yards of coars cloth which I could not get into the Trunk, and must stay till captain cushing goes who I hear this day has got his vessel clear. By him then I must write to those Friends, who will say, is there no letter for me? dont complain my dear Girls,[7] I will write you soon, and to Miss Betsy Palmer too, whom I have a long time owed. 3 months ago I began a letter to her,[8] whilst I was writing, the Melancholy News of the death of our Dear Aunt reachd me, I lay'd it by too melancholy to proceed. My Regards to all my Neighbours, my Respects await our good Parson. Good dr Price is in great affliction having lost mrs Price about 3 weeks ago. He has not preachd since; but wrote us word last week[9] that he hoped to on sunday next. What has become of mrs Hay, that I have never received a line from her since she left me. Remember me to Miss Payne when you see her. I would write her but really my correspondents are so numerous that I fear I write stupidly to one half of them.

Adieu my dear sister Heaven Bless you and yours is the Sincere wish of your affectionate Sister AA

RC (MWA:Abigail Adams Corr.).

[1] The reasons for the seizure of Cushing's ship are unknown; he was substantially delayed by it, however, not arriving back in Boston until mid-April 1787 (*Massachusetts Centinel*, 18 April).

[2] The resinous sap of the spruce fir, from the Neufchâtel region, applied as a plaster (*OED*).

[3] WSS, Susanna Boylston Adams Hall's grandson by marriage.

[4] James Thomson, *The Seasons: Spring*, lines 1137–1138.

[5] Alexander Pope, "Chorus of Youths and Virgins," from *Two Choruses to the Tragedy of Brutus*, lines 25–26.

[6] Charles Bulfinch, the architect, had met the Adamses when he arrived in England in July 1785 and saw them several times that year before beginning his tour of France and Italy in the winter and spring of 1786 (see vol. 6:162, 163).

[7] Elizabeth and Lucy Cranch.

[8] No letter from AA to Elizabeth Palmer has been found.

[9] Richard Price to JA, 5 Oct. (Adams Papers). Sarah Blundell Price, who had long been in ill health, died on 20 Sept. (Richard Price to JA, 21 Sept., Adams Papers; Caroline E. Williams, *A Welsh Family from the Beginning of the 18th Century*, London, 1893, p. 30–31, 59, 84–85).

Cotton Tufts to Abigail Adams

My dear Cousn. Boston Octobr. 14th. 1786

Your Favour of July 22d and Aug: 1st. and also Mr. Adams of July 4th. I recd by Barnard and Callihan, the former arrived the 5. Inst. and the Latter .[1]

In former Letters, I have expressed my Fears with Respect to the Stability of our Federal Government. Should this tumble, into Ruin, what is to be the Scituation of my Friend in Europe. But is not a Suspicion of this Nature, unwarrantable, Ought it ever to enter into the Heart of a Citizen, or even a Doubt be admitted of its Stability. The Security and Happiness however of my Friend is at all Times near my Heart, and that of my dear Country. I confess Our Scituation is far from being considered desperate and on the other Hand, there are strong Symptoms of Dissolution and unless some Strong Exertions are soon made, the Event will inevitably take Place.

Bror. Cranch has given you a particular Account of the Rebellion existing in some of the Western Counties.[2] Should the Constitution of this State be thrown down, all the Rest in the Union will probably follow. An Event which Heaven avert. A few Months, however will determine in my Opinion, whether it will stand or fall. Between the several Opinions in the Genl Court, whither coercive Measures in the first Instance, or coercive Measures joined with Lenient, or Lenient Measures in the first Instance shall be adopted a wretched Indecision remains. Newhamshire Government has I imagine crushed the Rebellion there in its Embrio.[3] Fortunate would it have been had we taken Measures here to have suppressed the rising Flame in its first Appearance. Time does not permit me to assign the Causes of this rebellious Spirit, this may be the Subject of a future Letter.

You may easily suppose from our present Scituation the difficulty of my collecting Monies from your Estate here for the Support of your Children, at present I am advancing in my own Stock and shall continue so to do at present, as it will suit me eer long to draw on Mr. Adams in favour of Mr Elworthy, from whom I shortly expect a Quantity of Goods. Mr. Morton who has repeatedly offered me Belchers Place, not long since urged me to make him an offer, I accordingly offered him £60, (You may recollect that the Number of Acres are 5 1/2, that part of the House is decayed much the Roof mostly gone and open to the Heavens). He refused it and said he had been offered £120. This might have been some Years a gone, But I am pretty certain, No one will give it at this Day, And I think no Inducement will carry the Price above £70 or 75. Nor should I have ventured even to such a Price, had I not recd Mr. Adams sentiments expressive of his Desire to have it although dear. Nothing further has turned up with respect to Verchilds Lands since I wrote you last. They will be sold as soon as the Agent here has recd a Copy of Verchilds Will.

Your Three Sons are at our University, all in the Enjoyment of Health and of the good Opinion of their Instructors. In the Beginning of this Month, the Overseers by their Committee visited the University. I had the Pleasure of seeing Mr John display his Talents in a forensic Dispute On the Inequality of Power in a popular Government, in which he did himself Honor as also our Cousin Cranch who was his Opponent. Master Thomas boards at Mr Sewalls is well accommodated. No Chamber in College could be obtained.

At Weymouth we are still without a settled Minister. Mr. Evans recd a Call from us, accepted the same, soon after married our Cousin Hulda Kent, went with her to Philadelphia, returned, preached with us 6 or 8 Sabbaths and a few Days since went to Portsmouth and left behind a Letter requesting the Parish to revoke their Call.—Time must unravel the Mystery.

My best Regards to Mr. and Miss Smith, May every Blessing attend them. Yours affectionately.

RC (Adams Papers).

[1] Blank in MS. Barnard arrived in Boston on 6 Oct.; Callahan reached Cape Ann on 8 Oct. and Boston on the 10th (*Massachusetts Centinel*, 7, 11 Oct.).

[2] Cranch to JA, 3–11 Oct., Adams Papers.

[3] On 20 Sept., 200 yeoman surrounded the statehouse in Exeter to demand that the legislature take up the issue of paper money. In response Gov. John Sullivan called up 2,000 members of the militia to quell the uprising. Some shots were exchanged but most of the yeoman, recognizing the disparity in numbers, fled into the woods. Of the few who were captured, five were tried for treason in military courts martial (David P. Szatmary, *Shays' Rebellion: The Making of an Agrarian Insurrection*, Amherst, Mass., 1980, p. 78–79).

Abigail Adams to Elizabeth Smith Shaw

London october 15 1786

And so my dear Sister all your Nephews have quitted your Hospitable Mansion for the university of cambridge but tho they have quitted your House; I know they Still possess a share of your Maternal care and tenderness, in a degree they have been "Plants of your Hand, and children of your care."

As they rise in Life, may they increase in knowledge and virtue, and never be unmindfull of the good examples and Friendly admonitions of those who have their best interests at Heart. I hope their places will be supplied to you by a like Number of virtuous Youths; the Success your Worthy Partner has met with in prepareing Youth for their admission at the university, shews him to be peculiarly adapted to "rear the tender Thought, and teach the Young Idea how to shoot"[1] whilst the benevolent Heart, and amiable Manners of his help Mate, by her precepts, and example confirms and Seconds the good advice and Maxims of her Friend. What are common Schools compared to a family where Manners and Morals are equally an object of attention, where Love, and not Morossness is the Preceptor. Mr Adams frequently wishes that he had Tommy here,[2] but this is rather the wish of a parent desiring to see a Son long Seperated from him; than his real judgment; for we are daily more and more confirmed in the opinion, that the early period of every Americans Education, during which the mind receives the most lasting impressions; ought to be in his own Country, where he may acquire an inherent Love of Liberty and a thorough acquaintance with the Manners and taste of the Society and country of which he is a Member. He will find a purity in the Government and manners, to which Europe has been long a stranger. He will find that diligence integrity Genius and Spirit, are the true Sources of Superiority, and the Sure and certain means of rising in the estimation of his fellow citizens; instead of titles Stars and Garters. Far removed be those pests of Society; those Scourges of a free Government, from our happier land. His object should be the Hearts of his Countrymen, which is of more importance to a youth, than the good opinion of all the rest of Mankind, without the first the Second is very rarely obtained. When the judgment is ripened and taste and habits formed, when the heyday of the Blood, as shakspear terms it,[3] is abated, then may a Gentleman visit foreign countries with advantages. But so forcible is custom So tyrannical fashion, so Syren like vice, "when Lewdness courts them in the shape of Heaven" which is too, too often the case, that a Youth must be something more or less than Man; to escape contamination. Chastity Modesty decency, and conjugal Faith are the pillars of society; Sap these, and the whole fabrick falls sooner or later; *sixty Thousand* prostitues in *one city*, Some of them; the most Beautifull of their Sex!!![4] "take of the Rose From the fair forehead of an innocent love, and Set a Blister there; make Marriage vows as falce as dicers' oaths."

Such with shame be it spoken, is the picture of Europe. Alass how many victims have I seen, sent here without Guide or Gaurdian, to improve their Manners, but disgracing their country, ruin ing their Health, waisting their fortunes,[5] till from Kings bench, or Newgate, a supplication comes to help them to their own Country;

the picture which Richardson drew of Mrs Sinclair he drew from Life, horid as it was.[6] What I once read as Romance I no longer conceive as a fiction.

The only News which I can write you from this quarter of the World, will be a phenominon indeed should it take place. I mean that France and England should from Natural Enemies become very good Friends, as the court runners give out, the late treaty of commerce Signed between the two powers is to have a wonderfull effect by cementing the two Nation in bonds of lasting peace and union. With regard to America, she has got her answer from this court, that when the Treaty shall be fully complied with on our part, then the post shall be evacuated the Negroes payd for &c. The conduct of our Country makes their service abroad very unpleasent, dignified conduct, and united measures, is the only basis of National Respectibility: and honesty is the best policy for a Nation, as well as an individual.[7]

Your Neice is very well and very happy, as she has every reason to be, from manly tenderness and unfeigned affection, from kind and assidious attention, from all those virtues of the heart which constitue a good Husband, from all those qualifications of the mind which form the Gentleman, the Man of letters the Patriot and the Citizen.

Present my Love to my dear Friend mr Thaxter with whom I most sincerely Sympathize,[8] remember me to Mrs Allen and to every inquiring Friend. Accept a triffel[9] for my little Neice to whom and her Brother give a kiss which tell them I sent in my letter. To mr Shaw, you may give an other if you please, from your ever affectionate Sister

A Adams

RC (DLC:Shaw Family Papers); endorsed: "October 15. 1786." Dft (Adams Papers), filmed at [1787?], Adams Papers, Microfilms, Reel No. 370.

[1] James Thomson, *The Seasons: Spring*, lines 1152–1153.

[2] In her Dft, AA writes, "but in this wish I cannot join him for I am more and more persuaded that the early period of every Americans Education. . . ."

[3] Shakespeare, *Hamlet*, Act 3, scene iv, line 69. AA's subsequent two quotations in this paragraph are likewise from *Hamlet*: Act 1, scene v, line 54, and Act 3, scene iv, lines 42–45, respectively.

[4] AA probably refers to Paris, where she had been offended by the large number of prostitutes (to Mary Smith Cranch and to Mercy Otis Warren, both 5 Sept., vol. 5:443, 447).

[5] AA's Dft finishes the paragraph: "and their Morals. These are chiefly southern Youth whose minds are Naturally more *elevated* than those of our cold Northern climate. They have been usd to cringing slaves. This gives them a Hateur not alltogether adapted to Republican Governments."

[6] Mrs. Sinclair was the madam of a brothel in Samuel Richardson's *Clarissa*.

[7] AA's Dft extends this paragraph considerably, adding: "and no Country or Person will Succeed long where this essential prop-

erty is lost in selfishness and tricking. It is the talant of Humane Nature to run from one extreem to an other. Those who read our publick papers, more particularly some of the instructions to the Representitives and the county conventions will be led to think that our Liberty is become licentiousness. Publick principal and publick ends cannot be promoted by these illegal assemblies. There must be some crafty leader, some sly insinuating Serpent difusing his venom upon a deceived multitude for common Sense and plain Reason could not pervert and mislead my countrymeen thus." This is AA's first extended comment on the unrest in Massachusetts that gave rise to Shays' Rebellion.

8 In her Dft AA wrote, "Mr Thaxter I sympathize with him. It is the first near affliction Stroke he ever experienced. The circumstances of it render it still more so. Such is Humane life we ought to know the tenure by which we hold it, and let nothing surprize or amaize us, happy for those who can attain this christian Resignation." The "Stroke" was the death, following childbirth, of John Thaxter Jr.'s sister Lucy Thaxter Cushing in June.

9 The Dft identifies this as "a peice of calico for a Slip."

Abigail Adams Smith to Lucy Cranch

London October 15th 1786

Your Letter my Dear Cousin from Haverhill[1] I received a few weeks since, and hearing of an opportunity to Boston I embrace it to acknowledge the receipt of and answer your Letter.

I think myself very unfortunate respecting my Letters which went by Mrs Hay, that by their very long delay I was prevented hearing from my friends, and Still more that those friends should *imagine themselvs forgotten*. It Convinces me that Candor is wanting amongst them, that they should *all* make observations so much to my disadvantage for *One* supposed omission towards them. If they had each lookd Back to the Numbers of my Letters and Compared them with their own, they might rather have Condemned themselvs, for I beleive I have written two to one to most of my Correspondents Since I left America. From *such* and other instances of want of Candor I have some times half a mind to place dependance upon, a very few.

I am quite of your opinion my Cousin that you nor I should derive no happiness with our present Sentiments from Birth or Titles. But we are so very incompetent to form any judgment of others that I would not venture to decide from what scource *anyone* could ensure it to themselvs. It is *a general* foult that we too often take upon us to judge for other People, where we can have no Laudable motive for so doing.

The Idea of Mammas returning so early as the spring is I imagine rather premature. My Pappa has talkd of the next Spring for his return every season since I have been in Europe. I now Consider it only as his wish which may for many Successive seasons prove in

Compatible with his actions. Therefore my Dear I would advise you and all other Friends who feel interested in their return, not to place such a dependance upon it as to be disappointed should it not take place for several years. It may so happen that you may see your Cousin before your Aunt, for whenever I return to America, I hope it will be in my power to pay *you* an early visit. But I know of nothing at present to Ground a Supposition of my speedy return, nor is it probable that it will be within a year or two perhaps more.

I regret my seperation from my Brothers more than any other Circumstance, and there are times when it makes me unhappy, but I indeavour again to reconcile myself to it as the result of inevitable necessity.

You my Dear Lucy are happy in never having been Seperated from any of your family for any length of time. It is an happiness which you cannot Sufficiently prize without having been deprived of it, and may you enjoy it for many Successive years. We may Congratulate ourselvs my Cousin that the Behavour of our Brothers has been thus far unexceptionable, that their Conduct is not marked with any of those youthfull follies which would tarnish the Brightest tallents. This is a Sattisfaction which I find superior to every other Consideration.

I thank you my Cousin for your wishes for my Happiness, and I doubt not but it will give you pleasure to hear from me that I am so. You justly observe that happiness depends upon the peace of our minds. I beleive mine to arrise in some degree from this scource for I know of no present couse to interrupt its tranquility. Connected by ties of Honour delicacy and affection to a Gentleman fully deserving my Confidence, who is esteemd and respected by all to whom he is known, the first wish of Whose Heart is to render your Cousin Happy. She cannot be otherwise, every principle and Sentiment Conspires to establish it upon a basis that Cannot be overthrown.

Mr Smith desires to be remembered to you as my friend and relation. Write me whenever you can find an oppertunity. Remember me to your Sister and family and beleive me at all times your friend and Cousin A Smith

RC (MWA:Abigail Adams Corr.); addressed: "Miss Lucy Cranch Braintree near Boston."

[1] Not found.

Abigail Adams to Isaac Smith Sr.

My dear sir London october 16 1786

Your favour of july 20th[1] repeated to me the melancholy tidings of my dear Aunts Death. The first information which we received of it, was by a Letter from Mr W. Smith by way of Liverpool in a very short passage, upon the receipt of which I immediately wrote you. No person my dear sir can more sincerely sympathize with you than your afflicted Neice, the kindness with which my dear Aunt always treated me, was truly Maternal. As a Parent I loved her, as a Friend and companion I esteemed her. Ever pleasent and cheerfull, she filld every Relation in life with a constant—punctuality, and a strickt regard to that future State of existance to which it has pleased Heaven to remove her, and where we have the best grounded hopes of her happiness. However painfull the loss of such a Friend is to the Survivours, the reflextion upon the excellent character and many virtues which adornd their Lives, is a consolation in the midst of sorrow, it is a healing balm to the wounded Heart,

"The sweet remembrance of the just
Shall flourish when they Sleep in dust."[2]

Your Children Sir Survive to comfort your declining Years, and you have every Satisfaction in them a Parent can desire. My most affectionate Regards to them. I am indebted to mr Smith for a letter and will write him by captain cushing.[3] I have addrest a small trunk to you sir by captain Folger who has promised to take particular of it, it contains some articles for my children and a suit of part worn cloths. I suppose their be no occasion of an entry of it at the custom house as there is no Bill of laiding of it, having bought and put up the things myself only for family use. I however inclose you the key if it should be call'd for. The Trunk you will be so good as to deliver to Mrs Cranch who has the care of the things. Dr Tufts will pay you any expence arising upon them. I inclose you a Prussian Treaty, and am dear sir with every Sentiment of Regard Your affectionate Neice

A Adams

RC (MHi:Smith-Carter Papers); addressed: "To Isaac Smith Esqr Boston"; endorsed: "London Oct. 86 A. Adams."

[1] Not found.

[2] A common paraphrase of Psalms, 112:6. Elizabeth Cranch used the same quotation in her letter to AA of 1 July, above.

[3] Probably Isaac Smith Jr. to AA, 8 July, above. AA replied to him on 30 Dec., below.

Abigail Adams to John Cranch

Dear sir London october 21 1786

A fine Salmon by the Exeter Stage; a week ago informd me that the Gentleman from whom I had before received a similar favour; was still mindfull of his Friends by his deeds, tho he seldom favourd them with his personal presence.

Accept sir my thanks, not only for the Salmon, but for the Partridges and woodcocks, which I presume came from the same quarter Last Spring,[1] tho you have not sufferd [yo]ur right hand, to disclose what your Left hand has perform'd.

It pains me to receive these repeated [in]stances of your politeness, and attention, having nothing to offer you by way of acknowledgment; unless a Literary American production, may prove agreeable to you.[2]

As I know you to possess a Liberality of sentiment, beyond many of your countrymen, I have taken the Liberty to offer to your acceptance, what a dread of Truth, and a just representation of facts, prevents the printer to whom they were sent for Sale, to offer to the publick.[3]

The conduct of Britain towards America in the late Revolution, though recorded by the pen of Truth, and the Spirit of candour, is considerd as a Libel upon the actors; who are too wealthy and powerfull, to suffer a just Representation of those very deeds, which they blushed not to perpetrate.

Adulation, and the Wealth of the East Indies may silence a venal age; but a Cornwallis and a Rawdon, will Still be recorded in the Historic page of America with all the dark Shades of their Characters.[4]

Mr Ramsey the writer of the Revolution of Carolina, is a Gentleman of fortune and respectable Character and was lately President of congress.

By my last Letters from America dated in August, I had the pleasure of hearing that our [friends] were well; I had promised myself the pleasure of visiting Devonshire during the Summer, but an unexpected [call] obliged mr Adams to go to Holland, whither I accompanied him, and returnd too late; to think of an other excursion this Season.

Whenever you come to London, be assured, Sir, that I Should be very happy to see you, mr Adams presents his compliments to you.

I am sir, with Sentiments of Esteem, your Friend & Humble Servant
A Adams

RC (NhHi:Presidential Autographs Collection [Dorothy Whitney]); addressed by WSS: "Mr. John Cranch attorney at Law at Axmister"; endorsed: "21. Oct. 1786. Her Excellency the Amer. embassadress." Some loss of text where the seal was removed. Dft (Adams Papers), filmed at [1787], Adams Papers, Microfilms, Reel No. 370.

[1] John Cranch of Axminster, Richard Cranch's nephew, had also sent gifts of game to the Adamses by the Exeter stage in Sept. 1785 (vol. 5:325, 326; 6:382–383).

[2] AA concludes this sentence in her Dft with "of the Poetick kind."

[3] AA was sending Cranch a copy of David Ramsay's *The History of the Revolution of South Carolina*. Ramsay had considerable difficulties getting the book published in London, where his agent, Charles Dilly, was reluctant to sell the book for fear that its anti-British content would provoke the public or the Crown. It was finally published there in 1787, but even then, it was not sold openly (Arthur H. Shaffer, *To Be an American: David Ramsay and the Making of the American Consciousness*, Columbia, S.C., 1991, p. 102, 303).

[4] Lord Cornwallis, commander of British forces in South Carolina in 1780–1781 as well as at Yorktown, had been named governor-general of India in early 1786. Francis Lord Rawdon (1754–1826) had served in various capacities in the British Army during the Anglo-American war. He was notorious for his harsh treatment toward American forces in the Carolinas and was particularly reviled for his decision to execute Col. Isaac Haynes in Aug. 1781 (*DNB*; Greene, *Papers*, 9:251–252).

Abigail Adams to Thomas Brand Hollis

october 21 1786
London Grosvenour Square

Sir

In my late visit to Holland I was present at the Grand ceremony of Swearing their New Elected Majestrates at Utrecht. I observed at the Breast of every soldier of the free choir, as they are term'd, a Medal. Curiosity led me to inquire the design of it, and upon viewing it I was so much gratified with it, that I got a Friend to procure me one, and I know not Sir to whom so properly to dedicate the triumph of Liberty, as to the Sincere votary of her. And mr Hollis will give me real pleasure by his acceptance of the Medal, and granting it a place in the Temple of Liberty, amidst the Selection already sacred to that Goddess.

Inclosed is the explanation of the Medal, from sir your Humble Servant
A Adams

ENCLOSURE

An explanation of the medal struck at utrecht March 20 1786

The Nymph of the city of utrecht is known by her crown and her

Arms upon her Breast. By her side is the Alter of Liberty known by the Hat, and the date of the year from whence their Liberty commences. Upon the Alter are laid the roman Rods and Hachet. A Letter with three Seals designates the rights of the city and the three Members of the State. The Nymph holds it with the fingers of her Left Hand to Shew the part which the city of utrecht hath taken and to testify how much every one is interested in keeping it. In her right Hand she holds a written paper unroled upon which are written the new Rules of Government for the city. She presents it to an officer. He receives it and administers the oath both to the officers and citizens, which is performd by raising the two fingers of the right hands, whilst the citizens behind conform to it by presenting their Arms. The Houses and the Towr of the church of [. . .] at a distance on the right, point out the Square of Neude where the Solemnity was performd. The Revers is a civic crown with these words Allegience of the Citizens of utrecht to the rules of the Government of the city 20 March 1786.

RC (CSmH:HM26330). The enclosure, in AA's hand, presumably a FC, is in the Adams Papers, filed at 20 March, and filmed at that date in Adams Papers, Microfilms, Reel No. 367.

Mary Smith Cranch to Abigail Adams

My dear Sister Braintree 22d of october 1786

Cousin Charles and I have stay'd at home from meeting to day, he to write to his Papa[1] and I because I was fatigue'd with runing about Boston Street for two days to pick up a number of things for our Sons. Mr JQA wanted a winter wastcoat and mr charles a Gown and a Pair of Breeches and little Tom a surtout. He had his Brother charless last winter and uses it, this to Answer the purpose of a Gown, the Freshman are not allow'd any. I have taken a coat of his Papas which you sent in the trunk to make him one of, but it is Scarcly so long as we wear surtouts here but I tell him it will do. The vacancy is half out already[2] and I have not been able to get my Tailor to work till yesterday. We must all set to work and help her. I beleive they play as hard as they Study by the appearence of their cloaths and I do not know but it is necessary. They make such a noise in the morning as would make you laugh. They all sleep in one chamber and poor Cousin JQA wants a mor[*n*]ing nap, but they will not let him take it. If he will it must be without Bed cloaths. I tell them Sometimes to be quiet, you will hear them. I can call them to order at any time when I think they have done enough. I often think how you would rejoice to see them all. It is a goodly sight—Four liklier Lads are seldom seen.

I wish you would send a piece of Cambrick proper to ruffle their Linnen which you sent them. We shall make it this winter, they will not want to wear them till the spring. I cannot get any cambrick proper for that Linnen here under three dollars a yard and I dare not ask the Doctor for money to purchase it at this price. It will not comport with his Ideas of Frugality. I can buy a little to ruffle their old shirts, and I think it is no matter if some of them are wore without especially in the Freshman year.

My dear Sister I have been oblig'd to do what gives me great pain. The troublesome times into which we are fallen has depriv'd mr cranch of the possibility of geting one shilling from the publick of what is due to him for his services in past years or the present, by which means I find it impossible to provide Food for our Family during the vacancys without taking Something for the Board of my dear Nephews. It has given me more dissagreable feelings than I can express. I hop'd it would have been in my Power to have in this way return'd some of the obligations I feel my self under to you. The dissapointment Sinks my spirits—and has caus'd me not a few tears.

I have charg'd Ten shillings a week for each of them, as provision is I believe it will take that to feed them. I believe I have told you that I have a washing and an Ironing woman to whom I give one and four pence a day. We generaly wash once in a fortnight Sometimes once a week, just as the Quanty of Linnen chanceth to be, this I thought the cheapest way to get their washing done. If I have your approbation I shall be happier.

I wish you to keep the affair of a certain Gentleman a secret, as it is yet uncertain Whether Law or Philosophy is to be charg'd with it.[3] The Split Peas are excellent, and I thank you for them. I did not know you had sent any till a few weeks since.[4]

Betsy will write this week. It has not been in her Power to write since she reciev'd yours and mrs Smiths kind Letters. Lucys being absent, her needle has been fully imploy'd. She sends her Duty and Love. Leanard White and her Freind Peggy are here. She is soon to be married to mr Bailey Bartlet, She says give my respect to mrs Adams and Mrs Smith—yours affectionaly M. Cranch

RC (Adams Papers); endorsed: "Mrs Cranch ocbr 22 1786."

[1] Not found.

[2] Harvard's fall vacation extended from 17–31 Oct.; the three Adams boys and William Cranch spent most of it at the Cranches' in Braintree (JQA, *Diary*, 2:116–120).

[3] That is, Royall Tyler's fathering Elizabeth Hunt Palmer's daughter Sophia (see Mary Smith Cranch to AA, 24 Sept., note 4, above).

[4] AA never mentioned the split peas in her correspondence with Cranch, but they were probably sent around the time of AA's 4 July letter, above, which Cranch received on 9 October.

Thomas Brand Hollis to Abigail Adams

Chesterfeild Street

Madam octo 22. 1786

I was most sensibly pleased, with the Sight of the Dutch Liberty medal which you was so obliging as to send me. I know not how to deprive you of it but in compliance with your commands and from the manner in which you express yourself.

Assuredly it shall have an interesting, place in my cabinet sacred to Freedom amidst the american medals.

If you and Mr Adams will come down to the Hide, you will increase my obligations, and see the Series of Heroes and of Patriots which as America promises to equal it may be of use to observe the manner of preserving their fame and portraits.

The Dutch can no longer be reproached—"with whom Dominion lurks from hand to hand undignified by publick choice,"[1] and I hope this is the begining of better times. They are indebted to the Americans who are become the preceptors of mankind as once the English were!

My intention was to have waited on you and Mr Adams before this but have been much engaged and detained at home. Shall be in town again soon and, renew my application. I am madam with the greatest regard your obliged, Friend T Brand Hollis

RC (Adams Papers).

[1] Mark Akenside, Ode VIII: "On Leaving Holland," *Odes on Several Subjects*, London, 1745, lines 24–25.

Thomas Welsh to Abigail Adams

Dear Madam Boston Octobr 27th 1786

Your esteemed Favor of July 22d did not come to hand untill Capt Callahan had arrived 12 Days, for which and its Contents accept our

Thanks. I shall see Dr Tufts and attend to the Directions of the Note.[1]

I am sorry to reflect that the Conclusions drawn in my last to you were so erroneous they were founded upon an opinion of Virtue which I am now convinced is [in?]suficiently possessed by the main Body of the People to govern their political Conduct. The Causes however of the Tumult have been laid in former Administrations.

For several Years the Militia of this Commonw[ealth] had been intirely neglected and with out Officers. The Peop[le] of the back Counties Suffered to neglect the payment of the[ir] Taxes these consequently had accumulated, and the Aversion to discharge increased in Proportion. The County Traders had obtained large Credits of the sea port Mercha[nts] and they in their Turns had obtaind Credits in Europe; prior Debts accumulated during and previous to the Warr; and add to this the Bounties promised to the Soldiers[2] being all demanded at the s[ame?] Time was too much for the Virtue of these People to [. . .] and afforded a Compleat Oppertunity for a Number of bold and designing Men to inflame and mislead others less informed than themselves. The Requisitions of Congress I ought to have mentioned as it is one of the principle Bones of Contention. In short every thing that has the Appearance of Government is matter of Complaint with them.

The present Governor has been exerting himself since his Appointment to get the Militia organized but the former Appointments were such as discouraged the Attempt in part and for the want of this it is generally thought the Insurgents were able to make any Way.

The Continent feels its Infirmity for the Want of committing that Degree of Power to Congress which she wants to regulate the Concerns of the whole and I am fully convinced we shall be a Contemptable People untill it is granted but whether it will ever be I know not.

The Genl Court are sitting and examining into the Causes of the Complaints of the People but I think They will have their Hands full and after they have done they will not be satisfied I am sure.[3] They ought not to be gratified but I suppose as they cry for nothing like froward Children they will be visited with a Rod. Blessed with a Constitution faulty only as it is too good they must expect no other th[a]n a m[or]e rig[orous?] Government in exchange for that [whi]ch they now dont know the Value of. I hope you will not in future be mislead by my Accounts from this Quarter. I am Sensible the Politics of the Country have got beyond my Reach. It is more easy for me to inform you of the little Events which occur in the domistic Circle. Mr Sullivan of Boston you have undoubtdly heard lost his Wife last Winter. He is now about to be married to Mrs Simpson of Portsmouth who made herself famous when the Wife of Mr Barrell of that Place in sueing for a Divorce which she obtained appearing h[erse]lf in open Court for that Purpose. She has 4 Children [and Mr] Sullivan seven a patriarchal number. Courage on both Sides, but She has a Fortune and it is said is accomplished.[4] Mrs Hayleys marriage is an old affair and Mr Jeffries keeps the Keys now of Course being head of the Family.[5] Mr Thos Russell is like soon to have his Family increased,[6] but as I think I must have exhausted your Patience I will now tire it no longer but do myself the Honor to subscribe with Sentiments of great Respect to Mr Adams and yourself your most Humle Ser Thomas Welsh

RC (Adams Papers); addressed: "His Excellency John Adams Esqr: Grovesnor Square London"; notation: "Ship letter"; stamped: "12 NEW RUMNEY"; endorsed: "dr Welch ocbr 27. 1786." Some loss of text where the seal was removed and at a torn margin.

[1] The 22 July letter is printed above from an incomplete Dft. It does not contain the directives to which Welsh refers.

[2] At this point Welsh struck out an entire line so thoroughly that it is illegible.

[3] The General Court sat from 27 Sept. to 18 Nov. (Mass., *Acts and Laws*, Resolves of 1786, Sept. sess., p. 347, 422).

[4] James Sullivan's first wife, Mehitable Odiorne, died 26 January. On 31 Dec., Sullivan married Martha Langdon of Portsmouth, N.H., a sister of New Hampshire's recent governor, John Langdon. Her first marriage, to William Barrell in 1765, had ended after just three months when she petitioned the New Hampshire legislature for divorce on the grounds that Barrell was "utterly incapable to satisfy the most virtuous and modest Feminine Inclination and is Impotent to render that due Benevolence which every married woman is warranted." She later married Thomas Simpson, who died at sea in 1784 (*DAB* [Sullivan and Langdon]; Lawrence Shaw Mayo, *John Langdon of New Hampshire*, Concord, N.H., 1937, p. 23–24; *Documents and Records Relating to the Province of New-Hampshire, from 1765 to 1776*, ed. Nathaniel Bouton, 7 vols., Nashua, N.H., 1875, 7:93, 97–98; Joseph Foster, *The Soldiers' Memorial. Portsmouth, N.H. 1893–1923*, Portsmouth, N.H., 1923, p. 46).

[5] Mary Hayley married Patrick Jeffery Esq. in Boston on 13 Feb. (Boston, *30th Report*, p. 413).

[6] Sarah Sever and Thomas Russell had a daughter, Sarah, on 1 Dec. ("An Account of the Russell Family of Charlestown," 1905, p. 26–27, MHi:Sullivan-Russell Papers).

Elizabeth Smith Shaw to Abigail Adams

My Ever Dear Sister Haverhill November 1st. 1786

Two Vessels arrived from London while I was upon my little southern Tour. It was in vain that I enquired after Letters directed to me. "You have received one from Mrs Smith."[1] Yes, It was a sweet Morsel, it informed me of her Marriage, but not half enough to reperuse by our chearful fireside, no *particulars of the proceedings*, to satisfy the Curiosity of an hundred inquiring Friends. I cannot say but what I feel Chagrined and should be much more grieved if *I could* entertain an Idea that my dear Sister thought *me* less interested than Others, in any Event, or in any Circumstance that could affect *her* Happiness.

She has a thousand avocations. She is treasuring up Knowledge, a Fund for the improvment, and entertainment of her Friends, Neices, and *Grand-children*. She will adorn, and make old-age honourable. She will smooth, and sweeten the decline of Life by her instructive Conversation. Her setting Sun, will diffuse chearfulness, light, and knowledge upon all around her.

She has many Correspondents. She needs an Amanuensis. She has been very good to me, and seldom has omited writing. Thus in the Multitude of my Thoughts I comforted myself.

Cousin William Cranch came last Week and carried Home my Neice Lucy, so that my Family is reduced now to quite a small one. I endeavour in every Situation of Life to be Content. But I think I never felt happier than when my Nephews were around me, and I fancied I was supplying their dear Mothers Place in some small Degree. And Cares, if not too great are always pleasing to the active Soul.

Cousin Lucy has been happier, in this Visit to Haverhill, than she has ever been before, for it has so happened that some one, or other of the Family has always been sick, but now she has escaped with my Children only having the Chin Cough,[2] and Hall Tufts a Lung Fever. She has fine Health herself, and is possessed of an excellent Temper. Her constitution will never be impaired by any voilent agitation of Spirits, for she is sensible, modest, gentle, tranquil, not greatly elated, or depressed. Perhaps not quite so sociable, and engaging to Strangers as her Sister; she rather withdraws, than obtrudes upon your Notice. But the more she is known, the more she is beloved, and esteemed. I have been particular because I think her Manners were not formed when you left America, and she is much likelier, and more improved now than when you saw her.

We had the pleasure of finding all our Friends comfortable, and well upon our Journey. My Father Shaw is still living, and makes old-age honourable by his chearful, and pleasant Conversation. It is indeed a Crown to such, who have fought, a good Fight. And I never saw a Man glide down the slope of Life with more ease, and fewer Complaints than he.[3]

The cheif Conversation in that part of the Country, (setting aside political matters) was relating to Mr Oaks Angier's Life, and Death. He died of a Consumption last September, after a few Months lingering Illness. What has he left is the question? Ten thousand pounds L M,[4] which he had amassed in the course of about fourteen Years Application to Buisness. Clear of every incumbrance. He made his Will, and divided it between his Wife and five Children. He spoke for his Coffin, and ordered every Affair, relating to their mourning. He advised his wife to marry again if she could with advantage charging her at the same time to get some able Lawyer to draw the marriage Articles, that she might not be tricked out of what he had given her.[5] He directed that his eldest Son should have a liberal Education,[6] after that, study Law with Mr Davis, and give him the same sum of Money, which Mr Davis had given his Father for the like purpose. The other Children were to live with their Mother, allowing her a Dollar pr week for their Board.

His two Daughters when they were of a proper age, were to be sent to Boston, and put to School there, three Summers, and directed them to have every advantage that could be obtained for them.[7] His own Brother, and his wives Brother are the Executors of his very particular last Will, and Testament.[8] I am very sorry, I cannot find the News Paper that I might give you his Character, as it was given to the Publick. But whatever Censure, or Eulogy the world may pass upon his Character—*You* know the Man.—In the course of a few years he had often said, that no Man had any *right*, or *buisness* to live after they were forty years old. And (perhaps) least he might view himself as a cumberer of the Ground, his Maker gave him leave to Depart just as he had entered his fortieth year.

People seem much divided in their Opinion, some suppose he was a real Convert, Others, that he was only frighted at the Idea of dying—and that, had he been restored to Health, he would have been the same scoffer, and despiser of Religion he was before.

It was not till the *last* week of his Sickness that he sent for Mr Reed, and beged him to propound him to the Church for full Communion, and his Wife for Baptism for herself and all their children. His Request was made known to the Church, while he lay a poor lifeless Corpse in his own House, and Providence did not suffer him to live, to be admited as a member here below. I hope he is received into the Church triumphant, and that he is made white in the Blood of the Lamb. But Oh my Sister! how terrible It is, for any one to leave the important Concerns of Eternity, to a Moment of *Time*.

He sent for every person who thought themselves abused, and ill treated by him, and desired their forgivness. He thanked God that he had been true to his Client, and wronged no man designedly. Thus ended the Life of a Man indefatigable in his Proffession, possessed of great Qualities, and great Faults.

November 3d.

We have had a remarkable pleasant Fall, almost as warm as July and August, without any long Storms as usual. Last Thursday we kept our Doors, and windows open, and a monday it snowed the whole afternoon.[9] So changeable is the Weather, but not more various than human Events. For last Night I received a Letter from my Sister Cranch, informing of Cousin Lucys return in fine health and Spirite, and making them all happy. But alas! there Joy was soon turned into mourning, for Mr Cranch came from Boston the same Evening, with a Letter in his Pocket which brought the melancholly Tydings of Mr Perkins Death. He was seized with a Fever upon his Lungs, and dyed last August, after a few Days Iillness. You know what a sincere affection my Sister Cranch had for this amiable, virtuous young Man—And cannot wonder if she is deeply wounded. But the gentle Eliza, I tremble for her. His virtues had of late taken full possession of the Heart of Eliza—Dear unhappy Girl—I hope thy better Days are to come.[10]

This Letter must go by Capt Marsh to Boston, for I hear a Vessel will certainly sail in a Day or two. I shall write to Mrs Smith and forward it to go in the same Vessel if possible. My Son made me promise I would ask Aunt Adams to send him the Childrens Friend.[11] I told him it was too large a Request for a little Boy to make. And Quincy she has set by and done half a dozen Letters up, full of Love she says to her Aunt, but you must accept the Will for the Deed. It is late—and I must bid you good Night—wishing you Health, and every Blessing. I hope to hear from you soon, and that you are not injured by your late Excursion to the Hague. Once more adieu yours affectionately Eliza Shaw

Mr Shaw sends his Love, and best Respects and thanks for the Book.

RC (Adams Papers).

[1] AA2's letter to Shaw has not been found.

[2] Whooping cough.

[3] Rev. John Shaw of Bridgewater was 78 years old and would live until 1791 (*Sibley's Harvard Graduates*, 8:627–629).

[4] Lawful money, that is, Massachusetts currency.

[5] Susanna Howard (or Haward) Angier (1751–1793) eventually remarried, to Jesse Fobes, in 1792 (same, 16:7; *Vital Records of Bridgewater Massachusetts to the Year 1850*, 2 vols., Boston, 1916, 1:141; 2:134, 472).

[6] Charles Angier (1774–1806), Harvard 1793 (*Harvard Quinquennial Cat.*).

[7] The Angiers had three daughters: Mary (b. 1776), Sarah (b. 1780), and Susanna (b. 1783). All three were still living in 1786 (same, 16:7).

[8] Oakes Angier's brother was Samuel Angier (1743–1805), Harvard 1763, who served as the second minister of the First Congregational Parish of East Bridgewater, following in the footsteps of his father, Rev. John Angier (same, 6:370; 15:350). Oakes had three brothers-in-law: Edward, Daniel, and Martin Howard (or Haward) (*Vital Records of Bridgewater*, 1:137, 139, 141).

[9] JQA noted that it "Snow'd all the morning" of Monday, 30 Oct., in Braintree (*Diary*, 2:120).

[10] Elizabeth Cranch was indeed deeply affected by the death of Thomas Perkins in Kentucky. She confided to her diary that "the *dreaded event has taken place*—and Heaven deprives me of the friend on whom my Heart lean'd" (MHi:Elizabeth Cranch Norton Diary, 21 Nov.).

[11] Arnaud Berquin, *The Children's Friend; Consisting of Apt Tales, Short Dialogues, and Moral Dramas*, 24 vols. in 12, London, 1783.

Thomas Brand Hollis to Abigail Adams

The 4th of November
The day of deliverance from Popery and Tyranny. 1786[1]

Mr Brand Hollis presents his compliments to Mrs Adams and desires her acceptance of two medals one on the execution of the counts Egmont and Horne two Dutch Patriots contrary to faith-given!

The other on the Murder of the first Prince of Orange

Base acts of a Tyrant![2]

Three common wealth coins[3] to record, what England once was.

Mrs Adams had the only copy of the right hand of Fellowship which was printed at that time[4] otherwise more would have been sent.

RC (Adams Papers).

[1] Guy Fawkes Day, 5 November.

[2] The "tyrant" was Philip II of Spain. Lamoral, Count of Egmont, and Philip de Montmorency, Count of Hoorn, prominent Catholic critics of Philip's rule in the Netherlands, were executed at Brussels in 1568 on the orders of Philip's lieutenant, the Duke of Alva. William I (the Silent), Prince of Orange, leader of the Protestant revolt in the Netherlands' northern provinces, was assassinated, with Philip's encouragement, at his home in Delft in 1584 (see JA, *Papers*, 10:108–110, 116, 117).

[3] Not identified.

[4] Not identified.

John Cranch to Abigail Adams

Madam Axminster, 7. Nov; 1786

Being much ignorant of the republican distinctions of preeminency in title, as well as of American etiquette in general, I must anticipate your pardon for any errors in that kind, while I acknowledge the honor of your Excellency's obliging letter and present of books: Both have afforded me great satisfaction; only the latter moving now and then, to some untempered gusts of resentment against those *Excorables*—Balfour, Cunningham, &c:[1] But the sentiments and actions of such beings as Rutledge, Greene, La Fayette, Gadsden, and others, soon allayed those little indignations; and The mind, lit up by such splendid examples of courage, generosity and divine patriotism, no longer perceived itself shaded by the feeble rancours of an expiring petty tyranny.

My notion about the war always was, that the ministry, [I don't at all consider the * * * *[2] in this hypothesis; because, *at least*, from the end of Lord Chatham's administration to the beginning of his son's, it is impossible to conceive his Majesty in any larger idea than that of *a respectable private gentleman in disagreeable circumstances.*][3] without much inclination of it's own, was urged to it, by a scotch-infested junto, consisting of the Navy, the Army, the Contractors, and a larger banditti than usual of plunder-inspired, profligate adventurers. The bountifull Head of the Treasury,[4] doubtlessly, intended to place and pension *all mankind*; but resources failing, the clamorous Disappointed found no difficulty in fixing his Lordship's views upon the goodly Goshen of America:[5] In all the subsequent proceedings, administration and this "quadruple alliance" mutually—(and it must be owned, with the utmost *propriety*)—supported and illustrated each other. Whether the *actors* of the British hostilities, who (according to my creed) were also the chief *authors* of them, were ever *serious* in their sentiments and designs; or whether the whole was but a *pretence*, and the supposed war only a stalking-horse for messrs. Avarice, Rapine and Plunder, the *generals* to whom the conduct of it seems to have been principally committed, I will not presume even to surmise; but certainly I never knew any Englishman, without the sphere of partial and undue *influence*, and who possessed common sense, but was capable of ridiculing the pretended *justice*, as well as the pretended *idea in* *general*, of subjugating America in the political circumstances in which that wild-goose chace was attempted.

But I should not thus, madam impertinently trespass on your attention; and I beg your pardon.

We had entertained hopes in the summer, that this country would be honored with at least a transitory presence of His Excellency and yourself (agreeably to the plan you mention to have been frustrated by your journey to Holland:) The season is slipped away, but our disappointed cottages will again be trimmed for your reception, at a more genial and auspicious season.

You charge me with *total* silence: When I sent some of the birds last winter, I meant to trouble our illustrious friend with a line of advice about them; and such a note was certainly carried to the post, though I must now conclude, by your imputation, that it miscarried: I am gratefully sensible of the honor His Excellency does me by his obliging remembranc: It is not unlikely that I shall be in London sometime this winter: If so, madam, be assured I shall accept the civilities you condescend to offer me, with great pleasure; and with the respect and gratitude which becomes Your Excellency's Most obliged Faithfull Humble servant J. Cranch

P.S. Accept my congratulations on the union of miss Adams and Colonel smith: [. . . .] peculiarly pleasing to the [. . . .] Liberty to observe their favorite [. . . .]—[pardon a jocular allusion][6] [. . . .] to administer the *Ecclesiastical gluepot* on that happy occasion.

RC (Adams Papers); addressed: "To Her Excellency Mrs Adams."; endorsed: "J Cranch Letter." Some loss of text in the postscript, and possibly in AA's endorsement, where the seal was removed.

[1] Nisbet Balfour (1743–1823), a Scottish officer under Cornwallis, served as commandant of Charleston and was responsible for raising a militia of over 4,000 Carolina loyalists (*DNB*). William Cunningham was a member of the British militia from South Carolina; David Ramsay accused him of committing various atrocities against settlers who supported the American cause (Ramsay, *The History of the Revolution of South-Carolina, from a British Province to an Independent State*, 2 vols., Trenton, N.J., 1785, 2:272–273).

[2] Thus in MS.

[3] This material was written at the end of the letter, following the postscript, with brackets around it, and marked for insertion here.

[4] Frederick Lord North.

[5] That is, a land of rich natural resources and abundant harvests like Goshen, where the Israelites lived from the time of Joseph until the Exodus (Genesis, 45–47; Numbers, 11:5).

[6] The brackets around "pardon a jocular allusion" are in the MS.

Abigail Adams to Elizabeth Smith Shaw

My Dear Sister London November 21 1786

Mr Sparhawk calld upon us a Day or two ago, and deliverd me your kind Letter of: july the 20th. It was of a latter date than any I had received from you tho near four months old. It was a little unfortunate for the Gentleman that mr Adams enterd immediately into an inquiry of him, respecting the State and commerce of the Massachusetts, of which be sure the Gentleman drew a most gloomy picture, and finishd the whole by saying; that the people in the united States were as much oppressed by taxes as they were in Europe. This being so wholy groundless it roused the quick feelings of mr A. who replied a little warmly–give me leave to tell you Sir, that people who hold this language, betray a total ignorance of the Subject. Name the article in this Country, even to the light of Heaven, the air you Breath and the water you drink, which is not taxed? Loaded down with accumulated burdens is this *Free people*. Yet the whole is not Sufficient to pay even the interest of the National Debt, and the Charges of government. Mr Pitts Surpluss is a vision, and new methods of taxation must be devised. Pray are our Farmers perishing in the midst of plenty, as in Ireland, are our Fishermen Starving? cannot the labourer find a subsistance? or has the price of labour fallen to 6 pence and subsistance risen to a shilling? or is it only trade that languishes? Thank God that necessity then will oblige those who have lived Luxuriously at the expence of others, and upon property which was not their own, to do so no longer. There is not a Merchant in England France or Holland, with capitals which could buy fifty of our most oppulent Merchants, that lives at half the expence which I have been informd many of ours run into during the War and Since.

By this time I had got into that part of your Letter which informd me that mr Sparhawk had been unfortunate in buisness. I knew mr Adams was a perfect Stranger to this and could design nothing against the Gentleman but Still I felt pained for him, as I presumed he had never had such a lesson before. He drew in his horns and was more upon his gaurd the remainder of the time. We ask'd him to dine with us the Next day but he was engaged. Mr Adams will return his visit, and then we Shall send him a card of invitation. In his Manners and address he appears much of a Gentleman, but his domestick conduct will allways make me regard him as an unhappy Man. His Brother lives here in affluence and splendour.[1]

We have had an other of your Parishoners to visit us, mr Blodget, a queer Soul you know, but a very great admirer of you. He has a project in his Head for rasing the Royal George, and has sent proposals to the Lords of the admirality and Lord How was inquiring his character of mr Adams the other day at the Levee, from which circumstance I fancy he is attended to.[2] But if he does not accomplish this, he is determined to travel through the different counties in England, and collect as much knowledge of agriculture as he possibly can, and by that he may render service to his own Country. He has a real good understanding, tho little cultivated.

The accounts you gave me of the Singing of your Birds and the prattle of your children entertaind me much. Do you know that European Birds have not half the melody of ours, nor is their fruit half so sweet, or their flowers half so Fragrant, or their Manners half so pure, or their people half So virtuous. But keep this to yourself, or I shall be thought more than half deficient in understanding and taste. I will not dispute what every person must assent to, that the fine Arts Manufactories and agriculture have arrived to a great degree of maturity and perfection. But what is their age? what their individual Riches when compared with us? Far removed from my mind may the National prejudice be, of conceiving all that is good and excellent comprized within the narrow compass of the united States. The Unerversal Parent has dispenced his Blessings through out all creation, and tho to some he hath given a more goodly Heritage than others, we have reason to believe that a general order and harmony is mantained by apportioning each their proper station. Tho Seas Mountains and Rivers are geographical boundaries, they contract not the benevolence and good will of the Liberal mind which can extend itself beyond the limits of Country and kindred and claim fellowship with Christian jew or Turk. What a lesson did the great Author of our Religion give to mankind by the Parable of the Jew and Samaritan, but how little has it been regarded. To the Glory of the present age, they are shaking off that narrow contracted Spirit of preistcraft and usurpation; which has for so many ages tyranized over the minds of Mankind; and deluged the World in Blood. They consider Religion not as a State Stalking Horse, to raise Men to temporal power and dignity, but as a wise and benevolent System calculated to Still the Boisterous passions, to restrain the Malevolent ones to curb the ambitions, and to harmonize mankind to the temper of its great Author who came to make peace, and not to destroy. The late act of toleration pass'd by Virgina is Esteemed here as an example to the World.[3]

Captain Folger by whom I wrote you is I hope arrived safe captain Cushing will make a winters voyage of it I fear. We are now really in the Gloomy Month of November Such as I have heard it described, but did not last year experience. Now we have it, all smoke fog and darkness, and the general mourning for the Princess Amelia adds to the Gloom of the Scene. I was yesterday at the drawing room for the first time Since her Death, and tho I cannot Say all faces gatherd Blackness, all bodies appear so. As she had given her fortune to her German Nephews it would have been absurd to have shewn any appearence of Grief.[4] Poor John Bull is vastly angry and mortified. Had it been given to the Prince of Wales, *his liberal hand* would soon have pourd forth the golden Shower, and as his Aunt acquired it all in this Nation, here it ought to have remained, Says john. But he cannot alter it, so he vents himself as usual in abuse and bellowing. Yours most tenderly A Adams

RC (Adams Papers). HA2, a trustee of the Adams Manuscript Trust, bought this letter from Goodspeed's Book Shop in March 1949 and placed it in the collection of family papers.

[1] Nathaniel Sparhawk Jr. was separated from his third wife, Deborah Adams, who was left to support Sparhawk's children from his previous marriages. In 1788 the Commission on Loyalist Claims granted Sparhawk a pension of £80 per year. He did not return permanently to America until 1809. His brother was probably Sir William Pepperrell, Harvard 1766, a Massachusetts loyalist who had inherited substantial wealth from his grandfather, Gen. Sir William Pepperrell (*Sibley's Harvard Graduates*, 16:235–237, 397–403).

[2] Samuel Blodget (1724–1807), a merchant and manufacturer in Haverhill, had invented a machine for raising sunken ships. He used it to raise cargo from a ship sunk near Plymouth in 1783 and proposed to do the same in Britain for the *Royal George*—a ship of the line that had capsized off Spithead with heavy loss of life in 1782—but was unsuccessful (*Appletons' Cyclo. Amer. Biog.*).

[3] The Virginia General Assembly passed the "Statute for Establishing Religious Freedom" that disestablished the Episcopal Church in early 1786.

[4] Princess Amelia Sophia Leonora, aunt of George III, died on 31 Oct. On 3 Nov., the London *Daily Universal Register* reported that Amelia had directed in her will that the proceeds from the sale of her lands and personal property should go to her nephews, the prince of Hesse Cassel and his brother, in Germany. In the following days, some newspaper reports criticized this decision, noting that "In the disposal of her fortune she most certainly has disappointed numerous expectants, and much is it to be regretted that a foreign partiality should have so entirely obliterated every trace of domestic concern" (London *Morning Post and Daily Advertiser*, 6 Nov.; London *Daily Universal Register*, 4 Nov.).

Abigail Adams to John Quincy Adams

My dear Son London November 22 1786

It is a long time since I received a line from you, or any other of my Friends, nor have we learnt with certainty whether your Brother Tommy was admitted Colledge. By captain Folger I wrote to you, and hope it went Safe to your hand, as the Letter containd Something more than words. As I know you will not wish to Spend any time Idle it may not be too early to consult you respecting the preceptor you wish to be placed with. Law I take for granted is the Study you mean to persue. Mr Lowel of Boston and mr Parsons of Newbury port, are both of them Gentleman Eminent in their profession, and I have made inquiry of mr Cutting who you know was with mr Lowel respecting the Situation of his office and the method persued in it. Mr Cutting has the highest opinion of mr Lowels abilities, and a great esteem for his private character, as every person acquainted with him must have. But he adds that mr Lowel has a natural Indolence about him, which prevents a pupils deriving all that information and advantage from him, which a more active Character would afford,[1] and in addition to this, a city is not the best calculated for study. Mr Parsons character is equally high as a Lawyer, and he has, as I have been informd an insatiable thirst for knowledge, and is never better pleasd than when he can meet with a Youth of Similar taste and inclinations. I own from the Character of both Gentlemen, and other circumstances, I am led to incline to mr Parsons. But you who are upon the spot, with the information and advice of your Friends, may be best able to judge upon the Subject. I know your Father means to leave it to your choice. You will inform yourself upon the Subject, and the Terms &c and communicate to us. Your Father will then write to the Gentleman.[2]

We are Still left in the Dark respecting our continuance here. Few decisive measures appear to be taken by Congress upon any Subject, indeed I fear they are so much embarressd as not to know what to do. I hope according to Parson Moodys doctrine, they will not do, they know not what, which has some times been the case.[3] The Treaty between France and England is ratified between the high contracting parties, it must come before Parliament and receive a Sanction there; whether it will meet with much opposition there; time only will determine. What is termd opposition here, is a very feeble party, who have not purses and concequently not power to carry any points of importance. It is rather Novel for this Nation to Court and cringe to a Country which they have ever affected to Hate and despise, but the Edicts of the King of France totally prohibiting British Manufactories, Effected what mr Crawford could not, by three years residence, and I dare Say the united States might have accomplishd the Same, if they would all have adopted the Massachusetts Navigation act, and abided by it.

It is a subject of much regreet to every Friend of America, and no small mortification to those in publick Character, to see the proceedings of some Counties and Towns, uneasy and wrestless under a Government in which they enjoy perfect freedom, they are taking effectual methods to create themselves a Tyrant e'er long. By wishing to abolish the Senate they are destroying that balance of power by which alone their Liberties are secured to them. The Printers in this Country Eagerly Seaize every paragraph of this kind and publish it, which they would not do, if they did not conceive they could injure America by it. They have given us in this days papers the proceedings of the County convention of Hampshire, which are a disgrace to our annals.[4] I have been thinking whether it might not be of use to our Country to have some Such Societys formed as there are in this Country, call'd debating Societies, in which a precident presides. The Question is publishd two Days or more before hand, admission is easy, only 6 pence a person, and any person who pleases may enter and speak to the Subject. And these Societies are the resort of all the Young Gentleman who wish to form themselves for publick Speaking; whether for the Law, divinity, or the House of commons. And sometimes Questions are discussed here in a masterly manner. A perfect Stranger has an equal freedom of Speach, with the best known, order and decency must be observed, but no questions are askd, who you are, or from whence you came. I will give you from this Days paper the Question for tomorrow Evening.

"Which of the three publick Characters in the present Situation of this Country, is most qualified by his abilities and integrity to fill the office of Prime Minister, Lord North, mr Fox or mr Pitt."[5]

This is a question of no small importance and delicacy. I think with judicious management Societies of this kind might be establishd at least in the different universities, and many benifical concequences result from them.

Your Father is much engaged in a work that may prove of no Small utility to our Country. It is an investigation into the different Forms of Government, both ancient and modern, Monarchical Aristocratical Democratical and Republican, pointing out their happiness or misery in proportion to their different balances. It appears to be a subject in which America is greatly interested, and upon which her future happiness depends. When compleated, he means only to publish a few for the present and those only for himself and Friends, but he is So much Swallowed up in the persuit of his Subject that you must not wonder if you do not receive a line from him. I think he enjoys better Health this fall than I have known him to have for Several years.

RC (Adams Papers); endorsed: "Mrs: Adams Novr: 22. 1786."; docketed "My Mother. 22. Novr: 1786."

[1] John Lowell trained numerous students over the years, but as Harrison Gray Otis noted, "He then rarely came to the office,—only for a few minutes at a time, then hurrying up to the court in session, to rush into the argument of some important cause. . . . His consultations with clients were principally at his own house in Roxbury, and in short interviews. He generally amused himself in his garden until it was time to hurry in to court,—where he never arrived too early" (*Sibley's Harvard Graduates*, 14:654).

[2] No such letter from JA to Theophilus Parsons regarding JQA's study of the law has been found.

[3] Samuel Moody (1675/6–1747), Harvard 1697, served as the chaplain to the garrison and minister of the First Church at York, Mass. (now Maine), for nearly fifty years. Something of a folklore character in Massachusetts, Moody was known for his ability to quote apt scripture. In one instance, where members of his church were having difficulty making decisions, he advised them to adjourn and pray for guidance. The following Sunday, he preached on the text "Neither know we what to do: but our eyes are upon thee" (2 Chronicles, 20:12). After introducing the text, he claimed for his own doctrine, "When a person or people are in such a situation that they know not what to do, *they should not do they know not what;* but their eyes should be unto the Lord for direction" (*Sibley's Harvard Graduates*, 4:356–364; Charles C. P. Moody, *Biographical Sketches of the Moody Family*, Boston, 1847, p. 70). See also JA's description of Moody at vol. 1:115–116.

[4] The Hampshire County Convention met 22 Aug. at Hatfield with fifty towns represented. Seventeen of the twenty-one articles the convention adopted were grievances, some of which could only be resolved by a new state constitution (Leonard L. Richards, *Shays's Rebellion: The American Revolution's Final Battle*, Phila., 2002, p. 8).

[5] Debating societies were both common and popular in late eighteenth-century London, covering an array of topics but most especially politics, religion, and philosophy. The one AA describes here took place on 23 Nov. at Coachmakers Hall (London *Morning Herald*, 23 Nov.; Donna T. Andrew, comp., *London Debating Societies, 1776–1799*, London, 1994, p. 191.)

Mary Smith Cranch to Abigail Adams

My dear sister — Braintree November 26th 1786

Come home my Sister, that Braintree may have some of its old inhabitants residing in it. Could you look in upon it, you would sigh over some of its desirted mansions. General Palmers Family mov'd last week to charlestown. They came here in a violent Snow-Storm; they had sent away all their Provision and had nothing to eat. The next day they Set off in much better Spirits than I expected. The salt Works is his Hobby Horse yet. I hope somcthing will be found at for him to do that may support the Family.[1] Cousins Polly and Betsy are greatly oblig'd for their Gowns. You desir'd me to give them skirts but as they had skirts, and no Gowns I knew you would had you been here added two yards more to have made them what would have been so much more necessary for them. I hope I have not done wrong.

Mr Alleyn has been gone ever since the spring to the West Indies. Able is not yet married. Mrs Quincy and Miss Nancy are gone out of Town the greatest part of their time and uncle Quincy has not been off his Farm since December. Betsy was at Haverhill all last Fall and winter and Lucy all the summer. She return'd in october vacancy. It is in the vacancys only that we have any gallants in Braintree, except for married *Ladies* and not for all those your sister is an exception.[2] *The Double Sleigh* begins to run.[3] Its owner has not shewn his Face in our House nor meeting House since May. Matters remain just as they did in Boston. He continues to Board in the Family and all the Town to fix the — upon him, and, laugh att the tame Husband. Not one of the Generals Family but himself and he only when business obliges him to; will go to the House.

A mr woodard has mov'd into the House which mr T. bought for him of mr Glover. I hear they are a pritty Family I design to visit them. I Shall stand a chance to meet mr T. there. I find he has *domesticated* himself already.

I Sent you a Short Letter by capt Barnard I had not time to do more. I find he has Sail'd.[4] I wrote you that I had been making a visit to Sister Smith a wedding visit at Medford, and spent a night or two at cambridge. I went into cousin Toms chamber for the first time, it is a very good one and look'd very nice. He loves to have every thing in its place, and takes very good care of his cloaths and conducts well in every respect, So far as I can learn. Cousin JQA is chosen one of the Theses collectors which does him honour. The Governeurs of the College speak well of them all. There is like to be a great disturbance in cambridge at, the seting of the court of common Pleas this week. There is an express come to the Governour to inform him that one Shays one of the Heads of the Incindiarys, (It is a many headed Beast) is determin'd to come with eighteen hundred men to stop the court. There will be force Sent to oppose them I suppose, and I wish there may not be Blood shed. Are we not hastning fast to monarchy? to Anarchy I am sure we are, unless the

People discover a better Spirit soon. We are concern'd for our children I assure you. The college company are wishing to be allow'd to march out in defence of Government but they will not be permited.[5] Mr cranch will go tomorrow and take care of them of our children I mean.

Teusday 28th

And a colder day I never knew in January. I hope it will cool the courage of the Insurgants. I am anxious to hear Mr Cranch went to cambridge yesterday he is too aprehensive to be happy.

wednesday 29th

Tis extreem cold yet and no news from cambridge. I have just heard that our Braintree captains have been round to order all the Militia to be ready to march at a minutes warning. How hostile the appearence! I hope'd to have seen peace in my day for the future, but from the present cloud which hangs over our affairs nothing can be expected but Storms and Tempests.

Six o'clock. About a quarter after four this afternoon We had a very sensible Shock of an earthquake.[6] I was in my chamber standing at a trunk, when my Chest of draws began to shake and the Brasses to rattle violently. It lasted but a few seconds and was not attended with any noise that I can learn. I was not a little alarm'd being almost alone made me feel more So.

thursday 30th

I have just receiv'd a Letter from mr cranch informing me that the Insurgents came no further than concord from thence, they Sent a Man to Bristol county to collect all the discontented there and to ingage them to meet those at concord. Chaise [*Shays*] was to come with his Gang from another Quarter, but the man from concord meeting with no success in Bristol county and upon his return not finding chaise arriv'd advis'd the Party to return. "That the Govr had call'd a counsel of war," at which he was invited. There were present Genls Lincoln and Prescott, Coll Hitchbourn 4 Counsilors and several other Gentlemen. That measurs were propounded and discuss'd with great prudence and wisdom, but that he was not at Liberty to mention the result. T[*he*] Insurgents at concord were about Sixty. They expected chaise would have brought three Thousand.

Satturday Decem. 2d

The Secrect is out, at least part of it. A Party of Light Horse all Vollentiers went from Boston on wednesday morning in pursuit of the Insurgents. They had warrants to take up a number of their leaders and a sad company they were. The Light Horse consisted of Lawyers Physicians and merchants and were Joind by a number of Gentleman from the country as they pass'd thro it. They were commanded by Colln. Hitchbourn and were in number about three Hundred. They went as far as Groton and return'd a Friday morning with three of the Leaders of the mob, Shaddock Parker and Page. Shaddock defended himself with his sword till he had like to have kill'd a mr Reed who Seiz'd him first and who was himself Tar'd and Feather'd in former times but is now for Submiting to the Powers that Be. As Shaddocks arm was lifted to give a wound that might have been fatal to Reed, Doctor Rand Struck him upon the knee with his Broad Sword, and brought him to the ground.[7] The others were taken without Sheding Blood. Cousin Willm. Smith was of the Party who went out. Another Party went out after another Set of them, but return without doing any thing. They did not think themselves strong enough to oppose such numbers as were collecting.

December 3d

I was very sorry I could not get a Letter aboard Davis, but I could not get one into Town Soon enough. Mr Cranch and the Doctor will write I hope. They can give you a better account of Publick matters than I. You may remember that in one of my Letters I mentiond our receiving Letters from mr Perkins who was at Kentucky. We receiv'd another Pacquit Last June in which he inform'd us that he was in very good Business but must stay a few years Longer, before he could think of returning, he must make a fortune. He went for that purpose and altho the hope of Settling among his Friends was almost the only thing that made Life desirable to him yet without sufficient to Set him above want he never would return. We had just sent answers away when mr cranch receiv'd a Letter from a Friend of his with an account of his Death. You my Sister who knew his worth: the goodness of his Heart, and how dear he had render'd himself to us, by his kindness and attention to this Family will easily judge how much we must be shock'd. The tender heart of my Eliza receiv'd a deeper wound than you would have supposed from what I told you before you went away. Tis no easey matter to withhold our affections from those who tenderly Love us. Mr Perkin's dy'd the 22d of August of a dessorder upon his Lungs. His Illness was thought to be but slight till the evening before he dy'd. He was then taken with violent nervous complaints which depriv'd him of his senses till he expir'd.

I think I told you in a former Letter of the Death of Prentis Cushing. His Parents are full of grief, they were very fond of him. He sustain'd an exellent character. We have this to comfort us, under our affliction in the loss of both. Mr Perkinss' Friend writes that he was universally belov'd and esteem'd while living and that his Death was greatly lamented. In almost every Letter I send I have to acquaint you with the Death of some of our Friends or acquaintance. I know you must rejoice with trembling whenever you receive a Letter from any of us till you have read it. It is thus that I am affected whenever I hear a vessel is arriv'd from England.

Your mother Hall Still lives as injoys a comfortable Share of health. She desires to be remember'd to all her children. Your Brothers Family are well he spent sunday evening with us. Your Neighbours are well but most Sincerely wish for your return they often come to inquire about you. Abdy and Phebe do very well and live very comfortably. She has her health better than She use'd to do. She washes for some of the Neighbours. She does So for me. She complains that she cannot get work enough to do. "He is always Puddering about but does not bring much to pass." Mrs H. Hunt sends her love and says if it was not for your kindness she could not afford herself a piece of meat all winter. She has taken Becca Field to live with her for company and the poor Girl has had a very bad sore on her neck which has been open'd. She has been confin'd with it above a month. The neighbours have been kind to her or she must have suffer'd greatly. She could not lay in her Bed. I went to see her and carry them a few comforts, but was surpriz'd to see how the poor creature was fallen away: She has not been able to swallow a bit of Bread for three Weeks.

5th.

This is the Seventh Snow Storm we have had and a dreadful one it is. The Banks are already even with the Fences, neither man nor Beast can turn out. The cold is also Severe—how many poor creatures may be in distress upon our coast. The Season has been so dry that I expect we Shall be loaded with Snow this winter. You never knew such distress for water as there is in this town, almost all the wells are dry, and the Brooks very low.[8]

8th

I have just heard of a Ships being cast upon point Shirley and that all the crew but one Perish'd. I fear I shall hear of more.[9] Much damage has been done in Boston by the high Tide.

Mrs Russel has a fine Boy I hear, and is very well. The affairs of our milton Freinds are I fear greatly imbarrass'd. Winslow is confin'd in Hartford.—He was oblig'd to find Bondsman when mr Codman took him, as he could not discharge the debt, he deliverd himself up. I am griev'd for the General and his Lady. I have not taken up your debt from them. I could never find any thing, that it would do to take it in.

If the vessel does not sail soon you Shall hear again from your affectionate Sister Mary Cranch

Cushing is not yet arriv'd by him I hope to hear from you.

RC (Adams Papers); endorsed: "Novbr. 26 1786 Mrs Cranch" and "Mrs. Cranch december 3. 1786."

[1] The Adamses had begun to express fears concerning Gen. Joseph Palmer's economic well-being as early as three years before (vol. 5:139, 140). For more on his salt works, see vol. 6:13.

[2] Possibly a reference to Richard Cranch's now living full-time in Braintree; in the past he had frequently traveled on business.

[3] For Royall Tyler's earlier difficulties with a sleigh, see vol. 6:94.

[4] Mary Smith Cranch to AA, 28 Sept., above. Barnard sailed for London around 17 Nov. (*Boston Gazette,* 20 Nov.).

[5] The first military company of Harvard students, the Marti-Mercurian Band, had been formed in 1769 or 1770, overturning a seventeenth-century ban on students' participation in military companies. While the company drilled occasionally (usually followed by liberal consumption of rum), it never saw service and was disbanded around 1787 (Samuel Eliot Morison, *Three Centuries of Harvard 1636–1936*, Cambridge, 1936, p. 28, 141). For JQA's description of and reactions to the possible attack, see his *Diary*, 2:133–136.

[6] On 2 Dec., the *Massachusetts Centinel* reported, "Wednesday afternoon [29 *Nov.*], about four o'clock, a small shock of an Earthquake was sensibly felt in this town." A later report indicated that the quake was strongest in the area of Oliver's dock, and west from there to Newton (*Massachusetts Centinel*, 6 Dec.).

[7] Sampson Reed of Boston led a company of twelve men in arresting Capt. Job Shattuck. Shattuck was wounded by a sword in the process, but Reed was apparently unharmed (Jacob Whittemore Reed, *History of the Reed Family in Europe and America*, Boston, 1861, p. 182; Lemuel Shattuck, *Memorials of the Descendants of William Shattuck*, Boston, 1855, p. 126).

[8] The Boston newspapers reported that the snowstorm of 4–5 Dec. was "as severe a snow-storm as has been experienced here for several years past.—The wind, at east, and north-east, blew exceeding heavy, and drove in the tide with such violence on Tuesday, as over-flowed the pier several inches, which entering the stores on the lower part thereof, did much damage to the Sugars, salt, &c. therein. The shipping in the harbour, we are happy to find, received but little injury: yet our apprehensions for the vessels which were daily expected to arrive, and which

were supposed to have been on the coast when the storm began, are great." On 9 Dec., another snowstorm hit the Boston area, adding to the accumulated totals, "so that with what fell the preceeding part of the Week, makes it nearly 4 Feet deep upon a Level; consequently travelling is very precarious" (Boston *Independent Chronicle*, 7 Dec.; *Boston Gazette*, 11 Dec.). See also JQA, *Diary*, 2:136–139, and JQA to AA2, 14 Jan. 1787, below.

[9] Due to the storm, the brig *Lucretia*, Capt. Powell, ran up on Point Shirley on the morning of 5 Dec. while trying to reach Boston Harbor. Of the eleven people on the boat, five made it to shore but could not reach shelter from the storm and thus died. Powell and five others stayed on board and subsequently reached safety (*Boston Gazette*, 11 Dec.).

Elizabeth Smith Shaw to Abigail Adams Smith

Haverhill November 27th. 1786

I must frankly acknowledge to my Dear Niece that I could not but wonder at her long Silence. I feared that my Letters had not reached her, or that I had inadvertenly written something that had wounded her feelings, and so had, in her estimation, forfeited that Love, and generous confidence which she had so kindly placed in me.[1] But when I recieved a Letter from your Mother last April, which announced to me her Daughters being upon the point of Marriage with a Gentleman whose Name she did not mention, and the next week to hear you were really married, you cannot wonder if my Mind felt *inquisitive*—hurried—and struck with amazement. By this I found that my Niece had been employed in adjusting matters of the utmost importance; and as she knew not how much she was beloved, nor how deeply I was interested in her happiness, I could not so *much blame her* for not sparing *one* Moment to acquaint, a most affectionate Aunt of her pleasing Prospects.

As you my Neice have given me a new Nephew, permit me to congratulate you both upon the Celebration of your Nuptials. May he who has so worthyly defended the Liberties of his Country, now dwell in Peace, and Harmony, and enjoy the delights of Friendship, and all the Sweets of domestic Life, and never have occasion again to reassume any Weapons of War. You my Niece who have so happily escaped the dangers, the whirlpools, and the quicksands of the single Life, and have safely arrived at the Haven of Matrimony, will find a new *Scene* open to your view. And that there are two very principal Characters in which *you* must become the *Actress*—[th]at [o]f Wife and Mistress—and before a much more *interested* Audience than you have yet ever beheld in a publick Theatre. I need not tell you, I mean your Husband, and your Family,—and perhaps e'er long, you may be called to act in a third, not less important, arduous and tender. That each have their several incumbent Duties, and that there are certain Traits requisite, without which a Lady of your Judgment, well knows a female Character must be exceedingly imperfect. A proper reverence of yourself—a dignity of Manners—joined with Meekness, and Condescention—gentleness, and sweetness of Temper—have most attractive Charms, and are the richest, and most valuable Ornaments, you can adorn yourself with. They with [*will*] render you lovely in Youth, and (I may venture to say,) forever ensure you the attention, the Love, and the best Affections of that Man, who is truly worthy of *you*.

The Woman who is *really* possessed of superior Qualities, or *affects* a Superiority over her Husband, betrays a pride which degrades herself, and places her in the most disadvantatious point of view.

She who values domestick Happiness will carefully gaurd against, and avoid any little Contentions—the *Beginnings* of Evil—as she would a pestilential Dissease, that would poison her sweetest comforts, and infect her every Joy. There is but one *kind* of Strife in the nuptial State that I can behold without horror, and that is who shall excell and who shall oblige the most. Since marriage is one of the most important Transactions of our Lives, you will excuse my suggesting to you several Things which I deem so Essential towards the *preserving* an happy Union, and imputing what I have said, to my Love, and solicitude for your Happiness and not to a fear, that you should be found wanting in any requisite. For she who has been a dutiful Child, seldom fails of becoming a most discreet, and obliging Wife. Sure I am Anything of the preceptive kind would be unnecessary to you who have a living, and a bright Example of the conjugal Virtues in your excellent Mother. There they shine with distinguished Lustre. She who in some measure overcame the ties of Nature, and crossed the wide Atlantic to sooth, and to relieve *him* whose labouring Mind was vexed, and oppressed with the mighty Cares of a rising Empire, must be possessed of Qualities, and Graces that would endear her, not only to her Husband, but to all who can properly estimate real Worth.

The sensations you experienced upon quitting your Fathers Family were such, as I can easily conceive. What I suffered myself upon the like occasion, Time can never efface. Even blessed with the kindest, and most assiduous Partner, and with the most flattering Prospects, it is at best, as you have well expressed it,

> "But a solemn Scene of Joy."

To bid adieu to our former Habitation, and to give up the kind Gaurdians of our youth, and place ourselves under quite a new kind of Protection, cannot but strike a reflecting Mind with awe, and the most fearful Apprehensions—as it is *the* important Crisis, upon which our Fate depends.

> "Happy the Youth that finds his Bride
> Whose birth is to his *own* ally'd
> The sweetest Joy of Life."[2]

Our News Paper has announced to us the Nuptials of Revd Mr Osgood, and Miss Breed. Dr Archelaus Putnam and Miss Bishop. Cupid I fancy got fast asleep in his Mothers Lap, and old Plutus, has yoked the Dove.[3] Not so with the amiable Peggy White. She is now happily connected with a Gentleman, who, I believe was her *first*, and her *last* attachment. Last Week I visited her. She was dressed elegantly, and in all the splendor of Bridal Innocence. She, and her worthy Partner Mr Bayley Bartlet[4] looked so happy, and complacent, as must have given pleasure to every beholder. There was always a sweetness, and a dignity in her Manners that I admired; but upon this occasion every Feature appeared more animated, and every Grace had received an additional Charm.

Mr Duncan has married, and brought home his third Wife. She appears to be a very discreet worthy Woman, and agreeable to all the Children. Miss Duncan has greatly recovered her health. When Mr T— and Miss B will enter *the* List, Or when Hymen will twist Blessings with *their Bands*, I cannot say. But I hope the Time is not far distant.

I have thought of you often, since I heard your Father and Mother were gone to the Haugue. I have longed to look in upon you. But all we can do at present, is to write to each other, which I hope you will never omit doing by every Opportunity, as it will exceedingly gratify her who wishes you every possibly degree of felicity, and though I am distant from you, am at all times, your truly affectionate Aunt

E Shaw

Dft (DLC:Shaw Family Papers); addressed: "To Mrs Abigail Smith London Wimpole Street."

[1] No letters from AA2 to Shaw have been found.

[2] Isaac Watts, "The Indian Philosopher," lines 43–45.

[3] Rev. David Osgood (1748–1822), Harvard 1771, pastor of the First Church of Medford, married Hannah Breed on 1 November. Osgood also himself performed the marriage of Dr. Archelaus Putnam and Abigail Bishop on 12 Nov. (*Sibley's Harvard Graduates*, 17:570–571, 579; *Massachusetts Gazette*, 14 Nov.).

[4] Bailey Bartlett (1750–1830), a member of

the Massachusetts state legislature and later a member of Congress, married Peggy White (1766–18[illegible]) [illegible] November [illegible], had thirteen children, nine daughters and four sons (Levi Bartlett, *Genealogical and Biographical Sketches of the Bartlett Family in England and America*, Lawrence, Mass., 1876, p. 22–24).

Abigail Adams to John Quincy Adams

My dear Son November 28 1786

Since I wrote you, the packet from N york has arrived after a passage of 43 days, and by that your Letter of August 30th came safe to hand, and upon reading it I was glad to find that your sentiments so nearly agreed with mine. You will inquire into mr Parsons' Terms and with the advise of Dr Tufts look out for Board. But I will get your Father to write you I had rather you should have his opinion directly than at Second hand.

I hope you will not apply so constantly to your Studies as to injure your Health: exersise is very necessary for you, but from the accounts from my Friends I fear you do not pay attention enough to it.

By captain Callihan you received your Books and Letters I presume. I am quite impatient to get Letters from my Friends, tho I know they will be such as to give me pain. The Newspapers and Letters from Newyork are filld with accounts of the most allarming Nature, and I could not refrain shedding tears over them, to behold my Countrymen who had so nobly fought and bled for freedom, tarnishing their glory, loosing the bands of society, introducing anarchy confusion and despotisim, forging domestick Chains for Posterity. For the experience of ages, and the Historick page teach us, that a popular Tyrranny never fails to be followed by the arbitrary government of a Single person. Who can refrain from anxiety, who can feel at Peace or set Idle, and see whole Bodies of Men giving into those very practices which are sure to work their destruction, breaking a constitution by the very same errors that so many have been broken before?

Common sense and plain reason will ever have some general influence upon a free people, and I will Still hope and believe that a Majority of our CountryMen will bear their testimony against such lawless proceedings, and that by wisdom and firmness they will be able to restore order and harmony without the dreadfull necessity of Shedding Blood. Rome had her Cæsars and her Pompeys, nor will America be less productive; civil dissensions never fail to spirit up the ambition of private Men; the Same Spirit which prompted Honestus to attack the order of the Lawyers, as he terms them, has diffused itself throughout Massachusets, His publications were calculated to sow the seeds of discontent, and dissention amongst the populace and to pull down the pillars of the State. Would to Heaven that none but such as himself, might be crushed by the fall.

I had flatterd myself with the hope that my Children would reap the benifits of an equitable and peaceable Government, after the many Perils and difficulties which their Father had pass'd through to obtain one. But if this is not like to be the case, I would enjoin it upon each of them to turn their attention and their Studies to the Great Subject of Government, and the Rights of Mankind, that they may be qualified to defend them, in the senate, and in the Feild if necessary. You have an Elder Brother whose Heroic Soul and independant Spirit, Breaths the ardour of a Hero and a Freeman, and I have reason to bless the hand of Providence which saved a beloved child from impending ruin, and gave her a Protector, in a Man of Honour and integrity. We are as happy, as the distance from our Friends, and the dissagreeable state of our Country will permit us to be.

I am glad to find by your Le[tter] your Brother Tommy is admitted colledge. I hope you [will] watch over him with the care of a parent, and the affection of a Brother. I fear their will be no passenger by this packet to whom we can commit our Letters, and if so I am wholy at a loss for a conveyance as Cushing is not like to get out till Spring.

December 3. 1786

I have a Letter or two for some other of my Friends but they must wait. I heard yesterday that Captain Sayer was arrived. I received one Letter only and that from Mrs Rogers dated 16 of october, which came up by the post.[1] I trust the captain is orderd to deliver his Letters himself. As the Wind is against his comeing up, it may yet be Several days before we get our Letters which you know is very mortifying to Your affectionate Mother A. A.

RC (Adams Papers); addressed by WSS: "Mr. John Quincy Adams Student at Cambridge near Boston in Massachusetts north America Pr. Packett"; stamped: "[. . .]/DE" and "POST A [. . .]"; mail notations: "2/3"; "6.16"; "post pad [2p—?]"; and "[J Q A?]"; endorsed: "Mrs: Adams. Novr: 28. 1786."; docketed: "My Mother. 28. Novr: 1786." Some loss of text where the seal was removed.

[1] Not found.

Thomas Jefferson to Abigail Adams

Dear Madam Paris [*November 1786*][1]

I am never happier than when I am performing good offices for good people; and the most friendly office one can perform is to make worthy characters acquainted with one another. The good things of this life are scattered so sparingly in our way that we must glean them up as we go. Yourself and Madame de Corny then must avail yourselves of the short time she will remain in London to make each other happy.[2] A good heart and a good head will ensure her a place in your esteem. I have promised it to her: and she has yet a better title, a high respect for your character. I asked her to carry me in her pocket, that I might have the pleasure of bringing you together in person: but on examining the treaty of commerce, she found I should be contraband; that there might be search—and seisur—and that the case would admit very specially of embarras. So instead of my having the honour of presenting her to you, she will have that of putting this into your hands, and of giving you assurances of her esteem and respect, with which permit me to mingle those of, dear Madam, your most obedient and most humble servant Th: Jefferson

FC (DLC:Jefferson Papers).

[1] The date is established by Jefferson to Maria Cosway, 19 Nov., in which he mentions Madame de Corny's upcoming visit to London (Jefferson, *Papers*, 10:542–543, 557).

[2] Anne Mangeot, Madame Ethis de Corny, was the wife of Louis Dominique Ethis de Corny (1738–1790), a French writer and administrator, and a friend of Jefferson's. Although Madame de Corny remained in London for over a year, it is unlikely that she ever met AA or that AA ever received this letter (Hoefer, *Nouv. biog. générale*; Jefferson, *Papers*, 11:569–570, 12:551).

Abigail Adams Smith to Thomas Jefferson

London December 2d 1786

Mrs Smith presents her Compliments to Mr Jefferson and is very sorry to trouble him again upon the Subject of the Corsetts, but not having received them, She fears Mademoisell Sanson has not been so punctual as she promised, if Mr Jefferson will permit Petit to inquire after, and forward them by an early opportunity, Mrs S will be much obliged.[1]

RC (MHi:Jefferson Papers); endorsed: "Mrs. Smith."

[1] This letter was enclosed in WSS to Jefferson, 5 Dec. (Jefferson, *Papers*, 10:578–579). AA2's earlier request for corsets has not been found.

Lucy Cranch to Abigail Adams

My dear Aunt Braintree. Decr. 7. 1786

Your obligeing Letter of July th' 20, was duly recieved—those repeated attentions to me deserve my earliest acknowledgments. Grateful indeed to my heart are those sentiments of affection which you so kindly express for me.

Tho in some things I may *appear* indifferent, yet in this I feel, that I am not. Smith says "that the cheif part of human happiness, consists in the consciousness of being beloved."[1] I believe he says true, the greatest pleasure I ever feel is derived from a consciousness that there are those, who feel a friendship for me and who I have reason to think are interested in my happiness. I am proud that among that number I am allowed to place my Loved my respected Aunt Adams. It shall ever be my study to deserve the continued honour of your Love.

You my dear Madam, are constantly laying me under obligations to yourself. I want words to express my thanks. I will endeavour by my actions to shew that I am not ungrateful.

The fashionable Magazine, is it possible that the Empire of Fashion is so great, that monthly publications issuing its decrees can find sufficient encouragement. When I first read the Preface, I thought it was ment for satire, but when I reflected on the great height to which folly has arrived, I supposed it was sober earnest. You could not have sent a Book that would have been in greater demand. I received it at Haverhill—the news was soon spread—that Miss Cranch had the fashionable magizine. *Gentlemen* and Ladies, all borrowed it. The dress of the Hair, the make of the Cap, the shape of the Waist, and the cut of the Coat, were examined with as much attention among the *Ton* of Haverhill, as a new theory of the Earth would be among the Academicions, of Cambridge.

The Treatise upon gardening, we have not had time to read, I think it must be entertaining. When I have read it I suppose I shall wish to have an ornamented Farm, at present our best way is to have a useful one.

Luxery and extravagance are taking hasty strides through our Land, if not soon checked they will prove our ruin. The Court have been adopting some, economical plans, in their last Sessions. The

Govr. and a number, of the members of both houses have entered into an agreement to discourage Luxery, and the excessive use of foreign articles, and to encourage our own manafactures, as much as is in their power within the circle of their influence.[2]

At present every thing is in disorder. I hope that the delusion which has spread among the people will be dispersed, before the consequences grow more serious, a war within ourselves is what I most dread. We trust for sucour in that omnipotent being, who bringeth light out of darkness and good out of evill.

I rejoice with you Madam and with my Uncle, in the addition it must be to your happiness, to see your amiable Daughter so happily united to the Man of her choise, a Man worthy of her tenderest Love. May they long be blessed in each other, and Live to be an example to the world, that the path of *rectitude* will always lead to happiness.

We shall expect in the next Ship, an account of your tour to Holland, from which we expect great entertainment.

Adieu my dear Aunt, may all happiness, attend you and yours, is the wish of her who is with every sentiment of respect and esteem, your grateful and affectionate, Neice, Lucy C—h

RC (Adams Papers); addressed: "Mrs Abigail Adams. Grosvenor-Square Westminster"; endorsed: "Lucy Cranch Decem 1 1787."

[1] Adam Smith, *The Theory of Moral Sentiments*, London, 1759, p. 87.

[2] On 17 Nov. 1786, the Massachusetts legislature approved a "Report of the Committee for Encouragement of Manufactures, &c. in this Commonwealth," which recommended "That the General Court should make a serious and determined Exertion, by Example and Advice, to inspire a due Regard to our own Manufactures; to the Fruits of our own Industry, and the Efforts of our own Genius, and at the same Time to discourage the Importation and use of foreign Superfluities." On the same day, the General Court passed "An Act to Raise a Public Revenue by Impost," which taxed various imports and completely banned others, "to give all due encouragement to the agriculture and manufactures" of Massachusetts (Mass., *Acts and Laws*, Resolves of 1786, Sept. sess., ch. 132; Acts of 1786, Sept. sess., ch. 48).

Thomas Jefferson to Abigail Adams

Dear Madam Paris Dec. 21. 1786

An unfortunate dislocation of my right wrist has for three months deprived me of the honor of writing to you. I begin now to use my pen a little, but it is in great pain, and I have no other use of my hand. The swelling has remained obstinately the same for two months past, and the joint, tho I beleive well set, does not become more flexible. I am strongly advised to go to some mineral waters at

Aix in Provence, and I have it in contemplation.[1] I was not alarmed at the humor shewn by your countrymen. On the contrary I like to see the people awake and alert. But I received a letter which represented it as more serious than I had thought. Mr Adams however restores my spirits; I believe him and I thank him for it. The good sense of the people will soon lead them back, if they have erred in a moment of surprize.[2] My friends write me that they will send my little daughter to me by a Vessel which sails in May for England. I have taken the liberty to tell them that you will be so good as to take her under your wing till I can have notice to send for her, which I shall do express in the moment of my knowing she is arrived. She is about 8. years old, and will be in the care of her nurse, a black woman, to whom she is confided with safety. I knew your goodness too well to scruple the giving this direction before I had asked your permission.[3] I beg you to accept assurances of the constant esteem with which I have the honor to be Dear Madam your most obedient & most humble servt. Th: Jefferson

RC (Adams Papers); endorsed: "Mr Jeffersons Letter december 21 1787."

[1] Jefferson hurt his wrist on 18 Sept., and his ability to write was hindered by the injury for several months thereafter. He visited Aix-en-Provence during an extended tour of southern France in spring 1787 but did not find the mineral waters helpful (Jefferson, *Papers*, 10:394; 11:31, 338, 426–427).

[2] John Jay wrote to Jefferson about the uprising in Massachusetts on 27 Oct., describing it as "more formidable than some at first apprehended. . . . If Faction should long bear down Law and Government, Tyranny may raise its Head, or the more sober part of the People may even think of a King. In short, my Dr. Sir; we are in a very unpleasant Situation." By contrast, JA's letter of 30 Nov. instructed Jefferson, "Dont be allarmed. . . . [A]ll will be well" (same, 10:488–489, 557).

[3] Mary (Polly) Jefferson arrived in London on 26 June 1787. The nurse Jefferson had intended to accompany her was unable to make the trip, so she came in the care of Sally Hemings. They remained with the Adamses in London for just over two weeks, after which they departed for Paris (same, 11:501–502, 592).

Abigail Adams to John Adams

Abbe Green, Bath decem 23 1786

We arrived here about four oclock a fryday afternoon,[1] after a very pleasent journey. The weather was somewhat cold, but a clear Sky and a fine Sun Shine was ample compensation. We found convenient apartments, Good Beaf Mutton and excellent fish for dinner; it was fortunate that we engaged Lodgings before we came, as every House is full. To day being rainy and fogy we have not made any excursion, or looked about us. We wanted a little remit after rising 3 mornings by candle light and riding through the cold. I hope an additional quantity of bed Cloaths will make you comfortable; we had the city Musick this morning to wait upon us, and welcome us to Bath. I Suppose we Shall have some more compliments of the Same kind. I think the Bath road has more of an American appearence than any I have traveld in this Country. The Stone Walls and the Hills and the Towns bearing the Same Names, Reading Malborough newburry all reminded me of New England. I think you would have been better pleasd if you had come with us, than you was when you traveld this road formerly,[2] in summer it must be delightfull. I think very often of your being alone, but whilst the Book lasts you will not want employment, tho you may amusement. Be so good as to let me hear from you, tell me how you do, and direct under cover to col Smith at mr [3] abbe Green. But why it is calld so I know not, as it is a small paved square and nothing Green to be seen about it.—A Good Nights repose to you tho more than a hundred miles distant my thoughts are very often in Grosveneur Square, and we drink your Health every Day. Mr and Mrs Smith present their Duty. Yours ever

AA

RC (Adams Papers); addressed by WSS: "To His Excellency John Adams Minister Plenipo: &c &c &c. Grosvenor Square"; stamped: "23/DE"; docketed by WSS: "Mrs. Adams"; and by CFA: "Bath. Decr 23d 1786."; notation by WSS: "at Mr. Marjrams abbe Green." Mathematical notation by JA, dividing 336 by 16.

[1] 22 December. This was AA's first letter to JA since 30 July 1784 (vol. 5:408–409).

[2] JA visited Bath with JQA in Dec. 1783 during their first stay in England (JA, *D&A*, 3:151–152).

[3] Blank in MS.

John Adams to Abigail Adams

My dearest Friend — Grosvenor Square Christmas Day

I hope you have had a Pleasant Journey and are happy in your tour. I am, in a state of Phylosophic Solitude, that has hitherto been very tolerable, because I know my Treasures are not far off. But, as soon as the Novelty of it, wears off, and my occupation shall cease it will grow tedious enough. Dont hurry yourself however nor your Friends, but improve the opportunity to see, whatever you have an Inclination to see. I shall receive the Benefit of your observations when We meet and with more Pleasure than I could have made them perhaps in Person. Love to the Coll and my Nabby Smith, and Compliments to all the Party.

A Letter from Squire Storer is in closed. Barnet is arrived somewhere but I have no letter yet, but one from Storer in which this was in closed.[1] Yours forever John Adams

RC (Adams Papers); endorsed: "december 25 Mr A. 1786."

[1] Probably Charles Storer to AA, 12 Sept., above, enclosed in Storer to JA, 16 Sept. (Adams Papers). The London *Daily Universal Register*, 25 Dec., announced the arrival of Captain Barnard at Plymouth on 21 December.

John Adams to Abigail Adams

My dearest Friend Grosvenor Square Decr 25. 1786

This moment returning from Mr Bridgen where I had been to deliver him a Letter to you, written this Morning I found your very agreable favour of the 23. Am very glad you are so well Situated, So much pleased with your Journey, and present Accommodation. Dont be solicitous about me. I shall do very well—if I am cold in the night, and an additional quantity of Bed Cloaths will not answer the purpose of warming me, I will take a Virgin to bed with me.—Ay a Virgin.—What? oh Awful! what do ⟨[. . .]⟩[1] read?

Dont be Surprized. Do you know what a Virgin is? Mr Bridget brought me acquainted with it this Morning. It is a Stone Bottle, Such as you buy with spruce Beer and Spa Water, filled with Boiling Water, covered over and wrapped up in flannel and laid at a Mans Feet in Bed. An Old Man you see may comfort him self with Such a Virgin, as much as David did with Abishay,[2] and not give the least Jealousy even to his Wife, the smallest grief to his Children, or any Scandal to the World. Tell Mr Bridgen when you see him that I am indebted to him for this important Piece of Knowledge, which I would not sell for a great deal of Money.

Tell Coll Smith I am half disposed to be almost miffed with him—for going off without giving me his Letter about the Indians.[3] And what compleats the Mischief is, that he has all the Books locked up in his Room—pray him to write me, if it is possible to get at the Letter or the Books—both are what I want. My Love to Nabby Smith and her Knight, and to all the Party. Mr Shippen is with you eer now—he was so good as to pick a bone with me once—and Mr Cutting is very good. We now talk Politicks all alone and are much cooler and more rational than when We dispute in Company.

Yours forever John Adams

RC (Adams Papers); addressed: "Mrs. Adams at Mr Marjrams abbe Green Bath"; endorsed: "Mr A. 25 decem 86."

[1] JA canceled "I" and two illegible letters here.

[2] Abishag, the young virgin who ministered to the aged King David in 1 Kings, 1:1–4.

[3] Not identified. This may have been a memorandum WSS was drafting in response to Lord Carmarthen's letter to JA of 11 Dec. concerning debts owed to British merchants by Creek and Cherokee Indians in Georgia and a related land claim (PCC, No. 84, VI, f. 371–372).

John Adams to Abigail Adams

My dearest — Grosvenor Square Decr 27. 1786

Mr Murray, whom I am glad to see out again will carry to Bath this Memorandum that We are all very well. He will arrive for what I know before Mr Bridgen. The Weath's is very cold, but by a good fire and a good Walk I have not yet been obliged to recur to my Expedient of an immaculate Virgin Bottle of hot Water. I sent Yesterday—Packetts to Coll Smith from Paris.[1]

The News from Boston is very well. The Court has set at Cambridge in great Pomp guarded by three thousand Men and a train of Artillery. The General Court have passed an Amnesty, with some Exceptions, to all who will take the oath of allegiance, in a certain Time. The Governor reviewed the Troops and made them a Speech. In short government appears now in its Majesty supported by those in whom all Majesty originally resides, the People. I have not seen the Papers but Coll Trumbul gives me this Account,[2] Coll Smiths Toast "common sense to the Common People" is already verified.

Make your observations, keep your Journal, and make Nabby Smith do so too, and let me see all when you return.

Yours evermore — John Adams

RC (Adams Papers); addressed: "Mrs Adams at Mr Marjrams abbe Square Bath favd by Mr Murray"; endorsed: "Mr A December 27."

[1] Presumably Thomas Jefferson to WSS, 20 Dec., including a twelve-sheet map of South America and possibly a lost letter to AA2 (Jefferson, *Papers*, 10:620).

[2] Not found. For the opening of the Middlesex County court in Cambridge on 1 Nov., see JQA, *Diary*, 2:120–121. The General Court's amnesty, "An Act Granting Indemnity to Sundry Offenders, on Certain Conditions, and Providing for the Trial of Such, Who Shall Neglect or Refuse to Comply with Said Conditions, and of Those Who Shall Be Guilty of Like Offences in Future," was approved on 15 Nov. (Mass., *Acts and Laws*, Acts of 1786, Sept. sess., ch. 44).

Abigail Adams to John Adams

My dearest Friend — december 30th 1786 Bath

I yesterday received your kind favour by mr Murry and the day before; yours by mr Bridgen. Mr and Mrs Rucker left us this morning, but I did not write by them knowing that the post would be much Spedier. You tell me to keep a journal, but you do not think what a task you impose or how every Hour is occupied at this place by those who stay only ten or twleve Days, and run the circle of amusement, or rather dissapation. The Young are delighted here, because they feel less restraint in their amusements and pleasures than in the city. The excercise they take, together with the clear sun shine and fine air of Bath tends to exhilirate the spirits. The aged and the infirm receive Health and Spirits from the Bethsadian pools and not a little satisfaction is derived to all parties from visiting a place of fashionable resort. As it may be more amusement to you in my absence to read a little detail of my excursion than if I brought home a journal to you, I will endeavour to recollect the events of the past week. You know I had but one acquaintance who resided here, and him I determined to find out and leave a card at his Lodgings. But on Sunday last, before I had made any inquiry for him, he heard of my arrival and came immediately to see me. He was wonderfully polite and civil to us, offerd us every attention in his power. We invited him to dine with us the next day, and the old Gentleman came. He told us that he had not for 3 years past been a Subscriber to any of the publick amusements the concert excepted, and to that he would have the honour of conducting us.[1] This he did the next Evening and procured us Seats to much advantage. The next Day he invited us to a Breakfast with him and entertaind us with great Elegance and Hospitality. He has taken such a prodigious fancy to col Smith that he has made him a confident in his private affairs. Col Smith brought a letter of introduction to mr Fairfax who is mr Boylstones most intimate Friend.[2] Mr Fairfax was Sick confined to his Chamber and his Lady quite an invalide but they have been very obliging to us, Sent us cards for the benifit Ball and yesterday we dinned with them. Tho mr Fairfax was not able to set at table, he deputed mr Boylstone to do the Honours of it, and the old gentleman appeard as happy as if he had, had so many of his children about him and mrs Fairfax said she had never Seen him in such Spirits in her Life. In the Evening we went to a party at Miss Hartlys, a musical Route I believe I must call it, as we had both vocal and instrumental, we had Stars and Garters Lords and Ladies present. Miss Hartly is quite a criple having lost one of her feet by a mortification, very infirm, and delicate but quite well bred polite and soft in her manners. Her mind seems much more cultivated than most of the Ladies we meet with. She is very fond of Musick and a performer.[3] She is moved about in a chair set upon wheels, quite helpless her hands excepted. She reads or hears a young companion whom she keeps with her, is very pleasent and cheerfull and was once a very handsome woman. I drank tea with her once before without company and it was then I made my observations. We have been to three Balls one concert one play, two private parties, to the publick walks &c and all this in one week is enough to surfeit one. The Ball to morrow Evening will conclude our amusements at Bath. We then propose a visit to the Hot well of Bristol.[4] That accomplished we set out for Grosvenour Square which we mean to reach on saturday next, perhaps on fryday, but as it is not convenient for all of us to travel fast; I rather think we shall make 3 or four Days of our return. I have lost my bed fellow to Day, but as the weather is so much moderated I think I shall do without an Abbe the remainder of my stay. You recollect in France that they are so polite to the Ladies as to accomodate them with an *Abbe*, when they give the Gentleman a Nun—even the Chaste and immaculate Dr, used to take a Nun to his Bed.

I am happy at the intelligence received from Boston, and hope all will be well.

Mr and Mrs Smith present their duty; Mr Cutting writes that he had dinned with you 3 times out of 8 Days. I wish I Could Send you some of the fine fish of Bath in which they greatly excell any part of England that I have visited. Small Bear Bread Mutton and fish are excellent here, but I begin to wish myself at Home notwithstanding. Having visited Bath once I am satisfied, as you have no fancy for that which makes it so delightfull to most people. I do not wonder that you preferd building up Republicks, and establishing Governments. Be so good as to let john and Esther know, that we Shall be at Home on Saturday next.

Ever yours.

RC (Adams Papers); endorsed: "Portia. Decr. 30. 1786."

[1] Among the entertainments at Bath were a regular concert series, held in the Assembly Rooms on Wednesdays during the winter and outside at the Spring Garden in the summer, and twice-weekly subscription balls. These formal balls were regulated by strict rules, separating participants by social rank for part of the evening, and ended promptly at 11:00 P.M. (*The New Bath Guide; or, Useful Pocket Companion for All Persons Residing at or Resorting to This Ancient City*, Bath, 1791, p. 23–24; Trevor Fawcett and Stephen Bird, *Bath: History and Guide*, Dover, N.H., 1994, p. 62; Graham Davis and Penny Bonsall, *Bath: A New History*, Staffordshire, Eng., 1996, p. 41–42).

[2] George William Fairfax (1724–1787) and his wife Sarah Cary, both originally from

Virginia, had moved to England in the early 1770s and eventually settled in Bath (Edward D. Neill, *The Fairfaxes of England and America*, Albany, N.Y., 1868, p. 135, 153–154, ante 209).

[3] Mary Hartley (1736–1803) was the half-sister of the British MP David Hartley, who had long corresponded with JA. Despite her continuing ill health, she managed his household and was also a noted linguist and artist (George Herbert Guttridge, *David Hartley, M.P.: An Advocate of Conciliation 1774–1783*, Berkeley, Calif., 1926, p. 234–235, 323–325).

[4] The Hot Wells was a resort spa in the village of Clifton, about a mile from Bristol, on the banks of the Avon River (*Leigh's New Pocket Road-Book of England and Wales*, 2d edn., London, 1826, p. 82).

Abigail Adams to Isaac Smith Jr.

My Dear sir London[1] December 30th 1786

Your Letter to me informing me of the Death of your dear Parent, and my much Loved Aunt, awakened in my Bosom all those tender and Sympathetick emotions, which my own and your loss united.

Twice in my Life it hath pleased Heaven that I should taste of a Similar affliction in the loss of a Father and a Mother. Time which has meliorated the poignant anguish; which attends a recent seperation, presents to my recollection, their numerous virtues, and their endearing characters; which are a constant Solace to me, and excite in my Heart the warmest gratitude to Heaven for having blest me with Such parents, and continued their Lives to me for so many years. And Such my Dear sir must be your consolation when your thoughts employ themselves upon a Parent, who fullfilld every Duty and every Relation in Life with a conscientious punctuality with a tenderness and benevolence that constantly testified the strict unison which Subsisted between her Duty, and her inclination. Next to my own Parents, was your Dear Mother in my affection and regard. The Law of kindness was always upon her Lips,[2] and it was from the abundance of her Heart, that her Mouth Spake.

Tho it hath pleased Heaven to take from me the flattering Idea of being welcomed by her, upon a return to my native Land and I now view with pain, that hospitable Mansion, once the Seat of pleasure, shorn of half its glory, and that Seat deserted; which was once filld with Smiles and with courtesy. I wipe the selfish tear from my Eye, "and look through nature up to Natures God"[3] and in that Mansion not made with Hands I view the Departed Spirit, disencumberd from the Clogs of Mortality, earnestly desirious of receiving and welcoming her Friends into those happy Regions of Security and Bliss where She is safely landed, and there perfecting all those virtuous Friendships which were but commenced on Earth.

"Angles from Friendship, gather half their joy"[4]

These are consolations which Christianity offers to the afflicted mind. You sir who have for a course of years made those sacred doctrines your study and delight cannot fail to find them a Support under your present affliction. Those doctrines do not call for a Stoical insensibily or forbid us to feel as Humane Creatures, but so to regulate and watch over our passion, as not to permit them to lead us into any excesses that would discover an impotence of mind, and a diffidence of providence.

Excuse me Sir that I have not written you before, my mind was too much agitated to write with that calmness which I wished for.

Present me in affectionate terms to your Worthy Father, and to your Brother and Sisters.

My dear Betsy, alass she knows not how much I have felt for her, but she is a child trained up in the way in which she should go.[5]

Mr Adams joins me in affectionate Regards to your family. Believe me dear Sir most Sincerely your Friend A. Adams

RC (MHi:Smith-Carter Papers); addressed: "To The Rev'd Isaac Smith Chaplain at Castle William Boston."

[1] This letter may have been written at Bath but was probably mailed from London following AA's return on 6 Jan. 1787.

[2] Proverbs, 31:26.

[3] Alexander Pope, *An Essay on Man*, Epistle IV, line 332.

[4] Young, *Night Thoughts*, Night II, line 574.

[5] Elizabeth Smith (1770–1849), the youngest child of Isaac Sr. and Elizabeth Storer Smith. The characterization of her upbringing is from Proverbs, 22:6.

John Quincy Adams to Abigail Adams

My dear Madam Cambridge December: 30th: 1786

Three months have now elapsed, since, I have received, one line from Europe; and the only information I have had in all that time, were a couple of paragraphs in the newspapers, the one mentioning your departure from London, and the other your return there;[1] I feel very impatient and anxious for letters, a vessel arrived a few days since; but, I do not hear, that she brought any: if I have been negligent in writing, I have surely had an excuse, and I hope my friends will not punish me, for an involuntary fault. For two complete months, I have not been two miles distant from the spot, where I now write; confined within the walls of a college; having day after day the same scene before my eyes, surrounded by the same objects, and pursuing the same course of studies, what matter could I find to fill up, a sheet of paper? As for public affairs, I have a great aversion, even to thinking of them, and near as we are to Boston, I should know nothing concerning them, if riots, insurrections, and anarchy, were not at this time the only topics of conversation. The people in four or five Counties of this State are distracted, and several hundreds of men, have repeatedly taken arms, and prevented the setting of the court of common pleas. In Worcester, Berkshire, and Hampshire, the people in general are said to be discontented, and to complain of taxation, of the court of common pleas, of the Senate, of the salaries of public officers, and of debts, public and private; all these are, they think, intolerable grievances, and they wish to abolish them. In the other Counties however the people, are quiet, and in general firmly attached to their constitution. Among the rioters that have appeared several times in opposition to the Courts of justice, there has not been one man, of any reputation in the State; and there have been consequently, a number of leaders; three of them, have lately been taken, and, it is probable the others, will soon share the same fate; the insurrections are not immediately dangerous, but our government, has not sufficient vigour and energy, to suppress them at once. There has appeared in the counsel, a degree of timidity and irresolution, which, does no honour to the executive power of a commonwealth. It is said to have arisen chiefly, from the second citizen in the State, who is now distinguished by the ludicrous nick name of *the old Lady*.[2] I am however in hopes that in two or three months the public tranquillity, will be perfectly restored: I suspect that the present form of government will not continue long; for while the idle, and extravagant, and consequently the poor, complain of its being oppressive, the men of property, and consideration, think the constitution, gives too much liberty to the unprincipled citizen, to the prejudice of the honest, and industrious; the opinion that a pure democracy, appears to much greater advantage, in speculation, than when reduced to practice, gains ground, and bids fair for popularity; I feared that by having received so large a share of my education in Europe, my attachment, to a republican government, would not be sufficient, for pleasing my Countrymen; but I find on the contrary, that I am the best republican here, and with my classmates if I ever have any disputes on the subject, I am always obliged to defend that side of the question.—But, you will have so much political news from other quarters, that I will say no more on that head.

I received about two months since, a box of books, for which I return, my most grateful acknowledgments: I have not as yet perused them all, but many of them, have been quite serviceable: among the rest were two volumes of a history of the late revolution, in French. I received much pleasure from them, as the author, appears to aim at impartiality, notwithstanding the dedication was to lord Percy: probably there will be a continuation of it, in which case I shall request to have the continuation; the manuscript marginal notes are peculiarly precious to me, and I hope they will not be discontinued in the future Volumes.[3] I have already wrote to beg a set of *Blair's* lectures upon rhetoric, and belles lettres; and have nothing further at present to ask, for myself. The government of the university intend to introduce, as a classical book, *Enfield's institutes of natural philosophy*;[4] they are contained in a small quarto volume, and they will be necessary for my brother Charles, about nine months hence, and afterwards for Thomas. I suppose Charles will write for them, himself.

My Brothers, and all the other students, except two or three of my classmates, are absent from college, as we are now in vacation time: the reasons which determined me to remain, here, and several other particulars concerning myself, you will find, in a letter which I am going to write to my Sister; for I address almost all my egotism, to her; and indeed seldom make mention to her of any thing or anybody besides myself. Charles, and Tom, behave, with prudence, and in such a manner as has acquired them the friendship of their classmates, and the approbation of our college government. They are economical in their expences, and attentive to their studies. I was in some fears lest Tom's youth and inexperience, should lead him into an idle, dissipated way, which is the case, with many of the younger students; but his conduct, ever since his admission, has been so uniformly steady, that I am convinced he will do honour to himself, and merit the applause of his friends, in his academical course.

January 11th. 1787.

I am informed that Callahan proposes to sail in a few days, and will therefore close this letter; I have nothing of any consequence to add, except acknowledging the receipt of your favour of Septr: 27th and Octr. 14. but I am still more anxious to hear again, than I was before these letters arrived, as both your letter and my Sister's, mention that you had been ill since your return from Holland. Another vessel is daily expected from London, and I am extremely impatient to hear that your health is perfectly restored: absence from my friends, I am so much inured to, that I can bear it; but when, a state of suspense with respect to their health is added, it becomes almost intolerable.

The account of your tour to Mr Hollis's seat, afforded me much entertainment: and I am very desirous to see that of your journey to Holland; but I know not when, I shall see Mrs Cranch: most probably not within two or three months. Mr: and Mrs: Dumas, I supposed, even before I received your letter, to entertain a more favourable opinion of me, than I am conscious of deserving:—and Miss, you say, look'd kind. Kindness and benevolence, are indeed her characteristics. I never concealed from you the esteem and *friendship*, which I had, and which I still retain for her; but, (notwithstanding, some shrewd hints, contained in several of my Sisters letters, in which she appears to suspect my independence,) a more tender sentiment than friendship, has not yet gained admision into my breast, and I trust my Reason will for at least seven years to come, preserve my heart as free, as it ever has been.

Will you present my duty to my Father, to whom I will write soon.[5] To Coll: Smith I wish to be remembered; I have attempted to write to him, but a certain awkwardness, in addressing a person whom I never saw, (though I condemn myself for it) has prevented. My Sister I intend, shall hear directly from me by this opportunity.

Your dutiful, and affectionate Son. J. Q. Adams

RC (Adams Papers); endorsed: "J Q Adams Janry 11 1787."

[1] The Boston newspapers regularly reprinted items from London detailing the activities of the Adamses in England. For the reports on their trip to the Netherlands and their return to London, see the *Massachusetts Centinel*, 28 Oct., and Boston *Independent Chronicle*, 30 November.

[2] Lt. Gov. Thomas Cushing.

[3] For François Soulés, *Histoire des troubles de l'Amérique anglaise*, see AA to JQA, 22 May, note 2, above. He dedicated the volume to Hugh Percy, 2d duke of Northumberland (1742–1817), who had commanded British troops at Boston from 1774 to 1776 despite his personal opposition to the war (*DNB*). When Soulés published a second edition of the work in Paris in 1787, he expanded it to four volumes; a copy of this later edition, with JQA's bookplate, is at MQA.

[4] William Enfield, *Institutes of Natural Philosophy, Theoretical and Experimental*, London, 1785.

[5] JQA may not have written to JA until 30 June 1787, which is the next extant letter from him to his father. In it, he apologizes for not writing for so long (Adams Papers).

Mary Smith Cranch to Abigail Adams

My dear Sister Braintree December 31d 1786

I reciev'd a few days since your Letter of Sepr. 12th and yesterday that of october the 12th and thank you most sincerly for them both.

Your account of Holland entertaind me much. You must have improv'd your time well to have visited so many places and notic'd so much. The fatigue was too great for you. It was this that made you sick. I was rejoic'd to find your dissorder whatever it was for you did not tell me what had left before I heard of it. I feel a sad pertubation of spirit whenever a vessel arrives till I can see your hand writing and read that all are living and well. Your Family have been preserv'd thro many dangers, and for valuable purposes I dare say, but I most sincerly wish you all Safe at home. I shall comply with your wishes relaiting to a particular subject. The Person would not have been So often mention'd if some circumstances had not taken place which had no reference to your Family.

Our dear uncle Smith has recover'd his Spirits much better than I expected he would, but a heavey Sigh often escapes him yet. He is So much alter'd in his Family and in his attention to his Friends that you would scarcly suppose him the same man he once was. He left those little matters to our Aunt which now he attend too himself. Cousin Betsy behaves with the utmost prudence and discretion. She has a most exellent disposition. I am Sure you would Love her more than ever was you here.

We have had another Snow Storm Since I wrote last. Such an one has not been Seen for seventy years. Many People were oblig'd to get out of their chamber window, upon the Banks. The roads have been impassable in many places for a fortnight, and yet the Fields and some of the Streets in this town are bare. The college was oblig'd to be deserted Several weeks before the vacancy usually begins, wood could not be got.[1] Your eldest Son chose to Stay and ran his chance for wood as he thought he could Study there better than at home, and he will take this time to collect his part of the theses for commencment. The class have petition'd for a private one and have Set forth their reasons in a long preamble to their Petition. The Scarcity of money and the difficulty many of them find to pay even thier quarter Bills, are among the number.[2]

January 5th

Letters have been falling in to one and another ever since Folger ariv'd but not one for mr Cranch is come to hand yet: "he wonders at it as he has written so largly both to Brother and Sister." Did you receive one from him? you have not mention'd it. He hopes it was not lost.[3] The Trunk you Sent is Salve in uncle Smiths Store it was got out without any difficulty or paying any Duty that I can hear off.

The Shirts for JQA came Safe last Fall as did the Linnin for your other Sons. The Shirts went immediately to Cambridge. I Supposed Cousin would have mention'd them or I Should. It was a long time before I could find Who had the Peice of Linning, which was the reason I did not say any thing about it at that time. When we Shall be able to get the Trunk which is just arriv'd I know not. There has been a great thaw within a few days which has render'd it almost impossible for a carriage to pass. A thousand thanks my dear Sister is all I can offer you for these renewed Instances of your kindness to me and my dear Girls, but I cannot bear you should let them be So expencive to you. Half worn Gowns Such as might not be proper for you to wear in your Situation, would have been receiv'd with the utmost gratitude by them and Would have been priz'd more for having been wore by an Aunt they So dearly Love. The Silk you have Sent I heard them say they should lay up till they were married, but you must come home and find them Husbands! there are but few with whom they could be happy. They have had an education which calls for Tast Learning and virtue and they could not be *happy* in partners destitute of these qualifications. They go but little into the World, and into the Gay part of it not at all. There are Some Ladies of whom one may know every thing that is to be known in one afternoon. The diffidence of others renders it not so easey to discover their characters.

Our cousin William Smith has at last found a Lady Sensible enough of his merit to accept him for a Partner for Life. Miss Hannah Carter is the Lucky girl. The matter is Settled I hear. They will soon be married.[4] I think you know her she is very Sensible, and has a much more improv'd mind than is commonly to be found among the gay world. Doctor Simon Tufts dy'd last Sunday. The calmness with which he left the world does honour to the Religion he profess'd and practic'd. He call'd all his Family round him and pray'd with them and in that Prayer expir'd. His Daughters Grief is excessive, you know the Strength of her Passions.[5]

I heard from Sister Shaw last week She and the Family were well. Whether she will be able to get a Letter to town Soon enough to Send is uncertain as the roads are so bad.

Your two younger Sons have been writing to you and will do so to their Sister if the vessell does not Sail So Soon as we hear it is too.[6] Betsy and Lucy will write also if they can. It is a busy season with us. Our young Gentlemen always come home tatter'd and torn. We have met with a great Loss in mrs Betsy Nash. She is married and is to leave the Town soon.[7]

RC (Adams Papers); the text appears to be incomplete.

[1] Officials at Harvard decided on 12 Dec. that they would close the school if more than half of the students lacked sufficient firewood. On 13 Dec., following morning prayer, they formally adjourned the school for an eight week vacation (JQA, *Diary*, 2:139).

[2] See JQA to AA2, 14 Jan., note 12, below.

[3] Richard Cranch had written to JA on 20 May and 3 Oct. (both Adams Papers). JA replied to Cranch's May letter on 4 July (MWA; LbC, Adams Papers), which Cranch acknowledged receiving at the end of his 3 Oct. letter. Cranch had also written to AA on 13 April and 5 July, both above, but no letters from AA to Richard Cranch have been found for 1786.

[4] AA's cousin William Smith, son of Isaac Smith Sr. and Elizabeth Storer Smith, would marry his cousin Hannah Carter of Newburyport on 13 June 1787 (*Vital Records of Newburyport, Massachusetts*, 2 vols., Salem, 1911, 2:78).

[5] Either Lucy Tufts (1752–1811), who married Benjamin Hall in 1777, or Catharine Tufts (b. 1754), who married Nathan Wyman of Woburn in 1772 (*Vital Records of Medford, Massachusetts*, Boston, 1907, p. 147, 150, 308, 310, 385).

[6] No letter from either CA or TBA to JA, AA, or AA2 has been found for 1786 or 1787.

[7] Elizabeth Nash of Braintree married Ralph Pope of Dorchester on 25 Dec. (*Braintree Town Records*, p. 869).

Cotton Tufts to Abigail Adams

My Dear Cousn — Weymouth Jany. 2d. 1787

By Capt. Folger who arrived here last Saturday, I recd. Your obliging Letter of the 10th. of Octobr. last, a Bill of the Books sent for Revd. mr Cutler, and your kind Present for which I return You my Thanks. The Bill for Papers procured by Mr. Adams at the Request Lt Govr. Cushing, which you refer to, has not been paid to me; not a Syllable has been said by him upon the Subject, nor have I mentioned it to him, supposing that an order on the Treasury, would be all the Pay (except in Discharge of that, an Order on some Collector of back Taxes). However it may be best (at least) to Hint the Matter to him, especially if there should be any opening for getting the Money—and you will also on your part furnish me with the Date of the Time when the Money was advanced &C. En passant—Ill give you a Hint which may not be unprofitable. Moneys advanced in Europe are not suddenly repaid here.

In a late Settlement with Mrs. Cranch, for purchases for your Children, Allowance was made for their Board during the Vacations and for washing. This I conceived would be agreable to you and am happy to find that I was not mistaken. The embarrassed state of Our Affairs, Mr Cranch has severely felt. The greater part of his Time for several Years past has been spent in Attendance in the Genl

Court and Committees, for which he has not been able to obtain but a very small part of his Pay, I suppose not much more than sufficient to defray his Expences at Boston (this has been the Case with the Members of Court in general for 15 or 18 Months past and for several Sessions they have not recd. any Money), that I feel not a little anxious for him. £300 or £400 is now due to him and he cannot realize above one third of it in money if necessitated to raise it.

My Acctt. to the 14th. of Augt. last was forwarded by Capt [1] but conclude you had not recd. it as You make no mention of it in your Letter. At that Time the Ballance in your Favour was £28.11.7. My Expenditures since have exceeded that Ballance between £80 and 90£. Belchers Place is bargained for @ £70. Verchilds also will probably in a few Days be agreed for. I have drawn on mr. Adams in favr. of mr Elworthy for £130.7.1 and must shortly draw for a further Sum, if these Bargains should be compleated. Although Belchers Place is not in my Opinion worth that Sum, yet I think mr Adams had better give Ten or even Twenty Pounds extraordinary, than to have the Place continue in its present State. Verchilds Place has a very considerable Quantity of Wood on it and in that respect must be valuable although the Pasture is of an indifferent Quality. It has been a Doubt with me whether your Interest would be promoted by making purchases of Land. It is very certain it would be much more so by vesting the same money in public securities, could we be assured of any Stability in our public Funds. They are so fluctuating and the public Faith so much sported with, that I have been tempted several Times to vest those of Mr. Adams in Eastern Lands.[2] For the Interest on his Loan Office Certificates, Indents have been paid, Part of these I have negociated for Pierces final Settlements,[3] and with these I propose to buy a Ticket in the Land Lottery which youll see an Acctt. of in Adams & Nourses Paper. The Committee for selling Eastern Lands dispose of the Land also at private Sale in Town Ships or smaller Lots from 3/ to 9/ payable in public Securities.[4] If the Securities should depreciate much more, perhaps it may be best, to vest them in these Lands. At present consolidated notes are sold from 4/ to 5/ pr. £ in Specie. Loan office (Appletons) notes[5] from 3 to 4/ Pierces final Settlements from 2/4 to 2/6.

Newhall has quitted your House, given his Note for almost 1 Quarters Rent; no money is the Cry. It is now let to Adams & Nourse, Printer, at the yearly Rent of £44. being the most that could be obtained.[6]

Mr. T—r has not yet closed his Acctt. such assurances were given as supported my Patience and made me hope soon to see a Period to repeated and fruitless Journies. I have been disappointed, but will suppress my Feelings and having already had as much Success as any that have had Business to do with Him, will persevere till the whole is accomplished.

The unguarded Conversation of S. T. which gave Ld. Gordon an opportunity to display his meddling Genius, gave much Uneasiness to the Friends of S. T more especially to his Father who was then in a languishing State, brought on by an Hemorrhage from his Lungs. As all the Letters which passed between Ld. Gn. and the Minister, between Ld Gn. and S. T. as well as the Denial of the Matter alledged, were published in several of our Papers, perhaps it will be unnecessary to insert any Thing further in the Papers on the Subject.

Billy Cranch this moment came in and handed me a Letter from Medford which informs me that my Dear Friend and Brother Simon Tufts Esq. departed this Life on last Lords Day. Oh how many of my dear Connections, within a few Years past have entered the gloomy Mansions of the Dead, whose Society and Friendship smoothed the rugged Paths of Life and afforded a constant Source of Comfort and Delight! And where is the Loss of tried Friends to be repaired? and is not the forming of new Connections, like forming a new Existence? But I forbear. All is well. Tis mine to fill up the remaining Span of Life with Propriety, the Scene will soon close. Eer long we shall mix with our kindred Spirits and partake of their Felicity. Oh happy Day, for this may We watch, pray look and long, till we recieve their Welcome.

Be pleased to remember me to Mr and Mrs Smith and accept of my sincerest Wishes for your present and future Felicity. And Am Your Affectionate Friend & Kinsman Cotton Tufts

RC (Adams Papers); addressed: "Madam Abigail Adams London"; endorsed: "Dr Tufts Janry 2 1787."

[1] Blank in MS. The account has not been found.

[2] That is, Passamaquoddy, the easternmost section of the district of Maine.

[3] Certificates issued to Continental Army troops by Paymaster General John Pierce in 1783 (see vol. 6:424).

[4] The Boston *Independent Chronicle*, 30 Nov. 1786, advertised a lottery for Maine, selling tickets at $200 or £60 each. The committee overseeing both the lottery and the sale of additional lands included Samuel Phillips Jr., Nathaniel Wells, John Brooks, Rufus Putnam, and Leonard Jarvis.

[5] Nathaniel Appleton (1731–1798), Harvard 1749, was a Boston merchant and chandler. He had been appointed Massachusetts' commissioner for the Continental loan office in 1777, a position he held until his death (*Sibley's Harvard Graduates*, 12:355, 358–359).

[6] Thomas Adams (1757?–1799) and John Nourse (1762?–1790), publishers of the Bos-

ton *Independent Chronicle*, replaced Andrew Newell as tenants in the Adamses' Court (formerly Queen) Street house in Boston. The house was located close to the *Chronicle's* offices (vol. 2:187–188, 6:259, 260; JA, *D&A*, 2:63–64; James C. Y. Shen, *Early Boston Newspapers*, Boston, [1978?], p. 133).

Elizabeth Cranch to Abigail Adams

Braintree Jany. 7th. 1787

I have not wrote you my dear Aunt for a long time, much too long I confess; and even now those motives which have prevented, continue in force: A barreness of Subject is of all preventives the most dissagreable and I find it is like to prevail and increase in me daily; motives however more powerful have overcome this; and I am induced to write—tho—I triffle.

Love, gratitude and esteem, I feel; You cannot doubt it; elaborate expressions of each of these affections of my mind, might prove a copious subject, and the goodness amiableness and many excellent virtues, which excite them, might if represented in their full perfection, adorn the purest Page, and give a fair example of female excellence. But there is a certain delicate sensibility which recoils at the direct commendations of its virtues, tho conscious of meriting them. And perhaps an endeavour, to immitate, and implant them; is a more flattering, and at the same time more delicate, and a worthier acknowledgement of them.

I have now to thank you for your last Letter of July 18th. and for the Book accompanying of it. I had not by any means, an adequate idea of the perfection to which they had brought the art of ornamenting their farms and grounds in England; I think they must be enchantingly beautiful; I felt when I had finished it, as if I almost regretted having read it: for having never before had Ideas of such perfection, in my mind, wherewith to compare what I saw, I could think these beautiful and they satisfied me; but now my standard is altered, and all appear uncouth and imperfect; I am wishing to alter this, pull down that, build up another, cut down this tree, and have an immediate spontaneous growth on that hill, turn the course of a rivulet, widen a brook, and a thousand other whims and impossibilities are coming into my mind, every time I look abroad; but alas all in vain! However perhaps possessing them, I might not be happier than now. I cannot help wishing to *see* those delightful places; even this must be denyed me. This however teaches me, what many, many, of the events of Life are constantly instructing me in, that my happiness depends more upon bounding my desires and wishes than in seeking earnestly to gratify them. Dissapointment is written upon many a *Page* of my Life; and strange as it may seem, experience had not made me wise eno', to prevent its appearing a conspicuous character in some of the latest.

Perhaps in this state of existance, our human faculties cannot attain to strength sufficient to enable us to repel the force of dissapointment; but in aid of their weakness, Religion offers powerful assistance, and Resignation her lenient balm. These can calm the tumult of the mind when dissapointment has broken in upon its fondest hopes and destroy'd its long concerted schemes of happiness; these can make us look beyond the present and give a firm assurance to the wounded heart, that almighty Goodness, "Scourges in mercy, and corrects in Love." Firmly perswaded of this, we may yet rejoice; contentment may preside at the heart and Gratitude for many present blessings, overcome all too anxious regret for past misfortunes.[1]

It is with real pleasure that I hear of my Cousins present happiness; long may she injoy it uninterruptedly; long may she live unhurt by numerous sarrounding evils; may each revolving year add to her blessings and her virtues; She does not, cannot know how much I love her, distance and absence prevent, and will I fear prevent my giving her any personal assurances of it; I hope she feels most perfectly assured of my regard, esteem and friendship; I could not be happy should there rest upon her mind any bias that had induced her *ever* to distrust either.

Your Sons are at present most [. . .] amiable Youths; each display their growing virt[ues by] a pleasing variety of effects. They all enjoy fin[e health?] and appear happy. Cousin John deprives us of the p[leasure] of his company this Vacancy, and devotes himself intirely to the Muses; he courts their patronage most assiduously, and I presume will be their favourite, and their Glory. Charles is also pursuing the same path with all the Loves and Graces in his train. Thomas is very good; his temper and disposition excellent; his faculties and capacitys are just expanding, before the invigorating rays of Science, and I doubt not the future fruit will amply repay the present culture.

I must beg you to present my most respectful regards to my Uncle—to Mr and Mrs Smith my Love, I intend writing her by the next Vessel. I am sure you will do me the justice to believe me with every sentiment of affection & the warmest gratitude your Neice

E Cranch

RC (Adams Papers); addressed: "Mrs Adams. Grosvenor-Square Westminster."; endorsed: "E Cranch's Letter Janry 7th." Some loss of text where the seal was removed.

[1] Cranch had recently learned of the death of Thomas Perkins, whom she had hoped to marry. See Elizabeth Smith Shaw to AA, 1 Nov. 1786, above.

John Adams to Charles Adams

My Dr. Charles — Jany. 10. 87

I have recieved with pleasure your letter of the 22d. of octr.[1] and agree with you that the times are such as to make it difficult for a young Gentleman, to determine upon a Profession, yet there is no reason to be discouraged, The Prospect will brighten. I have so well grounded a Veneration for the Law, that I shall never discourage any of my sons from pursuing the study of it, if their Genius and disposition incline them in favour of it. You should well consider that it is an arduous, studious and labourious course of Life, and will require the exertion of all your faculties. Think of it well enquire maturely and decide for yourself, if your final resolution should be in favour of it, I will do my utmost to assist you in your Preparations and Progress, if my Life should be spared. I hope you will apply yourself to your Studies and Business, and have less interruption from public avocations than your father has had. A Lawyer, who confines himself to his practice and is careful to preserve his honor Intigrity, Humanity, Decency, and Delicacy, may be as happy and useful a Citizen as any in society. But ambition will be his ruin. Launching into public Life even from Patriotism, will destroy his happiness, and not probably increase his real usefulness.

My Love to your worthy Brothers, and believe me anxious for the good Behaivour as well as success of all of you. Yours affect.

J. A.

LbC in WSS's hand (Adams Papers).

[1] Not found.

John Adams to John Quincy Adams

My dear Son — Grosvenor Square Jan 10. 1787

I am much obliged to you for the Copy of your Dialogue, which does you honour. I am the more pleased to learn that you are to collect the Mathematical Theses, as the Same part fell to my Share in the Year 1755.[1]

Your Reasons for preferring Newbury Port to Boston for the Study of the Law are judicious, and discover an Attention and a Consideration, which give sure Presages of your future Success. You must take Some opportunity to pay your Respects to Mr Parsons, and know his Terms; or pray Dr Tufts to write to him. It will be of great Importance, to your happiness to get into his Family, to board, if that be possible. But if it is not, you must pay a particular Attention to this point, in the Choice of a Situation and a Family to board in. I am very happy to hear that your Brother Thomas, behaves as well as his elder Brothers, and that all three are irreproachable. May you all continue, in a virtuous Course, and be happy. You must all attend to your health. All depends upon that. I found it difficult to persuade you, while in Europe, to take your fresh Air, and active Exercise regularly.

When you come into a Lawyers office, you will find it more necessary Still. At present, Attendance on Prayers, Recitations and public Exhibitions, and the Amusements of Conversation with your fellow Students, are instead of Exercise. But when you come to pore alone over Law, which is not very entertaining, you will find a difference.

But at all times and in all Places, above all Things, preserve the Sentiments and the delicate sensibilities of youth, throughout your whole Life. Honour and Integrity, Humanity and Modesty are natural to Man. Let not the Commerce of the World, ever wear them out or blunt the Edge of your sensibility of them.

Libertatem, Amicitiam, Fidem, præcipua humani animi bona, retinebis. According to your Friend Tacitus.[2] Riches and Grandeur are empty Baubles: but the moral Sentiments must be your Companions every hour of your Life: and infallibly your constant Comforters, or Tormentors. Consult your own heart, consult Experience, and History and they will all concur, with this Advice of your affectionate Father John Adams

RC (Adams Papers).

[1] For JQA's mathematical theses, part of the Harvard commencement exercises for 1787, see his *Diary*, 2:xii, 82–83, 256–257 (illustration). While JA left no record of his own mathematical theses for the 1755 Harvard commencement, he did record several mathematical exercises in his Diary; in his Autobiography, he further recalled his strong interest and ability in mathematics while at Harvard and his delight in teaching JQA mathematics in France in 1784 (*D&A*, 1:32, 107–108, 126–127, 177–178; 3:260, 262).

[2] A paraphrase of Tacitus, *Histories*, Book 1.15, lines 22–24: You will hold liberty, friendship, and fidelity as the highest goods of the human soul.

Mary Smith Cranch to Abigail Adams

My dear Sister Braintree January 10th 1787

I have sent one Letter on Board callahan,[1] but hope he has not yet sail'd, as I have much to say that I was oblig'd to omit then for want of time. Betsy has written to you also. By her Letter you will see the State of her mind better than by any thing I can Say, but I am Sure you will wonder how such a change in her affections took place. You may remember what I mention'd to you before you went from us. She then thought that Friendship and gratitude was all she could possible return him, but His absence soon became painful. She wanted the company of the Friend who had Study'd her Temper and disposition, and who never appear'd happier than when he could amuse or entertain her. She look'd around her, and say many who's manners were more polish'd than her Freinds, but none whos principles were better, morals purer, or heart more sincere. He was incountering dangers and difficulties to acqure a fortune without which he could not with propriety ask a return of her affections. In this part of the country he saw no prospect of gaining one suddenly, he therefore left it and was seeking it in a wilderness surrounded by Savages. It was a long time before She heard from him. So long that we thought he must have fallen a sacrifice to Savage brutality as many other Travellers had done about that time. This awakend all her tender Passions and distress'd her greatly. She felt altho innocent as if she was the cause of his Death. I did not know till this time that She had any attachment to him. She was soon reliev'd by receiving a very long Letter from him. We receiv'd others the past summer by which he appear'd to be in very good business and it is probable in a few years would have made a pretty fortune.[2] As soon as he had acquir'd Sufficient to set him above want he design'd to return and spend it with his Friends, "The thought of this (he says in a Letter to her) was almost the only thing that made life desirable to him." But heaven has seen it to be best that he should be cut off in the midst of his fondest hopes, and most pleasing prospect. His will be done is all we ought to say. "It is right, surpport me heaven" was all She did say, but her countinance distress'd me greatly, it was calm but solemn. She has recover'd her spirits much but the wound will not be soon heal'd. He was sick but a few days was not thought dangirous till the evening before he expir'd he then lost his reason and did not recover it again. The gentleman who Sent us an account of his death says, "He was greatly belov'd and esteem while Living and almost unversally lamented now dead."

Janu 12th

I yesterday reciev'd your Trunk and shall deliver the things as directed. Betsy and Lucy are greatly oblig'd for their silks. They are very good and very pretty. The Stockings are such as I wish'd, the price is I suppose Sterling. I shall give you credit accordingly. The pieces of cousin JQAs coats are well pattern'd. The remnant of course Linnin is come also. The suit of Cloathes of mr Adams will not do for your eldest son the Shirts and the coat are so short for the present Fashon that he will not have it I am sure. He would have had a Blue velvet of his Papas this winter if it had not been for this difficulty. They must be lay'd by till long wasts and short shirts are the mode. He is in no want of any new ones at present, he wears a coat very little. I think he will not want any stockings this summer. As to their Linnin, the children will make it. The two youngest grow so fast that before a measure could reach you it would not fit them. Thomas will soon out run Charles in height, and is no spindle shanks I assure you. He is the best shape'd of the Family. Such Cambrick as you have sent cannot be purchas'd here under 16/ Lawful. I shall this afternoon carry your mother Hall her Gown and the calico for the children, they will be highly gratified. Mrs Hall injoys fine health for one of her years. She is grown quite Fleshy. She din'd and spent the day with me and her grandchildren here about a week since. I sent our Sleigh for her. It look'd so much like what you use'd to do, that it afforded me and her I believe more pleasure than if she had made me a visit of her own motion. I told her What you said about her caps and offer'd to make some for her. I will send you a pattern, but will make some in the meantime out of some of the pieces which may be left of Cousin Charles Linnen, she will not want many.

I do not think of any thing your sons want which we cannot get here. I wish to know the price of those silk Hankercheifs, and what you can buy good mode for,[3] mode which will do to make cardinals of and what colour Is most commonly worn by young Ladles. I do not mean little misses. I should be glad of a Pattern to cut them by, our children must have new ones soon and I wish to know if I can get them cheaper with you than here. Cushing is not arriv'd. I wrote you some time since that mr William White, a merchant in Boston sent you the chocalate. He partly own'd the vessel. Mr Cranch went to put Some on boar'd but the capn. would not take it. Said he had enough already. After this mr White told me what he had done. Winslow W. is at home again. I know not how he was releas'd. I have not Seen the Family this winter.

Your youngest son designs to be a Farmer he told me the other day he may change his mind, but at present he seems determin'd.

RC (Adams Papers).

[1] Probably that of 31 Dec. 1786, above.

[2] For publication information on and a summary of the only known extant letter from Thomas Perkins to Elizabeth Cranch, see vol. 6:271–272, 275.

[3] A thin glossy silk, used for hoods and scarves (*OED*).

Mary Smith Cranch to Abigail Adams

[*post 10 January 1787*][1]

There is another vessel up which will sail soon. What I may have omited by this I shall write by that. Our uncle Quincy was well a few hours since is glad to see his Friends but cannot be perswaided out. Cousin Cotton remains the same he was, Flying from spray to spray without determining Where to chuse his Partner. If his Father should marry as he will certainly do as soon as he can get time to look round him,[2] He will find such a change in the Family as will interfere with his managment of Boiling the Pot and making the Pyes. If such an event should take place, I shall talk soberly to him. If he would wish to live happy he must have a Family of his own.

Your Nieghbours are well. Old Mrs Hayden desires me to thank you for your kindness to her.[3] Our Freinds at General Palmers are all Well I hear. I have not seen them since they remov'd to Charlestown. Miss Eunice has been at Newtown ever since the begining of the summer.[4] I believe she is well for her. If you have any old white silk Stockings and will send them to her I know they will be acceptable as she finds her Feet easer in them than in any others. If some of her Friends were not kind to her she would not have cloaths to cover her. I gave her two pair of cousin JQA old silk Stocking which he could not wear. She cut of the tops and made feet to them and told me I had made her happy for the summer.

My own health is much better but I am wrappd up in Flannel and stiff half my time notwithstanding but while my stomack and head is limber I mind it not. I thank you for your kind prescriptions.[5] I am sensible that Ironing hurts me and do not do it, but it is sometimes a great trouble to me that I cannot. I have made a charge of your sons Board in their vacancys and as to the washing and Ironing If you will only pay the washing and Ironing woman for a day's work once a week it is all I desire and much more than I am satisfied with. It look so like ingratitude, when you are continually loading us with favours that I do not know how to bear it. It is what I never design'd to do and what I never would if we could get any thing but orders from the Publick. We have been oblig'd to lose 15 dollars out of one of 50 dollars which we were oblig'd to sell in order to purchase necessarys for the Family. This feels hard when mr cranchs pay is so small, but if you do not think me ungratful I shall not be quite unhappy. I design'd this only for a cover but it seems I have fill'd it and have scarcly left a corner to tell you that I am your affet Sister M C

RC (Adams Papers); addressed by Elizabeth Cranch: "Mrs Abigail Adams. Grosvenor Square London"; stamped: "COWES SHIP LRE.s"; endorsed: "Mrs Cranch Jary 10. 178⟨6⟩7"; notation in another hand: "1786"; filmed at [*10 January 1786*], Adams Papers, Microfilms, Reel No. 367.

[1] The docketing and content indicate that the letter was written in 1787; presumably, Cranch used it as the cover for her letter of 10 Jan., above.

[2] Cotton Tufts Jr.'s mother, Lucy Quincy Tufts, had died in Oct. 1785; his father, Dr. Cotton Tufts Sr., did not remarry until 1789, to Susanna Warner.

[3] Mrs. John Hayden of Braintree, to whom AA made regular gifts of support (vol. 5:346; 6:107).

[4] For Eunice Paine, see vol. 5:386–388.

[5] AA had previously recommended to Cranch William Buchan's *Domestic Medicine; or, the Family Physician*, Edinburgh, 1769. Both Cranch and AA suffered from rheumatism (vol. 5:267, 363, 383–384; 6:60).

John Quincy Adams to Abigail Adams Smith

Cambridge January 14th: 1787

I determined about a fortnight agone, to sit down, and write you a letter, expressing my anxiety and surprize, that for three months I had not received one line from my friends in Europe; I did in fact in a letter to Mamma, make my complaint, but a day or two afterwards I was made happy, with two excellent letters, the one from her, and the other from you. But instead of making apologies for not writing more frequently of late, you call me to an account for my own neglect: in answer to which I can only repeat, what I have so frequently said; that the noiseless tenor of a college life, and the unvaried uniformity of circumstances, cannot furnish a subject, either for interesting relation, or brilliancy of sentiment. I have not however missed any opportunities for writing, of which I have been apprized; and you may be assured that I shall never fail in my duty, when I can see a possibility of fulfilling it. Now for journal. On the 17th: of October the fall Vacation began, and I went to Braintree. On the 1st: of November the Vacation being ended I returned to Cambridge. Remarkable events! are they not. "But" say you, "how did you spend your time at Braintree during that fortnight"? Why Madam, I read three or four Volumes of History, and Burlamaqui, upon Law:[1] I wrote a few Letters,[2] (but as they had not a voyage of 3000 miles to undertake, I was not at much trouble in equipping them;) I went a fowling once or twice, and had my labour for my pains. I prick'd off a few tunes, and blew them on the flute. And further the deponent saith not. But by the bye, since I have made mention of my flute, I must relieve you from your anxiety, concerning the effect it might have upon my health. It is now nine months since I first began to blow, and I have never experienced the least bad effect from it. I have consulted several persons, used to that instrument, and they have all told me; that unless a person be of a very slender constitution, the moderate use of a flute, cannot be hurtful. I have neither time, nor inclination to blow so much as to injure my health. But it has been since, my residence here, my greatest amusement, and the chief relaxation after study; and indeed it affords me so much pleasure, that I cannot think of giving it up, while I am sensible of no injury from it: thus far however I will promise you: that if I ever perceive myself hurt by it, I will immediately quit; before it can do any essential injury.

I now return to my history. For six weeks after my returning here, I went once to Mr Gerry's (he has bought a house and farm in this town, and came to live here about five month's since.)[3] Excepting this visit and two or three at Mr: Dana's,[4] I went no where.—Upon recollection, I must also except one dancing party, that we had with a number of the young Ladies in the town: I would describe it to you, and might possibly raise a smile, by characterizing the Ladies; but I must avoid it, for fear, of having *another lecture* for severity.—In December two violent Snow storms which happened in one week; stopp'd up the roads in the Country so effectually, that no wood came in town for three weeks. Many families in town, and two thirds of the Students, were entirely destitute. I was without any, four of the coldest days, we have had this Season. On Wednesday the 13th. of December, the students were dismissed, for eight weeks. The vacation commenced three weeks sooner than common, on account of the impossibility of procuring wood. I determined to remain here through the vacation, for several reasons. I thought that four of us going at once to Mr: Cranch's, would make it troublesome, and inconvenient to them: and although I have always been treated there with as much attention and kindness as I could possibly wish, yet it was not like home; the absence of my Parents and Sister, deprived Braintree of its chief attractions, and the place by reviving so frequently the idea of their absence, caused too many melancholy sensations, to be an agreeable residence. I knew that if I left Cambridge, I should be obliged to spend more than half my time in visiting here and there, and every where, which could be of no service to me, nor to any other person:—and besides this, I had engaged some time since, at the desire of my Class, in an undertaking, somewhat laborious; my avocations in Term time are such, that I cannot pay much attention then to this piece of work, and I cannot attend to it conveniently, except I be in Cambridge. The present leisure time afforded me an excellent opportunity; and I thought I should fail in my duty to the Class, if I did not improve it. I have employ'd a great part of my Time, to that purpose, and have got about half through the business.

It would have been disagreeable to remain in college, entirely alone; in this respect, I was very fortunate: a young gentleman, by the name of Bridge, whose character as a scholar and a gentleman is inferior to none, at this university, remained here likewise, and we agreed to *chum* together during the vacation. We keep a chamber in College, and board, at professor Wigglesworth's. This gentleman is equally free from the supercilious frown of the President, and the distant reserve of a Tutor. He treats us with an unaffected complaisance, which is not the most remarkable characteristic of all the governors of the university; he commands respect, but not by insisting on it, as an highwayman, who demands your purse. There are in his house two young Ladies; his niece, and daughter. I am happy that I can give you a few traits of their characters, without incurring your censure, for *severity*. Miss Catharine Jones, is just turn'd of eighteen. Her face is one of those, which without containing perhaps one beautiful feature, view'd seperately, yet taken all together, possesses a certain charm, which entitles her to the appellation of a beauty. Her person is large, though not inelegant; I would say she was *stout built*, if the expression, were not more applicable to a man of war, than to a young Lady. Her mind appears to partake of several of these qualities; if considered in a comprehensive manner, it may be called amiable, though an enumeration of every particular quality might be to her disadvantage. She has a share of wit, and a share of good nature, which is however sometimes soured, by a small tincture of caprice. She is not wholly exempt from Vanity; but as her understanding, rather than her person is the object of this Vanity, she endeavours to appear sarcastic, because she supposes, a satirical talent, must imply, an uncommon share of wit. To sum up my opinion of her; I could esteem her as a friend, I could love her as a Sister, but I should never think of her as the companion of my life.[5]

Miss Peggy Wigglesworth is two years older than her Cousin. Her complexion is of the browner order; but this defect, if a defect it be, is compensated, by a rosy variety of colour; her face is not beautiful, but is remarkable for expressing, all the candor, benevolence, and sincerity of her heart, her shape, would be genteel in France or England, though her size, would seem to give her the title of a *pretty woman* as Fielding expresses it. As to her mind, should I attempt to give you a just description, of its virtues, I fear you would suspect me of writing a panegyric, rather than a character. She does not make such a display of wit, as her cousin, but she has an open frankness, and a generous candor, infinitely more amiable in my opinion, than an incessant endeavour to appear smart, and as she is equally acquainted with the enjoyments, and the solicitudes, which attend great sensibility, she is intirely free from that Vanity, whose gratification, consists, in the mortification of others. The greatest imperfection, which the severest scrutiny of her conduct and sentiments could discover, would be a degree of sincerity and unreservedness, which is considered as a fault only because the taste of mankind is vitiated by dissimulation. Notwithstanding all this, she is almost universally the object of, friendship, and esteem, rather than of love.[6] I am sensible of this fact myself, and when I search my own mind to find the causes of it, I am reduced to condemn, either the Passion; of Love, or the sentiments by which it is produced.—The characters of these two ladies, you will perceive, are very different yet they are both very agreeable, and their conversation, affords us pleasing relaxation, after the toils, of study. There are a number of other families where we have visited in the course of the vacation, but excepting Mrs: Dana, and Mrs: Pearson, I believe you have no acquaintance here. I have frequently in the course of the vacation, been at Mr: Dana's: his Lady you know; she is very agreeable, and always in excellent spirits. Miss Almy Ellery, is with her: I think you have seen this young Lady. She is unfortunately somewhat deaf, but is uncommonly sensible, and, (what I am griev'd to say is still more uncommon in this country) her mind is much improved by reading: so that she can entertain a company with a large variety of conversation, without having recourse to the stale, and trivial topics of common-place, or to the ungenerous, and disgraceful topic of scandal. She is not handsome, and is I suppose 27 years old: yet if she was in company with twenty of the most beautiful young ladies in the State, and in this company, I had to choose my seat, it should certainly be by her side.[7] I have been endeavouring, my Sister, ever since I returned from Europe, to find a female character like this, united to great beauty of person. As yet my researches have been unsuccessful, and I begin to have the same prejudice against a beauty, as you have expressed in one of your letters against handsome men.

Sunday Feby: 5th: [*i.e. 4th*]

Callahan sailed a fortnight sooner than I had been led to expect, and I had not an opportunity, to send this Letter, before he went. Since I wrote the preceding pages, few circumstances have occurred, the relation of which could afford you any entertainment. One little party only, has given variety to the scene; there was nothing interesting in it, but such as it was, you shall hear. You must know in the first place, that in the town of Mystic,[8] about 5 miles from this, there are about thirty five young Ladies, of what is called the *ton*; and excepting two of my Classmates, who spend the vacations in that place, there are only two young gentlemen. You may judge, that in such a dearth of men, if any thing is going forward which requires their presence, volunteers must be hunted for in the neighbouring towns. About a fortnight agone, a dancing party being proposed there, one of the classmates aforesaid, came and invited Williams, (the professor's son, and likewise a Classmate) my Chum and me, to join them:[9] accordingly we went over one evening, and were introduced into a large company of Ladies, with whom we were entirely unacquainted. Many of them were handsome, but female beauty, is so universal in this country, that I pay little attention to it. We soon went to dancing, and this circumstance assisted me greatly to become acquainted with the Ladies. Where human beings are unacquainted with the ridiculous solemnity of formal ceremony, the social spirit which is natural to them, will always produce its effect. Before the evening was ended, I felt as free from restraint, as I could be in the most familiar company. It fell to my lot, at first, to dance with the handsomest lady in Company. I endeavoured to enter into conversation with her, but to every thing I could say, the only answers were, "yes," "no," "I think so," "indeed!" I was soon tired of her, and concluded she was too much occupied in thinking of herself, to give any of her attention to other people: we drew again for partners, and I found in a short time that I had made an advantageous exchange. One of these Ladies could only be seen, the other was likewise heard with pleasure.[10]

In your last Letter, (which I must observe by the bye, is dated September 1st:) you caution me against satirizing the heads of our university, and moreover threaten me with a syllogism, at Commencement. I have made it a rule ever since I entered college, to treat the government, with all the deference, and respect due to them, and I have reason to suppose, that no one of them, has any particular pique against me. If they had I should have perceived it, for their partialities are generally very conspicuous; and as to the syllogisms, it is by no means terrible to me, for I conceive I have as good a right to doubt of their judgment as they have to doubt of my capacity. . . . But I have some hopes that I shall not be subjected even to the temporary mortification of reading syllogisms, as there is some probability, that we shall not have a public Commencement. The expences of that day, to the Class which graduates, are said to amount upon an average to 1000£. In the present situation of the Country, this is a large sum, and the advantages derived from appearing in public are not adequate to it. The Class have unanimously signed a petition to the corporation, requesting a private Commencement, and we are in great hopes it will be granted.[11]

Friday. Feby: 9th:

The vacation closed the day before yesterday: our brothers and Cousin return'd from Braintree: but the weather has been so bad, that only a small number of the students have arrived. I went to Boston yesterday, for the first time since last October. Uncle Smith's family, Doctor Welch's, Mr: Storer's are well. Polly Storer has been ill several months, but is recovering. Mr. W: Smith is in a fair way of getting married, to a lady in Newbury. Strange things, will happen some times.[12] Dr: Tufts and Mr: Cranch are both in Boston attending the general Court; who assembled last week, and finally did, what might with propriety have been done four months past. That is, they have declared that a rebellion exists in the Counties of Worcester, Hampshire and Berkshire.[13] It is to be hoped that the government will now act with some spirit, but I suppose you see our newspapers regularly, and they will give you full accounts of all the late political occurrences.

Honestus has been attacked since his arrival from England, and accused of being an instrument in producing the rebellion:[14] his writings, which were preserved from the neglect, and contempt which they deserved, only by the temporary frenzy of popular prejudice, are now deprived even of that support, and will probably receive very little attention, henceforward from the public. They have not terrified me from the study of the Law, but with whom I am to study is not yet decided.

Captain Folgier proposes sailing the first fair wind. I am in hopes I shall be able to send this before he goes. I begin to be impatient for letters again. Cushing is expected every day; I shall depend upon hearing from you by him.

Remember me to Mr: Smith, and to our Parents. I should have written to my father, had I heard sooner of this opportunity, and if possible, I will yet write.

Your ever affectionate brother. J. Q. Adams

RC (Adams Papers); endorsed: "Mr J Q Adams Jan 14 87 answered july 11th 87."

[1] In his Diary, JQA indicates that he had finished reading the first volume of Jean Jacques Burlamaqui's *The Principals of Natural and Political Law* (transl. Thomas Nugent, 2 vols., London, 1763) on 15 Oct. and the second on the 24th. On the 26th, he noted that he was in the process of reading Claude François Xavier Millot's *Elemens d'histoire générale* (9 vols., Switzerland, 1778). JQA's own copy of Millot is at MQA (*Diary*, 2:116, 118–119).

[2] The only letter located is to JQA's Harvard classmate James Bridge, 22 Oct. (NjP: de Coppet Collection). In that, he indicates that he will next write to an unnamed "Lady."

[3] JQA visited Elbridge Gerry on 4 Dec. (*Diary*, 2:136).

[4] JQA visited Francis Dana on 26 Nov. and 7, 14, and 18 Dec. (same, 2:129, 137, 141–142)

[5] Catherine (Katherine) Jones of Newburyport (b. 1768) married Capt. William Brown in 1793 (*Vital Records of Ipswich Massachusetts*, 3 vols., Salem, 1910, 1:211; *Vital Records of Newburyport Massachusetts*, 2 vols., Salem, 1911, 2:256). For more of JQA's thoughts on her, see his *Diary*, 2:142–143.

[6] Margaret (Peggy) Wigglesworth (b. 1766) was the daughter of Hollis Professor of Divinity Edward Wigglesworth and a cousin of Catherine Jones. She married John Andrews of Newburyport in 1789 (Lucius R. Paige, *History of Cambridge, Massachusetts 1630–1877 with a Genealogical Register*, 2 vols., Cambridge, 1930, 2:813; *Sibley's Harvard Graduates*, 5:410).

[7] Almy Ellery (1759–1839), daughter of William Ellery and Ann Remington, married William Stedman, later a member of Congress (*NEHGR*, 8:318, 320 [Oct. 1854]).

[8] Malden, Mass., which was originally known as Mystic Side before it separated from Charlestown in 1649 (*Historical Data Relating to Counties, Cities and Towns in Massachusetts*, Boston, 1966, p. 41, 77, 83).

[9] For Samuel Williams Jr., see JQA, *Diary*, 2:242–243. JQA, Williams, and James Bridge were invited to the party by their classmate Ebenezer Learned (same, 2:150, 217).

[10] JQA describes this party and "Miss Dixey," whom he found beautiful but self-centered, in his Diary at both 19 and 21 Feb. (same, 2:150).

[11] The first of several petitions by the class of 1787 seeking a private commencement was approved by the seniors in Dec. 1786. School officials ultimately rejected the request but

did agree to have a simpler, more frugal public celebration (same, 2:136–137).

[12] The paragraph, to this point, was later covered by a strip of paper pasted over the text, probably by Caroline Amelia Smith de Windt, who omitted this text from her edited collection (AA2, *Jour. and Corr.*, 3:141).

[13] The "General Court's Declaration, That a Horrid and Unnatural Rebellion Exists within This Commonwealth" passed on 4 Feb. (Mass., *Acts and Laws*, Resolves of 1786, Jan. sess., ch. 5).

[14] See, for instance, Boston *Independent Chronicle*, 11, 18 January.

John Adams to Thomas Boylston Adams

My dr. Thomas — Jany. 15. 1787

I am glad to find by your Letter[1] that you are so well situated, at Mr. Sewalls, make my Compliments to that Gent. and thank him for the Kind present of his translation of Young—it appears to me to be well done. You will write to me from time to time, if you want Books, or any assistance in your studies, from this side the Water. I hear a good account of your Conduct, your studies you must pursue, literally for your Life. It is, generally benificial to begin early to think of a Profession, tho it is not proper to take unalterable Resolutions, before the time arrives when they become necessary. It is never amiss to reflect early on the subject. You may write me your thoughts. I have ever thought it the duty of Parents to consult the Genius and Inclination of Children in their future destination in Life, when their Characters are not vicious and their dispositions are not inconsiderate. It is a serious thing to determine for Life, and it is your happiness that is sought.

I shall find it difficult enough to provide for the Education of my sons, but as they behaive well and mind their studies, I will do all in my power to assist them and I would advise you to chuse that faculty, which you think will be most agreable to you, and in which you may be most useful to others.

We are not born for ourselves alone, Benevolence is really a part of our Nature, as self-Love, and man is never so happy as when he is conscious that he is useful to others.

I am my dr. son your Fr — J. A.

LbC in WSS's hand (Adams Papers).

[1] Not found.

Thomas Jefferson to Abigail Adams Smith

Paris Jan. 15. 1787

Mr. Jefferson has the honour to present his compliments to [Mrs.] Smith and to send her the two pair of Corsets she desired. He wishes they may be suitable, as Mrs. Smith omitted to send her measure. Times are altered since Mademoiselle de Sanson had the honour of knowing her.[1] Should they be too small however, she will be so good as to lay them by a while. There are ebbs as well as flows in this world. When the mountain refused to come to Mahomet, he went to the mountain. Mr Jefferson wishes mrs Smith a happy new year, and abundance of happier ones still to follow it. He begs leave to assure her of his esteem and respect, and that he shall always be happy to be rendered useful to her by being charged with her commands.

FC (MHi:Jefferson Papers); notation: "Smith mrs."

[1] A reference to AA2's pregnancy, which WSS had confirmed in his correspondence with Jefferson in Nov. (Jefferson, *Papers*, 10:479, 518).

Abigail Adams Smith to Cotton Tufts

Sir Grosvenor Square London Jany 16 1787

By a Letter to my Mother from you, I Learnt that you had in your Possession the Letters and Picture which I requested you to take the Charge of.[1] I now must once more trouble you upon the Subject, and request the favour of you, to address the Picture to Miss Margaret Smith at Jamaica on Long-Island New York,[2] and forward it by some safe Conveyance, under Cover to Mr. Daniel Mc.Cormick[3] No 39 Wall Street New York.

All the Letters I will request you Sir to Burn with your own Hands, after which I hope you will receive no further trouble on the Subject.

With much respect I am Sir your Humbl servt A Smith

RC (ViU:Special Collections, Adams Family Letters #7231-A); addressed: "The Honble Cotton Tufts Esqr. Weymouth Massachusetts"; endorsed: "Mrs. A. Smiths Lettr. recd April 19. 1787."

[1] Of 15 Aug. 1786, above. See also Tufts to AA, 6 July, above.

[2] Margaret Smith, named after her mother, was WSS's eldest sister. She later married Felix de St. Hilaire, the French vice consul for the port of Alexandria, Va. (*JCC*, 14:759; AA2 to Elizabeth Cranch Norton, 7 Feb. 1791, MHi:C. P. Cranch Papers).

[3] Daniel McCormick (d. 1834), born in Ireland, was a New York merchant and one of the first directors of the Bank of New York (Walter Barrett, *The Old Merchants of New York City*, 2d series, N.Y., 1863, p. 249, 252–253, 264–265).

Abigail Adams to John Quincy Adams

My dear Son London Janry 17 1787

I wrote you so largly by the Newyork December packet, that a few lines must now suffice. I cannot let a vessel sail without some token from me, and tho I do not insist upon Letter for Letter, you should recollect how dissapointed you used to be when your Friends omitted writing.

Your Aunt Cranch wrote me in the fall, that you had been unwell with a swiming in your Head. I know by experience how dissagreeable that complaint is for I was Seaizd with it on my return from Holland, to an allarming degree untill I was Bled which relieved me. As you and I both are inclined to corpulence we should be attentive to excercise. Without this a Sedantary Life will infallibly destroy your Health, and then it will be of little avail that you have trim'd the midnight Lamp. In the cultivation of the mind care should be taken, not to neglect or injure the body upon which the vigor of the mind greatly depends. Youth are seldom wise, but by experience, and unhappily few are so attentive in the first portion of Life as to remark with accuracy the causes of indisposition occasiond by excesses, either of food animal or Mental. A great Student ought to be particularly carefull in the regulation of his diet, and avoid that bane of Health late suppers.

I would advise you upon the approach of Spring to lose some Blood, the Headacks and flushing in your face with which you used to be troubled was occasiond by too great a Quantity of Blood in your Head. I know you will smile at these precautions, but if you do not heed them; repentance may come too late. Your Brothers Charles and Tommy will I hope be equally attentive, particularly the latter of Night damps and dews. Your sister I have had with me for these ten days suffering under a severe cold taken at Bath. I have not known her so sick since we left America. She is however getting better. With the *Beau mond*, we have made a Tour to Bath for a fortnight. We made up a party of ten or a Dozen Americans, Mr and Mrs Rucker and Miss Ramsey whom you know, were a part of the company. Your Pappa insisted upon my going, tho he could not, as the printers would have waited for him, not then having compleated his Book, I returnd to London quite surfeited with Balls concerts &c.

The seditions in Massachusetts induced your Pappa to give to the World a Book which at first he designed only for a few Friends. He thought it was a critical moment and that it might prove usefull to his Countryman and tend to convince them that salutary restraint is the vital principal of Liberty, and that those who from a turbulent restless disposition endeavour to throw of every species of coercion, are the real Enemies of freedom, and forge chains for themselves and posterity.

I send you by Captain Cushing half a dozen shirts. I shall have another half dozen ready for you by Barnard. Let me know if they fit.

To day we have a Clerical party to dine with us, amongst whom are the two American Bishops[1] dr Price dr Kippis dr disney[2] Dr Rees and several other Clergymen. Adieu my dear son, and accept my best wishes this and every succeeding year of your Life, for Health of body and peace of mind, "for peace o virtue!, peace is all thy own."[3] Affectionatly yours, AA

Inclosed is a little poetick peice written at the Hyde[4] and the particular description I gave You of the owner and the place, will explain the peice to you.

Accept the little coin inclosed if this and an other which I sent some time ago comes safe to your Hand, make a mark in your next letter thus .

RC (Adams Papers); endorsed: "Mrs: Adams. Jany: 17. 1787."; docketed at a later time: "My Mother. 17. Jany: 1787."

[1] Rev. William White of Philadelphia and Rev. Samuel Provoost of New York, both of whom were in London to be consecrated as bishops of the American Episcopal church on 4 Feb. (Clara O. Loveland, *The Critical Years: The Reconstitution of the Anglican Church in the United States of America: 1780–1789*, Greenwich, Conn., 1956, p. 213–217).

[2] Rev. John Disney (1746–1816) was a Unitarian minister, secretary of the Society for Promoting the Knowledge of the Scriptures, and eventual heir to Thomas Brand Hollis (*DNB*).

[3] Alexander Pope, *An Essay on Man*, Epistle IV, line 82.

[4] Neither the poem nor the coin mentioned in the next paragraph has been found. AA and JA visited Thomas Brand Hollis' home, The Hyde, in July 1786, and the coin may have been one that Hollis sent to AA on 4 Nov., above.

Thomas Welsh to Abigail Adams

Dear Madam Boston Jany 17th 1787

Being without any of your Favors unanswered I take the Liberty to write this in Advance.

The State of some Counties having been tumultuous to this Time notwithstanding the lenient Measures of Government has induced the supreme Executive to order a Military Force into the County of Worcester under Genl Lincoln;[1] I should blush for my Country was I not sensible that it is not uncommon under more established Governments than ours to have Ebullitions; but it is more natural to expect in proportion to the Degrees of Liberty in the Governments. I have not the least Doubt but the Force intended and which is indespensable will prove sufficient for the purpose. I have this Morning seen a Gentleman from Rutland who says that their prime Leader Shays was to hold a Counsell of his Leader at Barre yesterday to determine whether they should still persist in their Oposition to Government? This Deliberation is produced by the Dread of *Lincoln's* march to Worcester which will commence on Friday the 19th. The Court will sit on the 23d. I wish success to the Enterprize.

Another Match in the Family, Mr William Smith is paying his Addresses to Miss Hannah Carter of Newbuyry Port, a Young Lady of about 21 Years of age, tall light Complextioned, of amiable temper very sensible, of good Education eloquent and sociable to a most engaging Degree a Compleat Œconomist not Wastefull; but appears so upon Acquaintance; I believe she is known to Mrs Smith as She has tarried repeatedly in our Family, where Mr Smith had the good Fortune to see her often. Mr Carter will furnish her with one thousand Pounds to procure Furniture &c. This Match is highly pleasing to both Familys in short She is the most suitable Person for Mr Smith and he appears to be already transformed to a Lover and will be still improve mouldered by the hand of his intended Companion. The Marriage will probably take Place in June every Preparation being now making for that Purpose.

To Mr Adams Mr and Mrs Smith and to yourself may our Compts and Respects be acceptable and permit me to subscribe your obedt St Thomas Welsh

RC (Adams Papers); endorsed: "Janry 17. dr welch."

[1] On 4 Jan., Gov. James Bowdoin proposed the creation of a special army of 4,400 troops to be led by Benjamin Lincoln to put down the rebellion. Since Bowdoin acted

without legislative approval, funds for the troops had to be raised privately, largely from Boston merchants. On 19 Jan., the soldiers left Boston for Worcester (David P. Szatmary, *Shays' Rebellion: The Making of an Agrarian Insurrection*, Amherst, Mass., 1980, p. 84–90).

Abigail Adams to Mary Smith Cranch

Mr dear sister London Janry 20th 1787

Since the Sailing of captain Folger by whom I wrote you, I have received Letters from you of the following dates, Sepbr 24 and 28th 8th 9 and 22 of october and November 18th.[1] I cannot sufficiently thank you for the entertainment afforded me in them. Some accounts you give me respecting a certain family Shocked me. I should suppose that the peace and happiness of the family was totally destroy'd in a Country like ours, where conjugal infidelity is held in the utmost abhorrence, and brands with eternal infamy the wretch who destroys it. Had the Parties lived in France or Viena where the perplexing word reputation has quite an other meaning than what we have been accustomed to, the Husband might have lookd upon the Gallant as Men do upon their deputies, who take the troublesome part of the buisness off their Hands. But in a Country where the absolution of the Priest is not considerd a compensation for crimes, and Marriage is esteemed holy and honorable, the seducer should be considerd as the worst of assassins. But in this case it may be difficult to determine which was the Seducer, and I feel more inclined to fix it upon the female than the paramour. At any rate she is more Guilty, in proportion as her obligations to her Husband her children her family and the Religion of which she is a professer are all scandilized by her and she has sacrificed her Honour her tranquility and her virtue. Well might Mrs Guile say that she had not ink black enough to describe the vile story, and my Gentle Friend Mrs Rogers writes me, "I think my young Friend will ever have reason to bless the period when prior prospects terminated as they did."[2] The Letter you mention is proof that the *confident was the Author* of the distresses complaind of. But I quit a subject so painfull to reflect upon to give you some account of my late Tour to Bath, that Seat of fashionable Resort, where like the rest of the World I spent a fortnight in Amusement and dissipation, but returnd I assure you, with double pleasure to my own fire side, where only thank heaven, my substantial happiness subsists. Here I find these satisfaction which neither Satiate by enjoyment nor pall upon reflection, for tho I like Some times to mix in the Gay

World, and view the manners as they rise, I have much reason to be gratefull to my Parents that my early Education gave me not an habitual taste for what is termd fashionable Life. The Eastern Monarch after having partaken of every gratification and Sensual pleasure which power Wealth and dignity could bestow, pronounced it all Vanity and vexation of spirit,[3] and I have too great a respect for his wisdom to doubt his Authority. I however past through the Routine, and attended 3 Balls 2 concerts, one Play and two private parties besides dinning and Breakfasting abroad. We made up a Party of Americans, Mr and Mrs Smith mr and Mrs Rucker and Miss Ramsey, mr Shippen mr Harrison mr Murry mr Paridice mr Bridgen and a Count Zenobia a venition Nobleman.[4] These with our domesticks made a considerable train, and when we went to the Rooms we at least had a party to speak to. As I had but one acquaintance at Bath, and did not seek for Letters of introduction. I had no reason to expect half the civility I experienced. I was however very politely treated by mr Fairfax and Lady who had been in America and own an estate in Virginia, and by a sister of mr Hartleys, who tho herself a criple, was every way attentive and polite to us. Mr John Boylstone whom I dare say you recollect, was the acquaintance I mentiond. He visited us immediatly upon our arrival, and during our stay made it his whole study to shew us every civility in his power. We Breakfasted with him, and he dinned with us. He has very handsome apartments tho he lives at Lodgings. We drank tea and spent an Evening with him in a stile of great elegance, for he is one of the nicest Batchelors in the World, and bears his age wonderfully retaining the vivacity and sprightliness of Youth. He has a peculiarity in his Manners which is natural to him but is a Man of great reading and knowledge. He is a firm friend and well wisher to America, as he amply testified during the War by his kindness to the American Prisoners. And now you will naturally expect that I Should give you some account of Bath, the antiquity of it, and the fame of its waters having been So greatly celebrated. The story which is related of its first discovery is not the least curious part of it. A Certain King Bladud said to be a descendent from Hercules, was banishd his Fathers court on account of his having the Leporissa. Thus disgraced he wanderd in disguise into this part of the Country, and let himself to a swineherd, to whom he communicated the Disease as well as to the Hogs. In driving his Hogs one day at some distance from his home, they wanderd away to these Streams, of which they were so fond that he could not get them out: untill he inticed them with

Acorns. After their wallowing in them for several Successive days he observed that their Scales fell of, and that his herd were perfectly cured, upon which he determined to try the experiment upon himself, and after a few Bathings he was made whole. And Bladuds figure in stone is placed in the Baths known by the Name of the kings Bath with an incription relating his discovery of these Baths 863 years before Christ.[5]

Bath lies in a great vally surrounded with Hills. It is handsomely built, chiefly with free Stone, which is its own growth and is dug from the Sides of its Hills. The streets are as narrow and inconvenient for Carriages as those of Paris, so that Chairs are chiefly used particularly in the old Town. Bath was formerly walld in and was a very small place, but of late years it is much extended, and the New buildings are erected upon Hills. Since it has become a place of such fashionable resort it has been embellished with a circus and a Cressent. The parades are magnificient piles of buildings. The square is a noble one and the Circus is said to be a beautifull peice of architecture, but what I think the beauty of Bath; is the Cressent.[6] The front consists of a range of Ionic Colums on a rustick basement. The Ground falls gradually before it, down to the River Avon about half a miles distance, and the rising Country on the other side of the River holds up to it a most delightfull prospect. The Cressent takes its name from the form in which the houses Stand; all of which join. There is a parade and street before them a hundred foot wide and nothing in front to obstruct this Beautifull prospect. In this situation are the New assembly Rooms which are said to exceed any thing of the kind in the Kingdom both as to size, and decoration, but large as they were they were compleatly crouded the Evenings that I attended. There is a constant emulation subsisting between the New and old Rooms,[7] similar to the North and South end of Boston. It was said whilst I was there that there were fourteen thousand persons more than the inhabitants of Bath. By this you may judge what a place of resort it is, not only for the infirm, but for the Gay the indolent the curious the Gambler the fortune hunter and even for those who go as the thoughtless Girl from the Country told Beau Nash (as he was stiled,)[8] that She came *out of wantoness*. It is one constant scene of dissipation and Gambling from Monday morning till saturday Night, and the Ladies set down to cards in the publick rooms at they would at a private party. And not to spend a fortnight or Month at Bath at this season, of the year, is as unfashionable as it would be to reside in London during the summer Season. Yet Bath is a place I should never visit a second time for pleasure. To derive a proper improvement from company it ought to be select, and to consist of persons respectable both for their Morals, and their understandings. But such is the prevailing taste, that provided you can be in a crowd, with here and there a Glittering Star, it is considerd of little importance what the Character of the person is, who wears it. Few consider that the foundation stone and the pillar on which they Nest the fabrick of their felicity must be in their own Hearts, otherways the winds of dissipation will shake it and the floods of pleasure overwhelm it in ruins. What is the Chief end of Man? is a Subject well Worth the investigation of every rational Being. What indeed is Life or its enjoyments without settled principal, laudable purposes, Mental exertions and internal comfort, that sun shine of the soul, and how are these to be acquired in the hurry and tumult of the World; my visit to Bath and the scenes which I mixed in, instead of exciting a gayety of disposition, led me to a train of moral reflections which I could not refrain detailing to you in my account of it.

Upon my return I had a new scene of folly to go through which was prepairing for the Birth day, but as the fashionable Magizine will detail this matter I shall omit any account of Birth day dresses and decorations only that I most sincerely wish myself rid of it. It is a prodigious expence from which I derive neither pleasure or satisfaction. Mrs Smith did not go this year, for reasons you can Guess I suppose. We have advised col Smith to give up his House and return here again, as it will be vastly inconvenient to me to have her out of the family, no sister no cousin no Aunt who could be at all with her. So that in March they will remove here again, and in April tis probable your Sister may be a Grandmama.[9] New Relatives create new anxieties.

And now for a few domestick Matters. You will find that before I received your Letters I was uneasy and had written to you and Dr Tufts both upon the subject of Board; there can be no reason that you should be at any expence on their account and it would give me pain to know you were. It will be cruel indeed if our Country will not allow us enough to educate our children in the frugal manner we wish for, when for 12 years mr Adams has devoted himself and all his talants to their service, and if they have not reaped all the benifit they might from him, it is there own fault. He has not been laying up a fortune nor has he been squandering one away—nor is there an other Minister either in France England or Holland whose allow-

10. THE ROYAL CRESCENT, BATH, BY THOMAS MALTON JR., 1777

See page xvi

ence is not splendid to his. But I will not reflect upon our Situation. I will only say that my children Shall not whilst we remain here, live upon my friends or be chargeable to them. Whilst he resided in Holland and his allowence was better he was able to save a little but the publick have no right to expect that she [*he*] should expend that, any more then that he should run out the little estate he has in America.

I hope captain Folger arrived safe as well as my Trunk. I have sent you by captain Cushing a Hamper of 4 doz porter a double gloucester cheese for commencment, and a cask of Split peas. Be so kind as to Send Sister Shaw half a dozen quarts. I got mr Elworthy to procure them for me, and I dare say he has done his best. If the porter is agreeable it May save you some wine and make a variety. It mortifies me that I cannot do all I wish but take the will for the deed.

The Roits and dissentions in our state have been matter of very serious concern to me. No one will suppose that our situation here is renderd more Eligible in concequence of it, but I hope it will lead the wise and sensible part of the community in our state as well as the whole union to reflect seriously upon their Situation, and having wise Laws execute them with vigor justice and punctuality. I have been gratified with perusing many late publications in our Boston papers, particularly the Speach of the Chief justice which does him great honour.[10] Mr Adams you will see by the Books which captain cushing has carried out, has been employed in strengthning and supporting our Governments, and has spaired no pains to collect examples for them and shew them in one short comprehensive statement the dangerous concequences of unbalanced power.[11] We have the means of being the freest and the happiest people upon the Globe.

Captain Scot I hear is just arrived, but it may be a week, perhaps ten days before he will get up himself, so that whatever Letters he may have I shall not be able to get them before captain Cushing Sails. This is rather unfortunate as there may be something I might wish to replie to. As to India handkerchief I give 2 Guineys a peice here for them so that they are lower with you as well as all other India goods. I give more for an oz of spice than I used to for a quarter of a pound in America. Only think too of 5 shillings Sterling for every pound of coffe we use. O pray by the next oppertunity Send me a peck of Tuscorora Rice. Let it be sifted, I want it only to Scour my hands with. Tuscorora rice say you, why I suppose She means Indian meal. Very true my dear sister, but I will tell you a good story about this said rice. An Ancestor of a family who now hold their Heads very high is said to have made a fortune by it. The old grand dame went out to America when its productions were not much known here and returnd rather in Indigent circumstances.[12] After some time knowing the taste in all ages for cosmeticks, made out a pompus advertizement of a costly secreet which she possesst for purifying and beautifying the complexion, nothing less than Tuscorora Rice at a Guiney an oz. The project took like the olympian dew at this Day, and Barrel after Barrel was disposd of at the moderate price before mentiond, till one fatal day, a sailor whose wife had procured one Quarter of an oz was caught in the very act of useing it. The sailor very roughly threw away this darling powder upon which his wife exclamed that he had ruined her, as She could procure no more there being an unusual Scarcity at that time. The fellow examined the paper and swore it was nothing but Indian meal and that he would bring her two Barrels for a Guiney the next voyage he went. Upon this the imposture was discoverd and the good woman obliged to decamp. Now tho I do not esteem it so highly as the sailors wife I pronounce it the best antidote to sea coal cracks that can be found. One Friend and an other has supplied me ever since I have been here, but now I am quite destitute. It is an article in so small quantity that will not be an object for the custom house, so that it may come safely. Remember me most affectionately to all my Friends. I cannot write to half of them. My Neices shall hear from me by Bairnard—in the mean time be assured my dear Sister of the warmest affection of your Sister A Adams

RC (MWA:Abigail Adams Corr.).

[1] Probably a mistake for Cranch's letter on 26 Nov. 1786, above; all of the other letters are also above.

[2] Neither the letter from Abigail Bromfield Rogers to AA nor the source of Elizabeth Quincy Guild's comment has been found.

[3] The preacher in Ecclesiastes, traditionally identified as Solomon. See especially 1:14, 2:11.

[4] Alvise Zenobio was a Venetian nobleman living in England. In 1792 he published two English-language tracts, *The French Constitution Impartially Considered in Its Principles and Effects* and *An Address to the People of England, on the Part Their Government Ought to Act, in the Present War*, addressing constitutional issues raised by the French Revolution, and in 1794 he was deported from England for his radical associations (John Eglin, *Venice Transfigured: The Myth of Venice in British Culture, 1660–1797*, N.Y., 2001, p. 186–187, 233).

[5] AA's recounting of the history of the founding of Bath is similar to versions found in various editions of *The New Bath Guide; or, Useful Pocket Companion for All Persons Residing at or Resorting to This Ancient City*, a popular guidebook to the city that first appeared ca. 1762.

[6] The building of Queen Square, designed by John Wood Sr. and named for George II's Queen Caroline, began in 1729 and continued for seven years. Wood sought to create a palace front on the north side of the square, facing a garden, with symmetrical wings to the east and west. Builders had discretion to

design the interiors however they chose but had to conform to Wood's specifications for the outside, creating a unified appearance. The Circus façade was also designed by Wood Sr. but built by his son John Wood Jr. in 1754. While modeled after the Roman Coliseum, the Circus actually reverses the amphitheater design by facing inward although it retains a Roman decorative style (David Gadd, *Georgian Summer: Bath in the Eighteenth Century*, Bath, 1971, p. 39–42, 46–50). For the Royal Crescent, designed by Wood Jr., see the Descriptive List of Illustrations, No. 10, above.

[7] The Old Assembly House—also known as Harrison's Rooms, for their builder Thomas Harrison, and then later as Simpson's Rooms or the Lower Rooms—were the original social center of Bath, hosting balls and concerts, as well as offering a card room and tearoom. The New (or Upper) Rooms, built between 1769 and 1771, were designed by John Wood Jr. to accommodate the growing Bath population. The New Rooms first competed with, then slowly supplanted, the Lower Rooms, until the latter finally closed following a fire in 1820 (same, p. 28–29, 105–106).

[8] Richard "Beau" Nash (1674–1761) arrived in Bath in 1705, attracted by the gambling, but soon became active in developing the city into a true resort town. He served as master of ceremonies at Bath for 55 years. He brought order to the social life of the rapidly growing spa, instituting codes of conduct for dancing, bathing, gambling, and other social activities, and oversaw the building of some of Bath's most famous attractions, including the Pump Room (*DNB*; Gadd, *Georgian Summer*, p. 24–29).

[9] This is AA's first reference to AA2's pregnancy. After the birth of their son William Steuben Smith on 2 April, AA2 and WSS moved from Wimpole Street, where they had lived since July 1786, to Grosvenor Square, where they remained until their departure for America in 1788.

[10] The Boston *Independent Chronicle*, 16 Nov., reprinted in full the charge of the chief justice, William Cushing, to the grand jury of Middlesex County at the opening of the Supreme Judicial Court at Cambridge on 31 October. In the speech, Cushing strongly denounced the rebels and argued for the importance of the rule of law.

[11] The entirety of JA's *Defence of the Const.* deals with this topic, but AA may be referring to JA's summary in the final letter of the first volume, which concludes with the statement, "All nations, under all governments, must have parties; the great secret is to controul them: there are but two ways, either by a monarchy and standing army, or by a balance in the constitution. Where the people have a voice, and there is no balance, there will be everlasting fluctuations, revolutions, and horrors, until a standing army, with a general at its head, commands the peace, or the necessity of an equilibrium is made appear to all, and is adopted by all" (Letter LV, p. 382).

[12] Possibly Sybilla Masters, wife of Thomas Masters, a Pennsylvania merchant and former mayor of Philadelphia, who went to England in 1712 to obtain a patent for a process for milling "Tuscarora rice," a type of cornmeal, claiming it as a cure for consumption. She received the patent in 1715, the first issued to any American, although it was made in the name of her husband. The couple subsequently set up a water mill near Philadelphia to produce the ground corn in quantity, although it is not clear whether they ever successfully sold the product. Upon Thomas' death in 1740, his estate went largely to his brother William Masters, whose daughters Mary Masters Penn and Sarah Masters spent time with the Adamses in London (Samuel H. Needles, "The Governor's Mill, and the Globe Mills, Philadelphia," *PMHB*, 8:285–293 [1884]; AA2 to JQA, 22 Jan. 1786, notes 3 and 4, above).

Abigail Adams to Elizabeth Smith Shaw

My Dear sister London Janry 20 1787

You will see by the inclosed that I wrote you a long Letter, and that it has lain some time without meeting any opportunity of conveyance.[1] In the mean time, two kind Letters have reachd me from you. In the last you complain that I did not write you, but sure captain Callihan had a Letter for you.

I had heard for some time that Cushing would not sail till March, and I have been absent at Bath near 3 weeks, but upon my return I found he was to go by the 20th of Janry. I have many Letters to write and the Birth day of her Majesty to prepare for, alass I shall be behind hand. Mrs Smith very unwell too, a voilent cold taken at Bath attended with a good deal of fever. She is however better, and I will hasten to scrible you off a few lines. I send the Books which my Nephew requested, and beg his acceptance of them as a New Years gift from his Aunt. There has been as you will see a valuable addition of two more volms to them, and I think them well calculated to pour the fresh instruction over the mind, and to instill the best of principals. Mr Adams has directed one of his Books, the defence of the American constitutions, to be deliverd to mr Shaw, and I hope it will prove equally Serviceable to Children of a larger growth, who seem so much disposed to quarrel with their best Friends, the Laws and Government. I should like to know how the sentiments and doctrines are received. I have been much mortified and grieved I assure you to find mr Sparhawks accounts so well founded, tho at the time he gave them, I was disposed to think much better of my Countrymen. May the triumph of the wicked be short, and the fair fabrick of Liberty still be protected by Minerva, whilst Discord and faction those vile deamons are banishd to their Native Regions of Darkness.

I have Sent to my Neice some Silk which I have had died and scowerd. You may pick a shirt perhaps from it. As to any kind of milinary which your sister has worn, the Sea coal smoke and the hair Powder so totally distroys it, that even my maid cannot wear it till it is washd. With regard to any other articles of dress, you would not find your sister better drest here, than she used to be by her Braintree fireside. A calico or a chintz a muslin or a double Gauze handkerchief and Apron is her usual dress. Tis True her Hair suffers more torture than in America and the powder covers the venerable Gray. Tis time to think of being venerable when tis probable a few Months will make her a *Grandmamma* and she has now got to look out a Nurse and make Baby linnen &c &c. A thousand New cares and anxieties as well as pleasures attend new Relatives.

I was really shocked at the Death of mr Anger as I had never heard of his Sickness. Alass our Worthy Friend mr Perkins, he is gone too, to the Land from whence their is no return. But he was a virtuous well principald Man, and possessd that great ornament of society, Honesty, without which all the Graces and Embelishments of Life are but varnish and unsubstantial qualities which the artfull assume for purposes of deceit.

Adieu my dear sister. I dine abroad and must therefore quit my pen to dress. I shall write You again by captain Barnard who will sail in a few weeks. I have no time to coppy. You must therefore excuse every inaccuricy. My Regards to mr shaw to mr and Mrs Allen to my Nephew and Neice, and to every one who inquires after Your affectionate Sister A Adams

RC (DLC:Shaw Family Papers).

[1] Apparently AA enclosed her last letter to Shaw on 21 Nov. 1786, above, in this letter.

Abigail Adams to Cotton Tufts

Dear sir London Janry 24th 1787

I designd to have written you a much Longer Letter than I shall now be able to. The State of politicks in our Country is such as to give pain to every Friend and well wisher of it. I hope the pamphlet mr Adams has lately written and which captain Cushing carries out, will have a benificial influence if it comes not too Late. I inclose to you a ministerial publication which has past through four Editions in about ten days.[1] What he says with respect to the Kings popularity in the English Nation is at this present time stricktly true. His Characters are drawn with freedom, his intention is however to wash Some Etheops White.

This day col Franks arrived here with the Emperor of Morocos Treaty and will sail in the next packet for New York with it.[2]

Mr Adams has directed me to request you upon the receit of this Letter to purchase two hundred Guineys worth of congress Paper. We are told that it is sold at 2 and 6 pence pr pound. Do not be affraid, as the little he has is in publick Securities, it is as safe in one kind as an other, and if one sinks all must Sink, which God forbid. We are told here that the Name of the person must be enterd upon the Treasury Books, or the Name of a Friend, but you doubtless know the method. Our credit is not yet so low, but what Foreigners are eagerly tho Secretly buying up this paper. You will draw upon mr Adams for the Money—it will never be at a lower ebb than at present unless actual war takes place. You will find an account forwarded in mr Adams letter.[3] Scot is arrived but none of our Letters are yet come up. Inclosed is a letter from mrs Smith. It was only two small red coverd Manuscrip Books which the Gentleman had and not pocket Books. Will that House be to be sold do you imagine which he owns?[4]

Regards to all inquiring Friends from Dear Sir your ever affectionate Neice

A Adams

RC (Adams Papers); addressed by WSS: "The Honorable Cotton Tufts Esquire Boston"; endorsed: "Mrs. Ab. Adams rcd April 19. 1787."

[1] Sir Nathaniel William Wraxall, *A Short Review of the Political State of Great-Britain, at the Commencement of the Year One Thousand Seven Hundred and Eighty-seven*, London, 1787. Wraxall (1751–1831), a member of Parliament, published the pamphlet anonymously. In the first few weeks of publication, it went through six editions and sold roughly 17,000 copies in England (*DNB*).

[2] The Treaty of Peace and Friendship negotiated by Thomas Barclay for the United States and signed by the emperor of Morocco in June and July 1786. The English translations were signed and sealed by Jefferson in Paris on 1 Jan. 1787 and by JA in London on 25 Jan. (Miller, *Treaties*, 2:185–227).

[3] Probably JA to Cotton Tufts, 15 Jan. (Adams Papers), but the account has not been found.

[4] For an extended discussion of the Vassall-Borland House (Adams Old House) and Royall Tyler's aborted purchase of it, see vol. 3:264–266.

Abigail Adams to Thomas Jefferson

My dear sir

London Janry 29th 1787

I received by Col Franks Your obliging favour[1] and am very sorry to find your wrist Still continues lame. I have known very Salutary effects produced by the use of British oil upon a spraind joint. I have Sent a Servant to See if I can procure some. You may rest assured that if it does no good: it will not do any injury.

With regard to the Tumults in my Native state which you inquire about, I wish I could say that report had exagerated them. It is too true Sir that they have been carried to so allarming a Height as to stop the Courts of Justice in several Counties. Ignorant, wrestless desperadoes, without conscience or principals, have led a deluded multitude to follow their standard, under pretence of grievences which have no existance but in their immaginations. Some of them were crying out for a paper currency, some for an equal distribution of property, some were for annihilating all debts, others complaning that the Senate was a useless Branch of Government, that the Court of common Pleas was unnecessary, and that the Sitting of the General Court in Boston was a grieveince. By this list you will see, the materials which compose this Rebellion, and the necessity there is of the wisest and most vigorous measures to quell and suppress it.

Instead of that laudible Spirit which you approve, which makes a people watchfull over their Liberties and alert in the defence of them, these Mobish insurgents are for sapping the foundation, and distroying the whole fabrick at once. But as these people make only a small part of the State, when compared to the more Sensible and judicious, and altho they create a just allarm, and give much trouble and uneasiness, I cannot help flattering myself that they will prove Sallutary to the state at large, by leading to an investigation of the causes which have produced these commotions. Luxery and extravagance both in furniture and dress had pervaded all orders of our Countrymen and women, and was hastning fast to Sap their independance by involving every class of citizens in distress, and accumulating debts upon them which they were unable to discharge. Vanity was becoming a more powerfull principal than Patriotism. The lower order of the community were prest for taxes, and tho possest of landed property they were unable to answer the Demand. Whilst those who possesst Money were fearfull of lending, least the mad cry of the Mob[2] should force the Legislature upon a measure very different from the touch of Midas.

By the papers I send you, you will see the benificial effects already produced, an act of the Legislature laying duties of 15 pr cent upon many articles of British manufacture and totally prohibiting others.[3] A Number of Vollunteers Lawyers Physicians and Merchants from Boston made up a party of Light horse commanded by col Hitchbourn Leit col Jackson and Higgonson, and went out in persuit of the insurgents and were fortunate enough to take 3 of their Principal Leaders, Shattucks Parker and Page. Shattucks defended himself and was wounded in his knee with a broadsword. He is in Jail in Boston and will no doubt be made an example of.[4]

Your request my dear sir with respect to your daughter shall be punctually attended to, and you may be assured of every attention in my power towards her.

You will be so kind as to present my Love to Miss Jefferson, compliments to the Marquiss and his Lady. I am really conscience Smitten that I have never written to that amiable Lady, whose politeness and attention to me deserved my acknowledgment.

The little balance which you Stated in a former Letter in my favour,[5] when an opportunity offers I should like to have in Black Lace at about 8 or 9 Livres pr Ell. Tho late in the Month, I hope it will not be thought out of season to offer my best wishes for the Health Long Life and prosperity of yourself and family, or to assure you of the Sincere Esteem and Friendship with which I am Yours &c &c

A Adams

RC (DLC:Jefferson Papers); addressed by Col. David S. Frank. "His Excellency Thomas Jefferson Paris"; endorsed: "Mrs. Adams." Dft (Adams Papers).

[1] Probably Jefferson to AA, 21 Dec. 1786, above. Jefferson also wrote to AA on 7 Jan., but that letter has not been found (Jefferson, *Papers*, 11:24).

[2] The Dft has "the cry of the people" in place of "the mad cry of the Mob."

[3] In the Dft, the paragraph begins, "The disturbances which have taken place have roused from their Leathargy the Supine and the Indolent animated the Brave and taught wisdom to our Rulers."

On 17 Nov. 1786, the Massachusetts legislature passed "An Act to Raise a Public Revenue by Impost," which placed impost taxes ranging from 1 to 15 percent on various goods and prohibited outright the importation of others (Mass., *Acts and Laws*, Acts of 1786, Sept. sess., ch. 48). The paper was probably the Boston *Independent Chronicle*, 30 Nov., which reported this information.

[4] The Dft arranges the first three sentences found in the RC paragraph somewhat differently and identifies Lt. Col. (Jonathan) Jackson as a man Jefferson had met in France and Lt. Col. (Stephen) Higginson as a former member of Congress before closing with the sentence: "It is not unlikly that some examples must be made before the riots will be totally quelled and peace and good orderd restored."

[5] Probably Jefferson to AA, 9 Aug. 1786, above, showing a balance of £6.11.11 1/2 due to AA.

Cotton Tufts to Abigail Adams

Boston Feby 6th. 1787

Col. Jacob Davis not long since called upon me for the Payment of one of the Lots of Land in Vermont State which you recd. a Deed of and was not paid for, by his Brother Ebenr Davis whom he empowered for that Purpose. I accordingly paid it, he requested Interest from the Time the Deed was given, I did not conceive myself authorized to allow it as You did not give me any directions relative to it. He said it was customary and supposed You would allow it if present. As he desired me to mention it to You I wish You to write to me in your Next on the Subject. I also paid him £6. 8. 0 for Taxes on the Four Rights. The Tenure on which you hold these Rights, does not appear to me sufficiently secure. Mr. Davis could not give me any particular Information relative to them. I believe I must take Mastr. Charles or Thos in some Vacation and make a Tour there and see to the Safe recording &c of them. A very good Plan, but when shall I get Leisure.[1]

The Legislature have at length found it necessary to declare Rebellion existing in the Commonwealth. An Army under Genl Lincoln is employed to crush it.[2] A few Days will in great Measure determine whether We shall have the Constitution remain or not.

Whether we shall have Law and Justice administerd or not. A strange Infatuation has seized a great part of the People, Should I say two Thirds of the whole Body. It would not be far from the Truth. I flatter myself notwithstanding that their Eyes will be opened very soon and their Minds Yield to Conviction. ⟨*this Evil I have As*⟩ Sufficient Addresses have made to their Interests these have been in Vain. An Address to their Fears, is now tried, and I trust will be the only succesful Advocate.

Feby. 7th.

The Insurgents under Shays and the other ⟨*officers*⟩ Heads of the Army have not been much short of 3000. They have however crumbled away from Day to Day, since Genl Lincolns appearance in the Western Counties. After their Dispersion at Petersham (of which you have an Account in the News Papers new sent[3] and which News came to hand (this Moment)) their Number appeared to be about 940, and they were shaping their Course to the County of Berkshire. The March of Genl Lincoln last Saturday Evening from Hadley and reaching Petersham the next Morning by 9 oc was perhaps as great an Enterprize as as ever been undertaken. A Snow Storm when they set out, followed about One or Two Clock the same Night with a Shift of Wind and excessive cold the Wind blowing like a Hurricane, till they reachd Petersham, suffering more with the blowing of the Snow and the severe cold, than can possibly be conceived off but by those who have been in similar Circumstances; no proper Place to halt for Refreshment. Yet they persevered with out murmuring, till they reached Petersham, a March of 30 Miles. Many were frost bitten.

Feby 8.

Shays with about 100 Men is said to be at Chesterfield in Newhampshire State—the riot dispersed. Gen. Lincoln is gone into the County of Berkshire, with his Army. The Insurgents there will probably submit, without much Difficulty. We have ordered two or three Regiments to be kept up for 3 or 4 months. And I hope we shall by and by get into a more orderly State. Should this Insurrection or rather Rebellion have prevailed here, it would undoubtedly have run through all the States. As the Papers will give You a particular Acctt. of the doings of the Genl Court and of Genl Lincolns' Movements, I refer you to them for further Information.

9th.

Mr. John dind with me yesterday,[4] he is solicitous of knowing with whom he is to purrsue his Studies in the Law after Commencement. If Mr. Adams has any particular Instructor in view, that he would prefer before any other and will give timely Notice, We shall pursue his orders, otherwise we shall act according to our best Discretion. At present We think that at least Part of the Three Years Study, may be under some Gentleman in the Country (or rather out of Boston): the Expence Less, and Advantages equal. I have consulted with several Gentleman and shall make every Enquiry that I think necessary to form a Result beneficial to your Son and to your Interest.

The aforegoing has been wrote by Piece Meals, as I could catch an opportunity, and you must excuse the Errors of Your affectionate Friend and H sert C Tufts

Pray remember me to Mr Adams Mr and Mrs Smith.
Your Children here and all Friends well.

RC (Adams Papers). Tufts also produced "Minutes of a Letter wrote to Mrs. Adams" in which he summarized the details of this letter and added the note, "Sent this Lettr. by Capt Folger"; filmed at 8 Feb. 1787, Adams Papers, Microfilms, Reel No. 369.

[1] In early 1782, AA arranged to purchase five 330-acre lots in Salem Township (now Derby and Newport, Orleans County), Vt., from Col. Jacob Davis of Worcester, who headed a group settling the area. She paid for four of the lots then, and obligated herself to pay for the fifth "in a few months," holding off on making full payment until the title to the land could be made more secure (vol. 4:315, 316–317, 345; AA to Tufts, 29 April, Adams Papers).

[2] On 4 Feb., the same day that it formally acknowledged the existence of a rebellion in western Massachusetts, the General Court belatedly recommended to Gov. James Bowdoin that he authorize Gen. Benjamin Lincoln to either enlist new members or extend the enlistments of current members of the Massachusetts militia, so that it could continue its work of suppressing the rebellion (Mass., *Acts and Laws*, Resolves of 1786, Jan. sess., ch. 5, 6).

[3] Probably the *Massachusetts Centinel*, 7 Feb., which printed a 4 Feb. letter from General Lincoln at Petersham that had arrived in Boston on 6 February. The letter describes Lincoln's progress in dispersing the insurgents, who had begun to retreat after Lincoln took nearly 150 of them as prisoners.

[4] JQA dined with Tufts and Richard Cranch at James Foster's (*Diary*, 2:157, where he is misidentified as Joseph Foster).

Elizabeth Smith Shaw to Abigail Adams

My Ever Dear Sister Haverhill February 8th. 1787

My Uncle Smith has been so kind as to send me word this Morning, that a Nephew of Mr Gill's was to sail for London, in a Vessel from Boston next Saturday. Though I fear I shall not get a Letter into Town soon enough, yet I will write, a few Lines (though I have nothing very particular to communicate,) hoping I may meet with some favourable Conveyance.

The State of our publick Affairs engrosses attention of all Ranks, and Classes of Men. In every private Circle of Gentlemen, and Ladies I hear their several Opinions, dictated by Fear, Ignorance, Malice, Envy, and self-Interest the most powerful of all.

We all feel a Weight, which we could not but reasonably expect, and which the wise and Judicious say, may soon be lightened by Prudence, Industry, and good Oeconemy in our Families. But such is the Pride—the Idleness—the vanity, and extravagance which pervades every Order, that I am perswaded nothing but distress, and necessity will induce them to comply with this method, though I presume it is the only one, by which there is the least probability of obtaining Releif.

No One is willing to believe *themselves* the *Cause* of any Evil they feel, but attribute it, to the weakness, or the perfidy of Government—to the great Sallaries given to those in Office, or to the injustice of those *vile Wretches* the *Lawyers*.

Our excellent Govenor need not be envied, I am sure. He has enough upon his head, and his Heart to distract him. He will now try the Strength of Government, and I hope it will be found to have such a Basis, as the Collected Force of *Capt Shays* cannot overthrow.

Though I am situated far distant (at present) from the Seat of War, Yet I tenderly feel for those who are enduring the hardships of a winters Campaign, in this very cold Season. The ground has bean cheifly covered with three, or four foot of Snow ever since the beginning of November—So that it has rendered General Lincoln's March extremely difficult—and we hear that 5 hundred of his Men were touched with the frost.

Yesterday Orders came here for more men to be draughted—to day there are counter Orders.[1] The news is, Shays is fled, and that a general Pardon is all they sue for. *He* is gone to the State of new Hampshire.

But I will quit Politicks, and leave them to the Gentlemen, who I presume, give you a much more particular account.

I *fancy* sometimes to myself how *these matters*, will operate upon the Mind of *your Friend*. We think sometimes, he may do us more service *here*, than he can in his present Situation. We want his Wise Counsels, to direct our publick Weal.

But *He* who has the Hearts of *all* in his hands, will I hope inspire our Counsellors with *that* Wisdom which is from above, may Vigor, Courage, Unanimity, and Discision mark their Steps.

I received Your Letter of the 15th of October. Mr Shaw, and my little Ones thank you, for *all* your Tokens of Affection both Ideal, and material. Mr Shaw wishes, to draw upon *your Friend* for the like expression of Regard. He presumes, his Bill will not be protested.

Your two Children Charles, and Thomas spent a part of the long Vacation here. Mr Shaw would have bean quite displeased if they had not have come, we were very sorry Mr JQA did not accompany them.

Cousin Thomas could not help thinking it was home here yet, and no wonder—for it was almost three years, and half that he lived with us. He says he has a good Chamber at Cambridge, and the People of the House are very kind, and he can go to their Closet, with as much freedom as he used to here. I told him *my Pyes* were almost dried up, a waiting for him, for I expected they would have been here a fortnight sooner. Mr Shaw, and I have the pleasure of assuring you they behave well. We have taken particular Care to enquire of their Preceptors—for your Children do indeed, possess a very great share of our tenderest Love. Mr and Mrs Allen, and Cousin Sally Austin spent monday Evening here. I assure you we live in the most perfect amity, and good Neighbourhood. She has lately spent a fortnight in Boston, thinking she could not so conveniently again leave home. Mr Allen has *now*, I believe a prospect of additional Happiness in the domestic way,[2] and I can see, that he is not a *little* gratified. Our good Cousin William Smith will be married to Miss Hannah Carter the 1st of June. It is imposible for any thing to be more agreeable to *all* Parties. And it appears very strange, that what now gives so much satisfaction, could not have been thought of *before*. But this is the Year for happy Matches. I verrily believe some unusual lucky Star presides over the Hymeneal Torch. For I never knew half so many agreeable Connections formed as has been, within these twelve Months. I have written to my two Neices, telling them, I wish *its* benign Influences may be protracted, and the ensuing Months sweetly roll on, and smile as propitious upon them, as it has upon my other Friends.

Miss Carter is a Lady of real merit, and well deserving of the good

Husband (I presume) our Cousin will make. She is a Daughter in whom my Aunt Smith would have greatly delighted, had she still been living. This Lady is distinguished from the gay Trifflers of the age, not by Beauty, but by the more lasting Qualities of the Mind, for Virtue good Sense, Prudence Oeconimy, and an affable, modest Deportment mark her Character.

It gives me the greatest pleasure, that you appear to be so satisfied with your own Daughters Connection. It must be the Solace, and the Joy of your Mind. Long may they live, and be a Blessing to you.

Mr Thaxter *may* be married in the Course of the year,[3] but at present all Courts are stoped, and little or no buisiness can be done.

Mrs Marsh is still alive, and enjoys the Fruits of a good old age. The Fruit of good Government in her own Family, for her Children rise, and bless her.

Adieu! thou ever dear, & Much loved Sister—Accept this written in haste, from your E Shaw

RC (Adams Papers).

[1] On 29 Jan., Gov. James Bowdoin issued orders that members of the militia should prepare themselves to serve if the need arose. On 5–6 Feb., the General Court reiterated its support for a call-up of 2,600 men to reinforce the troops under General Lincoln working to put down Shays' Rebellion. Despite that, Bowdoin announced on 7 Feb., after positive reports from Lincoln of the success of his troops in dispersing the rebels, that he was countermanding the draft order (Boston *Independent Chronicle*, 1, 8 Feb.).

[2] Rev. Jonathan Allen and Elizabeth Kent Allen had a daughter, Betsey, who was baptized on 12 Aug. in Bradford (*Vital Records of Bradford Massachusetts*, Topsfield, 1907, p. 10).

[3] John Thaxter Jr. would marry Elizabeth Duncan on 13 November.

Mary Smith Cranch to Abigail Adams

Dear Sister Braintree February 9th 1787

If you have reciev'd our Letters by Capn Callahan you will be in Some measure prepair'd for the accounts which Capn Folger will bring you of the Rebellion which exists in this state. It had arisen to such a height that it was necessary to oppose it by force of arms. We are always in this country to do things in an extraordinary many [*manner?*]. The militia were call'd for, but there was not a copper in the Treasury to pay them or to support them upon their march. Town meetings were call'd in many places and promisses were made them that if the would inlist they would pay them and wait till the money could be collected from the Publick, for thier pay. And for their present Support People contributed as they were able and in this manner in less than a week was collected an army of five thousand men Who march'd under the command of General Lincoln to worcester to protect the court. The result you will see in the papers. The season has been stormy and severe our army have suffer'd greatly in some of their marches especially last Saturday night. Many of them were badly froze, they march'd thirty mile without stoping to refresh themselves in order to take Shays and his army by surprize. They took about 150 of them. Shays and a number with him scamper'd of and are got to new hampshire.

Shays and his party are a poor deluded People. They have given much trouble and put us and themselves to much expence and have greatly added to the difficulties they complain off. I think you must have been very uneasy about us. Shays has not a small party in Braintree but not many in this parish. They want paper money to cheat with. They call'd a Town meeting about a week since to forbid colln. Thayers attending the general court but they could not get a vote.[1]

It is now almost four months since I have heard from you. What is become of capn. Cushing, he has been long expected. This has been the longest winter I ever knew nothing but snow storms. The slaighing is fine and while our Lads were at home we did something at it, but now they are return'd to their studys and we are very lonely. No sister Adams to run too, no Germantown Freinds to visit:[2] mrs Quincy and nancy gone to spend the winter in Boston and if I turn my eyes to weymouth, there is not even the Docr. at this time to smile upon me. The Docr. is going to raise the roof of his House immediatly. What a pity that Josiah Quincy should have left his wife in such a manner, that She must quit it all if she marrys again. She is young and very agreable. Abel Willard has left a widow, not quite so young nor so comely but she is sensible amiable and benevolent to a great degree. She is also use'd to a country Life has no child and has a small fortune left her by her Father. Her Husbands went to the publick.[3] What think you, will either of these do. He says I must get him a wife he has not time to look about him, and one he must have soon. I want your assistance so please to nominate, and give your reasons but I will not promise that you will not be too late. What think you of our mrs Quincy for uncle Smith. If this should take place we should again feel as if we had an Aunt. I cannot but hope it. It is talk'd of, and that is one way to make it so. I have receiv'd a Letter to day from Sister Shaw. She is well, Billy has a troublesome cough. I was at cambridge sometimes in the vacancy to see

Cousin JQA. He Was well and quite a gallant among the Ladies. He promis'd to make us a visit but has been so ingag'd that he could not: Cousin Tom is a great favorite at mr Sewalls. He is neat loves order is very careful not to give any unnessary trouble, has scarcly any company and goes but little out. We cannot be thankful enough my dear Sister that our children are such as they are. Cousin charles is a lovely creature. He is so amiable and so attentive that he will be belov'd wherever he sets his Foot. Our children are so happy together that I can scarcly forbear a sigh When I think how soon they must be scatterd and yet it must and ought to be so.

Mrs Hall is well she spent the day with me this week and desir'd me to give her Love to her Son and you and her grandchildren. She charg'd me to thank you for what you had sent her and your Nieces. They look'd much pleas'd and beg'd me to thank their Aunt.

Mrs Allen has made a vissit to her Friends in Boston, but return'd without my seeing her. She is like to increase her Family which has sister Shaws says causd a complacenc in the countenance of her "own good man."

The newspapers will inform you that Doctor Clark dy'd very suddenly, but they will not tell you that he dy'd without a Will by which means miss Betsy Mayhew and her Brothers will have a fortune of four thousand pounds a piece. This is a great fortune for an american Lady enough certainly to bye her a Husband.[4]

Mr Evans is preaching where Doctor Gorden was settled, tis suppos'd they will give him a call.[5] Mr Norton is still at weymouth.

I went the other day to see our milton Friends. Mrs Warren is anxious for Henry. He went General Lincolns aid.

The musical society at Braintree return their thanks for those Scotch Peices of Musick whih you so kindly Sent them. They talk'd of chusing a committee to draw up a Letter of thanks but as they were not all present they deputed me to do it for them. They luckily came in the vacancy. They have had time to learn to sing and play several of them. You need not be concern'd about their playing upon a Flute they have not time to play enough to hurt them.

Uncle Quincy is as Well as usual. The roads have been so bad that I have not been to see him but onc this winter. Our Hingham Friends are well. Nancy looks quite *Stately*. Quincy is gone with General Lincoln. Good Doctor Gay lives yet and preaches every Sunday. Doctor Chancy is suppos'd very near his end but he has render'd himself immortal by his writings. Have you read his late publications. If you have not do get them of Doctor Price. They were printed under his direction. I scarcly ever read any thing with more pleasure.[6]

How does my new Nephew and my dear Niece. Well I hope. Does she begin to look *Stately* too. I wish I could look in upon them. When my Sister oh when will you return. I have had a Letter begun Six months ago for mrs Elworthy but I have not had time to finish it. Do you ever see her. If you do give my Love to her. Tell her sister Bond and Family were well a few days since. Mr Bond was in Boston. We had Letters from cousin Ebbit. Mrs Bond and her Sister are fine Women. I regret their living so far from us. I hope to visit them next Summer.[7]

Mrs Hay lives at Newbury. I have never seen her but once since she return'd. Why did she return without her Husband?[8] It looks strange.

Parson wibird visits us every other day almost. He still lives in that vile house. I told him the other day that nobody but he could live in and retain a moral character, that I was tir'd of vindicating his Character, where he was not known. That the House had become so Scandelous that if it was in Boston the Select men would pull it down and it is true. It is a vile house my sister but all I can say he will live there.

I hope you have not had a return of the dissorder which made you so sick.

Betsy and Lucy send their Duty to you and Love to their Cousins, will write by the next vessel. We did not hear of this till a day or two ago, and they are so busy that they cannot attend to their Pen at present.

Will you present my Love to mr Adams. To mr and Mrs Smith, and accept of the warmest Love & gratitude of your ever affectionate Sister

Mary Cranch

RC (Adams Papers); endorsed: "Mrs Cranch Febry 9th 1787."

[1] At a 29 Jan. town meeting, some Braintree residents attempted to recall Ebenezer Thayer as their representative to the General Court or to alter his instructions, but the motion was dismissed (*Braintree Town Records*, p. 569–570).

[2] Gen. Joseph Palmer's family, who had moved to Charlestown in the fall (Cranch to AA, 26 Nov. 1786, above).

[3] Abel Willard (1731/2–1781) of Lancaster, Mass., had emigrated with his wife, Elizabeth Rogers, to England as a loyalist refugee in 1776. He was subsequently proscribed under the Act of 1778 and his Massachusetts estate was confiscated. Following his death in 1781, his widow returned to Boston (*Sibley's Harvard Graduates*, 13:301–303).

[4] Dr. John Clarke, AA's fellow passenger and good friend on the *Active* in 1784 (see vol. 5:360–383 *passim*), was the uncle of Elizabeth Mayhew, daughter of the late Rev. Jonathan Mayhew and Elizabeth Clarke. Betsy's "brothers" were her half-brothers, John Clarke Howard and Algernon Sidney

Howard, sons of Elizabeth Clarke and the Rev. Simeon Howard, who had succeeded Mayhew as minister at Boston's West Church. Betsy Mayhew later married Peter Wainwright (*Sibley's Harvard Graduates*, 11:444, 469; 14:288).

[5] Rev. William Gordon, the patriot historian, had long been the minister of the Third Congregational Church in Jamaica Plain (Roxbury), Mass., prior to his return to England in March 1786. The church did not call another minister until 1793, when it chose Rev. Thomas Gray to be its pastor. "Mr Evans" was probably Israel Evans, for whom see Mary Smith Cranch to AA, 9 Feb. 1786, note 8, above (MHS, *Procs.*, 63 [1929–1930]: 303; Ellen Lunt Frothingham Ernst, *The First Congregational Society of Jamaica Plain 1769–1909*, n.p., 1909, p. 33–34).

[6] Rev. Charles Chauncy, the venerable Arminian pastor of Boston's First Church since 1727, died on 10 Feb. at age 82. His last important works, published in England, were *The Mystery Hid from Ages and Generations*, London, 1784, and *Five Dissertations on the Scripture Account of the Fall and Its Consequences*, London, 1785 (*DAB*).

[7] William and Hannah Cranch Bond lived in Falmouth (now Portland, Maine), as did Hannah's brother Ebbett (1750–1789) ("Extract from a Register of the Bond and Cranch Families, drawn up in the year 1852," MHi:Cranch-Bond Papers). Elizabeth Cranch Elworthy of London, wife of James Elworthy, was Hannah's sister and Richard Cranch's niece.

[8] Katherine Hay decided to return to the United States alone, rather than go with her husband, a ship captain, on a lengthy voyage or remain in England without him (AA to Mary Smith Cranch, 28 April, MWA:Abigail Adams Corr.).

John Adams to Richard Cranch

My dear Brother — London, Feb. 21, 1787

I believe there is not another Man in the World whose Life has been such a series of Remorses as mine. It seems as if there was a Destiny that I should never be paid. The time is drawing near, for eleven or twelve months will soon be round, when we embark for Home. This is an irksome undertaking—to break up a settled habitation and remove a family across the Seas, at any time of life is no small matter, but when people grow into years and are weary of changes it is more disagreeable. It is in vain to murmur, and we must submit.

In every Point of view, it would be impertinent for me to think of remaining longer in Europe. It would be some expence to the public, without any benefit, and a great torment to me, without any profit. I shall leave to future Conversations at your Fireside, all further revelations upon these subjects. It is idle to complain. If there is not some other Plan persued at home, no good can be done abroad.

I am extremely anxious about the wild Projects of Government both for the Confederations and for particular States that I am informed are in circulation.[1] Yet I can not but hope and trust that the Massachusetts will get better very soon of her own difficulties. The people I think cannot be so weak and misled as to continue their outrages against all Government.

I shall hardly find my homely house a Scene of tranquility or of Pleasure, but it can't be worse for myself or others, than to stay here. My tender affections to my Sister and all our Friends. Tho I have not had a Youth of Pleasures, I must reckon on an old age of Cares. These however will be softened by the Neighborhood and Society of my old Friends—in the cheering hopes of which permit me to subscribe myself, your affectionate and obliged Brother,

John Adams

RC not found. Printed from Paul C. Richards Cat., #47 [1970], Brookline, Mass.

[1] JA first received a report of a potential constitutional convention in Philadelphia from Rufus King, 2 Oct. 1786, who wrote, "The convention proposed to have been held at Annapolis in the last month on the subject of commerce has terminated without credit, or prospect of having done much good. . . . Whether the states will acceed to the proposition of a convention at Philadelphia, in May is yet uncertain" (Adams Papers).

John Adams to Cotton Tufts

Dear Sir London Feb. 21. 1787

Having determined to return to Pens hill, I begin to think in what a pitiful Condition I shall find my Meadow and Hill &c &c. Poor as a heath I Suppose, as I found them, but am determined they shall not remain long in such a contemptible plight. This is therefore to beg the favour of you to purchase for me Josh. Bracketts Heap at his stable[1] for a year, and desire my Brother or my Tenant to hire Boats and Teams to transport it to Braintree, and to bring a proportional Quantity of Marsh Mud and street Dust to be laid in heaps for manure. Belcher remembers the whole Proscess. Draw upon me, as soon as possible for the Cash to defray all Expences. I am determined not to remain an Hour in Europe after the Expiration of my Commission to this Court. So I shall embark in January or February 1788 for Boston, if possible, if not, for New York in the Packett.

I am, my dear sir, with much Affection your Friend

John Adams

RC (CtY:Franklin Papers); endorsed: "John Adams Esq. Feby. 21. 1787—respecting his Return."

[1] For Joshua Brackett's stable, see vol. 4:259–261; JA, *D&A*, 3:194.

Thomas Jefferson to Abigail Adams

Dear Madam Paris Feb. 22. 1787

I am to acknolege the honor of your letter of Jan. 29. and of the papers you were so good as to send me they were the latest I had seen or have yet seen. They left off too in a critical moment; just at the point where the Malcontents make their submission on condition of pardon, and before the answer of government was known. I hope they pardoned them. The spirit of resistance to government is so valuable on certain occasions, that I wish it to be always kept alive. It will often be exercised when wrong, but better so than not to be exercised at all. I like a little rebellion now and then. It is like a storm in the Atmosphere. It is wonderful that no letter or paper tells us who is president of Congress,[1] tho' there are letters in Paris to the beginning of January. I suppose I shall hear when I come back from my journey,[2] which will be eight months after he will have been chosen. And yet they complain of us for not giving them intelligence. Our Notables assembled to-day, and I hope before the departure of mr Cairnes[3] I shall have heard something of their proceedings worth communicating to mr Adams. The most remarkable effect of this convention as yet is the number of puns and bon mots it has generated.[4] I think were they all collected it would make a more voluminous work than the Encyclopedie. This occasion, more than any thing I have seen, convinces me that this nation is incapable of any serious effort but under the word of command. The people at large view every object only as it may furnish puns and bons mots; and I pronounce that a good punster would disarm the whole nation were they ever so seriously disposed to revolt. Indeed, Madam, they are gone. When a measure so capable of doing good as the calling the Notables is treated with so much ridicule, we may conclude the nation desperete, and in charity pray that heaven may send them good kings.

The bridge at the place Louis XV. is begun. The hotel dieu is to be abandoned and new ones to be built. The old houses on the old bridges are in a course of demolition.[5] This is all I know of Paris. We are about to lose the Count d'Aranda, who has desired and obtained his recall. Fernand Nunnez, before destined for London is to come here.[6] The Abbe's Arnoux and Chalut are well. The Dutchess Danville somewhat recovered from the loss of her daughter.[7] Mrs Barrett very homesick, and fancying herself otherwise sick. They will probably remove to Honfleur.[8] This is all our news. I have only to add then that mr Carnes has taken charge of 15. aunes of black lace for you at 9 livres the aune, purchased by Petit and therefore I hope better purchased than some things have been for you; and that I am with sincere esteem Dear Madam your affectionete humble sert

Th: Jefferson

RC (Adams Papers); endorsed: "Mr Jefferson Febry 22 1787."

[1] The new Congress, scheduled to convene in Nov. 1786, did not obtain a quorum until 17 January. It elected Arthur St. Clair of Pennsylvania as its president on 2 Feb., and John Jay informed Jefferson of this on 9 Feb. (*JCC*, 32:1, 11; Jefferson, *Papers*, 11:129).

[2] Jefferson left Paris on 28 Feb. for a tour of southern France and northern Italy, returning on 10 June, for which see his "Notes of a Tour into the Southern Parts of France, &c" (same, 11:415–464).

[3] Burrill Carnes, an American merchant at Lorient, carried letters to London for Jefferson in Feb. (same, 11:143, 188; vol. 6:200).

[4] The Assembly of Notables, proposed by Louis XVI's controller-general, Charles Alexandre de Calonne, opened on 22 Feb. after two postponements. Called to consult on France's financial crisis, and widely lampooned at its opening, it proved far more independent than expected and suggested various reforms. The assembly met until 25 May when Louis XVI dismissed them in the wake of their demand for a meeting of the full Estates-General to approve new taxes. Jefferson described the assembly to JA in a letter of 23 Feb. (Simon Schama, *Citizens: A Chronicle of the French Revolution*, N.Y., 1989, p. 227, 238–241, 259–260; Jefferson, *Papers*, 11:176–177). For an example of the satirical prints mocking the assembly that were prevalent in Paris in February, see Schama, *Citizens*, p. 241.

[5] Construction of the Pont de la Concorde, the bridge crossing the Seine from the Place Louis XV (later Place de la Concorde) and built in part with stones from the Bastille, began in 1787 and was completed in 1791. The plan to close the Hôtel Dieu, the oldest hospital in Paris, and build a new one on the outskirts of the city, never came to fruition under Louis XVI and was abandoned at the start of the Revolution. It was finally remodeled in the 1860s (Karl Baedeker, *Paris and Its Environs*, 19th edn., N.Y., 1924, p. 59, 62, 264; Howard C. Rice Jr., *Thomas Jefferson's Paris*, Princeton, N.J., 1976, p. 5–6, 25–26; Edward Planta, *A New Picture of Paris; or, the Stranger's Guide to the French Metropolis*, 10th edn., London, 1818, p. 264–265).

[6] Pedro Pablo de Abarca y Bolea, Conde de Aranda, was Spain's ambassador to France from 1773 to Sept. 1787. Carlos José Gutiérrez de los Rios y Rohan-Chabot, Conde de Fernán-Núñez, Spain's former ambassador to Portugal, replaced him in Dec. 1787 (*Repertorium*, p. 430–431, 438).

[7] Elisabeth Louise (1740–1786), daughter of Marie Louise Nicole de La Rochefoucauld, widow of Jean Baptiste Frédéric de La Rochefoucauld de Roye, Duc d'Anville (JA, *D&A*, 4:42, 66–67; *Dict. de la noblesse*, 17:366).

[8] The former Boston resident Nathaniel Barrett and his wife Margaret Hunt Barrett did not move to the port city of Honfleur, France, nor was she merely "fancying" her illness. She died on 6 June in Paris, probably of consumption (Jefferson, *Papers*, 11:276, 476; Boston *Independent Chronicle*, 13 Sept.).

Abigail Adams to Mary Smith Cranch

My Dear Sister London Febry 25 1787

Captain Davis called yesterday to let me know that he should sail in the course of the week. Captain Barnard will not be long after him, and I almost wish I was going to embark with him. I think I should not feel more anxious if I was in the midst of all the disturbances, than I do at this Distance, where Imagination is left at full Liberty. When Law and justice is laid prostrait who or what is Secure? I received your Letters which came by captain Scot just as I was going to step into the carriage to go into the City upon some Buisness. As I was alone I took them with me to read, and when I came to that part of your Letter, where in you say, that you had hoped to have seen only Peace in future, after surmounting the Horrors of one war the Idea was too powerfull for me, and the Tears invollumtary flowed. I was obliged to quit the Letter till I had finishd my Buisness. The thoughts which naturally occured to me, were for what have we been contending against the tyrranny of Britain, to become the Sacrifice of a lawless Banditti? Must our glory be thus shorn and our Laurels thus blasted? Is it a trifling matter to destroy a Government, will my countrymen justify the Maxim of tyrants, that Mankind are not made for freedom. I will however still hope that the Majority of our fellow citizens are too wise virtuous and enlightned to permit these outrages to gain ground and triumph. Solon the wise lawgiver of Athens, published a Manifesto for rendering infamous all persons, who in civil Seditions should remain Spectators of their Countrys danger by a criminal Neutrality.[1] The Spirit shewn by the Gentleman vollunteers and the capture of Shattucks does honour to our State. More energy in Government would have prevented the evil from spreading so far as it has done.

> "Mercy but gives Sedition time to rally
> every soft pliant talking busie Rogue
> Gathering a flock of hot braind Fools together
> can preach up new Rebellion
> Spread false reports of the Senate working up
> their Madness to a Fury quick and desp'rate
> till they run headlong in to civil discords
> And do our buisness with their own destruction."[2]

This is a picture of the civil dissentions in Rome, and to our mortification we find that humane nature is the same in all ages. Neither the dread of Tyrants the fall of Empires, the Havock and dessolation of the Humane Species, nor the more gloomy picture of civil Discord, are sufficient to deter Mankind from persueing the Same Steps which have led others to ruin. Selfishness and spight avarice and ambition, pride and a *levelling* principal are qualities very unfavourable to the existance of civil Liberty. But whatever is to be the fate of our Country, we have determined to come home and share it with you. Congress have never given mr Adams a recall from Holland and he is vested (with mr Jefferson) with powers to form treaties with Several other Countrys. His commission to this Court will terminate this time twelve Months, and he has written to Congress his fixd and full determination to resign his commissions and return at that period, if not before.[3] So that my dear sister I most joyfully accept your invitation and will come home God willing e'er an other Year expires. Dissagreeable as the Situation of my Native State appears, I shall quit Europe with more pleasure than I came to it, uncontaminated I hope with its Manners and vices. I have learnt to know the World, and its value. I have seen high Life, I have Witnessd the Luxery and pomp of State, the Power of riches and the influence of titles, and have beheld all Ranks bow before them, as the only shrine worthy of worship. Notwithstanding this, I feel that I can return to my little cottage and be happier than here, and if we have not wealth, we have what is better, Integrity.

Feb'ry 27 1787

I had written you thus far with an intention of sending by Davis, but received a card to day from captain Barnard that he will sail at the same time which is a fortnight sooner than I expected. I have concluded to send by him. Captain Callihan arrived at Cows in a very short passage of less than 30 days, and your Letter of Janry 10 and 12 came up by the post, one from uncle Smith and one from my eldest son.[4] The rest are still on Board, nor do I know when we shall get them, as captain Callihan Stays I suppose to repair, having lost his Mast in a gale of wind. I was very happy to find that Folger had arrived safe as we were anxious for him, on account of the severe weather. I wrote you by captain Cushing, on Board of whom I got mr Elworthy to put a small present for you, but was much mortified a day or two after to find by a Boston paper that they were prohibited articles. I hope you will not meet with trouble on account of them. I cannot but approve the Spirit which dictated the measure.[5] The causes which gave rise to it, must be deplored, for it is evidently a work of necessity rather than choice. The Luxery which had made Such rapid Strides amongst our countrymen was more criminal than that which is founded upon *real wealth*, for they have Roited upon the property which belonged to others. It is a very just observation, that those who have raised an Empire, have always been grave and Severe; they who have ruined it, have been uniformly distinguished for their dissapation. We shall wait with impatience for the result of General Lincolns expedition. Much depends upon his Success. Government seem affraid to use the power they have, and recommend and intreat where they ought to *Command*, which makes one apprehend that the evil lies deeper than the Heads or Hands of Shaise or Shattucks. From letter received here both from Boston and Newyork it is to be feared that Visionary Schemes, and ambitious projects are taking possession of Men of Property and Science. But before so important an Edifice as an Established Government is alterd or changed, its foundation should be examined by skilfull artists, and the Materials of which it is composed duly investigated.[6]

The defence of the American constitutions is a work which may perhaps contribute to this end and I most Sincerly wish it may do the good intended.

I lament with you the loss of a Worthy Man, for such indeed was the Friend of my dear Eliza. Our own duration is but a Span, then shall we meet those dear Friends and relatives who have gone before us and be engaged together in more elevated views, and purer pleasures and enjoyments than Mortality is capable of. Let this Idea Sooth the aflicted mind, and administer Balm to the wounded Heart; all things are under the Government of a supreeme all wise director, to him commit, the hour the day the year. I will write my dear Neice as soon as I get her Letter.

I fear if Barnard sails so soon I shall find myself tardy. I have been much engaged in assisting Mrs Smith. I wish for a sister as the time draws near. I shall find myself of little use. She seems to have good Spirits and knowing nothing fears nothing. Dr Jeffries is our family Physician, and is really an amiable benevolent Man tho formerly he took a different side in politicks.[7]

You inquire the price of Mode. It is of various prices the widest and best five shillings sterling. As to the fashion sattin cloaks of all coulours except Black are worn in winter in Spring black mode, in Summer Muslin and Gauzes linned with blew pink or white Sasnit [*sarcenet*] like one which was made by my Millinar and sent to Mrs Russel by Cushing, but I will endeavour to get a Pattern for you. What new fashions may be introduced by the admission of French Millinary during the summer, is past even the art of devination, but as that is a matter which my Country women will concern themselves very little with *I hope*, a Monthly magizine may serve their purpose instead of a daily volm which we may soon expect to See.

Pray what has become of Mrs Hay I have never received a line from her since she left this Country? You did perfectly right in adding the two yds more for Gowns for the Miss Palmers. The moths I hope will not plunder what little Wollens I have particularly my Scarlet cloth and my carpet. As to what other things I have, I consider them as a usefull deposit for family service should I live to return. Amongst them I think I have a large parcel of threads which my Neices will repair to when they have occasion to make linen for their cousins. As to any thing else, I had rather have it purchased for the children than taken from thence. I wish you would be so good as to look into my draws and you will find a green Lutestring Gown and a brown ducape a pattern of each I wish you to send me, as they will never be of Service to me unless I can match them. I have sent by captain Barnard a peice of Linen for the children, it is addrest to mr Cranch. I did not know whether they wanted yet but thought it would do no harm as Moths will not eat that. Within the Linnen you will find the trimming for it, *Smuglled a little* but that you will be mush about. Dont even tell that wise and good Senator your Husband. Take enough of it for cousin William half a dozen pr of. I have also sent the other half dozen shirts for JQA, so that he will not want for these twelve Months. Mrs Payne shall not be forgotten.

My dear sister say not one word about being ungratefull in charging the Board of your Nephews. I am sure it is your Duty to do it and it would pain both mr Adams and me exceedingly if you did not. Dr Tufts will pay you quarterly and for their washing and Ironing. I know that there are a thousand cares for which you cannot be paid only by the gratefull acknowledment of your sister.

You have hinted to me Several times as tho our good uncle Tufts was looking him a wife. Pray is there any particular person you think of. Our Friend Mrs Quincy has been in my mind for one or the other of our uncles. So cousin William has at last found one sensible Girl. Tis a Shame that a solid young fellow, should be so little to the taste of the young Ladies. I am always glad to hear every thing pleasing of my Friends, and I begin now to feel as if I should See them again.

Mrs Smith sits by the table working as fast as her needle can fly and is so buisy that I do not think She will write a line by this opportunity.

Let mrs Feild know that Esther is well as usual, a weakly creature at best, requires as much care as a Young Turkey. John is not much better, never well, but an excellent Servint, honest and trust worthy.

Thus have I told you a domestick tale and my scond sheet warns me to close, but not untill I present my Love to Brother Cranch to my Nephew and Neices, to all my kin however wide, to my Neighbours and Friends, from their and your affectionate AA

RC (MWA:Abigail Adams Corr.).

[1] Solon (ca. 7th–6th century B.C.), the "Lawgiver," was a statesman, poet, and archon of Greece ca. 594–590 B.C. Plutarch's *Lives* cites a law of Solon that a person refusing to take sides during times of division would be disenfranchised (Ivan M. Linforth, *Solon the Athenian*, Berkeley, Calif., 1919, p. 3–4, 27; Plutarch, *Life of Solon*, XX, para. 1).

[2] Thomas Otway, *The History and Fall of Caius Marius*, London, 1680, Act III, lines 7–10, 70–73.

[3] JA made his intentions known to Congress in a letter to John Jay of 24 Jan. (PCC, No. 84, VI, f. 392–395).

[4] The letter from Isaac Smith Sr. to AA has not been found; the letter from JQA is that of 30 Dec. 1786, above.

[5] AA was sending porter and cheese, both of which had been prohibited under the new Massachusetts impost (AA to Thomas Jefferson, 29 Jan., above; Mary Smith Cranch to AA, 22 April, Adams Papers).

[6] By this time, the Adamses had received a number of letters from Boston and New York not only discussing the troubles in Massachusetts but also outlining the activities of the Annapolis Convention and consideration of a new federal convention in Philadelphia. See, for example, letters to JA from Rufus King, 2 Oct.; Benjamin Hichborn, 24 Oct.; and Samuel Osgood, 14 Nov. (2d letter) (all Adams Papers).

[7] Dr. John Jeffries (1744/5–1819), Harvard 1763, had studied medicine at Aberdeen but then returned to Boston to practice. He sided with the loyalists, however, and became a doctor in the British Army, first in Nova Scotia and later in Savannah and then New York. In 1780, he migrated to London, where he continued to practice medicine and also became interested in aeronautics, particularly balloons. He served as the Adamses' family physician throughout their time in England (*Sibley's Harvard Graduates*, 15:419–427).

Abigail Adams to John Quincy Adams

My dear son London Febry 28th 1787

Your Letter to me by captain Callihan came safe to hand, that to your Sister and others from my Friends are yet with him at Cowes where he put in having lost his Mast. I think single Letters are better put into the Bag, Newspapers given to the captains.

Blairs lectures were purchased for you last fall and left at the New England coffe house for captain Barnard to take with him, and we thought that you had received them. If they have mist, an other set will be procured for you. Enfields institutes will also be Sent, but captain Barnard going a fortnight sooner than we expected, am not ready for him. I have requested him to take the remaining half dozen of your shirts which are done up in a bundle like those I sent by cushing and addrest to you; the volms you mention receiving of French History, were written by a very needy Man, a mere Chevalier d'Industry, who has since been in Newgate and as they were much too impartial to Sell in this country I Suppose he could not pay the printing.[1] He Swindled us out of ten Guineys and has dissapeard. There is nothing that is American, is or can be in vogue here. They cautiously avoid bringing our country into view. Indeed she does not at present exhibit the most pleasing picture, but to make us believe that she is of no kind of concequence to them they do not even retail our disturbances, or comment upon them. If they had Money I should suppose they were willing to keep up our quarrels and would lend a hand to sow dissentions, but they are as much distresst for ways and means as we are, and those who form conjectures of this kind know little of the finnances of this Country. The day is fast approaching when we have determined to quit it. God willing I once Set my foot on American ground not all the embassies to Europe consolidated into one shall tempt me again to quit it. I do not wonder at your longing to return, and I have many induceme[nts] which you had not, not one single one to remain here. My dear lads you know that we shall return poor, but at the same time you know what have been the Services of your Father. You know his honour and his integrity that shall be your inheritance. If we can get you all through colledge, the World is all before you, and providence your guide.[2] You will do better I doubt not than if you had been led to expect wealth.

You will apply my son to mr Parsons and get fixed with him I hope. If we live to return to you we shall be able to look after your Brothers.

I am rejoiced to find there conduct so good. This is a balm amidst all the publick calamities. Pray attend to your own Health, I have written you before upon this Subject. Mine is better than in the fall, tho as the Spring approaches I find a return of my Rhumatick complaints. I am obliged to write you in great haste as Barnard is to Sail tomorrow, and my Letters must go to him this Evening. Col Smith says he has the same feeling which you express, that he wrote you long ago but has never Sent it. Your sister is well and will write you as soon as she gets her Letter.

Adieu and believe me most tenderly you[rs] AA

Love to your Brothers.

RC (Adams Papers); addressed by WSS: "To Mr John Quincy Adams Student at Cambridge near Boston"; endorsed: "Mrs: Adams Feby: 28 1787."; docketed: "My Mother. 28. Feby: 1787." Some loss of text where the seal was removed.

[1] François Soulés.

[2] Milton, *Paradise Lost*, 12:646–647.

Appendix

Appendix

LIST OF OMITTED DOCUMENTS

The following list includes twenty documents that have been omitted from volume 7 of *Adams Family Correspondence*. Each entry consists of the date, correspondents, form in which the letter exists (Dft, LbC, RC), location, and publication, if known. All copies that exist in some form in the Adams Papers are noted. The list also includes one letter that has come to the editors' attention since the publication of the volume in which it would have appeared. This item is marked with an asterisk.

1784

14 May*	John Adams to Richard Cranch, RC (NHi:Gilder Lehrman Coll., on deposit).

1786

3 Jan.	Richard Cranch to John Adams, Dft (MHi:Cranch Family Coll.).
10 Jan.	Charles Storer to John Adams, RC (Adams Papers).
11 Jan.	Richard Cranch to John Adams, RC (Adams Papers).
16 Jan.	Lucy Ludwell Paradise to John and Abigail Adams, RC (Adams Papers).
22 Jan.	John Thaxter to John Adams, RC (Adams Papers).
26 Jan.	John Singleton and Susanna Clarke Copley to John and Abigail Adams and Abigail Adams 2d, RC (Adams Papers).
4 Feb.	John Thaxter to Abigail Adams, RC (Adams Papers).

11 Feb.	Lucy Ludwell Paradise to Abigail Adams, RC (DSI: Hull Coll.).
20 Feb.	Abigail Adams 2d to Lucy Cranch, RC (MWA).
12 March	John Adams to Isaac Smith Sr., RC (MHi:Smith-Carter Papers).
[*ante* 30 *March*]	Jean Balthazar, Comte d'Adhémar to John and Abigail Adams and Abigail Adams 2d, RC (MQA).
21 April	William Vaughan to John and Abigail Adams and Abigail Adams 2d, RC (Adams Papers).
26 May	John Adams to Richard Cranch, RC (Private owner, 1957); LbC (Adams Papers).
20 June	Ann Torkington Jebb to John and Abigail Adams, RC (Adams Papers).
4 July	John Adams to William Smith, RC (MHi:Smith-Carter Papers); LbC (Adams Papers).
3 Oct.	Richard Cranch to John Adams, RC (Adams Papers).
21 Dec.	John Adams to William Stephens Smith; PRINTED: John Adams, *A Defence of the Constitutions of Government of the United States of America,* 3 vols., London, 1787–1788, 1:372–382.

1787

15 Jan.	John Adams to Richard Cranch, RC (NN:Presidents' Papers); LbC (Adams Papers); PRINTED: JA, *Works,* 1:432–433.
15 Jan.	John Adams to Cotton Tufts, RC (Adams Papers).
5 Feb.	Anna Quincy to Abigail Adams, RC (Adams Papers).

Chronology

Chronology

THE ADAMS FAMILY, 1786–1787

1786

4 Jan. – 8 Feb.: CA, a Harvard freshman, spends his winter vacation in Braintree and Haverhill, where JQA and TBA are being tutored by their uncle, Rev. John Shaw.

10 Jan.: JQA visits New Hampshire for the first time on an evening sleigh ride to Hampstead.

9 Feb.: AA and AA2 attend the queen's birthday celebration, accompanied by Col. David Humphreys, and the birthday ball, with WSS, at St. James' Palace.

16–20 Feb.: JA meets with Ambassador Sidi Haggi 'Abd-ur-rahman Aga of Tripoli to negotiate a commercial treaty.

21 Feb.: WSS departs London for Paris, dispatched by JA to confer with Thomas Jefferson on the treaty negotiations with Tripoli.

28 Feb.: Lord Carmarthen responds to JA's Nov. 1785 demand that British troops be withdrawn from U.S. territory, stating that Britain will fulfill its treaty obligations when America does the same.

11 March: WSS and Thomas Jefferson arrive in London, the latter coming to help negotiate commercial treaties with Tripoli, Portugal, and Great Britain.

14 March: JQA leaves Haverhill for Cambridge. On the 15th he is examined and admitted to Harvard as a junior sophister.

15 March: JA presents Jefferson to King George III.

18–22 March: JQA visits the Cranches in Braintree.

22 March: JQA takes up residence at Harvard College.

4–10 April: JA and Jefferson tour English gardens, countryseats, and historic sites, including Stratford-on-Avon where they carve a souvenir sliver from what is said to be Shakespeare's chair.

11–26 April: JQA and CA spend the Harvard spring vacation at Braintree.

17 April: JA acquires eleven acres in Braintree's New South Precinct, now Randolph, in settlement of a loan to David Sloan.

19 April: JA meets Joseph Priestley.

20 April: The Adamses and Jefferson visit the countryseats of Sion House and Osterley Park in Brentford.

24 April: The Adamses, WSS, and Jefferson visit the British Museum.

25 April: JA and Jefferson conclude negotiations for a commercial treaty with Portugal, a treaty that neither country ever ratified.

29 April: In a diplomatic slight, JA is excluded from the annual Royal Academy dinner for foreign ministers.

9 May: JA publishes an anonymous letter in a London newspaper denying a report that his salary is paid by the French government.

12 May: Commissions held by JA and Jefferson to negotiate commercial treaties expire.

11 June: AA2 and WSS are married at the U.S. legation in Grosvenor Square.

17 June: CA and his cousins William, Elizabeth, and Lucy Cranch attend the dedication of the bridge connecting Boston and Charlestown. JQA remains at Harvard.

20–24 June: The Adamses visit Portsmouth, stopping at the countryseat of Painshill in Surrey and Windsor Castle.

30 June: AA2 and WSS depart Grosvenor Square for a residence on Wimpole Street.

13 July: Harvard's summer vacation begins, and JQA and CA go to Braintree.

20–26 July: TBA visits Braintree.

24–28 July: JA, AA, AA2, and WSS visit the Essex estate of Thomas Brand-Hollis.

26 July – 5 Aug.: JQA and CA visit Haverhill, participating in a sea-turtle banquet on a Merrimack River island on 28 July.

27 July: JA and AA visit Braintree, England, for "the Gratification of Curiosity."

2 Aug.: JA attends a levee with the king to announce his departure for The Hague. On the same day, the king escapes an assassination attempt by a knife-wielding Margaret Nicholson.

3 Aug. – 6 Sept.: JA and AA travel to The Hague for the signing of the Prussian-American treaty. While in Holland, the Adamses visit Rotterdam, Leyden, Haarlem, Amsterdam, Delft, and Utrecht.

16 Aug.: JQA returns to Harvard for the fall quarter, following CA, who arrived in Cambridge five days earlier to prepare their rooms.

17 Aug.: Frederick the Great of Prussia dies and is succeeded by his nephew, Frederick William II.

22 Aug.: TBA is examined and admitted to Harvard's freshman class; he boards with Prof. Stephen Sewall in Cambridge.

25–28 Aug.: AA2 and WSS visit Salt Hill in Buckinghamshire and Staines in Middlesex.

29 Aug.: Shays' Rebellion begins when 1,500 farmers protest rising taxes and foreclosures by occupying the Northampton courthouse.

Sept.: JA begins writing what would become his three-volume *A Defence of the Constitutions of Government of the United States of America.*

11 Sept.: The Annapolis Convention convenes in Maryland to consider federal regulation of commerce but fails to reach a quorum.

26 Sept.: JQA and William Cranch debate "Whether inequality among the citizens be necessary to the preservation of the liberty of the whole" at a Harvard College exhibition.

Oct.: JA publishes a series of letters he wrote in 1780 to Hendrik Calkoen, an Amsterdam lawyer, as *Letters.* The book is later retitled *Twenty-Six Letters, upon Interesting Subjects, Respecting the Revolution of America.*

17 Oct.: The Adams sons spend the Harvard vacation in Braintree. CA returns to Cambridge on the 30th; JQA and TBA on 1 November.

17 Nov.: The Massachusetts legislature approves bills encouraging domestic manufacture and taxing imported goods.

13 Dec. – 7 Feb.: Harvard vacation begins early due to a massive snowstorm and shortages of wood. JQA elects to stay at the college.

22 Dec. – 6 Jan.: AA, AA2, and WSS visit Bath while JA remains in London.

1787

20 Jan.: AA announces to family in the United States that AA2 and WSS are expecting their first child, William Steuben Smith, born 2 April.

24 Jan.: JA informs Congress that within a year he will resign his commissions and return to the United States.

25 Jan.: JA signs a Treaty of Peace and Friendship with Morocco.

21 Feb.: Congress approves a proposal to hold a Constitutional Convention in Philadelphia in May.

27 Feb.: Shays' Rebellion ends with a final skirmish in Sheffield, Mass.

Index

NOTE ON THE INDEX

The index for volume 7 of the *Adams Family Correspondence* is designed to supplement the annotation, when possible, by furnishing the correct spellings of names, supplying forenames when they are lacking in the text, and indicating dates, occupations, and places of residence when they will aid in identification. Markedly variant spellings of proper names have been cross-referenced to what are believed to be their most nearly standard forms, and the variant forms found in the MSS are parenthetically recorded following the standard spellings. Cross references under maiden names are used for women who were single when first mentioned in the text and were married subsequently but before March 1787.

In a change from previous indexes of *The Adams Papers*, subentries appear in alphabetical order by the primary word of the subentry. Abbreviations are alphabetized as if they were spelled out, thus "JQA" is alphabetized under "Adams."

The Chronology, "The Adams Family, 1786–1787," has not been included in the index.

The index was compiled in the Adams Papers office.

Index

Index

Index

¶The *Adams Family Correspondence* was composed in the Adams Papers office using Microsoft Office Professional with style sheets and programs created by Technologies 'N Typography of Merrimac, Massachusetts. The text is set in eleven on twelve and one half point using the Linotype-Hell Postscript revival of *Fairfield Medium*, a design by Rudolph Ruzicka that includes swash characters especially designed for *The Adams Papers.* The printing and binding are by Edwards Brothers of Ann Arbor, Michigan. The paper, made by Mohawk Paper Company, is a grade named *Superfine.* The books were originally designed by P. J. Conkwright and Burton L. Stratton.